D1074787

REFERENCE GUIDE TO SCIENCE FICTION, FANTASY, AND HORROR

Reference Sources in the Humanities Series
James Rettig, Series Editor

Communication and the Mass Media: A Guide to the Reference Literature. By Eleanor S. Block and James K. Bracken.

Journalism: A Guide to the Reference Literature. By Jo A. Cates.

Judaism and Christianity: A Guide to the Reference Literature. By Edward D. Starkey.

Linguistics: A Guide to the Reference Literature. By Anna L. DeMiller.

Music: A Guide to the Reference Literature. By William S. Brockman.

On the Screen: A Film, Television, and Video Research Guide. By Kim N. Fisher.

Philosophy: A Guide to the Reference Literature. By Hans E. Bynagle.

Reference Guide to Science Fiction, Fantasy, and Horror. By Michael Burgess.

Reference Works in British and American Literature: Volume I, English and American Literature. By James K. Bracken.

Reference Works in British and American Literature: Volume II, English and American Writers. By James K. Bracken.

REFERENCE GUIDE to SCIENCE FICTION, FANTASY, and HORROR

Michael Burgess
California State University, San Bernardino

LIBRARIES UNLIMITED, INC.
Englewood, Colorado
1992

LIBRARIES UNLIMITED, INC.
P.O. Box 6633
Englewood, CO 80155-6633

Library of Congress Cataloging-in-Publication Data

Burgess, Michael, 1948-
  Reference guide to science fiction, fantasy, and horror / Michael
Burgess.
    xv, 403 p. 17x25 cm. -- (Reference sources in the humanities series)
    Includes bibliographical references and index.
    ISBN 0-87287-611-X
    1. Reference books--Science fiction--Bibliography.   2. Science
fiction--History and criticism--Bibliography.   3. Reference books-
-Fantastic fiction--Bibliography.   4. Fantastic fiction--History and
criticism--Bibliography.   5. Reference books--Horror tales-
-Bibliography.   6. Horror tales--History and criticism-
-Bibliography.   I. Title.   II. Series.
  Z5917.S36B87   1992
  [PN3433.5]
  016.8093'876--dc20
                                                    91-44853
                                                       CIP

For my youngest brother,
Scott Alan Burgess,
whose maiden voyage,
The Work of Reginald Bretnor:
An Annotated Bibliography & Guide,
was launched in 1989

CONTENTS

PREFACE

Science fiction has, from its very beginnings as a literary genre in 1926, attracted an inordinate amount of fan interest, and these fans have, in turn, contributed a large number of indexes, bibliographies, and other books about the field, far more than in the comparable genres of mystery and western fiction. Beginning in the late 1950s, fantastic literature also began receiving the serious attention of academic critics, who have added their own fair share of critical monographs and reference materials, leaving the genre with a vast amount of coverage for its size. This bibliography is one small attempt to provide the librarian, researcher, and fan with a path through the labyrinthine maze of amateur and professional reference materials in the related fields of science fiction, fantasy, and horror.

Included herein are annotations for all the major (and most minor) SF reference volumes published through the fall of 1991, plus some items from 1992. The books are grouped in sections by type, then listed alphabetically by main entry. Each entry provides complete bibliographical data, a description of the book's organization, content, and purpose, and an evaluation of how well the author met his or her stated objective. Material enclosed in brackets in some entries indicates data that were not provided by the publisher but were supplied by the author (such as the editions in entry #40). I have tried in every instance to synthesize general critical reactions to the volumes covered, showing each book's weaknesses and strong points, with a balanced summation. I have rated or compared similar volumes when such comparison seems appropriate; and I have also provided suggested core collection lists for librarians and scholars at several different interest levels. The indexes at the end of this volume provide complete access to the individual monographs by author, title, and subject correlated to item number.

For the record, my own publications have been listed and evaluated (I hope objectively) with the rest; to exclude them, or those of any of my colleagues, would eliminate a significant percentage of the listings. The world of SF criticism is a small one indeed, involving no more than a few hundred individuals, most of them having some near or distant acquaintanceship with each other. No evaluation has been inflated or deflated based on my knowledge of the author. My sole purpose here has been to dissect these publications in such a way that their construction becomes obvious to all and then to provide some clear idea of how well each has met its objectives and how useful each may be to the librarian or scholar.

Readers may also wish to know something about the critical perspective I bring to this book. I believe that reference volumes should normally include certain apparatus. Except for those works which already consist of nothing but an author- and/or title-arranged data base, all books should be indexed, and I will invariably mention the absence of same. Bibliographies and literary guides should include paginations and other significant bibliographical data for both monographic and periodical works, and I will reduce my evaluation of any book which lacks them. I expect reference books to be well and consistently organized, with data obviously and conspicuously arranged and displayed so that even a casual user will be able to tell at a glance how the volume works and what it contains. I will not hesitate to point out these types of deficiencies. The overuse of abbreviations is the sure sign of an amateur at work, and I will criticize those works which employ them too frequently. I will also point out obvious physical deficiencies with the book, including faint printing, poor binding, and other substandard production values. I do not state or imply that there is only one way to organize data, for in fact there are as many ways to construct a reference volume as there are bibliographers and indexers; but if a work requires forty hours of classroom time before it can be used, then there are obvious (to me, at least) construction problems present. I regard my function here as a guide to the uninitiated, pointing out the obvious and not so obvious, the good points and the bad of each of the works evaluated, with occasional pithy comments tossed in to enliven the tour. I have tried to apply these same standards throughout this work—evenhandedly, fairly, consistently.

The primary sources for the books have been my own collection, which includes ninety-eight percent of the items annotated; the J. Lloyd Eaton Collection of Science Fiction and Fantasy Literature at the Tomás Rivera Library, University of California, Riverside; and the John M. Pfau Library at California State University, San Bernardino. My special thanks to Dr. George Edgar Slusser, Curator of the Eaton Collection at UCR; Arthur E. Nelson, Library Director at CSUSB through spring of 1988; Marty Bloomberg and Johnnie Ann Ralph, Acting Library Directors in 1988; and Dr. William Aguilar, University Librarian from 1989, for their generous accommodation. A tip of the hat also to Robert E. Briney and Edward Wood for their pioneering work *SF Bibliographies* (Chicago: Advent, 1972), which covers many early fan productions now virtually impossible to locate. Finally, thanks to Hal W. Hall of the Texas A&M University Libraries, who took the time to preview significant portions of the manuscript and who also provided last-minute photocopies of hard-to-locate pamphlets and books; his input made this a better book than it would have been otherwise. Also to Paul David Seldis, Mary A. Burgess, and Daryl F. Mallett, who independently proofread the final manuscript, and to Chickie Huizar, who obtained additional monographs on interlibrary loan.

My thanks also to the publishers who sent review copies of their books, particularly: The American Library Association, The Borgo Press, Carroll & Graf Publishers, Creatures at Large Press, Crossing Press, Drumm Books, Facts on File, Galactic Central Publications, Gale Research Co., Garland Publishing Co., Greenwood Press, Harper & Row, Haworth Press, Hypatia Press, Kent State University Press, Locus Press, McFarland Publishing Co., Meckler Publishing, Niekas Publications, Oryx Press, Salem Press, Scarecrow Press, Charles Scribner's Sons, SFBRI, Soft Books, Starmont House, and University of Iowa Press. Finally, my gratitude to Dr. Fran J. Polek, who gave me the opportunity to work on my first bibliography during my senior year at Gonzaga University; to Neil Barron, Fred Lerner, Daryl F. Mallett, Ted Taylor, and Marsh Tymn, for their assistance in locating specific items;

and to Buckley Barrett, Ned Brooks, Charlie Brown, Scott Burgess, Bill Contento, Lloyd Currey, Jack Dann, Barry Levin, Doug Menville, Bill Nolan, Mark Owings, and Leslie Kay Swigart, who have, over the years, always been willing to "talk shop." Thanks also to my long-suffering editor, Jim Rettig, of the Swem Library, College of William & Mary, who has conscientiously reviewed every part of this manuscript and provided many valuable suggestions; and to all the good people at Libraries Unlimited, particularly David V. Loertscher. Finally, my love to my wife, Mary, who lets me play with these things—when I should be doing something else!

Additions and corrections are welcome and should be sent to the author at P.O. Box 2845, San Bernardino, CA 92406.

—Michael Burgess
1992

HOW TO USE THIS BOOK

To locate a specific book, please check the title or author index and use the item number of the volume to locate it in the text. The monographs included herein are numbered consecutively throughout the entire book. Index references correlate to item numbers only. Specific books may also be found by broad type: all encyclopedias and dictionaries, for example, are located in one chapter, arranged alphabetically by main entry. Similarly, author bibliographies are grouped together into one section, organized by the name of the writer being covered. The subject index at the end of this book will give the reader still another access point.

Please note that material enclosed in brackets in bibliographic entries indicates data that were not provided by the publisher but were supplied by the author (such as the editions in entry #40).

ABBREVIATIONS

Assoc. = Associate

Ed. = Editor or edition

Eds. = Editors

Exp. = Expanded

Pbk. = Paperback

Rev. = Revised

SF = Science fiction

ENCYCLOPEDIAS AND DICTIONARIES

SCOPE NOTE: This chapter includes all those publications that call themselves encyclopedias of fantastic literature, plus dictionaries of critical or fan terminology. Character dictionaries are listed under the section of that name later in this book.

1. Ash, Brian, ed. **The Visual Encyclopedia of Science Fiction**. London & Sydney, Pan Books, 1977. 352 p. (pbk.). Also: New York, Harmony Books, 1977. 352 p. index. LC 77-7036. ISBN 0-517-53174-7; ISBN 0-517-53175-5 (pbk.). Also: London, Triune Books, 1978. 352 p. ISBN 0-85674-077-2.

A highly eclectic reference book masquerading as an encyclopedia, Ash's work jumps widely all over the literary landscape, although its organization is not quite as eccentric as might appear on the surface. The first section of the book, "Program," is a sixty-page timeline of science fiction, listing prominent books, authors, stories, magazines, awards, and fan events, in year-by-year order, with numerous mini-illustrations scattered throughout. Ash's chronology is unique in the SF field for its detail and extensive development. Part Two, "Thematics," is a series of nineteen ten-page articles, each focusing on a particular SF theme, such as "Spacecraft and Star Drives," "Galactic Empires," "Cities and Cultures," or "Religion and Myths," all apparently penned by Ash himself. Each of these essays is prefaced with an original 500-word introduction by a famous SF author, one per chapter; Ash then provides a popular history of the subgenre or theme, giving background material and touching on many different stories and novels and authors involved with the particular theme. Individual bibliographies (there is sometimes more than one in a particular chapter) focus on stories and novels employing the featured subject(s). The book is copiously illustrated throughout with magazine and paperback cover reproductions and drawings and photos of the authors, many in color. Also inserted into each chapter are such miscellanea as the timelines from the future histories developed by Poul Anderson and Robert A. Heinlein for their stories and novels in the section "Future and Alternative Histories."

Section Three, "Deep Probes," includes essays by three SF writers on "Interface," "Science Fiction as Literature," and "Recurrent Concepts." The fourth and last section, "Fandom and Media," focuses on fandom, SF art, SF cinema, SF magazines and comics, including lists of awards, a timeline of major SF films, and a brief checklist of SF anthologies (by editor). At the front of the book is a checklist of SF themes, keyed to page number; detailed separate author/title and artist indexes complete the work.

The Visual Encyclopedia is a fascinating book to browse through, filled with eye-catching illustrations, hundreds of details, and marvelous mini-vignettes by many of the field's best-known writers. As a reference work, however, it lacks obvious organizational keys for the casual or serious reader, skipping from theme to theme without any clear pattern. Also, the mini-bibliographies, while organizing hundreds of stories and novels by subject, nonetheless miss a great many works that could (or should) have been included; and because they are fragmented into dozens of examples scattered throughout several hundred pages of material, the biblios are useless except as very general guides to further reading. Ash never pretends otherwise, stating in his introduction: "There is something [here] for everyone." That's just the problem.

2. Davis, Richard, ed. **The Encyclopedia of Horror**. London, Octopus Books, 1981. 192 p. index. ISBN 0-7064-1507-8. Twickenham, England, Hamlyn, 1987. 192 p. ISBN 0-600-55359-0 (pbk.).

This companion volume to Holdstock's 1978 *Encyclopedia of Science Fiction* (see #5) is similar in organization and style to the earlier book. Contents: "Foreword," by Peter Cushing; "Introduction," by Richard Davis; "Evil Monsters," by Tom Hutchinson; "The Frankenstein Saga," by Michel Parry; "The Devil's Army," by Richard Cavendish; "Vampires & Werewolves," by Basil Copper; "The Supernatural," by Michael Ashley; "The Undead," by Richard Davis; "Travelling Beyond," by Douglas Hill; and "The Catalogue," by Richard Davis and Denis Gifford. As with Holdstock, this volume is actually a well-illustrated coffee-table history of weird and supernatural horror in literature and film. The quality and coverage of each subject vary widely from chapter to chapter, with more than half of the text consisting of black-and-white, tinted, or (occasionally) full-color reproductions of motion picture stills, drawings, and book and magazine covers. There are separate chronological lists of horror comic books and films at the end of the book; the film list also includes year of production, title, director, principal star(s), and distribution company (and country where produced); none of these lists are anywhere near comprehensive. The index references all persons and titles mentioned in the text, with very scanty subject access. Lightweight and forgettable.

3. Franson, Donald. **A Key to the Terminology of Science-Fiction Fandom**. Heiskell, Tenn., The National Fantasy Fan Federation, 1962. [17] p. (Fandbook, no. 1). (pbk.).

This brief mimeographed dictionary is designed to be used by the "neofan" ("new fan, usually only such for a few months") or the "faaan" ("fan who is interested more in fans and fandom than in stf" ["stf"=SF]) and includes, in addition to common fan terminology, acronyms and initialisms used by the major fan groups and conventions. The latter are now somewhat out-of-date, but many of the terms themselves remain in current use. An updated and expanded guide and study to the peculiar word usage of SF fandom is long overdue.

4. Gunn, James, ed. **The New Encyclopedia of Science Fiction**. New York, Viking, 1988. xix, 524 p. LC 87-40637. ISBN 0-670-81041-X.

With the prolonged delay in the preparation of a second, revised edition of the Nicholls/Clute *Encyclopedia* (see #7), Gunn's book was eagerly awaited by the science fiction world; unfortunately, it has generally received poor reviews, for reasons that become all too apparent upon close examination. Like Nicholls's, the book is arranged alphabetically by main entry, including science fiction writers and artists, plus individual entries on major SF films and magazines. Basic entries range in size from 100-1,500 words (averaging 400-500); interspersed throughout the text are an additional ninety-six mini-essays (ranging from 1,000-2,000 words in size) on somewhat broader topics (e.g., "Alien Worlds," "Children's Science Fiction," "Cyberpunk," "Scientists and Science Fiction," "Utopias and Dystopias," etc.). A typical author entry includes the name under which the author is best known, middle name or real name (if the main entry is a pseudonym), years of birth and death, nationality, a brief chronological evaluation of the writer's life and career (focusing on his or her works), plus selected "Other Works." The 250 film entries include: title, year of production, director, photographer, screenwriter, film musician, principal actors, running time, an indication whether the picture was made in color or black and white, plot summary, and significance. The general essays are usually chronological assessments of the particular topic, subgenre, or subject. The book is profusely illustrated throughout with author photographs, paperback and magazine cover illustrations, and movie and TV stills; there are also sixteen pages of color cover reproductions inserted into an unpaged signature at the center of the book.

Comparisons with Nicholls are inevitable. Although *The Science Fiction Encyclopedia* is not significantly longer than Gunn's work, it actually contains almost twice the text due to differences in layout and type size. Thus, while Gunn includes writers and films that have become prominent only in the 1980s (and that therefore are not in Nicholls), the latter actually has far more entries covering a much broader range of subjects and personages, including many peripheral figures of importance to the field. Entries in Gunn are also usually shorter than their Nicholls counterparts, particularly for lesser-known writers. For example, the essays on Raymond Z. Gallun and Daniel F. Galouye, neither of them household names, average in Gunn 100 words each, with evaluations of two books by Galouye and one story by Gallun (plus a barebones listing of five additional titles); in Nicholls, Gallun's entry is 300 words and Galouye's 400, with many more works evaluated, plus see references to other entries in which both writers are mentioned and a further reference in the Galouye essay to an interesting attack on "new wave" SF that he contributed to an important reference work. (Not all of this is Gunn's fault; reportedly, the publisher drastically cut the projected length of the book long after essay assignments had been made, forcing many last-minute parings of both text and entries.)

Both works use outside contributors, most of them acknowledged experts in the field, but Gunn relies on more than 100 such critics, while Nicholls uses just thirty-four; and even this figure is deceptive, because a large percentage of the entries in the latter were actually contributed by Nicholls and Clute, the editors, by John Brosnan (for films, often in collaboration with one of the principals), or by the two contributing editors, Malcolm Edwards and Brian Stableford—these five men account for 80-90% of the text in Nicholls, giving it overall a much stronger editorial focus. The lack of such guidance in Gunn's work becomes clearer when one examines typographical and textual errors, with which the book overflows in profusion, and the lack of cross- and see-also references (or index). One must also question some peculiar editorial standards for the inclusion and exclusion of specific personages and films—why, for example, if space was such an obvious problem, does the book provide so many entries on relatively worthless and unknown films while excluding such important figures as David G. Hartwell, a prominent book editor of the 1970s? *The New Encyclopedia* is better laid out, more attractive physically, and more current than its principal competitor, but in every other respect, Nicholls's work is by far the superior.

5. Holdstock, Robert, consultant ed. **Encyclopedia of Science Fiction**. London, Octopus Books, 1978. 219 p. ISBN 0-7064-0756-3.

A coffee-table picture book masquerading as an encyclopedia, this colorful British production includes thirteen chapters contributed by such well-known (mostly British) critics and SF writers as Brian Stableford, Patrick Moore, Mike Ashley, Alan Frank, Harry Harrison, and Christopher Priest, on the following topics: "Locations" ("a modern perspective of science fiction"), "Marriage of Science & Fiction," "Major Themes," "Pulps & Magazines," "Screen Trips," "Machine as Hero," "Alien Encounter," "Art & Artists," "Fiction to Fact," "Outer Limits," "New Wave," "Yesterday, Today & Tomorrow," and a "Catalog" section, which includes brief essays on collecting SF, fandom, SF pseudonyms, major awards, a table of SF magazines (title, dates of publication, number of issues published, general subject evaluation [e.g., "SF"=science fiction], including many foreign titles), a brief alphabetical table of major SF films (listing title, date, director, nationality), and a table listing the world science fiction conventions through the mid-1970s. None of these lists are in any way complete or comprehensive, and all are now very much outdated. A detailed author/title index completes the book.

The essays are popularly oriented and written and tend to jump from title to title and writer to writer without any evident guiding plan for the book as a whole. However, the volume is well designed and illustrated, filled with full- and partial-page color illustrations reproduced from book and magazine covers and cover paintings, plus a few color stills from prominent motion pictures. Light, fun, pretty, Holdstock's book is also utterly worthless as a reference tool.

See also the companion volume on horror (see #2).

6. Naha, Ed. **The Science Fictionary: An A-Z Guide to the World of SF Authors, Films, & TV Shows**. New York, Seaview Books, 1980. xii, 388 p. LC 80-5195. ISBN 0-87223-619-6. Also: New York, Wideview Books, 1981. xii, 388 p. LC 80-16748. ISBN 0-87223-629-3 (pbk.).

The Science Fictionary focuses primarily on SF films and television programs, with only marginal attention to science fiction authors and other topics. After brief introductions by Naha, the book is divided into four major sections: "Films," "Television," "Authors," and "Awards, Magazines, Themes." The first chapter, by far the longest in the volume (237 pages), is an alphabetical guide to the major and minor motion pictures of the genre. Each entry includes title, nationality (if other than U.S.), date, black-and-white or color format, running time, plot summary, and lists of the production crew and cast (other than those mentioned in the annotation). The essays range in size from 20-400 words, averaging 50-100, and tend to be light and breezy, focusing on plot rather than content. The second chapter adds fifty pages of similarly arranged material on fantastic television programs. In both of these sections, "science fiction" is loosely defined to include fantasy and horror productions, as well as classic "sci-fi" videos.

The "Authors" section is a sixty-page who's who of the field, arranged alphabetically by surname, including writers mainly identified with a strict definition of the SF genre. A typical entry provides name (including middle name), years of birth and death, brief biographical data (in some entries non-existent), plus a chronological account of the author's career which mentions major works, with years of publication and occasional one-sentence summations. The evaluations seem fair and "centrist" but provide little material that cannot be found in other, more complete reference sources. The final chapter includes lists of the Hugo and Nebula award winners through 1978; the Oscars awarded to SF films; a description of other awards presented in the field (but no mention of winners); an alphabetical guide to the major SF magazines, with brief histories giving lists of editors, numbers of issues published, years published, and other data; and a wholly useless list of twelve major science fictional themes, with fifty-word descriptions. The book is illustrated throughout with small black-and-white inset photographs and film stills. The absence of a title index makes access more difficult than it should have been.

The motion picture and television data are remarkably complete and concise, but the remaining sections appear to have been added almost as afterthoughts: the chapter on SF writers accounts for less than one-sixth of the entire text. Under such circumstances, one wonders why it was included at all.

7. Nicholls, Peter, ed., John Clute, assoc. ed. **The Encyclopedia of Science Fiction: An Illustrated A to Z**. London, Granada, 1979. 672 p. LC 80-480051. ISBN 0-246-11020-1. Also: London, Toronto, Panther Books, Granada, 1981. 672 p. ISBN 0-586-05380-8 (pbk.).

As: **The Science Fiction Encyclopedia**. Garden City, N.Y., Doubleday & Co., 1979. 672 p. LC 77-15167. ISBN 0-385-13000-7.

An encyclopedic dictionary in one volume, Nicholls and Clute's work is arranged alphabetically by main entry, with individual entries on major and minor authors, general themes, motion pictures, publishers, series, television and radio programs, original anthologies, comics, science fiction and fantasy in various countries, terminology, awards, fanzines and fandom, and miscellanea. Contributions were solicited from thirty-four critics (including the editors), many of them British; the great majority (more than 90%) of the entries, however, were written by the two editors and three other critics: John Brosnan, Malcolm Edwards, and Brian Stableford. The biographical entries, comprising the greater part of the text, typically include the person's name (in boldface), years of birth and death, a brief summary of the person's career (with minimal biographical material), and brief evaluations of his or her principal works and/or contribution to the field, with dates of publication of the former but no other publication data. Anyone who had written a book with fantastic content through the late 1970s is included, as are numerous writers prominent in the pulp era; also covered are the major foreign-language authors in the field, particularly those who have had at least one of their works translated into English; artists; film directors; major fans; and many other figures associated with the genre. The book is copiously illustrated with photographs, film stills, and reproductions of book and magazine covers. An acknowledgments page provides a brief bibliography of major sources.

The book includes an enormous amount of material on science fiction, virtually everything one would want to know in a quick-reference volume. Even comparatively minor writers receive generous 300- to 400-word entries evaluating their careers and major works and always mentioning any secondary sources in book form. Although the book lacks an index, this deficiency is partially exculpated through numerous see and see-also references embedded at the end of almost every entry. The *Encyclopedia* has been criticized for its slightly pro-British and pro-new wave slant, for its failure to include a comprehensive title index, and for disparities in the lengths of entries on certain authors. Despite these comparatively minor caveats, and the fact that it now needs revising (a new edition is reportedly underway for publication in 1992/93), Nicholls and Clute's book remains a thoroughly sound piece of work, outstanding in its conception and execution, the most comprehensive single-volume reference guide to science fiction and related fields, and certainly one of a handful of volumes that can truly be called "essential" to libraries and researchers everywhere. The original editions are out-of-print, but remaindered copies of the American reprint (which is identical internally to the British original) can still be obtained through Locus Press. Compare Gunn's *New Encyclopedia* (see #4).

8. Rovin, Jeff. **The Fantasy Almanac**. New York, E. P. Dutton, 1979. 312 p. LC 79-11757. ISBN 0-525-47600-8 (pbk.).

Another misnomer, Rovin's book is *not* an almanac (nor does it deal strictly with fantasy) but a dictionary of persons, events, places, and characters significant in the folklore, literature, comic books, television, films, and other media of the SF and fantasy genres. This poor man's version of *Brewer's Dictionary of Phrase and Fable* is arranged alphabetically by main entry. Each essay averages between 100-200 words and includes topic name, classification key (e.g., "FT"=Fairy Tale, "U"=Unexpected, etc.), description and background material (the bulk of the entry), and see references to related topics. The book also includes numerous black-and-white line drawings, a one-page "Key to Classifications," and a brief "Selected Bibliography." Some author entries are interfiled with the rest.

Rovin's annotations are straightforward, readable, and easy to digest, but he fails to cite any sources for his material (other than the general bibliography at the end of the book) and gives no indication anywhere in the book of the criteria used in selecting the entries—or why certain authors and their creations were intermingled with figures from classic Greek and Roman mythologies while other myths and authors remained untapped. The casual reader will thus find essays on Edgar Rice Burroughs, Ray Bradbury, Mr. Ed, Prince Ivan, Tribbles (cuddly critters from "Star Trek"), the Incredible Hulk, Batman, the *Galactica* (from the TV series "Battlestar Galactica"), Fu Manchu, Brigadoon, and Aphrodite, to cite but a few, all jumbled together into one alphabetical sequence. Why? Random records do not a reference work make.

9. Sullivan, Jack, ed. **The Penguin Encyclopedia of Horror and the Supernatural**. New York, A Promised Land Production, Viking, 1986. xxviii, 482 p. LC 85-40558. ISBN 0-670-80902-0.

This first attempt at a true encyclopedia of horror film and literature includes contributions from sixty-four major and minor critics and fiction writers. Contents: "Editor's Foreword" (by Sullivan); "How to Use This Book" (by Sullivan); "Contributors" (in alphabetical order, with brief bio squibs); [List of Major] "Essays"; Introduction: "The Art and Appeal of the Ghostly and Ghastly," by Jacques Barzun; the encyclopedia proper, with items arranged in alphabetical order by main entry; "Checklist of Film and Television Entries"; and "Illustration Credits and Acknowledgments." As with Gunn's *New Encyclopedia of Science Fiction* (see #4), the book includes three different types of entries: critical biographies (of authors, artists, film makers, etc.), motion pictures critiques, and major theme essays.

Biographical entries range in size from one short paragraph to several pages and typically include name (bold caps), middle names or real names (in parentheses), years of birth and death (where known), brief biographical data, an analysis of his or her writings or contributions to the horror genre, and a list of major "Works" (titles and years of first publication only); most essays focus on the person's contributions rather than his or her life. Film or television entries include title, year(s) of production, basic credits (names of the director, script writer, major actors, etc.), running time, whether produced in color or black-and-white, plus a summary of the picture's story line, and brief critique; film entries typically average two-to-three paragraphs in size. The fifty-four major essays cover such diverse topics as "Arkham House," "B Movies," "Ghosts," "Japanese Cinema," "Opera," "Sex," "Writers of Today" and vary from 1,000-8,000 words in length. Each entry in the book is signed with the contributor's initials. Internal see-also references in the articles to related topics are indicated by putting the [sur]name or film or subject referenced in all caps; the volume also includes a few see references throughout the main alphabetical sequence to authors or topics covered elsewhere—but no overall index. The book is attractively designed and illustrated with black-and-white photographs, stills, and drawings taken from a wide variety of sources.

Sullivan's work displays many of the same problems as Gunn's *New Encyclopedia* (see #4), most of them due to loose editorial control. Any reference work compiled from contributed entries must have strong, consistent direction from the top or it will inevitably fail in execution. Such failures become evident when one examines the small discrepancies in style and form that permeate both Gunn and Sullivan. For example, some entries in Sullivan record the middle or full names of their subjects while others do not, for no apparent reason—R. Chetwynd-Hayes's first name is readily known, as are Agatha Christie's middle and married names; J. Sheridan Le Fanu's first name [Joseph] is given, but not his second middle name; Theodore Sturgeon is *not* a pseudonym of Edward Hamilton Waldo but the legalized version of his stepfather's name—to cite but a few examples.

There is a greater difficulty, however, in the original editorial choice of entries and subjects. Several of the major essays, particularly "Writers of Today," are used as "dump" entries to cover large numbers of comparatively minor writers; see references to these writers are then made in the main alphabetical sequence (e.g., "McCAMMON, ROBERT R.: see WRITERS OF TODAY"). One may use this approach, but it inevitably results in questions concerning the placement of certain writers (for example, are Clive Barker or Dean R. Koontz, each of whom has one paragraph in "Writers of Today," really lesser writers [by any definition] than R. Chetwynd-Hayes, who has a four-paragraph entry in the main sequence?). As employed by Sullivan, this particular format is both badly and inconsistently applied. Michael McDowell and James Herbert, for example, are listed in *both* sections, the former with overlapping, single-paragraph articles that essentially duplicate each other; other writers very little known have short, single-paragraph entries in the main text no greater in length or treatment than the "lesser" authors covered in "Writers of Today." And the alphabetical see references do not really help the situation: the "Writers of Today" section is one of the longest in the book, exceeding 8,000 words; without an index, quick or easy access to the material in this essay is virtually impossible. Finally, there are great inconsistencies in coverage between, say, the authoritative articles on early supernatural writers contributed by Everett F. Bleiler (a well-known authority) and the detailed coverage by Kim Newman of such minor films as *The Howling* and *I Walked with a Zombie*, which receive three paragraphs each. This lack of editorial balance permeates the text.

Sullivan's book is better proofread than Gunn and lacks the latter's obvious typographical and textual errors; but as a reference book, it must be placed somewhere between the Isles of Mediocrity and Lackadaisia, a far lesser work than it should have been.

10. Tuck, Donald H. **The Encyclopedia of Science Fiction and Fantasy Through 1968: A Bibliographic Survey of the Fields of Science Fiction, Fantasy, and Weird Fiction Through 1968**. Chicago, Advent:Publishers, 1974-82. xxviii, 920 p. in 3 v. index. LC 73-91828. ISBN 0-911682-20-1 (v. 1); ISBN 0-911682-22-8 (v. 2); ISBN 0-911682-26-0 (v. 3). Previously published in shorter and somewhat different form as **A Handbook of Science Fiction and Fantasy**. Hobart, Tasmania, Tuck, 1954. 151 p. LC A55-3612 (pbk.). And: **A Handbook of Science Fiction and Fantasy: A Collection of Material Acting As a Bibliographical Survey to the Fields of Science Fiction and Fantasy (Including Weird), Covering the Magazines, Books, Pocket Books, Personalities, Etc., of These Fields up Through December 1957**. Hobart, Tasmania, Tuck, 1959. viii, 396 p. in 2 v. LC 60-40710 (pbk.).

Tuck's massive compilation had two previous self-published incarnations as oversized paperbound volumes, but since neither of these achieved much circulation and both were completely superseded by subsequent editions, they will be mentioned only in passing here. Volumes 1-2 of the *Encyclopedia* are an A-Z listing of the major and minor writers in the field and their works, incorporating all known monographs (and their writers) published in fantastic literature from 1945-1968, with selected works prior to that time. A typical entry includes the writer's name in bold caps, middle or real name(s), dates of birth and death (when known), a one- to three-paragraph biographical (when data are available) and critical summary, an annotated bibliography of the major books in alphabetical order by title (including all monographs published in the field between 1945-68), giving title in boldface type (e.g., "C"=collection), publisher, place of publication, year, pagination, stock number, original price, and similar data for all known reprint editions through 1968, plus foreign translations (with foreign-language titles), contents (if a collection or anthology) with original magazine publication data, and a one-sentence story summary (for novels). Anthologies and nonfiction books on fantastic literature appear in their own alphabetical sections after the listing of the author's fictional monographs. A comprehensive title/author index completes the two-volume who's who set.

Volume 3 contains five sections, the first of which covers the SF magazines, with a complete A-Z listing of all professional periodicals in the field, including many peripheral publications; a typical entry provides title, nationality, type (e.g., "weird"), number of issues published, dates, physical size, usual page count, usual price (with dates in effect), editor(s) (with time spans), publisher(s) (with time spans), frequency of issue (with time spans), major cover artists, a short critique and history, notable fiction published by the periodical (chronologically), a table of issues, dates, and volume numbers actually released (for long-running publications such as *Galaxy*), plus a summary of overseas editions by nationality.

The second section of Volume 3 is a guide to paperback publications in the genre through 1968, indexed first by author and title, giving publisher, stock number, year of publication, pagination, price, and type (e.g., "J"=Juvenile); second by publisher, giving publisher, place of publication, price codes, and a year-by-year summary of the publisher's paperback books (both trade and mass market) in order by stock number, author, and title; and third by title and author. The third part of Volume 3 lists pseudonymous authors, first by pseudonym and real name, then reversed. The fourth chapter, "Series, Connected Stories, and Sequels," lists references to the appropriate entries in Volumes 1-2 for books and an actual list of stories (with magazine title and dates of issues) in order of publication for short periodical series—all series listed also include the author's name. The final section includes miscellanea such as television series, major SF films, awards listings and histories, comic books, and related topics.

Tuck includes such an incredible amount of raw data that it is difficult to see how any serious researcher could work in the genre without having access to these volumes. One obvious problem with the books is currency: although the final volume was not published until 1982, the cut-off date for all material except death dates was 1968, making the set now more than two decades out-of-date and excluding much of importance in modern science fiction. Tuck promises in his introduction to provide supplements at five- or six-year intervals, but none has been forthcoming to date (or seem likely to appear). Another difficulty with the set is a certain "fuzziness" in focus, since much of the data were derived second-hand from Tuck's correspondents; one wonders whether certain of the books and authors included really belong in an encyclopedia of fantastic literature, by whatever definition one is using (and that vision of imaginative fiction is never articulated by Tuck anywhere in these volumes, leaving us to wonder whether he did, on occasion, throw in the proverbial kitchen sink). Yet, despite these minor carpings, most of the material *is* sound, well-organized, easy to use, and filled with prime research data; and there is no doubt whatever that these volumes are "must" purchases for academic institutions everywhere. Let us hope they are updated at regular intervals in the future.

11. Versins, Pierre. **Encyclopédie de l'Utopie, des Voyages Extraordinaires, et de la Science Fiction**. Lausanne, Switzerland, L'Age d'Homme, 1972. 997 p. LC 73-327497. Also: [Rev. ed.] Lausanne, Switzerland, L'Age d'Homme, 1984. 1,037 p. No ISBNs.

This French-language volume is the only foreign encyclopedia of science fiction and fantasy yet published, and, as might be expected, its coverage of European SF far surpasses that of any other one-volume source. Versins includes in one alphabetical sequence hundreds of biographies of major and minor figures in the field, as well as historical and critical articles on magazines, SF fandom, the history of SF, the subgenres, major fictional characters and some fictional places, countries, films, and other topics of interest. Personal surnames which are the subject of biographies are listed in all caps; real and imaginary places appear in boldface all caps; other topic heads run in small letters with initial capital letters only. The book is illustrated throughout with black-and-white cover reproductions, line drawings, and many old woodcuts, some of them full-page.

Versins covers a large number of writers, American and European, including many on whom very little information is available in the United States. The critiques range from 50-5,000 words in size, averaging 200-300, and typically include minimal biographical information (years of birth and death, plus one or two sentences of background data), with a focus on the writer's career, covering the major books (listed in boldface) in roughly chronological order. For minor writers, a list of additional titles is sometimes given at the end of the entry without critical comment.

The book is particularly strong in its coverage of seventeenth- through nineteenth-century fantastic literature, in its lists of major French science fiction publishing series, and in its critical evaluations of many writers whose works have never been translated into English. Versins shows no consistency, however, in his citations of English-language works, sometimes using the original titles but often citing only French translations of those titles without further reference. Since the original title is not always obvious, even to those fluent in French, he should, perhaps, have included the original appellation in parentheses when using French translations. The numerous antique illustrations are marvelous. The 1984 edition updates and corrects the original but adds no significant amount of new information. This wide-ranging reference work should grace the shelves of every major American university library. See also Gunn (#4) and Nicholls/Clute (#7).

12. Wolfe, Gary K. **Critical Terms for Science Fiction and Fantasy: A Glossary and Guide to Scholarship.** New York, Westport, Conn., Greenwood Press, 1986. xxxvi, 162 p. index. LC 86-3138. ISBN 0-313-22981-3.

This first true dictionary of fan and critical terms relating to fantastic literature is a carefully considered compilation and analysis of those words and phrases which have special meaning to the genre. Wolfe's lengthy introduction discusses the history of SF scholarship and the problems scholars have had in agreeing upon common definitions when discussing science fiction and fantasy literature. He then provides a comprehensive A-Z listing of the major terms used by fans and scholars, with copious see and see-also references. A bibliography and an index to the authors mentioned in the definitions complete the book. Most entries quote from or cite other published sources from the list of 218 works provided in the "Works Consulted" section at the end of the book. The roughly 700 terms range in size from 15-2,000 words in length (the longest covers "science fiction" itself), averaging 100 words, and are balanced, authoritative, and readable, although oriented toward the scholarly rather than the popular. Indeed, Wolfe's book is as much a guide to the development of SF scholarship in the 1980s as it is a dictionary of science-fiction terminology, and as such it should be read and consulted by any student of fantastic literature. By defining these terms, he helps define the genre itself. A most valuable and enlightening scholarly synthesis.

ATLASES AND GAZETTEERS

SCOPE NOTE: Included in this chapter are general atlases of fictional universes, map books of specific created worlds, and volumes which call themselves gazetteers of fantastic geography, general or specific. Character dictionaries are included in the section of that name later in this book.

13. Falconer, Lee N. **A Gazeteer [*sic*] of the Hyborian World of Conan, Including Also the World of Kull, and an Ethnogeographical Dictionary of Principal Peoples of the Era, with Reference to the Starmont Map of the Hyborian World**. West Linn, Ore., Starmont House, 1977. xiii, 119 p. LC 77-79065. ISBN 0-916732-19-3; ISBN 0-916732-01-0 (pbk.). Also: San Bernardino, Calif., The Borgo Press, 1980. xiii, 119 p. LC 80-19671. ISBN 0-89370-031-2.

Falconer, a pseudonym of popular SF author Julian May, provides a brief introduction explaining the difficulties of elucidating the geography of Robert E. Howard's invented mythos and details the history of previous attempts by fans to prepare maps of the Hyborian World (including her own separately published map for Starmont House). The main section of the book (102 pages) is an A-Z guide to the people, places, and kingdoms mentioned in the entire Conan and Kull sagas (through 1977), including the non-Howard contributions to the series. A typical entry includes a description of the place in one or more paragraphs (as paraphrased from Howard's writings), with occasional parenthetical remarks by May plus an indication at the end of the entry of the story/stories in which the name appears (cited in italics). The appendices provide a chronological checklist of the Conan and Kull stories, including the non-Howard novels; "Notes on Various Peoples of the Hyborian Age," by Robert E. Howard; "Notes on Hyborian Heraldry and Cartography"; and "Source Maps of the Hyborian World," with reproductions of previous attempts to map Howard's intricate fictional world (the separately published map by May herself is not included here, however).

This type of work has the same value (primarily entertainment) to the reader and researcher as the numerous character dictionaries included elsewhere in this volume; May's contribution is readable, tastefully and attractively designed, and could certainly be useful to the scholar interested in Howard's literature or in the development of series fiction by hands other than the original creator.

14. Fonstad, Karen Wynn. **The Atlas of Middle-Earth**. Boston, Houghton Mifflin Co., 1981. xiv, 208 p. index. LC 80-22132. ISBN 0-395-28665-4.

This was the first of Fonstad's atlases, and it set the pattern for all the rest. A general introduction provides background material on J. R. R. Tolkien's Middle-Earth, the created universe of *The Lord of the Rings* Trilogy, and includes a key to map symbols. Because Tolkien's world covers a timespan of many thousands of years, encompassing wholesale changes in the historical geography of Middle-Earth, Fonstad divides her coverage into several different periods corresponding with Tolkien's time-line of The First Age, The Second Age, and The Third Age. Following these three sections are additional chapters providing regional maps of Tolkien's fictional geography, maps dealing specifically with the events chronicled in *The Hobbit* and *The Lord of the Rings*, and thematic maps (population, climate, languages, etc.). End matter includes an appendix listing major mountain chains, river systems, inland lakes and other bodies of water, and major political divisions; "Notes" providing the sources of quotations and other data included in the main text; "Selected References"; and an "Index of Place Names," giving name, map coordinates, and page number(s) (primary page number references are shown in italics, and site maps are underlined).

Each chapter of the atlas includes a general introduction giving background historical and geographical data and is then subdivided into several sections (ranging from 5-31 in number), each corresponding to major events or characters or places in Tolkien's world. These subchapters typically include one to three pages of background textual material accompanied by an illustrative map or maps occupying one-half to four pages. The descriptive material is taken directly from Tolkien's writings, including many quotations straight from the master's pen; all such citations are footnoted, with exact page references being given in the notes section at the end of the book. The maps themselves are carefully and exquisitely rendered (and attractively reproduced) in black and brown ink.

A superbly researched and excellently drawn volume, Fonstad's book will be of equal interest both to the Tolkien fan and the serious researcher, providing a very careful synthesis of the entire Tolkien corpus through *The Silmarillion*. See also the Strachey atlas, *Journeys of Frodo* (#20).

15. Fonstad, Karen Wynn. **The Atlas of Pern**. New York, A Del Rey Book, Ballantine Books, 1984. xvii, 169 p. index. LC 84-6511. ISBN 0-345-31432-8; ISBN 0-345-31434-4 (pbk.). Also: London, Corgi Books, 1985. xvii, 169 p. ISBN 0-552-99148-1 (pbk.).

The second in this series of guides to major science fiction and fantasy worlds focuses on Anne McCaffrey's Dragonriders of Pern series. Following a general introduction to the geography of the world Pern as described in McCaffrey's series of books, Fonstad includes three different types of maps: detailed regional maps of those parts of Pern articulated by McCaffrey in her novels; a novel-by-novel chronology and geography, with each locale, "hold," and set of buildings mapped in great detail (again, based on descriptions from the series); and finally, a set of thematic maps, including a depiction of Pern's eccentric orbital path, climates and ocean currents, land use and occupation, and population density. Each map is accompanied by descriptive text based around (and frequently quoting from) McCaffrey's original prose. Completing the book are notes referencing these descriptions to appropriate passages in the original novels by volume and page number; a selected bibliography; and an index of place names coordinated to page numbers of the maps in question, with latitude and longitude.

The maps are well drawn, clear, and distinctly reproduced in black and brown ink, with easy-to-follow keys and guides. Any fan of McCaffrey's series, or researcher into her fiction, will want this well-researched and executed atlas.

16. Fonstad, Karen Wynn. **The Atlas of the DRAGONLANCE™ World**. Lake Geneva, Wis., and Cambridge, England, TSR, Inc., 1987. xx, 168 p. index. LC 86-51273. ISBN 0-88038-448-4 (pbk.).

The fourth of Fonstad's atlases pictures the proprietary universe of DRAGON-LANCE™, a series of interactive games and separately published novels developed by the staff of TSR, Inc. Contents: "Introduction" (including map key); "The South"; "The East"; "The West"; "The North"; "Paths and Battles"; "Thematic Maps" (i.e., climate, population, etc.); "Footnotes"; "References"; "Index of Place Names." Each chapter includes a general introduction plus additional chapters on places of interest in those regions. A typical entry includes one to two pages of descriptive text, including numerous quotations from DRAGONLANCE™ games and literature, and one or more maps illustrating structures, cities, or locales. Quotations are cited in the "Footnotes" section at the end of the book. The maps are clearly reproduced in blue, black, and reddish brown ink. The index correlates place names with page numbers and map coordinates; site map page references are underlined, primary locations are listed in italics.

The potential audience for this atlas is much more limited than with Fonstad's previous three books due to the proprietary nature of this series; as usual, however, her research is impeccable and her draftsmanship clear, competent, and straightforward. Recommended.

17. Fonstad, Karen Wynn. **The Atlas of the Land**. New York, A Del Rey Book, Ballantine Books, 1985. xix, 201 p. index. LC 85-6203. ISBN 0-345-31431-X; ISBN 0-345-31433-6 (pbk.).

The third in Fonstad's map guides to science fiction and fantasy universes is arranged much like its companions. A general introduction describes the map keys and symbols and gives some background material on Stephen R. Donaldson's *Chronicles of Thomas Covenant the Unbeliever*. The book follows Thomas's journeys into the Land by dividing its geography into four roughly equal quarters and then detailing the sites described in the two three-volume sets of *Chronicles* (Covenant's two journeys to the Land are separated by thousands of years of relative time; however, the geography changes little over the eons). Accompanying each map are descriptive paragraphs quoted or paraphrased directly from Donaldson's novels, with footnotes. End matter includes a detailed chronology of both series, a section referencing the notes to Donaldson's books, a selected bibliography, and an index of place names keyed to the page number of the specific map with coordinate numbers to find the locale.

The maps are attractively printed in black and brown ink, the drawings legibly produced, and the entire volume easy to read and follow, with clearly indicated guidelines. Fonstad's books have little general reference value, but this atlas will appeal to fans of Donaldson's work and to scholars interested in the development of his fiction.

18. Manguel, Alberto, and Gianni Guadalupi. **The Dictionary of Imaginary Places**. New York, Macmillan Publishing Co., 1980. 438 p. index. LC 80-11128. ISBN 0-02-579310-1. Also: Expanded ed. San Diego, New York, A Harvest/HBJ Book, Harcourt Brace Jovanovich, 1987. 454 p. LC 86-26063. ISBN 0-15-626054-9 (pbk.). Also: London, Granada, 1981. 438 p. ISBN 0-246-11560-2. Illustrated by Graham Greenfield, maps and charts by James Cook.

This *Baedecker* of imaginary geography includes in one A-Z listing a selection of invented cities, countries, volcanoes, islands, deserts, and other places located in a wholly fictitious geographical setting. Excluded are fictional depictions of Heaven or Hell, places with a future setting, or locales which are "disguises" for existing real-life places, such as Proust's Balbec or Hardy's Wessex. A typical entry includes place name (in bold caps) and description and history (ranging in size from 50-3,000 words, averaging 200-400), with background data paraphrased from the text of the original works, which are cited by author, title, publisher, and date at the end of each annotation. A comprehensive author/title index completes the book; each author listing also includes (in all caps) a list of the geographical entries included in the *Dictionary*, referenced by book title. The expanded edition inserts an eleven-page A-Z addendum of newly-discovered fictional locales after the main text, plus a two-page separate author/title index for these entries after the main index, but is otherwise identical to the original (in fact, the text does not vary through the first 424 pages). The book is beautifully illustrated throughout with original maps and line drawings, some full-page, and is very attractively designed and printed.

One major source cited by these European authors is Versins's *Encyclopédie de l'Utopie, des Voyages Extraordinaires, et de la Science Fiction* (see #11), the use of which results in a number of entries referencing older, rather obscure (to U.S. readers) Continental works of imaginative literature, many of which have never been translated into English. And while all the standard fantasy classics are included (Tolkien is well represented here, as are the works of Edgar Rice Burroughs, Richard Adams, E. R. Eddison, Ursula K. Le Guin, and others), one might still have wished for a more catholic selection, or even for a more thorough coverage of the geographies actually included. Where, for example, is The Commonwealth of John Myers Myers's *Silverlock* or the later (or earlier) history of Leonard Wibberley's Duchy of Grand Fenwick (only two of the five "Mouse" books are cited here), or the land of Zimiamvia (there are ten geographical entries from E. R. Eddison's fantasy world, but not the place itself), or Hentzau from Anthony Hope's *The Prisoner of Zenda* and *Rupert of Hentzau* (only two entries are included for these books)? The text as presented is well written and illustrated, but one is struck by how much more could have legitimately been included (by the authors' own definitions) from modern fantasy literature, and by how many of the existing entries could have been omitted from an American edition without the reader or researcher ever missing them.

19. Post, J. B. **An Atlas of Fantasy.** Baltimore, Md., The Mirage Press, 1973. xi, 283 p. LC 73-75640. ISBN 0-88358-108-6; ISBN 0-88358-011-X (pbk.). Also: Rev. ed. New York, Ballantine Books, 1979. xiv, 210 p. index. LC 79-63506. ISBN 0-345-27399-0 (pbk.). Also: London, Souvenir Press, 1979. xiv, 210 p. index. ISBN 0-285-62424-5 (pbk.).

Jeremiah Post, former Map Librarian at the Free Library of Philadelphia, compiled this volume as a labor of love, collecting over a hundred maps of imaginary and invented lands dating from a map of Eden devised in the year 776 and continuing through the medieval Utopia to the modern fantasy worlds of Stephen R. Donaldson, Katherine Kurtz, and Anne McCaffrey. The original volume is 8.5" x 11" in size, the revised edition a more workable 11" x 8.5" (i.e., lying on its side), reducing the size of some maps in the latter by as much as a third (others, however, remain unchanged). A typical entry in both books places the map on the right-hand page and a description of the place, author, artist, on the facing left-hand page. Some maps in the original edition were dropped or reshot from clearer copies in the Ballantine version and a handful of newer maps added. The latter also has a very useful index of artists not included in the first edition. It's worth noting that some of the maps included represent authors and books not usually associated with fantasy or science fiction, particularly Raintree County, from Ross Lockridge's book of the same name, and Jefferson and Yoknapatawpha Counties, Mississippi, from the works of William Faulkner.

While Post makes no claim of having compiled a *complete* atlas of fantasy lands, this is an attractive, well-presented, and entertaining guide to some of the more interesting iconographies of fantastic literature. An expanded, updated edition covering some of the newer fantasy writers and their created worlds would be greatly appreciated.

20. Strachey, Barbara. **Journeys of Frodo: An Atlas of J. R. R. Tolkien's The Lord of the Rings.** London, Boston, George Allen & Unwin, 1981. [110] p. ISBN 0-04-912016-6; ISBN 0-04-912011-5 (pbk.). Also: New York, Ballantine Books, 1981. [110] p. LC 80-70523. ISBN 0-345-29723-7; ISBN 0-345-29633-8 (pbk.).

A straightforward series of fifty-one maps in 7.5" x 9.5" format, the first of which gives an overview of Middle-Earth based upon the maps originally drawn by J. R. R. Tolkien for his fantasy trilogy, the rest taking the reader on a step-by-step journey through various parts of the land as Frodo and his companions make their epic journey from Hobbiton. Each map is reproduced in black and red and faces a page of descriptive text by Strachey, who cites specific chapters from Tolkien's novels as authorities. Unlike the Fonstad volumes, which take a more systematic approach to the fantasy worlds they depict, this volume is less a reference work than a traveler's guide to Middle-Earth, designed to be used with a reading of Tolkien's popular novels. However, it should be noted that Fonstad's atlas of Middle-Earth (see #14) is much more detailed and thus much more useful to the scholar.

CATALOGING GUIDES

21. Burgess, Michael. **A Guide to Science Fiction & Fantasy in the Library of Congress Classification Scheme**. San Bernardino, Calif., The Borgo Press, 1984. 86 p. index. (The Borgo Reference Library, Vol. 8). LC 80-11418. ISBN 0-89370-807-0; ISBN 0-89370-907-7 (spiral-bound pbk.). **A Guide to Science Fiction and Fantasy in the Library of Congress Classification Scheme**. 2nd ed. San Bernardino, Calif., The Borgo Press, 1988. 168 p. index. (Borgo Cataloging Guides, No. 1). LC 87-6308. ISBN 0-89370-827-5; ISBN 0-89370-927-1 (pbk.).

A professional university cataloger, Burgess prepared these guides for librarians using the Library of Congress classification scheme to catalog SF books and materials, for students seeking to know more about the way the LC classification arranges books, and for researchers examining the development of subject specialties in the SF genre. Some familiarity with cataloging theory and practice is presumed, particularly in the first edition.

Contents (first edition): "Subject Headings," "Author Main Entries and Literature Numbers," "Artist Main Entry and Artist Numbers," "Motion Picture Main Entries and Classification Numbers," "Subject Classification Numbers," "Index to Subject Classification Numbers." Bibliography numbers are included for those authors who have them. The second edition adds these additional chapters: "LC Literature Tables," "Television and Radio Program Main Entries and Classification Numbers," "Comic Strip Main Entries and Classification Numbers," "About the Author"—in addition to expanding and revising those previously included.

In the first edition, Burgess tried to anticipate some of the changes wrought by the adoption of the second edition of the *Anglo-American Cataloging Rules* (AACR2), with mixed results, since some were never actually implemented by LC. This first edition also fails to include sufficient see references from pseudonyms to the main entries established by the Library of Congress and is clearly designed for the technician, limiting its usefulness for the casual user.

The second edition was extensively revised to make it more accessible to non-professionals. In addition to doubling the size of the author base, with the inclusion of many more see and see-also references, Burgess also added extensive introductions to each section to better explain LC usage and practice, literature tables to demonstrate how author numbers are generated, plus several new sections. He also closely examined the changes in name forms resulting from LC's adoption of AACR2 in 1980 and returned all other main entries to the forms used prior to AACR2 until (and if) new versions are actually generated by the Library of Congress. The result is a current, accurate rendition of modern LC cataloging practice as it relates to fantastic literature in all its complexities and contradictions, but with sufficient explanations to make it useful not only to the professional but also to the serious fan and researcher.

22. Cameron, Alistair. **Fantasy Classification System**. St. Vital, Canada, Canadian Science Fiction Association, 1952. 52 p. index. LC 53-33139 (pbk.).
Cameron uses a decimal-based cataloging scheme to classify fiction, particularly short stories, by theme. Following an introduction in which he defines fantasy literature and elucidates his cataloging theory, the author outlines his classification system, then expands upon it in much greater detail. Concluding sections cover "The Literary Information Profile," and profiles for "Single Stories," "Collections and Anthologies," and "Non-Fiction";

"Using the Classification Scheme"; "Examples of Classification"; "Index to Classification Numbers" (by subject and number); and "Some Remarks on Indexing." The schematic is really an attempt to define and analyze fantastic literature in all its myriad forms in very great detail and as such will certainly be of interest to those scholars interested in the theory of science fiction and fantasy. But it is clear from the examples he provides that Cameron's classification scheme fails in any practical demonstration, producing very long, cumbersome numbers that could never actually be used to organize a collection of monographs. Thus, as with Lerner (see #23), Cameron's system at best remains an interesting intellectual curiosity.

23. Lerner, Fred. **"The Cataloging and Classification of Science Fiction Collections,"** in *Science/Fiction Collections: Fantasy, Supernatural, & Weird Tales*, ed. by Hal W. Hall. New York, The Haworth Press, 1983, p. 151-170.

Although Hall's book is covered elsewhere in this book (see #106), Lerner's article has been extracted because it is the only known development of a classification scheme specifically designed for science fiction and fantasy literature and for the many nonfiction books published about these genres. Lerner, a well-known academic librarian, first discusses existing classification schemes, particularly the Dewey Decimal and the Library of Congress systems (as well as Cameron's book, listed above), and how they treat literature in general and SF in particular. His essay, though brief, is thorough and illuminating, clearly indicating the difficulties of housing an SF collection intermingled with other literatures. He then proceeds to extrapolate an LC-based classification scheme, the "PX" class, "Fantastic Litera-ture" (PX is currently unused by the Library of Congress), specifically to arrange a large science fiction and fantasy collection. His development is logical, elegant, and thorough, employing a typical LC literature arrangement, with applications and subsidiary tables designed to handle the peculiarities of the genre, plus plenty of room for expansion. While it seems unlikely that any library will actually employ Lerner's scheme, the fact that it exists is testimony in itself to the field's growth and to the serious interest many academics are now devoting to its study.

YEARBOOKS, ANNUALS, AND ALMANACS

SCOPE NOTE: This chapter includes literary annuals, yearbooks, and annual almanacs. Excluded are annual periodical indexes (listed in the "Periodical Indexes" section) and barebones annual bibliographies of the literature (these can be found in the "General Bibliographies" chapter). Descriptions are based on the latest years published.

24. Brown, Charles N., and William G. Contento, eds. **Science Fiction, Fantasy, & Horror: A Comprehensive Bibliography of Books and Short Fiction Published in the English Language**. Oakland, Calif., Locus Press, 1984-DATE. Annual. index. LC 88-645572. ISSN 0898-4077. (The first *published* volume in the series was called **Science Fiction in Print: 1985**).

Charlie Brown, publisher and editor of *Locus*, the standard monthly news magazine of the SF field, has joined with William Contento, author of the standard guides to stories published in SF anthologies (see #117), to develop the first true literary annual of English-language fantastic literature. Initiating the series with the 1985 annual (published in 1986), Brown and Contento have continued to add subsequent volumes at regular intervals and have also released a retrospective volume for 1984 (published in 1990—however, no further annuals prior to that date are currently planned).

The editors have attempted to compile a complete descriptive (and partially annotated) book and periodical bibliography for each calendar year, plus additional features on topics of interest to the fan, professional, and researcher. Typical contents include (1988 annual) "Preface," by William G. Contento; "Author List: Books"; "Title List: Books"; "Author List: Stories"; "Title List: Stories"; "Contents List: Books [and] Magazines"; "Research Index," by Hal W. Hall, including "Subject List" and "Author List"; Appendices: "Book Summary," by Charles N. Brown; "Magazine Summary," by Charles N. Brown; "Cinema Summary," by Frank M. Robinson; "1988 Review," by Ed Bryant; "U.K. Year in S.F.," by Phil Stephensen-Payne; "Recommended Reading," by Charles N. Brown, Faren Miller, Tom Whitmore, Carolyn Cushman, Dan Chow, and Mark Kelly; "Awards," by Harlan McGhan; "Publisher Addresses"; and "Abbreviations."

Much of the bibliographical data is taken from monthly listings in *Locus* (with corrections and emendations), but many of the summaries (and the secondary source bibliography) are original. The primary "Books" section is listed alphabetically by author or editor; a typical entry includes author (all caps), series and title (boldface), publisher, ISBN number, month and year of date first seen (plus similar data for actual publication date, if different, in brackets), price, pagination, format (e.g., "pb"=paperback), reprint/reissue information (with mention of publisher and year of first edition), book type (e.g., anthology, novel, original anthology, etc.), brief annotation (usually one sentence), additional series information and/or data on related editions or books. Books are listed under the pseudonyms which appear on the title pages, but Brown and Contento have included see-also references from known pennames to others used by the same author.

Similarly, short stories published in magazines or books are listed alphabetically by author's name, with a typical entry including name (all caps), title (regular type), format abbreviation (e.g., "ss"=short story), source (i.e., the earliest known publication of the piece if this appearance is not original, with title of original anthology or magazine in which it appeared, plus publication date), magazine abbreviation (e.g., "F&SF"=*The Magazine of*

Fantasy & Science Fiction) or book title (for collections and anthologies, in boldface), and date of publication. Anthology entries also include editor and publisher in addition to year of publication. The title indexes correlate titles and authors only. The "Book Contents" section provides complete contents of story collections and anthologies, with editor (all caps), title (boldface type), bibliographical data, and a list of the stories as they appear in the book, including beginning page numbers for each item included, and title and author. The "Magazine Contents" chapter provides similar data for each magazine issue published throughout the year, arranged by periodical title (italics), then by volume and issue number and date, with editor's name, publisher, price, pagination, format (e.g., "pb"=paperbound), and a complete contents listing, arranged by page number, with title and author.

Hall's research index (beginning with the 1988 book), a continuation of his *Science Fiction and Fantasy Reference/Research Index* (see #93), includes all known essays, indexes, bibliographies, and monographs published throughout the world relating to the study of fantastic literature. The first part of this section is arranged by subject, author, and title, with complete bibliographical data; the second part rearranges the same data by author. The appendices provide statistical tables, lists of awards, reading lists, and other material of interest.

These books are well designed and presented, attractively and legibly typeset in an 8.5" x 11" double-column format, and bound in sturdy library cloth editions. The 1988 edition includes 471 pages of closely packed data. While the bibliographies are not 100% complete, they include the vast majority of fictional publications actually released each year, missing only very peripheral or minor items; and the addition of Hall's secondary source lists in the newer annuals will provide a valuable adjunct for researchers in the genre. Brown and Contento's series is rapidly and justifiably becoming a standard part of any SF reference shelf. Highly recommended.

25. Collins, Robert A., and Robert Latham, eds. **Science Fiction & Fantasy Book Review Annual**. Westport, Conn. & London, Meckler, 1988-1989. Annual. index. LC 89-642022. ISSN 1040-192X. New York and London, Greenwood Press, 1990-DATE.

When *Fantasy Review*, then the leading SF review magazine in the field, ceased publication in the summer of 1987, its editors, Collins and Latham, reincarnated its essence in this annual series of literary guides to the primary and secondary literature of science fiction and fantasy. The first of these books, published in 1988, covers the year 1987; the second volume (with 1988 reviews) did not appear until 1990, and a third annual was published by Greenwood at the end of 1991.

SF&FBRA is both similar and dissimilar to its ancestral periodical. The first edition includes the following introductory sections: "Author of the Year: Orson Scott Card," by Mark Van Name; "The Year in Fantasy," by Charles de Lint (with "Recommended Reading List"); "The Year in Horror Literature," by Michael Morrison (with "Recommended Reading List"); "The Year in Science Fiction," by Michael Levy (with "Recommended Reading List"); "The Year's Research & Criticism," by Neil Barron (with "Bibliography"); and "Award Winners in 1987." These general survey essays summarize the literary highpoints of the year, covering both monographs and short fiction, as well as publishing, magazines, and the specialty press, with suggested readings lists of the best fiction of the year. Neil Barron's learned but dispiteous analysis of the major critical works published in 1987 includes some material not covered in the review section, plus a bibliographical checklist of the works (including author, title, publisher, pagination, price, and ISBN number); unfortunately, the number "9" was transcribed by the typesetting program as "6" throughout his bibliography in Volume One, making hash of the data.

The bulk of the 1988 volume, "Reviews of 1987 Books," is broken into three sections: "I. Fiction"; "II. Young Adult Fiction"; "III. Non-fiction." Each of these is arranged alphabetically by author, then by title. A typical entry includes author (boldface), title (italics), publisher, place of publication, month and year of publication, pagination, price, ISBN number, and a contributed review. The reviews themselves range in size from 100-1,000 words, averaging about 300. Reviewers include both well-known and unknown critics, academics, professionals, and fans, and the quality of the material varies widely, as might be expected. Generally, about half of a typical entry summarizes the plot or content of the book, with a paragraph or two of analysis and summary, including mention of related books or authors. Most are at least readable; the best provide flashes of literary insight into the author and his work. The title index correlates title, author, and page number(s) for every book and film title mentioned in the volume (including those buried in the introductory essays and those mentioned in passing in the bodies of each review), providing comprehensive access to the casual reader.

In their general introduction, the editors acknowledge some gaps in coverage, but the great majority of noteworthy SF titles published in 1987 are reviewed in this nearly 500-page volume. The book is attractively designed and typeset, well bound in a library cloth edition, and is exceptionally easy to read and use (save for the glitches in Barron's article). Although *SF&FBRA*'s overall impact and its value to SF scholarship remain to be seen, the first three annuals have at least provided a promising beginning.

26. Lester, Colin, ed. **The International Science Fiction Yearbook 1979**. London, Pierrot Publishing; New York, Quick Fox, 1978. 394 p. ISSN 0143-1390. ISBN 0-905310-16-0 (pbk.).

The first volume in what was intended to be an annual series includes a large amount of rather dated material arranged very peculiarly. Contents include "How to Use the Book"; 1. "Introduction"; 2. "The Year in Fantasy Fiction"; 3. "New Works, New Worlds: A Survey of SF in Latin America"; 4. "The State of the Art in Determining & Delimiting SF"; 5. "Obituaries"; 6. "Book Publishing"; 7. "Magazines"; 8. "Organizations"; 9. "Fanzines"; 10. "Agents"; 11. "Anthologies"; 12. "Criticism, Commentary, Bibliography"; 13. "Translators"; 14. "Libraries"; 15. "Book Clubs"; 16. "Booksellers"; 17. "Pseudonyms"; 18. "Conferences & Workshops"; 19. "Conventions"; 20. "Awards"; 21. "Artists"; 22. "Films"; 23. "TV"; 24. "Radio & Drama"; 25. "Music & Recordings"; 26. "APA's"; 27. "Miscellaneous Services"; 28. "Name-Interests" [summaries of critical and associational material available on six major names' in the field—e.g., Robert E. Howard]; 29. "Fringe Interests."

Lester compiled a huge amount of data for this book, derived both from direct-mail questionnaires and a network of correspondents worldwide; the coverage is international, although a great many of the listings perforce reflect English-language sources and publications. Many chapters include a descriptive introduction, then an alphabetical arrangement of the data. Much of the information is presented in abbreviated form, keyed to boldfaced numbers buried in each paragraph, with the description of the key located after the textual material at the beginning of each chapter. The presentation is unnecessarily confusing and frequently difficult to elucidate, even for the experienced researcher: the text often seems to run together on the page, and one must constantly flip back and forth to decipher each entry. Also, the choice of a double-column format with no running page heads is particularly unfortunate in this type of publication, as is the utter absence of an index (which was not, however, the fault of the compiler; Lester prepared a comprehensive index rejected by the publisher). These major design flaws, plus the absence of any bibliographical details, and the fact that much of the material was originally oriented toward fans (and is now wholly out-of-date), render this work almost useless a decade after the fact.

27. Stewart, Elke, and Alan Stewart, eds. **The SF Yearbook 1976**. London, BSFA Ltd., 1976. 57 p. (pbk.).

This very amateurish chapbook from the British Science Fiction Association summarizes happenings in the SF world (with particular attention to UK events) during the calendar year 1975. Contents: "Foreword," by Kenneth Bulmer; "Introduction," by Alan Stewart. Articles: "Books in 1975," by Philip Stephensen-Payne; "Magazines in 1975," by David Ross; "Films in 1975," by Andrew Tidmarsh; "Television in 1975," by Graham Poole; "Fandom," by Elke Stewart; "Writing SF," by David Penny (essay); "Story of a Group," by Sonya Porter. Reference: "Awards of 1975"; "Publications"; "Booksellers"; "Publishers"; "Clubs and Groups"; "Past Conventions"; "Future Conventions." Artwork: Front Cover by Andrew Stephenson; Back Cover by David "Shep" Kirkbride. This pamphlet was clearly intended for fans and contains very little of library interest—and much of that is outdated. The book is shot from photo-reduced (and often hard-to-read) typed copy and is saddle-stitched in plain (flimsy) paper covers. There is nothing here that can't be found elsewhere.

ANNUAL DIRECTORIES

SCOPE NOTE: Included herein are the annual membership directories of professional and fan societies. Descriptions are based on the latest years published.

28. Hopkins, Harry, and Mariane S. Hopkins, eds. **Fandom Directory**. Various cities [currently Springfield, Va.], Fandata Publications, 1979-DATE. Annual. ISSN 8756-8349.

Published annually since 1979, the *Directory* was originally edited by Harry Hopkins then jointly edited with his wife, Mariane, and then edited solely by Harry. Contents (of No. 11, 1989-1990 Edition): "Foreword"; "Status & Interest Codes"; "Geographic Distribution"; "Contributing Artist Credits"; "Fan Publications Index"; "Convention Index"; "Fan Club Listing"; "Research Libraries of Interest to Fandom"; "Retail Stores Index"; "Alphabetical Listing"; "Last Minute Additions"; "Artists' Gallery"; "Zip Code Listing"; "Advertising Rates"; "Classified Advertisements"; "Artwork Contest Information"; "Fandom Directory Order Form"; "International Fan Location Service"; "Fandom Directory Data Form"; "Index to Advertisers"; "Customer Response Forms."

Major features include a current alphabetical list of SF fan magazines (fanzines), giving title, type of contents (e.g., "Star Trek fiction and humor"), frequency, price, publisher, and address; conventions announced for the year by date, with dates, title, featured programming, sponsor, address, and telephone number; an alphabetical directory of fan clubs with name, interests, frequency of meeting, publications, organization name or coordinator, and address; major research libraries arranged by state then alphabetically by institution name, with a description of holdings, date of survey (e.g., "6/85"=June, 1985), contact person or curator, address, and phone number; an index of retail stores selling materials of interest in SF, comics, and related fields arranged by state then alphabetically by store name, with name, address, and phone number; an alphabetical index to all persons and organizations mentioned including interested fans who have submitted data sheets on themselves, giving name (personal or institutional or society), state, and zip code (to find more information, one must look in the zip code directory); a zip code index arranged by state and then by zip code number listing name, address, city, state, zip code and phone number (for about two-thirds of the addresses), and codes giving status (e.g., "D"=Mail Order Retailer) and interests (e.g., "FK"=filking). Canadian listings follow the United States directory by province and postal code; fans living in other foreign countries are listed following the Canadian directory, in alphabetical order by country, then alphabetically by main entry. The directory also includes a portfolio of fan art selected from pieces submitted by budding artists in the field; prizes are awarded by a panel of five judges to the best of the lot.

The *Fandom Directory* is particularly useful as a very current guide to fan publications, conventions, and groups; librarians and researchers may also find the retail store and library collection directories helpful for bibliographical control and interlibrary loan purposes.

29. Horror Writers of America Membership Directory. Eugene, Ore., Horror Writers of America, 1986-DATE. Annual.

HWA is a relatively new organization, having been founded in 1986 by Dean R. Koontz and others, and its annual directory of members is somewhat less formal than those of its rival organizations, consisting of stapled 8.5" x 11" sheets. The approximately 330 members are arranged alphabetically by surname, international members being located in a small separate alphabetical section at the end of the list. A typical entry includes name, address, phone number, and status (e.g., "AC"=active) only. With the expansion of the horror field into a separate paperback genre in the 1980s, HWA has rapidly increased its membership over the last few years and seems destined to grow even further. The directory is restricted to members only, and membership qualifications are currently much more stringent than for many other writers' organizations, including SFFWA. Researchers should note that there is very little overlap between the membership of this organization and Science Fiction and Fantasy Writers of America (see #32).

30. International Association for the Fantastic in the Arts Membership Directory. Boca Raton, Fla., International Association for the Fantastic in the Arts, 1986?-DATE. Annual.

This rival organization to the Science Fiction Research Association (see #31) was founded by well-known critic and bibliographer Marshall B. Tymn about 1985. The directory is arranged alphabetically by surname and lists roughly 300 scholars interested in the serious study of fantastic literature and art. A typical entry includes name, address, phone number, and a brief statement of the individual's scholarly interests. The front flyleaf lists the IAFA executive board members and IAFA division heads, and the final page provides a brief chronological directory of the IAFA awards presented since 1985. Since many academics belong to only one of the two organizations, both directories are necessary to follow current research trends in SF and fantasy.

31. Science Fiction Research Association Annual Directory. Palatine, Ill., Science Fiction Research Assoc., 1971?-DATE. Annual. index.

This directory of approximately 300 scholars interested in serious research into fantastic literature has been published annually by the association since about 1971. The main section lists members alphabetically by surname, typically including name (surname in caps), address, phone number, plus a one- or two-sentence description of the member's interest in the genre (e.g., "teaching SF at secondary level"). A geographical index at the end of each directory arranges the members by state or country, then alphabetically by surname. A third section reproduces the SFRA bylaws. The directory is available to members only, but institutions (including libraries) are invited to join. This is a very useful annual guide to the major scholars in the field and their current research interests. See also the directory of a rival organization, IAFA (#30).

32. SFWA Membership Directory. West Columbia, S.C., Science Fiction and Fantasy Writers of America, Inc., 1965?-DATE. Annual.

This organization of professional science fiction writers has published an annual directory (consisting of roughly 850 writers and institutional members) since its inception. Names are arranged in alphabetical order by surname; a typical entry includes name, address, phone number, status (e.g., "A"=active), and a three-letter code referring to the author's agent. Following the main directory is a list of agents arranged by letter code, including name, address, and phone number. A third section provides a geographical listing of members arranged by state (or country) and surname. There is also a one-page pseudonym list. The final section includes members with computer timesharing access numbers indexed by service and access number or code. The first two pages of the directory give the officers of the organization, with addresses and phone numbers. The directory is available to members only, but libraries may join as institutional members. Most currently active American SF writers belong to SFWA, (pronounced "Séfwa"), plus some thirty Canadian authors and fifty more from nineteen other countries.

STATISTICAL SOURCES

SCOPE NOTE: Included herein are books made up largely of tables, statistical charts, and comparative lists relating to the study of fantastic literature.

33. Ashley, Mike. **Illustrated Book of Science Fiction Lists**. London, Virgin Books, 1982. 190 p. ISBN 0-907080-45-6 (pbk.). As: **The Illustrated Book of Science Fiction Lists**. New York, Cornerstone Library, Simon & Schuster, 1983. 190 p. LC 83-235099. ISBN 0-346-12628-2 (pbk.).

Ashley, a well-known British bibliographer, divides his book into four sections: "A. What Is This Thing...?," including fifty lists on the best or most noteworthy stories and novels in the genre, the best magazines, artists, and films, and novels about specific topics (e.g., mutations, matter transmission, other dimensions, etc.); "B. Expert Opinion," forty-four lists generated by various experts in the field (SF writers, artists, and editors) on their favorite works in particular categories (for example, "Stephen R. Donaldson's 10 Favourite Fantasy Novels"); "C. The Recordholders," comprising thirty-four statistical lists on the most prolific, oldest, youngest, and most award-winning writers, the highest advances paid in the field for particular SF titles, and many other similar renditions; and "D. Oddities and Entities," with thirty-eight lists providing odd statistics or facts about SF writers (e.g., "10 SF Writers Whose Careers Were Cut Short," "10 Pen Names That Hide the Identity of Two or More Authors," etc.).

Ashley's lists are authoritative, and he frequently provides annotations that enlighten the reader further about the author or his records or that give further illuminations about the book or story or magazine in question. The very detailed contents pages help substitute for lack of an index. Section C, "The Recordholders," includes a number of statistical tables unavailable in any other source and could provide a valuable launching point for further sociological analyses of the genre and its writers. A second edition would definitely be warranted.

34. Jakubowski, Maxim, and Malcolm Edwards. **The Complete Book of Science Fiction and Fantasy Lists**. London, Granada, 1983. 350 p. ISBN 0-586-05678-5 (pbk.). As: **The SF Book of Lists**. Expanded ed. New York, Berkley Books, 1983. 384 p. LC 83-237697. ISBN 0-425-06187-6 (pbk.).

Jakubowski and Edwards's book appeared almost simultaneously with Ashley's and covers much of the same material. The book is very loosely organized, without division, into specific subject lists covering the works, the awards, the authors, and the films of science fiction literature. The heart of the book is the ninety-page section called "The Years of Futures Past," which attempts to identify the major stories and novels of the field chronologically by compiling major award winners in the field, award nominees, stories selected for "Best of the Year" anthologies, and prevailing critical opinion for the very early periods, before specific SF awards existed. This is a uniquely valuable guide to the literature of the genre.

The rest of the book is often interesting and fun to read but is so loosely arranged that, without either an index or contents page, it cannot really be used as a reference tool. The American edition is identical to the British through page 350, adding thirty-four pages of further lists, except that the final list, on pages 382-384, repeats verbatim the list on pages 347-350, with which the British version ends. Comparisons with Ashley (see #33) are inevitable, since the books were released within months of each other in the United States, and since they cover much of the same material (indeed, the premises, although not the contents, of many lists overlap wholly or in part). However, while Ashley's volume clearly works better as a reference tool and includes statistical material not found in Jakubowski/Edwards, the latter has its own unique and very detailed chronicle of the best SF from its beginnings to modern times and incorporates many more tables in a much larger number of pages; and both books include contributions by major SF authors and critics. Thus, while each work has value in its own right, neither really displays any marked advantage over the other.

35. Pickard, Roy. **The Hamlyn Book of Horror and S.F. Movie Lists**. London, Hamlyn Paperbacks, 1983. 223 p., [16] p. of plates. ISBN 0-600-20778-1 (pbk.).

Pickard's volume focuses specifically on fantastic films and is arranged in alphabetical order by topic. Despite its superficial aura of superior organization, Pickard's book, like Jakubowski/Edwards's (see #34), is really a potpourri of popularly oriented associational items, sequels, directors' lists, and other miscellanea, as can be gleaned from a sampling of the chapter heads: "Awards," "Ray Bradbury," "Budgets," "Curses," "Peter Cushing," "Hammer Films: All of Them," "George Lucas," "The Most Popular Science-Fiction Films of the 1950s," "Priests," "Star Trek," "Unusual Names," and "Last List," a chronological checklist of the major events in the development of science fiction, fantasy, and horror films. There are sixteen pages of plates reproducing black-and-white stills from various pictures mentioned in the book (but uncorrelated to the text). The book is fun and readable, but very slight; the lack of an index makes it almost unusable as a reference work.

AWARDS LISTS

SCOPE NOTE: This chapter includes monographs consisting largely or entirely of lists of science fiction and fantasy awards. It should be noted that most general guides to the literature include some awards listings, although none are as complete as those covered below.

36. Franson, Donald, and Howard DeVore. **A History of the Hugo, Nebula, and International Fantasy Awards.** Dearborn Heights, Mich., Misfit Press, 1985. 185 p. index. LC 71-25327 [1971 ed.] (pbk.). At least nine editions of this book were issued between 1969-85, many of them not clearly labeled, but each is slightly larger than the last; no attempt has been made to list the earlier versions here.

A basic guide to the three premier awards in the genre, Franson and DeVore's book includes short histories of the awards, sample pictures of the trophies, and chronological listings of the nominees and winners, the latter being listed in boldface type. Very detailed records of the nominees are provided for the Nebulas, usually representing both the first and second ballots, while only the single, final ballot for the Hugo Award is shown. The index lists winners (authors, motion pictures, magazines, publishers), but not individual titles, referencing page numbers plus an abbreviation (e.g., "N" [boldfaced]=Nebula winner, "N"=Nebula nominee) denoting winners and nominees, but without indication either of the years or titles for which an award was received or considered. These restrictions make the index somewhat difficult to use for authors such as Harlan Ellison who have been nominated for (and have won) dozens of awards. Also, many of the pages in the earlier sections of these books, which have been reproduced verbatim from one or more previous editions, are faint and difficult to read. Now largely superseded by Reginald (see #38), which does not, however, list nominees who did not actually win an award.

37. Reed, Donald A., and Patrick Pattison. **Collector's Edition: Science Fiction Film Awards.** La Habra, Calif., ESE California, 1981. 107 p. ISBN 0-912076-39-9; ISBN 0-912076-40-2 (pbk.).

Reed founded The Count Dracula Society in 1962 to promote the study of horror films and literature and a decade later created the Academy of Science Fiction, Fantasy and Horror Films to promote "the arts and sciences of science fiction, fantasy, and horror films." The first annual "Science Fiction Film Awards" were presented by the Academy later that year (1972). This 8.5" x 11" volume lists the award-winners from 1972-80 inclusive, with numerous film stills and pictures of the actors and actresses nominated for the awards, as well as photographs from the awards ceremonies. The text also provides career summaries for the winners and plot summaries and background data on the best films of the year. There is a complete chronological list of the winners at the end of the book, but no alphabetical index, making location of specific data unnecessarily difficult. A new, updated edition (with index) would be appreciated.

38. Reginald, R. **Science Fiction and Fantasy Awards, Including Complete Checklists of the Hugo Awards, Nebula Awards, Locus Awards, Jupiter Awards, Pilgrim Awards, International Fantasy Awards, Ditmar Awards, August Derleth Awards, World Fantasy Awards, Eaton Awards, Gandalf Awards, British Fantasy Awards, John W. Campbell Memorial Awards, Milford Awards, Prometheus Awards, and Selected Foreign**

Awards, with a Complete Index to Winners, a List of Officers of the Science Fiction Writers of America from the Beginning of That Organization, a Checklist of World Science Fiction Conventions and Their Guests of Honor, and Detailed Statistic Tables. San Bernardino, Calif., The Borgo Press, 1981. 64 p. index. (Borgo Reference Library, Vol. 2). LC 80-10788. ISBN 0-89370-806-2; ISBN 0-89370-906-9 (pbk.). Mallett, Daryl F., and Robert Reginald. **Reginald's Science Fiction and Fantasy Awards: A Comprehensive Guide to the Awards and Their Winners**. 2nd ed. San Bernardino, Calif., The Borgo Press, 1991. [248] p. index. (Borgo Literary Guides, No. 1). LC 87-6305. ISBN 0-89370-826-7; ISBN 0-89370-926-3 (pbk.).

The original version of this comprehensive guide to science fiction awards was arranged alphabetically by award name (a few minor awards were inserted into conveniently blank places in the book, but these can readily be identified through the table of contents) and then chronologically by year. Two years are given for each award, the first being the year of qualification, the second (in parentheses) the year in which the award was actually presented; this system was necessary because there is no uniformity in the way these awards are popularly regarded or described (for example, the two major awards in the field, the Hugos and the Nebulas, are generally labeled by the year of qualification and the year of presentation, respectively, the 1980 Hugos thus being equivalent to the 1981 Nebulas). Under each award year, the awards are listed by category, the most prestigious category being listed first, plus title and author of the winner. A "Personal Name Index" repeats the data by author name. In addition to the major and minor awards in the field, including some foreign awards, the book also includes a chronological list of the elected officers of the Science Fiction Writers of America, the major professional organization in the field; plus a chronological list of the world science fiction conventions, with formal name, site, and guests of honor—these honors are also included in the name index. Four statistical tables correlating the highest number of winners (overall, for all fiction categories, for the Hugos, and for the Nebulas), complete the book.

The second edition was updated by Daryl F. Mallett and edited by Reginald and quadruples the data from the first version. In addition to bringing previously existing sections down to mid-1991, many new awards have been added (including foreign) plus a title index, a history of each award, the rules governing the presentation of the awards, and an indication of what the presentation includes (trophy, plaque, scroll, etc.). All those awards proprietary to the science fiction world are listed in alphabetical order by name of award, then chronologically by date; however, the basic format of the book is the same as the original. Foreign awards and those awards that have honored SF writers for accolades outside the genre of fantastic literature are grouped together into two appendices, again alphabetically by award name. Also included in the end matter are lists of the officers of the Science Fiction Writers of America, Horror Writers of America, and Science Fiction Research Association. The statistical data have also been expanded (by Reginald). The amount of data in this volume (covering 126 separate awards) far exceeds anything available on SF awards even in the major reference tools, and the detailed tables provide prime material for further sociological study. With the cessation of Franson/DeVore (see #36), Reginald/Mallett must perforce become the standard guide on the subject.

PSEUDONYM LISTS

SCOPE NOTE: Included herein are monographs consisting primarily of lists of science fiction pseudonyms and their real authors. Partial lists can be found in many other general guides and bibliographies.

39. Bates, Susannah. **The PENDEX: An Index of Pen Names and House Names in Fantastic, Thriller, and Series Literature**. New York & London, Garland Publishing, 1981. xii, 233 p. index. LC 80-8486. (Garland Reference Library of the Humanities, Vol. 237). ISBN 0-8240-9501-4.

The PENDEX includes pseudonyms used by authors working in both fantastic literature and in the mystery and detective genre. After a brief introduction by Bates, the book is organized into five sections. "Real Names" includes the author's real name in capital letters, with middle names and years of birth and death (where known), followed by the writer's penname(s) in regular type, indented two spaces. Some pseudonyms include the following letter codes after the name: "CPN"=Collaborative Pen Name; "HN"=House Name; "SSN"=Stratemeyer Syndicate Name. The second section includes "Pen Names," in which the *noms de plume* appear in all caps, with real names in regular letters indented two spaces, preceded by the letters "RN" (i.e., "real name"). The third chapter lists "Collaborative Pen Names," that is, a pseudonym used by two or more authors in collaboration, listed by name (in all caps), with the real names of the authors in ordinary letters, indented two spaces. The fourth section includes "House Names," with a similar arrangement, listing all known author(s) using the name. The final section covers the Stratemeyer Syndicate, which produced adolescent series novels under house pseudonyms. Two appendices cover "Pulps & Digests: Some Working Definitions" and "Round Robin Serials," in which each author would contribute one or more chapters. A brief bibliography of sources consulted is followed by a complete index to real names (in capital letters) and pseudonyms (in regular type).

Bates covers roughly 1,700 pseudonyms of some 950 authors, a figure appreciably smaller than McGhan (see #40), particularly when one realizes that she is also attempting to include the pennames of mystery writers. Her source list demonstrates that she has missed all the major reference tools of fantastic literature published in 1979 and 1980, thereby losing many identifications first made in those publications; for example, she only catches half of Fanthorpe's pennames. More disturbing by far than this lack of focus or understanding of the genre is the large number of outright errors: Frank Aubrey is consistently listed as "Aubray"; Fanthorpe's pseudonym is given as "Ziegfried" when it should be "Zeigfreid," and it is *not* a house name (but Karl Zeigfried, which is not listed, *is*); several well-known names of Don Pendleton, particularly Dan Britain, are not included in his entry; only one penname is listed for Lauran Paine, when he has used dozens on his SF, mystery, and western novels; Greye La Spina is misspelled "Greya"; Frederic Arnold Kummer is listed as "Frederick"; Edmond Hamilton is misspelled "Edmund"; Harlan Ellison's pseudonym Cordwainer Bird is spelled "Cortwainer"; Fairman did indeed write five Lester del Rey novels, but not all were juveniles, and not all were published by Scholastic; Brûce Elliott is misspelled Elliot, "Julain" (actually Julian) Chain is *not* a pseudonym of May Dikty (Bates confuses Julian May, or "Judy" Dikty, with real-life author Julian Chain, a mistake also made by McGhan); and so on, in endless permutations.

The proliferation of omissions and commissions is inexcusable, particularly given the large number of resource persons and volumes readily available; it reflects a carelessness and inattention to detail that must inevitably damn this book to the Bibliography Hall of Shame. Such errors also make the work completely untrustworthy; although McGhan's production values and binding are shoddy by comparison, his book (and Robinson's) are 100% more reliable.

40. McGhan, Barry. **Science Fiction and Fantasy Pseudonyms**. Dearborn, Mich., Misfit Press, 1979. vi, 77 p. LC 72-176242 [1971 ed.]; LC 74-161774 [1973 ed.] (pbk.). At least seven editions of this book were published between 1971-79, but the earlier versions have not been listed here.

McGhan provides a comprehensive list of 1,581 SF pennames and the roughly 1,000 real authors behind them in one alphabet, real names being given in boldface, house pseudonyms being indicated with the letters "*h ps*" prior to the name. Following each name is a number in parentheses, referencing a bibliography of seventy-one items at the front of the book, indicating every source used to verify a pseudonym (roughly a quarter are marked "private communication" from a specified individual)—this enables the researcher to follow McGhan's scholarly footsteps. The 1979 version is identical to the 1976 edition through page 70, except for the addition of further sources on introductory pages v-vi and a separate alphabetical "1979 Supplement" on pages 71-77; some pages were faint in the three editions examined, and the book uses a loose, saddle-stitched binding. Only SF authors are included in this book, but some of the pennames listed were used solely for non-SF publications, although McGhan makes no distinction between them; it is also impossible to determine which names were used on monographs and which on stories. A new edition taking into account the many major reference works released in 1979 and the early 1980s would definitely be welcome.

41. Robinson, Roger. **Who's Hugh? An SF Reader's Guide to Pseudonyms**. Harold Wood, Essex, Beccon Publications, 1987. 173 p. LC 89-146783. ISBN 1-870824-01-6; ISBN 1-870824-02-4 (pbk.).

Who's Hugh is the most current and comprehensive guide to SF pennames, covering roughly 3,200 *noms de plume* of an unknown number of real-life authors (Robinson's format makes an estimate impossible). Like McGhan, Robinson documents his work by citing ninety-nine previously published (or oral) sources (including McGhan as the ninety-ninth, but missing both Bates and Mossman's *Pseudonyms and Nicknames Dictionary*) noted in a four-page bibliography at the front of the book; unlike Bates and McGhan, his work takes into account the numerous SF reference works published in the late 1970s and early 1980s. Robinson uses a somewhat complicated format, perhaps unduly so, running his data in three columns on facing pages, pseudonyms on the left-hand page, "usual names" on the right; by "usual," he means either the author's real name or the name under which he or she is best known, even if this is itself a pseudonym. The information is arranged so that the same sections of the alphabet are covered on both pages, even if this means that one page's copy will be very short.

The pseudonym list, running on left-hand pages only, is arranged in alphabetical order by surname or by the last element of the name (e.g., The Lord Commissioner is filed under "C"); the pseudonyms occupy the first left-hand column position on the page. Pennames used on books are printed in all caps; those used on short fiction or nonfiction run in lower case, with initial capitalizations. The second column on the left-hand page includes the "usual name" by which the author is known or under which he or she commonly writes.

Those names which are in themselves pennames are prefixed with an asterisk; a question mark prior to a name indicates the attribution was unverifiable; a question mark without a name indicates the real name of the writer is unknown; a "+" following a (list of) name(s) means that other authors also used the penname; a name or publisher name in parentheses means the pseudonym was employed as a house penname. The third column provides a list of numbers referring the user to the bibliography of sources at the front of the book.

The right-hand page lists the "usual name" by which the author is known in the first column, with a list of the pseudonyms the writer has employed in the second column, followed by a third column citing references from the bibliography of sources in the book's introduction. If the author's "usual name" is itself a penname, an asterisk appears before the name. In the second column, book pseudonyms run in all caps, house pseudonyms are enclosed by parentheses, and a "+" before a name indicates others have used it as well. A "#" sign on either page indicates the name is not really a pseudonym but results from a publisher's typographical error. This complicated system results in much paging back and forth in the volume. For example, Rex Gordon is the usual name of writer Stanley Hough, who also wrote under the name Bennett Stanley. Both facing pages have entries for Rex Gordon: on the left-hand page, we learn that his real name is Stanley Hough; on the right-hand page the entry for Gordon mentions his pseudonym, Bennett Stanley. Elsewhere in the book, on a right-hand page, we find Hough's real name listed, with a see reference to Rex Gordon. Under Bennett Stanley, however, we find a reference only to Rex Gordon. Is this *really* necessary? Could not the arrangement have been simplified into one alphabet?

There are the usual errors and omissions here: Robinson also misidentifies Julian May with Julian Chain (as do Bates and McGhan), and he lists A. A. Glynn consistently as Glyn, and Don Pfeil as Pfiel. The identification of David Wright O'Brien with David O'Brien, a British paperback writer of the early 1950s, is questionable. Ballantine Books is misspelled "Ballentine." As might be expected, Robinson's sources for modern British writers are stronger than for their American counterparts, but his work is generally sound throughout and certainly more complete and up-to-date by far than the two volumes mentioned above. Unfortunately, the book is virtually unavailable in America and only had a small printing in England; a second edition is promised, however.

BIOGRAPHICAL AND LITERARY DIRECTORIES

SCOPE NOTE: This chapter includes who's who-type publications, bio-bibliographical directories, and literary dictionaries arranged alphabetically by author, whose focus is as much biographical as it is critical. Readers' and critical guides to SF authors and their books can be found in a later section of this book.

42. Ash, Brian. **Who's Who in Science Fiction**. London, Elm Tree Books, 1976. 220 p. LC 77-361941. ISBN 0-241-89383-6. Also: New York, Taplinger Publishing Co., 1976. 220 p. LC 76-11667. ISBN 0-8008-8274-1; ISBN 0-8008-8279-2 (pbk.).

Ash provides biographical and critical evaluations of about 400 writers listed in alphabetical order by surname. The biographies have been adapted in very abbreviated form from previously published books and other sources, particularly Tuck's *Encyclopedia of Science Fiction and Fantasy* (see #10) and Reginald's *Science Fiction and Fantasy Literature* (see #182), as acknowledged in the author's introduction. Typical entries run between 50-1,000 words, averaging 100-200. While his biographical material is clearly derivative, Ash's comments on the writers' major works (book titles and dates are provided, but no bibliographical data) typically include pithy one-line annotations, with some attempt at appraisal. A "Select Bibliography of Books on Science Fiction" completes the book.

Ash's purpose, to provide a brief guide to the major SF writers and their works, is a worthy one, but his book suffers by comparison with the many other biographical and critical tools released during the late 1970s and early 1980s, particularly *The Encyclopedia of Science Fiction* (see #7), *Science Fiction and Fantasy Literature* (see #182), *Twentieth-Century Science-Fiction Writers* (see #47), and *The New Encyclopedia of Science Fiction* (see #4). His work has generally been dismissed by the critics as weak and second-hand and is now, of course, largely out-of-date. A title index would have been helpful. See also the companion book on horror (see #43).

43. Ashley, Mike. **Who's Who in Horror and Fantasy Fiction**. London, Elm Tree Books, 1977. 240 p. LC 78-309133. ISBN 0-241-89528-6. Also: New York, Taplinger Publishing Co., 1978. 240 p. LC 77-4608. ISBN 0-8008-8275-X; ISBN 0-8008-8278-4 (pbk.).

This companion volume to *Who's Who in Science Fiction* (see #42) is based upon Ashley's original research and is much less derivative, both in biographical details and critical comments, than the Ash work. Following a brief introduction by Ashley, the book includes a chronological list of the genre's major works by year, title, and author; biographies of major and minor writers in the field, arranged alphabetically by surname; and five appendices: "An Index to Key Stories and Books," arranged by title, with selected annotations; "Selected Weird Fiction Anthologies," by title, with selected contents listings; "Weird and Horror Fiction Magazines," by title, with dates of publication, editors, nationality, and listings of major authors and stories published; "Awards" (the August Derleth Award and the World Fantasy Award), with winners listed chronologically by year. A short bibliography of nonfiction sources (now out-of-date) completes the book.

Ashley frequently includes biographical details and other tidbits not found in any other source and his inclusion of a large number of classic horror writers of the eighteenth, nineteenth, and early twentieth centuries makes his book valuable even more than a decade after its original publication, unlike the Ash volume on SF writers. He also manages to mention and intelligently evaluate thousands of books and stories while commenting on the authors' lives and careers. A title index would have been helpful. This concise and authoritative guide is a good example for would-be compilers of "popular" reference works to follow.

44. Cowart, David, and Thomas L. Wymer, eds. **Twentieth-Century American Science-Fiction Writers**. Detroit, Mich., A Bruccoli Clark Book, Gale Research Co., 1981. xv, 306, ix, 346 p. in 2 v. (Dictionary of Literary Biography, Vol. 8). LC 81-4182. ISBN 0-8103-0918-1 (set).

Cowart and Wymer's volume follows the standard *DLB* format, including critical essays by forty-one contributors on the lives and works of ninety-one American SF writers, arranged alphabetically by surname. A typical entry includes author's name, critic's name and academic affiliation, brief biographical data on the author, awards received by the author, a selected bibliography of the author's books, and the essay itself followed by a selected list of secondary sources. Most entries also contain at least one author photo (some have several), and many include a sample page from one of the writer's manuscripts or reproduction(s) of one or more magazine or paperback covers featuring the author's work. At the end of Volume Two are six appendices: "I. Trends in Science-Fiction," including essays "The New Wave" and "Science Fantasy"; "II. The Media of Science Fiction," including "The Iconography of Science-Fiction Art," "Paperback Science Fiction," and "Science-Fiction Films"; "III. Fandom and SFWA," including "Science-Fiction Fandom and Conventions," "Science-Fiction Fanzines: The Time Binders," "Science Fiction Writers of America and the Nebula Award," and "Hugo Awards and Nebula Awards" (a chronological checklist); "IV. A World Chronology of Important Science-Fiction Works (1818-1979)," a brief list by year, title, and author; "V. Selected Science-Fiction Magazines and Anthologies," including three sections: "Magazines," listing selected titles by title, with dates published, editors and years served, and major works published; "Reprint Anthologies," by title, giving editor(s), publisher, place, year of publication, and brief annotation (only sixteen titles are listed); "Original Anthologies," by title, with the same information as the previous section (listing just seventeen titles); "VI. Books for Further Reading," with four pages of secondary sources but no annotations. Most of these mini-essays have short secondary bibliographies attached.

The critical essays range in size from 1,500-15,000 words (averaging 2,500) and focus primarily on the author's work, although biographical details are often incorporated into the beginning paragraphs of each piece. The critiques touch upon the author's major fictions, roughly chronologically, with plot summaries and individual evaluations plus a one-paragraph summation. The longer essays, relatively few in number, have the space to comment at length on the author's *oeuvre* and are distinctly superior to their 1,500-word counterparts (the bulk of those included); all, however, are at least readable and seem sound and balanced in their perceptions, well within the mainstream of SF critical thought. The appendices provide roughly 5,000 words each of illustrated comments by different critics on specific SF themes and movements; these too are at least interesting, if not particularly deep. One wonders, however, why certain topics were selected for this section and other subjects which could just as easily have been included were not. The chronology is too brief to be useful, and a general author/title index would have been appreciated.

This volume's chief rival, Bleiler's *Science Fiction Writers* (see #56), covers sixteen fewer writers but has a better mix of nationalities and time periods (Cowart and Wymer, following the series format, deliberately restrict their coverage to twentieth-century American writers). The essays in the former volume are generally longer and more illuminating, although certain essays in Cowart/Wymer (the piece on Robert A. Heinlein, for example), are considerably longer (and therefore touch upon more works in greater depth) than their Bleiler counterparts. Bleiler uses fifteen fewer critics, and as a group, they are generally better known and more authoritative than those in Cowart/Wymer; curiously, there is not one overlap between the two lists. Both are equally current in their coverage of the same writers; the addition of photographs and illustrations in *Twentieth-Century American Science-Fiction Writers* is a nice embellishment but unnecessary for the serious reader. On balance, both are worthy additions to the body of SF critical literature, and while each has its strong points, neither set has any significant advantage over the other.

45. Green, Scott E. **Contemporary Science Fiction, Fantasy, and Horror Poetry: A Resource Guide and Biographical Directory.** New York, Westport, Conn., Greenwood Press, 1989. xviii, 216 p. index. LC 89-16966. ISBN 0-313-26324-8.

Green's volume is the first guide to the prominent persons and publications of a subgenre which grew rapidly in popularity during the 1980s. A preface defines the different categories of SF and fantasy poetry and cites major sources for the book; other front matter includes a brief acknowledgments list and an introduction, "A Brief History of Science Fiction, Fantasy, and Horror Poetry Publishing in America," all by Green. The primary text is divided into three major sections: "I. Poetry in Magazines"; "II. Poetry in Genre Anthologies"; and "III. Biographical Directory of Poets." Part I is further subdivided into "Commercial and Newsstand Genre Magazines" and "Small-Press Genre Magazines," each organized in alphabetical order by magazine title. A typical entry provides title (in bold italics), brief history and market orientation, editorial personnel, and a comprehensive listing of the poets who have appeared in each publication, in alphabetical order by surname, with specific dates and issues in which their poems appeared. Those poets who have appeared in SF prozines which did not normally feature verse are listed in a catch-all section at the end of the first chapter, in alphabetical order by poet, with the magazine title and specific date ("3/56"=March 1956) of each appearance.

Part II is divided into four chapters: "Key Anthologies and Anthology Series," "Historical Anthologies," "Additional Anthologies," and "Single-Author Collections"; the "Key" and "Historical" chapters are arranged alphabetically by book title, a typical entry providing title (in bold italics), editor, place of publication, publisher, year of publication, annotation (100-250 words summarizing and evaluating the contents), with a complete checklist (in alphabetical order by author) of the poems and poets appearing in each anthology. The "Additional Anthologies" section provides skeletal lists (in alphabetical order by anthology title) of anthologies including one or two poems amid other material (usually short stories); the "Single-Author Collections" section, arranged alphabetically by author of the collection, similarly lists those books including a handful of verse contributions embedded among short stories by one author.

The "Biographical Directory of Poets" comprises half the text, listing SF and fantasy poets currently active in the field alphabetically by surname, giving name (in boldface), address, a summary of the author's career as a poet (50-300 words), with lists of the major magazines and anthologies that have printed the writer's verse. An appendix provides a chronological list of the Rhysling Awards for SF poetry. Two very comprehensive general and poem title indexes complete the book. The volume is well-designed, typeset, and bound to library standards.

Green's directory will undoubtedly become the standard guide to its field, particularly if maintained through regular future editions. The only significant data lacking here are paginations, both for books and periodicals, and while enough material is provided to enable even the casual user to locate specific poems and publications, the addition of complete bibliographical information would be helpful in a second edition. Despite this minor *caveat,*

Green is both authoritative and definitive, and his guide can be recommended without reservation to any library with an interest in twentieth-century American verse.

46. Reginald, R. **Stella Nova: The Contemporary Science Fiction Authors**. Los Angeles, Unicorn & Son, 1970. [358] p. index. LC 79-282012. (pbk). As: **Contemporary Science Fiction Authors, First Edition**. Rev. ed. New York, Arno Press, 1975. 365 p. index. LC 74-16517. ISBN 0-405-06332-6.

Reginald was a college student when he put together the original version of this book in 1968, compiling it from direct-mail questionnaires and his own research. *Stella Nova* incorporates bibliographies of 483 SF writers active between 1960-68, with biographies of the 308 who responded to his queries. A typical entry includes author's name (in caps); bibliography of the writer's science fiction books in descending chronological order by date of publication (giving book number in order of publication [i.e., 1, 2, 3, etc.], publisher, year of publication, book title, and a code letter indicating format [paper or cloth] and type [collection, anthology, etc.]); first professional sale (with bibliographical data); works in progress (in 1969/70); biography (including information on the author's careers and a list of awards won); and (occasionally) an original statement by the author responding to the compiler's questions.

The original edition included a quirky and largely unusable title index keyed to the author's entry number; the Arno edition reworked this into a more normal title/author format, added a list of pseudonyms cross-referenced with the authors' real names, substituted a new introduction and abbreviations list (the latter was accidentally omitted from the first printing of the revised edition but was added to all subsequent printings), and made several other minor corrections. Most of the biographical data remained untouched, although a few additional see references were included where appropriate. The book eventually evolved, with a much different format, into *Science Fiction and Fantasy Literature* (see #182).

Both bibliographical and biographical entries are a bit too cryptic or concise to work very smoothly, although the format becomes somewhat clearer when one reads the introduction and actually uses the material. It is not always obvious, for example, that a particular piece of data is a marriage record, or a list of children, or some other, similar detail, without checking its position in the entry. Despite such format problems, this first attempt at producing a who's who of science fiction and fantasy includes an amazing amount of original, primary data, the collaborative result of the authors' own contributions and responses and Reginald's tenacious research; one can understand this better by examining Stella Nova's influence on later biographical directories of SF authors, all of which borrow from this seminal work to a greater or lesser degree (some shamelessly and without acknowledgment). In a number of key cases, such as "John Norman," the only "hard" data available on the author's life is the material in the original Stella Nova, endlessly repeated elsewhere, including other works of Reginald himself.

47. Smith, Curtis C., ed. **Twentieth-Century Science-Fiction Writers**. London: Macmillan, 1981. xviii, 642 p. index. ISBN 0-333-31945-1. Also: New York, St. Martin's Press, 1981. xviii, 642 p. index. LC 81-8944. ISBN 0-312-82420-3. 2nd ed. Chicago & London, St. James Press, 1986. xviii, 933 p. index. LC 87-180709. ISBN 0-912289-27-9. 3rd ed. Watson, Noelle, and Paul E. Schellinger, eds. Chicago & London, St. James Press, 1991. xxvi, 1,016 p. Index. ISBN 1-55862-111-3.

This bio-bibliographical and critical guide to science-fiction authors, a companion volume to similarly titled volumes on mystery, western, and romance writers, is divided into three sections: English-language writers (532 authors in the first edition, 571 in the second), foreign-language writers (thirty-five authors in the first, thirty-eight in the second), and major fantasy writers (the same five authors in both), and then alphabetically by surname. Some writers covered in the first edition were dropped from the second, and many others (especially newer authors) were added. In both editions, Smith relied upon a board of advisors (the same twenty writers and critics were used in both books, with one additional name in the revised version) to suggest a basic list of writers to be covered. The critical essays were then assigned to a long list of contributors (146 in the first book, 173 in the second).

A typical entry includes author's name (in boldface, including middle or real name[s]), nationality, brief biographical and career data (in one paragraph); a complete bibliography of the author's books, science fiction publications being listed first, then all other books (the entries provide book titles in italics, with series information, places of publication, publishers, years of publication, and corresponding data on the first U.K. or U.S. edition), as well as all uncollected short stories (including magazine or anthology of publication, place of publication, and date of issue or year of publication [for an anthology]), lists of monographic works about the author (including critiques and bibliographies), plus an indication if the author's manuscripts are housed in a library collection; commentary by the author himself (for about a third of the modern entries); plus a critical essay by a contributing critic. The critiques range in size from 300-2,500 words (most average 500-1,000) and include a short summation of the author's contributions to the genre, with commentary on the principal works, including a paragraph of plot summary and a sentence or two of critical analysis. With so many critics involved in the project, the quality of the material varies widely from essay to essay, as might be expected, but is always at least readable; the limitation on length does not allow for any serious examinations of the writers in question, but for many lesser-known writers, the brief commentaries in these volumes are the only analyses currently available.

Although the title suggests a modern focus, in fact the volumes include all major SF writers (and many lesser-known ones) who lived and/or died in the twentieth century; however, a number of historical figures were dropped from the revised edition to make room for newer authors, so both books should be retained by libraries and researchers. The biographies were compiled through direct-mail questionnaires and from other previously published sources; the authors' comments are original to these volumes, although many were repeated verbatim in the second edition; at least one-third of the entries have minimal (or no) biographical data. The bibliographies were updated where necessary in the 1986 version, and some (but not all) of the essays for active writers were either reworked by the original critics or rewritten from scratch by completely different contributors. Both editions include an introduction by the editor giving a brief background history of the genre plus a general "Reading List" of nonfiction works which unfortunately includes a few "ghost" titles. This is followed by lists of each book's advisers, contributors, and authors covered. There are brief biographies of the critics at the end of each volume, and the revised version includes a much-needed title/author index.

Smith's book tries to be all things to all researchers, and it succeeds about as well as any of its competitors. Its chief rival, Gunn's *New Encyclopedia of Science Fiction* (see #4), although slightly more current, contains generally smaller entries and much less specific biographical and bibliographical data for each of the writers covered. Reginald's *Science Fiction and Fantasy Literature* (see #182) has more detailed biographical material but will not be current until the new edition is published in 1992; Nicholls's *The Encyclopedia of Science Fiction* (see #7) is also a decade out-of-date, although a new edition is underway. One wonders why certain writers were included and others of apparently equal importance omitted and also why the same five fantasy writers were sequestered (in both editions) in a separate little ghetto of their own at the end of each volume. If these particular fantasy authors are worthy of inclusion in what purports to be a science-fiction volume, should not others have been covered? There are no answers to these questions. A third edition was published at the end of 1991.

48. Weinberg, Robert. **A Biographical Dictionary of Science Fiction and Fantasy Artists**. New York and Westport, Conn., Greenwood Press, 1988. xvi, 346 p. index. LC 87-17651. ISBN 0-313-24349-2.

The first biographical directory specifically devoted to SF artists, Weinberg's book includes two short introductions; an abbreviations list; a thirty-one-page essay by Weinberg, "Science Fiction Art: A Historical Overview"; a biographical directory of roughly 250 artists arranged alphabetically by surname; a closing essay by Weinberg, "Science Fiction Art: What Still Exists," on the collecting of SF artwork; a chronological checklist of the Hugo and World Fantasy awards for best artist by year awarded; a bibliography; an index of biographical entries; and an author/title index, which does not, however, include books listed in the bibliographical sections of the artist biographies but does mention the artists themselves (duplicating somewhat the previous section). A typical entry includes the artist's name in bold caps; date of birth if known (a question mark appears if the date is unknown); nationality; an account in narrative form of the artist's life and career; and a selected bibliography of published works, primarily paperback covers, hardcover dustjackets, and magazine covers (the book titles appear in italics with two-digit terminal years of publication in parentheses [e.g., "80"=1980] arranged alphabetically by title, while the magazine publications are keyed to a two- to four-digit letter code [e.g., "GXY"=*Galaxy Magazine*], with the years of publication written out and the months of publication indicated in numerical form in parentheses thereafter [e.g., "11"=November]). Weinberg states in his introduction that the listings of magazine cover lists are nearly complete for most artists but acknowledges that the bibliographies of book covers are often incomplete.

The essays, many of them penned by Weinberg himself (Richard Dalby wrote most of the British and French entries with the assistance of Mike Ashley and Philip Harbottle— their contributions, amounting to one-fourth to one-third of the total, are signed), normally include some brief biographical data and a lengthier career assessment, although many of the entries on artists from the pulp period provide very few details about the artist's life. The critiques range in size from 50-1,500 words and are readable, authoritative, and appear conversant with standard art techniques, forms, and media, with the science fiction world in general, and with pulp and paperback publishing in particular. Some of the essays include much more information than others, however, depending on Weinberg's ability to contact the artist or to locate other source materials; compare, for example, the entry on modern SF artist Gray Morrow (weak and derivative at 150 words) with that for Rowena Morrill (which discusses in a 600-word essay her unique style of painting and provides much background material on her interesting life). References to other artists covered in the book are noted with asterisks following each name as they are mentioned in an entry, often as influences on the style or work of the artist being critiqued. Several reviewers have noted some errors of fact in the book, but this was probably inevitable given the pioneering nature of the work.

Although SF artists are covered to a limited degree in other major references tools (Nicholls's *Encyclopedia of Science Fiction* [see #7] mentions about fifty names), Weinberg touches upon so many more artists, at much greater length, that his volume is sure to become the standard guide to the subject.

49. Yntema, Sharon K. **More Than 100: Women Science Fiction Writers**. Freedom, Calif., The Crossing Press, 1988. [vi], 193 p. LC 88-3600. ISBN 0-89594-301-8. Cover title reads *More Than 100 Woman* [*sic*] *Science Fiction Writers: An Annotated Bibliography.*

Yntema's bio-critical directory includes entries for 104 mostly twentieth-century, mostly English-speaking, female writers of the fantastic. A typical entry provides name, date of birth, place of birth (country, state, city, in that order), pseudonyms, annotation, awards won by the author, a very limited bibliography of secondary sources (absent for many entries, often consisting of a handful of book reviews), a list of the author's fictional books in chronological order by publication year (series are grouped together under the series title), a chronological checklist of significant short stories (with publication dates plus magazine titles and/or anthology titles and editors where appropriate), and nonfiction (or other genre) monographs. Eight appendices list "170 Additional Names of Women Science Fiction and Fantasy Authors with Titles and Dates of Their Books" (an alphabetical list of women SF writers with a chronological checklist of their books), "Authors of Science Fiction and Fantasy for Children and Young Adults" (a barebones list of thirty-three authors), "Where Were They Born?" (a checklist of the authors by country of birth), "When Were They Born?" (a chronological checklist of the authors by year of birth), "Which Authors Are No Longer Alive?" (a chronological checklist of the authors by their years of death), "Who Are Their Literary Agents?" (a very brief register of thirty authors and their agents, with agents' addresses), "Recommended Science Fiction Books by Women" (an alphabetical list by author and title), and "Other Resources" (an annotated list of fourteen secondary sources plus nine additional undescribed books).

The textual part of each entry ranges from one to three short paragraphs and provides brief biographical data and a summary of the writer's career, including passing mention of the author's major stories and books. Yntema's style is populist rather than literary, and her comments are often thin and unilluminating. No less than seventy-one of her entries (68.3%), for example, begin with the words "[author's name] is a/an...," with many of the other entries substituting "was" for "is." Unfortunately, the book is also filled with factual and typographical errors: Evangeline Walton's fantasy series should be "Mabinogion," not "Mabinagian"; Thea Von Harbou is actually Thea von Harbou, and her name (befitting her German origin) should be filed under "H"; C. L. Moore's middle name is spelled with one "L"; Zoë Fairbairns uses an umlaut over the "e" in her first name; Jessica Amanda Salmonson's original given name (unmentioned here) was Amos; and so on. Yntema's bibliographical data are nonexistent, her so-called list of secondary sources for each writer woefully incomplete, her biographical material very scanty. Her selection criteria must also be questioned, since she seems to have included only those writers on whom information was readily available, relegating the rest to the limbo of her appendices; such well-known women SF writers as Julian May are unmentioned in either section. On the plus side, the book is well-designed and typeset and bound to library standards.

Yntema's idea—a bio-bibliographical directory of female writers of the fantastic—is an excellent one, particularly given the fact that women authors virtually dominated the genre during the 1980s; but her execution leaves much to be desired, and the resulting hodgepodge can scarcely be called a "reference" book of any kind. Compare Roger C. Schlobin's *Urania's Daughters* (see #236), which provides far more bibliographical entries but fails to include biographies, annotations, or critical commentaries.

READERS' AND CRITICAL GUIDES

SCOPE NOTE: This section includes literary and critical guides whose intent is to recommend or criticize a selected list of authors, titles, or groups of authors in one or more subgenres of fantastic literature. Bibliographies intended to record an *entire* genre or subgenre or national SF literature in some systemic way are listed in the bibliographies chapters, even when extensively annotated.

50. Allen, L. David. **Science Fiction: An Introduction**. Lincoln, Neb., Cliffs Notes, 1973. 187 p. index. ISBN 0-8220-1169-7 (pbk.). As: **Science Fiction Reader's Guide**. Lincoln, Neb., Centennial Press, 1974. 299 p. index. ISBN 0-8220-1611-7 (pbk.).

These two nearly identical versions of the same book were originally published in the Cliffs Notes series, with the typical CN orientation toward plot summary rather than exegesis. The first section includes detailed analyses of fifteen classic SF novels followed by chapters "Toward a Definition of Science Fiction," "A Way of Reading Science Fiction: Another Look at 'Dune'," "Guidelines for Reading Science Fiction," "Verisimilitude in Science Fiction," "Awards for Science Fiction," "A Selected Bibliography of Science Fiction," "A Selected Bibliography of Works About Science Fiction" (the latter three sections now badly out-of-date), and an author/title index. Mediocrely written and of marginal interest, Allen's book is included here only because the title of the reprint promises something more than it can actually deliver.

51. Barron, Neil, ed. **Anatomy of Wonder: Science Fiction**. New York, R.R. Bowker Co., 1976. xxi, 471 p. index. LC 76-10260. ISBN 0-8352-0884-2. **Anatomy of Wonder: A Critical Guide to Science Fiction**. 2nd ed. New York, R.R. Bowker Co., 1981. xiv, 724 p. index. LC 81-4391. ISBN 0-8352-1339-0; ISBN 0-8352-1404-4 (pbk.). **Anatomy of Wonder: A Critical Guide to Science Fiction**. 3rd ed. New York, R.R. Bowker Co., 1987. xvii, 874 p. index. LC 87-9305. ISBN 0-8352-2312-4.

Barron's *Anatomy* has generally been accepted as the standard readers' guide to science fiction literature. The three editions follow the same general format, with coverage of fiction broken into three or four chapters, each dealing with a specific, somewhat arbitrarily defined period of the genre's development, plus additional chapters on juvenile SF, nonfiction, and (in the later editions) on foreign-language SF. Each section is authored by a different critic who contributes a lengthy introductory essay framing the subject, then provides brief annotations of each work covered, in alphabetical order by author and title. A typical entry includes item number (e.g., "4-551," item 551 in Chapter 4), author, title (in boldface), publisher of the first edition, year of publication, two- or three-sentence annotation, mention of book(s) with similar themes, and a letter code indicating whether the work has been nominated for or has won an award. Alternate titles or original titles (for translations), with translators, are given as part of the collation, as are middle names (or real names) of the authors. The annotations are descriptive and sometimes evaluative and tend to be somewhat longer for acknowledged classics of the field. The item numbers begin with the number one in each new chapter and are completely different from edition to edition.

The evolution of *Anatomy* can be seen in the contents pages of each version. The first edition includes, with front matter, the following chapters: "Science Fiction: From Its Beginnings to 1870," by Robert M. Philmus; "The Emergence of the Scientific Romance, 1870-1926," by Thomas D. Clareson; "The Gernsback Era, 1926-1937," by Ivor A. Rogers;

"The Modern Period, 1938-1975," by Joe De Bolt and John R. Pfeiffer; "Juvenile Science Fiction," by Francis J. Molson. Also included are sections by Barron, "History, Criticism, and Biography," "Bibliographies, Indexes, and Teaching Aids," "Magazine and Book Review Indexes," "Periodicals," "Literary Awards," and "Core Collection Checklist," and a final section that includes "Library Collections of Science Fiction and Fantasy," by H. W. Hall, and "Directory of Publishers," "Author Index," and "Title Index." The indexes in this edition *only* are keyed to page number; in all later editions, they refer to item number.

The second edition includes the following sections: "The Emergence of Science Fiction: The Beginnings to the 1920s," by Thomas D. Clareson; "Science Fiction Between the Wars: 1918-1938," by Brian Stableford; "The Modern Period: 1938-1980," by Joe De Bolt and John R. Pfeiffer; "Children's Science Fiction," by Francis J. Molson; chapters on German, French, Russian, Italian, Japanese, and Chinese science fiction by experts from those countries; plus the chapter "Research Aids," most by Barron: "Selection, Acquisition, and Cataloging of Science Fiction," "Indexes and Bibliographies," "History and Criticism," "Autobiography, Biography, and Author Studies," "Science Fiction on Film and Television," "Science Fiction Illustration," "Classroom Aids" by Marshall B. Tymn, "Science Fiction Magazines" by H. W. Hall, "Library and Private Collections of Science Fiction and Fantasy" by Hall, and "Core Collection Checklist," with author and title indices.

The third edition includes five chapters on English-language SF: "The Emergence of Science Fiction: The Beginnings to the 1920s," by Thomas D. Clareson; "Science Fiction Between the Wars: 1918-1938," by Brian Stableford; "The Early Modern Period: 1938-1963," by Joe De Bolt and John R. Pfeiffer; "The Modern Period: 1964-1986," by Brian Stableford; and "Children's and Young Adult Science Fiction," by Francis J. Molson. The foreign-language chapters are much expanded, including sections on German, French, Russian, Japanese, Italian, Danish, Swedish, Norwegian, Dutch, Belgian, Romanian, Yugoslav, and Hebrew SF, all by experts on those literatures. Research aids (most by Barron) include "Science Fiction Publishing and Libraries," "General Reference Works," "History and Criticism," "Author Studies," "Science Fiction on Film and Television," "Science Fiction Illustration," "Teaching Materials" by Muriel R. Becker, "Science Fiction Magazines" by H. W. Hall, "Library and Private Collections of Science Fiction and Fantasy" by Hall and Barron, and "Core Collection Checklist," with author/subject and title indices.

Because different critics contributed sections covering different periods of time in each edition, access to all three versions is desirable. For example, Clareson's section on the beginnings of SF was trimmed from 182 listings in the second edition to 108 books in the third, making it much less comprehensive than comparable chapters in previous versions; while Stableford's second chapter, on the period from 1918-38, was expanded by sixteen books, with some entries being recast but many remaining exactly the same. The somewhat arbitrary breaking of the modern period into two sections for the third edition results in many well-known authors' works being split between the two chapters, making an overall critical perspective difficult for the user. However, despite a slight British bias in the Stableford chapters, most of the evaluations seem fair, balanced, and current. Coverage of untranslated foreign-language SF is extensive and unrivaled: for most of the works and authors evaluated, *Anatomy* is the only critical source in English. The comments on secondary sources and research aids tend to be learned but quirky, sometimes focusing on such extraneous elements as cost (over content); and it is here that the lack of specific bibliographical data (particularly paginations) is most heavily felt, since comparisons between similar critical works or bibliographies do not always mention their lengths. The core collection lists are useful for libraries and critics with limited budgets and are generally well-chosen and well-balanced, with a good mix of basic authors and themes.

Unlike many of the works evaluated in this book, *Anatomy* has continued to grow and evolve through three successive editions, each version larger than the last, making it perhaps the most useful single-volume guide to science fiction literature, with fair, current, comprehensive coverage of all the major books in the field. However, the rationale for breaking coverage of English-language fiction into chronological sections which vary with each edition is unclear beyond the immediate need to pay each contributor for his or her chapters; a more logical and useful arrangement for future editions might be a single alphabetical sequence for English-language authors, excepting juvenile fiction, or a grouping of authors (rather than titles) into specific periods of development acknowledged by the critical experts, so that one writer's works would not be spread over more than one section. Despite this small *caveat*, Barron remains a vital and essential reference tool for every library collection, as well as for every SF critic's personal library. See also the companion volumes on fantasy and horror (see #52 and #53).

52. Barron, Neil, ed. **Fantasy Literature: A Reader's Guide**. New York & London, Garland Publishing, 1990. xxvii, 586 p. index. (Garland Reference Library of the Humanities, Vol. 874). LC 89-23693. ISBN 0-8240-3148-2.

Intended as both a companion to *Anatomy of Wonder* (see #51) and *Horror Literature* (see #53) and as a replacement for Tymn/Zahorski/Boyer (see #77), this guide is organized very similarly to the other two books in the series, into broad chapters contributed by individual critics, each covering successive stages of the genre's development, then further subarranged alphabetically by author's name and by his or her individual works.

Contents: "Preface" (by Barron); "Contributors" (brief biographical squibs); Introduction, "Children Who Survive," by Michael Bishop. "Fantasy Literature": "1. Development of the Fantastic Tradition Through 1811," by Dennis M. Kratz; "2. The Nineteenth Century, 1812-99," by Brian Stableford; "3. From Baum to Tolkien, 1900-56," by Stableford; "4A. Modern Fantasy for Adults, 1957-88," by Maxim Jakubowksi; "4B. Modern Fantasy for Young Adults, 1950-88," by Francis Molson and Susan G. Miles. "Research Aids": "5. Fantasy and Horror Fiction and Libraries," by Barron; "6. General Reference Works," by Barron; "7. History and Criticism," by Gary K. Wolfe; "8. Author Studies," by Richard C. West; "9. Fantasy on Film and Television," by Michael Klossner; "10. Fantastic Art and Illustration," by Walter Albert; "11. Fantasy and Horror Magazines," by Mike Ashley; "12. Library Collections," by Randall W. Scott; "13. Core Collection, Awards, Organizations, Series," by Barron. "Author Index"; "Title Index"; "Theme Index."

The five major chapters on the literature comprise 350 pages (out of 586) and cover 1,129 items as compared to 222 books in Tymn *et al.* (see #77), providing vastly greater (and ten years more current) coverage; however, it should be noted that the focus of Tymn's work is on core collection materials only, that the annotations in Tymn are much longer (averaging nearly a full page each as compared to three sentences for Barron), and that Tymn generally contains much more analysis of the individual works, the authors of those works, and their place in the history of fantastic literature. As with *Anatomy of Wonder*, authors whose works fall into more than one period will have their works split into two chapters without cross-references, making an overview of a particular writer's fantastic fiction sometimes difficult. The reviews themselves are fair and balanced, and the overall coverage includes all the recognized classics of the field, plus representative titles from some lesser-known writers, and a few books that are relatively little-known. A new and very attractive feature of both *Fantasy Literature* and *Horror Literature* (as compared to *Anatomy of Wonder*) is the inclusion at the head of each author's entry of a series of two- to three-letter codes referencing twenty of the best-known bio-bibliographies and readers' guides in the field;

however, the abbreviations list is somewhat awkwardly buried in the middle of the preface when perhaps it would have been more obvious to casual users if listed on a separate page prior to the introductory material. The indexes reference item numbers only, but in general provide thorough access to all materials listed.

Barron's work will surely become the standard readers' guide to its subject, although Tymn's book of the same title is still useful as a guide to fantasy classics and should not be carelessly discarded. A "must" buy for all library collections.

53. Barron, Neil, ed. **Horror Literature: A Reader's Guide**. New York & London, Garland Publishing, 1990. xxvii, 596 p. index. (Garland Reference Library of the Humanities, Vol. 1220). LC 89-27454. ISBN 0-8240-4347-2.

The resurgence of weird and supernatural fiction in the 1980s, beginning with the enormous popularity of author Stephen King, resulted in the establishment of a separate paperback genre with its own packaging format and its own group of proprietary authors (who in turn formed their own writers' organization). Thus, it is highly appropriate that this new readers' guide, a companion volume to Barron's *Anatomy of Wonder* (see #51) and *Fantasy Literature* (see #52), and intended partially as a replacement to Tymn's *Horror Literature* (see #78), has now been published.

Horror Literature is arranged similarly to its two companions, with chapters contributed by individual critics, each covering successive stages of the genre's development, then further subarranged alphabetically by author's name and by his or her individual works. Contents include "Preface" (by Barron); "Contributors"; Introduction: "Children Who Survive," by Michael Bishop; "Horror Literature": "1. The Early Gothic, 1762-1824," by Frederick S. Frank; "2. The Later Gothic Tradition, 1825-96," by Brian Stableford; "3. Early Modern Horror Fiction, 1897-1949," by Stableford; "4. Contemporary Horror Fiction, 1950-88," by Keith Neilson. "Research Aids": "5. Libraries and Fantasy/Horror Publishing," by Barron; "6. General Reference Books," by Barron; "7. History and Criticism," by Michael A. Morrison; "8. Author Studies," by Morrison; "9. Horror on Film and Television," by Michael Klossner; "10. Fantastic Art and Illustration," by Walter Albert; "11. Fantasy and Horror Magazines," by Mike Ashley; "12. Library Collections," by Randall A. Scott; "13. Core Collections, Awards, Organizations, Series," by Barron; "Author Index," "Title Index," "Theme Index."

The four major chapters on the literature comprise 326 pages (out of 596) and cover 792 items as compared to 1,094 books in Tymn (see #78). Barron provides a thorough coverage of the vast explosion of the field during the past decade, describing books and authors unknown in 1981, while Tymn's work includes a far greater examination of the roots of the field in the gothic horror movement of the late 1700s and early 1800s and in general covers more books in somewhat greater depth. The disparity becomes even larger when one realizes that as many as *half* of the entries in Tymn are not described in Barron. As with *Anatomy of Wonder*, authors whose works fall into more than one period will have their works split into two chapters without cross-references, making an overview of a particular writer's horrific fiction sometimes difficult; however, *Horror Literature* evinces far less such overlapping than its two companion works, perhaps because the period divisions in *Horror* better reflect the actual development of the genre and not just an arbitrary splitting of the literature into more digestible units. The reviews themselves are fair and balanced, and the overall coverage includes all the recognized classics of the field, plus representative titles from some lesser-known writers, and a few books that are relatively little-known. A new and very attractive feature of both *Fantasy Literature* and *Horror Literature* (as compared to *Anatomy of Wonder*) is the inclusion at the head of each author's entry of a series of two- to three-letter codes referencing twenty of the best-known bio-bibliographies and readers' guides in the field; however, the abbreviations list is somewhat awkwardly buried in the middle of the preface when perhaps it would have been more obvious to casual users if listed on a separate page prior to the introductory material. There is considerable overlapping between the nonfiction chapters in these two guides (*Fantasy* and *Horror*), as might be expected; many entries are identical, although each book includes some unique references. The indexes refer to item numbers only but in general provide thorough access to all materials listed.

Barron's work will surely become the standard readers' guide to its subject, although Tymn's volume of the same title is still useful, particularly as a guide to the gothic period and the many lesser-known writers (and their works) of the nineteenth and early twentieth century not covered in Barron. With its companions, the Barron trilogy should be available in all library collections.

54. Bleiler, Everett F. **The Guide to Supernatural Fiction: A Full Description of 1,775 Books from 1750 to 1960, Including Ghost Stories, Weird Fiction, Stories of Supernatural Horror, Fantasy, Gothic Novels, Occult Fiction, and Similar Literature, with Author, Title, and Motif Indexes**. Kent, Ohio, The Kent State University Press, 1983. ix, 723 p. index. LC 82-25477. ISBN 0-87338-228-9.

Well-known critic, editor, and bibliographer Bleiler attempts nothing less than a comprehensive annotated survey to the supernatural in fiction through 1960, and he succeeds magnificently.

Materials are organized in alphabetical order by main entry (usually by author but under title for anonymous works), then chronologically by publication date. Works are listed under the byline appearing on the book, with appropriate see or see also references for pseudonyms; this sometimes results in a particular writer's work being split between two or more pennames. A typical author entry includes author's name (all caps, with middle names in brackets), years of birth and death, a one-paragraph critical biography (when known, mentioning nationality and summarizing the author's career), and a chronological list of the writer's supernatural fictions followed (where applicable) by a chronological list of the author's edited volumes of supernatural stories. A typical book entry includes item number, title (all caps, underlined), publisher of first edition, place of publication, year of publication, format (e.g., "paperbound") but no paginations, and an annotation. Entries are numbered consecutively throughout the volume from 1-1,774 (one less than the title indicates). The summaries are both descriptive and evaluative and range in size from 50-2,700 words, 250 being average. The annotations follow a standard format, with a prompt at the beginning of the entry indicating its content (e.g., "what-would-happen-if," "semiallegorical short novel set in 4th century Rome"), mention of alternative or original titles (if translated) followed by a detailed plot summary, and a brief evaluation. Bleiler does not hesitate to trash poorly written fictions, to praise those who deserve kudos, or to label run-of-the-mill books "routine." A few works published in the 1960s are included.

Most significantly, the author also covers in great detail the hundreds of anthologies and single-author collections produced in this genre, annotating and evaluating *every story* with supernatural content; stories are lettered in order of appearance from "a-z," "aa-zz," etc.; those reprinted in more than one publication (a not uncommon occurrence) are annotated once, with all other appearances being referenced back to the first. Thousands of tales are thus summarized, providing an immeasurably rich treasure trove for future scholarship. Finally, Bleiler includes at the end of his book an "Index of Motifs and Story Types," enabling the researcher to gain access to the material (both novels and stories) through very detailed subject breakdowns correlated to item numbers. The "Author Index" references authors, titles (novels in all caps, stories in lower case letters), and item numbers for all appearances; the "Title Index" correlates titles and authors only, requiring the user to refer back to the "Author Index." A brief closing essay, "The Phenomenology of Contranatural Fiction," completes the work. The book is shot from legible but light two-column typed copy (in 8.5" x 11" format) and bound to library standards.

Bleiler's coverage is remarkably thorough, delineating works from the gothics of the late eighteenth and early nineteenth centuries (but only those with supernatural elements) to the early modern period. As usual, his work is authoritative, his research sound, his judgments middle-of-the-road and generally supported by both the history of the literature and by the prevailing critical opinions on each writer. The principal problem with the book is its internal layout: Bleiler provides one-line breaks between author entries but none whatever between monographic records; for prolific writers, this tends to create page after page of somewhat light, massed-together copy, with only the occasional two-line left extent of the item number to break the mass of text. On many pages one is hard pressed to distinguish specific items in the body of the material without reading the sometimes lengthy entries in their entirety. It is also unfortunate that the title index lacks entry numbers and that paginations were omitted. These are small *caveats*, to be sure. The data themselves, the lifelong effort which has gone into producing this labor of love, everywhere speak to us of the knowledge, the sympathy, the understanding which the author has brought to this book. *The Guide to Supernatural Fiction* is a great achievement, even for Ev Bleiler, and that is saying a great deal indeed. See also the companion volume on early science fiction (see #55).

55. Bleiler, E. F., with Richard J. Bleiler. **Science-Fiction, the Early Years: A Full Description of More than 3,000 Science-Fiction Stories from Earliest Times to the Appearance of the Genre Magazines in 1930, with Author, Title, and Motif Indexes.** Kent, Ohio, and London, Kent State University Press, 1990. xxiii, 998 p. index. LC 90-4839. ISBN 0-87338-416-4.

Bleiler (and son) have once again produced a magnificent reference tool, one which is unlikely to be duplicated by any other researcher. The author examined every prose work of science fiction (periodical as well as monographic) with a publication date prior to 1930, which Bleiler uses as the demarcation point for the beginning of SF as a modern publishing genre. Materials are listed alphabetically by author's name, then chronologically by title. A typical author entry includes author (all caps boldfaced), years of birth and death (if known), brief biography (if known, giving nationality, career summation, and other notable accomplishments).

A typical fiction entry provides item number, title (boldfaced all caps), publisher, place of publication, year of publication, pseudonym (where applicable), illustrator, plus similar data for other significant editions, and annotation. Periodical entries (interfiled with the books) give magazine title (italics) and month and year of publication but otherwise are similarly handled. The annotations range in size from fifty-word paragraphs for short fiction to several pages of text (roughly 2,500 words) for major works and are largely plot oriented with a single-line summation/evaluation at the end and occasional bibliographical notes added on. Short SF stories within a collection are each covered individually. Completing the text are two additional sections, the "Addenda" and "Background Books" chapters. The materials are numbered consecutively throughout the book (including the "Addenda" section, but not the "Background Books") from 1-2,475.

Five indexes cover every conceivable access point: "Motif and Theme Index," "Date Index," "Magazine Index," "Title Index," "Author Index," all keyed to item numbers. The first of these provides extraordinarily detailed analyses of the works, listed alphabetically by subject (e.g., "Islam, sacred objects stolen. 679" or "Mercury, geography of," further subdivided into "Hot and cold zones, but habitable: 524, 1979," etc.). Would that such access were available for more modern works of fantastic literature! The "Date Index" records first publication dates of the works keyed to item number; one must examine the item to determine the author and title. The "Magazine Index" is arranged alphabetically by periodical title, then chronologically by year and item number. The "Title Index" lists titles (books in all caps, short stories with initial caps only) and authors but (curiously) no item numbers. The "Author Index" correlates authors, titles (using the same style as the "Title Index"), and item numbers. A two-page bibliography at the end of the book lists reference works alphabetically by author's name. The book is shot from very clear word-processed copy and bound to library standards.

There are several design problems with this bibliography that were perhaps inevitable given the amount of material included. The volume is laid out in an 8.5" x 11" double-column format, with one line break between each author but only a three-space paragraph indentation delineating new entries (for those authors who have more than one). This layout works well on those pages where there are three or more author entries and where the entries are relatively frequent and short; the single-line spacing which separates each writer also breaks up the text as the eye runs down the page. However, the entry for Jules Verne runs a dozen pages, with several more pages of collaborative entries, many of the entries occupying a full column or more; and it is here that the reader experiences problems. The absence of running heads and the absence of any paragraph indentations except at the start of a new entry combine to run the text together into one indivisible mass on the page, making the delineation of individual entries (or even the determination of the author's name) unnecessarily difficult.

However, in this particular instance the quality of the material clearly overrides the format quirks. Simply stated, there is no other work available or likely to become available in the future which provides so much important source material on the beginnings of science-fiction literature. Many of the books and stories covered here are totally inaccessible to modern scholars; some are known to exist in only ten or twenty copies, and many others will soon vanish due to oxidation of paper and bindings. This is not just an important reference tool; any future researcher investigating the origins of science fiction as a genre *must* have access to Bleiler's guide or forever be damned to a literary Hades. Copies should be held by all academic libraries. A companion volume on horror fiction (see #54) is also available.

56. Bleiler, E. F., ed. **Science Fiction Writers: Critical Studies of the Major Authors from the Early Nineteenth Century to the Present Day**. New York, Charles Scribner's Sons, 1982. xv, 623 p. index. LC 81-51032. ISBN 0-684-16740-9.

Bleiler is best known for his bibliographies and critiques of fantastic and criminous literature, but this book demonstrates his further abilities as an editor. *Science Fiction Writers* is divided into seven major sections: "Early Science Fiction," "Primitive Science Fiction: The American Dime Novel and Pulp Magazines," "Mainstream Georgian Authors," "American Science Fiction: The Formative Period," "The Circumbellum Period," "The Moderns," and "Continental Science Fiction." The book consists of seventy-five full-length essays by twenty-six contributors (including Bleiler himself) ranging in size from 4,000-8,000 words (most in the lower range), arranged in alphabetical order by surname of the author being critiqued (for chapters five and six), and in no discernible order for the rest. Each entry includes a brief biography, extensive commentary on the author's works (specifically and generally), a critical summation, an assessment of the author's place in the history of science fiction literature, and a selected bibliography of primary works (in chronological order) and secondary works (in alphabetical order by author), often including brief annotations. The focus here is on "classic" writers, the youngest author included (Samuel R. Delany) having been born in 1942. Bleiler contributes a brief introduction, and an extensive author/title index completes the book.

The essays reflect the abilities of the individual critics but are generally authoritative, well-considered, and longer than those available in any other reference set. The arrangement by chapters, each reflecting a specific period or movement, is the only major flaw in the book, since more than half of the entries (forty) fall into "The Moderns," and three chapters (four through six) out of seven account for fifty-eight of the seventy-five entries. It would make more sense in some future edition simply to arrange the authors being covered by surname, thus enabling the reader to access the material immediately. Also, many of the primary bibliographies are deliberately incomplete, an unfortunate choice given the ready accessibility of this information in other published sources. Even with these minor problems, however, *Science Fiction Writers* is a valuable one-volume critical guide to the classic writers of the SF genre, an essential purchase for anyone even marginally interested in the field. See also Bleiler's companion volume on supernatural writers (see #57) and Cowart and Wymer's *Twentieth-Century American Science-Fiction Writers* (see #44).

57. Bleiler, E. F., ed. **Supernatural Fiction Writers, Fantasy and Horror.** New York, Charles Scribner's Sons, 1985. xix, 1,169 p. in 2 v. index. LC 84-27588. ISBN 0-684-17808-7 (set).

This companion volume to *Science Fiction Writers* (see #56) is similarly arranged and presented. One hundred forty-seven essays by sixty-two critics are organized into fifteen chapters representing specific periods and nationalities: Volume One: "Early Writers," "French Writers," "German Writers," "British Gothic and Romantic Writers," "British Victorian Writers," "British Fin-de-Siècle Writers," "British Early-Twentieth-Century Writers"; Volume Two: "British Writers of the Interbellum Period," "British Postwar Writers," "American Early-Nineteenth-Century and Victorian Writers," "American Fin-de-Siècle Writers," "American Mainstream Writers of the Early to Middle Twentieth Century," "Early American Pulp Writers," "American Pulp Writers of the Circumbellum Period," and "British and American Modern Writers." Each entry ranges in size from 3,000-7,000 words (averaging 4,000) and typically includes a brief biography, an extensive commentary on the author's major works, a critical summation, an assessment of the writer's place in the history of fantastic literature, and a selected primary and secondary bibliography. Bleiler himself contributes a brief introduction and thirteen of the critical essays; a detailed author/title index and brief general bibliography complete the book. Coverage is considerably broader than in *Science Fiction Writers*, with one-third of the essays covering nineteenth-century writers of the supernatural, many known only to experts and literary historians, and the inclusion at the other end of the scale of several writers born in the late 1940s.

As in *Science Fiction Writers*, the quality of the material varies with the abilities of the many individual critics but is generally high. The short author bibliographies, which include only the writers' more important books with selected nonfiction sources and occasional one-sentence annotations for the latter, are at best of limited usefulness—they could easily have been expanded into more complete (and more valuable) listings. The arrangement by individual chapter and thereafter alphabetically by author surname (for the last two chapters—the modern period—only; the other, smaller chapters have no discernible internal arrangement) is unnecessarily confusing; a more logical arrangement for a second edition might be one alphabetical sequence for the entire book. This problem is exacerbated by the failure of the publisher to repeat the table of contents at the beginning of Volume Two. Even with these difficulties, however, Bleiler's book is a major modern source for critical evaluations of writers of the fantastic; in particular, his coverage of little-known but important nineteenth- and early twentieth-century authors of weird and supernatural literature is unparalleled. Bleiler's firm editorial hand is evident throughout, the judgments of the critics generally fair and balanced, the book well designed, bound, and presented. A necessary addition to the library of any would-be researcher of horror literature.

58. Budrys, Algis. **Benchmarks:** *Galaxy* **Bookshelf**. Carbondale, Ill., Southern Illinois University Press, 1985. xxvi, 349 p. index. (Alternatives). LC 84-10518. ISBN 0-8093-1187-9.

Budrys, a well-known science fiction writer, produced this series of fifty-four book review columns for the February 1965-November/December 1971 issues of *Galaxy Magazine*, covering 161 books released during this particularly fertile and energetic period in SF publishing and touching upon many other books and authors peripherally. The columns are reproduced in the same order as originally published, with little editing but occasional sidenotes to explain particular references or to comment further on the book(s) being reviewed. Introductions by Frederik Pohl, former editor of *Galaxy*, by Catherine L. McClenahan, and by Budrys himself frame the material; a comprehensive author/title index and a separate "List of Books Reviewed Index" complete the volume and provide complete access to the material covered.

Budrys shines while pointing out the literary deficiencies of the giants of the genre, as in his review of Frank Herbert's *Dune*, generally considered a modern classic of science fiction:

> But we are not yet the omnipathetic departed, and we have to simply read the words. What we find, dulling the fine creation and shrouding it as surely but not as stingingly as the storms of Paul's Arrakis, are the words—the twisting, sub-plotted, ravelled edge of unhemmed selvage at the margins of the strong whole cloth. Herbert has chucked MacLeanism, he has chucked Kipling's mistake; but instead of seeing his own mistake he has elaborated it. Being intelligent and sophisticated, he has made the elaboration most enjoyable. But if he thinks—if you think—that the reason *Dune* turns flat and tails off at the end is because even four hundred pages cannot encompass it properly, please consider instead the possibility that 200 pages would have sufficed even for an epic. *The Odyssey* is not that long. Nor *Beowulf*, nor the narrative of the New Testament.

The critic's pointed, pithy remarks, never intended to be anything but opinionated, rarely fail to illuminate and are always entertaining and enlightening. And while this collection is not a readers' guide in its organization or original intent, Budrys touches on so many important writers and books in his six years of commentary that *Benchmarks* achieves very near the same purpose.

59. Cawthorn, James, and Michael Moorcock. **Fantasy: The 100 Best Books**. London, Xanadu Publications, 1988. 216 p. index. ISBN 0-947761-24-1. Also: New York, Carroll & Graf, 1988. 216 p. index. LC 88-9510. ISBN 0-88184-335-0.

The second in the "100 Best Books" series includes a hundred 800-word essays on classics of fantastic literature arranged chronologically by date of first publication (with some anomalies), beginning with *Gulliver's Travels* in 1726 and including books published as recently as 1987. Several of the pieces cover more than one item, bringing the total number of books actually critiqued to 110. Each entry includes author, title, publication data (publisher, place of publication, and year of publication) for both the first edition and the first U.S. or U.K. edition (depending on where the book was originally published), plus critical commentary consisting in roughly equal measures of background data (often mentioning the author's other prominent works), plot summary, and evaluation and summation. A brief pair of introductions by the editors and an author/title index complete the book.

This type of work stands or falls on the validity of its selections, as well as the soundness of the authors' critical judgments. "Fantasy" is loosely interpreted here to include horrific, gothic, fantastic, surrealistic, and science fictional literature; several of the choices, such as Herman Melville's *Moby-Dick*, are only marginally fantastic under the widest possible definition of the field. The blurring of genre lines is somewhat unfortunate given the fact that two companion books in this series already cover horror and science fiction (see #63 and #73); and, in fact, several titles overlap between the horror and fantasy volumes. Still, the eighty-four books listed prior to 1960 are all acknowledged classics of fantastic literature, with few exceptions, over whose merits no critic could much quibble. The selections for the modern period (1961-87) remain much more controversial, however, demonstrating a clear pro-British bias (eighteen out of twenty-six volumes covered) and including several books and authors little known in the United States while omitting other acknowledged classics that should perhaps have been included (Stephen R. Donaldson's *The Chronicles of Thomas Covenant the Unbeliever*, for example).

The essays themselves are pointed, sure, illuminating, always transcending the need to include plot summations without becoming either dreary or bogged down in philosophical ruminations. One is left with a real desire to read or revisit these books, a true measure of Cawthorn and Moorcock's ability to delineate their essences. Thus, even with its selection problems, *Fantasy: The 100 Best Books* remains one of the more readable and enlightening of the four published volumes in this series. Compare Pringle's *Modern Fantasy* (see #72).

60. Crawford, Joseph H., Jr., James J. Donahue, and Donald M. Grant. **"333": A Bibliography of the Science-Fantasy Novel**. Providence, R.I., The Grandon Co., 1953. 80 p. index. LC A55-8667 (pbk.). Also: New York, Arno Press, 1975. 80 p. index. (Science Fiction series). LC 74-15959. ISBN 0-405-06324-5.

The Grandon Company was a short-lived SF specialty imprint that presaged the later and much better-known company, Donald M. Grant, Publisher. This guide includes plot summaries of 333 gothic, horror, science fiction, fantasy, lost race, and associational novels published through 1950. The book is arranged alphabetically by author, then by title. A typical entry includes author (surname in all caps), title (italics), place of publication, year of publication, publisher (in parentheses), an indication whether the book is "illustrated," category (e.g., "lost race," "oriental," "fantastic adventure"), and summary. The annotations range from 75-150 words in length, and are descriptive rather than analytical. A title/author index completes the book. The text is typeset (an unusual feature for reference works of this period), and both printings are clear and legible.

Crawford *et al.* emphasize "classic" works of fantastic literature, and indeed, very few of the works described will be unknown to serious researchers, most also being covered in Barron's three guides (see #51, #52, and #53) and in other works. However, the very lucid plot summaries in *"333"* (some of which are longer and more detailed than those found in any other source) still make this a useful guide for scholars interested in early fantasy, horror, and science fiction. The original version is now scarce, and the Arno reprint was withdrawn shortly after publication (in a dispute over rights) with only a handful of copies being distributed, making it even harder to find than the Grandon edition.

61. Fletcher, Marilyn P., ed.; James L. Thorson, consulting ed. **Reader's Guide to Twentieth-Century Science Fiction**. Chicago and London, American Library Association, 1989. xiv, 673 p. index. LC 88-7815. ISBN 0-8389-0504-8.

In the first sentence of her introduction, Fletcher rhetorically poses the question, "What prompts the need for yet another science fiction reference book?" and it is her failure adequately to answer her own query that defines the problems with this book.

Fletcher offers 130 bio-critical essays (on 131 writers) contributed by thirty-eight critics. Entries range in size from 1,000-3,000 words, averaging 2,000, and generally are divided into four sections: "Life and Works" (250-750 words), "Themes and Style" (150-500 words), "Plot Summaries of Major Works" (the bulk of each entry), and "Biographical/Bibliographical Readings" (a short paragraph of secondary sources, without annotations, including articles, interviews, critical studies, and bibliographies, usually comprising no more than two to ten entries total). An acknowledgments page, three-page introduction, list of contributors, two appendices ("A: Science Fiction Magazines and Critical Journals"; "B: Nebula and Hugo Award Winners"), a half-page list of sources, and a title index complete the book.

All of the major SF authors are covered, of course, but it is in her selection of secondary writers, those who have yet to attain generally acknowledged fame outside of genre circles, that Fletcher begins to go awry. The focus of the book is stated to be twentieth-century writers, the earliest figure included being H. G. Wells, and Fletcher limits her coverage to no more than six items per author (although even this rule is fudged with specific entries). Fair enough. But in what sense is Anatoly Dneprov the equal, say, of Thomas M. Disch, either as craftsman or *littérateur* or science-fiction writer? How, precisely, does the career of horror writer H. P. Lovecraft fit into a book ostensibly about SF authors? Are we to presume, by virtue of the fact that her entry is equal in length to those of Heinlein and Wells, that the life and works of Marta Randall are of *equal* significance? These are troubling issues, scarcely satisfied by the introductory material.

The quality of the material also varies widely. Some of the critics—Sam Moskowitz, Michael Collings, Stephen Potts, Jay Rawlins, Richard Bleiler—are well-known researchers and acknowledged experts on the history of fantastic literature, or at least on specific writers and/or movements. The vast majority, however, are not; included among their number are a graduate student, many librarians, an environmental water specialist, several lecturers, etc. This is not to impugn any specific critic's profession—I am myself a librarian, as is Richard Bleiler—but only to suggest that Ms. Fletcher failed to draw extensively upon a well-established stable of academics and other experts who are readily available to contribute to this type of publication. As a result, while some of the critics transcend the format limitations, weaving summaries of the author's major books into critical mosaics illuminating the major themes of the writer's career, all too many are constrained into producing potboiled plot summaries that scarcely tell us more than "so and so" did "such and such." The secondary-source lists at the end of each entry are vastly incomplete, as is the source bibliography on page 663, which misses the standard genre biblios as well as major biographical sources.

Yet even mediocre reference books sometimes have their uses, and this particular volume does contain commentaries on some specific works at lengths that might be difficult to locate elsewhere, at least in a one-volume guide. Also, Fletcher might well prove useful in the small or medium-sized public library, where resources are limited and only a few books can be purchased on specific subjects. One wonders, however, why the major American librarians' organization, which has done so much good work in the field, continues to churn out so many half-baked reference guides. Perhaps too many cooks spoil the broth.

62. Holdom, Lynne. **Capsule Reviews**. Lake Jackson, Tex., Joanne Burger, 1977. 51 p. index. (pbk.). Also: San Bernardino, Calif., The Borgo Press, 1980. 51 p. index. LC 80-20445. ISBN 0-89370-056-8.

This amateurishly produced guide covers roughly 450 science fiction and fantasy novels from the 1950s-70s, arranged alphabetically by author, then by title. A typical entry includes title (all caps), author, summary, and series notation (where applicable). The annotations range from one to three sentences and are mostly descriptive, with occasional one- or two-word analytical comments. The title index lists titles and authors only. The book is shot from typed copy. The vast majority of these books can be found in Barron's three guides (see #51, #52, #53) and in similar works with better annotations and bibliographical data (none of which are provided in Holdom's work). Largely useless.

63. Jones, Steve, and Kim Newman, eds. **Horror: 100 Best Books**. London, Xanadu Publications, 1988. x, 256 p. ISBN 0-947761-37-3. Also: New York, Carroll & Graf, 1988. x, 256 p. LC 88-7351. ISBN 0-88184-417-9.

The editors of the third volume in the "100 Best Books" series, unlike its two companions, invited the world's leading horror writers to select their favorite books in the genre and then provide a 700-word essay on each item. Several previously published critical pieces by Edgar Allan Poe and M. R. James were also reprinted. The entries are arranged chronologically from the earliest (*Doctor Faustus*, 1592) to the latest (1987). Each entry provides a 150-word plot summary in italics, including brief background material on the author followed by the critic's commentary. The contributors are mostly well-known horror and fantasy writers in their own right. Two brief introductions by the editors and by Ramsey Campbell, biographies of the contributors, and a six-page chronologically arranged "List of Recommended Reading" complete the volume.

Although the editors restricted the selections to a previously prepared list of "classics," many of these titles were perforce not chosen by the participants and therefore not included in this book except in the recommended reading section. Thus, *Horror: 100 Best Books* does not really include the *best* books of the genre under any set of criteria but 100 individual selections of a *best book*, reflecting the idiosyncrasies of the critics and including a number of items which are questionably fantastic or which have already been covered in the science fiction and fantasy volumes in this series. There is also a much greater focus in this book on the modern period to the detriment of truly time-tested "classics"—of the 100 selections, more than half were published after World War II, more than a third after 1970, and almost a fifth in the 1980s. One must question how so many "classics" could have appeared among us so quietly unheralded.

The quality of the essays also varies widely, from "gee whiz, that's great!" meanderings to profound literary insights from the likes of Brian W. Aldiss, Colin Wilson, and Brian Stableford. Most are at least entertaining, however, which is all this quasi-guide can be. The absence of an index is dismaying.

64. Kies, Cosette. **Supernatural Fiction for Teens: 500 Good Paperbacks to Read for Wonderment, Fear, and Fun**. Littleton, Colo., Libraries Unlimited, 1987. xii, 127 p. index. LC 87-3228. ISBN 0-87287-602-0 (pbk.). **Supernatural Fiction for Teens: More than 1300 Good Paperbacks to Read for Wonderment, Fear, and Fun**. 2nd ed. Englewood, Colo., Libraries Unlimited, 1992. ix, 267 p. ISBN 0-87287-940-2.

This handy guide selectively annotates 500 works of horror and fantasy suitable for the young adult reader, books that have also been issued in inexpensive, paperback form. Kies's introduction explains her criteria and includes a short seven-item list of secondary sources (all dealing specifically with the literature of horror and the supernatural). The main bibliography includes 463 novels and collections, arranged alphabetically by author. An additional thirty-seven items are included in a separate anthologies section, alphabetically by editor's name. The appendices include a list of books in series (by series name, with author and title); an index to movies (motion pictures mentioned in the primary bibliography, by film title and item number); a directory of paperback publishers, with addresses; "Title Index" (title and item number); and "Subject Index" (by broad subject—e.g., Fairies, Zombies, Paranormal Abilities, etc.—and item number).

A typical entry includes item number, author, title (boldface), place of publication, publisher, year of publication, pagination, ISBN number, original publisher and date if previously published, series, category (a single, boldfaced letter: "**A**"=Written for Teens; "**B**"=Written for Younger Teens; "**C**"=Written for Adults; "**D**"=Classic [tales of the supernatural from nineteenth- and early twentieth-century sources]), "Other works" of interest by the author, information on movie adaptations (with title [if different], production date, director, and major stars), brief annotation, and subject (keyed to the subject index). The annotations consist of one- to three-sentence plot descriptions. Short story collections (in the main section) and anthologies include complete contents listings (story titles and authors), except for series anthologies (*The Year's Best Horror Stories*, for example), where only the latest published volume is annotated. The text is well designed and typeset, easy to read, and well indexed.

Compared to Lynn's *Fantasy Literature for Children and Young Adults* (see #67), *Supernatural Fiction* surprisingly includes a great many titles (more than half of the 500 listed) annotated in no other source. Kies covers a few books which might more appropriately be categorized as "high fantasy," but the vast majority of the titles covered are original or reprint horror paperbacks published for the adult and young adult markets. Authors such as William W. Johnstone, Shaun Hutson, John Halkin, William Schoell, J. N. Williamson, and other rising stars of modern horror are scarcely mentioned elsewhere; also unique is her coverage of Bantam's Dark Forces Series, Dell's Twilight Series, Ballantine's Find Your Fate books, and Pacer's The Zodiac Club, all designed as original fantasy/horror adventure novels published only in paperback. Kies's work should become a standard guide for public librarians. A second expanded edition was released in the spring of 1992.

65. King, Betty. **Women of the Future: The Female Main Character in Science Fiction**. Metuchen, N.J. & London, The Scarecrow Press, 1984. xxi, 273 p. index. LC 83-20130. ISBN 0-8108-1664-4.

King provides an historical and critical guide to female characters in science fiction (written by both male and female writers), the primary emphasis being on twentieth-century fantastic literature. The book is broken into seven main sections plus three appendices: "1.

Historical Perspective—1818 Through 1929"; "2. The 1930s"; 3. "The 1940s"; "4. The 1950s"; "5. The 1960s"; "6. The 1970s"; "7. The 1980s"; "Appendix A: Collections and Anthologies of Stories about Women Characters"; "Appendix B: Women Characters in Erotic Science Fiction"; "Appendix C: Amazon Women."

The thirty-seven-page first chapter includes, in narrative form, a chronological summary of the major works of the pre-modern period in fantastic literature. The remaining sections each provide a brief summary paragraph for the decade and then list, in alphabetical order by author's name, the major works of short and long fiction published during that ten-year period. A typical entry includes author (in all caps with middle names in parentheses and real names in lower case in parentheses where applicable), story title (in quotes if a short story, underlined if a novel), and bibliographical data. For shorter works, King provides magazine where first published (underlined), month and year of publication, and a list of the collections or anthologies in which the story has appeared, with title (underlined), place of publication, publisher, and year of publication. Only those stories which have been reprinted in book form are included. For novels, King includes place of publication, publisher, and year of publication, plus similar information on known reprints in English. No paginations are provided.

The annotations include main characters, with their physical characteristics and mental/emotional characteristics, and "story particulars" (i.e., plot summaries) ranging in size from 300-700 words, averaging 500; even short stories are covered in great depth, and most of the descriptions include at least a one-sentence summation of the work's effectiveness. Each of the six later chapters includes an "Additional Reading List" in alphabetical order by author, then by title, giving author, title (underlined), place of publication, publisher, and year of publication, but no annotations. One hundred four works are annotated in the main sections, with many hundreds of other titles being mentioned in the end pieces. The first appendix lists seven anthologies of stories with women characters, arranged alphabetically by editor's name, with bibliographical data as above and a one-sentence annotation. The second appendix provides a few paragraphs of very incomplete and largely irrelevant text (in narrative form) on so-called erotic female SF characters. The last appendix lists novels and stories featuring "amazon"-type SF characters, in alphabetical order by author, then by title, with bare-bones bibliographical data. King also provides a two-page bibliography of sources; an "Index of Physical and Mental/Emotional Characteristics of Characters in the Synopses," in alphabetical order by characteristic, then by page number; an "Index of Story Particulars in the Synopses," by location, societal structure, themes, and time setting, then subdivided by topic and page number; and an "Index of Titles and Authors," not cross-referenced, which lists title or author and page number(s) only, with an asterisk following the page numbers of title records indicating an annotated entry—none of the appendices are indexed, however. The book is shot from clearly reproduced typed copy and bound in library cloth.

The structural arrangement of *Women* makes it unnecessarily difficult to use, artificially dividing authors and stories into ten-year segments that sometimes make very little sense. Thus, works by Andre Norton, for example, are referenced (in the author/title index) to four sets of page numbers, including one annotated work from the 1960s (on pages 126-27), one unannotated book from the same period (on page 139), eight unannotated novels from the 1970s (on pages 195-96), and two unannotated works from the 1980s (on page 234)—but there is *no way* to tell from the index exactly how many works by Norton are covered, what they are, or whether or not they are annotated. Further, while King covers a great many works, one wonders about her selection criteria; how could any modern researcher of women SF characters miss, for example, D. G. Compton's highly acclaimed novel, *The Continuous Katherine Mortenhoe*? Nor are there comparisons between one work and another, or one author and another, and no easy way to make such evaluations, even though the clear intent of this work is to cover a very selective list of stories and novels.

Yet, even with these *caveats* King does provide a treasure trove of descriptive and analytically indexed material found in no other source in this form, and researchers and library collections specializing in the study of women characters and authors in fantastic literature will find this book a useful starting point.

66. Lewis, Naomi. **Fantasy Books for Children**. London, National Book League, 1975. 46 p. LC 76-357468. ISBN 0-85353-240-0. Also: Rev. ed. London, National Book League, 1977. 61 [actually 55] p. LC 78-312430. ISBN 0-85353-260-5 (pbk.).

This slim British paperback annotates 214 fantasy novels, collections, and novel series suitable for pre- and early-teen readers. Books are arranged alphabetically by author's name and book title; a typical entry includes item number, author or editor, title (bold caps), translator (where appropriate), (British) publisher, year of publication, price (in 1977), pagination, illustrator, ISBN number, and description. Annotations typically run 50-375 words in length, averaging 150, and include both plot description and evaluation. There is also a list of then-current publishers' addresses. The books selected by Lewis include many nineteenth-century "classics" and well-known twentieth-century works, in equal measure, plus a scattering of 1970s titles (twenty-to-thirty volumes) which have had little circulation in the United States. Many of the latter are not in Lynn (see #67); Lewis's annotations are also considerably longer and more evaluative than Lynn's, making her brief guide worth consulting by children's librarians and students of juvenile fantasy.

67. Lynn, Ruth Nadelman. **Fantasy for Children: An Annotated Checklist**. New York & London, R. R. Bowker Co., 1979. ix, 288 p. index. LC 79-21401. ISBN 0-8352-1232-7. **Fantasy for Children: An Annotated Checklist and Reference Guide**. 2nd ed. New York & London, R. R. Bowker Co., 1983. xiv, 444 p. index. LC 83-11868. ISBN 0-8352-1732-9. **Fantasy Literature for Children and Young Adults: An Annotated Bibliography**. 3rd ed. New York, R. R. Bowker, 1989. xlvii, 771 p. index. LC 88-8162. ISBN 0-8352-2347-7.

Since the first two editions of this continuing work were almost completely subsumed into the much expanded third edition, only the latter will be considered here. *Fantasy Literature for Children and Young Adults* has quickly become the standard guide to its field. Contents: "Preface"; "Guide to Use"; "Abbreviations of Books and Review Journals Cited"; "Introduction"; "Outstanding Contemporary Books and Series"; "Part One: Annotated Bibliography." "1. Allegorical Fantasy and Literary Fairy Tales," "2. Animal Fantasy": "A. Beast Tales," "B. Talking Animal Fantasy," "3. Fantasy Collections," "4. High Fantasy": "A. Alternate Worlds or Histories," "B. Myth Fantasy," "C. Travel to Other Worlds," "6. Humorous Fantasy," "7. Magic Adventure Fantasy," "8. Time Travel Fantasy," "9. Toy Fantasy," "10. Witchcraft and Sorcery Fantasy"; "Part Two: Research Guide." "11. Reference and Bibliography," "12. History and Criticism," "13. Teaching Resources," "14. Author Studies"; "Author and Illustrator Index"; "Title Index"; "Subject Index."

Lynn's introduction provides a broad history of the fantasy genre; her "Outstanding Contemporary Books and Series" lists those publications considered by library reviewers (and by Lynn) to be particularly noteworthy, arranged by subject category and then by author. The main section of the book, comprising 365 pages, lists 3,300 fantasy volumes (novels, collections, anthologies) suitable for children, teenagers, and young adults, arranged by subject chapter and then by author. A typical entry includes scope and recommendation codes ("C"=books appropriate for children in grades 3-6; "C/YA"=those appropriate for grades 5-8; "YA"=those appropriate for grades 7-12; "R"=recommended title [those receiving three-to-four favorable reviews in the literature]; "O"=outstanding titles [those receiving five or more such reviews]); author (last name in all caps); title (italics); grade level; brief annotation (one to two sentences) with skeletal plot summary; references to related volumes, sequels, or prequels; citations of reviews of the book appearing in the library media or in standard reference guides (including title abbreviation [the abbreviations list appears on pages xvii-xviii], volume number, and page number); bibliographical data (publisher, year of publication, pagination, in-print status ["o.p."=out of print] for all known English-language editions of the book, including paperbacks). Books which could fall into more than one subject category are described in the chapter considered by Lynn to be the most appropriate, with see references from all other related chapters.

The second half of the book, the "Research Guide," is vastly expanded from the previous editions, incorporating 280 pages of unannotated secondary sources, also arranged by general subject chapter, then by main entry. Included in these sections are reference books, critical monographs, and published articles on children's literature, on children's fantasy, and on fantastic literature written by and for more adult readers. The chapter "Author Studies," consisting of 245 pages out of 280, includes interviews, feature articles, bibliographies, critiques, and reference sources on 600+ authors, arranged by the name of the writer being covered, then alphabetically by main entry; Lynn records (for monographs) author, title (in italics), place of publication, publisher, and year of publication; for shorter pieces, the following bibliographical data are mentioned: author, title (in quotes), book or magazine title (in italics), editor, place of publication, publisher, and year (for anthologies), or volume number, year, and pagination (for journal articles). These entries seem both complete and current. The indexes correlate authors/illustrators, titles, and subjects with page numbers.

The introduction states that *Fantasy Literature* focuses primarily on twentieth-century fantasy published in the United States; a few nineteenth-century classics of children's fantasy are covered if still in print, and some foreign and British titles with American editions are also listed, but these are by no means complete (Lewis's guide to children's fantasy [#66] includes a number of British fantasies published from 1960-75 not in Lynn). While Lynn eschews science fiction and horror, in fact her book covers many works that traditionally have been classed in those genres, including time travel fiction, ghost stories, alternate histories, and "science fantasy." The third edition also adds a great many works suitable for older teens, including novels published for the adult market and authors (in the "Research Guide" section) generally considered "adult" writers of fantastic literature; at the same time, a number of books suitable only for very young readers (grades 1-4) are also annotated in some sections, making real comparisons between works difficult, if not impossible. The line between juvenile and adult fantasy has become increasingly blurred as Lynn's volumes have progressed, marking a similar change in the publishing and critical world at large (books released in cloth for young adults are now often reprinted for the adult mass market audience).

A major problem with Lynn's book is its awkward format. The primary bibliography is broken into thirteen sections, each with its own alphabetical sequence; the works of one author are frequently spread over two, three, or more chapters, making any correlation difficult without constant reference to the author index. Undeniably, access by subject can sometimes be useful, particularly for the young reader, but this could have been accomplished more easily through a general category index. A more utilitarian arrangement might have been one general alphabetical sequence or a breakdown by age levels. Also, the use of code symbols of varying sizes in the left-hand margin results in a ragged textual line, making individual entries unnecessarily difficult to pick out: the eye has a tendency to skip entries with one code letter ("C," for example), which are indented two spaces, in favor of those with two or three ("C/YA"), which are flush left. The entries in the "Reference Guides" section, which are flush to the left-hand margin and which use hanging indents, are much more readable and easy to spot. Had the authors' names in the Annotated Bibliography been run in boldfaced characters, flush left with hanging indents for the rest of the paragraph and the codes embedded at the end of the collation, the resulting text would have been much easier to follow.

With all these caveats, Lynn remains the most comprehensive and current guide to juvenile fantasy now available, including such a large number of both primary and secondary sources that it perforce must be the first stop for any librarian or researcher even marginally interested in this subgenre.

68. Magill, Frank N., ed.; Keith Neilson, assoc. ed. **Survey of Modern Fantasy Literature**. Englewood Cliffs, N.J., Salem Press, 1983. xviii, 2,538, li p. in 5 v. index. LC 83-15189. ISBN 0-89356-450-8 (set).

This companion set to *Survey of Science Fiction Literature* (see #69) was actually edited by Neilson in the standard Magill series format. Neilson used a board of six consulting editors to determine the initial list of titles to be surveyed, then assigned the approximately 500 essays to 102 critics. "Fantasy" is loosely interpreted here to include weird and supernatural fiction, surrealistic literature, traditional fantasy, sword-and-sorcery adventures, juvenile works, and even a few books which are arguably not fantastic (for example, *Camino Real*, a play by Tennessee Williams). As with all the Magill volumes, this book is arranged in alphabetical order by the title of the work being critiqued; the essays range in size from 1,000-10,000 words, 2,000 being average. Series are often covered under the series title, rather than individual book title; also, there are many entries grouped together under the heading "The Short Fiction of [author's name]," covering those writers who have made major contributions to the genre with less than novel-length fiction. A typical entry includes title, author's name, year of birth, year of first book publication, type of work (e.g., "novel"), the time or era in which the book is set, the locale where the plot is set, a brief single-sentence plot summary in italics, a list of principal characters, with brief descriptive annotation; the critical essay itself; a brief bibliography of secondary sources relevant to the work in question.

The quality of the pieces varies widely, but most are usually at least readable, and, although the series format demands much attention to plot description, many are surprisingly perceptive, the overall level of these volumes being much higher than standard Magill fare. This particular set also includes several noteworthy innovations: at the end of Volume 5 are an additional nineteen general essays on specific aspects of fantastic literature (e.g., "Arthurian Legend and Modern Fantasy" and "Modern Fantasy and Marvel Comics"), plus a year-by-year "Chronology of Modern Fantasy Literature" listing major authors and titles, a short annotated bibliography of secondary sources, a bibliography of major fantasy anthologies (by editor), and a detailed author/title index covering every reference in the entire five-volume set, an unusual bonus for a Magill book (most Magill sets index the major essays only, by author and title).

Coverage is extensive and comprehensive, touching upon almost every work ever labeled a "classic" in this genre and many others besides; however, the Magill format makes an overall evaluation of any one author's works difficult if that author has penned more than one "classic" volume (this is a somewhat lesser problem with fantasy writers, many of whose works are covered under general series titles, than with authors included in other Magill sets). Also, although the mini-bibliographies of secondary sources at the end of each essay are somewhat more comprehensive in this set than in the SF volumes, they still seem scanty, with many entries listing no sources whatever. Coverage of foreign-language titles hitherto untranslated into English is much less extensive in this set as compared to the *Survey of Science Fiction Literature*. The high price tags on these sets limit their potential market largely to libraries, but they should be standard purchases for any academic institution worthy of the name.

69. Magill, Frank N., ed.; Keith Neilson, assoc. ed. **Survey of Science Fiction Literature: Five Hundred 2,000-Word Essay Reviews of World-Famous Science Fiction Novels with 2,500 Bibliographical References**. Englewood Cliffs, N.J., Salem Press, 1979. xxv, 2,542, vii p. in 5 v. index. LC 79-64639. ISBN 0-89356-194-0 (set).

The Survey, although credited to Magill, was actually edited by Neilson in the standard Magill series format. Neilson used a board of thirteen consulting editors to determine the initial list of titles to be surveyed, then assigned the approximately 500 essays to 131 critics, including sixteen from non-English-speaking countries. As with all the Magill volumes, this book is arranged in alphabetical order by the title of the work being critiqued; the essays range in size from 1,000-10,000 words, 2,000 being average. Series are sometimes covered under the series title rather than individual book title; also, there are many entries grouped together under the heading "The Short Fiction of [author's name]," covering those writers who have made major contributions to the genre with less than novel-length fiction. A typical entry includes title (plus original foreign language title if this is a translation or a translated title if the book has never been published in English), author's name, year of birth, year of first book publication, type of work (e.g., "novel"), the time or era in which the book is set, the locale where the plot is set, a brief single-sentence plot summary in italics, a list of principal characters, with brief descriptive annotation; the critical essay itself; a brief bibliography of secondary sources relevant to the work in question.

The quality of the pieces varies widely, as might be expected with contributed essays, but most are at least readable, although the series format demands much attention to plot description; the list of critics was drawn from a small number of academics working actively in the field, and their contributions are often surprisingly perceptive, much better than the usual Magill fare but generally not as good as those in the *Survey of Fantasy Literature*. Essays contributed by foreign critics not fluent in English were specially translated into English for this set. The standard Magill index at the end of Volume 5 references the major essays only, by author and title; a more comprehensive index, covering every author and title mentioned in the book, would have been preferable.

Coverage is extensive and comprehensive, touching upon almost every work considered a "classic" in this genre and many others besides; however, the Magill format makes an overall evaluation of any one author's works difficult if that author has penned more than one "classic" volume, as is often the case here. This set is unique in its coverage of many older science fiction titles from foreign countries, most of which have never been translated into English. The mini-bibliographies of secondary sources at the end of each essay, consisting mostly of book review citations, were widely criticized for their lack of comprehensiveness, being generally worthless for further study; consequently, a *Bibliographical Supplement* compiled by Marshall B. Tymn was later issued as a separate volume (see #102). The high price tags on these sets limit their potential market largely to libraries, but they should be standard purchases for any academic institution and all large public libraries. See also the companion set on fantasy (see #68).

70. Pfeiffer, J. R. **Fantasy and Science Fiction: A Critical Guide**. Palmer Lake, Colo., Filter Press, 1971. iv, 64 p. index. LC 73-159397. ISBN 0-910584-25-7 (pbk.).

Pfeiffer's poorly presented and organized bibliography of primary and secondary sources in fantastic literature includes a brief introduction, "An Annotated Critical Bibliography of Authors and Works After 1900," "Fantasy and Science Fiction Before 1900," "Selected Periodicals Publishing Fantasy and Science Fiction," "Special Anthologies," "Bibliographical Works," "History and Criticism," "Special Periodicals ('Fanzines')," and Title Index. The main section, focusing on SF after 1900, constitutes half of the book and is arranged alphabetically by author. Each entry provides author, author's pseudonyms (in parentheses), years of birth and death, nationality, representative book titles (all caps), year of publication, number of known printings (in parentheses), and a series of letter codes indicating subject content. Coverage is spotty with no obvious system for selection of titles other than the fact the author has read the book. The second chapter, which includes representative titles before 1900, is arranged roughly chronologically by century and then alphabetically by author; these titles are not categorized. The nonfiction sections sometimes include brief annotations (no more than one phrase) that tell the reader virtually nothing about the book in question; and these chapters are, of course, long since out-of-date. The book is reproduced from barely legible typed copy. Execrably rendered.

71. Pflieger, Pat; Helen M. Hill, advisory ed. **A Reference Guide to Modern Fantasy for Children**. Westport, Conn. & London, Greenwood Press, 1984. xvii, 690 p. index. LC 83-10692. ISBN 0-313-22886-8.

This curious volume is a combination readers' guide, character dictionary, gazetteer, and biographical and critical directory to thirty-six nineteenth- and twentieth-century American and British authors of fantasy books for children. The main section of the book consists of 622 pages of material interfiled into one alphabet. The thirty-six bio-critical entries run one to two pages each in length and typically begin with a one-paragraph biographical summary. Most of the author entries, however, focus on the writer's juvenile fantasy works, each annotation intermingling plot summary with exposition with a one-paragraph final summation of the writer's contributions to the history of children's and fantastic literature. A brief checklist of the author's books (adult as well as juvenile) and a selected bibliography of secondary sources (books and articles) complete the record.

The remaining entries cover a wide variety of topics, including individual novels, major characters, races (elves, for example), principal places, objects (e.g., magical swords), and virtually everything else of interest to the reader and student of these writers' works. Asterisks provide internal see references throughout the text to related entries (titles, characters, etc.). The several appendices include a short (three-page) checklist of books and articles about fantasy; a brief chronology of the authors and works included; and an index of principal illustrators of the books mentioned. A thorough index to all names, entries, and topics mentioned completes the book. The volume is well designed and typeset and bound to library standards.

This type of work stands or falls on the selection of authors and topics to be covered and the thoroughness and authoritativeness of the annotations. The earliest of the writers in Pflieger, Charles Kingsley, was born in 1819, and the latest, Jill Paton Walsh, in 1939. Most of the remaining authors produced at least a few works that are acknowledged classics of children's and young adult fantasy, although some are better known than others. One may quibble, for example, over the inclusion of Penelope Lively, Philippa Pearce, or Jane Louise Curry in the company of J. R. R. Tolkien, George MacDonald, and Edith Nesbit, but in the end the argument doesn't really seem to matter. All of these writers have a sufficient body of work (and sufficient claim) to merit inclusion in such a directory, and one finally regrets only those authors who perforce had to be excluded.

The entries themselves are learned without becoming didactic, readable while remaining informative, and display a knowledge, sympathy, and understanding rare in this type of work. Perhaps this is due to the unified viewpoint expressed throughout and the clear and elegant language in which the book is written. Helen Hill's foreword states: "Few reference works can be read just for pleasure, but this guide to modern fantasy for children is a book that can give pleasure to the general reader as well as to the specialist." Amen indeed. Highly recommended.

72. Pringle, David. **Modern Fantasy: The Hundred Best Novels: An English-Language Selection, 1946-1987.** London & Glasgow, Grafton Books, 1988. 278 p. index. ISBN 0-246-13214-0; ISBN 0-246-13420-8 (pbk.). Also: New York, Peter Bedrick Books, 1989. 278 p. index. LC 89-33072. ISBN 0-87226-328-2; ISBN 0-87227-219-7 (pbk.).

When Xanadu (U.K.) and Carroll and Graf (U.S.) chose to use Cawthorn and Moorcock's *Fantasy: The 100 Best Books* (see #59) rather than Pringle's own sequel to his earlier *Science Fiction: The 100 Best Novels* (see #73), perhaps due to Moorcock's name-recognition value, they did themselves a disservice, for while Cawthorn and Moorcock produced an interesting (if quirky) volume, Pringle consistently maintains a more balanced and readable effort.

As with his earlier selection, Pringle focuses on the postwar period, listing one hundred novels published from 1946 to 1987 in chronological order by publication date. A typical entry includes author, title, the critique (averaging 700 words each), bibliographical data (giving place, publisher, and year for the first British and American appearances plus an indication of the most recent edition available [in 1987]). The essays themselves each provide brief background material on the author and his *oeuvre* but quickly focus on the works being discussed. Pringle weaves plot summaries with quotations from the authors' own hands to provide intelligent, readable, and always interesting comments that not only tell us what the book is about but why it is significant to the history of fantastic literature. All of the acknowledged classics are covered, as are many other interesting works; few will be unknown to the informed reader, and even these may be deserving of further attention. The list is nicely balanced between U.S. and British writers and includes some books traditionally considered to fall into the horror or supernatural genre (Shirley Jackson's *The Haunting of Hill House*, for example).

Pringle's editorial and critical balance is superior to Cawthorn and Moorcock's (see #59), although both books are readable and illuminating. The latter tends to be somewhat quirky in its choices of books to be covered, with a decided pro-British bias, but covers the entire history of fantasy literature (beginning in 1726), providing a much wider scope. There is surprisingly little overlap between the two books: of the thirty-seven entries in Cawthorn/Moorcock that fall into the period from 1946 to 1987, only fifteen coincide with Pringle. Pringle invariably includes those books *acknowledged* to be modern classics, while Cawthorn and Moorcock tend to focus on items which they *personally found interesting*. Thus, the average reader is much more apt to locate the modern classics with which he or she is familiar in Pringle, but Cawthorn/Moorcock remains the better overall survey of the genre simply because it covers a much greater period of time. Both should be purchased by public and academic libraries.

73. Pringle, David. **Science Fiction: The 100 Best Novels: An English-Language Selection, 1949-1984.** London, Xanadu Publications, 1985. 224 p. index. ISBN 0-947761-

11-X; ISBN 0-947761-10-1 (pbk.). Also: New York, Carroll & Graf, 1985. 224 p. index. LC 85-32532. ISBN 0-88184-259-1.

The first in the "100 Best Books" series is also the most consistent, thematically as well as in execution. The idea for these books came from *99 Novels: The Best in English Since 1939: A Personal Choice*, by Anthony Burgess (London: Allison & Busby, 1984). Similarly, Pringle focuses on a hundred SF classics from the postwar period. The entries are arranged in chronological order by date of original publication in book form; each includes author, title, publishing data (place of publication, publisher, year of publication) for the first edition and first American or British edition (depending on where the book was originally issued) plus a 600- to 800-word critique consisting largely of plot summary with background material and critical summation. Introductions by Pringle and Michael Moorcock, a brief general bibliography, and a good author/title index complete the book.

Virtually every title on Pringle's list is deserving of attention, having been critically acclaimed in many other fora; his coverage is comprehensive, fair, and balanced, including a broad range of authors and themes, both British and American. His highly readable annotations often provide short, illuminating passages from the books themselves to buttress his arguments and are intended for the general reader, not the scholar. As a one-volume popular introduction to the best of modern science fiction, *Science Fiction: The 100 Best Novels* is unsurpassed among readers' guides currently available. Note also Pringle's companion volume, *Modern Fantasy* (see #72), and compare with Searles *et al.* (see #76).

74. Pringle, David. The Ultimate Guide to Science Fiction. London, Grafton Books, 1990. xx, 407 p. index. ISBN 0-246-13215-9; ISBN 0-246-13635-9 (pbk.). Also: New York, Pharos Books, 1990. xx, 407 p. index. LC 90-7968. ISBN 0-88687-537-4; ISBN 0-88687-536-6 (pbk.).

The author of two previous readers' guides to fantastic literature (see #72 and #73) has here produced evaluations of roughly 3,000 novels, collections, and anthologies, most of them published since 1950. Entries are arranged in alphabetical order by book title, giving title (boldfaced), year of publication, rating (ranging from no stars to four stars, four being best), type (e.g., "novel"), author's name, brief annotation (averaging fifty words, with summation), plus a mention of related titles, sequels, etc., and occasional verbatim quotes from other critics. The vast majority of titles covered derive from the modern period, although there is a scattering of important early classics (Wells's *The Time Machine*, for example) that have remained consistently in print or that are significant for other reasons. Pringle focuses his attention primarily on English-language authors, emphasizing science-fiction works; fantasy authors such as Katherine Kurtz are not covered, nor are individual fantasy titles by predominantly SF authors (for example, Poul Anderson's *The Broken Sword*). Coverage extends through 1989. The index correlates authors and titles only. The book is nicely typeset and designed, and the cloth versions are bound to library standards.

Compared to Pringle's guide, Wingrove's *Science Fiction Source Book* (see #82) rates some 2,500 works (including individual short stories) published through the early 1980s in four categories—readability, characterization, idea content, and literary merit—with only moderate success. Wingrove includes a broader range of titles, including some works of pure fantasy and a wider range of years but generally covers fewer works per author. All of the major books—and most of the minor ones—by well-known SF writers are included in Pringle, and on this basis alone, plus the relative currency of his book, *The Ultimate Guide to Science Fiction* is probably a better buy. There is a slight British bias evident in both books. On the whole, Pringle's conclusions seem sound, and his ratings tend to conform with prevailing critical opinion in the field (always a good sign). Recommended.

75. Searles, Baird, Beth Meacham, and Michael Franklin. **A Reader's Guide to Fantasy.** New York, Avon, 1982. 217 p. LC 82-7364. ISBN 0-380-80333-X (pbk.). Also: New York, Facts on File, 1982. xvi, 196 p. ISBN 0-87196-772-3.

The second book in a two-volume set of reader's guides to science fiction and fantasy written by the employees of the New York specialty bookstore, The Science Fiction Shop, is organized similarly to the companion volume on SF (see #76). An introduction by Poul Anderson and a brief guide to using the book precedes an A-Z listing of 171 major fantasy authors (including some known for their juvenile fiction), a suggested basic reading list, fantasy awards and their winners, listings of fantasy series and sequels, six lists of books arranged by rough subject type, and a brief, ten-page history of the genre.

As with the science fiction guide, the 100-1,000-word critiques are written for a popular audience, focusing on the author's contributions to the field with brief one-line annotations of the writer's major works. Some entries overlap with the previous reader's guide, but the focus here is always on the writer's fantasy output, "fantasy" being loosely defined to include some horror fiction as well as "high fantasy." Light and readable, but not to be mistaken for serious literary criticism. Even with the popular orientation, an index should have been included.

76. Searles, Baird, Martin Last, Beth Meacham, and Michael Franklin. **A Reader's Guide to Science Fiction.** New York, Avon, 1979. xv, 266 p. LC 79-51729. ISBN 0-380-46128-5 (pbk.).

The first of a two-part series of reader's guides on fantastic literature produced by the employees of New York's The Science Fiction Shop, a specialty bookstore, includes a brief introduction by Samuel R. Delany, a short guide to using the book, 202 pages of guides to the major SF authors and their works, twenty-five pages of lists of well-known SF series and sequels, a section on Hugo and Nebula Award winners, a suggested basic reading list of fifty books, and a closing, twenty-page essay outlining the history of science fiction.

The main section of the book includes short essays (ranging in size from 80-1,100 words) on the 200 best-known authors in the genre arranged alphabetically by surname of the writer. Each entry summarizes the author's contribution to SF with one- or two-sentence annotations of the major books and suggestions for further reading. The orientation is popular, not scholarly, the comments generally approbatory, skin-deep, and easy to read. Coverage is now ten years out-of-date, however, somewhat limiting the book's usefulness since it misses completely the "Cyberpunk" movement and the authors associated with it; a new edition would be warranted. A book to be read just for fun; it doesn't take itself too seriously and shouldn't be taken seriously in turn. An index would have been helpful. See also the companion book on fantasy (see #75).

77. Tymn, Marshall B., Kenneth J. Zahorski, and Robert H. Boyer. **Fantasy Literature: A Core Collection and Reference Guide.** New York & London, R. R. Bowker Co., 1979. xiii, 273 p. index. LC 79-1533. ISBN 0-8352-1153-3.

Intended as a companion book to Barron's *Anatomy of Wonder* (see #51), *Fantasy Literature* is actually organized very differently, perhaps due to the influence of Zahorski and Boyer, well-known academic critics of fantastic literature.

Contents include "Foreword," by Lloyd Alexander; "Preface"; "Acknowledgments"; "Part I. The Literature": "1. On Fantasy" (thirty-six-page introductory essay on the definition of fantastic literature); "2. Core Collection" (subdivided into two sections: "a. Novels and Short Story Collections," and "b. Anthologies," each arranged alphabetically by authors' or editors' names); "Part II. Research Aids": "3. Fantasy Scholarship" (subdivided into two sections: "a. History, Criticism, and Author Studies," and "b. Reference Works," arranged alphabetically by authors' names); "4. Periodicals"; "5. Fantasy Societies and Organizations"; "6. Literary Awards"; "7. Fantasy Collections in U.S. and Canadian Libraries"; "Core Collection Titles Available in the United Kingdom"; "Directory of Publishers"; "Index" (author and title in one alphabet).

The end matter is largely out-of-date and irrelevant at this point, but much of the central core of the book still retains validity and usefulness. A typical entry in the Core Collection sections includes author or editor (boldface type), title (italics), place of publication, publisher of the first edition, year of publication, and similar data on the latest paperback edition available (in 1979), plus an annotation ranging in size from 60-1,250 words (300 being average). The essays provide a brief historical content, plot summaries, critical summation, and mentions of other authors or books of a similar nature. The anthology section is unique in its detailed coverage of these important (but neglected) materials, often including complete contents listings as well as evaluative annotations of specific stories. The lengthy essay "On Fantasy" is an excellent general introduction to the study and history of fantastic literature, from its beginnings to modern times. The index correlates authors/titles to page numbers.

Barron's recent guide of the same title (see #52) covers vastly more titles (1,129 to 222) than Tymn and is a decade more current; but the more specific focus of Tymn/Zahorski/Boyer—on a core collection of undisputed fantasy classics—ensures its validity far longer than most reference works of this kind (except for those lists of reference materials, awards, etc., which are clearly dated). Moreover, Tymn's book is far more readable than Barron's, more informative on the books it covers, and not as staid. *Fantasy Literature* has been in no way superseded by the newer work and should be retained by both scholars and libraries.

78. Tymn, Marshall B., ed. **Horror Literature: A Core Collection and Reference Guide**. New York & London, R. R. Bowker Co., 1981. xviii, 559 p. index. LC 81-6176. ISBN 0-8352-1341-2; ISBN 0-8352-1405-2 (pbk.).

The third of the Bowker readers' guides to fantastic literature (see also #77 and #51) is organized very similarly to Barron's *Anatomy of Wonder* and to Barron's later work, *Horror Literature* (see #53), which was intended to replace Tymn. Like Barron, Tymn acted as overall editor of the work, with each chapter being contributed *en masse* by an outside critic.

The book is divided into three main sections: "Foreword," by Peter Haining; "Preface," by Tymn; "Contributors"; "Part I. Fiction": "1. The Gothic Romance, 1762-1820," by Frederick S. Frank; "2. The Residual Gothic Impulse, 1824-1873," by Benjamin Franklin Fisher IV; "3. Psychological, Antiquarian, and Cosmic Horror, 1872-1919," by Jack Sullivan; "4. The Modern Masters, 1920-1980," by Gary William Crawford; "5. The Horror Pulps, 1933-1940," by Robert Weinberg; "Part II. Poetry": "6. Supernatural Verse in English," by Steve Eng; "Part III. Reference Sources" (all by Mike Ashley): "7. Biography, Autobiography, and Bibliography"; "8. Criticism, Indexes, and General Reference"; "9. Periodicals"; "10. Societies and Organizations"; "11. Awards"; "12. Research Collections"; "Core Collection Checklist"; "Directory of Publishers"; "Author and Title Index."

Each of the main fiction chapters includes an introductory essay, ranging in size from ten to thirty-five pages followed by coverage of individual titles arranged alphabetically by authors' names. A typical entry includes item number (in boldface; "1-254"=item number 254 of Chapter 1), author, title (in boldface), nationality of author (if other than American), publisher and year of publication of the first editions in the U.S. and Britain (however, without cities of publication, one is left to guess which is which), but no paginations. The annotations range in size from 25-500 words (averaging 75-100 in the chapters covering twentieth-century works) and tend to focus on plot summaries with very brief critical evaluations, although the coverage of classic antecedents is very extensive in some instances. The critics are all well-known experts in their fields, and their introductions and annotations are generally unbiased and balanced. Much of the end matter is now outdated. The index correlates authors and titles with item numbers only.

Compared to Barron, Tymn covers many more titles (1,094 to 792 entries), and they are much more heavily concentrated toward the earlier periods in the history of horrific literature. While the chapter breakdown between the two works is not exactly comparable, a few examples may still prove illuminating: Barron's first two chapters, covering through 1896, occupy ninety-two pages of text; Tymn's initial two sections, through 1873, cover 220 pages, more than twice the wordage in Barron. Conversely, Tymn devotes less than 100 pages to the period from 1920-80, while Barron uses 166 pages (and provides considerably more annotations) in covering the growth of the modern horror genre from 1950-88. Barron's coverage of secondary sources and reference materials is also far superior (and far more current) than Tymn's. Thus, while Tymn's book has undeniably been supplanted as a *readers' guide* by Barron, ironically his material still retains enormous worth and validity as a synthesis of eighteenth-, nineteenth-, and early twentieth-century horror and gothic literature, and should be retained by both libraries and scholars for that purpose. Many of the books covered in the earlier sections in Tymn are analyzed in no other source.

79. Tymn, Marshall B., ed. **The Science Fiction Reference Book: A Comprehensive Handbook and Guide to the History, Literature, Scholarship, and Related Activities of the Science Fiction and Fantasy Fields**. Mercer Island, Wash., Starmont House, 1981. ix, 536 p. index. LC 80-28888. ISBN 0-916732-49-5; ISBN 0-916732-24-X (pbk.).

This laudable attempt at producing a readers' guide of interest to both a general audience and the scholar contains much of value but also much that could be improved. Following an introduction by Frederik Pohl and a brief preface by the editor are four sections: "Backgrounds," "Fandom," "Academe," and "Appendices," followed by a chapter on the contributors and a detailed author/title index. Each section includes four or five chapters, each contributed by a different critic (Tymn himself penned five of the eighteen chapters). The contributors are well-known critics who clearly know their subjects well.

The "Backgrounds" section includes "Toward a History of Science Fiction," by Thomas D. Clareson; "Children's Fantasy and Science Fiction," by Francis Molson; "Science Fiction Art: Some Contemporary Illustrators," by Vincent DiFate; "The Fantastic Cinema," by Vincent Miranda; and "Critical Studies and Reference Works," a bibliography by Tymn. The "Fandom" section includes "Science Fiction Fandom/A History of an Unusual Hobby," by Joe Siclari; "Writing Awards," by Harlan McGhan; "Literary Awards in Science Fiction," by Howard DeVore; and "Science Fiction and Fantasy Periodicals," by Tymn.

The "Academe" section includes "From the Pulps to the Classroom: The Strange Journey of Science Fiction," by James Gunn; "Masterpieces of Modern Fantasy: An Annotated Core List," by Roger C. Schlobin; "Outstanding Science Fiction Books: 1927-1979," by Joe De Bolt; "Science Fiction and Fantasy Collections in U.S. and Canadian Libraries," by Elizabeth Cummins Cogell; and "Resources for Teaching Science Fiction," by Tymn. The "Appendices" include "Doctoral Dissertations in Science Fiction and Fantasy, 1970-1979," by Douglas R. Justus; "Science Fiction Organizations and Societies," by Tymn; "Directory of Specialty Publishers," by Tymn; and "Definitions of Science Fiction and Fantasy," by Schlobin.

The Science Fiction Reference Book contains a large amount of valuable data, some now out-of-date, but suffers from a certain lack of focus, alternating between reference volume and critical history without ever centering on either. This kind of problem seems inherent in a reference work penned by many hands. For example, two central chapters by Schlobin and De Bolt provide annotated guides to classic fantasy and science fiction. Schlobin includes forty pages of annotations arranged by author and title (anthologies being grouped together in their own section after the novels and collections), while De Bolt arranges his eighty pages of annotations by year through 1979 and then seemingly randomly under each year. Why? Schlobin gives middle names of authors in brackets, clearly indicating the preferred byline of each writer; De Bolt gives full names without such indications. Why?

There are similar problems with other sections. The chapter on science fiction collections in libraries, while detailed and complete, uses a silly prefix code (e.g., MN1 for the first Minnesota library covered) that is meaningless and unnecessary; it is also badly out-of-date. The critical essays on children's F&SF and fantastic cinema are too cursory in their coverage to provide much information; the four introductory chapters in this section should perhaps have been organized in reference-book fashion rather than essay form, except possibly for Clareson's excellent short history. There is some overlap, of course, with Barron's *Anatomy of Wonder* (see #51), but there is also much information unique to this volume, and a second, updated edition would certainly be warranted, particularly with firmer editorial control. The seeds of a worthy rival volume to Barron have been planted; it remains to be seen if they will ever be harvested.

80. Waggoner, Diana. **The Hills of Faraway: A Guide to Fantasy**. New York, Atheneum, 1978. x, 326 p. index. LC 76-900. ISBN 0-689-10846-X.

Waggoner provides a curious hybrid between literary guide and bibliography, a kind of personal odyssey through the realms of fantasy literature.

Contents: Chapter One: "Theory of Fantasy" (twenty-five page introductory essay); Chapter Two: "Some Trends in Fantasy": "1. Mythopoeic Fantasy," "2. Heroic Fantasy and Adventure Fantasy," "3. Ironic Fantasy," "4. Comic Fantasy," "5. Nostalgic Fantasy and Sentimental Fantasy," "6. Horrific Fantasy"; "Appendix A: A Timeline of Fantasy, 1858-1975"; "Appendix B: Some Fantasy Award-Winners"; "Appendix C: Fantasy Illustration"; "Appendix D: Subgenres of Fantasy"; "Sources; A Bibliographical Guide to Fantasy" (the main part of the text); "Index of Names and Terms"; "Index of Titles."

The introductory essays are rather thin histories of each subgenre, intended for a popular rather than a scholarly audience and lacking any real critical perspective. The first appendix provides a brief two-and-one-half-page chronology of the history of fantasy literature by year, listing year, author, and book title. "Appendix B" is now completely outdated. "Appendix C" reproduces twenty pages of fantasy illustrations, poorly selected and reflecting no unified vision or understanding of this specialized field. "Appendix D" rearranges the books covered in the "Bibliographical Guide" by specific subjects (e.g., "Faerie Magic"), listing item number, author, and title only. The bibliography of sources includes five-and-one-half pages of nonfiction materials with author, title, and collation; this section is also now badly dated. These introductory materials cover 124 pages of text (out of 326).

The major portion of the book is an A-Z guide to the major fantasy authors and 996 of their better-known works of fiction. A typical entry includes author name (centered, in all caps, with dates of birth [and death] if known), item number (from 1-996), title (italics), city of publication, publisher of the first edition, year of publication, pagination, and a one-paragraph annotation. The latter range in size from 10-300 words (averaging 30-50) and tend to be very brief plot descriptions followed by a few pithy comments. A great many works originally published for the young adult and children's markets are included, although Waggoner claims to have prepared her book for an adult audience. The indexes correlate authors and titles to item numbers only.

Almost all of these materials are covered just as completely and competently in other sources, particularly in Lynn (see #67) and Barron (see #52), and Waggoner's mediocre effort now seems more dated than many of the other older guides covered in this section. It should be retained only by larger library collections and reference completists but is utterly dispensible for anyone else.

81. Wehmeyer, Lillian Biermann. **Images in a Crystal Ball: World Futures in Novels for Young People**. Littleton, Colo., Libraries Unlimited, 1981. 211 p. index. LC 80-26892. ISBN 0-87287-219-X.

Wehmeyer describes some 150 novels in this combination literary and teachers' guide to juvenile fiction dealing with future life. Contents include "Foreword"; "Part I. Working with Futuristic Fiction: Why and How"; "Part II. Futuristics and Futuristic Novels"; "Part III. Futuristic Novels Annotated"; "Part IV. Index of Themes and Motifs"; "Appendix: Novels Annotated in Part III"; "General Index."

The first chapter provides background information for teachers interested in the study of futuristic literature, including classroom and literary approaches. The second section describes general themes, ideas, and inventions common to the SF novel—i.e., the literary conventions of the genre. Wehmeyer contends "that teachers and librarians must insure a balance between optimism and pessimism in future-oriented units of study and in library collections of futuristic fiction."

The main section of the book, the annotations proper, occupies 110 pages of text arranged alphabetically by author, then by title. A typical entry includes author, title (boldfaced), place of publication, publisher, year of publication, pagination (haphazardly), grade level, summary, and notes. The annotations are both descriptive (in the "Summary" section) and evaluative (in the somewhat misnamed "Notes" section) and emphasize in the latter parts of each annotation major themes and their application to young people. The combined Summary/Notes range in size from 50-600 words, with the "Notes" part of the annotation occupying about one-third of each description. The first index provides very detailed access to the books by subject, author surname, and title only, including geographical subjects (e.g., "U.S.—Southwest (Setting)), genre categories ("Utopias"), time periods ("Twenty-Third Century"), and many others ("Vehicles, Electric-Powered," "Weather Control," "Slavery," etc.). The second index lists the novels covered in the guide by author, title, and page number. The "General Index" provides access to Parts I-II by subject, person, and title and to Part III by author, illustrator, title, and publisher, correlated with page number(s). The indexing in this volume is among the most comprehensive of any of the readers' guides covered in this section.

Images in a Crystal Ball only covers books published from 1964-79 (and still in print in the latter year), intended for readers in grade 8 or below, with no indication in the introductory material of why these limits were chosen. This choice creates such obvious lacunae as the complete absence of the Heinlein juveniles, considered classics of their kind, as well as the earlier adolescent SF novels by Andre Norton, and others. Most of the books and authors included *are* well known, and many (but not all) are mentioned in Barron's *Anatomy of Wonder* (see #51), with, however, fewer plot details. Thus, Wehmeyer's book remains a useful guide for grade and high school teachers and librarians alike, although it is now somewhat out-of-date and should be upgraded (and its coverage expanded backwards) with a second edition.

82. Wingrove, David, ed. **The Science Fiction Source Book**. Harlow, England, Longman, 1984. 320 p. Also: New York, Van Nostrand Reinhold Co., 1984. 320 p. index. LC 83-27338. ISBN 0-442-29255-4.

A strange conglomeration that never seems able to decide what it wants to be, *The Science Fiction Source Book* includes "Foreword," by Brian W. Aldiss; "A Brief History" of the genre, by Aldiss (eleven pages); "The SF Sub-Genres," by Brian Stableford, broken into mini-essays "Man and Machine," "Utopia and Dystopia," "Time Travel," "Aliens," "Space Travel," "Galactic Empires," "ESP," "Disasters," "Religion and Mythology," "Parallel Worlds and Alternate Histories," "Sex and Sensuality," "Alien Ecologies," "Magic," "The Media," and "Inner Space" (averaging three pages each); "The Science Fiction Writer at Work," one-page essays by twelve major SF writers on their own working methods; "Science Fiction Writers: A Consumers' Guide," with contributions by twelve British critics (185 pages); "First Magazine Publication of Leading Authors" (a one-page table); "Science Fiction Publishing" (eighteen pages), with essays on "The Science Fiction Magazines," by David Wingrove and "SF Publishing: The Economics," by Malcolm Edwards, and a six-page magazine checklist, listing editors and dates published (incomplete); "SF Criticism," with an introductory essay by Wingrove (three pages), and a checklist of reference and critical works (twelve pages); a brief "Afterword," by Kingsley Amis; and a detailed author/title index.

The center section of the book lists 880 science fiction authors arranged alphabetically by surname with the following data: author's name (including middle names and real name if a pseudonym), years of birth and death (if known), photograph (for roughly one writer in ten), nationality, a brief general appraisal of the author's contributions to the genre with very short mentions of major works or series, and separate listings of the writer's major fictional works, including short fiction (comprising 2,500 analyzed entries for the entire chapter) categorized by a five-star system (0-5, 5 being best) separately for readability, characterization, idea content, and literary merit. Most authors have at least one work analyzed; none has more than four. The critical summations range in size from 20-600 words, averaging about 80 words, and seem fair, if short. Virtually every writer publishing an SF book in the last twenty-five years is included (SF being broadly defined to include fantasy), plus many other authors whose books have been out-of-print for decades. The selection criteria for the analyzed works is unclear, however, covering a hodgepodge of novels and shorter works without any clear indication why story "X" was chosen over book "Y" or which of the twelve critics participated in evaluating each title (it seems exceedingly unlikely that all dozen read all 2,500 items). This results in many obscure and second- or third-rate books being evaluated, often by writers who had no more than one book published in their entire careers, while major books from major writers are often omitted.

The "Criticism Checklist" contains no annotations, and includes "ghost" titles never actually published. The magazine annotations list title, nationality, number of issues published, dates published, and editors with dates of service, but the chapter omits many lesser publications. The front sections of the book, while readable, interesting, and authoritative (both Stableford and Aldiss know whereof they speak), seem markedly out of place, literary orphans flung willy-nilly into the front of a reference volume to make it more "interesting." This section also includes a number of illustrations from representative books and films, added without any attempt to make them relevant to the text. *The Science Fiction Sourcebook* suffers from a lack of focus and editorial control; future editions, if there are any, should expand the author/book listings and dump much of the rest. Compare with Pringle's *Ultimate Guide* (see #74).

83. Winter, Douglas E., ed. **Shadowings: The Reader's Guide to Horror Fiction, 1981-1982**. Mercer Island, Wash., Starmont House, 1983. xi, 148 p. (Starmont Studies in Literary Criticism, No. 1). LC 83-21326. ISBN 0-916732-86-X; ISBN 0-916732-85-1 (pbk.).

Intended as the first of a series of annual or biennial guides to horror literature, this was the only volume actually published, for good reason: *Shadowings* is a hodgepodge of reviews, film critiques, and other miscellanea that never really gels as a reference work. A lengthy twenty-four-page introduction by Winter provides a summary of the major literary events of the two-year period. This is followed by thirteen essays by different hands on twenty-three major books published in 1981-82. Part II includes essays on four rising stars of the horror genre, and Part III follows with another four pieces on "Things That Go Bump in the Movies" (major films of the period), an essay on film director David Cronenberg, a forum on "Horror and the Limits of Violence" with seven horror writers, and an essay by Winter on the movie *Creepshow* and its relation to E.C. Comics. The final section, "The Year in Review," provides an unannotated list of major books, stories, films, and miscellanea published during 1981-82. "Notes on the Contributors" completes the book.

The essays vary widely in form and content, some being serious attempts to analyze the works in questions, others being sufficiently "airy" to float right off the page; most are at least entertaining if not particularly deep. The text is poorly reproduced, many pages being faint and difficult to read. The absence of an index is unpardonable. A worthy failure, but a failure nonetheless.

84. Wolf, Leonard. **Horror: A Connoisseur's Guide to Literature and Film**. New York & Oxford, Facts on File, 1989. 262 p. index. LC 88-11126. ISBN 0-8160-1274-1; ISBN 0-8160-2197-X (pbk.).

Wolf gives us a personal guide to his favorite novels, stories, verse, and movies in the horror and supernatural genre, stating (in his six-page introduction):

> In this book, the reader will find a partial record of my own lis-
> tening. Let me say at once that the entries that follow do not constitute a
> list of the best stories and films ever made. Then, why were they chosen?
> For three reasons: historical spread, thematic variety and fun. I have
> tried, as I made my selections, to keep in mind that my readers are
> connoisseurs, people who have, or are acquiring, a wide and an instructed
> experience of horror literature. But there is no connoisseur worthy of the
> name who is not also having fun.

And this is really the sum of Wolf's eclectic guide: a potpourri of good, mediocre, and bad (but entertaining) films and fiction, each covered in very well-written annotations ranging in size from 100-1,000 words (averaging 300). Wolf has a certain panache that deftly combines plot summary, historical background, and criticism into 380 scintillating mini-essays that clearly define a very personal vision of what the horror genre is—and what it should be. Short stories, novels, films, even poetry, are all intermingled into one alphabetical sequence.

A typical fiction entry provides title (bold caps), category (e.g., "short story," "novel"), author's name, nationality of author, year of first publication (for short stories) and an anthology in which it has recently been reprinted, or (for novels) year, place of publication, and publisher of first edition and similar information for a recent reprint edition, plus the annotation. A typical film entry gives title (bold caps), alternate titles, year of production, a code indicating color or black-and-white ("C" or "B&W"), nationality, running time, production company, director, producer, screenwriter, photographer, special effects technician, music, chief cast members (and the names of the characters they played), and annotation. The book is attractively illustrated throughout with black-and-white stills and author photographs. The index correlates authors and titles with page numbers, and a six-page bibliography provides a list of fiction and nonfiction for further reading.

Wolf's book cannot really be criticized as a reference work, since he makes no pretentions of it being anything more than a personal selection of some of his favorite works. Thus, quibbling over the inclusion (or omission) of specific novels, short stories, or motion pictures would be fruitless. Nor can *Horror* be compared to other reader's guides on the subject. One can only react personally to this work: Wolf's coverage of specific short stories is unparalleled, his knowledge and range (from the Gothic period to modern times) are impressive, and his guide is among the most entertaining and readable such works this critic has yet encountered.

GUIDES TO SECONDARY SOURCES

SCOPE NOTE: Herein can be found general bibliographies and literary guides of critical materials, book reviews, and reference monographs specific to the study of fantastic literature. Bibliographies of secondary materials on individual writers can be found in the "Author Bibliographies" section.

85. Anthony, Piers. **Index to Book Reviews in Science Fiction Magazines, 1926-1963**. Gainesville, Fla., Phyrne Bacon, 1966 (?). xvi, 119 p. (pbk.).

Intended as an adjunct to the Day/Metcalf/Strauss indexes to SF magazines (see #121, #128, #138), Anthony's guide includes "Abbreviations Used in the Index"; "Introduction"; "Reviewer Supplement" (i.e., alphabetical list of reviewers); "Partial Listing of Review Column Titles and Page Numbers"; and a 119-page printout of the books reviewed. A typical entry includes author of the book being reviewed, book title, single-letter subject code (e.g., "V"=science fiction novel), month and year of publication of magazine, and three-letter magazine code (e.g., "ASF"= *Astounding/Analog*), the latter adapted from Strauss's index (see #138). Anthony indexes reviews on all kinds of monographs, including general nonfiction works about science and cartoon books, in addition to SF materials. This book was photocopied or mimeographed in a very limited edition and is virtually impossible to find. Now wholly superseded by Hall (see #92).

86. Briney, Robert E., and Edward Wood. **SF Bibliographies: An Annotated Bibliography of Bibliographical Works on Science Fiction and Fantasy Fiction**. Chicago, Advent:Publishers, 1972. ix, 49 p. index. LC 72-86150. ISBN 0-911682-19-8 (pbk.).

This guide to bibliographies and indexes of science fiction and fantasy published through 1971 includes a brief introduction, with the text being divided into four sections: "I. Magazine Indexes," arranged in alphabetical order by book title (thirty-two titles covered); "II. Bibliographies of Individual Authors," with four general bibliographies arranged alphabetically by book title followed by thirty-one single-author bibliographies arranged by surname of the author being covered; "III. General Indexes and Checklists," including general and subject bibliographies arranged by book title (twenty-seven titles); and "IV. Foreign Language Bibliographies," including six volumes arranged by book title. An author/title index completes the book.

A typical entry includes title, author/editor, publisher, place of publication, year of publication, pagination, format (e.g., quarto), type of printing, type of binding, price (or an indication the book is out of print), edition limitation followed by a one- or two-paragraph essay. The annotations are brief (ranging from 20-200 words), descriptive, and evaluative. While Briney and Wood's judgments are sound, *SF Bibliographies* is so far out-of-date as to render it almost useless except as a guide to older small-circulation fan publications which are now almost impossible to find in any collection.

87. Clareson, Thomas D. **Science Fiction Criticism: An Annotated Checklist**. Kent, Ohio, Kent State University Press, 1972. 225 p. index. LC 71-181084. ISBN 0-87338-123-8.

Clareson's work was the first major attempt to identify and describe the many works of SF criticism which were starting to appear in the 1960s and '70s covering works published between 1926 and 1971. The book is divided into nine subject areas: "General Studies"; "Literary Studies"; "Book Reviews"; "The Visual Arts"; "Futurology, Utopia, and Dystopia";

"Classroom and Library"; "Publishing"; "Specialist Bibliographies, Checklists, and Indices"; and "The Contemporary Scene." Each section is arranged alphabetically by main entry (usually the author's surname, but by title if no author is shown). A typical entry includes item number (assigned in consecutive order from the number one with each new chapter), author, title (books are listed in italics, short essays in quotations), collation (for books, this includes place of publication, publisher, and year of publication but no paginations; for articles, Clareson lists the magazine or book in which the essay appeared [in italics], volume number, date [in parentheses], and page number); plus an annotation.

Clareson's comments range from 10-150 words and are almost wholly descriptive rather than evaluative, often in a kind of telegraphed English; for example, he notes that Bleiler's *Checklist of Fantastic Literature* "Lists 5,000 titles, British and American, from medieval period to 1947. Main listing by author is indexed by title. An 'annotated list of critical and historical reference works,' some sixty-five titles, focuses upon the Gothic and 19th century." This gives us basic information on how Bleiler's is organized and what it purports to contain, but it fails to indicate whether the book succeeds in its mission. An "Author Index of Entries" and an "Index of [other] Authors Mentioned" complete the book; both indexes cite name, chapter, and item number only, but since there are no running chapter heads, the indexes are virtually useless without constant referrals to the table of contents, a major flaw in this volume.

Dr. Clareson, one of the "grand old men" of science fiction criticism, founded *Extrapolation*, the first journal devoted to the study of fantastic literature (in which the early version of this book originally appeared as a series of articles in 1970-71); he clearly knows his sources well and has employed that knowledge fully here. While no book of this type is ever complete, *Science Fiction Criticism* includes a remarkably large number of entries for its period, including many studies that would prove difficult to locate even today. The work is supplemented by the several volumes of Tymn and Schlobin's *Year's Scholarship in Science Fiction and Fantasy* (see #105).

88. Crawford, Gary William, Frederick S. Frank, Benjamin Franklin Fisher IV, and Kent Ljungquist. **The 1980 Bibliography of Gothic Studies**. Baton Rouge, La., Gothic Press, 1983. ii, 20 p. (The Gothic Chapbooks, No. 1). ISBN 0-913045-00-4 (pbk.).

Two previous versions of this annual guide to gothic criticism were published in the periodical *Gothic* (in the December 1979 issue [for 1978 materials] and in December 1980 [for 1979]), but this was the first (and last) volume in the series to appear as a separately published monograph. Entries are broken into several sections—"I. Bibliographical and Textual Studies"; "II. General Studies"; "III. Author and Comparative Studies"—and within these chapters arranged alphabetically by author's surname. A typical periodical entry includes author, title (in quotes), magazine title (italics), volume number, pagination, brief (one- to two-sentence) annotation. A typical monograph entry provides author, title (italics), place of publication, publisher, and a two- to three-sentence annotation, but no paginations. The annotations are descriptive rather than evaluative. "Gothic" is here broadly defined to include modern horror fiction. Now completely superseded by Fisher (see #89) and Frank (see #90-#91).

89. Fisher, Benjamin Franklin IV. **The Gothic's Gothic: Study Aids to the Tradition of the Tale of Terror**. New York & London, Garland Publishing, 1988. xix, 485 p. index. (Garland Reference Library of the Humanities, Vol. 567). LC 88-18059. ISBN 0-8240-8784-4. Includes a loose errata page.

Fisher, a well-known critic and bibliographer of mystery and gothic fiction, here contributes an annotated guide to secondary sources on gothic writers and literature.

The book is divided into two major sections: "1. Authors" and "2. Subjects," the "Authors" section comprising the majority (299 pages) of the text. Part One is arranged by the name of the author being critiqued, in chronological order by the approximate date when the writer became known (these dates are never stated, only implied), and then alphabetically by main entry. A typical author entry gives the writer's name as a centered, boldfaced head in inverse order with dates and nationality (e.g., "Leland, Thomas (1722-1785): British") followed by a list of books and periodical articles about the author or his or her writings. A typical critical citation includes entry number, critic's name (uncredited materials are filed under "Anon.," in alphabetical order by title), title (in quotes for periodical articles, in italics for books), bibliographical data (for articles: magazine title [in italics], volume number, month and year of publication, pagination; for monographs: place of publication, publisher, year of publication, pagination only for those items where specific page numbers are referenced within the text [for those monographs which deal with the author's corpus *in toto*, no paginations are given]), and a one- to two-sentence descriptive annotation (e.g., "Scattered analyses of blending horror with humor."). Entries are numbered consecutively throughout the book from 1-2614. Part One also includes three small "dump" categories at the end of the section: "Miscellaneous American Gothics, Chronologically Arranged"; "Miscellaneous Later British Gothics, Chronologically Arranged"; "Miscellaneous Foreign Gothics, Chronologically Arranged."

Part Two (134 pages of text) is broken into broad and specific subject categories, including "Historical, General Critical, and Bibliographical Accounts: British and Continental"; "Historical, General Critical, and Bibliographical Accounts: American and Canadian" (these two sections occupy forty pages of text); and other miscellaneous categories such as "Orientalism," "Anti-Gothic Materials," "Faust," "Science Fiction and Fantasy," "Doubles," etc. (twenty-eight categories in all). Each of these chapters is arranged in alphabetical order by main entry with data similar to those in Part One. Some foreign-language authors and critical materials are included, although the general focus throughout remains on British and American literature. The book includes three very comprehensive indexes, all referencing item numbers: "Author, Artist, Subject Index"; "Title Index"; and "Critic Index"; and is attractively typeset and bound to library standards.

Despite the thorough indexing, there are some obvious problems here both with organization and selection criteria. In Part One, the organization of the 110 separate author sections is not obvious even to the most sophisticated of users, despite the fact that a complete list of the writers is provided in the table of contents. Nor is it clear why some writers were separated into their own categories, and others of potentially equal merit were dumped into the three miscellaneous categories at the end of the section. All of this makes access to the book unnecessarily difficult: for example, Ann Radcliffe's chapter runs from pages 16-27, including entries #86-158; the subject index lists over 200 other references with no indication what subjects or aspects these items may contain, requiring the reader to examine each one individually to determine content. An alphabetical arrangement of the authors in Part One would have been much more obvious: the user should have been able to go directly to the section on Radcliffe without searching either the contents page or index and should have been able to determine from the index specifically what subjects the other references to Radcliffe's work might cover.

One must also question the choice of authors and subject entries for twentieth-century materials. In precisely what sense, for example, is Carson McCullers a "gothic writer"—or John Hawkes, Margaret Atwood, Truman Capote, William Faulkner, and Stephen King?

Fisher includes King and H. P. Lovecraft, both well-known horror writers, but excludes most other twentieth-century writers of the supernatural. Why? Why include subject chapters on "Detective/Mystery Fiction," "Science Fiction and Fantasy," or "Racial Issues"? None of these questions are answered, none of the choices explained. It is also within these modern sections that one spots the most obvious lacunae in coverage: Fisher's coverage of Stephen King is laughable, consisting of two wholly minor entries from *People* magazine and *The New York Times Book Review* and ignoring dozens of widely available critical articles and monographs. Similarly, if Fisher includes Bleiler's *The Checklist of Fantastic Literature* (see #178), how can he ignore Reginald's *Science Fiction and Fantasy Literature* (see #182)?

The Radcliffe entries provide a good comparison between Fisher's guide and his four major competitors, since all include individual sections on this seminal gothic writer. Fisher includes seventy-three entries, Frank's *Gothic Fiction* (see #90) 123 entries, Frank's *Guide to the Gothic* (see #91) 121 entries, McNutt's *The Eighteenth-Century Gothic Novel* (see #98) 117 entries, and Spector's *The English Gothic* (see #100) 129 entries, with the second Frank volume and Spector also providing annotations that are generally longer than Fisher's. Overall, Fisher provides more entries than the largest of these other works, particularly the two Frank volumes, but exceeds these volumes only by a couple hundred items. All five books include at least a few entries in their Radcliffe sections not found in the other four. Fisher's strongest point is his coverage of materials on the early gothic, particularly isolated references to materials on a particular author in larger works on other writers or subjects: there are literally hundreds of such references here, many not caught in Frank's two works. For further comparisons, see the Frank entries (#90 and #91).

Nota bene: although Fisher's is the latest published of these five bibliographies, his coverage ceases with 1978, apparently on the theory that the annual volumes of *The Bibliography of Gothic Studies* (see #88) would provide sufficient coverage thereafter. Since these slim booklets are virtually unobtainable in university libraries and in any case ceased publication with the 1980 annual, one must question this editorial decision, along with so many others, and defer to Frank's two books, which operate under no such self-imposed limitations.

90. Frank, Frederick S. **Gothic Fiction: A Master List of Twentieth Century Criticism and Research**. Westport, Conn., Meckler, 1988. xv, 193 p. index. (Meckler's Bibliographies on Science Fiction, Fantasy and Horror, 3). LC 87-24705. ISBN 0-88736-218-4.

Frank is an acknowledged expert on the history of the gothic, particularly the classic gothic of the late eighteenth and early nineteenth centuries, so it is no surprise that his latest book, a comprehensive guide to secondary sources, is authoritative and complete; unfortunately, this is also one of its major problems. The book includes a brief introductory history of gothic criticism and bibliography, including analyses of all previous attempts to list secondary sources on the gothic. The bibliography itself is organized into (appropriately) thirteen chapters: "English Gothic Fiction: Primary and Secondary Bibliographies, Special Collections, Research and Reference Works"; "English Gothic Fiction: Literary Histories, Theories and Formal Definitions, Genre Studies"; "English Gothic Fiction: Individual Author Studies," including fourteen subsections on specific writers arranged by surname of the author being covered; "English Gothic Fiction: Special Subject Areas," with nine subsections such as "Gothic Parodies and Parodists" and "Pre-Gothic Tendencies and Graveyard Verse"; "American Gothic Fiction: General Histories, Critical Surveys, Definitions of Genre"; "American Gothic Fiction: Individual Author Studies," broken into ten subsections on specific writers, plus an eleventh section on "Later American Gothic (1820-1985), including Faulkner, Flannery O'Connor, Stephen King and the Popular American Gothic"; "The French

Gothic Novel or Roman Noir"; "The German Gothic Novel or Schauerroman"; "Other National Gothics and Comparative Gothicisms"; "Special Gothic Themes: The Evil Eye, Spontaneous Combustion, Science Fiction Gothic, Prominent Gothicists, Writing the Gothic Novel"; "The Wandering Jew and the Double Figure"; "Werewolfery and Vampirism"; and "The Gothic Film: A Selective Listing." A brief addenda of two items, and indexes of critics and of authors and artists, complete the book.

The 2,491 entries are numbered consecutively from the number one, the indexes referencing critics and authors with item numbers only. Entries are arranged in alphabetical order by main entry (usually author or editor), by section and/or subsection, depending on the chapter (as indicated above). A typical entry includes author, title (underlined for books, in quotes for articles), and bibliographical data (complete paginations for articles or essays included in anthologies, but no paginations for books). There are no annotations. Many foreign sources are listed in addition to the standard English-language works. The book was shot from word-processed copy but is generally clear and legible throughout. Entries as late as 1987 are included.

Frank is very thorough in his coverage of the early gothic novel; indeed, *Gothic Fiction* will undoubtedly become (with Fisher's work, #89) a standard source for secondary materials on this era. Frank's bibliography is better organized than Fisher's, with the author studies section being arranged more logically, but Frank also has the same problem as Fisher in defining twentieth-century materials and writers. One can make a legitimate case for including materials on the modern gothic developed as a paperback genre (with a very specific cover package) by Ace Books in 1960 and virtually dead by 1980, even though there is a vast difference in style, content, and intent between the two. The modern version at least hearkened back to the original literary tradition, although it basically followed the precepts and forms of the popular women's romance genre. But in what sense is H. P. Lovecraft, the twentieth-century American horror writer, a gothicist—or Stephen King, William Faulkner, Flannery O'Connor, or Russell Kirk? Like Fisher, Frank includes a few modern horror writers and ignores the rest, and as with his competitor's volume, his coverage of materials for the modern writers he *has* chosen is lamentably incomplete, missing major and minor sources obvious to any real student of modern horror literature.

Frank also makes the same unfortunate choices as Fisher in several other sections. In the first chapter, which includes bibliographies of gothic fiction, Frank lists such works as Bleiler's *The Checklist of Science-Fiction and Supernatural Fiction* (see #178), Hubin's *The Bibliography of Crime Fiction, 1749-1975*, and Tymn's *Horror Literature* (see #78) but omits Reginald's *Science Fiction and Fantasy Literature* (see #182), which parallels and exceeds Bleiler in coverage but is larger in size by far, as well as the second, much expanded edition of Hubin's bibliography (1984) and other similar works. Questions such as "Are all vampire and werewolf stories *per se* gothics?" are never answered, never even asked. Similarly, the admittedly incomplete listing of materials on the "gothic film" includes a wide variety of books and essays on Frankenstein films, vampire films, horror films in general, Dracula films, and werewolf films—are these also gothics? What is a gothic? Frank's (and Fisher's) responses to such questions seem to rely more on serendipitous encounters than on any reasoned definition of the genre. Finally, although the author indexes are comprehensive, the absence of a title listing in Frank is most unfortunate.

Frank's coverage of secondary sources for the classic gothic is about the same as Fisher's bibliography. Although both books include unique entries, and neither has any significant advantage over the other, the deficiencies of one cancel out those of its competitor. For the record, Fisher has a few hundred more entries and brief annotations, while Frank includes an extra decade of coverage without annotations (but Frank's earlier bibliography [see #91] *is* annotated). Scholars (and academic libraries) will need to maintain copies of all three bibliographies. A second edition of Frank should include a title index, and both authors need to rethink their basic definitions of the field before embarking on newer versions of their books.

91. Frank, Frederick S. **Guide to the Gothic: An Annotated Bibliography of Criticism**. Metuchen, N.J. & London, The Scarecrow Press, 1984. xvi, 421 p. index. LC 83-24507. ISBN 0-8108-1669-5.

Frank's interest in the bibliographical control of secondary gothic literature dates to at least 1973, when his article, "The Gothic Novel: A Checklist of Modern Criticism," appeared in the *Bulletin of Bibliography*. Much of the *Guide* overlaps with his later volume, *Gothic Fiction* (see #90), although this book does include annotations.

The *Guide* is broken into several major sections: "Previous Guides to the Gothic"; "English Gothic"; "Canadian Gothic"; "American Gothic"; "French Gothic"; "German Gothic"; "Other National Gothics"; and "Special Subject Areas." Most of these sections are further divided into chapters on specific writers (for the national gothics) and/or subjects. Under each subdivision, entries are arranged alphabetically by main entry. A typical entry includes item number, critic's name, title (periodical articles in quotes, books underlined), bibliographical data (for periodical articles: journal title [underlined], volume number, year of publication, and pagination; for monographs: place of publication, publisher, year of publication, but no paginations), and a one-paragraph descriptive annotation averaging fifty words in length. Entries are numbered consecutively from 1-2,508; some items are repeated in more than one section and are renumbered with each appearance, making a total count problematical. End matter includes a "List of Journals" (useless), "Index of Critics" (keyed to item number), and an "Index of Authors, Artists, and Actors" (also referenced to item number), but, astonishingly, no title index.

The arrangement of the authors is chronological as in Fisher's book (see #89), but unlike Frank's later volume, making access unnecessarily difficult for the casual user. As with these other two works, there are problems with definitions, scope, and coverage for the modern period (see the discussion in #90). The two Frank bibliographies contain very close correspondences in certain chapters, as one might expect; for example, the coverage of German gothics in *Gothic Fiction* includes seventy entries in one unbroken alphabetical sequence without annotations; in *Guide* the coverage is broken into nine subsections, seven dealing with an individual writer, also totalling seventy entries, but twenty-nine of these are see references to entries elsewhere in the book, although they are also numbered in sequence here. Since none of the unreferenced entries are missing from *Gothic Fiction*, the later book is clearly more comprehensive (and easier to use), but *Guide to the Gothic* does provide annotations longer than those in Fisher's bibliography, and its internal references, although occasionally irritating, could also be useful to the scholar by providing additional subject access while bypassing the index. The book is shot from occasionally faint typed copy.

As noted in the review of *Gothic Fiction* (see #90), none of these three works provides significantly greater access than either of the others, or any great advantages, and all contain unique materials not found in the others. Therefore, libraries should maintain copies of all three books. An amalgamation of the Frank volumes into one work, reorganized, updated, and reconstituted, would be most desirable.

92. Hall, Hal W. **Science Fiction Book Review Index, 1923-1973**. Detroit, Gale Research Co., 1975. xvi, 438 p. index. LC 74-29085. ISBN 0-8103-1054-6. **Science Fiction Book Review Index, 1974-1979**. Detroit, Gale Research Co., 1981. xx, 391 p. index. LC 81-1490.

ISBN 0-8103-1107-0. Hall, Hal W., and Geraldine L. Hutchins. **Science Fiction and Fantasy Book Review Index, 1980-1984: An Index to More Than 13,800 Book Reviews Appearing in Over 70 Science Fiction, Fantasy, and General Periodicals from 1980 to 1984 and Containing "Science Fiction and Fantasy Research Index," an Index to Secondary Literature, Providing Nearly 16,000 Subject and Author Access Points to Articles, Essays, and Books Featuring the History of, or Criticism on, Science Fiction and Fantasy Literature, Television Programs, Motion Pictures, and Graphic Arts.** Detroit, Gale Research Co., 1985. xxi, 761 p. index. LC 85-25219. ISBN 0-8103-1646-3. **Science Fiction and Fantasy Book Review Index, Volume 16, 1985.** Bryan, Tex., SFBRI, 1988. 69 p. index. LC 72-625320. ISBN 0-935064-20-6 (pbk.). Also: San Bernardino, Calif., The Borgo Press, 1988. 69 p. index. ISBN 0-89370-531-4. Previous annual editions were published beginning in 1970 by SFBRI in paperback, often with the title *SFBRI: Science Fiction Book Review Index*, and in 1980 in simultaneous library cloth editions by Borgo Press (including those released during the preceding decade).Volumes 17-19 were published by SFBRI in paper and by Borgo Press in cloth in the winter of 1992.

Hall's is the only work which attempts systematically to record book reviews on works of fantastic literature (and associated primary and secondary publications) in fan, professional, and library journals worldwide. Originally conceived as a series of annual volumes published by Hall himself under the SFBRI imprint, the first four books were cumulated and extended into a retrospective volume extending back to the beginnings of the field as an identifiable genre. From the very beginning Hall included all reviews appearing in the SF professional magazines, scholarly journals, and major fan publications, with selected coverage of SF books reviewed in the major library serials, particularly *Library Journal*, *Horn Book*, *Choice*, *Booklist*, and *Kirkus Reviews*, the major English literary journals such as *English Journal* and *Elementary English*, and such popular magazines as *Time* and *Newsweek*. The set is arranged alphabetically by author of the book being reviewed, then alphabetically by book title under each author, where more than one book by the writer has been reviewed.

A typical entry includes author or editor (in boldface beginning with the third Gale volume), title (underlined), place of publication, publisher, year of publication, pagination, LC card number (sporadically, in the first two volumes only), and a list of the reviews arranged alphabetically in descending order by one- to five-letter abbreviations identifying each publication in which the review appeared, with volume number (or issue number if the magazine issues are numbered consecutively without volume), issue number in parentheses (if the publication has a volume number), pagination (following a colon), date of issue, and reviewer (in parentheses, with the first name of the reviewer abbreviated to an initial letter). The abbreviations lists are provided in the front of each volume and also on the endsheets of the second and third Gale books; many of the initialisms are obvious to anyone familiar with library and SF publications. A title/author index completes each work. The second half of the third Gale cumulation is an early version of the *Science Fiction and Fantasy Reference Index* (see #93) and thus will not be annotated separately here. The first two Gale volumes were shot from typed copy, the third (and the recent annuals) from word-processed copy; all are legible and easy to follow, although boldfacing the authors' names in the more recent books does help make the entries stand out better.

It's difficult to imagine how any scholar even remotely interested in fantastic literature could bypass these volumes. Hall has gradually increased his coverage over the years to include a number of foreign publications difficult to find in the United States, some additional fanzines, and scholarly journals which rarely review SF materials. While no book of this type is ever complete, it is hard to see where large numbers of additional sources may be found. This is one of the major reference tools of fantastic literature.

93.   Hall, Hal W. **Science Fiction and Fantasy Reference Index, 1878-1985: An International Author and Subject Index to History and Criticism.** Detroit, Gale Research Co., 1987. xviii, xx, 1,460 p. in 2 v. index. LC 87-173. ISBN 0-8103-2129-7 (set). Hall, Hal W., and Jan Swanbeck. **Science Fiction and Fantasy Research Index, Volume 7.** San Bernardino, Calif., The Borgo Press, 1987. 197 p. index. ISBN 0-8095-6103-3. Hall, Hal W. **Science Fiction and Fantasy Research Index, Volume 8.** San Bernardino, Calif., The Borgo Press, 1988. iv, 68 p. index. ISBN 0-8095-6111-5. **Science Fiction and Fantasy Research Index, Volume 9.** San Bernardino, Calif. The Borgo Press, 1992. 97 p. Index. ISBN 0-8095-6112-3. Previous annual editions were published beginning in 1981 as *Science Fiction Research Index, Volume 1*, and *Science Fiction and Fantasy Research Index, Volumes 2-3*, by SFBRI (paper) and Borgo Press (cloth), *Volume 4* (by Hall and Geraldine Hutchins) by SFBRI and Borgo, *Volume 5* (by Hall and Hutchins) by Borgo only in cloth, and *Volume 6* (by Hall alone) by Borgo only in cloth; although still available separately, these were incorporated into the Gale volume, as was the second half of the 1980-84 cumulation of *Science Fiction Book Review Index* and will not be separately treated here. Beginning with the 1989 cumulation (1988 data), the annual volumes were merged into *Science Fiction, Fantasy, & Horror 1988* and following, by Charles N. Brown and William G. Contento (see #24). *Volume 9* is the last separately published volume of the series.

Hall's continuing reference series has become the standard guide to secondary sources in the field of fantastic literature (including science fiction, fantasy, and horror), particularly with the discontinuation of its chief rivals, Clareson and Tymn and Schlobin (see #87 and #105).

Hall divides his material into two sections: "Author Entries" and "Subject Entries." The first division arranges the data alphabetically by critic or bibliographer and includes author (as a boldfaced head), title (articles in quotes, books underlined), and bibliographical data—for books: place of publication, publisher, year of publication, pagination; for articles: magazine title (underlined), volume number, issue number (in parentheses), pagination, month and year of publication; for articles appearing in books: editor of book, book title (underlined), place of publication, publisher, year of publication, specific pagination of article within the volume.

The second section rearranges the material by subject, then alphabetically under each header by title. A typical entry includes subject heading (bold caps), title (articles in quotes, book titles underlined), author (where appropriate; many of the entries were anonymously contributed), and the same bibliographical data included in the Author Entries section. Entries may be indexed very specifically by proper name, and/or into such broader topics as "Science in SF," "Definitions," and "Romanticism." In general, the subject indexing seems at least adequate to allow the user access to the most obviously desired points of each essay. Also included in the Gale volume are a "Thesaurus of Science Fiction and Fantasy Indexing Terms (Proper Names and Movie Titles Excluded)" and "Lists of Sources" (with title [in italics], author, place of publication, publisher, year of publication, pagination).

The "Research Index" sections in the 1988 and 1989 Brown/Contento annuals follow the same basic format except that book titles are run in boldfaced type and magazine titles in italics. No annotations are provided in either the original versions or in Brown/Contento, and no indexes; however, Hall's volumes are among the easiest for the neophyte to use of any of the books annotated herein.

Although the Clareson/Tymn volumes include some entries not found in Hall, there is in fact a huge disparity in the number of entries that Hall lists as compared to all other published sources combined. His coverage of secondary materials for fantastic literature is quite simply unsurpassed, including thousands of entries from U.S. and foreign sources that are mentioned nowhere else; it is difficult to imagine how any researcher could possibly begin a critique or bibliography without first doing a literature search through these volumes. Also, the very specific subject indexing and the descriptive nature of the titles themselves somewhat alleviate the absence of annotations and the lack of an index, both of which would be desirable additions to future versions.

These are necessary purchases for all academic libraries and all large public libraries and for the personal libraries of all serious SF researchers.

94. Justice, Keith L. **Science Fiction, Fantasy, and Horror Reference: An Annotated Bibliography of Works about Literature and Film.** Jefferson, N.C. and London, McFarland & Co., Publishers, 1989. xiii, 226 p. index. LC 89-2841. ISBN 0-89950-406-X.

It is difficult to do justice to this work. On the one hand, the main title suggests a comprehensive bibliography of SF reference works, while on the other, the subtitle and contents actually provide something very different indeed. This curious dichotomy is symptomatic of a basic flaw at the heart of this work, an absence of focus and a certain muddiness in concept that combine to strangle this book before it ever achieves life.

Some of the problems become clear in Justice's introduction. He states:

> This bibliography was compiled to help librarians, collectors, researchers, and others with an interest in SF/fantasy/horror reference materials determine what books might be of use or interest to them or their library's patrons. The book is not comprehensive; however, it is the first book ever published which is devoted exclusively to listing and evaluating secondary materials (books) for the SF, fantasy, and horror genres.

The latter statement is not quite true, even in the sense that Justice intends, for while there indeed exists no other book *exactly* like his, there are in fact many other sources which evaluate SF secondary materials to a greater or lesser degree. But even if we accept his statement at face value, we soon begin wondering what exactly is included here—and why.

Justice annotates 305 books in nine sections: "1. General History & Criticism"; "2. Author Studies"; "3. General Bibliographies"; "4. Author Bibliographies"; "5. Biography, Autobiography, Letters & Interviews"; "6. Encyclopedias, Dictionaries, Indexes & Checklists"; "7. Television, Film & Radio"; "8. Comics, Art & Illustration"; "9. Anthologies, Collections & Annotated Editions." Three appendices include "I. Evaluations of Critical and Bibliographical Book Series"; "II. Critical and Bibliographical Book Series Title Listings"; "III. Suggested Core Collection Checklist." Three indices—by subject, title, and author/editor/compiler/major contributor—provide quick and easy access to specific item numbers only.

In each section, entries are arranged alphabetically by main entry (author, editor, or compiler); entries are numbered consecutively from 1-305. A typical entry includes item number and author (boldface type), title (italics), place of publication, publisher, year of publication, pagination, and a three-letter reference code to a basic list of five publications providing other annotations or sources (the master index to codes is buried in the introduction rather than on a separate page, making access more difficult than it should have been). The annotations are both descriptive and evaluative and range in size from 150-400 words, averaging 250. There is very little correlation between value and size of annotation: a six-page checklist on little-known British author Barrington Bayley receives as much notice as Aldiss and Harrison's major anthology of autobiographical essays, *Hell's Cartographers*. Justice's comments also vary widely in scope and content: he correctly analyzes some of the structural problems with Holdstock's *Encyclopedia* (see #5) and Ash's *Who's Who* (see #42) but completely misses the second and third Editions of Barron's standard guide, *Anatomy of Wonder* (see #51), which should be readily accessible to any researcher in the field, and thus also misses the many important changes in the evolution of that publication. Justice provides a good summary of Jakubowski and Edwards's *SF Book of Lists* (see #34) but clearly has no knowledge of Ashley's competing volume, which appeared virtually simultaneously.

This hit-or-miss anarchy pervades the entire volume: major and minor reference tools and other sources may or may not be covered, unpredictably and completely at random. Justice's haphazard selectiveness becomes even more apparent as we approach recent times, for, although this book was published in 1989, it misses many of the major works of the 1980s, particularly those published after 1985, and also fails to take into account numerous new editions, new developments in publishers' series, and significant new titles in general. For example, Starmont House had produced thirty-seven titles in its Starmont Reader's Guides (not Readers' Guides, as Justice has it) series of SF critiques through the end of 1988; Justice provides annotations for just ten, missing the very first book in the series, on Arthur C. Clarke, which went through two separate editions, while covering volumes 2-8, 18, 20, and 22. Where are the others? Similarly, Justice covers just twenty books (out of forty-one) produced in The Milford Series through 1988 and virtually misses coverage of the Masters of Science Fiction and Fantasy Series (which had ceased by 1984; see #263), reviewing just one title of these major author bibliographies (out of fourteen produced) on Robert Silverberg— and even there his few general comments on the Masters Series and on the Silverberg bibliography demonstrate a woeful lack of understanding of how and why and for what audience these books were produced.

Justice's volume also has a few structural problems. The format (alphabetically by main entry) works well for the general chapters but surely must be questioned in "Section 2: Author Studies" and "Section 4: Author Bibliographies," where the average reader would reasonably expect to find the material arranged by name of the author *being covered* instead of the author producing the book. The appendices seem dated and largely irrelevant, although the brief core collection list will be useful for public libraries.

One must not dismiss this book completely out-of-hand, however. Justice does provide annotations for some critical materials at lengths available in no other source, and his comments are generally fair and competent if not particularly deep. If reworked into a general readers' guide to critical materials, his volume has some future possibilities. Otherwise, it can be employed (with caution) as no more than a supplemental adjunct to the SF reference collection.

95. Justice, Keith L. **Science Fiction Master Index of Names**. Jefferson, N.C. and London, McFarland & Co., Publishers, 1986. vi, 394 p. index. LC 85-42533. ISBN 0-89950-183-4.

Justice indexes personal name references in 132 SF critical and reference works published between 1953-1984, centralizing them into one alphabet arranged by surname and keying each entry to a three-letter code representing the book title of the work cited, plus page numbers where appropriate. The book includes several introductions by Justice explaining how the book is organized, a list of the works cited arranged in alphabetical order by each book's three-letter code, the index itself (367 pages), and two checklists of the works cited by author and by title, the latter also including place of publication, publisher, and year of publication. Roughly 18,000 names are included whose citations range from one reference to several hundred for a writer such as Robert A. Heinlein, averaging five per writer. There are copious see and see also references to and from other pseudonyms used by the author; slight variations of one name are centralized under the most common variation. Middle names and years of birth and death are included when known.

Justice's index is a handy guide to many of the books annotated in this volume and, although it was shot from typed copy, is both legible and easy to use. Unfortunately, it suffers from a certain overzealousness, since not all of the works cited are comparable to the others either in design, function, status, or worth; and there is often no easy way to determine what the citation represents without looking at the original work. For example, the entry for Robert Reginald cites two reviews of a Reginald work, fourteen essays by Reginald on other writers, a contents list of an anthology edited by Reginald, a biography of author Robert Silverberg in a work compiled by Reginald, two biographies and one bibliography of Reginald, and a passing reference to a Reginald book. One might wish to have all of these citations if one were doing an extensive biography or bibliography of Reginald; however, the casual user who just wants a biography or other brief data would have a difficult time wading through these entries and discerning which is which. The situation is compounded a hundredfold with such major SF authors as Isaac Asimov, whose entry occupies nearly a full page of double-column text. The problem may be endemic to a work of this type but could have been helped with some annotations of the books themselves, indicating generally what each contains (this is not always obvious from the work's title). Also, there is no real indication (other than ready availability to Justice) why certain titles were analyzed and others presumably just as worthy were not. Major reference tools lie side by side with slim critical texts, each given equal weight here.

Despite these *caveats*, the *Master Index of Names* can be an extremely useful shortcut to the researcher or student who understands its limitations and who already has some basic familiarity with the major reference works in the field. It should certainly be continued and expanded with supplements or future editions.

96. Lerner, Fred. **An Annotated Checklist of Science Fiction Bibliographical Works**. East Paterson, N.J., Fred Lerner, 1969. [7] p. (pbk.).

A brief selected annotated bibliography of SF reference tools arranged in alphabetical order by title, with an appendix covering five additional titles. A typical entry includes author, title, bibliographical data (including paginations), and annotation. The essays are one paragraph in length, descriptive, with occasional evaluations. Lerner, a librarian and bibliographer, produced this now outdated but laudable effort as a library school project.

97. McGhan, Barry. **An Index to Science Fiction Book Reviews in** *Astounding/Analog*, **1949-1969,** *Fantasy and Science Fiction*, **1949-1969,** *Galaxy*, **1950-1969**. College Station, Tex., SFRA, 1973. vii, 88 p. index. (SFRA Miscellaneous Publication No. 1). LC 74-152723 (pbk.).

McGhan focuses on three of the better-known prozines of the 1950s and '60s, omitting brief mentions of SF books and reviews of non-book materials. Following a short preface, "On Book Reviewing," by Damon Knight, McGhan includes an introduction explaining the book's guidelines, a general guide to the review columns by magazine title, then chronologically by major period, covering the chief reviewers, the name of the column, exceptions to the standard reviewers, and issues not covered in this index. The major part of this book (63 pages) comprises an alphabetical list of the authors of the books being reviewed, with their publications listed alphabetically under each writer, referenced to the magazine title (a three-letter code: ASF, FSF, GAL) and date (in the form 10/62 for October, 1962). The title index correlates titles and page references to the first part of the book only; one must refer back to the author index to find complete bibliographical data. The book is shot from very legible typed copy. Mediocre mush, now completely superseded by Hall (see #92).

98. McNutt, Dan J. **The Eighteenth-Century Gothic Novel: An Annotated Bibliography of Criticism and Selected Texts**. New York & London, Garland Publishing, 1975. xxii, 330 p. index. (Garland Reference Library of the Humanities, Vol. 4). LC 74-22490. ISBN 0-8240-1058-2.

This was the first attempt to provide a systematic, comprehensive bibliography on the secondary literature of the classic gothic novel, and it remains a credible effort, if now slightly out-of-date.

McNutt organizes his book into thirteen chapters and an appendix: "1. Bibliographies and Research Guides"; "2. Aesthetic Background"; "3. Literary Background"; "4. Psychological, Social, and Scientific Background"; "5. Eighteenth-Century Gothic, in General Studies"; "6. Studies Devoted to Eighteenth-Century Gothic"; "7. The Gothic Legacy"; "8. Horace Walpole, 4th Earl of Orford (1717-1797)"; "9. Clara Reeve (1729-1807)"; "10, Charlotte (Turner) Smith (1749-1806)"; "11. Ann (Ward) Radcliffe (1764-1823)"; "12. Matthew Gregory Lewis (1775-1818)"; "13. William Beckford (1760-1844)"; "Appendix: Selected Foreign Language Items." Each of the main chapters is further subdivided into additional sections; Chapter 3, for example, is broken into four units: "a. Early Literary Theories"; "b. Verse Precursors"; "c. Prose Precursors"; "d. The Continental Background."

In each subdivision, materials are arranged alphabetically by main entry (usually author or editor). A typical entry includes author, title (periodical articles in quotes, books underlined), bibliographical data (for articles: magazine title [underlined], volume number, year of publication, pagination; for monographs: title [underlined], place of publication, publisher, year of publication, but no paginations), item number, and a descriptive annotation averaging sixty words in length but sometimes exceeding 200 words. The entry numbers run down the right-hand margin of each page, sometimes pushing the numbers on the left-hand (i.e., even-numbered) pages close to the gutter, making them unnecessarily difficult to read; entries are numbered consecutively from one in each chapter, in the form 12/1, 12/2, 12/3, etc., for the first few items in Chapter 12. The brief foreign language section (sixty-four entries) is unannotated. The index references authors' names and item numbers only, the authors' first names being abbreviated to initials (something unnecessary and irritating); the absence of a title index is unfortunate. The book is shot from occasionally faint typed copy.

McNutt covers 1,154 items, less than Fisher (see #89) and Frank (see #90 and #91), but his range is deliberately more restrictive. Unusually, he also lists and evaluates the major modern editions of the primary works of the several authors covered in Chapters 8-13, something which only Spector (see #100) among his competitors does on any systematic basis, and then only scantily. McNutt's annotations are also longer and more descriptive than those found in any of the books mentioned above, and his overall focus is sharper and more distinctive. Thus, despite the fact that his coverage only extends through 1974, McNutt's bibliography remains a very useful guide to the rapidly growing critical resources in this genre.

99. Science Fiction Book Reviews, 1969-1972. Sydney, Australian Science Fiction Association, 1973. 60 p. LC 77-354986 (pbk.).

No author is indicated for this book, but well-known Australian librarian and indexer Graham Stone may well have participated in its compilation. The index is broken into two sections: "Books Reviewed" by title and "Index" by author. The main section is arranged alphabetically by title of the book being reviewed, a typical entry including title (all caps), author, magazine title, month and year of magazine publication, pagination of review, reviewer's name; multiple reviews are arranged alphabetically by magazine title underneath the book title. The author index gives authors and titles only.

Now largely superseded by Hall (see #92), whose sets do not, however, include book reviews from *Science Fiction News* and the *ASFA Journal*, two fanzines which are covered in this index.

100. Spector, Robert Donald. **The English Gothic: A Bibliographic Guide to Writers from Horace Walpole to Mary Shelley**. Westport, Conn. & London, Greenwood Press, 1984. xiii, 269 p. index. LC 83-1443. ISBN 0-313-22536-2.

Spector's guide to the secondary literature of the classic gothic is presented in narrative form, very much akin to the style and format of *The Year's Work in English Studies*.

Following a preface, abbreviations list, and a critical/historical introduction to the genre, the book is arranged into five broad chapters: "1. Gothic, Gothicism, and Gothicists"; "2. The Beginnings: Horace Walpole and Clara Reeve"; "3. Sentimental Gothicism: Charlotte Smith and Ann Radcliffe"; "4. Schauer-Romantik: Matthew Gregory Lewis and William Beckford"; "5. The Inheritors: Charles Robert Maturin and Mary Shelley." Spector follows the same format in each chapter: in narrative style, he analyzes the major and minor works of the field, including the fictions of the gothic writers themselves, showing the development of each writer's career and the critical response to it both contemporaneously and subsequently; the narrative text is followed at the end of each chapter by a list of references arranged in alphabetical order by critic and broken into two divisions, each corresponding to one of the authors being covered. A typical bibliographical entry includes author, title (in quotes for journal articles, in italics for book titles), publication data (for periodical entries: magazine title or abbreviation [in italics], volume number, month and year of publication, pagination; for monographs: place of publication, publisher, year of publication, but no paginations). The index references both authors and titles to page numbers. The book is beautifully typeset and bound to library standards.

Spector covers a more restricted range of materials than his competitors, Fisher (see #89), Frank (see #90 and #91), and McNutt (see #98), but his intelligent, perceptive evaluations, which place both the authors and the criticism about them in historical perspective, make his bibliography far more useful to the scholar. When he writes of John Garrett's *Gothic Strains and Bourgeois Sentiments in the Novels of Mrs. Ann Radcliffe and Her Imitators* that "his major contribution is to distinguish between Radcliffe's attachment to eighteenth-century didacticism—her concern for the triumph of virtue over vice—and the often indulgent play upon the emotions exhibited by other Gothicists," we know immediately what Garrett says and, more importantly, how he says it and in what context. This type of evaluative commentary of secondary sources is badly needed in the related field of science fiction and fantasy, which has in recent years overflowed with an effluence of second-rate critical monographs. Spector is both knowledgeable and credible, and his guide is highly recommended.

101. Tymn, Marshall B. **A Basic Reference Shelf for Science Fiction Teachers**. Monticello, Ill., Council of Planning Librarians, 1978. 13 p. (Exchange Bibliography, No. 1523). LC 78-105377 (pbk.).

This work and its companion volume on fantasy (see #102) were the result of two conferences on teaching science fiction held at Eastern Michigan University (where Tymn was a Professor of English) in 1975 and 1976. Both works were designed to provide the teacher of fantastic literature with a core list of reference and critical works which might be useful in preparing classes or to which students could be referred for further study. This 8.5" x 11" booklet is divided into categories (e.g., "Preliminary Sources," "General Bibliographies," etc.), then arranged alphabetically by author. The annotations range from one to five sentences and are primarily descriptive rather than evaluative. All of the information included herein was later incorporated into *The Year's Scholarship* volumes (see #105).

102. Tymn, Marshall B. **Recent Critical Studies on Fantasy Literature: An Annotated Checklist**. Monticello, Ill., Council of Planning Librarians, 1978. 21 p. (Exchange Bibliography, No. 1522). LC 78-105385 (pbk.).

Unlike its companion volume on science fiction (see #101), this selective bibliography focuses primarily on critical materials about fantasy fiction and its authors and includes more articles than books. Tymn attempts to provide a basic list of materials suitable for the beginning teacher of fantastic literature. The arrangement here is by general category (e.g., "Critical Studies: Articles and Essays") and then alphabetically by author. Tymn's annotations are short (one brief sentence) and descriptive rather than evaluative. As with *A Basic Reference Shelf* (see #101), all of the data were later incorporated into Tymn and Schlobin's annual guide to secondary sources (see #105).

103. Tymn, Marshall B., Roger C. Schlobin, and L. W. Currey. **A Research Guide to Science Fiction Studies: An Annotated Checklist of Primary and Secondary Sources for Fantasy and Science Fiction**. New York & London, Garland Publishing Co., 1977. ix, 165 p. index. (Garland Reference Library of the Humanities, Vol. 87). LC 76-52682. ISBN 0-8240-9886-2.

Tymn/Schlobin/Currey cover much of the same territory as Clareson (see #87), albeit with an additional five years of data (covering through 1976). This new book is somewhat better organized, however, being broken into six major sections: "I. Preliminary Sources"; "II. Sources for Primary Materials"; "III. Sources for Secondary Materials"; "IV. Author Studies & Bibliographies"; "V. Periodicals; "VI. Sources for Acquisition," followed by a thirty-six page checklist of "Doctoral Dissertations in Science Fiction and Fantasy" by Douglas R. Justus (arranged alphabetically by author), and author and title indexes.

Each of the first three chapters is broken into two sections: "General" (sources outside the science fiction field [*Dissertation Abstracts International*, for example]), and "Science Fiction" sources. These latter sections are further subdivided into five or six other divisions (for example, the chapter "Sources for Primary Materials" includes the subdivisions: "1. General Bibliographies"; "2. Subject Bibliographies"; "3. Anthology Indices"; "4. Magazine Indices" [General and Individual]; "5. Film." The materials covered are numbered consecutively from 1-404 (the doctoral dissertations are not numbered or indexed, however); the author and title indexes refer to item number only.

In each section, materials are arranged alphabetically by main entry (usually author or editor) except for the long forty-page section on authors' studies, which is appropriately organized by name of the writer being covered, then alphabetically by name of critic or bibliographer. A typical entry includes item number, author, title (in italics), place of publication, publisher, year of publication, pagination, format ("paper"=paperback), and place of publication, publisher, and year of publication for any reprints. The annotations range in size from one short sentence to 300 words, averaging about seventy-five words, and are primarily descriptive, not evaluative, although occasional summations or pithy comments may be included. The separate checklist of dissertations remains a very thorough and useful starting point for these hard-to-locate, largely unpublished materials, although it is unfortunate that no attempt was made to index them with the rest of the items. Chapters 5-6 are now wholly out-of-date and useless.

Tymn's book differs from Clareson (see #87) in both coverage and arrangement: the latter includes hundreds of additional essays and articles broken into many more sections (not a benefit in this case), while *A Research Guide* restricts itself to separately published monographs (including chapbooks), is better organized, provides longer and more evaluative annotations, and includes five years more data. Neither really supplants the other. A new version of Tymn providing a current, up-to-date, completely annotated synthesis of the many critical monographs available in the field is badly needed; until one appears, this book, supplemented by Hall (see #93), Justice (see #94), and Tymn's annuals on SF scholarship with their cumulations (see #105), will have to do.

104. Tymn, Marshall B. **Survey of Science Fiction Literature: Bibliographical Supplement**. Englewood Cliffs, N.J., Salem Press, 1982. xiv, 183 p. index. LC 79-64639. ISBN 0-89356-185-1 (pbk.).

When the *Survey of Science Fiction Literature* (see #69) first appeared in 1979, it was primarily criticized for the relatively poor "Sources for Further Study" sections appended at the end of each essay (and not contributed by the authors of those essays). Subsequently, well-known critic Tymn was commissioned to produce this supplemental volume (a unique occurrence in the history of the Salem Press guides), providing much greater access to secondary materials for each of the works covered in the original five-volume set. The arrangement is the same as the original: by title of the work being covered, exactly reproducing the top matter at the beginning of each of the original essays (title, author, years of birth and death, type of work, one-sentence summation), followed by each mini-bibliography arranged alphabetically by name of critic. A typical entry includes critic, title of book or article, bibliographical data, and (inconsistently) specific paginations for the material within the book covering the specific work targeted in the original critical essay, plus a one-sentence descriptive annotation. Both books and magazine articles are included, as well as essays included in anthologies, but in general, Tymn's coverage of critical monographs and anthologies seems superior to his comprehension of the much vaster array of journal articles. An author index is included but references only those SF authors (and titles) on whom essays were written in the original set, correlated to the page number references in this new volume; none of the secondary materials are specifically indexed. The proprietary arrangement makes this book relatively useless without access to the *Survey* itself.

105. Tymn, Marshall B., and Roger C. Schlobin. **The Year's Scholarship in Science Fiction and Fantasy, 1972-1975**. Kent, Ohio, Kent State University Press, 1979. xvi, 222 p. index. (The Serif Series, Bibliographies and Checklists, No. 36). LC 78-21976. ISBN 0-87338-222-6. **The Year's Scholarship in Science Fiction and Fantasy, 1976-1979**. Kent, Ohio, Kent State University Press, 1982. ix, 251 p. index. (The Serif Series, Bibliographies and Checklists, No. 41). LC 82-16190. ISBN 0-87388-257-9 [*sic*]. Tymn, Marshall B. **The**

Year's Scholarship in Science Fiction, Fantasy, and Horror Literature 1980. Kent, Ohio, Kent State University Press, 1983. viii, 110 p. index. ISBN 0-87338-279-X (pbk.). **The Year's Scholarship in Science Fiction, Fantasy, and Horror Literature 1981**. Kent, Ohio, Kent State University Press, n.d. [1984]. viii, 103 p. index. ISBN 0-87338-301-X (pbk.). **The Year's Scholarship in Science Fiction, Fantasy, and Horror Literature 1982**. Kent, Ohio, Kent State University Press, n.d. [1985]. x, 107 p. index. ISBN 0-87338-302-8 (pbk.). Continued by annual supplements in *Extrapolation* and (beginning in 1989) by *Journal of the Fantastic in the Arts*.

Tymn's was intended directly to supplement Clareson (see #87) by providing comprehensive annotated coverage of all books and essays published in the fields of science fiction and fantasy for the specific years covered. Following two conferences that were held at Tymn's home instititution, Eastern Michigan University, in 1975 and 1976, Tymn and Schlobin prepared the first of their annual surveys for publication in *Extrapolation* and also simultaneously began work on the first of their cumulated volumes (1972-75). Beginning with the 1980 volume, Schlobin dropped out of the project to pursue other interests, and Tymn carried on the annual supplements himself (the last of these was published in the Fall 1988 issue of *Extrapolation*, covering 1987 publications).

The first of the cumulations, covering the four years 1972-1975, is something of a hybrid, containing elements of both Clareson and the later format that Tymn eventually developed. It organizes the book into four major sections: "I. General Studies"; "II. Bibliography and Reference"; "III. Author Studies and Bibliographies"; "IV. Teaching and Visual Aids," followed by author and title indexes. The major divisions are organized alphabetically by main entry (usually author or editor); the section on author studies is subdivided into "Collective Studies" and "Individual Studies" (eighty pages), the latter arranged by name of the author being covered. Each chapter or subchapter is numbered from the number one to the end; this arrangement works well enough except in the author studies chapter, where each individual subsection (the name of the author being covered) is also numbered from one. Since the indexes correlate item numbers only, this results in the very cumbersome reference III-B-xxxiii-1 for the sole interview on L. Sprague de Camp.

A typical book entry includes author, title (in italics), place of publication, publisher, year of publication, but no paginations. A typical essay entry includes author, title (in quotes), magazine title (in italics), volume number, year, and paginations (for a journal article), or book title, editor, place of publication, publisher, year of publication, and paginations (for an essay published in a book). A number of the books that could have been further analyzed were not: *Hell's Cartographers* is covered in the "Collective Studies" section of Chapter 3, but the individual autobiographical pieces are not mentioned under the respective authors' names in the "Individual Studies" subchapter. The annotations are generally very brief (one to three sentences, averaging one) and usually descriptive rather than evaluative.

Beginning with the 1976-1979 cumulation, Tymn began using a more standard format. The contents for that volume include "Foreword"; "Preface"; "A. General Studies"; "B. Bibliography and Reference"; "C. Collective Author Studies"; "D. Individual Author Studies"; "E. Art and Film"; "F. Teaching Resources"; author and title Indexes. In each of these chapters, materials are numbered from one to the end, preceded by the key letter for each chapter, and are organized alphabetically by main entry. As before, individual author studies are arranged by name of the author being covered; this section also includes numerous see references to materials analyzed elsewhere in the volume. The indexes correlate item numbers only.

Later annuals added still more subject chapters as the field continued to expand. The 1982 annual, for example, includes the following divisions: "A. Bibliography and Reference"; "B. General Surveys and Histories"; "C. Theoretical and Critical Studies"; "D. Subject Studies"; "E. Collective Author Studies"; "F. Individual Author Studies"; "G. Art; Media: Film, TV, Radio";"H. Writing and Publishing"; "J. Teaching Resources"—but otherwise follows the same general format.

Hall (see #93), Tymn's chief rival, has always had a far greater reach than Tymn and his main set (covering 1878-1985) is unrivaled as an initial source for further study, including hundreds, even thousands, more entries than the Clareson/Tymn sets for a comparable period, with many more specific subject analyses. However, Tymn/Schlobin and Clareson's annotations provide a dimension not available in Hall and include a few dozen items missed by Hall, for no apparent reason. Also, Tymn's arrangement is more accessible for certain kinds of research. Thus, scholars should consult both sets if they wish to conduct a thorough literary search.

Unfortunately, none of the later Tymn volumes have been cumulated or (after 1982) even published in book form, rendering access increasingly difficult. Tymn had been discussing the possibility of doing a completely new cumulation of the entire data base, but his near-fatal car accident in 1989 has put that project on indefinite hold. The 1989 annual was edited by his colleagues for publication in Tymn's *Journal of the Fantastic in the Arts*, and subsequent volumes may also be compiled by other hands.

LIBRARY CATALOGS
AND COLLECTION GUIDES

106. Hall, Hal W., ed. **Science/Fiction Collections: Fantasy, Supernatural & Weird Tales**. New York, Haworth Press, 1983. 181 p. LC 82-21355. ISBN 0-917724-49-6.

This interesting collection of essays focuses on nine special libraries of fantastic literature, seven public and two private, and was previously published as an issue of the journal *Special Collections*. Hall's introduction outlines the major SF collections known to exist in the world today, some of them not otherwise covered in this volume. This is followed by contributed essays on the collections of fantastic literature at the Library of Congress, the University of California, Riverside, Texas A&M University, Eastern New Mexico University, Syracuse University, the Toronto Public Library, and the M.I.T. Science Fiction Society, plus the private collections of Sam Moskowitz and Forrest J Ackerman. The pieces focus both on the history and the scope of the analyzed libraries, ranging in size from thirty-two pages (Moskowitz) to four pages (Syracuse), and have all been contributed by current or past employees of the libraries or by the owners (in the case of the two private collections). Several additional essays are also included: "Science Fiction Specialty Publishers," by Robert Weinberg; "Bibliographical Control in Fantastic Literature: An Evaluation of Works Published, 1941-1981," by Marshall B. Tymn; "The Cataloging and Classification of Science Fiction Collections," by Fred Lerner (annotated separately in this volume in the "Cataloging Manuals" chapter [see #23]); "A Checklist of Science Fiction and Fantasy Book Dealers," by David Aylward and Robert Hadji; and "A Brief Directory of Science Fiction Research Collections," by Hall.

These latter sections are all now out-of-date, but provide some useful information (particularly Lerner and Hall). The same is true to a lesser degree of the library histories, but their broader scope still provides the potential researcher with a real feel for what each library contains, its primary emphases, and how well each collection is being maintained, facts which are unlikely to have altered very much in the intervening years (UC Riverside is still the only academic collection that makes any real attempt to acquire all currently published materials in the field). This is one volume which should be read and studied by any scholar intending to do intensive research on a particular SF writer or movement.

107. Lewis, Arthur O. **Utopian Literature in the Pennsylvania State University Libraries: A Selected Bibliography**. University Park, Penn., The Pennsylvania State University Libraries, 1984. xxx, 230 p. index. (Bibliographical Series, No. 9). (pbk.).

This catalog, like the Negley work (see #108), is arranged alphabetically by author, then by title. A typical entry includes author's name (that under which he or she is best known), title (italics), place of publication, publisher, year of publication, and similar data for the various editions held by the library; since the bibliography describes only those books actually located in the library collection, the first edition of the work may not be included. No paginations are given, but brief descriptive annotations are included for most entries, ranging in size from one sentence to 500 words (averaging seventy-five). In addition, a few entries (for Sir Thomas More, Plato, Aldous Huxley, etc.) feature major bio-critical essays on the author, his life, and works, ranging up to 2,300 words in length. Many foreign-language books are covered. Lewis's fourteen-page introduction provides a brief but well-written history of the utopia genre. The title index references book titles and page numbers only. *Utopian Literature* also includes a one-page addendum, a pseudonym list, and reproductions of sixteen title pages and woodcuts from some of the books annotated. The book is shot from legible typed copy.

Lewis covers about 1,700 works, compared to 1,200 in the Negley catalog (see #108), and his sometimes lengthy annotations provide descriptions and other background material not found in the Negley or Sargent utopian bibliographies (see #231 and #232). His catalog is sufficiently important in its own right that it should be collected by the larger university libraries.

108. Negley, Glenn. **Utopia Collection of the Duke University Library**. Durham, N.C., Friends of Duke University Library, 1965. iii, 83 p. (pbk.). Also: S.l., Folcroft Library Editions, 1970. iii, 83 p.

Negley arranges this collection catalog alphabetically by author, then by title. A typical entry includes author's name, title, place of publication, year of publication, year of publication of the edition held by Duke University, but no publishers or paginations. Known pseudonymous works are referenced to the authors' real names. Completing the book is an eleven-page chronological checklist of the works by date of the first edition irrespective of the printing held by Duke, referencing author's name only (no titles). The book is shot from legible typed copy. Roughly 1,200 titles are included, including many rare English- and foreign-language editions. This catalog was later subsumed into Negley's larger bibliography of utopian literature (see #231).

109. University of California, Riverside. **Dictionary Catalog of the J. Lloyd Eaton Collection of Science Fiction and Fantasy Literature**. Boston, G. K. Hall, 1982. v, 558, 575, 568 p. in 3 v. ISBN 0-8161-0379-8 (set).

This catalog of the Eaton Collection at the University of California, Riverside Library is the only volume of its kind ever published in the field, barring several dealers' catalogs generated for the sale of specific private collections (and these vary greatly both in scope and in the kind of information they provide). Following a brief three-page introduction by Dr. George Edgar Slusser, curator of the collection, touching upon its history and outlining the types of materials the collection contains, the bulk of this oversized three-volume set is an exact reproduction of the shelflist cards in the Eaton Collection's card catalog in main-entry order (usually by author). Any errors—cataloging, typographical, or otherwise—included on the original cards are faithfully reproduced here; also, many books have more than one edition listed, since the intent of the library is to acquire all printing variations of any particular publication.

The Eaton Collection is the largest *cataloged* library of fantastic literature anywhere in the world, public or private; this volume includes card entries generated through 1981 covering about 20,000 volumes. Although some of this information is now available on a restricted or proprietary basis through OCLC and other sources, the value of this set should not be minimized, since it provides extensive bibliographical data on the books and organizes into one finding list the many obscure or hard-to-locate titles of this broadly based collection. Some of the volumes included herein have no other holdings records either in the *National Union Catalog* or in OCLC. All major academic libraries should acquire this set.

110. Wurfel, Clifford. **An Introduction to the J. Lloyd Eaton Collection of Science Fiction and Fantasy**. Riverside, Calif., University of California, Riverside Library, 1979. 13 p. (pbk.).

A short in-house guide to the major authors and works held by the Eaton collection by the librarian formerly in charge of Special Collections at UC Riverside, Wurfel's history of the collection notes that its core of 7,500 early volumes of fantastic literature was acquired from the estate of J. Lloyd Eaton, a medical doctor, in 1969 and that this early segment of the collection included many rare and obscure titles, as well as all the standard works in the field, through about 1956. The UCR Library has made significant efforts through the purchase of other collections (particularly the Douglas Menville library) to bolster its holdings for the "gap" between 1956 and 1969, to maintain the collection through ongoing purchases of all new SF publications, and to acquire large foreign-language holdings, particularly of French and other European SF. This basic introductory guide to the world's largest publicly accessible collection of science fiction and fantasy literature, now approaching 100,000 cataloged items, should definitely be expanded and brought up-to-date.

MAGAZINE AND ANTHOLOGY INDEXES

SCOPE NOTE: This chapter includes indexes and checklists of science fiction, fantasy, and weird fiction professional magazines, scholarly journals, and fanzines, plus indexes to monographic collections and anthologies and general cyclopedic guides to SF periodicals. Guides to specific publications are arranged in alphabetical order by periodical name at the end of this section.

CYCLOPEDIAS OF SF MAGAZINES

111. Tymn, Marshall B., and Mike Ashley, eds. **Science Fiction, Fantasy, and Weird Fiction Magazines**. Westport, Conn. & London, Greenwood Press, 1985. xxx, 970 p. index. (Historical Guides to the World's Periodicals and Newspapers). LC 84-11523. ISBN 0-313-21221-X.

Tymn and Ashley have compiled a comprehensive, authoritative, and exceptionally well researched A-Z guide to the major and minor professional periodicals in fantastic literature. The preface succinctly states: "Our purpose in compiling this volume is to provide scholars, researchers, and the general reader with a useful tool for evaluating the science fiction, fantasy, and weird fiction magazines as a historical and literary phenomenon, and to furnish a bibliographical apparatus for documenting the appearance of these magazines in all their various phases." And what a good job they do!

Thirty-eight well-known scholars in the field, including a number of the old-time editors themselves, have contributed hundreds of essays ranging in size from 200-20,000+ words (averaging 1,000). The magazines are listed in alphabetical order by title. A typical entry includes title, narration, footnotes, and two entry appendices: "Information Sources" and "Publication History." "Information Sources" may include the following items: "Bibliography" (reference sources specific to the magazine), "Index Sources" (places where the magazine is indexed, keyed to a set of letter codes referenced in an abbreviations list at the front of the book), "Reprint Sources" (derivative books and periodicals), "Location Sources" ([mostly academic] libraries currently holding substantial runs of the periodical). The "Publication History" section may include title (all title changes or variations, and subtitles), volume data (volume and issue sequence numbering, noting all errors, with magazine schedule and changes in schedule, and total number of issues published), publisher (publisher's name and place of publication, including locations of executive or other offices), editors (all editorial personnel responsible for selection of stories), format (the size and shape of the magazine, and the usual number of pages), price (cover price at the time of sale, with variations).

The essays vary widely in size depending on the importance of the publication in question, the entry on *Astounding/Analog* running over 20,000 words, and generally include background history (how and why the publication was founded and principal owners), some biographical and historical information on the editors, mention of the major authors and artists and stories featured in the magazine's run, reasons for decline and failure (where the publications have ceased), and a final summation of the periodical's importance to the history of fantastic literature.

Some of the material differs in quality, as might be expected with such a large number of contributors, but there is a sure editorial hand at work here, and the pieces never stray too far from their avowed purpose. Many of the histories include anecdotes, personal data, or other material that clearly derives from correspondence or interviews with the principals of the publications (and the sources are carefully cited). On the whole, the critiques seem fair, reliable, and historically sound. There are numerous internal see references to other titles covered in this volume.

End matter includes a section on "Associational English-Language Anthologies" (covering the hybrid "paperback magazine" series); "Academic Periodicals" and "Major Fanzines" (both of these chapters are arranged in separate alphabetical sequences by title); "Non-English-Language Magazines, by Country" (by country name, then alphabetically by title); "An Index to Major Cover Artists," alphabetically by artist name, showing major cover assignments (listing the magazine title and specific cover date of the artist's first SF cover assignment, then the total numbers of his covers for each magazine in descending order by number of assignments), followed by a list of the top fifty-five cover artists in descending order by total number of assignments; a general "Chronology" of the development of the SF magazine, showing years of birth for each publication listed herein; a "Bibliography" of all sources consulted, with author title and bibliographical data; and a comprehensive every-name index.

Tymn and Ashley have produced the standard guide to the SF magazines, one that is likely to stand the test of time for generations to come. It is difficult to imagine any serious researcher of these publications beginning his or her work without first consulting this volume. It should be on the shelves of every academic library.

GENERAL INDEXES AND CHECKLISTS

112. Boyajian, Jerry, and Kenneth R. Johnson. **Index to the Science Fiction Magazines: 1977-1984.** Cambridge, Mass., Twaci Press, 1981-85. 8 v. LC 82-641836. ISSN 0732-0655 (pbk.). **Index to the Semi-Professional Fantasy Magazines: 1982-1983.** Cambridge, Mass., Twaci Press, 1983-84. 2 v. LC 84-642059. ISSN 0743-4103 (pbk.).

The Twaci Press series of magazine indexes ceased with the 1984 annual but until that time was a well-established rival to the NESFA series (see #129). A typical annual includes a "Magazine Index" comprising two lists, both alphabetical by magazine title. The first index provides a chronological checklist of the issues, giving month, year, volume number, issue number, whole number, format (e.g., "D"=Digest sized), pagination. The second list is an issue-by-issue rendering of the magazine contents, giving magazine title, month and year of publication, title of each selection in the order presented in that issue, type when not a piece of short fiction (e.g., "art" or "verse" or "pt 1 of 3" for the first part of a serialized novel , author, page number where the selection begins).

The "Author Index" gives author, title of individual selections, magazine title, month of publication and is followed by a "Title Index" listing author and title only and an "Artist Index," which provides artist, magazine, paginations where the artwork appeared (or "cover" if the contribution was a cover illustration). Increasingly as the series developed more attention was paid to SF published in periodicals not generally regarded as genre publications (*Playboy*, for example, or *Omni*), and separate "Author Indexes" to these are provided in the later annuals.

The companion *Index to the Semi-Professional Fantasy Magazines* covers in identical format the many borderline fiction magazines which were founded in the 1980s (*Whispers*, for example), which published professional-level SF, fantasy, or horror without mass market distribution.

The Twaci series provided some minor information not found in the NESFA guides (the detailed listings of artists' contributions, for example) but clearly not enough to justify its continued existence in the face of its better-established competitor.

113. Cockcroft, T. G. L. **Index to Fiction in *Radio News* and Other Magazines**. Lower Hutt, N.Z., T.G.L. Cockcroft, 1970. 12 p. index. (pbk.). Based in part on two previous compilations: Evans, William H. **The Gernsback Forerunners**. Brooklyn, N.Y., Julius Unger, 1944. 5 leaves. (pbk.). And: Engel, Theodore. **Evolution of Modern Science Fiction**. [New York, Hugo Gernsback, 1952—publishing data speculative]. 12 p. (pbk.).

New Zealand fan Tom Cockcroft produced over a two-decade period a series of small but worthy indexes to fantastic literature in the early pulp magazines. This new booklet is based on a series of issue-by-issue checklists of the early Hugo Gernsback magazines previously produced by Evans and Engel (as noted above). Gernsback, who founded the first professional SF magazine, *Amazing Stories*, in 1926, had begun his career in publishing during World War I by inaugurating a group of popular science and radio periodicals, some of which published science and other speculative fiction, including his own seminal novel, *Ralph 124C41+*. Cockcroft's index covers six of these titles: *Modern Electrics*, *Practical Electrics*, *The Experimenter*, *Radio News*, *The Electrical Experimenter*, and *Science & Invention*. The basic index is arranged alphabetically by author surname, then by title, giving author (all caps), title, magazine abbreviation, month and year of publication, but no paginations. The title index includes title (all caps), author, magazine abbreviation, month and year of publication. There is a separate guide on page 2 to Clement Fezandié's series of stories, Dr. Hackensaw's Secrets, plus an index of those stories later reprinted in *Amazing Stories* and the other professional science-fiction magazines. As with all of Cockcroft's works, the book is shot from photoreduced but legible typed copy. Although difficult to locate, these brief indexes do provide a service to scholars and should ultimately be gathered into some more permanent form.

114. Cockcroft, Thomas G. L. **Index to the Verse in *Weird Tales*, Including *Oriental Stories*, and the *Magic Carpet Magazine*, and *The Thrill Book***. Lower Hutt, N.Z., Thomas G. L. Cockcroft, 1960. 16 p. + 1 unnumbered page on the inside back cover. index. (pbk.).

Cockcroft's booklet was a precursor to his *Index to the Weird Fiction Magazines* (see #115), covering many of the same titles. The major part of this guide is devoted to *Weird Tales*, indexing the poems appearing in that publication first by title, then by author, with months and years of publication but no paginations. Page 10 includes a brief guide to "Virgil Finlay's Poetry Series" in *WT* and a brief index to verse in *Oriental Stories* and *The Magic Carpet Magazine*. The inside back cover provides an index to the verse appearing in the sixteen issues of *The Thrill Book*. The book is shot from legible typed copy. Although the book is still useful as a one-volume guide to verse in the early fantasy pulps, much of this information is available in the more detailed indexes to *The Thrill Book* (see #171) and *Weird Tales* (see #176) covered elsewhere in this volume.

115. Cockcroft, T. G. L. **Index to the Weird Fiction Magazines**. Lower Hutt, N.Z., T.G.L. Cockcroft, 1962-64 (and 1967). 100 p. in 2 v. index. (pbk.). Also: New York, Arno Press, 1975. 100 p. index. (Science Fiction). LC 74-15955. ISBN 0-405-06322-9.

Since Day's index of the science fiction magazines (see #121) failed to include those pulps devoted to weird or supernatural fiction (specifically, *Weird Tales*), Cockcroft produced this supplemental index as a labor of love to record the stories published in these periodicals between 1923-1954 (when *Weird Tales* ceased publication).

The first volume provides a brief introduction, a checklist of magazines indexed (giving an issue-by-issue rendering of whole number published, year and month of publication, volume and issue number, cover artist, title of story featured on the cover), a list of editorial staff, a checklist of cover artists and the issues they illustrated, some general editorial notes, and a comprehensive index to the fiction published in these periodicals, alphabetical by title of each story, plus author and month and year of publication. Seven magazines are indexed other than *Weird Tales*, although the latter comprises the vast majority of the entries; *WT* listings are uncoded, while entries for fiction appearing in other publications are noted with a two- or three-letter code preceding the date (e.g., "GF"=*Golden Fleece*).

The second volume, issued in 1964 (and slightly updated in 1967), reworks the same material alphabetically by author and also provides a brief story series index and a note on "Translators and Translations." Both books were shot from typed copy; some pages in some copies are faint. The Arno Press reprint was shot facsimile from the original and produced as a one-volume amalgamation of the original.

Cockcroft has now largely been superseded by Parnell and Ashley (see #130), except that the latter fails to include a title index; also, three of the relatively minor magazines covered by Cockcroft (*Oriental Stories*, *The Magic Carpet Magazine*, and *Golden Fleece Historical Adventure*) are *not* indexed in Parnell, although some issues are covered haphazardly in Robbins (see #133) and Day (see #121), and the first two are mentioned in Jaffery/Cook's index to *Weird Tales* (see #176).

116. Cole, W. R. **A Checklist of Science-Fiction Anthologies**. Brooklyn, N.Y., W. R. Cole, 1964. xvi, 374 p. index. LC 65-1442. Also: New York, Arno Press, 1975. xvi, 374 p. index. (Science Fiction). LC 74-15956. ISBN 0-405-06323-7.

This was the first guide to stories in SF anthologies ever attempted, and as with many fan-produced indexes, a few organizational and production problems frame its large mass of data.

Following brief introductions by the author and by Theodore Sturgeon, we find a two-page "How to Use the Checklist," an "Abbreviations List," a brief list of the anthologies included in the *Checklist*, alphabetical by title (correlated with editor's names and the page numbers within this book on which the contents of each anthology are delineated), then the main "Alphabetical Listing by Editor." The latter section includes editor's name(s), anthology title, publisher, place of publication, number of stories included, pagination, price, date of publication (in most instances, to the month or day), and a list of the stories in the same sequence as they were published in the anthology. Each story listing includes story title, author, magazine in which the story was originally printed (where applicable), and month and year of original magazine publication. No paginations are included for the stories within the anthology.

There are separate indexes by story author and title, correlated with anthology title, magazine issue in which the story was originally published, and month and year of original periodical publication. Supplemental sections covering those anthologies produced in 1962-63 appear on pages 298-374 in their own alphabetical sequences. The book is shot from generally legible typed copy on strangely textured glossy paper.

The major problem with Cole's book lies in its initial section, the index by anthology, where the editor's name, anthology title, and story contents listings are all listed in capital letters, with the anthology title (but nothing else) indented five spaces from the left margin. The major entries are separated only by one full line break flanking the editor's name and title, making discernment of individual anthology listings difficult at first glance, particularly on pages where the anthologies are broken into two or more sections, each with their own half-titles. The author and title indexes do not share this defect, the data in these sections being clearly delineated through the use of hanging indents.

The Arno reprint reduced the physical size of the book from 8.5" x 11" to 5" x 8", with many pages appearing much fainter than the original (apparently the glossy paper did not reproduce well). Virtually all of the data in Cole have now been subsumed into Contento's continuing indexes (see #117), but it should be noted that Contento does not provide quite as much bibliographical detail for the anthologies themselves, omitting total paginations for the books and including only a skeletal series of codes for publisher and publication information.

117. Contento, William G. **Index to Science Fiction Anthologies and Collections**. Boston, G. K. Hall & Co., 1978. xii, 608 p. index. (A Reference Publication in Science Fiction). LC 78-155. ISBN 0-8161-8092-X. **Index to Science Fiction Anthologies and Collections, 1977-1983**. Boston, G. K. Hall & Co., 1984. xvi, 503 p. index. (A Reference Publication in Science Fiction). LC 78-155. ISBN 0-8161-8554-9. Partially continued on an annual basis by Brown and Contento's *Science Fiction, Fantasy and Horror* (see #24).

Contento's continuing series has become the standard guide to SF stories printed in anthologies, supplanting Cole's index (see #116); he was among the first researchers in the field to utilize the possibilities of the computer age. This is both the strongest and weakest point of the set.

Both volumes are organized similarly. The introduction provides a general description of what the books contain and is followed by a bibliography of sources consulted (including some, but not all, of the major SF reference tools, plus a few individual author bibliographies). This is followed by a brief "How to Use the Index" and an extensive abbreviations list (using two-letter codes for format and type, three-letter codes for publishers and periodicals, and seven-letter codes for anthology titles). There are almost 2,000 abbreviation codes in the second volume alone, requiring constant reference to and from the list. The "Checklist of Books Indexed" is arranged by title in the first volume and by main entry (usually editor, although at least one of the titles is referenced under the entry "Anonymous") in the second, and provides the following data: primary editor (second volume only), anthology title, primary editor (first volume only), type code (e.g., "AN"=anthology, "AC"=single author collection), format code (e.g., "Pa"=paperback), publisher code (e.g., "GOL"=Gollancz), year (or sometimes month/season and year) of publication.

The major section of each book, the "Author Index," provides a list of the stories anthologized, arranged alphabetically by name of author, including author's name, story title, type code (e.g., "SS"=short story), publisher/magazine code and date of original publication (e.g., "FSF"=*The Magazine of Fantasy & Science Fiction*), anthology title, anthology editor, type code (e.g., "OA"=original anthology [an anthology comprised of stories published for the first time]). The "Story Index" rearranges the same data alphabetically by individual story title. The final section, "Book Contents," is arranged alphabetically by anthology title and includes title, editor, type code, format code, publisher code, date of publication followed by complete contents listed in the same sequence as in the anthology (data include story title, author, type code, publisher code for the magazine or anthology in which the story first appeared, and the date of that original appearance). No paginations, either of the anthologies themselves or of the contents of those collections, are provided, making bibliographical citation of the stories impossible without actually viewing the books in question.

There's no doubt Contento correlates an enormous amount of data in these 8.5" x 11" volumes covering thousands of anthologies (including a few foreign-language volumes) and tens of thousands of individual stories, essays, and poems. But measuring the level of his completeness is extraordinarily difficult. Contento excludes some (but not all) collections of fantasy and horror fiction depending on the background of the authors (if they are associated with the science fiction field, he may include them); judging whether or not he has omitted an item because of content or because he is unaware of the volume is impossible to determine. Undoubtedly, he covers 95% or more of publications produced by the major trade and mass market firms; however, his coverage of lesser-known items appears more haphazard (for example, of nine anthologies produced by Menville/Reginald in the 1970s for the academic publishing house Arno Press, only one is indexed).

The physical appearances of these volumes and their basic organization also leave much to be desired. Both are produced from old-style computer-generated copy that has been substantially photoreduced in size to produce a double-column format. The copy is often difficult to read and follow, with the type all being in one face, and the extreme use of abbreviation codes is not just intrusive but frequently irritating and counterproductive. One can understand the need to conserve space in massive compilations of this kind, but when such conservation itself becomes a restriction on the average reader's ability to use these volumes successfully, one must question the utility of this kind of overcoded bibliomania. The use of codes should be severely restricted in any future editions.

Fortunately, the editor himself seems to have realized some of the problems with his format, because in the Brown/Contento annuals (see #24), he has provided a partial continuation of this series in the section entitled "Book Contents." Here the anthologies are arranged in alphabetical order by main entry (usually editors' names), providing editor (all caps), book title (boldface type), publisher, ISBN, date of publication, price, pagination, format (e.g., "hc"=hardcover), brief description ("Collection of 18 stories set in West Virginia"), and complete contents listings (these include the page numbers where each story begins, story title, author, type [e.g., "ss"=short story], and publisher and publishing date of the story's first appearance [if any]). The individual stories and their authors are then indexed in the "Title List: Stories" and "Author List: Stories" sections, respectively, together with stories and authors from the "Magazine Contents" chapter of the annuals. This is a much more readable and usable format than that used in the original Contento indexes; since the Brown/Contento books now extend from 1984-DATE, there are no gaps in coverage.

As for the original two-volume set, even with its structural defects it remains a wholly necessary tool for the serious SF scholar and should be acquired by all large university libraries. A huge, one-volume revision and update using the new format style from the Brown/Contento annuals is reportedly underway.

118. Cook, Frederick S. **Fred Cook's Index to the Wonder Group.** Grand Haven, Mich., Fred Cook, 1966. 239 p. [but some pages do not follow in sequence, and others are missing altogether]. index. LC 70-14090 (pbk.).

Cook's guide indexes a group of SF pulp magazines originally founded by entrepreneur Hugo Gernsback and later incorporated into the "Thrilling" pulp group after Gernsback lost control of his own creations. The guide covers *Air Wonder Stories, Science Wonder Quarterly/Wonder Stories Quarterly, Science Wonder Stories/Wonder Stories/Thrilling Wonder Stories, Wonder Stories Annual, Startling Stories, Captain Future, Fantastic Story Quarterly/Fantastic Story Magazine,* and *Space Stories.* Each of the publications is treated separately, in four sections: a one-page history of the magazine with a checklist of the publication dates of each issue (by year), physical description, price, and number of pages; a chronological checklist of each issue showing month and year of publication, volume and issue number, cover artist, and a list of the stories and authors appearing in each issue in the same order as they originally ran, but no paginations; an author index giving author's name (all caps), title, month and year of publication; a second author index showing the total number of stories written by each. The book is shot from very clear typed copy. The absence of an overall index severely limits the usefulness of this publication, and there is very little here (other, perhaps, than some of the brief historical data) that cannot be found in the general periodical indexes covered elsewhere in this section (see particularly Don Day's index, #121).

119. Day, Bradford M. **The Complete Checklist of Science-Fiction Magazines**. Woodhaven, N.Y., Science-Fiction & Fantasy Publications, 1961. 63 p. LC 61-19464 (pbk.).

Day lists all known professional science-fiction, fantasy, horror, and some peripheral magazines published in the United States, Canada, Great Britain, and Australia, plus a few foreign-language publications from continental Europe and Mexico. The periodicals are listed in alphabetical order by title, then chronologically by date of publication. Day uses a gridbox system, twelve boxes across (corresponding to the months of the year, with appropriate single-letter initials as running heads), each box down the page representing one year. Normally, two sets of numbers appear in each box (representing each issue of the magazine actually published); the top number is the volume number, the bottom number the issue number of that particular release. Quarterly publications are marked with single-letter codes next to these numbers indicating the season (e.g., "A"=Autumn). Bimonthly periodicals are so indicated by extending a series of hyphens across two boxes. In general, the schematic should be obvious at a glance even to the inexperienced user. The book is shot from clearly reproduced typed copy. Day lists data through the end of 1960; his work was continued by Desmond (see #122) and has now largely been superseded by Hall *et al.*(see #125), but Day does include some peripheral publications not indexed in other sources in quite this fashion.

120. Day, Bradford M., [and William H. Evans]. **An Index on the Weird & Fantastica in Magazines**. S. Ozone Park, N.Y., Bradford M. Day, 1953. 162 p. (pbk.).

One of the many bibliographies and indexes produced by this Long Island author during the period 1950-63, Day's guide is divided into three sections. Part I provides an issue-by-issue contents guide to eight pulp horror magazines of the 1920s-50s (*Weird Tales, Golden Fleece, Strange Tales, Oriental Stories, Magic Carpet, Tales of Magic & Mystery, Thrill Book, Strange Stories*), derived largely from an untitled series of magazine checklists produced in looseleaf format by William H. Evans in 1950. A typical entry provides editor's name (if it has changed from the previous issue), month and year of publication, size (if it has changed from the previous issue), volume and issue number, and a list of the material published in each issue with author names as they appeared in the original. Day has updated the *WT* list through the end of 1953 (the magazine died in 1954). A second section reproduces Evans's indexes to fantastic fiction published in the general adventure pulps (*The Argosy, Blue Book Magazine, Complete Stories, Romance Magazine, Popular Magazine, The Idler, All-American Fiction, All-Story Magazine, The Cavalier, Live Wire, Munsey's Magazine, Ocean*, and *Scrap Book*, with incomplete listings from thirteen other periodicals). The third section, "A Checklist of Fantastic Magazines," was a precursor to *The Complete Checklist* (see #119) published by Day in 1961 and follows the same format. The book is shot from generally clear typed copy, with the usual Day production problems (poor binding and proofreading). Now partly superseded by Parnell/Ashby (see #130) and Robbins (see #133), although many of the more obscure publications are not indexed in any other source.

121. Day, Donald B. **Index to the Science-Fiction Magazines, 1926-1950**. Portland, Ore., Perri Press, 1952. xv, 184 p. index. LC 52-41880. **Index to the Science Fiction Magazines, 1926-1950**. Rev. ed. Boston, G. K. Hall & Co., 1982. xv, 289 p. index. ISBN 0-8161-8591-3.

The *Index to the Science-Fiction Magazines* was the first serious attempt to produce a unified one-volume guide to the fiction published by the professional SF periodicals of the pulp era, and it marked an early high point in fan scholarship.

The main index is arranged alphabetically by author's name, then alphabetically by story title. A typical entry provides author (all caps), title, type (e.g., "s"=short story), a two- or three-letter abbreviation for the magazine title (e.g., "ASF"=*Astounding Science Fiction*), month and year of publication (in the form "Aug 42" for August 1942), and beginning page number. The title index gives story title (all caps), author, type, month and year of publication, and page number. A third section provides an issue-by-issue checklist of each magazine, chronologically in descending order, giving month and year of publication, volume and issue number for each issue published, physical page size (in inches), number of pages in each issue, and cover artist for each issue. A brief, two-page list of "Back Cover Pictures" completes the book; later issues also included a tipped-in errata sheet after the last page of text.

Day does not include *Weird Tales*, ostensibly because he lacked access to a complete set, but otherwise he covers all the major and minor prozines of fantastic literature from the founding of *Amazing Stories* in 1926 through the end of 1950. Some story series listings are embedded in the author entries. There are numerous see and see also references to and from known pennames and house pseudonyms to the real authors; in general, however, Day lists each story under the names actually used for publication. Day also indexes artists and magazine editors in the general alphabetical author sequence. The book is shot from sometimes faint typed copy.

G. K. Hall has done the SF world a service by completely resetting the book and updating the text from Day's own notes and from other corrections and addenda published in a wide variety of fan and professional sources. The result is an attractive, easy-to-use, authoritative guide to the nascence of the science fiction field. No serious student of the genre should be without it.

122. Desmond, William H. **The Science-Fiction Magazine Checklist, 1961-1972**. South Boston, Mass., Archival Press, 1973. 16 p. (pbk.).

Desmond's booklet was intended directly to supplement Day's *Checklist* (see #119) and uses a very similar format with slightly higher production values. Magazines are arranged alphabetically by title, then chronologically by year of issue. A boxed grid occupies each page, twelve boxes wide (corresponding to the months of the year), each descending box representing one year of issue. Desmond includes only those titles published between January 1961 and the end of 1972. Largely superseded by Hall *et al.* (see #125) and Wysocki (see #143).

123. Evans, William H. **Index of Science Fiction**. [Denver, Colo., Robert C. Peterson], 1949. 148 leaves. index. (pbk.).

Evans was an early indexer of the field whose work appeared in a variety of rather amateurish formats (this index was issued in looseleaf format); some of his work was later reworked into more professional guise by Brad Day (see #120). This guide indexes roughly thirty pulp SF magazines, providing complete contents listings on an issue-by-issue basis and covering issues produced through 1947 and 1948. Although most of his material has been superseded by Donald Day (see #121), Evans did attempt to classify the subject matter of each story through the Speer Decimal System, providing a unique subject access unavailable in any other source. Unfortunately, this index is itself virtually unobtainable, and most of Evans's pioneering work is now almost completely lost.

124. Frank, Howard, and Roy Torgeson. **The 1977 Science Fiction & Fantasy Magazine Checklist & Price Guide, 1923-1976.** Port Washington, N.Y., Science Fiction Resources, 1977. 50 p. index. ISBN 0-918364-00-0 (pbk.).

This checklist of SF and fantasy magazines is arranged alphabetically by title, then chronologically by year, showing each issue produced by year and by month, the latter being designated by its numerical equivalent (e.g., "12"=December). It provides general prices for copies of the issues in "good" condition. The checklist part of this booklet has been completely superseded by Hall *et al.* (see #125), and the pricing information is so far out-of-date as to be utterly useless except possibly as a general guide to value ratios.

125. Hall, H. W., Kenneth R. Johnson, and George Michaels. **The Science Fiction Magazines: A Bibliographical Checklist of Titles and Issues Through 1982.** Bryan, Tex., SFBRI, 1983. iv, 89 p. index. ISBN 0-935064-10-9 (pbk.). Also: San Bernardino, Calif., The Borgo Press, 1985. iv, 89 p. index. LC 84-11192. ISBN 0-89370-772-4.

Hall's checklist generally replaces all earlier efforts of this type, including Day (see #119), Desmond (see #122), Frank/Torgeson (see #124), and Robinson (see #134), with a few exceptions (Day lists some very peripheral titles not covered in Hall). The main section includes a complete alphabetical list of the professional science fiction and fantasy magazines published in English from 1924-82, excluding comic books and the broadly based adventure pulp magazines. Under each entry, Hall provides the following information: magazine title (all caps), total volume range published (e.g., "v.1-7 no.2," indicating that the magazine published issues from volume 1 through volume 7, issue 2), range of years published, place of publication and publisher (primary publisher or the latest publisher for active titles), an historical list of editorial personnel (by date), an historical list of publishers (by date), historical notes of interest, the two- or three-letter code commonly used for the magazine in the published indexes, a list of publications which have indexed the periodical, plus a comprehensive checklist of each issue published in descending order by publication date, including volume number, issue number, and month and year of publication. Hall notes title changes as interpolated line breaks when they occur and similarly records numbering errors (a frequent occurrence in the pulps) and other bibliographical data of interest.

End matter includes an "Editor Index" alphabetical by editor name and listing the publications and years served; "Indexes to the Magazines," a bibliography of published index sources; and an "Appendix: Non-English Language Magazines," which presents a skeletal listing of foreign prozines, arranged alphabetically by country, then by publication.

Hall's research is both sound and meticulous, and his checklist is a handy synthesis of the history of magazine publication in the field of fantastic literature. Note that Wysocki's checklist (see #143), although not as complete, does include several years' more data. A revised and updated edition with Daryl F. Mallett is currently in progress.

126. **Index to Fantasy & Science Fiction in Munsey Publications**. [S.l., s.n., n.d.]. 36 p. (pbk.).

This uncredited fan index, produced from mimeographed 8.5" x 11" copy circa 1950-55, provides a useful guide to fantastic stories and novels published in the following Munsey pulps: *Argosy Monthly, All-Story Magazine, The Cavalier, Munsey's Magazine, The Scrap Book, The Live Wire, Argosy All-Story Weekly, Argosy Weekly, All-Story Weekly*, and *All-Story Cavalier Weekly*.

The volume indexes the material alphabetically by author's name, then by story title. A typical entry includes author (all caps), title, type (e.g., "ss"=short story), subject code (e.g., "A"=Atlantis), magazine title abbreviation (e.g., "AS W"=*All-Story Weekly*), month (and day, where applicable) and year of publication. There is no title index. The booklet is shot from generally legible typed copy, although the publication itself is now yellowing with age. The subject codes, which are not universally applied, are still useful in determining what each story is about. Now virtually unobtainable.

127. Lewis, Al, [with various co-editors]. **Index to the Science Fiction Magazines: 1961-1963**. Los Angeles, Calif., Al Lewis, 1962-64. 3 v. index. (pbk.).

These three annual indexes to the SF magazines published during each calendar year include complete contents for each issue in chronological order by publication date plus author, title, and illustrator indices. The 1962-63 volumes also include an "Index to Book Reviews," a feature not incorporated into most other guides of this kind. However, virtually all of this data have now been subsumed into Metcalf (see #128) or Strauss (see #138) and the book review material by Hall (see #92), making these laudable early efforts now largely obsolete. Al Lewis should not be confused with Anthony R. Lewis, who edited many of the NESFA annuals (see #129).

128. Metcalf, Norm. **The Index of Science Fiction Magazines, 1951-1965**. El Cerrito, Calif., J. Ben Stark, Publisher, 1968. ix, 249 p. index. (pbk.).

Metcalf intended his index as a direct sequel and supplement to Donald Day's pioneering effort (see #121), and his guide follows much the same format as the earlier book.

Following a brief introduction on how to use the book, plus an abbreviations list (arranged two ways, by magazine title and inversely by abbreviation), the main section of the index is arranged in alphabetical order by author's name or pseudonym, then alphabetically by individual story title. A typical entry includes author's name (all caps), story title, word count (in the form "14.4" for 14,400 words), magazine title abbreviation (e.g., "ASF"=*Astounding Science Fiction*), and month and year of publication (in the form "Sep 61" for September 1961). As with Day, many story series listings are interpolated into the text, and the book is filled with see and see also references to other pennames of the authors. Editorial staff are indexed along with the rest, with appropriate periods of service; also included are references to photographs and biographical material. Finally, Metcalf also provides a general reference to authors covered in the earlier Day index (in the form "26-50" following the author's name).

The title index records story title (all caps), author (including mention of the author's real name where appropriate), word length, magazine title abbreviation, and month and year of publication. A separate index to illustrators (cover and interior) lists artist's name (all caps), magazine abbreviation, and cover and interior credits (by month and year of publication). An index to editorial staff provides a list of personnel by magazine, editor's name, and dates of service. A checklist correlating magazine titles, dates and years of publication, volume and issue numbers, and cover illustrators, completes the main text. An unpaged two-page corrigenda to Donald Day's earlier index is appended at the end of the book. The book is reproduced from very clear typed copy.

Metcalf's work is far more readable and legible than the computer-generated copy of Strauss (see #138) and is generally to be preferred; however, Strauss includes initial page numbers for all entries, data not found in Metcalf, while Metcalf includes series and pseudonym information and story lengths not in Strauss. Therefore, the avid bibliographer (and the academic library) should maintain copies of both books.

129. New England Science Fiction Association, Inc. (some volumes were edited by Anthony R. Lewis). **Index to the Science Fiction Magazines, 1966-1970**. Cambridge, Mass., New England Science Fiction Association, 1971. ix, 82 p. index. **Index to the Science Fiction Magazines, 1966-1969**. Cambridge, Mass., New England Science Fiction Association, 1968-70. 4 v. index. LC 75-650102. ISSN 0579-6059 (pbk.). **The N.E.S.F.A. Index [to] Science Fiction Magazines and Original Anthologies, 1971/1972-1986**. Cambridge, Mass., New England Science Fiction Association, 1973-88. 14 v. index. LC 75-646017 and LC 84-643001. ISSN 0361-3038 and ISSN 0747-7546 (pbk.). **The N.E.S.F.A. Index to Short SF, 1987**-DATE. Cambridge, Mass., New England Science Fiction Association, 1989-DATE. annual. index. (pbk.).

The NESFA volumes are intended directly to supplement Strauss (see #138). The 1966-69 annual volumes were cumulated (and added to) in the 1966-70 hardcover version; the later series evolved both in title and content through several permutations, gradually becoming more elaborate with the passing of years. Three of these volumes were published as two-year sets: 1971/72, 1977/78, and 1979/80.

The 1966-70 cumulation is virtually identical in style and format to Strauss, providing an abbreviations list, magazine checklist, and three indexes to the contents (by magazine issue, title, and author). A typical entry includes author, title, page number on which the piece begins, type (e.g., "S"=short story), month and year of publication (in the form "FEB 70" for February 1970), and a three-letter magazine code (e.g., "FSF"=*The Magazine of Fantasy & Science Fiction*). The book is shot in all capital letters from photoreduced computer-generated copy.

The latter annuals, beginning with the 1971/72 two-year cumulation, gradually began indexing (in addition to the dwindling number of professional magazines in the field) the many anthologies of original science fiction stories which began proliferating in the 1970s, assigning them six-letter abbreviation codes. The later volumes also include somewhat more elaborate formats, featuring some indentations of title data in the author section of the indexes and typeset introductory material (including expanded descriptions of the format and contents of the original anthologies), although the basic arrangement has stayed the same throughout. The books have also continued to increase in size, finally passing the 100-page mark with the 1987 annual (which further expanded coverage to *all* short SF fiction published in the year).

The NESFA indexes are essential supplementals to Donald Day's guide (see #121) and to the later Strauss and Metcalf indexes (see #138 and #128). One wonders, however, why no effort has been made by NESFA (or anyone else) to cumulate these volumes and produce a much more usable one- or two-volume index to modern short SF fiction. Until then, these stapled, somewhat amateurishly produced volumes will have to suffice.

130. Parnell, Frank H., and Mike Ashley. **Monthly Terrors: An Index to the Weird Fantasy Magazines Published in the United States and Great Britain**. Westport, Conn. &

London, Greenwood Press, 1985. xxvii, 602 p. index. (Bibliographies and Indexes in World Literature, No. 4). LC 84-19225. ISBN 0-313-23989-4.

This generally sound guide focuses on professional and semi-professional horror and fantasy magazines published in English from 1919-1983. Following brief introductions by Peter Haining and Parnell, Ashley contributes a six-page historical survey of the weird fantasy magazines. The "User's Guide" then provides a detailed summary of how the book is organized.

The major part of the book (300 of 602 pages), the "Issue Index," is arranged alphabetically by magazine title, each magazine's listings starting on a new page. A typical entry includes magazine title (centered in all caps), a brief historical summary, including publisher(s), publisher addresses, editor(s), title changes, and other vital data (all in italics), and an issue-by-issue contents listing (giving month and year of publication, volume and issue number, cover artist, and contents). The contents listings include title, type (if longer than short story length), and author. Major title changes are noted with appropriate see references at the end of the contents listings to the magazine under its new title.

The other major section, the "Author Index," includes: author's name (all caps), years of birth and death (if known), brief italicized description of the author's nationality and occupation (if known), and an alphabetical listing of the author's stories and other contributions (giving title, magazine title abbreviation, month [and/or issue number] and year of publication); stories under pseudonyms are listed under the author's real (or best-known) name, alphabetically by penname and then by title, with see references from the bogus name to the real one. Middle or additional names of authors are provided in parentheses. A separate Artist Index," also arranged alphabetically by name, lists the artists' cover and interior illustrations alphabetically by name of magazine (listed by abbreviations code), with year and month (or issue number) of publication. The "Editor Index" similarly lists editors correlated with position and time served, and name of magazine. The several appendices include an "Index to Series and Connected Stories," "Honorable Mentions" (borderline publications summarized in one or more paragraphs), "Chronological Checklist of Magazines" (by date of initial publication, showing entire range of publication dates), and a "Geographical Listing of Magazines," by state and country, then alphabetically by publisher, with name(s) of magazines issued by that publisher and publishing address. Completing the book is a two-page bibliography and an errata page. *Monthly Terrors* is reproduced from legible word-processed copy and is well bound in a library cloth edition.

As always with Ashley's publications, the historical notes and biographical squibs are thoroughly researched and indisputably sound. The book is well organized, clearly and logically laid out, and well indexed. However, the absence of a title index to the individual stories flaws what is otherwise a virtuoso performance and makes access to Cockcroft's index (see #115) still necessary. This error in judgment should be corrected in any future edition.

131.   Pavlat, Robert, and Bill Evans. **Fanzine Index, Listing Most Fanzines from the Beginning Through 1952, Including Titles, Editors' Names, and Data on Each Issue.** Flushing, N.Y., Harold Palmer Piser, Worldfare Publications, 1965. 141 p. LC 89-832232 (pbk.). Originally issued about 1953 by Pavlat and Evans as a series of fascicles.

Pavlat and Evans have provided an important checklist of the science fiction field's important but highly ephemeral fan publications, most of which are now nearly impossible to find. The index is arranged in alphabetical order by title of the periodical. A typical entry includes magazine title (with occasional see references to alternate titles), editor's name, and a chronological list of all known issues. For each issue, the authors have noted volume and/or issue number, month and year of publication (in the form "Jul 39" for July 1939), and a series of codes indicating (in order) page size, number of pages, and printing medium. All of this is valuable information, although an index of the editors would also have been desirable. The *Index* was shot from legible typed copy and mimeographed in paper covers (the paper now yellowing), and is itself now very difficult to locate. A comprehensive contents index of SF fanzines is badly needed, since so many SF professionals got their start with these publications. NOTE: the largest publicly accessible collection of science fiction fan magazines is located at the Eaton Collection, Rivera Library, University of California, Riverside, which purchased the 20,000-volume Terry Carr collection in the late 1980s.

132. Plum, Claude D., Jr. **The Terratoid Guide: A Checklist of Magazines Dealing with Fantasy, Science-Fiction and Horror Films**. Hollywood, Calif., Claude D. Plum, Jr., 1973. 18 p. (pbk.).

This A-Z guide lists professional and amateur magazines dealing with fantastic films. A typical entry includes title (all caps), publisher (or editor), and a list of known issues published (in the form "#1 to #30"), plus an additional notation if the magazine had "ceased publication" by 1973. A few foreign-language publications are listed. A second section provides publishers and their addresses (with the name[s] of the periodicals they produce) in alphabetical order by publisher name. The *Guide* is shot from very legible typed copy. Now largely out-of-date, although no comparable publication exists to supplant it.

133. Robbins, Leonard A. **The Pulp Magazine Index, First Series**. Mercer Island, Wash., Starmont House, 1988. x, 460, 882, 810 p. in 3 v. index. LC 88-20056. ISBN 1-55742-111-0 (set). **The Pulp Magazine Index, Second Series**. Mercer Island, Wash., Starmont House, 1990. viii, 583 p. index. LC 89-34752. ISBN 1-55742-162-5. **The Pulp Magazine Index, Third Series**. Mercer Island, Wash., Starmont House, 1990. xii, 639 p. index. ISBN 1-55742-204-4. **The Pulp Magazine Index, Fourth Series**. Mercer Island, Wash., Starmount House, 1991. xi, 567 p. ISBN 1-55742-241-9.

This massive continuing index to all known surviving pulp magazines includes many references to the SF, weird, fantastic, hero, and supernatural pulps in addition to those published in other genres.

Robbins employs a unique format that sometimes works against quick or logical access to his material. Each magazine indexed has been assigned an arbitrary one- to two-letter code (*Doctor Death*, for example, is "AT"), which is thereafter used to refer to that publication throughout the index. Since none of the codes are mnemonic, one must refer constantly back to the code list to determine a particular publication's title: they are not obvious.

The individual volumes/sets are all arranged similarly: the first section, "Special Remarks," lists discrepancies or variations in the data, reported in alphabetical order by magazine code, listing code letters, volume and issue numbers, and remarks (e.g., "Magazine TOC [i.e., Table of Contents] reflects B-3 in error"). These notes are themselves largely incomprehensible without reference to the main text. Following the remarks are lists of the magazines indexed, in alphabetical order by title, including title, price, page size, customary pagination, frequency, publisher's name, editor, and magazine code. The "Code Index" reworks the same information in alphabetical order by code.

The main index is arranged alphabetically by magazine code (not title) and provides the following data: code letter, issue date (in the form "04-1934" for April 1934), volume and issue number, initial pagination for the piece indexed, title of story or article, author of story or article, remarks (referring the user back to the "Remarks Index" at the front of the volume). Each issue of a particular periodical is indexed chronologically in order of publication, stories being recorded consecutively in ascending order by page number. The title and author indexes reorder the same data by title and author name, respectively. In addition, a separate "Artists File Report" indexes all known artwork used in these publications, alphabetically by artist name, giving artist, magazine code, volume and issue number, two columns labelled "Cover" [art] and "Int"[erior art] (an "X" is placed in the appropriate column), and the title of the story being illustrated. Finally, the "Character File Report" provides a list of chief characters associated with the stories, alphabetically by character name, including character, magazine code, volume and issue number, and story title. Following the character index is a short alphabetical guide to the characters' aliases and chief associates, referred back to their original names. The books are clearly reproduced from computer-generated copy and sturdily bound in library cloth editions.

There is a wealth of material here on a facet of American publishing that has now almost completely vanished. The first series alone indexes almost two hundred pulp titles, and the two additional volumes add another seventy periodicals. The very bulk of the material, however, combined with its division into four (and potentially more) units, and the arbitrary arrangement of the main indexes in all three sets, makes access more difficult than it should have been. All future series should include a complete magazine title and code index with see references to the appropriate volumes in which those periodicals are covered and an indication of what that coverage actually includes. Not all issues of all the periodicals mentioned may be indexed in one series, only those volumes or issues that were accessible to the compiler.

Even with these caveats, *The Pulp Magazine Index* provides a major new reference source for future scholarly research into American popular and SF literature, one that should be acquired by all large university libraries. Only a few hundred copies of each of these sets were produced, and they are not generally known or available outside the pulp collectors' market; once gone, they will themselves become highly desirable acquisitions.

134. Robinson, Roger. **Science Fiction and Fantasy Magazines, 1923-1980**. Harold Wood, Essex, England, Beccon Publications, 1984. 28 p. (Beccon Publications Collector's Checklist). (pbk.).

Robinson provides a brief checklist of all known professional SF and fantasy magazines published between the inception of *Weird Tales* in 1923 through the end of 1980, arranged alphabetically by magazine title. A typical entry includes title, nationality (e.g., "US"=United States), span of publication (e.g., "Mar52-Dec74" for March 1952 through December 1974), total number of issues published, and format (e.g., digest). Beneath this summary material is a chronological checklist of every issue published, by volume and issue number, in block paragraph format (e.g., "19/1,2,3,4" for volume 19, numbers 1-4), without correlation to months or years of publication. Similar data are provided for overseas editions.

Compared to Robinson, Hall's guide (see #125) includes considerably more data on the periodicals themselves (including editors' names, index references, publishers' names, and an exact correlation between months of publication and specific issue numbers) in a much more readable format with two extra years of material. Both volumes include titles not featured in the other, although there is considerable overlap, as might be expected. Robinson's smaller page size, however, makes his checklist much more convenient for actual use as a buying guide by collectors at conventions and book fairs. Libraries should prefer Hall.

135. Siemon, Fred(erick). **Ghost Story Index: An Author-Title Index to More Than 2,200 Stories of Ghosts, Horrors, and the Macabre Appearing in 190 Books and Anthologies**. San Jose, Calif., Library Research Associates, 1967. 141 p. index LC 67-30345.

Very similarly organized to the author's *Science Fiction Story Index* (see #136), Siemon's book indexes collections and anthologies of weird supernatural fiction. The first index correlates story authors and titles with anthology code numbers. The middle section of the book lists anthologies in alphabetical order by main entry (usually editor's name) with the following data: code number (in the form "A572" for an anthology by Pierre Andrezel), source code (e.g., "F"=*Fiction Catalog*), editor, title (underlined), place of publication, publisher, year of publication, and pagination. The final section gives story titles and authors only (last names and first initials). As with the companion volume on science fiction, the anthology codes are generated arbitrarily enough to require constant rechecking of the code/anthology index, and the absence of the codes from the title index requires the referencing of no less than three different sections of Siemon's book to locate the anthology in which a specific story appears. Such a remarkably poor design for a reference guide undoubtedly required much cogitation to devise. Siemon also misses nearly as many anthologies in this book as he did with his SF guide four years later. Yet, with the absence of any other work that systematically indexes horror anthologies, this very mediocre effort perforce holds the field.

136. Siemon, Frederick. **Science Fiction Story Index, 1950-1968**. Chicago, American Library Association, 1971. x, 274 p. index. LC 70-162470. ISBN 0-8389-0107-7 (pbk.). Fletcher, Marilyn P. **Science Fiction Story Index, 1950-1979**. 2nd ed. Chicago, American Library Association, 1981. xi, 610 p. index. LC 80-28685. ISBN 0-8389-0320-7 (pbk.).

Siemon's index is not so much a bad book as a mediocre one, which often amounts to much the same thing in the reference field. The author attempts to index SF short stories published in monographic collections and anthologies from 1950-68. The first section of the book indexes the stories alphabetically by author and then by title, correlating each entry with a series of code numbers referring to the anthology title (but with no paginations). The anthologies themselves are indexed in the middle part of the volume alphabetically by main entry (usually by editor's name, although some anonymously edited works are filed by title, and a few collections derived from magazines are listed under that periodical's name). A typical entry includes code number (e.g., "M275"), reference code (e.g., "F"=indexed in the *Fiction Catalog*), editor's name, title (underlined), subtitle (*not* underlined), author's statement (repeated), place of publication, publisher, year of publication, and pagination. The code numbers are generated from the main entry (the "M" in "M275," for example, corresponding to the first letter of the editor's name [in this case, Robert M̲agidoff]), each number interpolating the title in alphabetical order by main entry. There are often large gaps in the number sequences ("M455" is followed by "M570"), and the whole numbering system is so arbitrary that one must refer constantly back to the code/anthology section to check references from the author and title indexes. The title index correlates story titles and authors' names only; no references are made to the code numbers, requiring the reader to check *three* sections to locate a specific anthology from a story title; also, the author references only include the first *initial* of an author's name. Anthology titles are also interfiled in the title index with a reference to entry number (but anthologies are not otherwise readily distinguishable from the other titles listed).

Siemon himself acknowledges in his introduction missing almost a hundred anthologies or collections known to him, and indeed there are major lacunae in his volume;

both Cole (see #116) and particularly Contento (see #117) cover many more anthologies in much more usable formats with considerably more information (Contento, for example, lists original places of publication for all reprinted stories). Unfortunately, Fletcher's reworking of the *Index* does not help matters much.

Fletcher has placed the anthology list at the beginning of her book, which *is* a helpful move, and has expanded the code list from four digits to six (e.g., "BL0250" for an entry by Robert Bloch). Anthologies are again listed usually by main entry, although magazine-generated titles appear under the magazine name, and some titles, for no obvious reason, are filed by book title. The title index correlates story titles, authors, and code numbers; the author index lists authors, story or anthology titles (the latter followed by the appellation [anthology]), and code numbers. The book is reproduced from generally legible computer-generated copy, all entries running in all-capital letters. Again, Fletcher is far from complete, missing, for example, volumes 10-18, 20-25, and 27-30 out of the *New Writings in SF* series and including only the American edition of #7 (which has very different contents from the British original).

Both of these books have largely been superseded by the better-organized, far more complete volumes of Contento (see #117), which are much preferred. Evidently, the American Library Association itself acknowledged the ephemeral nature of these mighty tomes by releasing them only in paperback.

137. Stone, Graham. **Index to British Science Fiction Magazines, 1934-1953**. Canberra City and Sydney, Australian Science Fiction Association, 1977-80. 3 v. index. LC 74-491122. ISBN 0-9598342-2-2 (v.1), ISBN 0-9598342-4-9 (v.2), ISBN 0-9598342-3-0 (v.3) (pbk.). Originally issued in fascicles beginning in 1968 and also issued in a preliminary book version that year. Volume 2 of the 1977-80 set was issued after Volume 3.

Stone provides a necessary adjunct to Donald Day's index (see #121), Metcalf (see #128), and Strauss (see #138), which generally cover the major independent British magazines (such as *New Worlds*) but often miss the British editions of the major American SF periodicals, versions which usually had vastly different contents from their U.S. counterparts.

Volume 1 provides an issue-by-issue contents guide to the magazines, typically including magazine title (all caps), volume and/or issue number, month and year of publication, physical size (if it has changed from the preceding issue), total page count of the issue, an arbitrarily assigned consecutive issue number running from 1-503 (the total number of issues indexed in these volumes), and cover artist. The contents listings themselves include titles and authors in the same order as they appeared in each magazine issue; book review features include listings of the books (and their authors) being reviewed. Volume 2 indexes the material alphabetically by story author, including title, magazine, issue number appearing on the publication itself, and Stone's consecutive issue number. Volume 3 reworks the same data alphabetically by title, then author, magazine, issue number, and Stone's ID number, divided, however, into the following sections: "Fiction," "Verse," "Nonfiction," "Editorials," "Features," and "Reviews."

Since Volume 1 was originally issued in seven parts, individual magazines being covered as Stone was able to locate them, the cumulated version, which maintains the original order of the fascicles, follows no discernible arrangement except that most (but not all) of the journals are indexed in complete, consecutive runs. Individual periodicals can, however, be located through alphabetical tables of contents reproduced at the beginning of each volume. The books are shot from stenciled copy, which is faint on some pages of some copies; and the volumes themselves have rather amateurishly been gathered into signatures, stapled through the side, and glued into flimsy paper covers. The 1953 cutoff date is not always followed, with some (but not all) of the individual periodical runs arbitrarily being continued down through 1955.

Librarian Stone has shown with other volumes that he has the talent to do better than this "faanish" effort; a reworked, updated second edition, with better organization, production values, and a continuation of the data through the 1980s, would be highly desirable. In the meantime, this set is useful only as an adjunct to the major SF periodical indexes mentioned above.

138. Strauss, Erwin S. **The MIT Science Fiction Society's Index to the S-F Magazines, 1951-1965**. Cambridge, Mass., MIT Science Fiction Society, 1966. iii, 207 p. index. LC 73-174981. Cover title.

The MIT index was the first serious attempt to supplement Donald Day's pioneering 1926-50 index of SF magazines (see #121) and was among the first publications in the field to make use of computer technology to automate the indexing process. The result, although esthetically displeasing, is at least functional.

A brief introduction by the compiler is followed by an abbreviations list and a checklist by magazine (giving magazine title, abbreviation code, month and year of publication, volume and issue number, physical size, total page count, and cover artist). The main section of the book consists of the same data reorganized into three different indexes: by magazine issue, by title, and by author. The magazine issue index includes author, title, the page number on which the piece begins, content code (e.g., "S"=short story), month and year of publication (in the form "MAR 52" for March 1952) and a three-letter magazine code (e.g., "AMZ"=*Amazing Stories*). The title index reworks the same data by title, with the title listings still remaining in the *second* column of text. The author index reorganizes the same data by author.

All of the material is reproduced in all-capital computer-generated copy with no running heads or indentations to set off the text; while the multiple-column format does aid in identifying specific pieces of information (the authors are always listed in the first column and the titles in the second, etc.), the photoreduced typeface tends to run the copy together, and some of the copy is faint and difficult to read. Were it not for Strauss's inclusion of page numbers, Metcalf (see #128), which covers virtually the same material (but lacks this particular data), would be much preferred; as it is, however, both books are necessary adjuncts to the library of the serious researcher.

139.   Sween, Roger D. **Fanzine Publishing Record**. Kalamazoo, Mich., The Index Company, 1974-75 (?). 12 p. each. (pbk.). At least two trial issues and one regular issue were produced of this index.

Sween attempted to provide a complete contents listing for every fanzine issue being published in the United States in the mid 1970s. Entries are consecutively numbered from one in the first issue recorded for each year, apparently continuing until the final issue of that year. In each issue, fanzine issues are listed alphabetically by title. A typical entry provides item number, title (all caps), volume and issue number, editor, address, pagination, frequency, price, method of reproduction, and a complete contents listing (including artwork). The absence of indexes in the issues viewed makes access extremely difficult. Sween's idea was a worthy one, but his aborted attempt to provide bibliographical access to these hard-to-find publications is now itself just a footnote in the history of SF bibliography.

140. Tymn, Marshall B., Martin H. Greenberg, L. W. Currey, and Joseph D. Olander. **Index to Stories in Thematic Anthologies of Science Fiction**. Boston, G. K. Hall & Co., 1978. xiii, 193 p. index. (A Reference Publication in Science Fiction). LC 78-14287. ISBN 0-8161-8027-X.

This curious little guide indexes 181 anthologies of science-fiction stories by broad theme or subject category. The fifty categories include such chapters as "Alien Encounter," "Corruption," "Ethics," "Sports," "Women," and many others. In each chapter anthologies are listed chronologically by publication date (a rather strange choice for organization). The collections are numbered consecutively from 1-181. A typical entry provides entry number, title (underlined), editor, place of publication, publisher, year of publication, pagination, format ("paper"=paper-back), and a list of the stories and authors included in each book in the same descending order as they appear within the anthology. No specific paginations are listed. An author index references both story authors and anthology editors in one alphabetical sequence with the code numbers for the books in which their stories appear (code numbers for anthology editors are underlined) but no specific list of stories. The title index correlates story and anthology titles to the code numbers (the numbers for anthology titles are underlined) but no authors. The volume is shot from legible typed copy.

All of this material is available in Contento (see #117), and while the latter does not attempt to categorize anthologies by subject, most of the subject assignments are fairly obvious from the book titles. The indexing in Tymn *et al.* leaves much to be desired; readers seeking stories by such prolific writers as Isaac Asimov are left with a list of forty-four code numbers, all of which must be individually searched to determine the actual story titles. This is a particularly unfortunate choice for a guide which purports to index *stories*. Similarly, without appropriate author information the title index is virtually useless. A poor excuse for a reference volume.

141. Weinberg, Robert, and Lohr McKinstry. **The Hero-Pulp Index**. Hillside, N.J., Robert Weinberg, 1970. 54 p. index. LC 70-24788 (pbk.). **The Hero Pulp Index**. [2nd ed.]. Evergreen, Colo., Opar Press, 1971. 48 p., [16] p. of plates. index. (pbk.). McKinstry's name is listed first on the first edition.

The first version of this guide to the hero pulps (magazines which were named for a continuing character appearing in the lead novel-length story featured in each issue—e.g., *Doc Savage*) was an 8.5" x 11" mimeographed production rather amateurishly produced and distributed and difficult to read in spots. The second version was reduced in size to 5.5" x 8.5", shot from completely reworked typed copy, and illustrated throughout with sixteen full-page reproductions of the original magazine covers; despite its lesser page count and size it actually contains more text.

The main section of the book is arranged alphabetically by magazine title (i.e., character name). A typical entry includes magazine title (all caps), author (usually a house pseudonym followed in parentheses by the major author[s] known to have written under that name), and a chronological list of the issues published, giving whole number out of all issues published, volume and issue number, month and year of publication, and the title of the lead character novel for that issue. Title changes are also noted as well as the unpublished novel announced in the final issue for the next issue that never appeared. A brief author index lists the main house pennames in alphabetical order, with the authors known to have contributed entries under those names plus an alphabetical list of the real authors and the hero pulps they are known to have contributed fiction to (with the total number of such novels that have been attributed to them). A third section lists later reprints in book form from the hero pulps by character (i.e., title) name. The final section, "A Guide to the Hero Pulps," provides detailed summaries of the histories, backgrounds, associates, characteristics, enemies, and careers of the heroes themselves. The book is shot from legible typed copy; the second edition also has a loose errata page slipped into some copies.

Weinberg and McKinstry have produced a very worthwhile guide to these now vanishing monuments to American popular culture, and a third edition with better production values and an individual title index would definitely be warranted. It should be noted that, although many of the hero pulps were fantastic in nature, very few of these periodicals are indexed in other sources; this book also covers a number of mystery and western heroes not indexed elsewhere, although some are gradually being found in Robbins (see #133), but without the additional historical and background material.

142. Wood, Edward. *Journal of Science Fiction* **Magazine Index, 1951-1952**. Chicago, Edward Wood, 1952-53. 2 v. index. (pbk.). Wood, Edward, and Earl Kemp. **The *Destiny* Index of Fantasy—1953**. Chicago, Edward Wood, 1954. 64 p. index. (pbk.).

Intended to supplement Donald Day's 1926-50 index (see #121), Wood's three annuals were published as entire issues of the fanzines indicated (Vol. 1, No. 3 and Vol. 1, No. 4 of the *Journal*, and the Fall 1954 issue of *Destiny*). In both instances, Wood merely provided issue-by-issue contents lists of the SF magazines published in each calendar year; however, the third annual also included a brief five-page list of SF monographs published in 1953, plus "White Paper: 1953-1954," providing detailed statistics on the history of SF periodical publishing. All data except the latter have now been subsumed into other publications, particularly Strauss (see #138) and Metcalf (see #128).

143. Wysocki, R. J. **The Science Fiction, Fantasy, Weird, Hero Magazine Checklist**. Westlake, Ohio, R. J. Wysocki with cooperation from The Cleveland Science Fiction Connection, 1985. iv, 90 p. index. (pbk.).

Raymond Wysocki employs the same block format used by Brad Day in his 1961 checklist (see #119). Magazines are arranged throughout the guide alphabetically by title. Under each periodical, issues are listed chronologically, year by year, each year comprising one line of fourteen boxes across the page. The first box is reserved for the year itself, in the form "28" for 1928, the next twelve boxes for specific issue numbers, and the fourteenth box for running totals (total issues published during that year and total issues published through the end of that year for the entire run of the periodical); the empty space beyond the fourteenth box is reserved for notes. Across the top of each page are running heads listing the months of the year. In each box for which a corresponding issue was published, Wysocki puts the volume and issue number of that specific issue; quarterly publications also have added a one-letter code (e.g., "W"=Winter) for the season. Issues are recorded through January 1985. A brief magazine title index for publications with variant titles is located on page 90, followed by a tabular recapitulation on page 91 showing the total number of titles and issues published for each year from 1919-84. Wysocki's guide is the most current checklist of SF magazine issues available by several years but lacks the detailed historical, bibliographical, and other information provided by Hall's list (see #125), which is generally to be preferred.

INDEXES TO SPECIFIC MAGAZINES

Adventure

144. Bleiler, Richard. **The Index to** *Adventure Magazine*. Mercer Island, Wash., Starmont House, 1990. xii, 1,085 p. in 2 v. index. LC 90-10407. ISBN 1-55742-189-7 (set).

This magnificent guide surely must rank as among the most thorough indexes of one magazine ever compiled. Bleiler's forty-page introduction provides an excellent history of the founding and development of *Adventure*, which was possibly the best known (and one of the highest paying) of the "slick" pulp magazines from its founding in 1910.

The main part of Volume One is an issue-by-issue contents guide, from November 1910-April 1971 (881 issues). A typical entry includes month and year of publication, volume and issue number, editor for that issue, cover artist, interior artist(s), and a complete list of stories/articles and their authors in alphabetical order by author's name, plus continuing departments ("The Camp-Fire," for example). The first volume also includes an index of illustrators, alphabetical by name, giving artist's name, years of birth and death and brief bio squib (when known), and a list of the specific issues for which he produced cover and/or interior art (so specified).

Volume Two includes a 400-page author index, alphabetical by name, listing author, middle names (if known), years of birth and death and brief bio squib (if known), and an alphabetical list of the stories and/or articles appearing in *Adventure* with the specific issues in which they appeared. The title index correlates titles and authors only. A four-page bibliography lists sources for the biographical material. This 8.5" x 11" set is shot from very clear word-processed copy and is bound in sturdy library cloth.

Adventure included all kinds of fiction by major authors—fantastic, mystery, western, general adventure—which are now made accessible for the first time. It's a shame, however, that Bleiler did not choose to list the stories in the order in which they appeared in the magazines, with initial paginations, something which could easily have been added. On the other hand, the biographical material is unparallelled for a guide of this kind, reflecting a considerable amount of secondary and primary research by the author. This set was produced in a very short print run (several hundred copies) for the pulp collectors' market and is unlikely to remain in print very long; it should be purchased by all major academic libraries.

Air Wonder Stories

145. Okada, Masaya. **Illustrated Index to** *Air Wonder Stories* (Vol. 1, No. 1-Vol. 1, No. **11, July 1929-May 1930)** = Kuchu Kyoi Monogatari e-i Sakuin. Nagoya, Japan, Masaya Okada, 1973. 79 p. index. (pbk.).

Okada's tribute to this well-known Hugo Gernsback pulp SF magazine includes "I. Air Wonder Stories" (introduction in Japanese); "II. How to Use the Index" (in Japanese); "III. Index of Issues"; "IV. Index of Titles (Fiction)"; "V. Index by Authors (Fiction)"; "VI. Index by Authors" (nonfiction and miscellaneous); "VII. Aviation Forum"; "VIII. Aviation News of the Month"; "IX. Book Reviews"; "X. The Reader Airs His Views"; "XI. Front Covers by Frank R. Paul"; "XII. Principal Illustrations by Ruger, Leonard, Frank R. Paul"; "Postscript" (in Japanese). Except where noted, the text is in English with Japanese and English chapter heads. The index of issues lists story number (each fiction piece is numbered in order, from #1 in the first issue to #50 in the last), title (all caps), serial note (e.g., "1/4"=first part of four), author; nonfiction pieces are listed in normal case letters with initial capitals (e.g., "Future Aviation Problems"), and cover stories are so indicated by an asterisk following the story title. The title and author indexes provide similar data, plus issue and initial page number of the story (serialized pieces include such information only for the first part of the serial). In addition to the bibliographical material, much of which is found in Donald Day's index (see #121), Okada reproduces (in black and white) all of the eleven front cover illustrations and many of the major interior drawings, plus selected advertisements and small features which appeared in the magazine. Also included are twenty-four of the black-and-white drawings of the authors which ran in each issue, many of them of very obscure writers of whom little is known today. The book is shot from typed copy. Okada's guide to the magazine which many collectors regard as the best *looking* of the fantastic pulps is itself difficult to find but certainly of value to scholars seriously interested in the history of the early pulp era.

Analog/Astounding Science Fiction

146. Ashley, Mike, with the assistance of Terry Jeeves. **The Complete Index to** *Astounding/Analog*, **Being an Index to the 50 Years of** *Astounding Stories—Astounding SF & Analog*: **January 1930-December 1979, Together with the** *Analog Annual*, **the** *Analog Yearbook*, **& the** *John W. Campbell Memorial Anthology*. Oak Forest, Ill., Robert Weinberg Publications, 1981. [vi], 253 p. index. LC 80-53784. ISBN 0-934498-07-5. Jeeves, Terry. **A Checklist of** *Astounding Stories of Super Science, Astounding Stories, Astounding Science Fiction, Analog Science Fiction—Science Fact*. Sheffield, England, ERG Publication, 1965-70. 3 vols. LC 84-125630 (pbk.).

The self-published Jeeves checklist is included here because it was largely incorporated into the later work. Ashley and Jeeves's *Complete Index* is perhaps the best single-magazine index yet produced in the genre, providing every possible access point that the reader or reseacher might desire to search in this most significant of science fiction prozines. Contents: "Introduction"; "How to Use the Index"; "*Astounding* Analyzed" (title variations, publishers, schedule, format, page counts, cover prices, by issue date); "The People that Brought You *Astounding/Analog*" (list of editorial staff); "Issue Index"; "Author Index—Fiction"; "Author Index—Nonfiction"; "Title Index—Fiction"; "Title Index—Nonfiction"; "Series Index"; "Artist Index"; "Letter Index"; Appendices: "I. Total Number of Contents in ASF"; "II. Most Prolific Contributors"; "III. The Analytical Laboratory: A) Top Writers, B) Top Novels, C) Top Stories"; "IV. Most Prolific Artist"; "Errata" and "Addenda."

The main index lists each issue in order published, with date, volume and issue number, whole issue number, cover artist (and story illustrated), and then each issue's contents in order by internal pagination. Included are item number (each story or essay has been assigned a consecutive number from 1-4,239 beginning with the first piece in the first issue of the magazine to the last story in the *Analog Yearbook*, the last "issue" covered in the index); title; format (e.g., "s"=short story); author; initial page number; internal story artist (if any). Unnumbered but also mentioned at the end of each issue (where applicable) are the subjects of the "Biolog" Department (which provided a one-page biography of one of the authors featured in the magazine issue), and the title (and author, if not a regular columnist) of the "Reference Library" monthly book review column. Coverage is complete through the end of 1979; Ashley and Jeeves also list three original book anthologies which included "Analog" in their titles: these appear after the last magazine issue (December 1979) covered. The author index lists author (all caps), years of birth and death (if known), brief description (e.g., "US linguist and writer"), story number, story title (in alphabetical order), format, month and year of publication. The title index lists title (all caps), author, format, month and year of publication. The series index references series title and author(s) only. The artist index includes artist name (all caps), years of birth and death (if known), list of credits separated into covers and interiors, listed chronologically by year and month. The letter index lists persons who contributed missives to the monthly letter column, alphabetically by surname, with state or country of origin and a chronological list of years and months of contributions. The appendices include a complete breakdown of the periodical's output by year plus lists of the most prolific authors, most popular contributors, and most prolific artists. The book is shot from legible typed copy.

Ashley and Jeeves's guide is complete, accurate, well organized, and full of interesting details. The only additional data which might be of value to some future researcher are annotations; given the number of stories published in *Astounding/Analog*, such a guide is unlikely and, if ever produced, would be immense. A supplement covering the 1980s or a revised, updated second edition of this exceptionally well produced index would certainly be justified.

147. Boggs, D. W. *Astounding* **Story-Key, 1930-1951**. Minneapolis, D. W. Boggs, 1952. 18 p. (pbk.).

This brief alphabetical checklist indexes stories published in *Astounding Science Fiction* from its inception in 1930 through the end of 1951, citing story titles only, authors being cited by surname alone. Completely superseded by Ashley/ Jeeves (see #146).

148. Diviney, Jim, and Shirl Diviney. **Index** *Astounding Analog*, **British Edition, Nov. 53- Aug 63**. Brampton, Huntington, [1963?]. 41 p. index. (pbk.).

This guide to the British edition of *Astounding Science Fiction* (later *Analog Science Fiction/Science Fact*), which selected stories from various issues of the U.S. parent magazine, includes three indexes by issue number, author, and story title. Since the British editions of American SF magazines are *not* included in the standard indexes and the years indexed are not covered in Stone's guide (see #137), fan publications such as Diviney's provide a useful service for bibliographical completists. [not seen].

149. Lorenzen, Jan A. **"20 Years of** *Analog/Astounding* **Science Fiction*Science Fact, 1952-1971."** Avon Lake, Ohio, Locomotive Workshop, 1971. 40 leaves. (pbk.). Cover title.

The basic index in this brief guide to the premier American SF magazine of the period is by author (all caps), with each author's stories listed in chronological order by publication date under the main entry. There is no attempt to identify pseudonyms or provide other biographical data, and no title index. Also included is a chronological list of editorials, a similar index of cover symbols, a chronological checklist of nonfiction pieces and the "Department of Diverse Data," and a list of cover artists and the dates of the paintings they contributed to the magazine. Wholly superseded by Ashley/Jeeves (see #146).

150. Weinberg, Robert. **An Index to** *Analog* **(January 1960 to June 1965)**. [Chicago?, Robert Weinberg, 1966?]. [10] p. index. (pbk.).

Well-known SF historian and book dealer Weinberg analyzes six years of *Astounding/Analog* in chronological order by issue, with complete contents listings and an index by author. No title indexing is provided. Now wholly superseded by Ashley/Jeeves (see #146).

Authentic Science Fiction

151. Burgess, Brian. ***Authentic Science Fiction***. [England: s.n., 1960?]. 32 p. (p. 25-57). index. (pbk.).

Produced for a fanzine mailing, this index provides a complete guide to this little-known British SF magazine, with contents listings issue-by-issue and indexes by title and author. Now virtually unobtainable, Burgess's index has largely been subsumed into the cumulative magazine indexes produced by Strauss (see #138) and Metcalf (see #128).

Doc Savage

152. Clark, William J. **The Author Index to the *Doc Savage Magazine***. Los Angeles, M & B Publishers, 1971. 21 p. (pbk.).

Just as it says, Clark's brief guide provides access to the fiction published in this fantastic hero pulp magazine by author only, individual stories being listed in chronological order under each main entry. He also gives issue date and total pagination of each piece, identifications of pseudonyms (where known), and some cross references. *Doc Savage Magazine*, in addition to running one novel per issue featuring that superhero, also included three or more short stories per issue; Clark provides a valuable service in indexing this scarce pulp, but title, issue, and artist indexes would also have been helpful.

ERB-dom

153. Roy, John F., John Harwood, and Camille Cazedessus, Jr. ***ERB-dom*: A Guide to Issues No. 1-25**. Evergreen, Colo., Opar Press, 1964. 23 p. (pbk.).

A brief index to the first twenty-five issues of this fanzine devoted to the works of Edgar Rice Burroughs. [Not seen].

Fantastic Adventures

154. Gallagher, Edward J. **The Annotated Guide to *Fantastic Adventures***. Mercer Island, Wash., Starmont House, 1985. xxi, 170 p. index. (Starmont Reference Guide, No. 2). LC 84-16228. ISBN 0-916732-71-1; ISBN 0-916732-70-3 (pbk.).

Fantastic Adventures, a companion magazine to *Amazing Stories*, published 129 pulp issues between May 1939 and March 1953, including primarily fantasy stories with some science fantasy and weird supernatural tales tossed in. Contents: "Introduction"; "Annotated Story Guide"; "Appendix I—List of Issues"; "Appendix II—List of Departments"; "Appendix III—List of Biographies"; "Appendix IV—List of Illustrators"; "Appendix V—Story Motifs"; "Appendix VI—Editorial Personnel"; "Author Index"; "Title Index."

Gallagher's introduction provides an eighteen-page historical and critical overview of the periodical and its chief editors. The main index (139 pages) lists 852 fictional pieces included in the magazine, numbered in chronological order by date of publication. Each magazine issue includes volume and issue number and month and year of publication (as centered heads) followed by the stories included in each issue. A typical fiction entry lists item number, title (in quotes if a short story, underlined if a novel), author, real name (if the byline is a pseudonym), format (e.g., "novelette"), and a one-paragraph descriptive annotation. No paginations are provided for the individual stories. The appendices include lists of editorial staff, artists and item numbers of the stories they illustrated, a complete list of the 129 issues, including year, month, volume and number, total pagination, and cover artist(s), a motif index broken into seventeen general categories such as "war" (keyed to item number), and a list of the author biographies which appeared in the "Introducing the Author" department. The indexes coordinate authors and item numbers or titles and item numbers only, making it impossible to get a list of the stories penned by any one writer without constantly referring back to the main text. The book is shot from legible word-processed copy.

This very thorough guide to a rather mediocre magazine provides plot summaries for many hard-to-find fictions and much background information on the Ziff-Davis SF magazines; it should be of interest to both fans of the fantastic pulps and serious students of the SF pulp period. This is the first volume in a continuing series of magazine guides being produced by Starmont House (see also #170, #171, and #172).

Fantastic Novels

155. Dard, Roger. *Fantastic Novels*: **A Check List**. Perth, Australia, Dragon Press, 1957. 11 p. index. (pbk.).

Dard provides a chronological issue-by-issue contents guide to a well-received pulp magazine published between 1940-1951, which featured one reprint per issue of (an often abridged) classic novel of the fantastic. Largely subsumed into Donald Day's index (see #121) with Metcalf (see #128) and Strauss (see #138). [not seen].

Fantasy Review

156. *Fantasy Review*: **1984 Index to the Reviews, Volume 7, No.'s 1-11, Whole Numbers 64-74**. Boca Raton, Fla., College of Humanities, Florida Atlantic University, 1985 (?). 14 p. (pbk.). Cover title.

Originally called *Fantasy Newsletter*, *Fantasy Review* served during the mid-1980s as the principal review medium for science fiction books and related materials. This brief index (which may have been edited by Robert A. Collins) is arranged alphabetically by name of the author being reviewed, then by book title. A typical entry includes author's name (surname in all caps), title (boldfaced), reviewer's initials, and the review citation (in the form "68-24" for issue #68, page 24). The title index references titles (boldfaced) and authors' surnames only. The final page includes an alphabetical directory of reviewers' initials correlated with their complete names. All of this material has been subsumed into Hall's *SFBRI* (see #92).

Fiction

157. Valery, Francis. *Fiction*: **Domaine Français**. Cavignac, France, Auto Édition A&A, 1979 (?). 14 p. (Bibliographie des Revues Spécialisées, Volume 1). (Collection Documents SF). (pbk.).

The French magazine *Fiction*, started in the 1950s as a reprint vehicle for *The Magazine of Fantasy & Science Fiction*, soon began cultivating its own school of writers, which eventually formed the core of the developing literature of French science fiction, a very different style of SF than that popular in the United States. Well-known bibliographer Valery here provides a brief index of the original French-generated science fiction and fantasy published in this long-running prozine. The book is arranged alphabetically by author's name. A typical entry provides name (surname in reverse order, all caps, entire name underlined) and a chronological list of that writer's contributions with issue number, date (in the form "6/61" for Juin 1961), and title. Materials are included through Janvier

1979 (issue #297). A title index would have been helpful, and a comprehensive index to all of the stories and articles reproduced in this premier continental European SF magazine is badly needed.

Foundation

158. James, Edward. **Index to *Foundation*, 1-40**. Dagenham, Essex, Science Fiction Foundation, North East London Polytechnic, 1988. 108 p. index. (pbk.).

James's index covers the first forty issues (1972-87) of this well-known British scholarly journal in eight sections: "A. Dates of Issue"; "B. The Editorial Team"; "C. Author Index"; "D. Title Index"; "E. The Profession of Science Fiction" series"; "F. Books Reviewed"; "G. Lists of Books Received"; "H. Subject Index."

The main author index lists the writers in alphabetical order by surname, then alphabetically by title, giving author, title, issue number, pagination. The title index rearranges the same data by title, author, issue number, and pages. The index to book reviews is arranged alphabetically by author of the material being reviewed and includes author reviewed, title reviewed (in italics), reviewer's name, issue number, and pages. The subject index is organized alphabetically by topic (author, book title, movie title, subject) in one alphabet, giving topic and issue and page numbers (e.g., "22.49"=issue #22, page 49), with authors or topics receiving extended treatment (the focus of a full-length article, for example) listed in boldface together with boldfaced issue and page numbers for the piece in question. Section A provides a complete list of the magazine issues in release order, with publication dates; and B lists the editorial personnel who have worked on the journal, in alphabetical order by name, with titles and dates of service. The book is shot from generally clear word-processed copy (a few pages are fainter than others).

This is a very thorough and well-designed guide ·to this important academic publication, the only periodical of its type in Britain. All large university libraries should order a copy—and subscribe to *Foundation*.

G-8 and His Battle Aces

159. Carr, Nick. **The Flying Spy: A History of *G-8***. Chicago, Robert Weinberg, 1978. 160 p. LC 78-106443. (pbk.). Also: Mercer Island, Wash., Starmont House, 1989. 160 p. (Starmont Pulp and Dime Novel Studies, No. 3). LC 85-26231. ISBN 0-930261-72-0; ISBN 0-930261-75-5 (pbk.).

Carr's work is more a guide than an index, although a checklist of titles and dates published in this hero pulp magazine is also provided on pages 153-55.

Contents: "The Author," by Sid Bradd (biography of *G-8*'s author, Robert J. Hogan); "The Author," by Carr (another biography of Hogan); "Warrior of the Clouds" (a biography of the character "G-8," including a checklist of the wounds he received); "The Two Gladiators" (biographies of two of G-8's compatriots); "Portrait of an Extraordinary Englishman" (a biography of G-8's manservant); "The Necessities of Life" (implements used by G-8); "The Supporting Characters" (biographies of various characters appearing in the 110 G-8 novels); "A Bunch of Deceitful Rascals" (biographies of the principal villains [mostly German] opposing G-8, including a checklist of the issues in which they appeared); "The Little Fiend" (biography of another villainous character, Herr Doktor Krueger); "The Inventions of Madmen" (a list of the often fantastic inventions, machines, and devices used by G-8's opponents); "The War" (a history of World War I from G-8's perspective); "The Novels" (a checklist of G-8's 110 adventures); "Conclusion."

The book is illustrated throughout with reproductions of magazine covers and drawings of the G-8 characters and is reproduced from usually legible typed copy (a few pages are faint). An index would have been helpful.

Galaxy Magazine

160. Dollner, Karl. **The *Galaxy* Checklist, Covering the Period October 1950 to December 1958**. Cheltenham, Gloucester, England, British Science Fiction Association, 1961. 60 p. index. (pbk.).

One of a series of such booklets produced in the late 1950s and early 1960s by the BSFA, Dollner's guide analyzes *Galaxy Magazine* on an issue-by-issue basis, providing complete contents listings, including month and year of publication, volume and issue number, story title (all caps), type (e.g., "Nvt"=novelette), and author. The author index is arranged alphabetically by name, then by title, giving author (all caps), title, type, month and year of publication, with see references to co-authors. The title index rearranges the same data by title, type, author, and publication date. Largely subsumed by Metcalf (see #128) and Strauss (see #138).

161. **The Only Eleven-Year Cumulative Index to *Galaxy Magazine*, by Author and by Title, Oct. 1950-Dec. 1961, Complete, Including a Listing-by-Subject of Willy Ley's Science Articles**. [S.l., s.n., 1962?]. [22 leaves]. (pbk.). Cover title. Limited to 100 copies.

This uncredited index is arranged alphabetically by author, then by title. A typical entry includes author's name (all caps), title, and month and year of publication (in the form "10/58" for October 1958). The title index contains title, author, and month and year of publication. A detailed listing of the articles in Willy Ley's monthly science column is provided in the title section under the general heading "For Your Information" (the title of the feature), then arranged alphabetically by subject (e.g., "Greek Fire," "Dinosaurs," etc.). The 8.5" x 11" booklet was mimeographed and stapled through the spine, each copy being numbered in ink on the bottom right corner of the front cover. All of these data *except* the material on Ley's long-running nonfiction series are available in Metcalf (see #128) and Strauss (see #138).

Ghost Stories

162. Sieger, James R. ***Ghost Stories*: Stories of Ghosts**. Evergreen, Colo., Opar Press, 1973. [29] p. index. (pbk.). The author's name is given as "Seiger" on the cover and title page but is consistently mentioned as "Sieger" numerous times in the introduction and index credit.

This somewhat amateurishly produced booklet includes a brief introduction by Camille Cazedessus, an historical essay by Sam Moskowitz, a complete index of *Ghost Stories* by Sieger (fifteen pages), a reprint of a Robert E. Howard story (published in *GS* under the name John Taverel), and reproductions of other minor pieces and ads from the publication.

Sieger indexes his material alphabetically by author, providing author (all caps), years of birth and death and one- to three-word bio squib (if known), and a list of the stories/articles each writer has contributed, alphabetically by title, with months and years of publication. There are also supplemental lists of editorial staff, continuing "departments" and other features, cover artists, and reprint editions in book form, but no title index.

Ghost Stories is covered in Parnell/Ashley (see #130), but Sieger's guide does provide some minor biographical material not found elsewhere. Peripheral and unnecessary except for the most specialized collections.

The Magazine of Fantasy & Science Fiction

163. Durie, A. J. L. **Index to the British Editions of the '*Magazine of Fantasy and Science Fiction*', with a Cross-Reference to the Original American Edition**. Wisbech, England, Fantast (Medway) Ltd., 1966. 44 p. index. LC 66-71451 (pbk.).

Durie indexes the first (1953-54) and second (1959-64) series of the English versions of *Fantasy & Science Fiction*, which were actually selections from various issues of the American parent publication and not facsimile reproductions. Complete contents listings on an issue-by-issue basis are provided, plus indexes by author and title and an indication of when the story was published in the American edition of *F&SF*. These data are *not* available in the standard magazine indexes.

Nebula Science Fiction

164. Jakubowski, Maxim. *Nebula*: **An Index**. [England], British Science Fiction Association, 1963. 18 p. index. (pbk.).

One of a series of indexes to British SF magazines issued by the BSFA, this guide provides an issue-by-issue contents guide to *Nebula*, which was published between 1952 and 1959. Well-known historian Jakubowski also provides a brief history of the periodical and an author index. A title index would have been appreciated. Now largely subsumed by Metcalf (see #128) and Strauss (see #138).

New Worlds

165. Burgess, Brian. **A History and Checklist of *New Worlds***. [England], British Science Fiction Association, 1959. 33 p. index. (pbk.).

Burgess indexes the first eleven years of the premier British SF magazine (from 1946 to January 1957), with an introduction by founding editor John Carnell detailing its history and development. Complete contents guides are provided on an issue-by-issue basis, with author and title indexes. Although largely superseded by Metcalf (see #128) and Strauss (see #138), Carnell's brief essay does add some small significance to this booklet.

Operator #5

166. Carr, Nick. **America's Secret Service Ace: The *Operator 5* Story**. Chicago, Robert Weinberg, 1974. 63 p. (pbk.). Mercer Island, Wash., Starmont House, 1985. 63 p. (Starmont Pulp and Dime Novel Studies, No. 2). LC 85-26269. ISBN 0-930261-70-4; ISBN 0-930261-73-9 (pbk.).

One of a series of "pulp classics" published by Weinberg in the mid-1970s, Carr's literary guide to this fantastic hero pulp magazine includes a chronology of the life of Operator 5 (Jimmy Christopher), a biography of the character, biographies of "Alter Egos & Major Characters," biographies of the chief villains, guides to the supporting characters, a history of the invasion of America by the Purple Empire, biographies of the real-life authors of the novels, fantastic inventions and weapons used by the invading legions, and a chronological checklist of the feature novels correlated with issue dates. Also included are numerous reproductions of the magazine covers, of varying quality.

Carr provides a thorough introduction to this bizarre forty-eight-issue pulp, which featured a long-running invasion of the United States by a Germanic state and the Aztec Empire. As with the other volumes in this series, the book is shot from sometimes faint typed copy, and production values are low. The Starmont edition is a facsimile of the original. The absence of an index and the generally loose organization of the book (the chapter on villains, for example, lists them in no apparent order) hamper what could have been a worthwhile tribute to this most imaginative pulp.

Perry Rhodan

167. Lewis, Anthony R. **Index to *Perry Rhodan*, U.S. Edition 1-25**. Boston, New England Science Fiction Association, 1973. 12 p. (pbk.). **Index to *Perry Rhodan*, U.S. Edition 25-50**. Boston, New England Science Fiction Association, 1975. 18 p. (pbk.).

Produced in the same format as the NESFA magazine indexes (see #129), these two slight indexes provide author/title access to the fiction published in the first fifty volumes of the paperback magazine *Perry Rhodan* published in the United States by Ace Books. One wonders why this material was not incorporated into the NESFA annuals. Very peripheral.

Science Fiction Adventures

168. Peyton, Roger G. **A Checklist of *Science Fiction Adventures* (British Edition)**. [S.l., s.n., 1962?]. [13] p. index. (pbk.).

Peyton provides a brief issue-by-issue contents guide to the English version of the American SF magazine, which carried different contents from its U.S. parent publication (for issues #1-5), with indexes by title and author. After its first five issues, the British *SFA* began running original stories by British and American writers. Now subsumed into Metcalf (see #128) and Strauss (see #138).

The Shadow

169. Eisgruber, Frank Jr. **Gangland's Doom: *The Shadow* of the Pulps**. Chicago, Robert Weinberg, 1974. 64 p. (pbk.). Also: Mercer Island, Wash., Starmont House, 1985. 64 p. (Starmont Pulp and Dime Novel Studies, No. 1). LC 85-26069. ISBN 0-930261-71-2; ISBN 0-930261-74-7 (pbk.).

The first in a series of guides to the major hero pulp magazines, their characters and authors, Eisgruber's work includes an historical preface by Robert Weinberg, a discussion of The Shadow's "true" identity, biographies of his aliases, biographies of his major allies and associates, a description of the Sanctum, guides to the chief villains, the locales of the novels, a response to Philip José Farmer's theory of The Shadow's background, biographies of the real-life authors of The Shadow stories, and a checklist of the 325 Shadow novels, chronologically by publication date, with months and years of publication and identification of the authors (when not by Walter Gibson). Eisgruber's information seems generally sound, but the book as a whole is poorly printed, shot from sometimes faint typed copy and atrociously proofread. The numerous reproductions of *Shadow* magazine covers are also badly reproduced. The Starmont edition is an exact facsimile of the original.

As with the other books in this series (see #159 and #166), *Gangland's Doom* is a useful guide to a vintage American hero, synthesizing much information unavailable elsewhere (although some of the narrative is speculative). A revised edition—typeset, better organized, with additional details on the various later reprints in paperback and cloth— would definitely be warranted.

Startling Stories

170. Gammell, Leon L. **The Annotated Guide to *Startling Stories***. Mercer Island, Wash., Starmont House, 1986. 90 p. (Starmont Reference Guide, No. 3). LC 86-6012. ISBN 0-930261-51-8; ISBN 0-930261-50-X (pbk.).

The second of Starmont's magazine guides (see also #154, #171 and #172) provides much hard-to-find information embedded in a rather strange format.

The first section indexes the novels published in *Startling Stories*, chronologically by publication date. A typical entry includes author, title (all caps), month and year of publication, and an annotation ranging in size from 50-500 words (averaging 200). The summaries tend to be descriptive rather than evaluative, although the closing sentence sometimes includes critical remarks. Also mentioned are reprints in book form, with titles, publishers, dates, and motion picture versions of the novels.

The second part indexes short stories, again chronologically by issue date, giving month and year of publication, volume and issue number, author (underlined), title (all caps), type (e.g., "novelette"), and a one- to two-sentence annotation. At the end of each issue's entry Gammell lists the cover artist and featured story for that issue and the editor's name. The appendices provide contents listings of two anthologies derived from *Startling Stories* fiction and a series listing for Jack Vance's Magnus Ridolph stories, many of which first appeared in this periodical. The book is shot from very clear word-processed copy.

There are two problems with this guide: 1) Gammell unnecessarily divides the novels from the other contents of each issue, making a double reference necessary for the researcher who wants to examine the continuity of the periodical's publication; 2) the absence of any indexes, author or title, forces the user to page through the book to locate specific fictions and is utterly appalling in a purported reference guide. Hokum and humbug!

The Thrill Book

171. Bleiler, Richard. **The Annotated Index to *The Thrill Book*: Complete Indexes to and Descriptions of Everything Published in Street and Smith's *The Thrill Book***. Mercer Island, Wash., Starmont House, 1991. vii, 256 p. index. (Starmont Reference Guide, No. 18). ISBN 1-55742-206-0; ISBN 1-55742-205-2 (pbk.).

Academic librarian Bleiler, author of a previous guide to *Adventure Magazine* (see #144), here provides a comprehensive index to *The Thrill Book*, one of the rarest of the pulp magazines. This fourth volume in the Starmont magazine guide series includes a lengthy historical introduction by Bleiler, an issue-by-issue checklist, annotations, a title index, a subject/motif index, an illustrator index, and sixteen selected black-and-white cover reproductions.

Bleiler's authoritative twenty-eight-page introductory essay puts the periodical in perspective and provides what will surely become the standard critical view of this magazine. The contents list is a straightforward issue-by-issue index to everything published in *The Thrill Book* in the order in which the pieces appeared in the original issues, including date of publication (boldfaced), volume and issue number (boldfaced), price (boldfaced), editor, cover artist, interior artists, and complete contents (in descending order as published, with author, title (all caps), and specific paginations). So detailed are these listings that they even include advertisements! The third section of the book provides annotations for every story, article, and verse, editorials, fillers, and departments which appeared in the magazine, in alphabetical order by main entry (usually author). Items are numbered throughout the section, consecutively from the number one.

A typical entry includes author's name (including middle name and dates, if known), biographical details (one paragraph of varying size, depending on the status of the author and on the availability of information), and a detailed descriptive annotation of each piece published (plus a skeletal listing of stories announced for publication). Materials are listed alphabetically by title under each author's name; anonymous items are filed under title. Each entry also includes the issue date and specific pagination where it appeared. The title index references titles, authors, and item numbers; titles are listed consistently throughout all parts of Bleiler's book in all caps. The subject/motif index correlates situations, locations, and specific subjects with item numbers. The illustrator index is arranged alphabetically by artist name with a chronological list of the artwork each contributed to the magazine by issue date; biographical details are also provided where known. The cover reproductions add a touch of class to what is already a quintessential reference guide.

Bleiler has contributed another superlative effort, the perfect example of what a literary guide should be—and rarely is. Richard Bleiler is well on the way to establishing the same kind of reputation for quality and reliability as his father has already established as a bibliographer of fantastic literature. Highly recommended for all research libraries.

Unknown/Unknown Worlds

172. Dziemianowicz, Stefan R. **The Annotated Guide to *Unknown* and *Unknown Worlds***. Mercer Island, Wash., Starmont House, 1990. 212 p. index. (Starmont Reference Guide, No. 13). ISBN 1-55742-141-2; ISBN 1-55742-140-4 (pbk.).

The third of Starmont's magazine guides (see also #154, #170, and #171) focuses on the classic Street & Smith pulp *Unknown* (later *Unknown Worlds*), edited by John W. Campbell, Jr. as a fantasy companion to the better-known *Astounding Science Fiction*. (*Unknown* ironically helped launch the career of Scientology founder L. Ron Hubbard, who was a regular contributor to the magazine from its second issue.)

Dziemianowicz provides a lengthy introduction giving the history of *Unknown* during its thirty-nine-issue run from its founding in 1939 to its ultimate demise in 1943, a victim of the wartime paper shortages; this is the longest critical evaluation of this seminal fantasy periodical yet published. The main part of the book is an issue-by-issue index of *Unknown*'s fiction, nonfiction, and verse, in chronological order by date of publication. A typical entry includes (for the first story in each issue) cumulative issue number (in brackets, from 1 to 39), month and year of publication, volume and issue number, cover artist (individual cover art was discontinued with the July 1940 issue). For the individual pieces the entries include item number (numbered from one to the end), title, author, initial page number on which the story begins, word count (derived from Street & Smith's payment receipts), name of the artist who illustrated the story, original title of the story (if changed for publication), and an annotation. The material is arranged in the same order as originally published in each issue of the magazine; an asterisk before the title indicates the story was originally purchased for use in *Astounding*. The summaries range in size from 500 words (for some of the novels) to fifty words for short fiction and are both descriptive and evaluative (particularly for the longer works), providing much historical background and some indication of each piece's significance.

Eight appendices include "Unpublished Manuscript Inventory," "Stories Transferred to *Astounding Science Fiction*," "Inventory Dates of Purchase," "Story Index," "Author Index," "Letters Index," "British Edition," and "Reprints." The "Story Index" is arranged alphabetically by title, including author, date of publication, and item number. The "Author Index" rearranges the data alphabetically by surname, then by title, mentioning known pseudonyms, dates of publication of the stories, and item numbers. The correspondence index lists correspondents and the months and years of the issues in which their letters appeared. The book is produced from very legible word-processed copy and includes reproductions of a number of covers and interior illustrations from the periodical itself.

Unknown was among the most influential of all the pulp magazines despite its short run, with roughly half of the stories published in this periodical eventually being reprinted in book form; many of the major writers of modern science fiction cut their literary teeth on this publication and its sister magazine, *Astounding Science Fiction*. Dziemianowicz's guide is a superb work of research, much of it original to this book, well organized and presented, clearly a labor of love that every serious scholar of SF and fantasy will welcome. Highly recommended.

173. [Hoffman, Stuart]. **An Index to *Unknown* and *Unknown Worlds*,** by Author and by Title. Black Earth, Wisc., The Sirius Press, 1955. 34 p. (pbk.). Cover title.

This uncredited publication is among the most professionally produced of the early fan indexes. The first section of the book indexes *Unknown*'s fiction by author, giving name (boldface caps), title, type ("short"=short story), initial page number, volume and issue number (but no dates). The title index gives title (bold caps), author, type, page, volume and issue number, and a short annotation listing "Locale" and "Principal Characters." A third section indexes the principal characters by character name (bold caps) and story title. Unusual for this period, the book is typeset and housed in hard paper boards held together with a spiral plastic binder. A loose addenda page provides the otherwise missing correlation between volume/issue numbers and months and years of publication.

Most of this material has been subsumed into Dziemianowicz (see #172), but the character index still has some value (very few such guides are available in the field).

174. Metzger, Arthur. **An Index & Short History of *Unknown*.** Baltimore, T-K Graphics, 1976. [27] p. (pbk.).

Metzger provides a four-page historical introduction followed by an author index (in alphabetical order by writer's name, then by title, with months and years of publication), a title index (the same data reorganized by title, author, and publication date), a list of important reprints in book form, and brief lists of the cover artists for the first eight issues (after which pictorial cover art was discontinued). Now wholly superseded by Dziemianowicz (see #172).

Venture Science Fiction

175. Bishop, Gerald, and Bob Leman. ***Venture Science Fiction Magazine*: A Checklist of the First American Series, and the British Reprint Series, with an Index to Both of These by Author and Title; Also, an Index of the First Three Issues of the Second American Series.** Exeter, England, Aardvark House, 1970. [28] p. (pbk.).

This brief guide indexes the American and British series of the short-lived companion to *The Magazine of Fantasy & Science Fiction*. The first section provides an issue-by-issue contents list, beginning with the first American series (1957-58), continuing with the British series (1963-65), and ending with the first three issues of the second American incarnation (1969; the publication actually continued for three more issues into 1970 before folding a second time). It should be noted that the British series reprinted stories from various issues of the earlier *Venture* and *F&SF* and occasionally from other sources.

A typical entry includes cumulative issue number (beginning from one with each series, except that the second American series is properly considered an extension of the first); month and year of publication, cover artist, title, author, type (e.g., "short"=short story, with wordages indicated for any length beyond the short story level [for example, "16.5k"=16,500 words]). The second section indexes the material alphabetically by author's name, then by title, giving author, title, and publication dates (in two columns, one for the American series, the second for the British incarnation). The third part rearranges the same data by title, author, and publication dates. A two-page introduction by Bishop places the magazine in its historical perspective and provides a short publication history. The booklet is reproduced from generally clear typed copy.

Since neither Metcalf (see #128) nor Strauss (see #138) nor Stone (see #137) cover the British version of *Venture*, Bishop's index is a useful (though peripheral) guide to this reprint publication.

Weird Tales

176. Jaffery, Sheldon R., and Fred Cook. **The Collector's Index to *Weird Tales*.** Bowling Green, Ohio, Bowling Green State University Popular Press, 1985. 162 p. index. LC 85-71020. ISBN 0-87972-283-5; ISBN 0-87972-284-3 (pbk.).

Jaffery and Cook's index provides a handy one-volume guide to this influential horror fiction magazine.

The main section is an issue-by-issue contents listing. A typical entry includes month and year of publication, volume and issue number, cover artist, and a list of the stories, verse, and features in the order in which they appeared in each issue, with authors and illustrators. The author index lists the authors (bold caps) in alphabetical order by surname, with their stories organized in chronological order by publication date. A third section indexes poets and their verse, also in descending order by date. The fourth part lists cover artists with their artwork, in descending order by date, and the names of the stories illustrated (if known) or a description of the cover art (if no obvious attribution is made in the magazine issue). An appendix provides contents and author indexes for two *Weird Tales* competitors, *Oriental Stories* and *The Magic Carpet*. The second appendix includes a two-and-one-half-page essay, "Why *Weird Tales*?" A third appendix lists "Virgil Finlay's Poetry Series," a pictorial feature which ran from 1937 to 1940. The last appendix delineates in skeletal form the British and Canadian editions of the magazine. The book is attractively typeset and bound. A few amateurish black-and-white illustrations by current artists (not from the original publication) fail to capture the flavor of the original.

There are two design problems with this book: 1) the subsidiary indexes list their materials chronologically by publication date, not alphabetically, which is not a problem for short entries but can become irritatingly burdensome for a writer like Seabury Quinn, who contributed more than a hundred stories to the magazine; 2) this defect is compounded by the absence of a title index. Much of Jaffery and Cook's material can be found in Parnell (see #130), which also lacks a title index, although Jaffery/Cook *is* more detailed and explicit in its contents listings and uses a larger, more attractive, and much more readable typeface. *The Collector's Index* is a disappointment more for the expectations raised—and dashed— than anything else, because the authors clearly know their material and have done their research well and could have produced *the standard* guide to *Weird Tales*. And didn't.

GENERAL BIBLIOGRAPHIES

SCOPE NOTE: Included herein are all general bibliographies of fantastic literature. Bibliographies on specific national literatures, subjects, publishers, authors, or artists may be found in those sections, arranged alphabetically by topic. General literary guides are listed in the Reader's Guides chapter of this book.

177. Allard, Yvon. **Paralittératures**. Montréal, La Centrale des Bibliothèques, 1975. 728 p. index. (Sélections Documentaires, no. 2). LC 75-509636. ISBN 2-89059-000-3.

Allard has compiled a bibliography of French-language genre literatures in ten categories: "Mythe et Merveilleux," "Le Récit Fantastique," "Le Roman d'Aventures," "Le Roman Sentimental," "Le Roman Historique," "Le Roman d'Espionnage et de Politique Fiction," "Le Roman Western," "Le Roman Policier," "La Science-Fiction," "L'Humour."

Each chapter includes an introduction with a brief history of the genre, critical definitions, and a guide to what is included in that section's bibliography. Each bibliography is divided into several sections (using "Le Récit Fantastique" chapter as an example): "Études Historiques et Critiques," in turn broken into "Volumes" (i.e., books) and "Articles de Revues et Extraits de Volumes"; "Petit Dictionnaire d'Auteurs," giving biographical squibs (one paragraph) on each author mentioned; "Collections" (a list of major publishing series, with one-paragraph summaries of their programs); "Anthologies" (of fantastic literature), with complete bibliographical data and one-paragraph annotations; "Choix de Récits Fantastiques," an A-Z bibliography of major works listed alphabetically by author, then by title, with complete bibliographical data, original titles (if translated from English or other languages), and one-paragraph annotations; "Le Fantastique Occulte" (a bibliography of occult fiction, in the same format as the preceding section; "Annexes," broken into sections "Arts Fantastiques," "Cinéma Fantastique," "Les Meilleurs Nouvelles et Contes Fantastiques," and "Les 25 Chefs-d'Oeuvre du Roman Fantastique."

Similarly, the science fiction chapter is broken into "Ouvrages de Référence"; "Périodiques Spécialisés"; "Études Historiques et Critiques"; "Petit Dicionnaire d'Auteurs"; "Collections"; "Anthologies"; "Choix de Romans de Science-Fiction"; "Annexes." Typical entries include author, title, original title (if translated), translator (where appropriate), place of publication, publisher, year of publication, pagination, an indication whether the book is illustrated, series data, ISBN, price, and Canadian National Library card number. The annotations average two to three sentences of commentary and tend to be evaluative. Concerning David Lindsay's *A Voyage to Arcturus*, for example, Allard states: "Plus qu'un simple roman de science-fiction; il s'agit d'une allégorie métaphysique aux multiples interprétations, qui semblerait avoir inspiré C.S. Lewis pour sa fameuse trilogie. Un classique, vu sa date et son contenu." Each entry includes rating codes listed at the end of the annotation, as explicated on page three; these include symbols for age level suitability, knowledge level required (for the science fiction section only), and overall rating (on a scale of 3-5, 5 being best). Thus, the rating "J**A4" indicates that the novel is suitable for young adults as well as the general public and is "recommended." The Author Index correlates authors, titles, and page numbers; the title index includes titles and page numbers only.

Only a third of the volume deals with fantastic literature, but Allard's coverage of French-language materials, translations as well as original works, is unparalleled elsewhere, making this an important bibliographical source. A second, updated edition would definitely be warranted.

178. Bleiler, E. F. **The Checklist of Fantastic Literature: A Bibliography of Fantasy, Weird, and Science Fiction Books Published in the English Language**. Chicago, Shasta Publishers, 1948. xix, 455 p. index. LC 48-6709. Also: Naperville, Ill., FAX Collector's Editions, 1972. xix, 455 p. index. **The Checklist of Science-Fiction and Supernatural Fiction**. [2nd ed.]. Glen Rock, N.J., Firebell Books, 1978. xxii, 266 p. index.

Bleiler's book was the first attempt to provide a comprehensive bibliography of science fiction and fantasy literature, and it set the standards for its successors. A lengthy introduction describes how the book was compiled. The bibliography itself is arranged by author and title using the name of the primary author or editor as it appears on the title page; secondary authors appear throughout the bibliography with see references back to the main entries of the books they co-authored. Anonymously published books are gathered together in alphabetical order by title under the general heading "Anonymous." Authors writing under more than one name have their works split under each name, with appropriate see references. Each main entry provides title, publisher, place of publication, year of publication, pagination, and an indication whether the book contains illustrations. The title index includes short title and author only. Back matter includes "Notes," "Annotated List of Critical and Historical Reference Works," "A Few Associational Items," and "Bibliographical Sources."

The *Checklist* was started as a fan project prior to World War II; Bleiler took the notes and card files compiled by others and added considerable research of his own, as well as checking some bibliographical data on the original cards; no effort was made, however, to verify first editions. The communal nature of the project resulted in the inclusion of many books with questionable fantasy content and in some bibliographical errors that have been noted in subsequent reviews and fan articles. Nonetheless, Bleiler's original work was good enough to make it the standard guide to the field for over thirty years before it was finally supplanted by the deluge of bibliographies which began appearing in the late 1970s, including a revision by Bleiler himself (covered below). The original edition remains a valuable if somewhat idiosyncratic guide to pre-World War II fantastic literature (and, being the first book issued by the SF specialty publisher, Shasta Publishers, is itself highly collectible).

The revised edition follows the same general format as the original except that subject codes have been added after the pagination. Bleiler notes in his introduction that the data have been systematically rechecked whenever possible (about 95% of the entries), with proper first-edition information being inserted, that 600 entries from the original work have been removed, and that roughly 1,150 new books have been added. The coverage has also been extended slightly through the end of 1948 (the original included only a few titles from that year). Altogether, approximately 5,600 books are listed, 5,300 of them being subject coded.

The ninety subject categories range from the general ("science fiction") to the very specific ("revolt of animals") and are often combined in the text to indicate more than one subject. Since the codes are not obvious or alliterative, using them requires constant referencing back to the front matter; and since the book has no overall subject index, there is no easy way to find books with themes or subjects of a similar nature.

Yet, these are minor quibbles. Bleiler's knowledge of fantastic literature prior to the modern era is unsurpassed (he personally examined 95% of the titles included), and his bibliographical sense rates near the top of the field. This is a superb piece of scholarship, one that should be included in every collection of popular literature and on every SF scholar's bookshelf. A "must" acquisition.

179. Day, Bradford M. **The Supplemental Checklist of Fantastic Literature**. Denver, N.Y., Science-Fiction & Fantasy Publications, 1963. ii, 155 p. index. LC 64-46968. (pbk.). Also: New York, Arno Press, 1975. ii, 155 p. index. LC 74-15962. ISBN 0-405-06327-X.

Day intended this volume as a direct supplement to Bleiler's pioneering checklist (see #178) and thus organized it very similarly.

The main sequence lists titles alphabetically by author's name, then by title, providing author, title (all caps), publisher, place of publication, and pagination. The title index correlates titles and authors only. Anonymous works of fiction are grouped together under the heading "Anonymous"; anonymously edited anthologies appear under the heading "Anonymous Anthologies." Juvenile works are so indicated with the word "juv" after the pagination, verse with the appellation "poetry" after the pagination, and other notes or edition limitations noted in the same area. The book is shot from typed copy, generally legible but with occasional broken letters or faint spots, and stapled through the side in flimsy paper covers. The Arno reprint reproduces the original exactly, faint spots and all, in a much more permanent library cloth binding.

Day is less careful than Bleiler, and his book lacks the numerous see references and precise bibliographical data that the revised Bleiler contains. *The Supplemental Checklist* does attempt, however, to fill in lacunae in the original version of the Bleiler checklist (many of which have now been added to Bleiler's second edition), without noting the many items that should have been removed from the first edition. Day restricts himself only to cloth editions, reserving paperbound books to a companion volume (see #202); *The Supplemental Checklist* itself includes roughly 3,025 volumes. Now largely (but not totally) superseded by the revised Bleiler *Checklist* (see #178) and by Reginald (see #182).

180. Locke, George. **Ferret Fantasy's Christmas Annual for 1972**. London, Ferret Fantasy, 1972. 76 p. (pbk.). **Ferret Fantasy's Christmas Annual for 1973**. London, Ferret Fantasy, 1974. ii, 54 p. (pbk.).

These two booklets by a well-known British OP book dealer were intended as additional supplements to the Bleiler (see #178) and Day (see #179) checklists. The main index in both booklets is organized alphabetically by author's name, then by title. A typical entry includes author's name (underlined [in 1972 only]), title (all caps), place of publication, publisher, year of publication, pagination, plus an annotation.

The summaries for collections and anthologies generally consist of complete contents listings analyzed by brief subject appellation (e.g., "Maori legend," "murder story," "ghost story," etc.), although not all such collections are analyzed. The annotations for the novels average one to two sentences in length, summarizing the fantastical elements of each narrative (e.g., "Space opera of an inhabited solar system, set in the year 3020AD"). Both annuals also provide indexes to illustrators (if known) and a very useful index to themes by general category (e.g., "Future War," "The Interplanetary Theme"), then alphabetically by main entry.

In addition to the checklist additions, both books also provide articles on various bibliographical mysteries or puzzles, such as "The Christopher Blayre Trail," "British Paperback Fantasy, 1941-6," "Ghost Stories a la Mode." There are no overall indexes to the volumes and no title indexes to the bibliographies. Much of the checklists have been subsumed into the revised Bleiler (see #178) and Reginald (see #182), and some (but not all) of the entries into Locke's *A Spectrum of Fantasy* (see #181), but the annotations, subject guides, and miscellaneous articles are still of interest to the SF scholar and collector.

181. Locke, George. **A Spectrum of Fantasy: The Bibliography and Biography of a Collection of Fantastic Literature**. London, Ferret, 1980. vi, 246 p. LC 84-137321. Issued in limited cloth and pbk.

Partially reflecting Locke's earlier research on early SF and fantasy (see #180, #211, and #227), *A Spectrum of Fantasy* provides an A-Z annotated guide of roughly 3,600 works from the author's personal collection of science fiction, horror, and fantasy monographs. The book is arranged alphabetically by author; a typical entry lists author (boldface type), type code (e.g., "N"=novel), title (all caps), place of publication, publisher, year of publication, pagination, mention of illustrations or plates, illustrator's name, a description of the binding cloth and known bibliographical variations, and an annotation. The latter include a brief two- or three-sentence description of the book's fantasy elements and an indication of where and when Locke purchased the book, and sometimes why he regarded the acquisition as significant.

The result is a very personal view of fantastic literature as seen from the perspective of a sensitive and informed collector and bibliophile. Some of the books described date from as late as the 1970s, but the overall focus of the collection (and this bibliography) is on the pre-1950s period of fantastic literature with a heavy emphasis on British authors and publications. Since it is this very period which is the most difficult on which to find "hard" bibliographical data, Locke's descriptions are extraordinarily valuable additions to the literature of the field even though many of the bibliographical listings themselves can be found in Bleiler's revised *Checklist* (see #178) or in Reginald's bibliography (see #182).

182. Reginald, R. **Science Fiction and Fantasy Literature, a Checklist, 1700-1974; with, Contemporary Science Fiction Authors II**. Detroit, Gale Research Co., 1979. xi, 1,141 p. in 2 v., [28] p. of plates. index. LC 76-46130. ISBN 0-8103-1051-1 (set).

This is the largest bibliography of fantastic literature published to date (in Volume 1) and the largest single repository of SF biographical data (in Volume 2).

The major part of Volume 1 (583 of 786 pages) contains the bibliography proper, comprising 15,884 individually numbered monographs of fantastic literature in roughly 16,500 distinct entries (retitled entries are not renumbered, nor are co-authored entry numbers repeated a second or third time—such entries maintain the numbering of the original listing), arranged alphabetically by main entry (usually by name of author but occasionally [for anonymous works] by title or author appellation), then alphabetically by title.

A typical entry includes author's name (all caps), with middle names and years of birth and death (or real names if the author is pseudonymous) with a see reference to the biographical volume where appropriate (e.g., "biography included"); entry number (from 1-15,884, in consecutive order); book title (in italics), publisher, place of publication, year of publication, pagination, format (cloth or paper), type (e.g., Novel, Coll.[ection], Anth.[ology], etc.), series information (in brackets). An author's work is centralized under the name by which he or she is best known with appropriate see also references throughout the text. Pseudonymous or co-authored works are listed after those works individually authored. Retitlings of books are listed under the original title in descending chronological order, numbered with the original entry number followed by "A," "B," etc., with see references embedded at the point where that title would normally appear in the author's alphabetical title sequence.

The title index correlates titles and authors only; a series index is arranged alphabetically by series name, then chronologically by number (if the books are numbered) or date of publication, with titles, years of publication (in parentheses), and authors' names. End matter also includes an awards index, alphabetical by name of award and then chronological by award date (through 1978), and an Ace and Belmont Doubles Index. A list of the nine abbreviations used in the text (all fairly obvious even to the casual user) appears on page xi at the front of the book.

The 1,443 biographies in Volume 2 are arranged alphabetically by author's surname, then organized in the standard *Contemporary Authors* format with some minor modifications. In general, a typical entry is broken into several distinct paragraphs corresponding to the following data: personal details (full name, date and place of birth, parents' names, spouse and date of marriage, children's names); education, including degrees and honors; career, with details and dates of positions held; first professional sale, with bibliographical data; literary agent, with current address; honors, with names of works honored and dates of awards; memberships; avocations and interests; and direct comments by the writers. Inserted between pages 972-973 are twenty-eight pages of plates representing "A Short Pictorial History of Science Fiction and Fantasy Publishing," which, due to space limitations, is probably the weakest part of the entire set.

A book of this type stands or falls on the completeness and veracity of the data and on the strengths or weaknesses in the organization of that data. The published reviews on Reginald's checklist were generally approbatory, and the set has generally been accepted by many scholars as the standard bibliography of fantastic literature in both scope and completeness. Both Reginald's book and Bleiler's revised edition (see #178), which covers a more limited time period (monographs published through 1948), list works from comparable eras not found in the other. Part of the discrepancy is due to differing definitions of fantastic literature, Bleiler being slightly more liberal than Reginald in what he regards as "fantastic"; and part is undoubtedly due to the use of different source libraries, Bleiler's major sources being located on the East Coast and Reginald's in the West. Bleiler provides subject coding not found in Reginald's book, while Reginald generally has more data on title changes, authors' names and dates, and series. The best that can be said is that both books represent major bibliographical efforts on the part of their authors (Bleiler examined at least 95% of the entries included in his work, Reginald 98%), each supplementing the other while providing unique and valuable data.

Some criticism was levied at Reginald's biographical volume, *Contemporary Science Fiction Authors II* (Volume 2 of the set), which was partially adapted from his earlier work, *Contemporary Science Fiction Authors* (aka *Stella Nova*; see #46), and reworked using the format established by Gale Research Company's well-known continuing set, *Contemporary Authors*. Reginald compiled the work largely from primary sources—the authors themselves—via direct-mail questionnaires supplemented with a few biographies taken (with permission) from *CA*. Some critics called the data "dry," while others decried the content or volume of the personal comments supplied by the authors as not being matched to the author's so-called literary importance. Indeed, this was not the compiler's intention, since the sole criterion for inclusion was the publication of a single monographic work with fantastic content during the modern period; comments were solicited from all the writers: some responded, others didn't. Those who provided sidelights had them included in their entries irrespective of the author's importance. The true measure of the validity of Reginald's data can be seen in the extent to which later purported biographical directories of SF authors have liberally borrowed material (often without credit) from this volume and its predecessor.

Science Fiction and Fantasy Literature is a necessary purchase for all academic and large public libraries and for any serious SF researcher. A seventeen-year supplement covering the years 1975-91, and including an additional 20,000 more bibliographical records (more books than were published in the entire history of the genre through 1974) was published by the Gale Research Co. in the summer of 1992.

183. Tuck, Donald H. **Author's Works Listing**. Hobart, Tasmania, Tuck, 1960-62. 121 p. (pbk.). **Authors' Books Listing**. Lindisfarne, Tasmania, The Compiler, 1975. 32 p. (pbk.).

In the early 1960s Tuck, author of *The Encyclopedia of Science Fiction and Fantasy* (see #10), compiled a series of author bibliographies issued as fascicles, which were later cumulated into this guide and then reworked and updated as a brief bibliography of the works of seven science fiction writers (John Brunner, A. Bertram Chandler, Edmund Cooper, Philip José Farmer, Ursula K. Le Guin, Michael Moorcock, A. E. van Vogt) for the 33rd World Science Fiction Convention (held at Melbourne in 1975), at which Tuck was Australian Guest-of-Honor. Each writer's monographic works are arranged alphabetically by book title. A typical entry includes author (all caps) with middle names and dates of birth, book title (underlined), publisher of the first edition, place of publication, year of publication, and similar data for all subsequent editions (paperback versions being indicated with the letters "pa" after the date), and occasional annotations indicating earlier magazine publication, alternate titles, etc. Collections include complete contents listings. These booklets are shot from typed copy (and stapled into limp paper covers), and the reproductions are occasionally faint and hard to read. There are no title indexes. All of the author's books are listed, including those falling outside the SF genre; thus, although most of these data are available in Reginald's bibliography (see #182), a few items are not.

184. Wells, Stuart W. III. **The Science Fiction and Heroic Fantasy Author Index**. Duluth, Minn., Purple Unicorn Books, 1978. xxi, 185 p. LC 79-119071 (pbk.). ISBN 0-931998-00-X; ISBN 0-931998-01-8 (pbk.). Page 186, although numbered, is blank.

In the introduction to this volume, Wells states that his book

...is intended to be a compilation of every science fiction and heroic fantasy title published in America since 1945. It covers every novel and collection initially published or reprinted during this period in hardcover or paperback. Many earlier titles are included so that complete information is given for most authors. Anthologies are beyond the scope of this work as are pulp or magazine appearances of the various titles. Weird and horror stories are also omitted.

In fact, Wells includes skeletal checklists of roughly 5,000 titles by 1,000 authors. British and other foreign authors are listed along with their American counterparts, but only when editions of their works have been published in the United States. Thus, many of the bibliographies of major English writers are incomplete and/or lack proper first-edition information, while many very minor American writers are listed when perhaps they should have been dropped—if this book is intended for the collectors' market. And if this bibliography is not aimed at the SF collector, then for whom is it intended? Wells never seems to have asked—or answered—this vital question.

The authors are listed alphabetically by surname. A typical entry includes author's name (very large caps), title (small caps), type code (e.g., "N"=novel), publisher's abbreviation (e.g., "Pinn"=Pinnacle Books), stock number (for paperbacks), year of publication of the first American edition of the book, publisher codes and stock numbers (but no years of publication) for subsequent reprint editions in the U.S. but no paginations or other bibliographical data. Most of the books are listed alphabetically by title under each author's name; however, novels in series are listed in descending order under the blanket series title, chronologically by publication date; the author's other books then appear in alphabetical order by title after the series listings have been completed. The real names of pseudonymous authors appear after their pennames (e.g., "Peters, L. T.=Albert & Jo Ann Klainer"). All of the type in the checklist is in boldface, making discernment of individual data sometimes difficult, the pages tending to lump together before one's eyes.

Front matter includes a quick reference table of types of works excluded and included, an explanation of the symbols used, abbreviations of hardcover publishers, abbreviations of paperback publishers, author and co-author cross index (some see references are provided in the text, but not consistently), thirteen bibliographical notes. End matter includes novel winners for the International Fantasy, Hugo, and Nebula Awards (through 1978), comments, more notes, "Partial Bibliography of Recommended [nonfiction] Works" (ten items only), and an addendum. There is no title index.

Wells includes paperback stock numbers not listed in Reginald's bibliography (see #182) and some data for books published between 1975 and mid-1978 that will appear in Reginald's supplement (see #182). The list of reprints could be useful for bibliographical historians but is presented in such sketchy form as to be almost useless. The hit-or-miss nature of this mediocre effort makes one realize how truly useful an abridged checklist of modern fantastic *authors* and their works would be for the collector, and just how far Wells's *Index* misses the mark.

NATIONAL BIBLIOGRAPHIES

SCOPE NOTE: This section includes monographs which attempt to record all science fiction and fantasy books and/or fan and professional magazines published in a particular country, with occasional limitations by time period or broad genre.

AUSTRALIA

185. Stone, Graham. **Australian Science Fiction Index, 1939-1962**. Sydney, Futurian Society, 1964. 113 p. index. (pbk.). **Australian Science Fiction Index, 1925-1967**. Canberra, Australian Science Fiction Association, 1968. viii, 158 p. index. LC 72-367644 (pbk.). **Australian Science Fiction Index, Supplement, 1968/1975**. Sydney, Australian Science Fiction Association, 1976. vii, 48 p. index. LC 78-305781 (pbk.).

Well-known librarian Stone, author of an index to British science fiction magazines (see #137), has attempted in these volumes to provide complete bibliographical control over all SF books and periodicals published in Australia.

There are four major sections: "Magazines," "Numbered Series," "Unnumbered Series," and "Books." The magazines chapter includes seven titles, arranged by founding date, then chronologically, with issue-by-issue contents listings. A typical entry gives magazine title (underlined), issue number, month and year of publication, pagination, physical size, cover and interior artists, and a list of the stories and authors in each issue, arranged as they appeared in the publication. For the book series, Stone provides months and years of publication, authors and titles, and contents (where applicable). The books chapter includes all known monographs of fantastic literature published in Australia, both original and reprint, arranged alphabetically by author name, then by title, including author's name (surname in all caps), title (all caps, indented), publisher, year of publication, series title and number (if any), pagination, physical size. Middle names and years of birth and death of the authors are provided where known. The author index lists authors and titles with either magazine title and issue number (for short stories) or with publisher, publishing series and number, and year of publication (for books). The title index rearranges the same data by title and author. The eight-year *Supplement* is similarly arranged and produced.

The Australian Science Fiction Index is shot from generally legible but occasionally faint typed copy and bound with staples in flimsy paper covers. The data seem complete as presented, but the primitive production values sometimes make proper distinction of the material listed in the indexes difficult for the casual user. A revised, cumulated edition would definitely be useful.

CANADA

186. Colombo, John Robert, Michael Richardson, John Bell, and Alexandre L. Amprimoz. **CDN SF & F: A Bibliography of Canadian Science Fiction and Fantasy**. Toronto, Hounslow Press, 1979. viii, 85 p. LC 80-511063. ISBN 0-88882-036-4 (pbk.).

This annotated bibliography lists some 600 SF books by Canadian authors, including fiction titles with fantastic content, nonfiction books dealing with some aspect of Canadian SF or fantasy, plus fantastic literature by non-Canadian authors with Canadian settings. The book is arranged by subject, then by author and title. Chapters include "Science Fiction," "National Disaster Scenarios," "Polar Worlds," "Fantasy and Weird Tales," "French-

Language Science Fiction and Fantasy," "Children's Literature," "Non-Fiction" (including poetry, plays, prose, collections, criticism, and coverage of two fanzines), and "Canadian Interest" (i.e., books with Canadian settings). The annotations are often very brief, but occasionally quite helpful; previous editions under different titles or pseudonyms are mentioned when known. The section on French-language materials is particularly valuable, since information on these books is often hard to find. A title index would have been useful, and the book definitely needs a supplement or revised edition.

CZECHOSLOVAKIA

187. Olsa, Jaroslav, Jr. **Bibliografie Ceských a Slovenských Fanzinû do Roku 1987**. Praha, Ústrední Kulturní dûm Zeleznicárû-Klub Vedecké Fantastiky R.U.R., 1988. 4 v. index. (pbk.).

The *Bibliografie Ceských* is included in this section because it amounts to a partial national bibliography of short Czech SF, both translations and original works, as published in Czech fanzines (the only medium for both professional and amateur fiction). The first two volumes (the only ones examined) are an A-Z index to the authors and their works. Volume 3 was announced as a guide to reviews and Volume 4 to criticism.

The first volume includes an introduction in Czech, English, and Russian, followed by the main index to prose in alphabetical order by author, then title. A typical entry includes author (large type), nationality (a two- to three-letter abbreviation), title, original title (for translations), translator's name, magazine title (a two- to three-letter all-caps abbreviation), issue number, pagination. Volume One covers the authors whose surnames begin with the letters A-K, Volume Two, L-Z plus an A-Z listing of poets, a list of anonymously written poetry and prose (in alphabetical order by title), a general abbreviations list, and a list of magazine abbreviations. There is no title index. Data are included through 1987, although the author acknowledges that some of the more ephemeral publications may have been missed. The book is shot from legible word-processed copy.

A great many Western authors are included in the *Bibliografie* (British writer Brian W. Aldiss, for example, has a half dozen prose entries), making this index useful as both a contemporary portrait of one aspect of modern Czech literature and as a guide to translations of foreign SF authors into Eastern European languages.

DENMARK

188. Guld, Jens. **Bibliografi over Litteratur på Dansk om Science Fiction Indtil 1976**. København, Science Fiction Cirklen, 1977. 37 p. (Tangentserien, no. 5). LC 78-342552. ISBN 87-87662-08-6 (pbk.).

[Not seen.]

189. Schiøler, Carsten, and Erik H. Swiatek. **Dansk Science Fiction Guide 1974**. København, Science Fiction Cirklen, 1975. [Unknown] p. **Dansk Science Fiction Indeks, 1741-1976**. København, Science Fiction Cirklen, 1977. [125] p. (Tangentserien, No. 2). LC 78-376683. ISBN 87-87662-00-0 (pbk.?).

[Not seen.]

GREAT BRITAIN

190. Bishop, Gerald. **New SF Published in Great Britain, 1968, 1969**. London, British Science Fiction Assocation; Lake Jackson, Tex., Joanne Burger, 1970. 15 p. index. (pbk.). **New British Science Fiction and Fantasy Books Published During 1970 & 1971**. Lake Jackson, Tex., Joanne Burger, 1972?. 40 p. index. (pbk.). **Science Fiction Books Published in Britain, 1972 & 1973**. Winchester, Aardvark House, 1975. v, 33 p. index. LC 76-353013. ISBN 0-904756-10-6 (pbk.). **Science Fiction Books Published in Britain, 1974-1978**. Exeter, Aardvark House, 1979. vi, 82 p. index. LC 80-145464. ISBN 0-904756-11-4 (pbk.). Quarterly supplements were published through at least Vol. 7, No. 6 (January, 1985).

For over a decade Bishop produced a series of annual and cumulated indexes of fantastic literature published in England, some published under his own imprint, others released solely or jointly by Joanne Burger, publisher of a similar series on American SF books (see #198).

Using the last volume as a guide, the main section indexes authors alphabetically by surname then by title. A typical entry includes author, title (indented), publisher, price, year and month of publication (in the form "77.09" for September 1977), edition (e.g., "ne"=new edition), format (e.g., "pb"=paper-back), and ISBNs, but no paginations. Anonymous works are listed after the letter "Z" in alphabetical order by title, followed by a chronological checklist of publications issued by the Science Fiction Book Club (British version) and a separate author index to nonfiction works. The title index lists title and author only.

Bishop cast his net widely in an attempt to list all printings and editions of every SF book published in Britain and generally succeeded very well; the absence of his publication has been keenly felt by all bibliographers in the field. In recent years another Briton, Phil Stephensen-Payne, has produced a monthly bibliographical column in *Locus* that partially replaces Bishop, and these listings are now cumulated in Charlie Brown's annual publication, *Science Fiction, Fantasy, & Horror* (see #24).

191. Slater, Kenneth F. **British Science Fiction Book Index 1955**. Wisbech, Cambs., England, Fantast (Medway) Ltd., 1956. 14 p. index. (pbk.). **A Checklist of Science Fiction, Fantasy, and Supernatural Stories Available in Paperback in Britain, January, 1966**. Wisbech, Cambs., England, Fantast (Medway) Ltd., 1966. 30 p. index. LC 66-78086 (pbk.).

The first publication is a bibliography of monographs with fantastic content issued in Great Britain in 1955, arranged alphabetically by author surname with a title/author index. The second publication, a legal-sized booklet, is directly adapted from the catalogs issued periodically by Slater's book operation, Fantast (Medway) Ltd. (which specializes in new SF and fantasy materials), and amounts to a cumulative stocklist of works available at the time of issue. Unusually, Slater includes brief plot summaries and other information of note, plus complete bibliographical data (including paginations) and contents listings for anthologies. Thus, although much of this material has been subsumed into Reginald's checklist (see #182), the supplementary material still provides valuable descriptions of (primarily British) books now long out of print. A peripheral acquisition for all but the most specialized libraries and research collections.

HUNGARY

192. Csiszár, Jolán. **Utópisztikus Tudományos-Fantasztikus Müvek Bibliográfiája**. Miskolc, Hungary, [s.n.], 1970. 159 p. index. (pbk.). Bezerédy, Ágnes, and Jolán Csiszár. **Tudományos-Fantasztikus, Utópisztikus Fantasztikus Müvek Bibliográfiája**. [2nd ed.] Miskolc, Hungary, Rákóczi Ferenc Könyvtár, 1979. 434 p. index. LC 81-126692. ISBN 963-7571-32-9 (pbk.).

The standard guide to fantastic literature published in Hungary (translations from foreign literature, as well as original fiction and nonfiction), Csiszár and Bezerédy's bibliography is prefaced by introductions in Hungarian, English, and Russian, then divided into three main sections: "Szépirodalom" (i.e., Fiction and Literary Works), "Szakirodalom" (i.e., Nonfiction), and "SF Konferenciák, Klubok, Szövetségek."

The first part is itself subdivided into four sections: "Regények" (books), "Elbeszélések" (short fiction), "Versek" (poetry), and "Egyéb Müfajok"; and the second part into five sections: "Anticipáció, Fantasztikus Hipotézisek," "Tanulmányok az SF Témaköréböl," "Életrajzok, Könyvismertetések, Kritikák," "Biliográfiák," and "Fantasztikus Müvészet," which is further subdivided into "Filmmüvészet" and "Képzömüvészet."

In each section, materials are arranged alphabetically by main entry (usually author, although occasionally title in the nonfiction chapters), then by title. A typical book entry includes item number, author (all caps), title, series (in brackets), translator's name (in parentheses), place of publication, year of publication, publisher, pagination. A typical short fiction entry gives item number, author (all caps), title, type (e.g., "novella"), translator, magazine title (often *Galaktika*), issue number, place of publication, year of publication, publisher, and the specific pagination of that story. Items are numbered consecutively from 1-2,644. The author index references authors and item numbers only, the title index titles, author surnames (in parentheses), and item numbers only. The book is shot from very clear typed copy. Data are included from the 1800s through 1977.

There is no way to determine how comprehensively this bibliography covers its subject except to note that 2,600+ items are an extraordinary number of publications to be recorded from a small Eastern European country. However, future editions should include the original titles of translated literature following the Hungarian titles, since the user presently has no way of knowing for certain exactly what "Odakint," a story by Brian W. Aldiss, is; translations often undergo metamorphoses in titles as well as content, and access to dictionaries from the country in question will sometimes not help to identify a particular work's original incarnation. For larger SF collections.

NETHERLANDS

193. Spaink, A[rnold], G[eorges] Gorremans, and R[inus] Gaasbeek. **Fantasfeer: Bibliografie van Science Fiction en Fantasy in het Nederlands**. Amsterdam, Meulenhoff Nederland, 1979. [viii], 279 p. index. ISBN 90-290-1261-7 (pbk.).

This bibliography lists 5,600 SF works by 1,200 authors—original fictions as well as translations—published in The Netherlands through 1978, organized in a somewhat difficult format.

The main index is arranged alphabetically by author's name, then by title. A typical entry includes item number (items are numbered consecutively from one in each chapter, corresponding to each letter of the alphabet), author, title (the numbers, authors, and titles are slightly boldfaced; titles are preceded by a double hyphen), total page count (both for books and short stories), original title and original year of publication (for translations), and either bibliographical data (for books, including publisher, year of publication, series and series number, and pagination [in parentheses]) or a see reference to the publication (and to the item number elsewhere in the bibliography) in which the story or novel appears. There are hundreds, even thousands, of such references (in the form "B255" for item number 255 in the "B" section).

In the entry for American author Alfred Bester, for example, we find the novel *De Grote Onttakeling* (*The Demolished Man*) listed both as a separate publication (entry #B259) and referenced as part of the anthology *Science Fiction-Omnibus 2* (see #S106). The title index lists titles, authors' surnames, and item numbers only. End matter includes a chronological checklist of Dutch SF publishing series by series number, author surname, and title and a brief, one-page pseudonym/real name list. The book is shot from fairly legible typed or word-processed copy, with occasional faint spots.

There are two obvious structural problems with this book: 1) although each page carries a boldfaced running head for the letter of the alphabet in which that chapter falls ("H," for example), the numbers themselves do not include the letter prefixes used as see references throughout the work, and it is very easy to lose one's place; 2) the text runs throughout the book in double-column format, resulting in very tight internal columnar margins (for a 5.5" x 8.25" page size) that have forced the compilers to run the titles without obvious indentation except for the double hyphen that precedes each. Since the titles and authors are displayed in exactly the same typeface and size, and since the authors' names only appear once, it is very difficult on many pages to determine quickly what portion of the alphabet one has reached or, indeed, what author's works one is examining—the name of a prolific author may actually occur a page or two before the page being examined. The result is a mass of severely photoreduced text (to roughly an eight-point level) that tends to bunch together on the page. In their haste to save space, the compilers have produced a reference work that approaches the unreadable and unusable.

For those who wish to spend the time to dig them out, the data are here. The rest of us must wait for a (*mirabile dictu!*) completely redesigned second edition.

NEW ZEALAND

194. Rowe, Nigel. **The History of Science Fiction Fandom in New Zealand, Volume 3.** Auckland, New Zealand, Nigel Rowe, 1981. [21] p. (pbk.).

Volume Three of this multi-part work focuses on New Zealand fanzines, providing a complete chronological checklist of issues known to have been produced through May 1981. A typical entry includes year and month of publication, fanzine name, issue number, number of pages, size, reproduction medium, and editor(s) [surnames only]. The periodicals are listed in chronological order by publication date. The absence of any indexes severely limits the usefulness of this booklet. Reproduced from somewhat faint typed copy.

SOVIET UNION

195. Kerr, Stephen T. **A Bibliographical Guide to Soviet Fantasy and Science Fiction, 1957-1968**. New York, [Stephen T. Kerr], 1969. vi, 92 leaves. LC 78-20634 (pbk.).

Kerr adapted this bibliography of Soviet science fiction from his master's thesis (Columbia University, 1969). The main section of the book is arranged alphabetically by author's name, then by title. A typical entry includes author (surname in all caps), Russian title (stories in quotes, novels underlined), English-language translation (in brackets), bibliographical data (for monographs: place of publication, publisher, year of publication, and total pagination; for stories: anthology or collection name, volume number [where applicable], and specific paginations), with similar information on known reprints (both of stories and novels). Kerr also occasionally includes contemporaneous review citations. Anonymous anthologies are interfiled with the rest under title. Items are numbered consecutively from 1-1,485 throughout the book. Abbreviations are employed heavily for place of publication, publishers, and recurring book titles (most Soviet short stories were first published in original anthology series). A section at the end of the index lists "Special Bibliographical Sources on Soviet S.F." Appendix A provides a checklist of anthologies, alphabetical by English (for translated anthologies), then a separate listing by Russian title. There is no title index. The book is shot from generally clear typed copy.

Compared to Suvin (see #196), Kerr includes short stories which Suvin does not separately mention, but Suvin covers an additional seven years of data and provides a much broader list of Russian-language secondary sources. Both works will be necessary for the serious scholar.

196. Suvin, Darko. **Russian Science Fiction Literature and Criticism, 1956-1970: A Bibliography**. Toronto, "Secondary Universe 4" Conference, 1971. 35 p. LC 74-183207 (pbk.). **Russian Science Fiction, 1956-1974: A Bibliography: Original Books, Translated Books, and an Annotated Checklist of Criticism; with an Appendix on Criticism of Russian SF Before 1956**. Elizabethtown, N.Y., Dragon Press, 1976. vi, 73 p. LC 76-151334.

Yugoslavian academic Suvin (now a permanent resident of Canada) has produced a now-standard bibliography of Russian-language science fiction, divided into three sections: "Science Fiction Books in the Russian Language, 1956-1974"; "Russian Science Fiction in English and French Books"; "Criticism of Soviet Science Fiction, 1956-1970"; with "Appendix: Selective Bibliography of Critical Works on Russian Science Fiction to 1956" and an addendum.

The first section lists works alphabetically by author, then by Russian title. A typical entry includes author, title (underlined), place of publication (often abbreviated to "M"=Moscow or "L"=Leningrad), publisher, year of publication, pagination. Anonymous works are interfiled by title with the rest. The second chapter includes a similarly arranged list of translated titles in English and French, alphabetical by author, giving author, title (underlined), place of publication, publisher, and year of publication, but no paginations or original titles. Contents listings are also provided for anthologies (something not done in the first section). Part Three is a chronological (by year) annotated bibliography of criticism on Russian science fiction and its authors, in all languages; paginations are listed only for articles, not monographs. The appendix lists pre-1956 criticism by subject and main entry, broken into the following categories: 18th Century, 19th Century (subdivided into sections, "To 1860," "Chernyshevsky," "Dostoevsky"), 1890-1956 (subdivided into "Tsiolkovsky," "Bryusov," "Bogdanov," "Mayakovsky," "Zamyatin," "A. Tolstoy," "A. Belyaev," "Others, 1890-1930," and "Others, 1931-1956"). The book is shot from clearly reproduced typed copy.

A major problem with the work is the inconsistency in bibliographical format between the sections: why, for example, provide paginations in the first part and not in chapters 2-3? If the data are worth capturing for one, should they not be worth recording for all? Also, the absence of a title index and the utter failure to record the original Russian-language titles for the translations seriously hampers the potential researcher. The immense body of Russian SF, one of the largest such literatures outside the U.S. (and among the most important), cries out for an updated version of this book, one with full annotations and complete bibliographical data and an accurate, comprehensive guide to secondary sources. Until such a work appears, this somewhat lame bibliography will have to do.

SWEDEN

197. Lundwall, Sam J. **Bibliografi över Science Fiction och Fantasy, 1830-1961.** Stockholm, Lundwall, 1962. 58 p. index. (pbk.). **Illustrerad Bibliografi över Science Fiction & Fantasy, 1741-1973.** [2nd ed.]. Stockholm, Lindqvists, 1974. 338 p. index. LC 75-574749. ISBN 91-7090-115-5 (pbk.?).

Well-known SF writer and critic Lundwall has produced the standard guide to fantastic literature in Sweden (original works as well as translations) in this well-illustrated and presented bibliography.

Authors and titles are indexed together in one alphabetical sequence. Authors' names appear in boldfaced caps (quite distinguishable from the rest of the text). A typical author entry includes author, years of birth and death (if known), single-paragraph critical evaluation (one to three sentences), and a list of the author's books in alphabetical order by title. Title entries throughout the main text contain see references back to their authors; title entries within author entries include title (indented, in boldfaced type), original title (if translated), translator's name, series and series number, place of publication, publisher, year of publication, pagination, price, ISBN. Also included in the main alphabetical sequence are publishers' series listings arranged by publisher name, then numerically by series number with author and title but no bibliographical data (which are included with the author entries). The book is attractively typeset and illustrated throughout with author photographs and cover reproductions.

Lundwall's guide is one of the best organized and presented national bibliographies/cyclopedias yet produced and should definitely be updated to reflect the nearly two decades of data that have cumulated since this volume was published.

UNITED STATES

198. Burger, Joanne. **SF Published in 1967[-1977].** Lake Jackson, Tex., Joanne Burger, 1968-79. 11 v. index. LC 71-10701 (pbk.).

Burger began producing these bibliographies of all SF and fantasy books published in the United States as monthly and bimonthly checklists of forthcoming titles, including reprints and original works, which were then cumulated into annual indexes of those works that had supposedly actually appeared.

The main listing is alphabetical by author, then by title. A typical entry includes author, title (in italics in later volumes), publisher, stock number or ISBN, price, copyright date (if different from original publication date), type code (if not a novel; e.g., "a"=anthology), series number. Not all of the books listed have been viewed by Burger, and some are known not to have been actually published as scheduled. The title index lists title and author only. The 1977 annual also includes "Address[es] of Small Publishers," "Juvenile Books" (authors and titles only), "Art Books" (authors and titles only), "Non Fiction Books" (authors and titles only), and "Series Listings" (by author, with titles listed in chronological order). The books were produced somewhat amateurishly, reproduced from typed copy, and photocopied or mimeographed into stapled paper covers.

Burger was not always reliable, but her lists were brief, useful guides to the SF books scheduled to appear in the U.S. during each year. They now have been partially superseded by Reginald's bibliography (see #182) and have been continued by the monthly checklists of published SF works in *Locus* and by Charlie Brown's annuals (see #24) since 1984.

199. Clareson, Thomas D. **Science Fiction in America, 1870s-1930s: An Annotated Bibliography of Primary Sources**. Westport, Conn. & London, Greenwood Press, 1984. xiv, 305 p. index. (Bibliographies and Indexes in American Literature, Number 1). LC 84-8934. ISBN 0-313-23169-9.

Clareson is well known in the SF field for his essays and critical work and for having founded (and edited for three decades) the first academic journal devoted to science-fiction criticism, *Extrapolation*. Indeed, the first issue of that periodical, dated December 1959, featured Clareson's nineteen-page article "An Annotated Checklist of American Science-Fiction, 1880-1915," obviously the precursor to this larger work.

The book is organized in alphabetical order by author's name, then by title. Clareson uses the name by which the author is best known, even if it is a pseudonym, with no see references; thus, the works of "Harris Burland" and J. B. Harris-Burland (both the same man) are split, although the entry for the former does mention the author's real name. The entries are numbered in consecutive order from 001-838. A typical entry includes item number, author's name, title (underlined), place of publication, publisher, year of publication, but no paginations. The annotations are descriptive rather than evaluative and range in size from 10-300 words (100 being average). The author index lists authors and item numbers only; the "Short-Title Index" lists titles (but no subtitles) and item numbers only. The book is shot from very clear word-processed copy and bound in library cloth.

Clareson's 1959 article focused entirely on U.S. authors, and while the emphasis in this expanded version is still on writers of American descent, he also adds (somewhat randomly) works by British and other foreign authors if their works were regarded as influential in the history of American fantastic literature. Thus, nine works each by Wells and Verne are annotated, seven by George Griffith, and eleven by H. Rider Haggard (only one of which could be considered SF by the furthest stretch of the definition). Clareson's stated rationale for this decision, "to give a detailed and comprehensive overview of the field during the period from the 1870s to the 1930s," is a laudable one, but in so doing he opens a bibliographical barn door, in and out of which may wander all kinds of literary oddities, including many works with fantasy elements. One is left asking why some books were included while others were omitted, with no obvious answers except to say that they were.

Still, Clareson provides a gold mine of information on a period which is not well known or understood in the history of fantastic literature, and his annotations cover in detail a great many works described no where else. One might have wished for a better title index, a motif or subject index, and volume paginations, but these are relatively minor carpings. *Science Fiction in America* will undoubtedly become a prime source book for further research on these antecedent fictions and should be acquired by all academic libraries.

200. Tymn, Marshall B. **American Fantasy and Science Fiction: Toward A Bibliography of Works Published in the United States, 1948-1973**. West Linn, Ore., FAX Collector's Editions, 1979. ix, 228 p. index. LC 76-55151. ISBN 0-913960-15-2 (pbk.).

This little volume (4" x 7") was intended directly to supplement Bleiler's pioneering *Checklist* (see #178), following the same general format as that work and covering cloth hardcovers published in the United States between January 1948 and the end of 1973 (Bleiler's original edition includes some works published in 1948; his second edition covers through the end of 1948).

The main part of the bibliography is arranged alphabetically by author's surname, then by title. A typical entry provides author (all caps), title (italics), place of publication, publisher, and year of publication, but no paginations (unlike Bleiler). Some middle names and pseudonyms are listed for some authors, with appropriate see references throughout the text; illustrations, juvenile works, collections, and anthologies are so noted with abbreviations after the bibliographical data (e.g., "ill, juv" for an illustrated juvenile work). The title index lists titles and authors only. End matter includes fifty-four bibliographical notes, a thirteen-page list of "Borderline Titles" (arranged and presented in the same way as the main bibliography), and a list of first editions published by the Science Fiction Book Club (also alphabetically by author, although no mention whatever is made of the fact that first-edition SFBC books from this period bore the imprint "Nelson Doubleday"). The book is typeset, but the type has been photoreduced to about a six-point level, making it somewhat hard to read for middle-aged eyes.

About 2,250 books are listed in the main sequence, only a fraction of those published during the twenty-five year period which this bibliography ostensibly covers; and there are problems even with these data. Many of the books by British authors had English first editions not noted or acknowledged here; and many books which could or should have been listed are not mentioned. For well-known fantasy writer Robert Nathan, for example, Tymn lists five works published between 1951-72, when that author actually published fifteen novels with fantasy content between 1948-73, plus two new omnibuses of previously published books issued for the first time under those titles; by any accounting, Tymn has missed two-thirds of Nathan's relevant works. He is more certain (and complete) with well-known SF writers, but by omitting paperbacks, he deliberately ignores many first editions even from these authors. Finally, why provide a list of so-called "borderline titles"? If one cannot locate specific titles—or determine their fantastic content—then they should be omitted; dumping them into a miscellanea file simply trumpets one's own bibliographical shortcomings, of which, alas, there are just too many in *American Fantasy and Science Fiction*. All of these books, with complete bibliographical data, are listed in Reginald (see #182), which is much preferred.

201. Whyte, Andrew Adams. **The New SF Bulletin Index to SF Books 1974**. Boston, Spike MacPhee, Publisher, Paratime Press Publications, 1974. 42 p. (pbk.).

This one-shot was intended to rival Burger's bibliography (see #198) but failed for lack of a second—volume, that is.

The first section is "Comprehensive Listings: Original U.S. Novels—1974," arranged alphabetically by author, then by title. A typical entry includes author's name (surname in all caps), title (indented), type code (the abbreviations list at the front of the book is incomplete, making identification of the codes problematical at best), publisher (one word only), month of publication (in the form "04" for April). The rest of the index is broken into sixteen other mini-sections, each devoted to a very limited area ("Posthumous One-Author Collections," for example). Without an author or title index, the entire bibliography is essentially unusable unless one particularly enjoys reading such works word for word just before bedtime.

Amateurish mishmash/trash.

SUBJECT BIBLIOGRAPHIES

SCOPE NOTE: Included herein are bibliographies dealing primarily with specific subjects or themes, where the main intent is to provide a comprehensive list, annotated or not, of the books relating to that particular category. Books whose primary purpose is to provide readers with evaluative guides to broad genre categories (e.g., Barron's *Anatomy of Wonder*) may be found in the "Readers' and Critical Guides" section of this book. Background articles on specific subgenres of science fiction and fantasy literature may also be found in such works as Nicholls's *Science Fiction Encyclopedia*.

ADVENTURE FICTION

202. Day, Bradford M. **Bibliography of Adventure: Mundy, Burroughs, Rohmer, Haggard**. Denver, N.Y., Science-Fiction & Fantasy Publications, 1964. 125 p. LC 64-56055 (pbk.). Also: Rev. ed. New York, Arno Press, 1978. 125 p. (Lost Race and Adult Fantasy Fiction). LC 77-84282. ISBN 0-405-11019-7.

Well-known fan researcher Day here contributes the collected bibliographies of four writers of fantasy adventure, the first three of which were previously published by Day under his S-F&F imprint and updated for this edition (see #303, #388, #405).

The Mundy, Burroughs, and Rohmer sections are similarly organized: Day provides brief (two-page) biographical introductions to each writer, then lists the first editions of his books in alphabetical order by title, followed by the short fiction in chronological order by publication date. A typical book entry includes title (all caps), publisher, place of publication, year of publication, pagination, brief mention of known reprint publishers (with, however, no bibliographical data), a one-line quotation taken from the book, data on previous magazine serializations, if any (giving original title of the story, magazine title, and issue dates in which the piece appeared, but no paginations), and a description of the binding color and style on the first edition (e.g., "Cover red—black letters"). A typical short fiction entry provides title (all caps), magazine title, year of publication, month of publication, but no paginations. Also included in the short fiction section are serializations of the novels, thus providing double entries for some works later collected in book form. The Mundy bibliography also includes an appreciation and series listing by Dr. J. Lloyd Eaton, and the Burroughs section has an afterword delineating known newspaper serializations of Burroughs's works, a summary of comic strip appearances, a listing of Big Little Books adaptations, selected foreign-language translations, and a list of ephemera.

The Haggard bibliography, original to the 1964 edition, lists first editions of Haggard's books only, in chronological order by publication date. A typical entry includes title (all caps), publisher, place of publication, year of publication, pagination (the exact numbered page count—e.g., 3-242), description of binding style and cloth, number of copies printed, exact publication date (if known), and similar information on the first U.S. (or first British) edition. At the end of the checklist Day provides two other lists: the reading sequence of the Allan Quatermain series, and a correlation between U.S. and U.K. title variations. There are no indexes. As usual with Day's publications, the original book was reproduced from typed, mimeographed copy and bound in flimsy covers, and the first edition copies are now yellowed and brittle. The Arno reprint is an exact facsimile of the original, with minor corrections, bound to library standards.

The Burroughs section has now been superseded by Heins's more complete bibliography (see #305), the Haggard by Whatmore (see #342), and the Mundy by Grant (see #388). No complete or current bibliography of Rohmer exists, however, leaving Day's guide the most recent work available.

ALTERNATE HISTORIES

203. Hacker, Barton C., and Gordon B. Chamberlain. **"Pasts that Might Have Been, II: A Revised Bibliography of Alternative History,"** in *Alternative Histories: Eleven Stories of the World As It Might Have Been*, edited by Charles G. Waugh and Martin H. Greenberg. New York & London, Garland Publishing, 1986. p. 301-363. LC 85-45130. ISBN 0-8240-8659-7.

Although it is not the intent of this book to cover works within works, Hacker and Chamberlain's bibliography is so unique and well executed that omitting it would itself be a bibliographical crime. Originally published in *Extrapolation* in 1981, this revised and expanded version of "Pasts That Might Have Been" provides an annotated guide to alternate histories, imaginative variations on real-life historical events (for example, what might have happened if Germany had won World War II). Entries are arranged in alphabetical order by author, then by title. A typical item includes author (surname in all caps), title (stories in quotes, novels in italics), bibliographical data (for short stories: magazine title, and month and year of publication, or book title [if the first appearance was in an anthology] and editor's name [the anthology is usually also covered in a separate entry]; for monographs: publisher and year of publication, but no paginations for either category). Some information is provided on subsequent editions and reprintings. Each entry is accompanied by a one-sentence annotation (up to forty words) giving a brief description of where the history of the story varies from real-world events. There are also copious see references to related works in the bibliography.

Hacker and Chamberlain make too much use of publisher/periodical abbreviations and probably should have provided title and subject indexes, but the latter may have been beyond the scope of the two publications in which this bibliography appeared. Separate book publication of this very comprehensive guide, with additional bibliographical data, would definitely be warranted.

ARCHITECTURE

204. White, Anthony G. **Science Fiction and Architecture: A Selected Bibliography**. Monticello, Ill., Vance Bibliographies, 1979. 12 p. (Architecture Series: Bibliography, no. A-74). LC 79-120247 (pbk.).

White's brief annotated guide deals with architectural structures, particularly the depiction of futuristic cities, in fantastic literature. His booklet is divided into two sections: "Non-Episodal Literature" (nonfiction and art books) and "Episodal Literature" (i.e., fiction), and arranged in alphabetical order by author's name in each section. A typical entry includes author's name, title (shorter works in quotes, books not otherwise marked), bibliographical data (for short works: magazine title, volume and issue number, month and year of publication, and pagination; for monographs: place of publication, publisher, year of publication, but no paginations. No data are provided for subsequent reprints. Each entry also includes a descriptive annotation ranging from single-sentence notes in section one to 30-100 words in part two. Sixteen works are described in the first bibliography, forty in the second. There are no title indexes. The book is shot from generally clear typed copy.

Science Fiction and Architecture provides a beginning point for studies on this very specialized topic, but it is hardly definitive and badly needs updating and expansion.

ATLANTIS

205. Eichner, Henry M. **Atlantean Chronicles**. Alhambra, Calif., Fantasy Publishing Co., Inc., 1971. [x], 230 p., [16] p. of plates.

The first half of this posthumously published book (through page 132) is a rather amateurishly concocted rehash of legends, myths, tales, and speculations relating to the Atlantis story in history. Of much more importance are the several bibliographies compiled by Eichner on the Atlantis theme in literature, divided into two sections: "English Literature" (eighty-three pages) and "Foreign Literature" (twenty-five pages).

The English Literature section is organized in alphabetical order by author surname, then by title. A typical entry provides author's name, title (all caps), publisher, year of publication, but no paginations, and a one- to two-paragraph descriptive annotation. At the end of the main section are several subsidiary bibliographies: "Addenda," "Pocketbook Novels on Atlantis," "Pocketbook Novels on Lemuria," a list of books whose titles suggest they might be about Atlantis (but are not), "Motion Pictures of Atlantis," "Magazine Stories on Atlantis and Lemuria" (in alphabetical order by magazine title, then chronologically by issue date). The "Foreign Language" section is unannotated and arranged haphazardly by language, then alphabetically by author's name. A typical entry includes author, title, English-language title (occasionally), publisher, place of publication, and year of publication. There is a separate bibliography of works consulted. The book is typeset, although not very well proofread, and includes a sixteen-plate set of glossy reproductions of well-known book and magazine covers.

Eichner's comments are occasionally cutesy, and he is far from a polished writer, but his lifelong obsession with the Atlantis theme is evident in this book, which is by far the most complete compilation of such materials ever gathered into one source. A more professorial reworking and updating of this bibliography would certainly be justified.

BRAILLE AND LARGE PRINT BOOKS

206. Science Fiction: A Selected List of Books that Have Appeared in *Talking Book Topics* and *Braille Book Review*. Washington, Library of Congress, 1979. 61 p. index. LC 79-15071. ISBN 0-8444-0287-7 (large print pbk.). Also available in disc and braille formats.

This nonbylined bibliography lists science fiction novels, anthologies, and young adult discs, cassettes, and braille books published for the blind and reviewed in the publications listed in the title (and housed in the collection of the National Library Service for the Blind and Physically Handicapped). Each of the three sections is divided into three parts, each corresponding to the medium in question, with materials listed in each alphabetically by title. A typical entry includes title (boldfaced), order number (boldfaced), author, narrator (where appropriate), number of discs, cassettes, or volumes, a one-paragraph descriptive annotation, and year of original publication. The index correlates authors, titles, and editors with page numbers in one alphabet and also includes order numbers. A library order blank is provided at the end of the book.

This type of work is intended more as a service to its library customers than as a literary guide, but it is astonishing to see the popularity of the genre reflected in the numerous SF titles (over 550 works) that had been made available to the blind and visually handicapped through 1979. An updated version is badly needed.

DRUGS

207. Silverberg, Robert. **Drug Themes in Science Fiction**. Rockville, Md., National Institute on Drug Abuse, 1974. vii, 55 p. index. (Research Issues, 9). LC 75-601268 (pbk.).

Well-known SF writer Silverberg produced many nonfiction books in the earlier stages of his career, this bibliography being among the last such works before the author turned his talents exclusively to more lucrative fantastic fiction. A six-page introduction provides an overview of drug themes in science fiction. The bibliography proper is broken into three sections: "Primitive Period" (1900-1935), "Predictive Period" (1935-1965), and "Contemporary Period" (1965-date). Within each section stories and novels are listed chronologically by publication date. A typical entry includes author, title, publisher and place of publication (for books) or magazine title (underlined), volume and issue number, pagination, and publisher (for short stories), date of publication, format (e.g., novel or short story), descriptor (e.g., "drugs as intelligence enhancers"), and a one-paragraph descriptive annotation (averaging 100 words). Eight items are listed in the first section, twenty-five in the second, and forty-two in the third. Materials are dated as late as 1973. An author/title index referencing page numbers completes the book. The monograph is shot from very clear typed copy. It's impossible to determine the completeness of this work, although the small number of total citations (seventy-five) may signify a less than comprehensive survey. Still, Silverberg's inherent intelligence and literacy shine through *Drug Themes*, and it does provide a sound starting point for future scholarship. This would be a good project for some budding bibliographer to rework and bring up to date.

FANTASY FICTION

208. Schlobin, Roger C. **The Literature of Fantasy: A Comprehensive Annotated Bibliography of Modern Fantasy Fiction**. New York, Garland Publishing Co., 1979. xxxv, 425 p. index. (Garland Reference Library in the Humanities, Vol. 176). LC 78-68287. ISBN 0-8240-9757-2.

Schlobin's book is the first and thus far only attempt to compile a complete bibliography of modern adult fantasy, a category virtually created in paperback form by Ballantine Books during the 1960s and '70s, with its publication of the Tolkien Trilogy and the Adult Fantasy Series edited by Lin Carter. Schlobin's twenty-page introduction provides a critical and historical summary of the genre's development from publication of George MacDonald's *Phantastes* in 1858 through the end of the 1970s (the book includes materials published through May of 1979). Seven hundred twenty-one novels, 244 collections, 100 anthologies, 3,610 short stories collected in those volumes, and 165 author bibliographies are cited and indexed.

The main part of the bibliography (268 pages) records novels and collections, arranged alphabetically by author, then by title. A typical entry includes author's name (centered, all caps), item number, title (italics), place of publication, publisher, year of publication, similar data for noteworthy recent reprints, and an annotation, but no paginations. The summaries range in size from one brief sentence to 300 words, averaging sixty words, and are primarily descriptive, with occasional critical comments. Schlobin also makes an effort to note special apparatuses that might enhance reprint editions (new introductions, for example) and cites bibliographies consulted at the end of each author's overall entry. Short stories are mentioned only as parts of book collections or anthologies and are not separately annotated. Entries are numbered consecutively throughout the book, from 1-1,249. Anthologies are listed in a separate section at the end of the volume, arranged alphabetically by primary editor name, then by title; similar data are provided for these publications, but without annotations. Two indexes complete the book, both correlated with entry numbers: "Author, Compiler, Editor, and Translator Index"; and "Title Index." The book is reproduced clearly from legible typed copy, and bound to library standards.

If we compare Schlobin with his chief rival, Barron's *Fantasy Literature* (see #52), we see that the latter work covers 945 items published through 1988, with annotations of roughly comparable size contributed by three different critics, while Schlobin's bibliography lists 300 more books with nine years' less data. Barron includes many early mythical or antecedental works not found in Schlobin, although Schlobin is more complete in his coverage of the modern period. *Fantasy Literature* provides copious "theme" references to books of a similar nature, even when they're not penned by the same writer, and also cites vastly more references to nonfiction sources about the authors and their literature. However, both books include numerous listings not found in the other, thus requiring libraries and researchers to have access to both. One problem with Schlobin is his insistence on using the real names of pseudonymous writers as the major reference point for their entries, thus putting, for example, Piers Anthony's books under Piers Anthony Dillingham Jacob, with an appropriate see reference. This creates real irritations for both the casual and heavy user, since one is constantly having to flip back and forth through the book looking for writers in places where one does not expect to find them. Barron's work also provides such information but files entries under the names commonly used by the writers, a much more logical arrangement. Still, *The Literature of Fantasy* is a worthy initial effort at establishing bibliographical control over a rapidly growing and extremely popular genre and should be expanded into a second edition with paginations included.

FIRST EDITIONS

209. Bell, Joseph. **First Editions: "A Thousand and One Nights of Reading."** Toronto, Canada, Soft Books, 1988. 82 p. in 2 v. (pbk.). 200 numbered copies.

Canadian book dealer Bell here provides bibliographical descriptions of approximately 1,050 first-edition monographs of fantastic literature, including science fiction, fantasy, and horror. Items are arranged in alphabetical order by author, then by title; nonbylined works are grouped together in volume one under the label "Anonymous." A typical entry includes author, title (boldfaced), imprint, stock number (where applicable), description of binding (if a cloth edition), format (e.g., "dw"=dust wrapper), edition statement, year of publication, type (e.g., "coll"=collection), price, but no paginations. Bell reproduces the title as given on the title page, in capital or small letters, and similarly lists the edition statement (on the title or copyright page) exactly as printed in the original book. Pseudonymous works are listed under the real names of the authors, with appropriate see references. The 8.5" x 11" volumes are shot from legible word-processed, laser-generated copy and bound in paper covers stapled to the text. The set also includes seven full-page black-and-white reproductions from dust jackets and paperback covers. There is no title index.

The major problem with these volumes is the utter absence of any selection criteria beyond the author's personal tastes. Old and new authors, major and minor works, paperbound and cloth editions, are all intermingled willy-nilly, with nary a thought as to why or how. As one might expect, the majority of the books covered were published during the last three decades; but even these newer writers have only a fraction of their works delineated. For example, just six works of Isaac Asimov are covered, and only two of these could be considered "major" first editions. Thus, while Bell's data seem sound (although there are a number of typographical and other minor errors), the eclectic nature of his selections render this work almost useless. Although Currey's guide (see #210) is much preferred, Bell includes many books and authors, older and newer, not mentioned in the former.

210. Currey, L. W., with the editorial assistance of David G. Hartwell. **Science Fiction and Fantasy Authors: A Bibliography of First Printings of Their Fiction and Selected Nonfiction**. Boston, G. K. Hall & Co., 1979. xxix, 571 p. LC 79-18217. ISBN 0-8161-8242-6.

Currey's guide has become the standard bibliography of science fiction first editions since its initial release, with good reason: it is precise, authoritative, and complete for the authors and books listed. Currey is, like his two competitors, Bell and Locke, a dealer in science fiction and fantasy books, and his knowledge of first editions and points, particularly in the modern period, is unsurpassed.

The author's introduction discusses purpose, scope and coverage, arrangement, and terms of description. The bibliographies proper are listed in alphabetical order by the author's real name, and although the front matter includes a master pseudonym/real name index, this format still can create problems for the casual user (for example, well-known author Piers Anthony is filed under his legal name, Piers Anthony Dillingham Jacob). Each writer's monographs are broken into several sections: fiction, edited fiction, nonfiction (dealing with the fantasy genre only), edited nonfiction (dealing with the fantasy genre only), prose adaptations, associational, letters, and reference (i.e., monographic critiques and bibliographies about the author). In each subsection, books are listed in alphabetical order by title. A typical author entry provides the author's full name and years of birth and death. A typical book entry includes title (small caps), place of publication, publisher, year of publication (but no paginations), binding style (e.g., "wrappers"=paperback; cloth bindings are described in detail), printing format, dustjackets, identification of printing and edition (including edition, printing, state, and issue), priority of issue, mass-market paperback book stock number and price, numbered series, and serial publications. The intent here is to enable the collector, scholar, and bibliographer to properly identify the first printing states of a particular title's first edition. No contents listings are provided for collections or anthologies, and no general nonfiction books are included for very prolific authors like Asimov and Silverberg (but associational books about fantastic literature are covered); however, fictional works outside the genre (mystery novels, for example) are covered with the rest of the author's novels and collections. With few exceptions, later reprints of the same title are unmentioned unless they must be distinguished from the original or unless they represent first hardcover appearances of the works. There are no indexes. The book is beautifully typeset and bound to library standards. Books published through 1977 are included.

Currey covers every major writer of the genre (215 authors) from H. G. Wells through Vonda N. McIntyre and Stephen King, who became prominent in the mid-1970s. His work has generally been accepted, by both collectors and dealers, as definitive for the period covered. However, the omission of page numbers from monographic listings was an unfortunate bibliographical choice, since the presence of such information is one of the ways a collector, for example, may readily distinguish between a first edition of a novel and the book club reprint. An updated edition covering the 1980s and adding a title index and paginations is badly needed.

211. Locke, George. **Science Fiction First Editions: A Select Bibliography and Notes for the Collector**. London, Ferret, 1978. 96 p. LC 80-483930 (pbk.).

Like Bell (see #209), Locke is a well-known dealer specializing in out-of-print science fiction and fantasy books, and his bibliographical knowledge was derived from years of handling and vending scarce first-edition materials. Unfortunately, this book also shares the major shortcoming of Bell's bibliography, being little more than a potpourri of bibliomania mixing old works with new with no apparent selection criteria other than the fact that Locke possessed them at the time this book was prepared and was simultaneously offering copies for sale. The data are arranged alphabetically by author surname, then by title. A typical entry includes author, title (all caps), place of publication, publisher, pagination, number of illustrations, illustrator, and a detailed description of first edition points; at the end of each entry is a one-line description of the copy or copies actually being offered for sale, with an item number attached for ordering purposes. Two hundred forty-seven such items are recorded, and perhaps fifteen less records are actually described (several of the entries have two or three copies for sale). The books covered by Locke do tend to have more importance than those recorded in Bell's work (see #209), and Locke is more precise and more bibliographically correct in his discernment and description of points. Some of the books and authors covered in Locke are not mentioned in Currey's definitive work (see #210).

More important perhaps than the bibliography proper are the two addenda: "Notes for the Collector" and "The Bookcase of Morlock Tomes." The first section discusses the collecting and identification and pricing and importance of Ace Books and "Ace Doubles," Avalon Books, Ballantine Books, Doubleday, dustwrappers, film and television linked books, first hardcover editions, Grosset & Dunlap and A. L. Burt, letters, limited editions, manuscripts and typescripts, modern science fiction, proof copies, remainders, science fiction book club [editions], science fiction speciality publishers, signed copies, and single author short story collections. This twenty-two page essay should be reproduced and distributed by the thousands to every OP book dealer in the Western world, for it succinctly and precisely summarizes Locke's genuine bibliographical knowledge of these materials and his philosophy of the art of collecting. The third section, "The Bookcase of Morlock Tomes," a Sherlock Holmes pastiche, is a witty fictional account of the ratiocinative processes necessary to delineate the priorities or printing states of five major works of fantastic literature, including H. G. Wells's *The Time Machine*. Step by step the art of bibliographical detection is revealed clearly and precisely. A virtuoso performance.

FUTURE TALES

212. Clarke, I. F. **The Tale of the Future, from the Beginning to the Present Day**. London, Library Association, 1961. 165 p. index. LC 63-4922 (pbk.). **The Tale of the Future, from the Beginning to the Present Day: An Annotated Bibliography of Those Satires, Ideal States, Imaginary Wars and Invasions, Political Warnings and Forecasts, Interplanetary Voyages and Scientific Romances—All Located in an Imaginary Future Period—That Have Been Published in the United Kingdom Between 1644 and 1970**. 2nd ed. London, Library Association, 1972. 196 p. index. LC 73-157454. ISBN 0-85365-046-2 (pbk.). **Tale of the Future, from the Beginning to the Present Day: An Annotated Bibliography of Those Satires, Ideal States, Imaginary Wars and Invasions, Coming Catastrophes and End-of-the-World Stories, Political Warnings and Forecasts, Interplanetary Voyages and Scientific Romances—All Located in an Imaginary Future Period—That Have Been Published in the United Kingdom Between 1644 and 1976**. 3rd

ed. London, Library Association, 1978. xvii, 357 p. index. LC 79-310478. ISBN 0-85365-550-2 (U.S. ISBN 0-8389-3225-8) (pbk.).

Each of the three editions of this bibliography have built upon the previous, adding new entries throughout the text and correcting older entries, and each has been organized identically, so only the most recent version will be considered here. The intent of Clarke's work is to record any fictional titles published in England with a futuristic setting or background.

The books are arranged in chronological order by year of publication, then alphabetically (within each year) by author, then by title. A typical entry includes year of publication (running down the left-hand margin), author's name (boldfaced, with initials only given for first and middle names), title (italics), publisher, pagination, and a one-phrase annotation (e.g., "Mysterious spaceships invade earth."). Single-author collections and multi-author anthologies are also included, with contents not otherwise delineated save to list the total number of stories. Books previously published in the United States are so noted with the appellation "[U.S., {date}]" after the annotation. Books with a publication date through 1976 are included in the third edition. A comprehensive short title index references book titles, authors' surnames (in parentheses), and years of publication, and the author index lists complete authors' names (unlike the main text), short titles, and years of publication for the third edition only (previous editions listed authors' first names as initials, identically with the main bibliography). Roughly 4,000 books are covered in the 1978 edition. The book is professionally typeset but is only available in an impermanent trade paperback binding.

There are several problems with Clarke's work: his annotations are at times so cryptic ("a young Russian tells the truth") that they provide little indication of why they were selected; and the selection criteria themselves seem at times to question Clarke's basic definition of the "tale of the future." In what way, for example, is Stephen King's horror tale *Carrie* futuristic? Many political thrillers are also included whose premises are at best open to interpretation and whose background settings may not be definitively future-oriented. Clarke frequently seems to opt *for* rather than *against* such borderline cases, thereby tainting the very foundations of his bibliography. Also, one must question his decision to limit the scope of his work to monographs published in the British Isles. Many mid-level American SF titles are no longer reprinted in the declining British book market, both for cultural and financial reasons, and by omitting such works, Clarke deliberately shortens his bibliography by at least a third, possibly more, leaving out thousands of works at least as significant as some of the very obscure paperbacks and vanity press items included herein. Finally, this reader, at least, finds the use of initials in place of author's first names both irritating and occasionally obfuscating. A new edition building upon Clarke's original work but correcting some structural flaws would definitely be warranted.

FUTURE WAR FICTION

213. Clarke, I. F. **Voices Prophesying War, 1763-1984**. London, Oxford University Press, 1966. x, 254 p. index. LC 66-77284. Also: London, Panther Arts, 1970. x, 254 p. index. ISBN 0-586-03278-9 (pbk.).

Clarke's interest in futuristic fiction has already been examined in his continuing *Tale of the Future* (see #212). This bibliocritical text examines the "future war" genre from its inception in 1871 with the publication of *The Battle of Dorking*, Sir George Chesney's xenophobic reaction to the establishment of the German Empire (a few seminal works prior to this date are also covered). Chesney's influential work sparked discussions in Parliament and a flood of sequels, responses, and counterscenarios, culminating in a rash of publications leading up to the outbreak of World War I. Thereafter, matched against the horrors of real-life battle, the genre declined somewhat but has never been wholly extinguished, with new popular successes (*The Third World War*) appearing through the 1980s.

Clarke provides a narrative analysis and description of the major future war scenarios published through the early 1960s, including reproductions of a number of illustrations from the original publications. Three major bibliographies are included: "A. Principal Works Consulted"; "B. Select List of War Studies, 1770-1964"; and "C. Check List of Imaginary Wars, 1763-1965." The latter is arranged chronologically by year of publication, then alphabetically by main entry. A typical entry includes year of publication, author's name, and title, but no bibliographical data. The list is noteworthy for its inclusion of many European publications (particularly French and German) not found in any other source, although the lack of publishing information could limit the ability of researchers to locate actual copies of the volumes. Two indexes, to books and periodicals and to authors and subjects, complete the work.

Although the bibliography proper lacks annotations, in effect Clarke does the same thing, at least for the better-known works, through his extensive analyses in the main part of the text. In general his book has been accepted as authoritative, clearly reflecting a broad-based knowledge of the subject. There is very little overlap between Clarke's critical bibliography and Newman/Unsworth's more modern work (see #214). It appears unlikely at this juncture that Clarke will himself revise or update *Voices*, which is a great pity. No serious scholar of the future war genre could even contemplate beginning their researches without access to this seminal text.

214. Newman, John, and Michael Unsworth. **Future War Novels: An Annotated Bibliography of Works in English Published Since 1946**. Phoenix, Oryx Press, 1984. x, 101 p. index. LC 83-43245. ISBN 0-89774-103-X.

Newman and Unsworth describe 191 future war novels produced in the post-World War II period, arranged chronologically by year of publication, then alphabetically by author's name. A typical entry includes item number, author's name, title (italics), place of publication, publisher, pagination, LC card number, ISBN, and a one-paragraph description averaging 150 words in length. Books are numbered consecutively throughout the volume from the number one. Bibliographical data are provided for both the original editions and all known reprints (including paperbacks) in the U.S. and England. The annotations (written by Newman only) are largely descriptive, with occasional one-sentence summations or commentary. Author and title indexes, referencing item numbers only, complete the book. The text is nicely typeset and the book is bound to library standards.

Only about half of the entries covered by Newman and Unsworth in the years through 1965 are mentioned in Clarke (see #213) and vice versa, posing an interesting question: is the absence of coverage in both books due to the ignorance of the authors (Newman and Unsworth do mention *Voices Prophesying War* in their introduction) or to differences in definition and nationality (Clarke lives and works in the British Isles)? The authors *are* more restrictive in one sense, insisting that works be tied directly to present-day events and not be dressed with such science-fictional conventions as alien or far-future cultures. Nonetheless, by whatever definition this book seems to miss a great many titles which could justly have been included (see the comments on Brians's *Nuclear Holocausts* [#220]), and one must ask if the net was cast widely enough. Perhaps an expanded future edition of *Future War Novels* will settle the conflict.

GOTHIC FICTION

215. Frank, Frederick S. **The First Gothics: A Critical Guide to the English Gothic Novel**. New York & London, Garland Publishing, 1987. xxxi, 496 p. index. (Garland Reference Library of the Humanities, Vol. 710). LC 86-27092. ISBN 0-8240-8501-9.

Frank, author of several bibliographies of secondary resources on the literature of the gothic revival (see #90-#91), here provides an annotated guide to 500 of these extraordinarily rare novels of terror and the supernatural, all from the classic period of gothic literature (1758-1832).

Materials are arranged alphabetically by author, then by title (but nonbylined novels, of which there are many, are interfiled in the main sequence by title). A typical entry includes item number, author, title (all caps), place of publication, publisher, and year of publication of first edition, similar data on modern reprints, "Gothic Type" (e.g., "Gothified history"), biographical and research data, and annotation. The secondary sources mentioned in the "biographical and research data" reference the "Selected Bibliography of Critical Sources on the English Gothic Novel" in Appendix Two, citing authors, titles, and specific page numbers, and generally adding a very useful dimension to the entries. The annotations are both descriptive and evaluative and range in size from 50-1,500 words, averaging 300. Frank makes some comparisons between similar works, and his comments are informed, literate, and to the point. End matter includes "Appendix One: Glossary of Gothic Terms" (very useful); "Appendix Two" (noted above); "Appendix Three: Annual Chronology of the First Gothics, 1758-1832" (giving years, titles [all caps], and item numbers); "Index One: Index of Gothic Authors" (referencing authors and item numbers, but no titles, with primary records [i.e., those annotated] underlined); "Index Two: Index of Gothic Titles" (giving titles and item numbers only, with primary entries underlined); "Index Three: Index of Critics" (citing critics and item numbers only). The book is shot from legible typed copy and bound to library standards; fourteen full-page reproductions of illustrations from the gothics themselves add a touch of spice to the text. Frank's twelve-page historical introduction provides a good general introduction to the history of the literature.

Compared to Tracy's *The First Gothics* (see #218), which covers 500 titles, *The Gothic Novel* includes 208. However, only a few titles are unique to Tracy's volume (perhaps twenty books), and Frank makes some attempt at evaluating the titles, while Tracy only supplies straightforward plot summaries. Thus, while serious scholars will probably want access to both books, most libraries can satisfy the needs of their patrons, academics included, with copies of Frank's authoritative bibliography. Locating copies of the gothics themselves is almost an impossible task, for the vast majority have never been reprinted; most exist in less than ten or twenty copies, and some survive with just one known example; other titles mentioned in various contemporaneous lists and in Summers's bibliography (see #217) apparently do not survive. Frank estimates that as many as 4,500-5,000 gothic novels may actually have been published in the seventy-year period between 1760-1830.

216. Radcliffe, Elsa J. **Gothic Novels of the Twentieth Century: An Annotated Bibliography**. Metuchen, N.J. & London, The Scarecrow Press, 1979. xix, 272 p. LC 78-24357. ISBN 0-8108-1190-1.

In 1960 the late Donald A. Wollheim and Evelyn Grippo, editors of the paperback house Ace Books, created the modern gothic as a mass market category by developing a distinctive series package for several romance novels they had recently purchased for reprinting. This unique cover design, later adopted by many rival companies who developed gothic lines of their own, featured a young woman fleeing from a castle or old house at night, a look of horror or fear on her face, and one lone light flickering at the window of the decaying manse. The popularity of these first few releases sparked the rapid development of the category from the mid-1960s through the early '70s, when the genre rapidly began to wane. The aptly named Radcliffe has published the first bibliographical guide to this modern publishing phenomenon.

Gothic Novels is organized alphabetically by author surname, then by title. A typical entry includes author's name (all caps), biographical data (one brief paragraph; data are present for only about a third of the authors), entry number, title (underlined), rating (using the grade school letter grades of A, B, C, D, F), place of publication, publisher, year of publication, LC card number, paperback stock number (haphazardly), and similar data for known reprints, and a descriptive annotation (for about half of the entries) averaging forty words in length. No paginations are provided. Title entries are unified under the best-known pseudonym (or real name) of each writer, with see references throughout the text and an indication after each title which name was used on that book. Thus, the writings of Canadian writer W. E. D. Ross, who produced at least a hundred gothics, are centralized under his real name, with references from his thirteen gothic pennames to his real name. The entries are numbered consecutively from 1-1,973. Works are included through at least 1977. The title index references titles and item numbers only. There is also a list of works consulted at the beginning of the book. As usual with Scarecrow books, the bibliography is shot from very legible typed copy and bound to library standards.

Some of Radcliffe's comments are overly cute, and her bibliographical data are far from definitive; most of the novels she cites, for example, are known to have been pseudonymous (many were written by male writers under female names), with only a partial list of identifications being provided by her work. There are similar questions about her comprehensiveness (Radcliffe herself mentions in passing works by authors already included in her book which appear to be gothics but which she has been unable to verify; these novels are not included in the number count), about her selection criteria (in what way are the two fantasies by Peter S. Beagle gothics?), and about the uniformity of application of these criteria to the works at hand. On the other side, however, the gothic genre was itself so ill-defined (and bibliographical data on these books so difficult to find) as to present major problems to any potential bibliographer, since the paperback publishers, in their initial desperate search for material, threw into this category any work which could be even remotely construed as fitting the "gothic mystique." Radcliffe does cover at least adequately a majority of the books produced during the fifteen-year rise and fall of the modern gothic revival, providing some initial basis for future scholarship; perhaps her bibliography, as mediocre as the fiction it indexes, is the best we can hope for under the circumstances.

217. Summers, Montague. **A Gothic Bibliography**. London, Fortune Press, 1941. xx, 621 p. LC 41-3676. Also: New York, Russell & Russell, 1964. xx, 620 p. LC 64-8918.

Summers was a well-known critic and bibliographer with a particular interest in the gothic and horror novel. His guide to the classic gothic was so well regarded on publication that it has never been supplanted or even updated.

A Gothic Bibliography is divided into two major sections: "Index of Authors" and "Title Index," with a brief addendum similarly subdivided. The author index is arranged alphabetically by author surname. A typical entry includes author's name (surname in large caps, remainder of the name in small caps), biographical information (ranging from nothing [more than half of the entries] to mini-essays of 400 words), and a chronological list of the author's gothics, giving title (italics) and year of publication but no other data. The title index is actually the major focus of the volume, listing works in alphabetical order by title and giving title (italics), author, year of publication, place of publication, publisher, variant titles, number of volumes or pagination, size (e.g., "8vo" for octavo), price, and an occasional one-line descriptive annotation. Not all entries have the same level of data due to lack of sources (some of these books no longer survive with any known examples); many items lack paginations, for example. Similar information is provided on all known reprints. An extraordinary number of French, German, and other foreign gothics are included in the bibliography, some with English-language translations.

Summers's work is both authoritative and definitive; indeed, it is difficult to imagine any current researcher redoing his work or having sufficient resources even to begin such a project. This bibliography should be owned by all university libraries.

218. Tracy, Ann B. **The Gothic Novel, 1790-1830: Plot Summaries and Index to Motifs**. Lexington, Ky., The University Press of Kentucky, 1981. vii, 216 p. index. LC 79-4013. ISBN 0-8131-1397-0.

Given the difficulty in locating surviving copies of the novels produced during the classic gothic period of the early 1800s, Tracy provides a valuable service to the scholarly world by summarizing the plots of 208 of these rare and extraordinarily intricate fictions.

The Gothic Novel is arranged in alphabetical order by main entry (usually author, but occasionally title if no author is known), then by title. A typical entry provides item number, author, title (all caps), number of volumes or pagination, place of publication, publisher, year of publication, and an annotation. Tracy's summaries are descriptive rather than evaluative, ranging in size from thirty words (for several of the pamphlets) to 750 words, and are very detailed and explicit. The books are numbered consecutively throughout the book from the number one. The title index references titles and page numbers. Tracy also provides two other valuable indexes: to motifs and to characters, both referenced, curiously, to item numbers (it seems illogical and unnecessarily confusing to index titles one way and everything else another way). The book is shot from legible typed copy.

Students of the gothic revival will welcome this guide to the major gothic authors and their works. Although Tracy makes no attempt to evaluate the works in question or even to suggest a reading list, all of the major titles are here, and many minor ones; the only useful addenda which could conceivably be added in the future are summaries of other novels not heretofore covered. Compare with Frank's major complete guide (see #215).

IMAGINARY VOYAGES

219. Gove, Philip Babcock. **The Imaginary Voyage in Prose Fiction: A History of Its Criticism and a Guide for Its Study, with an Annotated Checklist of 215 Imaginary Voyages from 1700 to 1800**. New York, Columbia University Press, 1941. xi, 445 p. index. (Columbia University Studies in English and Comparative Literature, No. 152). LC 41-6604. Also: New York, Arno Press, 1975. xi, 445 p. index. (Science Fiction). LC 74-15972. ISBN 0-405-06328-8.

Gove's book deals with a now defunct subgenre of fantastic literature, the imaginary voyage to a mythical (and often fantastical) island, continent, or country (*Gulliver's Travels* is the best-known example), which became the rage of early eighteenth-century literature, then gradually faded into oblivion as the farther reaches of the world were actually explored (a later offshoot is the lost race novel, now also consigned to the ashheap of literature).

The first half of this book (178 pages) is "A History of the Criticism of the Imaginary Voyage," in which Gove succinctly and carefully summarizes critical reactions to the genre. Part Two, an "Annotated Check List of Two Hundred and Fifteen Imaginary Voyages from

1700 to 1800," is arranged chronologically by year of publication. A typical entry includes year of publication, author (with years of birth and death, if known), title, place of publication, publisher, and similar data for all known reprints through the year 1800 (but no paginations), a list of libraries in the United States known to have copies of the items in question (using the library symbols from the *Library of Congress* [later *National Union*] *Catalog*), and an annotation. The descriptions vary widely in length, some being very perfunctory, others providing much background data on editions, history, and other details; very few contain actual plot summaries or any literary evaluation of the texts. Gove also provides a separate bibliography of works consulted and a detailed author/title index correlated to page numbers. Works from all languages are covered (including almost as many original French and German editions as those in English) in almost a thousand separate printings. The book is attractively typeset, and both editions are bound to library standards (the Arno version is a facsimile reprint of the original).

The widespread acceptance of Gove as the standard work on the subject can be seen by the fact that no significant revision or upgrade of *The Imaginary Voyage* has ever been undertaken despite the passage of half a century. While his standards are undoubtedly high, it would have been helpful to have had paginations for these very rare publications and some indication of plots or motifs. These are minor points; however, this well-wrought critical bibliography should be available in all academic libraries.

NUCLEAR WARFARE

220. Brians, Paul. **Nuclear Holocausts: Atomic War in Fiction, 1895-1984**. Kent, Ohio & London, The Kent State University Press, 1987. xi, 398 p. index. LC 86-10685. ISBN 0-87338-335-4.

This critical bibliography is divided into two sections. The first half (ninety-four pages) provides a history of nuclear warfare in literature in five chapters: "1. The History of the Holocaust"; "2. The Causes of Nuclear War"; "3. The Short-Term Effects of Nuclear War"; "4. The Long-Term Consequences of Nuclear War"; and "5. Avoiding the Holocaust." Essentially these sections evaluate and compare (through the broad categories into which they fall) the fictions mentioned in the bibliography. A six-page intermediate section, "Sources," discusses and compares in narrative form the many secondary sources, both books and articles, on atomic energy and warfare in modern fiction.

The major part of the book (350 pages) is an annotated guide to the literature of nuclear warfare, arranged alphabetically by author, then by title. A typical entry includes author's name (boldfaced), title (italics), place of publication, publisher, and year of publication, but no paginations; similar data are provided for known reprints. Both novels and short stories are covered. The entry annotations range in size from one brief sentence (ten words) to 1,500 words, 100 being average, and tend to be descriptive with occasional one-line evaluations. End matter includes "Timeline," a chronological checklist of the materials covered by year, giving author and title; "Supplementary Checklists" of closely-related books and stories, including "Near-War Narratives," "Doubtful Cases," "Nuclear Testing," and "Reactor Disasters"; each of these brief sections is arranged alphabetically by author, then by title, the entries providing authors, titles, and years of publication only. There are also title and detailed subject indexes keyed to page number (the title index provides authors after each title). The book is very professionally and attractively designed and typeset and bound to library standards.

In comparing Brian's guide to Newman/Unsworth's *Future War Novels* (see #214), one would expect to find all of the works mentioned in the former for the years 1946-83 included in the latter but in fact at least half are missing. It is difficult to make exact comparisons, but Brians includes roughly 780 titles, not all of them with full-length entries; of these, perhaps 40% are short fiction, and another sixty or so were published before Newman/Unsworth's 1946 cutoff date, leaving about 400 novels in Brians compared to 191 in *Future War Novels*. Brians's reach is clearly much longer and his knowledge of the literature much broader. There are also, however, a few problems with the selection criteria in *Nuclear Holocausts*: a very small number of entries (for example, Mitchell Wilson's *Live with Lightning*) deal realistically with the development of the atomic bomb in the 1940s or with some other aspect of nuclear physics and are not clearly futuristic or fantastic. They seem out-of-place in the midst of so much fictional destruction. Barring such minor quibbles, Brians's bibliography is a thoroughly good piece of work and should be continued with subsequent editions.

PAPERBACKS

221. Day, Bradford M. **The Checklist of Fantastic Literature in Paperbound Books**. Denver, N.Y., Science-Fiction & Fantasy Publications, 1965. 128 p. index. LC 66-342. (pbk.). Also: New York, Arno Press, 1975. 128 p. index. (Science Fiction). LC 74-15961 ISBN 0-405-06326-1.

Day intended this book as a companion volume to his *Supplemental Checklist of Fantastic Literature* (see #179), which included only cloth volumes, and ultimately as a supplement to Bleiler's *Checklist of Fantastic Literature* (see #178), and it is organized very similarly to both.

The main section of the book organizes the literature in alphabetical order by author, then by title, anonymous works being centralized under the headings "Anonymous" or "Anonymous Anthology." A typical entry includes author, title (all caps), publisher, year of publication, pagination, and an indication (using the words "Book: same" or "Book: [original title]" beneath the entry) whether the work was previously published in cloth (original paperbacks have no such appellation). The title index references title and author surnames only. As is usual with Day's self-published works, the text is reproduced from sometimes faint typed copy and bound through the side with staples; the edges of some pages are beginning to yellow. The Arno Press edition is a facsimile of the original, photoreduced from 8.5" x 11" to 5" x 8" (which does help concentrate the text into a more legible format) and bound to library standards.

Day includes materials largely from the period 1948-64, although some earlier original paperbacks missed by Bleiler in his 1948 *Checklist* have been added. Now largely superseded by Reginald's *Science Fiction and Fantasy Literature* (see #182).

222. Stephens, Christopher P. **The Science Fiction and Fantasy Paperback First Edition: A Complete List of Them All (1939-1973)**. Hastings-on-Hudson, N.Y., Ultramarine Publishing Co., 1991. 143 p. index. ISBN 0-89366-162-7 (pbk.).

Chris Stephens, author of twenty-five other bibliographies on topics as diverse as science fiction, the literature of the Vietnam War, and the writings of P. C. Wren, has been very active in the last half decade. This new bibliography attempts to list all SF paperback first editions published from the inception of the mass market paperback in June of 1939 to the end of 1973.

Materials are arranged alphabetically by author's surname, then chronologically by title. A typical entry includes author (surname in all caps), item number, title (underlined), publisher, stock number, price, year of publication, pagination, cover illustrator, information on later cloth editions (where applicable), and other bibliographical notes. Materials are numbered consecutively from 1-1,655. Authors are listed under their real names when known, with see references from their pseudonyms to their birth names; this can create confusion for users attempting to find authors who have only written under one very well-known pen name. The index correlates titles with authors and years of publication, not item numbers. Books which the author has not actually seen are so indicated by an asterisk placed before the item number. The book is shot from typed copy and stapled through the spine into stiff paper covers.

Much of these data can already be found in Reginald's more complete bibliography (see #182) or in Tuck's *Encyclopedia* (see #10); however, Stephens does include information on stock numbers, cover illustrators, and subsequent cloth editions for the period 1969-73 that are not readily found elsewhere, and his guide will prove useful for bibliographers and researchers studying the golden age of paperback originals.

PSEUDONYMOUS AUTHORS

223. Rock, James A. **Who Goes There: A Bibliographic Dictionary, Being a Guide to the Works of Authors Who Have Contributed to the Literature of Fantasy and Science Fiction, and Who Have Published Some or All of Their Work Pseudonymously**. Bloomington, Ind., James A. Rock & Co., 1979. viii, 201 p. LC 79-125345. ISBN 0-918736-04-8; ISBN 0-918736-05-6 (pbk.).

This is a strangely realized bibliography, its basic premise being the listing of all fantastic literature written by authors who have penned at least one work pseudonymously in whatever forum. The main section of *Who Goes There* is arranged alphabetically by author's name, then alphabetically by penname, then chronologically under each name by title. A typical entry includes author's name (bold caps), years of birth and death and place of birth (if known), author's pseudonym (boldface), the first story published under this name in a periodical (plus magazine title [italics] and month and year of publication), then a chronological checklist of the author's science fiction and fantasy books under this name, giving titles (italics), places of publication, publishers, years of publications, paginations, an indication of illustrations, and binding ("paper"=paperback). The arrangement is repeated for each penname in alphabetical order by name. Rock also provides a representative selection of the authors' nonfiction and non-SF fiction monographs, if such exist, and references other known or unverified pseudonyms outside the field, without, however, providing examples of works under those names. The index coordinates pseudonyms (boldfaced) to real names and page numbers, but does not index titles. The book also includes a source bibliography and a six-page illustrated essay, "Notes on Collecting." The text is clearly typeset in double-column format and printed in an oversized 9" x 12" format.

There's a great deal of data here, but Rock's book is filled with inconsistencies, stretched examples, and skewed logic. For example, author Leo P. Kelley is included solely on the basis of a typographical error on the cover of one of his paperback novels, which misconstrued his middle initial as "F." *This* is a pseudonym? Chad Oliver is included because the fuller form of his name, Dr. Symmes C(had) Oliver, appeared on an anthropological text. Andy Offutt is listed because some half-stewed magazine editor left the second "T" off his last name, another clear instance of a typo slipping through. One can play such games, of course, but ultimately one must ask what purpose this bibliography serves. The only answer is irretrievably stuck between a bibliographical Rock and a hard place.

RECURSIVE SCIENCE FICTION

224. Lewis, Anthony R. **An Annotated Bibliography of Recursive Science Fiction**. Cambridge, Mass., NESFA Press, 1990. 56 p. index. ISBN 0-915368-47-1 (pbk.). The running title throughout the book is *Recursion!: Science Fiction Stories About Science Fiction*.

Lewis, one of the principals behind the NESFA magazine indexes (see #129), here provides an annotated bibliography of SF and other fictions using science-fiction authors, SF fandom, or other science-fictional backgrounds or settings as an integral part of their stories.

The main part of the book is organized alphabetically by author's name, then by title. A typical entry includes author (boldfaced), title (boldfaced, in quotes for short stories, in bold italics for novels), genre for works which are not in themselves fantastic (boldfaced, run to the righthand margin), annotation, and bibliographical data (publisher or magazine title, series, ISBN number [where appropriate], month and year of publication [with paginations provided on an inconsistent basis for short story appearances only] for all known editions and reprints). The annotations are descriptive rather than evaluative, focusing on the recursive elements in each story and averaging about eighty words each. The introduction incorporates a bibliography of "References" consulted. Included at the end of the book are separate sections on "Graphics" (comic books); "Performing Arts" (plays, musicals, teleplays, and films); a two-page addendum of "Items That Didn't Quite Make It Into the Bibliography" (all three sections are arranged in similar format to the main bibliography); "Cross Reference by Title," giving titles and authors only (plus, inconsistently, a few appellations such as "[film]" referencing titles in the three addendum sections); and a "Listing by Date of First Appearance," arranged by year, month (where known), author, title, and magazine title or publisher. Materials are covered through October 1990. The book is reproduced from excellent laser printer-generated copy on 8.5" x 11" sheets and stapled through the spine in typical NESFA fashion.

Lewis's coverage seems reasonably thorough (roughly 220 items), his list of reprintings valuable, and his annotations very readable; one might have wished, however, for complete paginations for all items included, instead of the hodgepodge actually provided. Moreover, the title index does not always distinguish between books, graphic publications, and media productions, and the books in the borderline chapter are not indexed at all. These inconsistencies need to be resolved in any future edition. Despite the book's title, Lewis also includes mysteries, romances, and other works with settings in the SF field (for example, Anthony Boucher's *Rocket to the Morgue*) interfiled with the rest but distinguished with category tags; these add a valuable adjunct to the main listings. For specialized collections.

SERIES

225. Cottrill, Tim, Martin H. Greenberg, and Charles G. Waugh. **Science Fiction and Fantasy Series and Sequels: A Bibliography, Volume 1: Books**. New York & London, Garland Publishing Co., 1986. xix, 398 p. index. (Garland Reference Library of the Humanities, Vol. 611). LC 85-45121. ISBN 0-8240-8671-6.

Cottrill *et al.* provide a very useful guide to the seemingly interminable spate of sequels and series that have plagued all genre literatures from their very beginnings.

The basic arrangement of the book is alphabetically by author's name (or by series name if more than one author has contributed separate items to the series—for example, "Star Trek"), then by series title. A typical entry includes author (all caps), years of birth and death (if known), series title (underlined), and a numbered list of the novels in the order of their publication (although additional numbering is sometimes provided if there are major sequential problems) coordinated with years of initial publication and publishers' names (often abbreviated). The multi-authored series volumes such as "Star Wars," "The Man from U.N.C.L.E.," and "Star Trek" may provide several numbering sequences for different subseries; these sections also include the names of each author after the titles they authored, in parentheses. A second section of the book lists anthology series arranged by editor, then listed by title, in chronological order by issue date, with the same data as above. Two indexes, to series titles and book titles, referenced to author surnames and page numbers, complete the book, with brief addenda and corrigenda sections and a bibliography of sources consulted. The book is shot from very clear typed copy and bound to library standards. A detailed abbreviations list appears at the front of the book.

Cottrill's reach is vast, and he and his co-authors cover every major (and most minor) SF series published in the English language through 1985. Roughly 5,200 books are covered. The only problem with the bibliography is the extensive use of publisher abbreviations, which are totally unnecessary (the book has plenty of white space running down the middle of each page), often obtrusive and irritating, and occasionally misleading for lesser-known firms. This problem should be fixed in any future edition. A second volume devoted to short fiction was announced but has not been published.

SEXUALITY

226. Garber, Eric, and Lyn Paleo. **Uranian Worlds: A Reader's Guide to Alternative Sexuality in Science Fiction and Fantasy.** Boston, G. K. Hall & Co., 1983. xxvi, 177 p. index. (A Reference Publication in Science Fiction). LC 82-21198. ISBN 0-8161-8573-5. **Uranian Worlds: A Reader's Guide to Alternative Sexuality in Science Fiction and Fantasy.** 2nd ed. Boston, G. K. Hall & Co., 1990. xxvi, 286 p. index. LC 90-37434. ISBN 0-8161-1832-9.

Garber and Paleo here contribute a very interesting series of bibliographies on homosexuality and other alternative sexual lifestyles mentioned in fantasy and science fiction stories and novels. The main part of the book is organized alphabetically by author, then by title. A typical entry provides item number, author's name (all caps), title (italics), place of publication, publisher, year of publication (but no paginations), subject code letter (e.g., "F"="Lesbianism or female bisexuality is a major component within a work"), and a brief descriptive annotation ranging in size from one sentence (ten words) to 200 words, fifty being average. Short story entries include author, story title, magazine or anthology title (italics), month and year of publication (for periodical appearances) or place of publication, publisher, and year of publication (for book appearances), but no paginations. Interpolated throughout the text are biographical notes on major writers, set off from the rest of the text by line rules and printed in smaller boldfaced type; these sections include author's name, year of birth (and death, if appropriate), career highlights as a writer, and an assessment of the writer's contributions to alternative sexuality in fantastic literature. Also listed in these sections are sources for additional information (bibliographies, critiques, etc.). The book annotations include plot summaries with the rationale for inclusion in the bibliography (sometimes the alternative lifestyle is a very minor part of the fictional framework of the novel or story, sometimes it dominates the narrative). The entries are numbered consecutively throughout each volume from the number one: the first edition contains 568 items, the second edition 935. Garber and Paleo also cover in the main sequence a handful of nonfiction articles about homosexuality and lesbianism in fantastic literature.

The second edition adds three appendices: "Selected Anthologies," listed alphabetically by title, giving title (italics), editor, place of publication, publisher, year of publication, and a one-sentence annotation which mentions the stories featuring alternative sexualities (which in turn are covered as separate items in the main text); "Selected Films," also alphabetical by title, giving title (italics), director's name, country of origin, year of production, subject code (as above, for the main part of the book), and a two-sentence annotation summarizing plot elements, mentioning the homosexual aspects of the motion picture, and giving the names of the chief characters (and the actors/actresses who play them); and "Selected Fan Organizations," giving organization name (all caps), description and purpose, address.

Both books also include a chronological index rearranging the data year by year, then alphabetically by author, a typical entry including year of publication, author's surname, title (italics), and item number; and an alphabetical title index correlating titles, author surnames, and item numbers only. The first volume is shot from typed copy, while the second is attractively typeset, providing a great improvement in general readability; both are bound to library standards.

Uranian Worlds is one of the few instances in this book where an effort has been made to maintain and expand an existing bibliographical data base. The original volume was a worthy effort; the 1990 version expands these listings by almost forty percent, including both the great and very obscure and certainly covering the vast majority of works which presently exist. The only modifications which might be desirable for future editions would be the addition of paginations to the bibliographical data and of full author names to the two indexes. We look forward to a third edition of this exceptionally well-wrought bibliography being produced in the mid-1990s.

Note also Donald Palumbo's edited volume, *Erotic Universe: Sexuality and Fantastic Literature* (New York & Westport, Conn., Greenwood Press, 1986), which includes a short annotated bibliography of fiction, nonfiction, and film SF and fantasy (pages 257-89) featuring sexual themes, including some works not mentioned in Garber/Paleo (but falling outside of their stated parameters).

SPACE VOYAGES

227. Locke, George. **Voyages in Space: A Bibliography of Interplanetary Fiction, 1801-1914.** London, Ferret Fantasy, 1975. 80 p. index. (Ferret Fantasy's Christmas Annual for 1974). LC 76-365519 (cloth and pbk.).

Two earlier, more general bibliographies by Locke bore the title *Ferret Fantasy's Christmas Annual for 1972* and *...1973* (see #180), but this particular volume was the first in the series to have a specific title and focus.

Locke's learned introduction discusses definitions and format. This is followed by a nineteen-item preliminary list, "What Had Gone Before: A Chronological Survey and Select Bibliography of Interplanetary Fiction up to 1800," which, except for the chronological arrangement, includes the same type of data as the main section. The primary bibliography is itself divided into two sections: "1. Books" and "2. Periodicals, Boys' Novelettes, Etc." In each section materials are arranged alphabetically by author, then by title (nonbylined works being filed under the appellation "Anonymous"). A typical entry provides item number, author's name, title (all caps), place of publication, publisher, year of publication, pagination, illustration note, and a brief descriptive annotation ranging in size from twenty-five to seventy-five words (averaging forty), followed by a detailed description of the first edition binding cloth, priority points, notes on reprint editions, etc. Items are numbered consecutively from 001-019 in the preliminary section and from 1-263 in the main bibliography (both parts together). The short stories mentioned in section two include story title (in quotes), place of publication, magazine title (italics), month and year of publication, and occasionally total (but no specific) paginations. A postscript includes statistic tables and graphs (e.g., "Flights to and from Earth") and a brief checklist of further secondary reading sources. The index correlates authors with titles and item numbers, but there is no separate title index; since the main organization of the book is by author, this seems a fruitless waste of space. The book is shot from attractive and legible typed copy, and the cloth edition is sewn to library standards.

Locke's immense knowledge of early science fiction is clearly reflected here; his book is filled with rare, seminal works, many of them described for the first (and only) time in this volume. Researchers interested in the antecedents of modern SF would find their time well spent examining Locke's very authoritative bibliographies, and all major research collections should own copies.

228. Smith, Lynn S. **Space Voyages, 1591-1920: A Bibliography of Works Held in the Library of the University of California, Riverside**. Riverside, Calif., University of California, Riverside Library, 1979. 45 p. (pbk.).

This very brief guide was produced to highlight books held in the J. Lloyd Eaton Collection of Science Fiction and Fantasy housed in the Rivera Library at the University of California, Riverside, whose complete collection catalog is covered elsewhere in this volume (see #109). Smith lists 131 mostly fictional voyages to outer space dated from 1591-1920, with a heavy emphasis on the pre-industrial era. A typical entry includes call number, author, title (underlined), place of publication, publisher, year of publication, a one- to two-sentence descriptive annotation, and a reference citation to one of three works: Locke (see #227), Bleiler (see #178), or Majorie Hope Nicolson's classic historical survey, *Voyages to the Moon* (New York: Macmillan, 1948). The book is shot from typed copy and includes several full-page illustrations taken from the works annotated. For scholars interested in this very limited topic, and wishing to examine copies of the works in question, this is a useful introductory guide; students of the very early antecedents of the science fiction genre may also find this bibliography of interest.

STAR WARS FICTION

229. Sheldon, Lita. **An Author List of Star Wars Fan Fiction**. Tsaile, Ariz., Lita Sheldon, 1984. [i], 33p., 4 leaves. index. (pbk).

The three *Star Wars* films spawned a rabid fan following that reached almost the level of the *Star Trek* fandom before suddenly dissipating after *Return of the Jedi* was released. During its heydey, *Star Wars* fans, like their *ST* counterparts, produced reams of stories, novellas, novels, and plays. Some were published in *SW* fanzines; others appeared as separate monographs or in *SW* anthologies. Such publications are technically violations of the copyright law, of course, since both created universes are proprietary properties owned and leased by the film companies that produced the original motion pictures and television programs. However, this has not stopped the fans, who have produced scores of derivatory fictions distributed in small numbers of copies to other fans.

Sheldon's guide is arranged alphabetically by author/illustrator's name, then by title. A typical entry provides author/illustrator, title, type (e.g., "story," "play," etc.), universe (e.g., "SW"=*Star Wars*), fanzine/book title, page numbers. A separate section indexes fanzine/book editors and addresses. The book is photocopied from sometimes faint computer-generated printout and bound with two staples through the side (without covers). Although useful as a guide to these very ephemeral materials, Sheldon's bibliography is necessary only for the most specialized collections.

TITLE CHANGES

230. Viggiano, Michael, and Donald Franson. **Science Fiction Title Changes: A Guide to the Changing Titles of Science Fiction and Fantasy Stories Published in Magazines and Books**. Seattle, Wash., National Fantasy Fan Federation, 1965. 47 p. LC 66-6551 (pbk.).

This straightforward guide lists variant titles of SF stories and novels correlated with author names. The basic arrangement is alphabetical by title; a typical entry lists first title and second title (all caps, separated by slashes), followed by a [-] and the author's name. The second title will appear in reverse order later in the index. The book is shot from legible typed copy. One problem with the guide is the absence of any indication of which title was used first or in what forum: magazine and book titles are jumbled together willy-nilly with no distinction. Also, an author index would have been useful. Now out-of-date, although the data remain valid for the period prior to 1965; a revised edition is badly needed.

UTOPIAN FICTION

231. Negley, Glenn. **Utopian Literature: A Bibliography, with a Supplementary Listing of Works Influential in Utopian Thought**. Lawrence, Kans., The Regents Press of Kansas, 1977. xxiii, 228 p. index. LC 77-8265. ISBN 0-7006-0164-3.

Negley's bibliography derived in part from his earlier guide to the *Utopia Collection of the Duke University Library* (see #108). The main section of the book is arranged alphabetically by author, then by title. A typical entry lists item number, author's name, title (italics), place of publication, year of publication, pagination (*but no publishers!*), and a very useful list of codes (the abbreviations list appears on page xxiii) noting libraries at which copies of the books may be found. This is followed by a bibliography, "Works Influential in Utopian Thought," similarly organized, "Short-Title Index" (referencing titles and entry numbers only), and a "Chronological Index" (listing works by years and item numbers only). Books are numbered consecutively throughout the book from 1-1,608; however, it should be noted that the numerous see references scattered throughout the bibliography are *also numbered* with the rest, as are subsequent editions, making an assessment of the real number of items included impossible; 1,200 are mentioned in the introduction. The latest book covered is dated 1963.

There are some major problems with this book. The deliberate omission of publishers' names, while perhaps appropriate for books published in the seventeenth century, is a serious error for later periods, as is the decision to number separately reprint editions and name references in sequence with the main entries. One must also question the index formats, particularly the chronology, which fails to include either authors or titles, but lists only the item numbers, requiring the user to refer constantly back and forth to different sections of the text. This type of amateurish mishmash severely reduces the integrity of the work. For a comparison with Sargent's competing work (#232), see below.

232. Sargent, Lyman Tower. **British and American Utopian Literature, 1516-1975: An Annotated Bibliography**. Boston, G. K. Hall & Co., 1979. xxvi, 324 p. index. (A Reference Publication in Science Fiction). LC 78-11086. ISBN 0-8161-8243-4. **British and American Utopian Literature, 1516-1986: An Annotated, Chronological Bibliography**. New York

& London, Garland Publishing Co., 1988. xix, 559 p. index. (Garland Reference Library of the Humanities, Vol. 831). LC 88-2546. ISBN 0-8240-0694-1.

These two volumes represent the development of a continuing bibliography on English-language utopian literature. Sargent's books are arranged chronologically by year of publication, then alphabetically by author name, then by title. A typical entry includes year of publication, author's name, title, place of publication, publisher (but no paginations), library location symbols, and a one-line annotation (e.g., "machine dystopia," "aliens bring eutopia to earth through conscience gas," "communist takeover of the U.S."). Sargent also includes short fiction, listing year, author, title (in quotes), magazine title, volume and issue numbers, month and year of publication, and specific pagination. Similar data are presented for all known reprints in English. Short stories appearing originally in anthologies give year, author, title (quotes), anthology title, editors, place of publication, publisher, and specific pagination. Materials are filed under the authors' real names, with both names being referenced in the author index. The author index correlates authors with titles and years of publication; the title index lists titles, author surnames, and years.

There are major differences between the two editions: the original version provides a 124-page bibliography, "Secondary Sources on Utopian Literature," subdivided into three sections, "Books," "Articles," and "Unpublished Materials" (usually dissertations). Each section is arranged alphabetically by author's name, then by title. A typical book entry includes author's name (boldfaced), title (italics), place of publication, publisher, year of publication, but no paginations. The "Articles" section provides author (boldfaced), title (in quotes), magazine title (italics), volume number, month and year of publication, and pagination. The third part of the secondary sources bibliography lists author (boldfaced), title (in quotes), and description (usually the name of the university and year the thesis was approved). All of these materials were dropped from the second edition, an extremely unfortunate choice. Also, this is the first time this critic has encountered a revised version of a reference work from a major publisher in which the production qualities have significantly declined. The first edition is attractively typeset and designed; the Garland version is shot from much less readable typed copy; both books are bound to library standards.

Negley's utopian bibliography (see #231) includes foreign-language utopias, while Sargent only lists English-language materials (many [but not all] of the foreign works were translated into English, however). Sargent's work is much more current, the second edition extending the data base through 1985; the latest book in Negley is dated 1963, and his bibliography contains very few works published after 1949 (forty-five monographs), while Sargent lists hundreds. Negley also appears to use a much more restrictive definition of "utopia" than Sargent, thereby limiting his scope to more traditionally accepted forms, while Sargent includes "dystopias" and many other somewhat peripheral items. Sargent also includes short fiction, while Negley restricts his coverage to monographs. Finally, Sargent provides at least a brief annotation, while Negley has no indication of content other than the title. *British and American Utopian Literature* includes roughly 1,650 records published through 1975 in the 1979 version, and approximately 2,580 in the 1988 edition. All three books will be needed by utopian scholars; this includes Sargent's first edition, which possesses a vital secondary sources index not found in any other source.

The guide to secondary materials should be restored with any third edition, or, if this is not possible, should be updated and separately published. The addition of paginations to the bibliographical data would also be appreciated. If a choice must be made, libraries should prefer Sargent's second edition.

VAMPIRE FICTION

233. Carter, Margaret L. **The Vampire in Literature: A Critical Bibliography**. Ann Arbor, Mich. & London, UMI Research Press, 1989. viii, 135 p. index. (Studies in Speculative Fiction, No. 21). LC 89-31932. ISBN 0-8357-1998-7. **Vampire Bibliography Annual Update No. 1 (January, 1990)**. Annapolis, Md., [Margaret L. Carter]. 1990. 18 p. (pbk.). **Vampire Bibliography Annual Update No. 2 (January, 1991)**. Annapolis, Md., [Margaret L. Carter]. 1991. 30 p. (pbk.).

The lowly vampire continues to exert an uncanny influence on modern readers, filmgoers, and scholars, resulting in the publication of no less than three bibliographies on vampire fiction within the past decade.

Carter's guide is both a critical introduction to vampiric literature and a bibliography of primary and secondary sources. Chapter One, "The Study of Vampirism in Literature," examines and evaluates in narrative form the major critical and bibliographical studies of the literature (both essays and monographs). The second chapter, "The Vampire in Legend, Lore, and Literature," contributed by Dr. Devendra P. Varma (a well-known expert on the gothic revival) discusses the folklore of vampirism and major early literary contributions. Chapter Three, "An Anatomy of Vampirism," delineates the major physical characteristics of fictional vampires as revealed in some of their fictional depictions. These narrative chapters occupy forty-four pages of text.

The remainder of the book (eighty-eight pages) contains the bibliography, broken into the following sections: "Chapter 4. Key to Annotations"; "5. Vampire Fiction in English"; "6. Anthologies of Vampire Fiction and Verse"; "7. Non-English Vampire Fiction in Translation"; "8. Dramatic Works on Vampires in English"; "9. Nonfiction: Books"; "10. Nonfiction: Articles." In each section, materials are arranged alphabetically by author's name, then by title. A typical novel entry includes author, title (italics), place of publication, publisher, year of publication (but no paginations) and subject code(s). A typical short fiction entry includes author, title (quotes), magazine title (italics), volume and issue number, month and year of publication (but no paginations), and subject code(s). A short fiction piece appearing originally in a collection or anthology also lists title of the book (italics), author or editor, place of publication, publisher, and year of publication, but no paginations. First appearances only are noted. The subject codes, delineated in Chapter 4, analyze the stories into very specific categories (e.g., "Rob"=robot, android, or cyborg vampire; "Pl"=blood-drinking or energy-draining plant); more than one code may be attached to a particular item. The anthologies are arranged in alphabetical order by editor's name, then by title, and typically include editor, title (italics), place of publication, publisher, year of publication, but no paginations or attempts at coding.

Chapter 7, on translations, similarly does not attempt to code the entries but does try to provide the original foreign-language title (and original publication data), where known, in addition to the first known translation into English. The "Drama" section lists plays in alphabetical order by playwright, then by title, with similar publication data and subject codes. The two chapters on secondary sources are arranged similarly to the fiction sections and provide the same kinds of data (except that Chapter 10 does include paginations), without coding. The index covers the narrative chapters only; astonishingly, there is no title index (however, a separately printed title index is available from the author). Roughly 1,150 titles are listed in the forty-eight-page main bibliography (Chapter 5); perhaps a third of these are short stories. Fifty-four secondary monographs are listed in Chapter 9, and seventy-nine articles in Chapter 10. The book is attractively typeset and bound to library standards.

Carter's bibliography on vampire literature is the most complete and current available; the self-produced annual supplements (beginning in 1990) are organized similarly to the original and will eventually be subsumed into future cumulations. Any such second edition should include an author/title index, paginations for all bibliographical citations, and a record of all known reprints for stories and novels alike. Until then, *The Vampire in Literature* will prove to be a necessary starting point for all scholars interested in these most fascinating of fictional creatures. Compare with Riccardo's *Vampires Unearthed* (see #235).

234. Cox, Greg. **The Transylvanian Library: A Consumer's Guide to Vampire Fiction**. San Bernardino, Calif., The Borgo Press, 1992. [256] p. index. (Borgo Literary Guides, No. 8). LC 88-36553. ISBN 0-89370-335-4; ISBN 0-89370-435-0 (pbk.).

This comprehensive annotated guide to vampire fiction arranges materials chronologically by year of publication, then alphabetically by author. A typical entry includes item number, author, title (italics), place of publication, publisher, year of publication, pagination, and a lengthy annotation. The summaries range in size from 50-1,500 words, averaging 300, and are light, pithy, and heavily opinionated, filled with witticisms and comparisons to other novels or stories. All items are rated at the end of each entry on a scale from "one bat" to "four bats," four being best. Monographs and short fictions are interfiled without distinction except for the bibliographical data; all entries are numbered consecutively throughout the text from the number one. Roughly 350 fictions are described, evaluated, and rated. End matter includes "Appendix I: The Un-Read" (items not viewed by Cox); "Appendix II: The Blood Countess on Film"; "Bibliography of Works Consulted"; "Author Index"; "Title Index." The indexes refer the user to item numbers only.

Cox provides the first extended examination of individual vampire fictions, and his work is sure to be welcomed by scholars and fans alike. While not as comprehensive as Carter's bibliography (see #233), *The Transylvanian Library* does cover all the major (and many minor) works and includes paginations which Carter's guide lacks. Since the books complement each other, researchers should have access to both.

235. Riccardo, Martin V. **Vampires Unearthed: The Complete Multi-Media Vampire and Dracula Bibliography**. New York & London, Garland Publishing, 1983. viii, 135 p. index. (The Unexplained, the Mysterious, and the Supernatural, Vol. 2) (Garland Reference Library of Social Science, Vol. 177). LC 82-49261. ISBN 0-8240-9128-0.

Riccardo attempts to record all known references to vampires in "Fiction" (Section One), "Dramatic Media and Performing Arts" (Section Two), "Nonfiction" (Section Three), and "Journals and Clubs" (Section Four).

Each of the four major sections are further subdivided into chapters: Section One: "1. Vampire Anthologies"; "2. *Dracula*," by Bram Stoker; "3. Vampire Novels in a Series"; "4. Vampire Novels"; "5. Short Stories of Vampires"; "6. "Children's Literature on Vampires"; "7. Vampires in Comic Books." Section Two: "8. Written Works on Vampires in the Dramatic Media: Movies, Theater, and Television"; "9. American Television Series with a Vampire"; "10. Vampire Plays"; "11. Vampire Movies"; "12. Vampire Records and Recordings"; "13. Vampire Poetry and Songs." Section Three: "14. General Nonfiction Works on the Vampire Mythos"; "15. The Vampire as an Unearthly Reality"; "16. Human Blood-Drinking (Hematomania)"; "17. Vlad Tepes, the Historical Dracula"; "18. Biographies of Figures Connected with Vampirism"; "19. Vampire Bats"; "20. Vampire Jokes and Humor"; "21. Vampire Cookbooks"; "22. Other Miscellaneous Vampire Material." Section Four: "23. Magazines and Periodicals with Vampire Material"; "24. Clubs and Organizations with Interests in Vampires"; "25. Sources for Further Research."

Most sections are organized alphabetically by author, then by title. A typical book entry includes item number, title (italics), place of publication, publisher, year of publication, paginations (lacking for some paperback entries), format (e.g., "p"=paperback), and similar data on known reprints. A typical shorter work entry gives item number, author, title (quotes), magazine title (italics), issue number (irregularly), month and year of publication, but no paginations; stories and essays first appearing in collections or anthologies give, in addition to the first three elements, editor's name, title (italics), place of publication, publisher, year of publication, and total page count for the book (but not of the individual piece). Items are numbered consecutively throughout the book from 1 to 1,116. The movie listings are arranged alphabetically by title and include item number, title (italics), director's name, nationality, year of production, principal characters and the actors who play them. Three indexes, "Alternate and Foreign Film Titles," an authors and editors index, and a very brief one-page guide to selected subjects and characters, all referenced to item numbers, complete the book. There is, however, no overall author/title index. The book is shot from legible typed copy and bound to library standards.

Riccardo's scope is much larger than Carter's (see #233), including film media and nonfiction works on vampire folklore, but he records (proportionately) far fewer items. Carter focuses specifically on vampires as literary characters, including works published through 1988; Riccardo lists titles with dates as late as 1982. Riccardo lists 106 vampire novels, plus another sixty-four novels in series, 172 short stories, and twenty-three juvenile pieces, for a total of 365 fictional works; Carter lists some 1,150 items in the same categories, and while some small measure of the increase is due to another six years of data, such a wide variation suggests to even the most casual observer that Carter has cast a much wider net. Also, Carter's listings are subject coded, providing such assistance to the researcher. However, Riccardo does include monographic paginations (which Carter's book lacks) and much data on peripheral vampiric infestations outside of Carter's scope. Both books will therefore be required for most library collections.

WOMEN WRITERS

236. Schlobin, Roger C. **Urania's Daughters: A Checklist of Women Science-Fiction Writers, 1692-1982**. Mercer Island, Wash., Starmont House, 1983. xiii, 79 p. index. (Starmont Reference Guide, No. 1). LC 83-2467. ISBN 0-916732-57-6; ISBN 0-916732-56-8 (pbk.).

Well-known critic Schlobin, past editor of the Starmont Reader's Guide series of critical monographs, here contributes a generally sound guide to science fiction and fantasy novels and story collections produced by female writers. The basic arrangement of the book is alphabetical by author surname, then by title. A typical entry includes author (boldfaced), title (underlined), place of publication, publisher, year of publication, but no paginations. Series entries under each author are listed in descending chronological order under the boldfaced series title. The title index gives titles and author surnames only. Authors are listed under their legal names; a "Directory of Pseudonyms, Joint Authors, and Variant Names" at the front of the book refers the user to the proper heading. The book is shot from legible word-processed copy.

Schlobin's bibliography seems reasonably complete for its period; most of the roughly 950 titles included were published in the modern period (since World War II), and no obvious omissions have been spotted by this critic. Any future edition should consider the addition of paginations, brief biographical details on the writers (at least years of birth and death), and a more complete title index. Even in this somewhat skeletal form, *Urania's Daughters* should prove a useful starting point for scholars interested in researching the influence of women writers on modern fantastic literature or on modern American literature in general. Compare with Yntema (see #49).

PUBLISHER BIBLIOGRAPHIES

SCOPE NOTE: This section includes bibliographies which delineate the science-fiction publications of one specific publishing company or works which focus on a group of SF specialty houses. Excluded are publishers' stock lists or catalogs. Additional information on SF publishers and their books may be found in such works as Nicholls's *The Science Fiction Encyclopedia* (see #7), Tuck's *The Encyclopedia of Science Fiction and Fantasy* (which includes dozens of SF paperback lists arranged by publisher, year of publication, and stock number; see #10), the many general bibliographies of science fiction and fantasy included herein, Reginald and Burgess's *Cumulative Paperback Index, 1939-1959*, and Hancer and Reginald's *The Paperback Price Guide* (now in its third edition).

GENERAL WORKS

237. Owings, Mark, and Jack L. Chalker. **Index to the Science Fantasy Publishers**. Baltimore, Md., The Anthem Series, 1966. 78 p. (pbk.). **The Index to the Science-Fantasy Publishers: A Bibliography of the Science Fiction and Fantasy Specialty Houses**. 2nd ed. Baltimore, Md., The Anthem Series, 1966. viii, 74 p. cloth and pbk. **The Science Fantasy Publishers: A Critical and Bibliographic History**. 3d ed. Westminster, Md., Mirage Press, 1991. xxviii, 744 p. index. ISBN 0-88358-204-X. The first printing [edition] was rejected, and very few copies were actually circulated.

Owings and Chalker compiled this bibliography as a guide to the SF specialty publishers which began with Arkham House in 1939 and which rapidly expanded following World War II to produce cloth editions of publications which had previously only been available in magazine form. Most of these publishers were forced out of business by the mid-1950s by the entrance of the large New York-based trade publishers into the regular production of science-fiction novels.

The basic arrangement of the book is alphabetical by publisher, then chronological by date of production. A typical publisher entry includes a one-paragraph historical survey of the house, with a list of the principals and dates of founding and cessation. A typical book entry gives title (all caps), author, year of publication, pagination, price, number of copies printed, brief (one-sentence) annotation, status (e.g., "O.P."=out of print, used for most entries), jacket and/or interior illustrator. To qualify for inclusion, the publisher had to have issued at least one cloth volume and to have specialized only in fantastic literature. End matter includes a two-page section on "The Almost-Ran," houses which failed before they even began; "Cross-Index," correlating authors, titles, and page numbers; "Appendix A: Geographic Breakdown" [of publishers]; "Appendix B: Numbers of books published by each publisher." There is no title index. The book was shot from typed copy and the paper editions (the bulk of the print run) stapled through the side.

The Index to the Science-Fantasy Publishers has been criticized for occasional historical or bibliographical inaccuracies and for a number of outright errors; for example, some of the data on total copies printed for each book were apparently estimated from the imperfect recollections of surviving staff members of the companies involved and have been demonstrated in individual cases to have been skewed far below or above the actual printings; moreover, printing figures may be deceptive, since in some cases not all copies printed were actually bound and distributed. Still, in the absence of any other guide to these influential publishers, Owings and Chalker's work will have to do. Portions of a third edition were serialized in *Fantasy Review* in the mid-1980s, then cumulated in book form at the end of 1991 amid much controversy over the editors' statements and assertions.

BIBLIOGRAPHIES OF INDIVIDUAL PUBLISHERS

Ace Books

238. Corrick, James A. **Double Your Pleasure: The Ace SF Double**. Brooklyn, N.Y., Gryphon Books, 1989. 85 p. index. ISBN 0-936071-13-3 (pbk.).

Well-known paperback historian Corrick here focuses specifically on the Ace Doubles, a publishing gimmick developed by Ace in 1952, in which two separate category novels (usually by different writers) were bound upside down to each other, with two covers. The first SF Double was published in 1953, the last original title in 1973, almost twenty years later. Corrick provides a brief historical introduction to the series, then lists the books in chronological order by publication date. A typical entry includes Ace stock number, month and year of publication, first book title (all caps), author, second novel title (all caps), second novel author, cover artist, and a summary of all known previous (magazine serializations and cloth publications) and subsequent printings of the books in English. No paginations are given. There are separate author and title indexes, both referring the user to Ace stock numbers. The book is shot from generally clear type and illustrated throughout with partial and full-page illustrations from the book covers. This is the best single guide to the Ace SF Doubles yet published; a second printing would benefit from better typography and a more professional appearance.

239. Dillon, Peter C. **An Ace Alpha-Numeric Annotated Science Fiction Checklist**. Richmond, Calif., Peter C. Dillon, 1973. 29 p. (pbk.).

Dillon lists Ace SF double and single novels through the early 1970s, in order by stock number with a separate record of the Edgar Rice Burroughs reprints published by Ace in the 1960s. A typical entry includes stock number, title, author (surname only), year of publication, former title (in parentheses), plus any previous magazine serialization (with months and years of original publication and a two- to four-letter abbreviation for the periodical; the abbreviations list appears at the end of the book. This amateurishly produced volume is shot from legible typed copy. However, the absence of full author names, paginations, exact months of issues, and indexes of any kind severely limit the usefulness of this index.

240. Massoglia, Marty. **Checklist of Ace SF Through 1968**. East Lansing, Mich., Marty Massoglia, 1969 (?). 11 leaves. (pbk.).

Ace Books seems to have attracted more amateur bibliographers than any other publishing line. This checklist lists Ace SF books in numerical order by price series and stock number. A typical entry includes year of publication (e.g., "55"=1955), stock number, author's name, title, and references to previous stock numbers under which the volume may have been issued by Ace. An erratum page is tacked on to the end. Poorly edited and produced on faint legal-sized sheets stapled together through the corner. Prefer Corrick (see #238).

241. Robinson, Roger. **Ace Science-Fiction Double Books**. Harold Wood, Essex, Beccon Publications, 1987. 16 p. index. (Beccon Publications Collectors' Checklists). (pbk.).

British fan Robinson provides a simple checklist of the Ace SF Doubles, two books bound upside down to each other, with two separate covers. The books are listed chronologically by publication date and stock number. A typical entry includes stock number, authors' surnames only, and book titles. The author index correlates authors and stock numbers only; there is no title index. The final page of this brief guide also covers three other "double" series: the Belmont Doubles, the Dell Binary Star series, and Galaxy Magabooks. Prefer Corrick's more detailed bibliography (see #238).

242. Spelman, Dick. **Science Fiction and Fantasy Published by Ace Books (1953-1968)**. North Hollywood, Calif., Institute for Specialized Literature, 1976. [ii], 62 p. index. (pbk.).

One of a series of checklists issued by Spelman in the mid-1970s, this particular volume is typical of the lot. The main index organizes Ace's science-fiction and fantasy publications in chronological order by stock number, arranged alphabetically by the letter preceding each number (after 1960 Ace assigned a letter code signifying price to each number; all books with that price and letter code were then numbered in order in a separate series). A typical entry includes stock number, author(s), title(s), a reference to any previous Ace stock numbers, note code (e.g., "*"=Ace Special Edition, "1"=Ace Double Novel, etc.), and year of publication. The author index correlates authors, titles, and stock numbers (more than one for some titles), while the title index provides titles, authors, and numbers. The book is shot from very clear typed copy. Spelman's ignorance of Ace's numbering system is shown by the fact that he lists the handful of novels published in the 1950s with an "S" prefix separately, when in fact they were issued as part of the "D" series. A definitive guide to Ace's science fiction publications has yet to be issued.

Arkham House

243. Derleth, August. **Arkham House: The First Twenty Years, 1939-1959: A History and Bibliography**. Sauk City, Wisc., Arkham House, 1959. liv p. (pbk.). **Thirty Years of Arkham House, 1939-1969: A History and Bibliography**. [2nd ed.]. Sauk City, Wisc., Arkham House, 1970. 99 p., [8] p. of plates. LC 76-121892.

August Derleth founded Arkham House, the oldest continuously operated publishing house specializing in fantastic literature, in 1939 to publish a collection of tales by the late H. P. Lovecraft. During his life Derleth prepared two bibliographies of Arkham's publications, the second building on the first. In both books entries are arranged chronologically by date of publication, with the books of the associated imprints, Mycroft & Moran and Stanton & Lee, being listed separately at the end of each volume. A typical entry includes item number, title (all caps), author, publisher, place of publication, year of publication, pagination, price, number of copies printed, contents (for collections or anthologies), and cover artist. Books are numbered consecutively in order from the number one, separately for each imprint; the 1970 edition lists ninety-eight Arkham House books and fourteen each from the associated imprints. There are no indexes. The books are professionally typeset, and the second edition was bound to library standards in typical black AH cloth. Derleth's sixteen-page introduction to the second edition provides much background and historical details about the founding and maintenance of the imprint and includes eight glossy pages of photographs of Lovecraft, Derleth, and other authors associated with the imprint tipped in to the center of the book. Now supplemented and supplanted by Jaffery (see #244).

244. Jaffery, Sheldon. **Horrors and Unpleasantries: A Bibliographical History & Collectors' Price Guide to Arkham House**. Bowling Green, Ohio, Bowling Green State University Popular Press, 1982. 142 p. LC 82-73849. ISBN 0-87972-219-3; ISBN 0-87972-220-7 (pbk.). **The Arkham House Companion: Fifty Years of Arkham House: A Bibliographical History and Collector's Price Guide to Arkham House/Mycroft & Moran, Including the Revised and Expanded Horrors and Unpleasantries**. [2nd ed.] Mercer Island, Wash., Starmont House, 1989. xv, 184 p. index. (Starmont Reference Guide, No. 9). LC 89-31701. ISBN 1-55742-005-X; ISBN 1-55742-004-1 (pbk.).

Both of these bibliographical guides are organized similarly except that the revised version, in addition to its extended data base, also includes a detailed index.

The basic arrangement of both books is chronologically by publication date, generally following the format established by Derleth in his two bibliographies of Arkham House (see #243). A typical entry includes item number, title (italicized in the original, boldfaced in the second edition), author's name, publisher, place of publication, year of publication, pagination, price, number of copies printed, cover artist, contents, an annotation, and current estimated value on the OP book market. The annotations average 300 words in length and include background information on the authors and their books, bibliographical tidbits, and other ephemera of interest. Items are numbered consecutively throughout the book from 1 to 180. Unlike the Derleth guides, Jaffery interfiles Mycroft & Moran titles with regular Arkham House productions but strangely does not mention the other AH imprint, Stanton & Lee. End matter includes "Appendix I: The Unpublished Titles"; "Appendix II: Sponsored Books"; "Appendix III: Horror Literature Core Collection, Arkham House Entries," taken from Marshall B. Tymn's *Horror Literature* (see #78); "Appendix IV: The Illustrated Lovecraft"; "Author/Title Index," correlating major entry authors and their books with entry numbers; and a very thorough "General Index," also referencing item numbers. The books are shot from very clear word-processed copy; the 1982 version was produced in 5" x 8" format, the 1989 volume in 8.5" x 11" style.

Although Derleth's earlier bibliographies (see #243) do provide some personal and other historical comments of interest by the founder of AH, *The Arkham House Companion* largely replaces those volumes with an authoritative, complete, excellently researched, and very well presented reference guide. Jaffery's work will be of interest to collectors and researchers alike and should be purchased by all major university libraries. Recommended.

245. Spelman, Dick. **Science Fiction and Fantasy Published by Arkham House and Mycroft & Moran (1939-1976)**. North Hollywood, Calif., Institute for Specialized Literature, 1977. 10 leaves. index. (pbk.). Rev. ed. North Hollywood, Calif., Institute for Specialized Literature, 1978. 10 leaves. index. (pbk.).

The final volume in Spelman's publisher checklist series is arranged very similarly to the others. The main part of the book organizes the data by imprint, then alphabetically by author's name and title. A typical entry includes author, title, year of publication, page count, number of copies printed, and price. The title index lists titles, authors, and imprint codes (e.g., "AH" and "MM") only. The book is shot from typed copy. The revised edition adds a few titles but otherwise is the same as the original. Now completely subsumed into Jaffery's much more detailed and complete guide (see #244).

Avalon Books

246. Spelman, Dick. **Science Fiction and Fantasy Published by Avalon Books and Bouregy & Curl**. North Hollywood, Calif., Institute for Specialized Literature, 1977. 10 leaves. index. (pbk.).

One of a series of publisher indexes prepared by SF fan Spelman in the mid-1970s, this brief guide indexes the 136 books produced by Thomas Bouregy & Co. under the imprints Avalon Books (the vast majority of the titles) and the earlier Bouregy & Curl. The main part of the book arranges the data alphabetically by author's name, then by title. A typical entry includes authors, title, date of publication (in the form "12-56" for December 1956), page count, dust jacket artist, and price. The title index lists titles, authors, and imprints only. The book is shot from typed copy. Although this is a very simple checklist, it does include the entire SF output of this collectible imprint and provides a useful guide until a fully annotated list appears.

Ballantine Books

247. Aronovitz, David. **Ballantine Books: The First Decade: A Bibliographical History & Guide of the Publisher's Early Years**. Rochester, Mich., Bailiwick Books, 1987. x, 107 p. index. LC 87-11504. ISBN 0-9618295-0-8.

Although Aronovitz's bibliography is not limited to science-fiction works, the early history of Ballantine Books is so intertwined with the SF genre, and its publications were of such importance to the development of fantastic literature as a *book* category in the 1950s, that this excellent guide to the Ballantine dual editions (simultaneous paper and cloth) will become a necessary adjunct to studies of this most vital period.

The bibliography is arranged alphabetically by author, then by title. A typical entry includes author's name, title (all caps, boldfaced), publisher of the cloth edition (usually Ballantine, but occasionally other houses), year of publication, price of the cloth edition, stock number, but no paginations; some entries also include bibliographical notes. Aronovitz's sixteen-page "Introduction" and "History" provide necessary background data on the development of Ballantine Books between 1952 and 1961 (the period covered by this guide). Two indexes, by genre subject (then alphabetically by main entry) and by publishing imprint (then alphabetically by main entry), both correlating entries with page numbers, complete the volume. The book is attractively typeset, printed in a small 4" x 7" format and bound to library standards. Nicely done, although a complete guide to this major publisher's SF and fantasy publications has yet to be countenanced.

248. Spelman, Dick. **A Preliminary Checklist of Science Fiction and Fantasy Published by Ballantine Books (1953-1974)**. North Hollywood, Calif., Institute for Specialized Literature, 1976. 42 leaves. (pbk.). **A Preliminary Checklist of Science Fiction and Fantasy Published by Ballantine Books (1953-1977)**. [Rev. ed.]. North Hollywood, Calif., Institute for Specialized Literature, 1977. 76 p. index. (pbk.).

Spelman's guide to the SF published by Ballantine Books is arranged chronologically by stock number. A typical entry provides number, edition (e.g., "1st"), author, title, publication date (in the form "12-54" for December 1954), price. The book is shot from sometimes faint typed copy. The first version of this checklist is unindexed. The revised edition extends the data base through February 1977 and includes an author index giving authors, titles, and stock numbers for each Ballantine printing. Prefer Aronovitz's more detailed guide (see #247) for the early years of Ballantine Books; a definitive index to the science fiction and fantasy publications of this important paperback house has yet to be produced.

DAW Books

249. Covell, Ian. **An Index to DAW Books**. Albuquerque, N.M., Galactic Central, 1990. 58 p. index. (Galactic Central Publisher Checklists, Vol. 1). (pbk.).

The main part of this bibliography indexes DAW Books in chronological order by date/stock number, giving stock number, date of publication (in the form "0472" for April 1972, the first month of DAW's publication), DAW book number (in addition to the standard stock number, DAW also assigned each of its releases a consecutive "collectors" number beginning at "1"), price, author, title (all caps). An asterisk before the first stock number signifies an original DAW publication, and a "@" before the author indicates an anthology. Reprints with the same stock numbers are also indicated, with printing information (e.g., "3"=third printing) and the symbols "RP" after the DAW book number. Personal names in quotes are pseudonyms; the handful of titles not assigned individual DAW book numbers are so indicated with the symbol "+++." No paginations are listed. Books are recorded through #781, published in May, 1989. Also included is an author (but no title) index giving author's name, book titles, DAW number, date of issue, and stock number; authors are listed under their real names, with appropriate see references. The final page also includes a brief checklist of the four DAW hardcovers and trade paperbacks issued through mid-1989. The book is shot from very clear word-processed copy. Compare with Jaffery's guide (see #250).

250. Jaffery, Sheldon. **Future and Fantastic Worlds: A Bibliographical Retrospective of DAW Books (1972-1987)**. Mercer Island, Wash., Starmont House, 1987. xiii, 297 p. index. (Starmont Reference Guide, No. 4). LC 87-9901. ISBN 1-55742-003-3; ISBN 1-55742-002-5 (pbk.).

DAW Books was founded in 1972 by the late editor Donald A. Wollheim (hence the name) as the first exclusive science-fiction paperback house. Well-known critic Jaffery, author of a previous guide to Arkham House publications (see #244) and other reference works, arranges the main part of this guide in chronological order by DAW book number and issue date. A typical entry includes DAW book number (boldfaced), author's name, title (italics), stock number, edition and printing data, month and year of publication, pagination, cover artist, price, mentions of previous or subsequent printings from other publishers, annotation, and series or other bibliographical notes (where appropriate). The annotations are descriptive rather than evaluative, heavily plot oriented, with occasional light, pithy, even flippant comments; entries for collections and anthologies include complete contents listings. Items are included through #707, published in May 1987. The book is shot from very clean word-processed copy and attractively printed and laid out.

Jaffery has produced another definitive and very useful publisher bibliography, one which should be maintained with future supplements or newly updated editions. All major research libraries should acquire this book.

251. Robinson, Roger. **DAW Science-Fiction Books**. Harold Wood, Essex, Beccon Publications, 1987. 20 p. index. (Beccon Publications Collectors' Checklist). (pbk.).

One of a series of checklists produced by British fan Robinson, this booklet indexes DAW Books in chronological order by issue date and book number. A typical entry includes DAW book number, author, and title, but no other bibliographical data (including publication dates). Books are listed through #710 (1987); the fifteen Cap Kennedy novels, which were not numbered in the main sequence, are listed after the principal bibliography and numbered from CK1-CK15. The index correlates authors and book numbers only; there is no title index. The guide is shot from legible word-processed copy. Prefer Jaffery's definitive bibliography (see #250).

Editrice Nord

252. Editrice Nord. **Editrice Nord: Quindici Anni di Fantascienza in Italia: Catalogo Ragionato delle Opere Pubblicate Fino al Dicembre 1985**. Milano, Editrice Nord, 1985. [116] p. index. (pbk.).

One of the larger popular publishing houses in Italy, Editrice Nord issued this bibliographical catalog to celebrate the fifteenth anniversary of its SF program. The book is arranged by publishing series and number. Each section includes a précis of the series as a whole, its intent and content. An individual book entry gives series code and number (e.g., "CA1"=volume one of the Cosmo Collana di Fantascienza series), title (bold caps), author (boldfaced), and a hundred-word plot summary of the book. There are occasional see references at the end of some entries to other works of interest, but most of the bibliographic data are included in the detailed author index, which is almost a separate guide in itself. A typical index entry gives author (bold caps), title (small bold caps), original title (if a translation), date and place of original publication, series number, month and year of publication by Editrice Nord, translator, and a list of awards (American and Italian) the work has received, but no paginations. The book is nicely typeset. Information on European translations of English-language SF (which constitute the majority of entries here) is always hard to find; bibliographers will welcome this catalog and hope that other companies will follow suit.

Robert Hale Ltd.

253. Robinson, Roger. **Hale & Gresham Hardback Science Fiction**. Harold Wood, Essex, Beccon Publications, 1988. 16 p. index. (Beccon Publications Collectors' Checklist). (pbk.).

Robert Hale Ltd. published (and still publishes) several series of category novels for the public library market in Great Britain, including a lengthy SF line produced between 1968 and 1982. Many of these books were original publications featuring authors not well known in the United States. This booklet indexes the "Hale SF" line alphabetically by author, then by title. A typical entry provides author's name (all caps), year of publication, and title. Also included are a pseudonym guide and a brief addendum. The pamphlet is shot from legible word-processed copy and stapled through the spine. This is the latest of the four collectors' guides produced by British fan Robinson.

Morrigan Press/Kerosina Press

254. Stephens, Christopher P. **A Checklist of Morrigan Press and Kerosina Press**. Hastings-on-Hudson, N.Y., Ultramarine Publishing Co., 1991. 18 p. index. ISBN 0-89366-165-1 (pbk.).

One of a series of checklists by Stephens on collectible publishing houses (see also #255 and #259), including four bibliographies on publishers not associated with the SF field, this new guide is broken into two sections corresponding to the imprints covered. In each section materials are arranged by publication date. A typical entry includes year of publication (as a running head), item number, author (surname in all caps), title (underlined), pagination, number of copies issued, description of binding, price, and similar data on all known variant issues. Materials are numbered from 1 to 8 (Morrigan) and 1 to 14 (Kerosina); variant editions are numbered, for example, 2b, 2c, 2d, etc. The index correlates authors/titles to years of publication, not item numbers. The booklet is shot from very legible typed copy and bound with staples into stiff paper covers. Although these two British imprints are not well known in the United States, the quality of their lists makes them future targets for the collectibles market.

Phantasia Press

255. Stephens, Christopher P. **A Checklist of Phantasia Press**. Hastings-on-Hudson, N.Y., Ultramarine Publishing Co., 1991. 19 p. index. ISBN 0-89366-201-1 (pbk.).

Phantasia Press has become one of the more collectible SF specialty publishing houses since its inception in 1978. Stephens's bibliography lists Phantasia's forty-nine books chronologically by publication date in entries numbered from 1-49. A typical entry includes year of publication (as a running head), item number, author (surname in all caps), title (underlined), series, number of copies issued, pagination, description of binding, cover illustrator, price, and similar data for all known variant issues (which are numbered, for example, 16b, 16c, 16d, etc.). The index correlates authors and titles (in one alphabet) to years of publication, not to item numbers. The book is shot from typed copy and bound with staples into stiff paper covers. Collectors will appreciate this succinct and well-organized guide. Future editions should reference index entries to the existing item numbers; an introduction giving a brief history of Phantasia Press, its styles and practices, would also be useful to the target audience.

Soft Books

256. Bell, Joseph. **Soft Book Publications: First Five Years, 1981-1986**. Toronto, Canada, Soft Books, 1986. 7 p. (pbk.).

This small Canadian house, the publishing arm of Bell's O.P. bookselling operation, specializes in producing books, pamphlets, and broadsides relating to the modern horror genre. Bell's brief checklist lists twenty-one items in chronological order by publication date. A typical entry includes item number, title (boldfaced), publisher's address, pagination, physical size, binding style, cover style, paper color, limitation notice, in-print status (with month and year when the book went out-of-print, if it did), series note, price, month and year of publication (boldfaced), and a complete contents listing, with bibliographical notes. Of interest primarily to collectors of modern horror fiction.

John Spencer & Co.

257. Ashley, Michael. **A Complete Index and Annotated Commentary to the John Spencer Fantasy Publications (1950-66)**. Wallsend, England, Cosmos Literary Agency, 1979. 54 p. index. (Fantasy Readers Guide, No. 1). (pbk.). Cover title.

John Spencer & Co. Ltd. produced several series of paperbound genre books during the two-decade period from 1950 to 1970, including both science fiction and supernatural horror short stories and novels. Among their publications were several supposed magazines that were actually collections penned by one writer per issue contributing stories under a variety of pseudonyms; two writers, Robert Lionel Fanthorpe and John Glasby, produced 95% of this publisher's SF and horror paperbacks between 1958 and 1967, when the last "issue" of *Supernatural Stories* appeared. Well-known bibliographer and literary historian

Ashley provides a brief history of Spencer and then lists each series and "magazine" in chronological order by series number and publication date. A typical entry gives series number, month and year of publication, book title (all caps) and author (for monographs), and complete contents and authors (for magazine issues). There are also brief guides to books reprinted by other publishers and to story series. The author index gives authors, titles, and book numbers, together with brief biographies of the principals. Ashley also provides a brief statistical chart and more extended biographies of Fanthorpe and Glasby, plus sample stories by E. C. Tubb and John Glasby. Reproduced from typed copy. This should be the last word on the subject.

Roy A. Squires

258. Squires, Roy A. **The Private Press of Roy A. Squires: A Checklist of Imprints**. Glendale, Calif., [Roy A. Squires], 1970. [4] p. (pbk.). **The Private Press of Roy A. Squires: A Descriptive Listing of Publications, 1962-1979**. [2nd ed.]. Glendale, Calif., [Roy A. Squires], 1987. [24] p. LC 88-113413 (pbk.).

The late Roy Squires was a well-known California collector and book dealer who in his spare time served as publisher and proprietor of the SF field's only true modern private press. In a shed in his back yard, Squires would spend hundreds of hours carefully hand setting the type for his distinctive booklets of poetry and prose, imprinting each sheet individually, then tying copies together with his distinctive flair and often housing them in specially imprinted envelopes. Squires's authors included Ray Bradbury, Clark Ashton Smith, H. P. Lovecraft (previously unpublished letters and poems), and many others. Un-usually, none of his books bore an imprint of any kind, only a place of publication (Glendale, California) on the bottom of each title page. Squires printed his first booklet in December 1960 in an edition of ninety-six copies; few of his publications ever reached runs higher than 300 copies, and none, of course, were ever reprinted, since the type was reused and reset after each series of impressions was finished. His booklets have been highly collectible from their first issue and will continue to appreciate in value as bibliophiles everywhere appreciate the care with which they were prepared.

The first of these checklists lists each of the works in order of publication. A typical entry includes item number (the materials are numbered consecutively from 1 to 30, number 30 being the bibliography itself), title (small caps), author, date of publication, number of copies produced. There is no index. The second version is believed to be the last work produced from Squires's press, printed long after the publisher had ceased to print works regularly. The format is identical to that of the original guide. No indexes are provided. These lists will themselves become collectors' items, having been produced and typeset to the same high standards as the rest of the printer's publications. What a shame we will see no more.

Tor Books

259. Stephens, Christopher P. **A Checklist of the Tor Doubles**. Hastings-on-Hudson, N.Y., Ultramarine Publishing Co., 1991. 18 p. index. ISBN 0-89366-194-5 (pbk.).

Like Ace Books before it, Tor began issuing a series of "double books" in 1988 (with a preliminary volume published in 1985), packaging the stories back-to-back and upside down to each other. Stephens lists the books in order by series number and year, giving the following information: year (as a running head), series number, author (surname in all caps), title (underlined), pagination, previous publication particulars, cover artist, plus similar data on the second short novel, and price. Discrepancies in the series numbering are also noted. The author/title index correlates each with series number. The pamphlet is shot from typed copy and stapled into stiff paper covers. This is a handy short guide to a popular publisher's series, one which fans and collectors will appreciate.

AUTHOR BIBLIOGRAPHIES

SCOPE NOTE: This section includes bibliographies of one author published in one monograph, or up to three authors where all of the authors covered are mentioned in the book title, and where each of the writers is covered individually within the book in his or her own section. Arrangement is by name of the author being covered. Bibliographies published in magazine format are included only where an entire issue of the journal consists of the bibliography of one author. Other potential sources for bibliographical data on science fiction and fantasy authors include author directories, encyclopedias, readers' guides, general bibliographies on fantastic literature or any of its many subgenres, and critical monographs about one or more SF authors. At the beginning of this section are listed series of author bibliographies consisting of at least five published volumes packaged under a common series title with standardized formats. Books included in these series are also covered individually.

BIBLIOGRAPHY SERIES

260. Bibliographies of Modern Authors. Boden Clarke, Series Editor. San Bernardino, Calif., The Borgo Press, 1984-DATE. 28 v. indexed. cloth and pbk. ISSN 0749-470X.

The intent of this series is to provide complete, comprehensive, current guides to the authors' lives and works. The books are designed to be upgraded into new editions every three to five years for active writers. Paginations range in size from 60 to 500 pages in 5.5" x 8.5" format, prices for the library cloth editions varying from $20-$50 each, with the trade paperback versions running $10.00 less per book depending on page count (most of the recent releases have averaged between 100 and 200 pages in length and have cost between $20-$30 each in cloth). The volumes are edited to strict series guidelines, and the series editor is directly and intensively involved in the preparation of individual monographs, sometimes adding data or reworking the manuscripts.

Thus, each work in the series closely resembles the others in format. Each author's works are divided into separate subject categories, the first of which is always Chapter A., the writer's "Books." Subsequent sections may include (in this order): "Short Fiction," "Short Nonfiction," "Poetry," "Drama, "Editorial Credits," "Other Media," "Screenplays," "Teleplays," "Radio Plays," "Unpublished Works," "Interviews, Secondary Sources," "Miscellanea," "Quoth the Critics" (selected critical opinions on the author's work), "Title Index," with additional chapters being generated as necessary to fit each writer's interests. Works in each section are listed chronologically, from the earliest to the latest, and numbered consecutively item by item, beginning at the number one and continuing to the end of each chapter; since each section is assigned a key letter in alphabetical order, the author's books will always be numbered "A1," "A2," "A3," etc., in publication order, his short stories "B1," "B2," etc., and so forth. Complete bibliographical data are provided, both for the primary edition and all known reprints, new editions, or anthologizations, including foreign-language publications. Annotations are provided for all books and any other noteworthy stories or materials.

There are two distinct stylistic periods in the development of this series. The first series, running from 1984 to 1987, originated the basic series format, but the absence of line breaks combined with the somewhat primitive computer-generated printout make some entries hard to read or find on the rather crowded pages. Beginning with *The Work of William F. Nolan* (October 1988), the basic format was upgraded to include lists of book reviews on individual monographs, and the overall internal and external design of the volumes was improved with the interpolation of line breaks and the use of near typeset quality (laser printer-generated) copy. All recent volumes also include detailed biographical chronologies and critical introductions and many have afterwords by or interviews with the authors themselves commenting on their lives and careers. The books are largely unillustrated, the bibliography on Nolan being the one exception (it included eight pages of cover reproductions). The cloth editions are bound to library standards. The first of the second editions of previously published works in the series appeared in late 1990 with the publication of revised bibliographies on George Zebrowski and Charles Beaumont; both of these volumes were extensively upgraded, the page count virtually doubling in size from the earlier versions.

This is by far the most comprehensive and current series of author bibliographies being produced in the genre today; it should be noted, however, that 1) these are *literary*, not collectors', guides, and they do not generally provide first edition points, descriptions of bindings, or signature collations; and 2) the series is not *per se* limited to science fiction and fantasy, although most of the books published to date have been on authors at least peripherally associated with fantastic literature.

261. Drumm Bibliographies. Chris Drumm, Series Editor. Polk City, Ia., Chris Drumm Books, 1983-DATE. 8 v. indexed. (pbk.).

These very basic chronological checklists of science fiction and fantasy authors, most of them written by Drumm himself, are primarily intended for a fan audience. Materials are organized chronologically by publication year, all of the author's works being interfiled into one straightforward list. Some bibliographical data are provided, plus an index keyed to title and page number. The books range in size from 8 to 63 pages (averaging 30 p.) and sell for $1.50-$4.00 each in 4" x 7" stapled paperback editions. The earlier books in the series were shot from somewhat primitive typed copy; later volumes have much more legible laser-generated text. These are skeleton guides to the authors' work only; secondary materials are mentioned only in the most recent books in the series.

262. Galactic Central Bibliographies for the Avid Reader. Gordon Benson, Jr. and Phil Stephensen-Payne, Series Editors (and publishers). Albuquerque, N.M., and Leeds, England, Galactic Central Publications, 1982-DATE. 40 v. ISSN 1049-6386 (pbk.).

This long series of copublished author checklists has been produced in two distinct styles. The earlier editions were shot from very cramped typed copy, with text tightly compressed into a small number of pages and often extending into the inner and outer margins, making many of the books difficult to read and use and (for libraries) impossible to rebind without losing text. Beginning in 1989, the books were progressively reworked as newer editions and volumes were released, by increasing the use of line breaks, white space, and margins and by using clearer and more legible word-processed copy as opposed to typed text; this has resulted in longer, roomier bibliographies, much more pleasing to the eye, with some attempt in the British-generated editions (constructed by Stephensen-Payne) to add secondary sources and other peripheral data. Also added was a nine-page standardized series introduction, identical in each book, providing a guide to the series format, section by section, and listing a two-page bibliography of works consulted.

The basic arrangement of these books is alphabetical by title, the author's works being broken into specific subject sections; these have been standardized in the revised format to the following sections: "A. Stories"; "B. Fiction Books"; "C. Series"; "D. Poems, Songs, and Plays"; "E. Poem, Song, and Play Volumes"; "F. Articles"; "G. Miscellaneous";

"H. Non-Fiction Books"; "I. Books and Magazines Edited"; "J. Media Presentations"; "K. Articles on [the author]"; "L. Reviews"; "M. Books About [the author]"; "N. Phantom and Forthcoming Titles"; "O. Related Books by Other Authors"; "P. Textual Variations"; "Q. Chronological Index." The volumes lack title indexes. The earlier books range in size from 5 to 50 pages, the later editions from 10 to 150 pages, the latter being priced at $2.00-$15.00 each in an 8.5" x 11" stapled paperback format. Each biblio is updated at least biennially (sometimes more frequently). This series includes about the same level of material as the Drumm Booklets, in somewhat greater bibliographical detail, but the books do not attempt to approach the depth of the Bibliographies of Modern Authors (see #260) or Masters of Science Fiction and Fantasy (see #263) series. Although intended primarily for the fan market, these checklists still provide concise and up-to-date starting points for scholars and researchers interested in the work of the authors in question. Note: only the latest editions of these frequently revised bibliographies are covered herein.

263. Masters of Science Fiction and Fantasy. L. W. Currey, Series Editor. Boston, G. K. Hall & Co., 1980-84. 14 v. cloth.

This excellent series of fourteen bibliographies on eighteen writers (two of the books cover three writers each, in separate sections) was edited by a well-known SF bibliographer and O.P. book dealer who extensively reworked (and added material to) many of the books. Each volume is divided into four sections: "A. Fiction"; "B. Miscellaneous Media"; "C. Nonfiction"; "D. Critical Studies," with comprehensive indexes keyed to title and item number. Materials are arranged chronologically, from the earliest publication to the latest, and each work is numbered by chapter and item in the same manner as the Bibliographies of Modern Authors series (see #260), except that a couple of the books also number reprints of the writer's monographs in the same sequence as the rest. Many of the volumes also include excellent extensive biocritical introductions to the writer's work. Physically, the books range in size from 100 to 400 pages, in 5.5" x 8.5" or 6" x 9" cloth format, selling for $20-$60 each; most were shot from typed copy with no illustrations and bound to library standards. As with the Borgo series, these were literary guides and did not include first-edition points. The Masters series was well edited and soundly based, by far the best set of SF bibliographies published through the mid-1980s, covering many of the classic SF authors; the individual volumes contain few factual errors, are current through the late 1970s, and provide much useful information on the authors' lives and works. However, no more books will be published in the series, and those which were released are now gradually going out-of-print and out-of-date.

264. Ultramarine Checklists. Christopher P. Stephens, Editor. Hastings-on-Hudson, N.Y., Ultramarine Publishing Co., Inc., 1987 (?)-DATE. 20 v. (pbk.).

Stephens has authored or co-authored all of the books in this continuing series of author checklists, of which fifteen have been compiled on science-fiction authors and another half dozen on other writers. All of the books follow the same basic format, materials being organized in chronological order by publication date and numbered anew from the number one in each section. Complete bibliographical data are provided for all English-language editions and printings of the author's monographs, and similar data for the short works (except that Stephens does not include paginations for any of the shorter work entries). A brief index at the end of each volume correlates titles and years of publication only. The books are all shot from typed or word-processed copy and bound with staples into stiff paper covers. The booklets are frequently updated, approximately once every two years, making them relatively current for the authors covered. These are very basic guides, of use primarily to collectors, but a number of the books cover authors for whom no other bibliography is available.

BIBLIOGRAPHIES OF INDIVIDUAL AUTHORS

Brian W. Aldiss

265. [Aldiss], Margaret Manson. **Item Forty-Three: Brian W. Aldiss: A Bibliography, 1954-1962**. Birmingham, England, Dryden Press, 1962. [24] p. (pbk.). Aldiss, Margaret. **Item Eighty-Three: Brian W. Aldiss: A Bibliography, 1954-1972**. Oxford, England, SF Horizons, 1973. 40 p. LC 79-10344 (pbk.).

This pair of basic checklists of Aldiss's work by his wife are similarly arranged in three sections: "A. Fiction"; "B. Nonfiction and Miscellanea"; "C. Edited Volumes," with materials being organized alphabetically by title in each part. A typical entry includes entry number (List A only, numbered in order); title; description (e.g., "novel," "8 story collection"; the short fiction section includes an estimated word count for each story); publication data (magazine, issue number, and date for short fiction; contents for collections; publisher, city [foreign only], year of publication, and pagination for books); and similar data for all known reprints. It is clear from both of these books that Aldiss has always been exceptionally careful in keeping track of his own work. All of these data except the word counts have been subsumed into Margaret Aldiss's later bibliography (see #266).

266. Aldiss, Margaret. **The Work of Brian W. Aldiss: An Annotated Bibliography & Guide**, by Margaret Aldiss. San Bernardino, Calif., The Borgo Press, 1992. [350] p. index. (Bibliographies of Modern Authors, No. 9). LC 87-746. ISBN 0-89370-388-5; ISBN 0-89370-488-1 (pbk.).

Preliminary guides to this important British author's works were published by the bibliographer (the author's wife) in 1964 and 1972 (see #265). This new work completely updates and revises the earlier books and rearranges the data in a more logical, legible, and easier-to-use format.

Contents: "Foreword"; Introduction: "Map and Territory," by David Wingrove; "A Brian W. Aldiss Chronology"; "A. Books" (with Annotations by Brian W. Aldiss); "B. Short Fiction"; "C. Nonfiction"; "D. Poetry"; "E. Other Media"; "F. Papers"; "G. Editorial Credits"; "H. Unpublished Works"; "I. Honors and Awards"; "J. Secondary Sources"; "K. Miscellanea"; "Quoth the Critics"; "Index."

In each section, materials are arranged chronologically and numbered consecutively, chapter by chapter, beginning at the number one (for example, Aldiss's second published book is "A2," his third short story "B3," etc.). All titles are boldfaced. A typical entry includes item number, title, byline, place of publication, publisher, year of publication, pagination, format, type of publication, and full bibliographical data on reprint editions, translations, republications, anthologizations, etc. The books are fully annotated, with complete contents listings, plot summaries, and other pertinent data; entries from other sections are selectively annotated as needed. Each of the books also includes a list of "Secondary Sources and Reviews," listed alphabetically by main entry (critic, title, or magazine), with bibliographical data. Wingrove's introduction provides background material on Aldiss's life and works. The chronology provides a year-by-year account of the author's professional and personal life in block paragraph format. "Secondary Sources" includes all known works about the author. "Miscellanea" includes information on pen names, book dedications, memberships, Library of Congress cataloging data, career highlights, and similar information. "Quoth the Critics" includes selected excerpts of reviews and other comments by leading critics on the author's work. The index correlates titles and item numbers only.

Aldiss's bibliography is one of the most impressive in this series, containing over a hundred published books, 300 short stories, and many other works, with huge numbers of subsidiary editions listed in every section; the story "Who Can Replace a Man?" for example, records two pages of reprints in languages as diverse as Polish and Estonian. Much of the material in this bibliography, as with Margaret Aldiss's two earlier checklists (see #265), derives from Brian Aldiss's extensive personal library, which includes copies of the vast majority of the known foreign-language editions of his own works. The book is beautifully designed and typeset, and the cloth edition is bound to library standards. Coverage is complete through mid-1991.

This particularly comprehensive and well-organized bibliography will become *the* major starting point for all future scholarship on this important writer's work. Highly recommended.

267. Stephensen-Payne, Phil. **Brian Wilson Aldiss, a Man for All Seasons: A Working Bibliography**. 2nd ed. Leeds, West Yorkshire, England & Albuquerque, N.M., Galactic Central, 1990. 9, 138 p. (Galactic Central Bibliographies for the Avid Reader, Vol. 26). ISBN 1-871133-00-9 (pbk.).

This basic checklist of primary and secondary works is arranged similarly to Margaret Aldiss's *Item* volumes (see #265). The nine-page standard series introduction (numbered separately from the rest) provides a general description of categories, organization of the bibliography, and a bibliography of works consulted. The first page gives the author's full name, date and place of birth, pseudonyms, and a chronological checklist of Aldiss's awards by year, award name, and work being honored. The bibliography proper is divided into subject categories, materials being listed in alphabetical order by title in each section.

Contents include "A. Stories"; "B. Fiction Books"; "C. Series"; "D. Poems, Songs, and Plays"; "E. Poem, Song, and Play Volumes"; "F. Articles"; "G. Miscellaneous"; "H. Non-Fiction Books"; "I. Books and Magazines Edited by Brian Aldiss"; "J. Media Presentations"; "K. Articles on Brian Aldiss"; "L. Reviews" (in alphabetical order by book being reviewed, then by publication in which the review appeared); "M. Books About Brian Aldiss"; "N. Phantom and Forthcoming Titles"; "O. Related Books by Other Authors" (none—this is an empty category); "P. Textual Variations"; "Q. Chronological Index" (listed in order by year and month [but month is not listed], with books and stories interfiled).

A typical shorter work entry gives item number, title, category ("ss"=short story, "nt"=novelette, etc.), magazine or book in which the item appeared, month and year of publication and issue number (for British titles only) for materials published in magazines, or editor's last name, publisher, and year of publication (for anthology listings), plus similar data for all known reprints, including some foreign-language materials, but no paginations. A typical monograph entry includes item number, title (all caps), contents (for story collections, giving a list of item numbers correlated to other sections in the bibliography), publication data (publisher, LC or British Library card number [inconsistently], stock number, month and year of publication [in the form "10-59" for October 1959], pagination, and price, plus similar data on all known reprints and reissues, including some foreign-language editions [with foreign titles]. Entries are numbered from one to the end in each separate chapter, prefixed by the identifying chapter letter (e.g., A1, A2, A3, etc., for the "Stories" section). There is no general title index. The book is shot from very clear word-processed copy and reproduced in an 8.5" x 11" size, stapled through the spine. Data are complete through 1989.

Although never intended to be more than a checklist, this volume provides a surprising amount of information in compact form. There are a few problems, however: Stephensen-Payne's book does not provide complete paginations for shorter works, and the series' "shorthand" style, which makes copious use of abbreviations to save space, could cause problems for the casual user. Nonetheless, this is an attractive, inexpensive alternative to Margaret Aldiss's more complete and detailed work (see #266); the latter will be preferred by serious scholars and academic libraries.

Lloyd Alexander

268. Zahorski, Kenneth J., and Robert H. Boyer. **Lloyd Alexander, Evangeline Walton Ensley, Kenneth Morris: A Primary and Secondary Bibliography**. Boston, G. K. Hall, 1981. xvi, 291 p. index. (Masters of Science Fiction and Fantasy). LC 81-6219. ISBN 0-8161-8055-5.

These bibliographies of three highly regarded fantasy authors provide a great deal of new information for the student and researcher. Contents: "Preface" (discussing the book's arrangement); "Acknowledgments"; individual bibliographies on Lloyd Alexander, Evangeline Walton Ensley, and Kenneth Vennor Morris; and indexes. In each section, the authors provide a lengthy critical and biographical introduction to the writer's work (averaging 25-30 pages), the bibliography proper being subdivided into four chapters: "Part A: Fiction"; "Part B: Miscellaneous Media"; "Part C: Nonfiction"; "Part D: Critical Studies." Completing the book are two indexes, "Works by the Authors" and "Works About the Authors."

Each of the author bibliographies is arranged chronologically, from the earliest published material to the latest, and numbered consecutively by section from the number one (e.g., A1, A2, for each author's fictional works). Books and shorter pieces are interfiled; reprints of books and stories are grouped as subsidiary entries under their first edition or appearance, chronologically by year of reprint; reprint editions of short stories include editor of anthology, title, place of publication, publisher, year, format (e.g., "paper"), but no paginations. Book entries give title (underlined), place of publication, publisher, but no paginations. Each shorter work entry lists title (in quotes), magazine, volume number, issue number, date, pagination; or, for those published originally in books, book title, book editor, place of publication, publisher, format, and paginations. Story collections include complete contents listings, plus the years in which the original stories were published. A few entries in Sections A-C include bibliographical notes but no other annotations.

"Part B: Miscellaneous Media" includes screenplays, teleplays, interviews, recordings, poetry, and other material which does not specifically fit the other three categories; only one item total is included for all three authors. "Part C: Nonfiction" includes all the author's nonfiction publications arranged chronologically by publication date. "Part D: Critical Studies" includes author, title, bibliographical data, and extensive subject annotations for book reviews, fan commentaries, critiques, bibliographies, and other secondary works. The indexes cite title and item number only, or author or title plus item number for the indexes to critical studies, with small letters prefixing the number crossreferencing entries in each of the three individual author sections (e.g., "kmC12"=item "C12" in the Kenneth Morris bibliography). The book is reproduced from legible typed copy and bound to library standards. Foreign language reprint editions are mentioned when known, but, curiously, none of the foreign-language titles are given.

Of the fourteen volumes published in this series, Zahorski and Boyer's is one of the best, and certainly the least likely to become outdated: all three authors had essentially completed their careers by the time the book was published, with two of them (Morris and Walton) having undergone significant rediscoveries of their work in the 1970s. The critical introductions provide readable, authoritative, even important summaries of the writers' lives and contributions to fantastic literature, as valuable in their own right as the bibliographies themselves. It is difficult to imagine how any future researcher of these writers' works could ignore this excellent volume.

Poul Anderson

269. Benson, Gordon, Jr., and Phil Stephensen-Payne. **Poul Anderson, Myth-Master and Wonder-Weaver: A Working Bibliography**. 5th ed. Leeds, West Yorkshire, England & Albuquerque, N.M., Galactic Central, 1989. 9, 123 p. (Galactic Central Bibliographies for the Avid Reader, Vol. 1). ISBN 0-912613-03-3 (pbk.). Also: San Bernardino, Calif., The Borgo Press, 1990, 9, 123 p. (Galactic Central Bibliographies for the Avid Reader, Vol. 1). LC 90-1934. ISBN 0-8095-4700-7.

Benson and Stephensen-Payne's basic checklist of this well-known science-fiction writer's works is arranged by subject category, then alphabetically by title. Contents: Author's name, date and place of birth, lists of awards won by the author (in chronological order, giving year, name of award, and title of work being honored), and his pseudonyms; "A. Stories"; "B. Fiction Books"; "C. Series" (including separate chronologies of the Technic Civilization and the Psychotechnic Series); "D. Poems"; "E. Poem & Song Collections"—none (blank section); "F. Articles"; "G. Miscellaneous" (including introductions and afterwords by Anderson, letters, and interviews with the author); "H. Non-Fiction Books"; "I. Edited Books"; "J. Media Presentations"; "K. Articles on Poul Anderson"; "L. Reviews" (of Anderson's books, alphabetically by title of the book being reviewed, then by magazine title, giving date and reviewer); "M. Books About Poul Anderson"; "N. Phantom and Forthcoming Titles"; "O. Related Items by Other Authors"; "P. Textual Variations"—none (section blank); "Q. Chronological Index" (by year and month [but months are not actually listed], and title).

In each section the material is arranged in alphabetical order by title; materials are numbered consecutively from one in each chapter (for example, B1, B2, B3, etc., for the author's books). Shorter work entries include item number, title, category ("ss"=short story, "nt"=novelette, etc.), magazine or book in which the item appeared, month and year of publication (for magazines in the form "2-68" for February 1968) or year of publication (for books), a list of subsequent reprints (for which title, publisher, year, and editor's last name are given), but no paginations. For book-length works, Benson and Stephensen-Payne provide item number, title, contents (if a collection, by item number), publication data (publisher, stock number, month and year of publication [if known, in the form "10-59" for October 1959], pagination, price), cover artist, plus similar data for known reprints. There is no title index. The series listings are especially helpful for Anderson, who has based so much of his work around a very detailed "history" of the future. The book is shot from very clear word-processed copy and stapled through the spine in an 8.5" x 11" paperback edition; the Borgo edition is bound in library cloth.

Poul Anderson is the most current and accurate guide to this important author's work yet produced. An index would have been helpful, as would the addition of paginations for the short fiction sections. However, Benson and Stephensen-Payne's data are sound, and the book well-organized and presented; their bibliography is a necessary starting point for all future scholarship on Anderson's many fictions.

270. Owings, Mark. **Poul Anderson: Bibliography**. Baltimore, Md., Balticon VII, T-K Graphics, 1973. [15] p. (pbk.).

Owings was a major bibliographer of the field during the late 1960s and early '70s before dropping out of fandom. His brief checklist of Anderson's work, produced for distribution at a science fiction convention, arranges the author's writings in one straight alphabetical list, book titles being underlined. For short fiction, Owings gives magazine of publication, date (in the form of "6/65" for June of 1965), and a basic list of subsequent reprints, but no paginations. Book entries include title, publisher, place of publication, date, pagination, price, and known reprints, including some foreign-language editions (information on which is very difficult to find). Owings is both careful and accurate: foreign cities of publication, for example, are listed exactly as they appear in their original languages. The book is shot from usually legible typed copy, mimeographed on 8.5" x 11" sheets, and stapled through the spine. This is a sound piece of work despite the limited production values, but it is now very much out-of-date and has mostly been superseded by Benson and Stephensen-Payne (see #269), who do not, however, include the foreign-language reprints.

271. Peyton, Roger G. **A Checklist of Poul Anderson**. Birmingham, England, [Roger G. Peyton], 1965. 26 p. (pbk.).

Peyton provides a brief checklist of Anderson's science-fiction publications, omitting works in other genres. Now superseded by Benson/Stephensen-Payne (see #269).

[Not seen].

Piers Anthony

272. Stephensen-Payne, Phil. **Piers Anthony: Biblio of an Ogre: A Working Bibliography**. Leeds, West Yorkshire, England & Albuquerque, N.M., Galactic Central, 1990. 9, 45 p. (Galactic Central Bibliographies for the Avid Reader, Vol. 35). (pbk.).

One of a series of basic checklists of the works of science fiction and fantasy authors, *Piers Anthony* is arranged by subject category, then alphabetically by title. Contents: Author's complete real name, date and place of birth, lists of awards won by the author (by year of award, also listing award name and title of work being honored), and Anthony's pseudonyms (including "Piers Anthony" itself).

The bibliography proper includes "A. Stories"; "B. Fiction Books"; "C. Series" (keyed to entry number from the B section; no titles or years are listed, forcing the user to refer back to the previous chapter for hard data); "D. Poems, Songs & Plays"; "E. Poem, Song and Play Volumes"—none actually listed; "F. Articles"; "G. Miscellaneous" (including author's notes, book reviews by Anthony, forewords, introductions by Anthony, letters, and interviews with the author); "H. Non-Fiction Books"; "I. Books Edited by Piers Anthony"; "J. Media Presentations"—none (section blank); "K. Articles on Piers Anthony"; "L. Reviews" (of Anthony's books, alphabetical by title of the book being reviewed, then by magazine title, giving issue number, date of publication, and reviewer); "M. Books About Piers Anthony"; "N. Phantom & Forthcoming Titles"; "O. Related Items by Other Authors"; "P. Textual Variations"; "Q. Chronological Index" (by year and month [but months are not actually listed], and title).

In each section the material is arranged in alphabetical order by title; materials are numbered consecutively from one in each chapter (for example, A1, A2, A3, etc., for the author's stories). Shorter work entries include item number, title, category ("ss"=short story, "nt"=novelette, etc.), magazine or book in which the item appeared, month and year of publication (for magazines in the form "2-68" for February 1968) or year of publication (for books), a list of subsequent reprints (for which title, publisher, year, and editor's last name are given), but no paginations. For book-length works, Benson and Stephensen-Payne provide item number, title, contents (if a collection, by item number), publication data (publisher, stock number, month and year of publication [if known, in the form "10-59" for October 1959], pagination, price), cover artist, plus similar data on all known reprints. There is no title index. The book is shot from generally clear word-processed copy and stapled through the spine in an 8.5" x 11" paperback edition.

Given Anthony's enormous popularity in the 1980s and '90s, it's strange that Stephensen-Payne's bibliography is the first separately published guide to the author's many novels and stories. Future editions should incorporate an overall title index and add specific paginations for those sections which do not have them. In general, however, this is a well-constructed if occasionally cryptic bibliography, one which will be very useful to all students of Piers Anthony's work.

Isaac Asimov

273. Miller, Marjorie M. **Isaac Asimov: A Checklist of Works Published in the United States, March 1939-May 1972**. Kent, Ohio, Kent State University Press, 1972. xiii, 98 p. index. LC 72-76948. ISBN 0-87338-126-2.

Miller's straightforward bibliography lists Asimov's works in chronological order by publication date. A typical entry provides title, place of publication and publisher (for books), or magazine title, volume number, month of publication, and paginations (for shorter works) followed by a list of known reprints in the U.S., England, and Canada. No foreign-language editions are shown, and no paginations are provided for books. An "F" in front of an entry designates a fictional title. Some abbreviations are used for magazines ("*F&SF*"=*The Magazine of Fantasy and Science Fiction*); an abbreviations list is located at the front of the book. Coverage is complete through May 1972.

The second section of the book, "Selected Criticism and Works about Asimov," consists of just over six pages of entries arranged in alphabetical order by author, providing bibliographical data similar to that included in the main section, plus a two- to five-sentence evaluative annotation. This chapter is noticeably *passé*.

The title index correlates titles and dates only, making location of specific items difficult for the average user, particularly in those years where Asimov produced a great many titles (which, for this particular author, is *most* of them). Miller's coverage seems thorough, but her book is now so seriously dated that it can be no more than a starting point for future scholarly research. Clearly, a more detailed and expanded bibliography of the author's work is long overdue.

274. Tepper, M. B. **The Asimov Science Fiction Bibliography**. Santa Monica, Calif., The Chinese Ducked Press, 1970. [89] leaves. index. LC 79-21922 (pbk.).

This amateurishly produced fan checklist of Asimov's works includes "Adult Science Fiction Novels," "Juvenile Science Fiction Novels," "Straight Mystery Novel," "Collections," "Omnibuses," "Science Fiction Stories," "Straight Mystery Stories," "Poems," "Spoof Articles," "Plays," "Comic Strip Continuity," "Notes," "Alternate Title Index." Each section is arranged chronologically by publication date, with book entries restricted to one a page. A typical monograph entry provides title, publisher, year of publication, and complete contents (either a list of the stories included or a reproduction of the chapter heads). The short stories are grouped one year to a page, then listed by title, magazine, month of publication, and size (i.e., novel, novella, novelette, short story, short-short story). No other bibliographical data are provided. Tepper omits Asimov's many science articles and the few anthologies he had then edited. Coverage is complete through 1969, with a few titles with 1970 dates. Now largely superseded by Miller (see #273), whose bibliography does not, however, include Tepper's size categorizations.

J. G. Ballard

275. Pringle, David. **J. G. Ballard: A Primary and Secondary Bibliography**. Boston, G. K. Hall, 1984. xxxvi, 156 p. index. (Masters of Science Fiction and Fantasy). LC 83-18528. ISBN 0-8161-8603-0.

Pringle, editor of the British magazines *Interzone* and *Million* and an acknowledged authority on Ballard's work, here provides the first comprehensive guide to the works of this highly regarded English writer of the fantastic.

Contents: "Preface" (discussing the book's arrangement); "Introduction" (twenty-three pages of critical and biographical background on Ballard); a chronological "Checklist of Books" by the author; an original "Interview with J. G. Ballard"; and the bibliography proper, divided into several sections: "Part A: Fiction"; "Part B: Miscellaneous Media"; "Part C: Nonfiction"; "Part D: Critical and Bio-Bibliographical Studies." Two appendices list known foreign-language editions of Ballard's books by language, in chronological order by date of publication. Three indexes at the end of the book cover "The Writings of J. G. Ballard" (by title and item number), "Critics, Reviewers, and Interviewers" (by surname and item number), and "Persons Referred to by Ballard and His Critics" (by surname and item number).

Each section of the bibliography is arranged chronologically by publication year, and numbered consecutively by section and item (e.g., A1, A2, A3, etc., for the author's fiction). Books and shorter works are interfiled together; reprints of books and stories are grouped as subsidiary entries under their first editions or appearances, chronologically by year of reprint. Each book entry provides title (underlined), place of publication, publisher, but no paginations. Each shorter work entry gives title (in quotations), magazine, volume number, issue number, date, pagination; or, for works published originally in books: book title, book editor, place of publication, publisher, format, and paginations. Reprint editions of short stories include anthology editor, title, place of publication, publisher, year, format (e.g., "paper"), but no paginations. Story collections include complete contents listings, plus the years in which the original stories were published. Some entries, particularly in Sections B-C, include bibliographical or descriptive notes but no other annotations; all of the entries in Part D are extensively annotated.

"Part B: Miscellaneous Media" largely consists of Ballard's verse. "Part C: Nonfiction" covers the author's nonfiction publications arranged chronologically by publication date. The "Critical Studies" section includes major reviews and all known articles and books about Ballard arranged chronologically, with author, title, bibliographical data, and summaries. Coverage is complete through 1982. The book is reproduced from generally legible typed copy and bound to library standards.

Pringle's book was one of the last two volumes published in this series, and while his work is now somewhat out-of-date (missing Ballard's most successful novel [and movie], *Empire of the Sun*), it remains a sound, thoroughly comprehensive, well-framed guide to the writer's *oeuvre*. The critical introduction is an excellent starting point for future scholarly studies, and the interview conducted in 1979 reveals much of Ballard's unique personality and character. In particular, the coverage of secondary sources in this volume is among the best in the series, including 167 references, many of them difficult to locate, with particularly thorough and analytic annotations. This is a first-class bibliographical effort that should definitely be maintained with future editions.

Clive Barker

276. Bell, Joseph. **The Books of Clive Barker.** Toronto, Canada, Soft Books, 1988. [18] p. (pbk.).

    Canadian book dealer Bell provides a collector's bibliography of the works of this rising British horror writer, arranged in chronological order by publication date. A typical entry includes title (large bold type), publisher, address, exact collation, first edition statement, number of copies printed, edition priority states, price, cover artist, exact date of publication (as close as possible), contents, and similar information on all known reprintings and subsequent editions. Bell also provides a one-page chronological checklist of all Barker's editions (including reprints), but no index. A one-page addendum is inserted into the basic bibliography. The book is nicely designed and typeset, printed in 8.5" x 11" format, and stapled through the spine. This checklist is clearly intended for collectors, and does provide much data of interest to the bookman; however, one might hope that a future edition would also feature more information about the *content* of the books, plus an index and some basic biographical information on the author.

Barrington J. Bayley

277. Ashley, Mike. **The Writings of Barrington J. Bayley: A Bibliography Prepared Specially for Beccon.** [Harold Wood, Essex, England: Beccon Committee], 1981. [7] p. (pbk.).

    Ashley is a well-known British bibliographer. This brief checklist of Bayley's work was originally prepared for distribution at Beccon, the major annual English science fiction convention. Data are organized into three sections: "A. Books"; "B. Short Fiction"; and "C. Of Further Interest." The first two parts are each arranged alphabetically by title. A typical book entry includes item number (e.g., A1, A2, A3), title, notes (e.g., "collection of 13 stories"), publisher, place of publication, year of publication, pagination, format ("pb" and "sc"=paperback, "hb"=cloth); similar data are provided for all subsequent reprints. Short story collections also include complete contents listings, plus references to the short fiction section. A typical "Short Fiction" entry includes item number, title, magazine or book title, pseudonym (where appropriate), issue number and date (for magazines); or publisher, place of publication, and year (for books); similar data are provided for all known reprints. No paginations are listed for short fiction. "Of Further Interest" mentions an article by Bayley and an essay *on* Bayley's work by another writer. Coverage is complete through 1980. A photo of the author appears on the front cover. Complete and thorough, if somewhat condensed in format; a more elaborate and attractive version would certainly be justified.

Charles Beaumont

278. Nolan, William F. **The Work of Charles Beaumont: An Annotated Bibliography & Guide.** San Bernardino, Calif., The Borgo Press, 1986. 48 p. index. (Bibliographies of Modern Authors, No. 6). LC 85-460. ISBN 0-89370-385-0; ISBN 0-89370-485-7 (pbk.). **The Work of Charles Beaumont: An Annotated Bibliography & Guide.** 2nd ed., rev. and exp. San Bernardino, Calif., The Borgo Press, 1990. 92 p. index. (Bibliographies of Modern Authors, No. 6). LC 90-15043. ISBN 0-8095-0517-7; ISBN 0-8095-1517-2 (pbk.).

Charles Beaumont burst like a shooting star on the science fiction world, beginning his brief career in 1950, then quickly moving to the high-paying slick magazines, and finally finding an outlet for his enormous energies in such award-winning television programs as *The Twilight Zone*. Sadly, after a brilliant ten-year career, Beaumont contracted Alzheimer's disease, prematurely dying at the age of thirty-eight. Nolan was Beaumont's close friend and frequent collaborator, and because they so frequently wrote in tandem, he kept meticulous notes on Beaumont's publications.

Contents (first edition): "Introduction"; "A. Books"; "B. Short Fiction"; C. Nonfiction"; "D. Screenplays"; "E. Teleplays"; "F. Comics"; "G. Letters"; "H. Unpublished Stories"; "I. Awards"; "J. Artwork"; "K. Editorial Posts"; "L. About the Author"; "Title Index." Contents (second edition): "Preface to the Second Edition"; "Introduction to the First Edition"; "Chronology"; "A. Books"; "B. Short Fiction"; "C. Nonfiction"; "D. Screenplays"; "E. Teleplays"; "F. Comics"; "G. Letters"; "H. Unpublished Works"; "I. Verse"; "J. Honors and Awards"; "K. Artwork"; "L. Editorial Credits"; "M. About the Author"; "N. Miscellanea"; "Quoth the Critics"; Afterword: "My Grandmother's Japonicas," by Charles Beaumont; "Index"; "About William F. Nolan."

Materials are arranged chronologically, section by section, and numbered consecutively from one in each chapter (e.g., Beaumont's sixth book is numbered "A6," his first short story "B1," etc.). A typical book entry includes item number (boldfaced), title (boldfaced), byline, place of publication, publisher, month and year of publication, pagination, format (e.g., "paper"), type of publication (e.g., "anthology"), and full bibliographical data on all known reprint editions and translations. The second edition also lists book reviews for each monograph, arranged alphabetically by main entry (usually critic's name), with complete bibliographical data. The books are fully annotated, with complete contents listings and/or plot summaries; entries in the other sections are selectively annotated, mentioning television adaptations, awards, or signficance. A typical shorter work entry provides item number (boldfaced), title (in quotes, boldfaced), byline (if a pseudonym was used), magazine title (italics), volume number, month and year of publication, and pagination; stories appearing first in collections or anthologies also include book title (italics), editor, place of publication, publisher, month and year of publication, format (e.g., "cloth"), and pagination; similar data are provided for all known reprint editions and translations. Nolan's introduction gives a brief history of Beaumont's life and career, and the six-page chronology in the second edition provides a detailed survey of Beaumont movements, publications, and the highlights of his brief career. "About the Author" includes all known secondary works arranged chronologically by publication date, with complete bibliographical data. The title index correlates titles and item numbers only. The media sections include such details as air and production dates, director, major actors (for motion pictures), production company, etc. Nolan acknowledges that the section on Beaumont's television work is incomplete and likely to remain so, since neither he nor Beaumont's family have complete records on his work outside *The Twilight Zone*.

Appreciation for Beaumont's legacy has been growing in recent years, and Nolan's bibliography is probably the most complete record now possible of his many writings. This well-organized and presented publication will be an essential starting point for all future research on this fantasy writer's life and career.

Michael Bishop

279. Nee, Dave. **Michael Bishop: A Preliminary Bibliography**. Berkeley, Calif., The Other Change of Hobbit, 1983. ii, 34 p. (+4-page supplement). index. (pbk.).

Nee, proprietor of the science-fiction bookstore The Other Change of Hobbit, has compiled a short checklist of this author's work, arranged by category, and then alphabetically by title. Major sections include "Preface and Acknowledgments"; "B. Books"; "C. Anthologies Edited"; "F. Fiction"; "N. Non-Fiction/Criticism" (i.e., secondary sources); "P. Poetry"; "R. Reviews" (of Bishop's works); "X. Source Books" (for stories of Bishop reprinted in other volumes); "Title Index"; "Chronological Index." Materials are numbered consecutively in each section from the number one. The "Books" section includes item number, title, the author's dedication in each book (reprinted verbatim), complete bibliographical data for all editions, including place of publication, publisher, ISBN, price, pagination, size in centimeters, cover artist, and exact date of publication (when known). The short fiction section lists item number, story title, magazine, date, pagination, plus all known reprints, with title of the reprint anthology, date of publication, and pagination. The "Non-Fiction/Criticism" section includes articles, biographies, and review essays on Bishop, and interviews with the author, but does not mention the book(s) being reviewed; reviews *by* Bishop are included in the "Reviews" chapter. Section X, "Source Books," gives complete bibliographical data (in a format similar to Section B) on the anthologies and other works *not* actually authored by Bishop but mentioned somewhere in the bibliography. The indexes cite title and item number only. The book is reproduced from 8.5" x 11" computer printout, using hanging indents to set off specific data, and stapled through the spine into paper covers. A four-page supplement, also dated 1983, was inserted in some copies. Nee's volume includes a surprising amount of data for this type of checklist, particularly on reprint editions; however, the volume numbers of periodicals are omitted. A revised edition is currently in preparation. See also the companion volume on Thomas M. Disch (see #332).

Algernon Blackwood

280. Ashley, Mike. **Algernon Blackwood: A Bio-Bibliography**. New York, London, Greenwood Press, 1987. xx, 349 p. index. (Bio-Bibliographies in World Literature, No. 1). LC 87-17808. ISBN 0-313-25158-4.

This absolutely superb bibliography on a classic British writer of the supernatural is a paradigm of what a bibliography should be: well-organized and comprehensive with virtually everything that one might want to know about the author.

Contents: "Foreword," by Ramsey Campbell; "The Why and the Wherefore: An Introduction"; "Acknowledgements"; "User's Guide"; "The Biography"; "The Bibliography." The biographical section contains a thirty-four-page essay by Ashley giving many little-known details about Blackwood's life and career; a chronology summarizes the salient points into a four-page table.

The bibliography proper is organized into four major sections: Part I. "Works by Blackwood"—"A. Books"; "B. Short and Serial Fiction"; "C. Non-Fiction": "CA. Essays and Sketches," "CB. Book Reviews"; "D. Poetry and Songs"; "E. Plays and Dramas": "EA. Stage Plays," "EB. Radio Plays"; "F. Radio Broadcasts": "FA. Stories," "FB. Talks," "FC. Interviews and Discussions"; "G. Television Broadcasts": "GA. Stories and Talks," "GB. Interviews and Discussions"; H. Films"; "I. Recorded Works"; "J. Unpublished or Un-broadcast Manuscripts"; "K. Untraced Items."

Part II: "Adaptations by Others"—"L. Stage Plays"; "M. Radio Broadcasts": "MA. Stories, Talks and Poetry," "MB. Radio Plays"; "N. Television Adaptations"; "O. Recorded Works and Editions for the Blind": "OA. Stories," "OB. Poetry and Songs," "OC. Plays," "OD. Books in Braille." [N.b.: There is no Section P.] Part III: "Works About Blackwood"—"Q. Selected Secondary Bibliography"; "R. Reviews of Blackwood's Books"; "S. Radio Documentaries About Blackwood"; "T. Portraits and Photography." Part IV: "Source Indexes"—"U. Index to Books by Publisher"; "V. Index to Magazines and Periodicals"; "W. Index by Anthologist"; "X. Index to Books Reviewed by Blackwood"; "Y. Index to Secondary Bibliography by Periodical." Appendixes: "I. Translated Books and Foreign Editions"; "II. Library Holdings": "A. By Library," "B. By Book"; "III. Archive Holdings"—"Manuscripts and Letters." Indexes: "I. Index to Locale and Theme"; "II. Chronological Index to All Works"; "III. Alphabetical Index to All Works"; "IV. Index to Personal Names": "1. Actors and Narrators"; "2. Artists and Designers"; "3. Writers and Critics"; "4. Friends and Acquaintances."

Each section is arranged chronologically by date of original publication. Materials are numbered consecutively from one in each new section, in the left-hand margin of the page; further printings of books are numbered from one through as many printings as are noted (e.g., "A.1.4" is the fourth British edition of Blackwood's first book). A typical book entry includes title (in boldface), description (novel or collection), total wordage for the book; contents (for a collection) or three- to four-sentence plot description (for a novel), the author's dedication (verbatim), a list of the British editions of the book in chronological order, a list of the American editions in chronological order, and see references. Bibliographical data include place of publication, publisher, year of publication, month of publication, format, physical size (in centimeters), exact pagination, description of binding and other "points," price, date of contract between author and publisher, description of reissues by the same publisher.

The "Short and Serial Fiction" section and similar chapters include title (in boldface), total wordage, one- to two-sentence plot description, bibliographical data (magazine, volume number, issue number, date, pagination, mention of illustration and illustrator's name), subsequent reprints (stories in Blackwood's own collections are crossreferenced by title and year; those appearing in other anthologies include title, editor, place of publication, publisher, date, and pagination). The media sections include all details known about the production companies, writers, actors, air times, etc. The indexes are enormously thorough, reworking the data through a wide variety of access points keyed to item number. The book is shot from occasionally faint word-processed copy.

Ashley is to be congratulated on producing perhaps the finest—and certainly the most comprehensive—bibliography ever compiled on an individual writer of fantastic literature organized into a very accessible and logical format. Future researchers will find a literary gold mine in these pages. Highly recommended, not just to students of Blackwood's life and literary career but to potential bibliographers.

281. Colombo, John Robert. **Blackwood's Books: A Bibliography Devoted to Algernon Blackwood**. Toronto, Canada, Hounslow Press, 1981. 119 p. index. LC 83-128835. ISBN 0-88882-055-0 (pbk.).

Colombo, best known for his checklist of Canadian science fiction (see #186), originally prepared this bibliography of Blackwood's books to assist in the compilation of a new collection of the author's horror stories. Blackwood's monographs are arranged alphabetically by title. A typical entry includes book title (boldfaced), place of publication, publisher, year of publication, author's dedication (reproduced verbatim), edition statement, other material of interest, and a complete contents list (for story collections) recording the fictions in the same order in which they appeared in the book. Also mentioned are place of publication, publisher, and year of publication for all known reprints and subsequent editions. Each of Blackwood's books is recorded on a separate page. Appendices include "I. List of Books by Year of Publication"; "II. Alphabetical List of [152] Stories with Locations" [in Blackwood's collections]; "III. Brief Life of Blackwood"; "IV. The Canadian Years" (i.e., Blackwood's adventures in Canada); "V. Theatre, Radio, and Television" [productions]; "VI. Master of Horror" by Walter Gillings (a critical essay on Blackwood's life and fiction); "VII. Select Bibliography" [of works consulted]. Colombo's arrangement may sometimes seem more quickly accessible for the casual reader than Ashley's *Algernon Blackwood: A Bio-Bibliography* (see #280), but there is very little here that Ashley did not subsume into his masterful bibliography.

James P. Blaylock

282. Stephens, Christopher P., and Tom Joyce. **A Checklist of James P. Blaylock**. Hastings-on-Hudson, N.Y., Ultramarine Publishing Co., 1991. 17 p. index. ISBN 0-89366-199-6 (pbk.).

Stephens and Joyce's guide is organized chronologically by publication date, materials being numbered consecutively from one in two sections covering the author's books (A1-15) and stories (B1-13). A typical book entry provides year (as a floating head), item number, title (underlined), pseudonym, publisher, stock or ISBN number, pagination, format (e.g., "paperback original"), cover illustrator, price, and similar data for all known reprints (which are numbered, for example, A2a, A2b, A2c, etc., in descending order by publication date). The chapbook is shot from legible typed copy and bound with staples in stiff paper covers. The index correlates titles with years of publication only. Blaylock is a rising star in the science-fiction field; this brief guide will be of interest primarily to his fans.

James Blish

283. Blish, Judith Lawrence. **"Bibliography of the Works of James Blish,"** in *The Tale That Wags the God*, by James Blish, edited by Cy Chauvin. Chicago, Advent:Publishers, 1987, p. 197-290. index. ISBN 0-911682-29-5.

This final collection of essays on science fiction written by SF author James Blish under his academic pseudonym William Atheling, Jr. also includes a nearly definitive bibliography of his works by his widow, J. A. Lawrence (Judith Blish), in a separate section following the index to the main text.

Materials are arranged into twelve subject categories: "Books," "Short Stories," "Anthologies," "Short Story Collections," "Science Fiction Criticism" (subdivided into "The Issue at Hand," "Column and Books"), "Literary Criticism," "Book Reviews," "Articles and Interviews," "Introductions," "Poetry," and "*Star Trek* Books." In each section materials are arranged alphabetically by title. A typical book entry includes title (italics, all caps), series title, original magazine serialization (where applicable, giving title, volume and issue number[s], months and years of publication, and publisher), publisher, nationality of publisher, year of publication, and similar data on all known reprints, listed in order by nationality, then by date, with variant and foreign-language titles. No paginations are listed. A typical short fiction entry includes title (in quotes), total wordage, pseudonym (where applicable), magazine title (italics), volume and issue number, publisher, nationality of publisher, month and year of publication, but no paginations. Similar data are provided for all known reprint editions, including anthology appearances and translations. Shorter works in other sections do not include word counts. There are separate title and name indexes referencing the page numbers on which the titles or persons are mentioned. The book is attractively typeset and bound to library standards.

This will obviously be the first stopping point for all students of Blish's work; among others, the data on the author's numerous translations are virtually unobtainable in any other source. However, it would have been helpful to have had paginations for all entries (and they should be added to any future edition) placed in a somewhat more standardized format. Lawrence's bibliography will likely remain current almost indefinitely; Blish's 1975 death means that any future additions to this guide will probably be rehashes or reprintings of old work.

Robert Bloch

284. Flanagan, Graeme. **Robert Bloch: A Bio-Bibliography**. Canberra City, Australia, Graeme Flanagan, 1979. 63 p. (pbk.).

Flanagan provides a tribute to Bloch together with a checklist of his works. Contents: "Introduction"; "Robert Bloch: A Few Words of Friendship," by Harlan Ellison; "Biography"; "The Robert Bloch Collection" (describing the collection of his manuscripts at the University of Wyoming Library); "Mr. Weird Tales," by Robert Weinberg; "Interview One: Mostly Concerning Weird Tales"; "'When Screwballs Meet...,'" by Fritz Leiber; "Interview Two"; "Bibliography"; "Radio, Television and Motion Pictures"; "My Weird Little Brother," by Mary Elizabeth Counselman; "Acknowledgments."

The miscellaneous articles and interviews provide much background material on Bloch and his work. The bibliography proper is organized into the following sections: "A. Short Stories—First Magazine Printings"; "B. Non-Fiction Published in Magazines"; "C. Novels"; "D. Collections—Short Stories"; "E. Collections—Non-Fiction"; "F. Short Stories and Non-Fiction Published in Anthologies"; "G. Short Stories and Non-Fiction Reprinted in Magazines"; "H. Foreign Translations"; "I. Miscellanea," including "Introductions/Afterwords," "Speeches," "Interviews," and "Biographies" (secondary sources in magazines). Sections A and B are arranged in chronological order listing title, magazine, and date only, but no paginations. Most of the remaining parts are listed in alphabetical order by title. A typical book entry includes title, publisher, place of publication, year of publication, pagination, and price for all known editions. The secondary sources are scanty at best. The other media section includes works by Bloch as well as screenplays and teleplays adapted by others from his work. The volume is shot from typed copy and is illustrated throughout with photographs of the author and a few book and magazine cover reproductions. While some of the background material remains interesting—and unique to this volume—the bibliography itself has been almost totally subsumed into Larson's book (see #286).

285. Hall, Graham M. **Robert Bloch Bibliography**. Tewksbury, England, Graham M. Hall, 1965. 32 p. index. (pbk.).

This mimeographed checklist of Bloch's publications lists them in straight chronological order by publication date. Reprints reappear as new entries throughout the list, making any kind of correlation between items unnecessarily difficult. The shorter works in the list are indexed at the end of the book by title of the magazine in which they were originally published, and also by anthology name (neither of these provide particularly helpful access points). There is also the usual guide to the Lefty Feep stories (a lengthy series of humorous SF tales penned by Bloch) and a short, very incomplete listing of Bloch's teleplays, radio work, and screenplays and film adaptations. Now completely outdated and superseded by Larson (see #286).

286. Larson, Randall D. **The Complete Robert Bloch: An Illustrated International Bibliography.** Sunnyvale, Calif., Fandom Unlimited Enterprises, 1986. x, 126 p. index. LC 85-82410. ISBN 0-9607178-1-1 (pbk.). Also: San Bernardino, Calif., The Borgo Press, 1987. x, 126 p. index. LC 87-20858. ISBN 0-8095-6106-9.

This nicely illustrated bibliography was compiled by the same critic who penned a well-received critique on *Robert Bloch* for Starmont House. Contents: "Preface"; "Introduction," by Bloch; "Robert Bloch: The Man with the Heart of a Small Boy," by Larson; "Main Bibliography"; "Fanzine Bibliography"; "Supplemental Bibliographies" (i.e., indexes); "Themes and Variations: A Categorical Guide to the Short Stories and Novels of Robert Bloch." The Main Bibliography is further subdivided into: "1. Short Stories"; "2. Novels"; "3. Collections"; "4. Non-Fiction"; "5. Introductions & Afterwords"; "6. Verse"; "7. Radio, Television & Motion Pictures"; "8. Bibliographic & Biographic Material" (secondary sources); "9. Miscellany."

In each section materials are listed alphabetically by title. A typical short story entry provides title (boldfaced), wordage, magazine title, date, and known reprints in order by date of publication (magazine titles are underlined, book titles are capitalized), but no paginations. A typical book entry includes title (bold caps), wordage, place of publication, publisher, year, format abbreviation (e.g., "hb"=hardcover, "pb"=paperback), but no paginations, plus a list of all known reprint editions, American versions being listed first, with similar types of publication data. No paginations are provided. For media presentations, Larson gives title or program title, year, network or production company, and (for motion pictures) director. The indexes rearrange the data by magazine and date of publication; also included are lists of Bloch's unanthologized short stories, the Lefty Feep series, collaborative stories, and pseudonymous stories. The themes and variations section provides a guide to Bloch's works by specific subject category.

The book also includes illustrations of book and magazine covers, title pages, and interior drawings on virtually every page plus a few stills from Bloch's screen- and teleplays and is generally very attractively presented. The coverage of foreign editions is particularly strong. However, one would hope in any future edition for both a general title index and paginations, the lack of which detract from what would otherwise be *the* definitive guide to Bloch's life and works.

Anthony Boucher

287. Christopher, J(oe) R., with D(ean) W. Dickensheet and R(obert) E. Briney. **A. Boucher Bibliography.** [White Bear Lake, Minn., Allen J. Hubin], 1969. [34] p. index. (pbk.). Bound with *A Boucher Portrait: Anthony Boucher as Seen by His Friends and Colleagues*, edited by Lenore Glen Offord.

Anthony Boucher, the well-known science-fiction and mystery writer, editor, and critic, died in 1968 at the age of fifty-seven. This memorial bibliography, reprinted from its original serialization in Volume 2 (Nos. 2-4) of *The Armchair Detective*, records materials from all of Boucher's writing worlds.

Materials are organized into specific series and subject categories: "I. Alias Watson: The Memoirs of Martin Lamb"; "II. The Casebook of Fergus O'Breen" (plus a separate section of "Related Stories"); "III. The Pride of Sister Ursula, O.M.B." (plus "Related Stories"); "IV. Noble Obliges: The Adventures of Detective Lt. Donald MacDonald,

L.A.P.D."; "V. Usuform Robotics" (plus "Related Stories"); "VI. Non-Sequence Stories"; "VII. Collected Fiction"; "VIII. Holmesian Material"; "IX. Essays and Other Non-Fiction"; "X. Verse"; "XI. Items in Special Interest Publications" (subdivided into: "a. Mystery Writers of America Periodicals"; "b. Opera Periodicals and Programs"; "c. Science Fiction 'Fanzines'"); "XII. Anthologies Edited"; "XIII. Reviewing Series"; "XIV. Magazine and Book-Series Editing"; "XV. Introductions to Non-Series Volumes"; "XVI. Translations"; "XVII. Biographical and Autobiographical Material"; "XVIII. General Addenda"; "Combined List of Subject Headings and Index" (to titles and item numbers).

In each section, materials are listed chronologically by publication date, novels and short fiction being interfiled together. A typical book entry includes item number, title (underlined), place of publication, publisher, year of publication, but no paginations; similar data are provided for all known reprints in English. A typical short fiction entry provides item number, title (in quotes), magazine title (underlined), month and year of publication, but no paginations, plus a list of known reprints in anthologies and collections (for which book title, editor, place of publication, publisher, and year of publication are included). Every fiction entry includes a descriptive annotation ranging in size from 50-300 words (averaging 150). Materials are numbered in each section or subject from the number one, using small roman numerals; thus, *The Case of the Seven of Calvary*, part of the Martin Lamb series, is numbered "i." in section "I." and should have been referenced in the title index as "I.i." (but the index misses this novel); those chapters which are divided into two or three parts (Sections II. and III., for example) are numbered from the small Roman numeral "i." in each subsection, preceded by an identifying letter (for example, "Mystery for Christmas" is referenced in the index as "II.b.i.," being the first item of the "Related Stories" section of Chapter II.). If this seems overly cumbersome, consider the last entry of Chapter VI., "The Smoke-Filled Locked Room," which is numbered "VI.xxxviii." The 8.5" x 11" booklet is shot from occasionally faint typed copy and stapled through the side.

The compilers acknowledge the incompleteness of the later sections of the bibliography, which record secondary sources and peripheral items by and about the author. The fiction chapters are much more complete, but the unnecessarily confusing format and poor production values make access difficult for the casual user. Very few copies of this guide were distributed, and the early issues of *The Armchair Detective* are themselves rarities. A definitive bibliography of this influential *littérateur* of the 1950s and '60s has yet to be produced.

Leigh Brackett

288. Arbur, Rosemarie. **Leigh Brackett, Marion Zimmer Bradley, Anne McCaffrey: A Primary and Secondary Bibliography.** Boston, G. K. Hall & Co., 1982. xlviii, 277 p. index. (Masters of Science Fiction and Fantasy). LC 81-4216. ISBN 0-8161-8120-9.

This tripartite bibliography of primary and secondary sources on three American women science fiction writers of the twentieth century includes "[About] the Author"; "Preface" (describing how the book is arranged); "Abbreviations and Other Minutiae"; "Introduction" (providing broad biographical and critical backgrounds for all three authors); the bibliographies proper, in three separate parts: "Leigh Brackett"; "Marion Zimmer Bradley"; "Anne McCaffrey"; "Indexes." In each chapter, the author's works are subdivided into four sections: "Part A: Fiction"; "Part B: Miscellaneous Media"; "Part C: Nonfiction"; "Part D: Critical Studies." The indexes grouped at the end of the book are similarly broken into six sections, one each covering the writer's primary and secondary works.

Each bibliography is arranged chronologically, from the earliest published material to the latest, and numbered consecutively from one in each section (e.g., A1, A2, A3, etc., for each author's fiction). Books and shorter works are interfiled; reprint editions of books appear as new entries under their respective years, with see references from one to the other. Reprints of stories are listed under the main entry, chronologically by year of reprint, with editor of anthology, title, place of publication, publisher, year, and format (e.g., "paper"=paperback). Each book entry lists title (underlined), subject category (e.g., "mystery"), place of publication, publisher, but no paginations. Each shorter work entry gives title (in quotations), magazine, volume number, issue number, date, pagination; or, for those published originally in books: book title, book editor, place of publication, publisher, format, paginations. Story collections include complete contents listings, plus the years in which the original stories were published. Many entries include bibliographical notes, but few other annotations for Parts A-C.

"Part B: Miscellaneous Media" includes screenplays, teleplays, interviews, recordings, poetry, etc. "Part C: Nonfiction" includes all nonfiction publications, with brief subject annotations. "Part D: Critical Studies" includes author, title, bibliographical data, and extensive subject annotations for book reviews, fan commentaries, critiques, bibliographies, and other secondary works, arranged chronologically by publication date. The indexes correlate titles and item numbers only, or authors, titles, and item numbers for the indexes to critical studies. No foreign language editions are included. The book is reproduced from typed copy and bound to library standards.

The decision to list exact reprints of previously published books as new entries under the appropriate year is unfortunate, since it tends to result in endless repetitions of the same titles over and over again (Arbur does provide see references, however); it would have been more useful to include subsidiary printings under the first edition of each book, as is true with most of the other volumes in this series. Coverage is complete only through 1980, making the sections on Bradley and McCaffrey, both still active as writers, very much out-of-date (but Brackett's section remains fairly current, the author having died in 1978). Finally, having six indexes to one volume, one after another, is cumbersome, to say the least; these should have either been combined into two indexes, as with the other tripartite volume in this series (on Lloyd Alexander/Evangeline Walton/Kenneth Morris; see #268), or included in place immediately after each author's bibliography. Even with these minor caveats, further editions of both Bradley and McCaffrey, who remain both active and popular, would certainly be justified.

289. Benson, Gordon, Jr. **Leigh Douglass Brackett and Edmond Hamilton: A Working Bibliography**. Leeds, West Yorkshire, England & Albuquerque, N.M., Galactic Central, 1988. i, 25 p. (Galactic Central Bibliographies for the Avid Reader, Vol. 20). ISBN 0-912613-05-X (pbk.).

Brackett and Hamilton comprised one of several husband-and-wife writer teams in science fiction, although they rarely collaborated with each other; they died a year apart in the late 1970s. Benson's checklist is arranged by category, then alphabetically by title; Brackett's list occupies pages 1-8, Hamilton's 9-25. Contents (for each author): author's full name, date and place of birth and date of death, lists of awards won by the author, pseudonyms, brief list of biographical sketches and obituaries. Bibliographical contents for Brackett include "A. The Stories"; "B. The Books"; "C. The Series"; "Addenda"; "Screenplays"; for Hamilton: "Abbreviations List"; "A. The Stories" (Excluding "Captain Future"); "B. The Series" (including the Captain Future stories and novels); "C. The Other Books"; "Additions and Corrections." In each section the material is arranged in alphabetical order by title, items being numbered consecutively from the number one in each section. For shorter works, Benson gives item number, title, category ("ss"=short story, "nt"=novelette, etc.), magazine or book in which the item appeared, month and year of publication (for magazines, in the form of "4-42" for April 1942) or year of publication (for books), a list of subsequent reprints (for which title, publisher, year, and editor's last name are given), but no paginations. Typical book entries include item number, title, contents (for collections, by item number), publication data (publisher, stock number, month and year of publication [in the form "10-59" for October 1959], pagination, price, with dates of reissues by the same publisher), cover artist. There is no index and just a minimal list of secondary sources. The series listings are very helpful, particularly for Hamilton, who produced many works for the hero and SF pulps. The book is shot from fairly legible typed copy, and some of the text runs into the right margin, making potential rebinding difficult for libraries. Future editions should include a title index and detailed paginations of short story appearances and their reprints, as well as more information on Brackett's screen and television work, which is given minimal play here; still, Benson's book is a useful starting point for the researcher interested in the Golden Era of the pulps. Note: this bibliography has not yet been revised into the new format for this series.

Ray Bradbury

290. Albright, Donn. **Bradbury Bits & Pieces: The Ray Bradbury Bibliography: 1974-88.** Mercer Island, Wash., Starmont House, 1992. [140] p. index. (Starmont Reference Guide, No. 15). LC 89-26108. ISBN 1-55742-151-X; ISBN 1-55742-150-1 (pbk.).

This sequel and supplement to Nolan's *The Ray Bradbury Companion* (see #291) was based on Albright's extensive collection of Bradburyana and is more of a collection catalog than a formal literary bibliography. Albright includes any items published before 1974 not listed in the *Companion* (roughly four pages), arranged in Nolan's original format; Bradbury fiction published after 1974 is organized chronologically in one list, novels and stories intermingled. No bibliographical data are included. Other sections cover fanzine items published between 1937-57 that were not in Nolan; Bradbury stories that have never been collected in book form; a checklist of 100 unpublished Bradbury tales, listed alphabetically by title; mimeos produced by Bradbury himself, including operas, playscripts, screenplays, teleplays, radio plays, and stage plays; adaptations of Bradbury stories by other hands in various media; first book appearances of Bradbury short stories (items Nolan missed, plus new material); books of special interest, 1958-1989, including Book Club editions, Canadiana, other reprint editions not mentioned by Nolan; pamphlets published since 1974; limited editions, 1947-1989; proofs and galleys (about forty items) of Bradbury books; British editions of the author's books (the contents of which in many cases are different from their American equivalents); foreign-language editions (about 450 items), listed chronologically; Bradbury fiction reprinted in English-language periodicals (1946-89); a list of stories that have been rewritten, and similar listings for nonfiction and verse; endorsements made by Bradbury, 1953-88; title changes from Bradbury's original titles; drama performances, 1974-89; corrigenda to Nolan; a selected list of secondary sources, 1945-89; a complete bibliography of books and pamphlets devoted to Bradbury and his works; a list of books dedicated to Bradbury. The book also includes a new introduction by Bradbury, a preface by Nolan, plus pieces of Bradbury stories which have never appeared in these forms elsewhere. Format size is 8.5" x 11"; the book is attractively designed and typeset and the cloth edition bound to library standards.

Albright estimates that three times as much Bradbury material was published during the fifteen years covered by this book than in all of the writer's preceding career. The volume also features original Ray Bradbury sketches throughout the book, and black-and-white reproductions of Bradbury paintings on the front and back covers. Although all serious researchers of the author's life and career will want this guide, *Bits & Pieces* has the feel of a literary hodgepodge and is certainly *not* the definitive one-volume bibliography that we might have expected on this major writer of the fantastic—and which the world of literature still badly needs.

291. Nolan, William F. **The Ray Bradbury Companion: A Life and Career History, Photolog, and Comprehensive Checklist of Writings with Facsimiles from Ray Bradbury's Unpublished and Uncollected Work in All Media.** Detroit, Mich., A Bruccoli Clark Book, Gale Research Co., 1975. xiii, 339 p. index. LC 74-10397. ISBN 0-8103-0930-0 (boxed).

Nolan, a well-known SF writer in his own right, became interested in Bradbury's work at an early age (see also his *Ray Bradbury Review* [#292]). This magnificently designed and produced 7.5" x 10.5" book was issued as a boxed volume and beautifully illustrated with full-page reproductions of manuscript pages, title pages, dust jackets, paperback covers, and photos of the author and his family.

Contents include "The Inherited Wish: An Introduction," by Bradbury; "Preface"; "Ray Bradbury Photolog"; "The Life and Career of Ray Bradbury—A Chronology"; "Facsimiles from Ray Bradbury's Unpublished and Uncollected Work in All Media"; "The Writings of Ray Bradbury" (the bibliography proper); "Writings About Ray Bradbury"; "Index to the Writings of Ray Bradbury."

The introductory sections, and particularly the photolog and chronology, provide extensive background material on Bradbury's life and career, the latter running thirty-one pages (through 1973). The bibliography proper is divided into sections: "Books and Pamphlets" (eighty out of 202 pages); "Bradbury's Magazine"; "Fiction"; "Articles and Miscellaneous Non-Fiction"; "Verse"; "Introductions"; "Reviews"; "Published Speeches"; "Published Plays"; "Stage Productions"; "Films"; "Television"; "Radio"; "Published Letters"; "Interviews"; "Anthology Appearances"; "Comic Book Appearances"; "Bradbury in Sound"; "Book Dedications"; "Bradbury Pseudonyms."

The books section is arranged in chronological order by year of publication and includes data on all U.S. and British first cloth and paperback editions and on all known reprints; foreign-language editions are listed only for *The Martian Chronicles*. For each first edition, Nolan provides complete collations, contents, and bibliographical data, as well as known print runs. For subsequent editions, only place of publication, publisher, and book I.D. number are given, with occasional notes citing title or contents variations from the original. Included in this section are facsimiles of most of the title pages (and many of the covers) of the first editions.

Other sections of the book provide less detailed information. Bradbury's short stories, for example, are listed in chronological order by date of publication, with titles, magazines, and dates listed, but no paginations. Nolan uses two-letter codes (e.g., "SS"=*S Is for Space*) to indicate the Bradbury book collections in which these stories have been included, noting briefly those stories anthologized elsewhere, with the title and year of the anthology (further details on these reprints are rather cumbersomely provided in the "Anthology Appearances" section, which is arranged in chronological order, with story title, anthology title, editor, place of publication, and publisher, but no paginations). The media sections include both works by Bradbury and adaptations of his work, with all known air dates, production companies, program titles, etc. The secondary bibliography is broken into two sections covering books and magazine/newspaper articles, both arranged in chronological order with title, author, and bibliographical data (but no paginations). Nolan provides short annotations of the monographs only. The index covers Bradbury's titles and other persons and titles mentioned by page number. Data are complete through 1973.

This is one of the best-*looking* single-author bibliographies ever produced in the genre, with extraordinarily high production values, but it also includes a wealth of details on the writer and his works. One might have hoped for a few more specifics (such as paginations) on the magazine and anthology appearances of Bradbury's stories, but other than this quibble, Nolan's work stands as a monument to one of the most popular and enduring writers of the fantastic. Albright's supplement (see #290) picks up where Nolan's work ends, adds some material omitted by Nolan, and corrects some very minor errors.

292. Nolan, William F. **"Ray Bradbury Index,"** in *Ray Bradbury Review*, edited by William F. Nolan. San Diego, Calif., William F. Nolan, 1952. p. 46-63. index. (pbk.). Also: Los Angeles, Graham Press, 1988. p. 46-63. index. A supplement (under the same title) appeared in *Shangri-LA* (Fall/Winter, 1953): 14-26.

This distant precursor to *The Ray Bradbury Companion* (see #291) is broken into eight sections: "Published Books," "Original Stories in U.S. Magazines," "Radio and Television Adaptations," "Articles," "Anthologies," "Reprints," "Scheduled Stories," "Index Addenda and Totals." A typical book entry includes title (all caps), publisher, year of publication, pagination, and contents. The short fiction section is arranged by magazine title, then chronologically by publication date. A typical entry includes magazine title (all caps), story title, type (e.g., "s.s."=short story), month of publication, year of publication. The "Anthologies" section is arranged in chronological order by date of publication of the anthology, giving book title (all caps), editor, year of publication (but no publishing data), and story title(s). This 5" x 8" booklet is shot from generally clear typed copy and stapled through the spine. The 1988 cloth edition is a facsimile of the original. Now outdated and subsumed into Nolan's later bibliography of Bradbury (see #291).

Marion Zimmer Bradley

Arbur, Rosemarie. **Leigh Brackett, Marion Zimmer Bradley, Anne McCaffrey: A Primary and Secondary Bibliography.** *See the entry of Leigh Brackett* (see #288).

293. Benson, Gordon Jr., and Phil Stephensen-Payne. **Marion Zimmer Bradley, Mistress of Magic: A Working Bibliography**. Albuquerque, N.M. & Leeds, West Yorkshire, England, Galactic Central Publications, 1991. 9, 51 p. (Galactic Central Bibliographies for the Avid Reader, Vol. 40). (pbk.).

Bradley has been widely acclaimed for her Darkover stories, which combine the best of science fiction with fantasy and psi elements. This new checklist of her works is complete through early 1991.

Bradley's works are organized alphabetically by title within broad subject categories: "A. Stories"; "B. Fiction Books";" C. Series"; "D. Poems, Songs & Plays"; "E. Poem, Song & Play Volumes"; "F. Articles"; "G. Miscellaneous"; "H. Non-Fiction Books"; "I. Books Edited by Marion Zimmer Bradley"; "J. Media Presentations" (none known); "K. Articles on Marion Zimmer Bradley"; "L. Reviews"; "+. "Books About Marion Zimmer Bradley"; "N. Phantom & Forthcoming Titles"; "O. Related Items by Other Authors"; "P. Textual Variations"; "Q. Chronological Index." A typical short fiction entry includes item number

(A1-A65), title, type (e.g., "NT"=novelette), magazine title and month and year of publication (e.g., "9-54"=September 1954), or, for those stories first appearing in anthologies or collections, book title (all caps), editor, publisher, and year of publication, plus similar data for all known reprints. No paginations are given. A typical book listing provides item number, title (all caps), publisher, format (e.g., "pb"=paperback), stock number, month and year of publication, pagination, price, and cover artist surname (in parentheses), with similar data on all known reprints and reissues in chronological order by issue date. The chronology groups Bradley's fiction year by year, then monthly by publication date (but the individual months are not actually listed). The book is shot from very legible word-processed copy and is easy to read and use.

In comparing Benson/Stephensen-Payne's checklist with Arbur's bibliography (see #288), the former is a decade more current, while the latter includes many more secondary sources, all of them annotated. Arbur also provides paginations for original short story appearances, data that Benson lacks; but Arbur fails to list the paginations for Bradley's monographs which Benson includes. Thus, serious scholars and libraries will need to retain both works; fans may be content to own just this more recent checklist.

Gary Brandner

294. Brandner, Martine Wood. **The Work of Gary Brandner: An Annotated Bibliography & Guide**. San Bernardino, Calif., The Borgo Press, 1992. [160] p. index. (Bibliographies of Modern Authors, No. 23). ISBN 0-8095-0519-3; ISBN 0-8095-1519-9 (pbk.).

Brandner is best known as the author of *The Howling* series of werewolf books and films and other very popular works of modern horror fiction. This new guide by his wife provides a thorough examination of the author's literary and screen work.

Contents: Introduction: "The Hemingway of Horror," by Martine Wood Brandner; Preface: "Gary Brandner: 'Oh Yeah?'" by Richard Laymon; Foreword: "My Introduction to Gary Brandner," by Kim Greenblatt; "A Gary Brandner Chronology"; "A. Books"; "B. Short Fiction"; "C. Short Nonfiction"; "D. Screenplays"; "E. Screen Adaptations"; "F. Series Detectives and Others"; "G. Panel Discussions and Classes"; "H. Committees"; "I. Footnotes and Insights"; "J. Interviews"; "K. Brandner on Brandner"; "L. Publicity on Projects that Went Awry"; "M. Publicity for Successful Projects"; "N. Secondary Sources"; "O. Miscellaneous"; "Quoth the Critics"; Afterword: "An Interview with Gary Brandner"; "Treatment of *Cameron's Closet*," with "Comments" by Gary Brandner; "Index."

In each section, materials are arranged chronologically by publication date. A typical book entry includes item number (boldfaced), book title (boldfaced), pseudonym (where applicable; Brandner has penned a number of novels under house names such as Nick Carter), place of publication, publisher, month and year of publication, pagination, format (paper or cloth), type (e.g., "horror novel"). Similar data are provided for all known reprints and variant editions, including foreign-language versions, in chronological order by publication date. Also included are lengthy plot descriptions, averaging 200 words each, and a list of known book reviews in alphabetical order by reviewers' name, with complete bibliographical data. Materials are numbered from one in each section, prefaced by the identifying letter for that chapter (e.g., C1, C2, C3, etc., for the author's nonfiction).

A typical shorter work entry includes item number (boldfaced), title (in quotes, boldfaced), magazine title (italics), volume number, month and year of publication, pagination, and similar data on all known reprints in anthologies or foreign-language periodicals. Screenplays and screen adaptations of Brandner's works mention director, production company, year of production, principal actors, and other similar data. "Quoth the Critics" includes excerpts of major critical reactions to the author's work. The introductions, chronology, and afterword provide detailed introductions to Brandner's personal and creative lives. Several special features enhance this bibliography, including a lengthy original interview, a reproduction of the author's screen treatment for *Cameron's Closet*, and an index to all the major characters in Brandner's novels. In addition, there is the standard series index correlating titles and item numbers. The book is shot from attractive laser printer-generated copy, and the cloth edition is bound to library standards.

It is interesting to use this book as an example of how the Bibliographies of Modern Authors series has developed. The first few books in the series, on Elliot (see #334) and May (see #379) were rather plain-looking volumes, filled with dry data but somewhat cramped in style. *The Work of Gary Brandner* not only includes a wealth of material about the writer's works (the chief *raison d'être* for any bibliography) but also provides a series of glimpses through the windows of the man's soul—in the eyes of his friends and compatriots, in the minds of the critics, through his own words. The physical appearance of the books has continued to improve together with their scope, and what we have in these latest volumes is nothing less than a summation of the writer's entire creative existence, attractively and logically and succinctly presented. There are individual bibliographies that match or even better the best of the books in the Bibliographies of Modern Authors series, but there is no group of single-author bibliographies in this or any other literary genre that comes close to matching their overall accuracy and completeness. Highly recommended.

Reginald Bretnor

295. Burgess, Scott Alan. **The Work of Reginald Bretnor: An Annotated Bibliography & Guide**. San Bernardino, Calif., The Borgo Press, 1989. 122 p. index. (Bibliographies of Modern Authors, No. 8). LC 85-31405. ISBN 0-89370-387-7; ISBN 0-89370-487-3 (pbk.).

Bretnor is well-regarded as an American SF and mystery writer, military historian, and critic, although he is perhaps best known for his Feghoots, short SF pun-stories featuring that debonair space- and time-travelling adventurer, Ferdinand Feghoot.

Contents: Introduction: "The Ghosts We Share," by Judith Merril; "A Reginald Bretnor Chronology"; "A. Books"; "B. Short Fiction"; "C. Nonfiction"; "D. Feghoots"; "E. Verse"; "F. Editorial Credits"; "G. Unpublished Works"; "H. Honors and Awards"; "I. About the Author"; "J. Miscellanea"; "Quoth the Critics"; "Through Time and Space with Ferdinand Feghoot #118" (an original story by Bretnor); "On the Proper Perpetration of Feghoots" (an original essay); "Through Time and Space with Ferdinand Fedhoot #119" (an original story); Afterword: "Debts and Acknowledgments," by Bretnor (an original essay); "Index."

In each section, the author's works are arranged chronologically and numbered consecutively, chapter by chapter (e.g., A1, A2, for Bretnor's first two books). A typical entry includes item number (boldfaced), title (boldfaced), byline (for pseudonymous works), place of publication, publisher, year of publication, pagination, format (paper or cloth), type of publication (e.g., "novel"), and similar data for known reprint editions and translations. A typical shorter work entry includes item number (boldfaced), title (in quotes, boldfaced), magazine title (italicized), volume number, month and year of publication, pagination, and similar data for all known reprints, including foreign-language titles. Book entries also include secondary sources and reviews listed alphabetically by main entry with full bibliographical data. All monographs are annotated, with complete contents listings and/or plot summaries; entries in other sections are selectively annotated as needed, providing information on award nominations, significance, etc. Merril's introduction is a poignant look at the author's life and works. The chronology provides a year-by-year account in block paragraph format of the author's professional and personal life; Bretnor is known for his reticence about personal details, some of which are revealed here for the first time. "About the Author" includes all known secondary works. "Miscellanea" include information on pen names, book dedications, memberships, Library of Congress cataloging data, and similar data. The "Quoth the Critics" section reproduces selected excerpts of comments by the leading critics on the author's work. The index cites titles and item numbers only. Bretnor's afterword notes his debt to the literary community and to his two deceased wives, both of them writers themselves. The book is shot from very attractive word-processed copy and the cloth edition bound to library standards.

Burgess worked very closely with Bretnor (a neighbor), using the author's personal collection of his own works to construct this very comprehensive bibliography. Coverage is complete through the Fall of 1989. Bretnor's humor is aptly demonstrated in the two Feghoots original to this volume, and his concluding essay (also an original work) reveals some of his personal and literary antecedents. The humanity of his fiction makes him a prime potential target for future scholars; this well-presented and -executed guide to his work will become a necessary starting point for all researchers.

Fredric Brown

296. Baird, Newton. **A Key to Fredric Brown's Wonderland: A Study and an Annotated Bibliographical Checklist.** Georgetown, Calif., Talisman Literary Research, 1981. 63 p. index. LC 81-52422 (cloth and pbk.).

Baird's interesting, attractive, well-designed 8.5" x 11" tribute to this well-regarded SF and mystery writer and his work includes "Preface" (about this book), "A Key to Fredric Brown's Wonderland" (biographical and critical introduction), "Chronology of Fredric Brown"; "Fredric Brown: My Husband," by Elizabeth C. Brown; "The Early Career of Fredric Brown," by Harry Altshuler; "It's Only Everything," a short autobiographical piece by Brown himself; "An Annotated Bibliographical Checklist of Fredric Brown's Writing" (the bibliography proper); "Index."

The introductory sections provide interesting background material on the author and his work. The bibliography itself is broken into subject sections: "A. Books"; "B. Foreign Anthologies by Brown Not Published in the U.S."; "C. Parts of Books by Brown"; "D. Short Stories"; "E. Poetry"; "F. Other Contributions to Periodicals"; "G. Radio Adaptations of Stories by Brown"; "H. Television Adaptations of Fiction by Brown"; "I. Film Adaptations of Fiction by Brown"; "J. Phonograph Recordings of Fiction by Brown"; "K. Parts of Books About Brown"; "L. Articles, Parts of Articles, and Published Letters About Brown"; "Appendix." Each of the sections other than K and L (which are organized alphabetically) are arranged in chronological order by date of publication.

A typical book entry includes title (in italics), place of publication, publisher, year of publication, pagination, and similar data for all known reprints, including foreign editions (with foreign titles mentioned); a 50-100-word annotation or contents listing (for collections); and a list of contemporaneous reviews of the book. A typical story entry gives title (in boldface), magazine (in italics), and date of publication, with no paginations. Reprint editions, including some foreign reprints, are also mentioned (for anthology listings, Baird provides editor, title, publisher, and date, no paginations). Section C includes an SF anthology edited by Brown and Mack Reynolds and an article included in a writers' "how-to" book. The media listings include title, program, broadcast dates, director, writer, cast, and other data. The secondary source listings seem complete through 1980. The appendix quotes several letters about Brown, includes a list of heroes, heroines, and anti-heroes in his fiction, tallies point-of-view methods in his novels, provides a list of his pseudonyms, and lists the stories he wrote in collaboration with Mack Reynolds. The index is comprehensive, correlating titles and authors to page numbers. The volume is nicely produced and printed and illustrated with a score of author photos and magazine and book cover reproductions.

This is a superior tribute to this late writer's work, one which should have received wider circulation at the time (only a few hundred copies were produced). Since Brown ceased writing in the mid-1960s, Baird is virtually complete except for a half dozen recent collections of Brown's pulp mystery stories exhumed and reprinted by Dennis McMillan. A new edition or printing would definitely be warranted.

John Brunner

297. Benson, Gordon Jr., and Phil Stephensen-Payne. **John Brunner, Shockwave Writer: A Working Bibliography.** 3rd ed. Leeds, West Yorkshire, England & Albuquerque, N.M., Galactic Central. 1989. 9, 79 p. index. (Galactic Central Bibliographies for the Avid Reader, Vol. 11). ISBN 0-912613-06-8 (pbk.).

This well-respected British author's works are arranged by broad category, then alphabetically by title. Contents: Author's full name, date and place of birth, lists of awards won by the author (in chronological order by year, with name of award and title of work being honored), and his pseudonyms. The bibliography proper includes "A. Stories"; "B. Fiction Books"; "C. Series"; "D. Poems & Songs"; "E. Poem & Song Collections"; "F. Articles"; "G. Miscellaneous" (including letters, prefaces, notes, etc.); "H. Non-Fiction Books"; "I. Edited Books"—blank section; "J. Media Presentations"; "K. Articles on John Brunner"; "L. Reviews" (on Brunner's books, alphabetically by title of the work being reviewed, then by magazine title in which the review appeared, giving month and year of publication, and reviewer's name); "M. Books about John Brunner"; "N. Phantom and Forthcoming Titles"; "O. Related Items by Other Authors"—blank section; "P. Textual Variations"—blank section; "Q. Chronological Index" (in order by year and month [but month is not recorded], giving titles only).

In each section materials are arranged in alphabetical order by title, items being numbered consecutively from the number one in each chapter (for example, A1, A2, A3, etc., for Brunner's stories). A typical shorter work entry provides item number, title, category ("ss"=short story, "nt"=novelette, etc.), magazine or book in which the item appeared, month and year of publication (for magazines, in the form "6-74" for June 1974), or year of publication (for books), and a list of subsequent reprints (for which title, publisher, year, and editor's last name are given), but no paginations. For book-length works, Benson and Stephensen-Payne give item number, title, publication data (publisher, stock number, month and year of publication [if known, in the form "10-59" for October 1959], pagination, price), cover artist, and similar data for known reprints. There are numerous see references to Brunner's many alternate titles. There is no overall title index. The series listings include books, articles, and short stories. The book is shot from very legible word-processed copy and stapled through the spine in an 8.5" x 11" format.

Brunner is a notoriously difficult writer on which to construct a bibliography, having produced numerous variant, rewritten, and upgraded editions of his works. Benson and Stephensen-Payne have done a good job of tracking these items through a maze of bibliographical chaos, although a general title index and paginations would have been helpful. This series is beginning to develop into something more than just a typical hodgepodge of fan-generated checklists, and it is interesting and encouraging to see some worthwhile reference guides emerging from the haze.

Algis Budrys

298. Drumm, Chris. **An Algis Budrys Checklist**. Polk City, Ia., Chris Drumm Books, 1983. 16 p. index. ISBN 0-936055-03-0 (pbk.).

This 4.25" x 7" checklist of this noted American SF writer's works is organized into one chronological sequence, books and short stories being interfiled. Drumm provides a short outline of Budrys's life and a list of his pseudonyms before proceeding with the bibliography itself. Entries are grouped by year and under each year by month; those titles for which a month is not known appear at the end of each year's listings; items are numbered in order from the number one (through 147). Books are underlined, short stories appear in quotation marks. A typical short fiction entry includes item number, title, magazine, category code (e.g., "s"=short story), month of publication (or book title, if an anthology, editor, publisher, year of publication). Subsequent reprintings are grouped under the original edition, with similar data provided. No paginations are included. A typical book entry gives item number, title, category code ("n"=novel), publisher, stock number, month of publication (if known), pagination, price, and format (e.g., "pb"=paperback). There are numerous see references (by item number) to alternate or incorporated titles. Some major secondary materials are mentioned in passing in their appropriate years. The index is by title and item number only. Data are complete through 1982; a one-leaf corrigenda sheet was also inserted in some copies. The book is shot from typed copy; some text runs too close to the right margin to allow rebinding by libraries. In a major omission, Drumm does not include references to Budrys's long-running monthly review columns in *The Magazine of Fantasy & Science Fiction*. This is a useful, inexpensive starting point for research on the author's work; an expanded, updated version with better production values and more bibliographical details would certainly be justified.

Kenneth Bulmer

299. Robinson, Roger. **The Writings of Henry Kenneth Bulmer**. Harrold Wood, Essex, England, Beccon 83. 1983. 51 p. index. (pbk). **The Writings of Henry Kenneth Bulmer**. Rev. and updated ed. Harold Wood, Essex, Beccon Publications, 1984. 51 p. index. ISBN 1-870824-00-8 (spiral-bound pbk.).

Robinson, author of *Who's Hugh?*, the standard pseudonym guide of the genre (see #41), here contributes a valuable checklist on the works of the prolific British writer Kenneth Bulmer. Contents (both versions): "Editor's Notes"; "On the Pen-Name Trail," by Bulmer; "Ken Bulmer: An Appreciation," by John Clute; "Pseudonyms and Collaborations"; "Alphabetical Listing of Fiction"; "Alphabetical Listing of Non-Fiction"; "List of Edited Works and Miscellaneous Items"; "Career Schematic; Book Series"; "Story Series"; "Chronological Listing of All Work with Publication Details." The latter is actually the main section of the book, listing all of Bulmer's works year by year (novels and stories interfiled), then month by month; items whose months of publication are unknown are grouped at the end of their respective years. Each item is numbered by year (e.g., "54"=1954) and then consecutively from one: ("54.1," "54.2," etc.). A typical short fiction entry includes item number, month, category code ("S"=story, "N"=novel, etc.), title (in quotes), byline (Bulmer frequently used pseudonyms, so every byline is listed verbatim), an indication whether Robinson has actually seen the item in question ("+"=seen), magazine, issue number, and other notes, but no paginations. A book entry consists of item number, month (if known), category, title (all caps), byline, previous publication data, place of publication, publisher, year of publication, pagination, format ("pa"=paperback), price, with similar data for all subsequent editions and reprintings. See references in the alphabetical lists and internally in the chronological list are always to item number.

The main difference between the two versions (other than the vast disparity in physical size) is that the revised edition includes nearly two extra years of data, covering items published through October 1984 (the last item in the first edition is dated December 1982), plus corrections. Both books are shot from generally readable word-processed copy, although the typeface in the second edition is much larger and more readable. Clute's introduction provides a short but valuable guide to Bulmer's major works; Robinson's "Career Schematic" of Bulmer's work charts his literary output (some 135 books) year by year from 1952-1984 (the last year of data for this bibliography). Robinson clearly had help from Bulmer himself, particularly for his pulp publications, and his bibliography is thorough and competent. Future editions should include short story paginations.

Edgar Rice Burroughs

300. Adkins, P. H. **Edgar Rice Burroughs Bibliography & Price Guide**. New Orleans, La., P.D.A. Enterprises, 1974. ii, 25 p. (pbk.).

Adkins's brief checklist and price guide contains "Editions" (information on Burroughs's publishers), "Format" (i.e., how to use the bibliography), "Pricing" (how prices were determined), "Condition" (rating system used), and the bibliography proper. Burroughs's books are listed in alphabetical order by title. A typical entry includes publisher, year of publication, cloth color, pagination, numbers of plates or an indication that the book is illustrated, first edition indicators, and suggested prices for good, fine, etc., copies of the volumes. Similar data are provided for all subsequent editions, including paperbacks (paperback listings include stock number of first printing). Page 25 includes a series listing. This booklet is shot from dark, photoreduced (to about an eight-point level) typed copy; the pricing data are wholly out-of-date. Prefer Bergen (see #301).

301. Bergen, James A., Jr. **A Reference and Price Guide to U.S. Books Written by Edgar Rice Burroughs**. Tualatin, Ore., Bergen, 1989. 46 p. LC 90-197302 (pbk.). **Price and Reference Guide to Books Written by Edgar Rice Burroughs**. [2nd ed.]. Beaverton, Ore., The Golden Lion, 1991. vii, 214 p. (pbk.)

Bergen's booklet is a synthesis of recent prices actually charged for Burroughsiana by eight U.S. book dealers, plus basic first (and later) edition identification data for Burroughs's books. Contents: "Birth Certificate" (of Edgar Rice Burroughs), "Reference and Price Guides Used," "General Information on Prices," "The Author" (on Bergen himself), "References," and "Cover Art," "Editions Published by ERB Publishers," "Big Little Books," "Biographical and Bibliographical Books on ERB," "Chronology of Tarzan Books," "Tarzan Editions" (book by book in chronological order by publication date), "Chronology of Mars Books," "Martian Editions" (book by book in chronological order by publication date), "Venus Editions" (ditto), "Earth's Core Editions" (ditto), "Unrelated Editions" (alphabetically by title), "First Edition Paperbacks Published by Ballantine"; "First Edition Paperbacks Published by Ace," "First Edition Paperbacks from Other Publishers," "Authorized Professional Sequel(s)," "Authorized Amateur Sequels," "Unauthorized Amateur Sequels," "Burroughs Fanzines," "Active ERB Fanzines," "Death Certificate" (of ERB, reproduced from the original).

A typical entry includes a summary of edition points for each printing of the book which has resale value, including book title (centered, boldfaced), item number (the printings of each particular title are numbered in order from one), alternate title (if any, boldfaced), publisher, year of publication, binding color, pagination, number of plates, first edition statement (if any), cover artist, price range (e.g., $100 to $250), and other bibliographical data of interest. Although the book has no index, the contents page serves essentially the same purpose. The volume is shot from occasionally faint word-processed copy and stapled through the spine. There are a few reproductions of Burroughs' covers and too many amateurish black-and-white illustrations by Bergen himself.

Bergen admits in his introduction that he is not himself an expert book dealer or *littérateur*, but his guide, by synthesizing the actual sale prices of Burroughs' books from a variety of sources, provides a useful composite of current market values for fans and collectors alike. An expanded second edition appeared at the end of 1991.

302. Cummings, David George. **An Edgar Rice Burroughs Checklist.** [s.l.], Savage Press in Association with Comma Publications, 1974. 31 p. (pbk.).

This poorly organized guide is divided into three sections covering Burroughs's hardcover books, paperback books, and magazine serializations. The author's preface, "Hardcover Notes," describes in very general terms, on a company-by-company basis, the main publishers of Burroughs's cloth fiction, with some information on the identification of first editions. A similar essay, "Papercover Notes," covers Ace, Ballantine, and the other Burroughs reprinters. Most of the book consists of a general schematic listing the books in series order, together with their publishers, in descending order by publication date (however, none of the dates are given), and a blank chart for the collector to describe the condition of his or her own copy of that work. There is also a brief checklist of the magazine issues in which Burroughs stories appear, in alphabetical order by periodical title, giving story title, issue date, and year, but no other data. The final section of the checklist includes three pages of "story lines," one-sentence plot descriptions of each of the novels. The book is shot from barely legible typed copy. Prefer Bergen (see #301).

303. Day, Bradford M. **Edgar Rice Burroughs Biblio: Materials Toward A Bibliography.** South Ozone Park, N.Y., Science-Fiction & Fantasy Publications, 1956. 28 p. (pbk.). **Edgar Rice Burroughs: A Bibliography.** [2nd ed.]. Woodhaven, N.Y., Science-Fiction & Fantasy Publications, 1962. 45 p. LC 62-3803 (pbk.).

Day's brief checklist of this American science fiction and fantasy author's fiction is organized similarly to his bibliographies on Haggard, Mundy, and Rohmer (see #202, #388, and #405). The book section is arranged alphabetically by title. A typical entry includes title (all caps), categorization (e.g., "stone age adventure," "Inner-Earth"), publisher, place of publication, year of publication, pagination, cover copy quote, brief mention of reprint editions (by publisher's name only) and/or magazine serialization (with magazine name and dates), plus binding color style. The short fiction section is arranged in chronological order by date of publication and lists title (caps), magazine title, year of publication, month of publication, list of reprints in Burroughs's books, but no paginations. There are also checklists of stories serialized in the *New York Evening World* and books included in the Big Little Books series, plus a brief list of foreign-language editions (giving foreign-language titles only—no bibliographical data). The book is mimeographed (1956 edition) or offset (1962 version) from occasionally faint typed copy and stapled through the spine. The basic bibliography was slightly updated in Day's later compilation, *Bibliography of Adventure* (see #202).

304. Harwood, John. **The Literature of Burroughsiana: A Listing of Magazine Articles, Book Commentaries, News Items, and Related Items Concerning the Life and/or Works of Edgar Rice Burroughs.** Baton Rouge, La., Camille Cazedessus, 1963. 105 p. (pbk.).
[Not seen.]

305. Heins, Henry Hardy. **A Golden Anniversary Bibliography of Edgar Rice Burroughs.** Albany, N.Y., [Henry Hardy Heins], 1962. 122 p. index. LC 63-336 (pbk.). **A Golden Anniversary Bibliography of Edgar Rice Burroughs.** Rev. ed. West Kingston, R.I., Donald M. Grant, 1964. 418 p. index. LC 63-13900.

Both of these bibliographies quickly assumed the status of collectors' items upon publication, almost immediately went out-of-print, and now sell for hundreds of dollars each. The first edition was published by Heins himself as an 8.5" x 11" paperback (150 copies), mimeographed from typed copy on green paper and pinned through the spine. Its data (and format) were subsumed, updated, and expanded into the more elaborate 7" x 10" Grant hardcover, the first book released under that highly successful specialty imprint.

Contents (Grant edition): Part One: "1. Foreword to the Revised Edition"; "2. Editor's Preface"; "3. The Master Story-Teller: An Appreciation"; "4. How I Wrote the Tarzan Books," by Burroughs; "5. Newspaper Appearances of Early ERB Stories"; "6. Chronology of the Stories, by Magazine Appearance"; "7. Mr. Burroughs' Publishers"; "8. The A. C. McClurg & Co. Trade Lists"; "9. The Dedications of the Books"; "10. Entertainment Is Fiction's Purpose," by Burroughs; "11. The A. L. Burt and Grosset & Dunlap Catalogues"; "12. Explanation of the Format"; "13. The Bibliography"; "14. The First Book Reviews of *Tarzan*"; "15. Special Note on the Grosset & Dunlap Reprints"; "16. The Red-Cover Tarzanas"; "17. The McLeod Titles"; "18. Copyright Data on the 'Big Little Books'"; "19. The Tarzan Clans of America"; "20. One Other Tarzan Book—And a Tarzan Booklet"; "21. Tarzan Series—Recapitulation"; "22. The Tarzan Theme," by Burroughs; "23. The 1958 Fire at Edgar Rice Burroughs, Inc."; "24. Mars Series—Recapitulation"; "25. Pellucidar Series—Recapitulation"; "26. Venus Series—Recapitulation"; "27. Other Works of Fiction—Recapitulation"; "28. Who's Who in the Titles"; "29. Other Published Writings of Edgar Rice Burroughs"; "30. Burroughs' Literary Activities During World War II"; "31. Radio Scripts by Burroughs"; "32. Mr. Burroughs Describes His Publishing Methods," by Burroughs; "33. The Officers of Edgar Rice Burroughs, Inc."; "34. The Munsey Magazine Dates"; "35. Burroughs in Foreign Translation"; "36. The Literature of Burroughsiana"; "37. It Runs in the Family"; "38. The Burroughs Bibliophiles"; "39. Other Fan Magazines"; "40. Burroughs Bibliographies"; "41. Related Items"; "42. Index to the Burroughs Chapter Titles"; addenda to Part One: "43. New Book Releases"; "44. Unpublished Manuscripts"; "45. Some Unusual Titles"; "46. Pseudonyms"; "47. Poetry by Burroughs"; "48. The Burroughs Story That Was Based on a Poem"; "49. Out There Somewhere," by Burroughs; "50. The Notebook of Edgar Rice Burroughs"; "51. Supplements." Part Two (in Grant edition only) includes "Illustrations and Advertisements" (161 pages of facsimile reproductions of book and magazine covers and of publisher catalog advertisements), plus an "Index" and an "Abbreviations List."

The bibliography proper is arranged by novel series (the Tarzan books, for example) then in chronological order by publication date. A typical entry includes title (underlined caps), copyright registration number, dedication, one- to two-sentence annotation; cover and interior illustration artist; a list of every edition and printing known to exist, with specific printing dates, original book prices, paginations, collations, binding colors and textures, and any other information necessary to identify edition states and priorities. Similar data are listed for British editions. At the end of each series section Heins summarizes the data for the series in a table running sideways down the page, giving page number where the book is covered in Heins's bibliography; series number; title code; title (with magazine title[s], if different); date of book publication, start of magazine serialization, and actual dates when written (as taken from Burroughs's master notebook); first edition publisher, magazine publisher, Burroughs's story number (derived from his notebook).

In addition to the bibliographical data, Heins provides a wealth of other sidenotes and details on Burroughs, his work and life, and related topics and many quotations from the master's work. The illustrations section, completely new to the Grant edition, provides very clear black-and-white reproductions of Burroughs's book and magazine covers (some of the book covers are also reproduced in the main bibliography section), interior magazine illustrations, and catalogs featuring Burroughs novels. The index correlates titles, publishers, and other names to their appropriate page numbers. The abbreviations list includes the letter codes Heins arbitrarily assigned to each Burroughs work, which he uses throughout these books for see" references.

At the time this book appeared, a renaissance of Burroughs's works had just begun, and while some of the soon-to-be-released "new" titles are mentioned by Heins, most, of course, are not, except in manuscript form (some of Burroughs's then-unpublished manuscripts were issued by Canaveral Press, Ace Books, and Ballantine Books between 1963-1970). Thus, while Heins is remarkably complete through the early 1960s, he misses perhaps eight original Burroughs titles released after 1964. Also, few foreign-language titles are mentioned, as Heins himself admits. It should be noted that the interior production values of this early Don Grant book do not match the elaborate, beautifully designed collector's items of later years; most of the text is shot from typed copy, although the numerous illustrations are faithfully and carefully reproduced. *A Golden Anniversary Bibliography* was out-of-print within two months of publication and has curiously never been reprinted or updated since; most copies went to fans, and relatively few found their way into library collections. Copies of both versions now routinely sell for $400 each. This means, unfortunately, that much of Heins's carefully gathered data are inaccessible to the average scholar. A new edition, updated and expanded (and reset), is badly needed.

James Branch Cabell

306. Brewer, Frances Joan. **James Branch Cabell: A Bibliography of His Writings, Biography, and Criticism.** Charlottesville, Va., University of Virginia Press, 1957. 206 p. index. LC a58-5622. Also: Freeport, N.Y., Books for Libraries Press, 1971. 206 p. LC 76-157325. ISBN 0-8369-5785-7.

This book and Bruccoli's collection guide (see #307) were issued simultaneously as a matched set and cataloged as one record in the *National Union Catalogue*. Cabell's books are listed by series name (e.g., *Biography of the Life of Manuel*), then by series number (or in chronological order by publication date, whichever is appropriate). A typical entry includes item number, title (all caps), place of publication, publisher, year of publication, pagination, physical size (in centimeters), description of binding cloth, points, and total printing of the first edition, contents, previously published excerpts or serialization, a list of contemporaneous reviews, and mentions of subsequent American and first British editions. Revised editions are covered as part of the entries for the original versions.

Part II: "Contributions to Books and Magazines" arranges the author's shorter works by title, a typical entry providing item number, title (small caps), magazine or book title (also in small caps), month and year of publication (periodical entries) or year of publication (book entries), but no paginations. Similar data are provided for all known reprints, including those in Cabell's own books. Cabell's works are numbered in order from No. 1 (the first book) through No. 276 (the last short piece). The third section lists "Biography [and] Criticism" on Cabell, arranged alphabetically by author but including data similar to that of Part II. Secondary works are numbered from A1-A257. There is also a "Chronology of Books and Contributions to Books and Magazines" (by Cabell), arranged in order by year and month and giving date, title, type (e.g., "m"=magazine [contribution]), and item number. Supplementary material includes a complete checklist of book dedications by Cabell to other persons, cited to item number(s), and a separate listing of "Bibliographies of the Works of James Branch Cabell," in alphabetical order by author, with complete bibliographical data. The index references authors, titles, and subjects to item numbers. The book is nicely typeset and bound to library standards.

Cabell died in 1958 shortly after this volume was published, so Brewer's guide is essentially complete for primary works. One laments, however, the lack of paginations for shorter works; also, Brewer's organization of the books section is unnecessarily confusing, particularly towards the end of the chapter, where works appear almost jumbled together haphazardly (there is, in fact, some order here [miscellaneous materials are arranged chronologically by publication date], but it is not obvious to the casual user); some of these organizational problems are offset by the detailed index. This bibliography supplements but does not supplant Brussel (see #309), who provides more detailed descriptions of individual monographs. Prefer Hall (see #308).

307. Bruccoli, Matthew J. **Notes on the Cabell Collection at the University of Virginia.** Charlottesville, Va., University of Virginia Press, 1957. 178 p. index. (James Branch Cabell: A Bibliography, Part II). LC a58-5622 [*sic*].

Produced as a companion volume to Brewer's bibliography of Cabell's works (see #306), *Notes* is a straightforward description of the books, manuscripts, and letters by James Branch Cabell held in the Alderman Library of the University of Virginia at Charlottesville. Books are listed in the same order as in Brewer's bibliography, with the same identification number, and indexed alphabetically by title in the table of contents. A typical entry includes item number, title (all caps), plus detailed descriptions of any copies of the manuscripts, galley proofs, and printed copies available in the Alderman collections. The second section, "Notes on Special Material," mentions secondary sources about Cabell and describes the Cabell manuscript collection (detailed physical descriptions of these materials are given in the first part under their respective book titles; however, a few of the manuscripts covered here are shorter works not mentioned in Section One). Also included are "Cabell's Notes on His Printed Books" (in two parts, by Cabell). Section Three, "Notes on the Cabell Letters," provides a detailed rendering of the Cabell correspondence (to and from) held by the University of Virginia, listed chronologically by date of letter with a one- to two-sentence description of the contents. The very complete index correlates authors and titles with page numbers. The book is attractively typeset and bound to library standards. Since the Alderman Library remains the largest single repository of Cabelliana, all scholars seriously interested in studying this influential writer's life and works will want access to this volume. This catalog is also interesting to the student of bibliography as being one of the early works of Matthew J. Bruccoli, who later developed so many major literary reference guides for Gale Research Co. and other companies, including his own firm, Bruccoli Clark Layman Inc. For larger academic library collections.

308. Hall, James N. **James Branch Cabell: A Complete Bibliography, with a Supplement of Current Values of Cabell Books,** by Nelson Bond. New York, Revisionist Press, 1974.

xi, 245 p. index. LC 74-23476. (The James Branch Cabell Series). ISBN 0-87700-208-8. Limited to 200 copies.

Hall's bibliography was prompted by a resurgence of popular interest in Cabell's work during the early 1970s, when Lin Carter reprinted a number of JBC's novels in his Ballantine Books Adult Fantasy paperback series. His book is arranged similarly to Brewer's guide (see #306). Part 1 separates Cabell's monographs into their respective series (for example, "The Nightmare Has Triplets"), then lists them in volume order. A typical entry includes item number, book title (all caps), ID code (mnemonic, consisting of two or three capital letters [e.g., "BL"=*Beyond Life*] followed by a hyphen and a printing ID number [e.g., "BL-A2"=the second printing of the first edition of *Beyond Life*]), publisher, printing statement reproduced from the copyright page of the book, pagination, and a complete description of binding cloth and other edition and printing points. Every known printing of the book, including translations into foreign languages (with foreign-language titles), is listed. The books are numbered consecutively from 1-43.

Part 2 lists shorter works by Cabell broken into four sections: "Original Material by Cabell," "Magazine Reprints in Books," "Reprint Material in Books," and "Selected Contributions to Periodicals." Materials in each section are organized chronologically by publication date. A typical anthology entry includes item number, book title (all caps), editor's name, place of publication, publisher (variously; not all entries include publisher's name), year of publication, and the specific item contributed by Cabell, with exact paginations and literary antecedents (previous appearances elsewhere) for all known printings of the books. Section IV, "Selected Contributions to Periodicals," includes only those items never reprinted in book form. Materials in each of these four subchapters are numbered from the number one, prefixed by the letters A, B, C, or D (corresponding to Sections I, II, III, and IV).

Part 3, "Cabelliana—About Cabell," is divided into five sections: "Books About Cabell and His Works," "Bibliographies," "Cabellian Art," "Cabellian Magazines," and "Miscellaneous," arranged chronologically by publication date and providing information comparable to the earlier chapters. Items in these sections are also numbered consecutively from one, prefixed by the letters E, F, G, H, and K, respectively. Appendix A "Where to Find It," correlates specific title and printing codes for Cabell's books with location symbols of libraries which have copies in their collections, followed by detailed one- to two-paragraph descriptions of academic libraries with major book and/or manuscript holdings of Cabelliana; this is a very useful tool for the scholar, although the heavy use of abbreviations, many of which require constant reference to the front of the book, is unnecessary, often irritating, and even counterproductive. Bond's afterword on valuing Cabell's books as collectors' items uses a similar code system but at least inserts book titles throughout the text; this section would have been better arranged alphabetically by title. The very detailed index correlates authors and titles to page numbers. The book is shot from sometimes light typed copy and bound to library standards.

James Branch Cabell: A Complete Bibliography is not quite the definitive work that Hall obviously intended it to be. It lacks the very careful title page descriptions provided by Brussel (see #309), omits some publisher data in Part 2, and uses too many abbreviations in subsidiary sections. One might also have wished for better production values internally. However, these are minor points: Hall does record in authoritative detail every printing of every book that Cabell ever produced and the vast majority of all other works of interest, including secondary materials, and his bibliography will prove quite sufficient for the vast majority of scholars.

309. Johnson, Merle. **A Bibliographic Check-List of the Works of James Branch Cabell, 1904-1921**. New York, F. Shay, 1921. 27 p. (pbk.). Holt, Guy. **A Bibliography of the Writings of James Branch Cabell**. Philadelphia, The Centaur Book Shop, 1924. 73 p. (The Centaur Bibliographies, No. 3). LC 24-9701. Brussel, I. R. **A Bibliography of the Writings of James Branch Cabell: A Revised Bibliography**. [2nd ed.]. Philadelphia, The Centaur Book Shop, 1932. 126 p. (The Centaur Bibliographies, No. 11). LC 32-14209. Also: London: Folcroft Press, 1970. 126 p. All three books were issued in very limited editions averaging fewer than 500 copies each.

Cabell, whose name is accented on the first syllable, attained early notoriety with publication of his satirical fantasy *Jurgen* in 1919. His fame generated great fan interest beginning in the 1920s, resulting in these three bibliographies, each pyramided on its predecessor(s).

Both Holt and Brussel (Holt loosely based his work on Johnson's brief guide) list Cabell's books chronologically by publication date. A typical entry includes item number (the books are numbered in order from the number one), title (all caps), exact publication date (to the day), an exact description of the title-page copy, complete collation, detailed description of the binding cloth and inscription(s), variations in later printings, original magazine publication date (where applicable), plus a brief description of the first British edition (if any). Many of Cabell's books were heavily revised or rewritten, sometimes under new titles; these are treated as variants of the original edition in Brussel (Holt records them as separate entries) and listed after them under separate entries, numbered, for example, "1a," "1b," etc., for each significant alteration in text. Twenty-nine books are listed in Holt, and thirty-one numbered entries (through *Some of Us*, published on Oct. 10, 1930) are described in Brussel, with a thirty-second title, the eighteen-volume Storisende Edition of *The Works of James Branch Cabell*, capping the sixty-eight-page main section.

Other chapters record Cabell's "Contributions to Books," "Contributions to Periodicals," "Studies and Reviews of James Branch Cabell" (broken into two sections: "I. In Books and Pamphlets," and "II. In Periodicals"). An appendix in Brussel reproduces a one-page letter by Cabell denying authorship for the literary hoax *Poor Jack* plus a reproduction of that play's title page and facsimiles of two pages from a pair of pirated editions of Cabell's works. Cabell's "Contributions to Books" are also listed in chronological order by publication date of the book, giving book title (small caps), author, place of publication (but no publisher), binding style, pagination, title of Cabell's work (in italics), and specific pagination of Cabell's contribution to the work. The "Contributions to Periodicals" chapter is much less helpful, being organized in chronological order in Holt but in alphabetical order by magazine title in Brussel, then chronologically by publication date. Both books list (in different order) story or article title, magazine title, and month and year of publication (but no paginations). Secondary sources are listed in chronological order by publication date, with complete bibliographical data except for names of publishers (a serious omission). There are no indexes. Both bibliographies are beautifully typeset and designed, with a (different) photograph of Cabell pasted opposite each title page and an original introduction by the master himself commenting on the "first edition" phenomenon.

Brussel's careful bibliographic description of Cabell's most popular novels (particularly the title-page copy) has not been totally superseded by any of the more recent works described above (see #306, #307, #308), and his bibliography retains sufficient value for scholars and researchers that it should be retained by all academic libraries. Hall's guide (see #308) remains, however, the most definitive modern bibliography of Cabell's work.

Ramsey Campbell

310. Ashley, Mike. **Fantasy Readers Guide to Ramsey Campbell**. Wallsend, Tyne and Wear, England, Cosmos Literary Agency, 1980. 62 p. (pbk.). Also: San Bernardino, Calif., The Borgo Press, 1980. 62 p. LC 80-22744. ISBN 0-89730-098-3.

The second book of this two-volume bibliography series (see also Ashley's guide to the publications of John Spencer & Co. Ltd. [#257]) focuses on well-known British horror writer Campbell. Contents: "Unshackled from Shadow," by Ashley (background material on Campbell's life); "As Far As I Can Recall...," by Campbell (autobiographical reminiscences); "Where It All Began," by George MacDonald (an extract from *The Princess and the Goblin* which inspired the author); "Before the Storm," by Campbell (an original short story); "Ramsey Campbell: An Appreciation," by T. E. D. Klein (a survey of Campbell's early writings); "Ramsey Campbell: Premier Stylist," by Jack Sullivan (a survey of the author's most recent work); "Ramsey Campbell: An Editor's Dream," by Hugh Lamb (profile and tribute); "The Gap," by Campbell (story); "The File on Ramsey Campbell," by Ashley (the bibliography itself).

"The File" is divided into three parts: Sections A and B, in flanking columns, give the author's fiction in order of writing and in order of publication by year, title, and item number, entries in one column being cross-referenced to those in the other. Section C, the primary bibliography, is also subdivided into three parts: "1. Short Fiction"; "2. Books"; "3. Non-Fiction"; in each section Campbell's work is arranged alphabetically by title. A typical short fiction entry includes title (in caps), year of composition, magazine or anthology title, date of publication, editor and publisher (for anthologies), and similar data on known reprints. No paginations are listed. A typical book entry lists title (in caps), date of composition, publisher, year of publication, reprints (with similar data), and complete contents (for collections). The non-fiction section includes a miscellany of items (letters, editorials, reviews). Some foreign-language editions are listed in all sections. Ashley also appends a note on Campbell's series, and Campbell himself adds a list of bowdlerized editions (with corrections!). The Cosmos edition is shot from generally legible typed copy and stapled through the spine; the Borgo facsimile version is bound to library standards.

Campbell has been very active in the past decade, making this checklist, which covers material published as late as 1980, now woefully out-of-date. A newly revised edition with paginations, better production values, and expanded details about each novel and story would certainly be warranted.

Orson Scott Card

311. Collings, Michael R. **Card Catalogue: The Science Fiction and Fantasy of Orson Scott Card**. Eugene, Ore., Hypatia Press, 1987. 15 p. (pbk.).

This brief guide to the works of a rising SF star was prepared as a booklet to be inserted in the signed, limited edition of Card's 1987 collection, *Cardography*. The *Catalogue* focuses on his fiction and nonfiction in fantastic literature, omitting his many religious publications but including articles, poems, and plays, and also his technical essays on computer science. Contents: "I. Novels"; "II. Collections"; "III. Short Fiction"; "III [*sic*]. Poetry"; "IV. Edited Volumes"; "V. Non-Fiction," in two sections, "Books and Articles." In each section and sub-section, Card's writings are arranged in alphabetical order by title; complete bibliographical data are provided for the short fiction and short nonfiction, but only place of publication, publisher, and year for book-length works. No reprint editions are listed for monographs. Award winners and nominees are mentioned, but few other annotations are provided. While this is a useful beginning checklist of Card's science fiction publications through 1987, it can in no way masquerade as a full-fledged bibliography and has now been totally subsumed into Collings's second, much reorganized expanded bibliography of Card's works (see #312).

312. Collings, Michael R. **The Work of Orson Scott Card: An Annotated Bibliography & Guide**. San Bernardino, Calif., The Borgo Press, 1992. [160] p. index. (Bibliographies of Modern Authors, No. 19). ISBN 0-8095-0516-9; ISBN 0-8095-1516-4 (pbk.).

Collings has authored a number of other critiques and bibliographies on science fiction and fantasy authors, including major guides to the works of Stephen King (see #356 and #357); this new literary bibliography delineates the fiction and nonfiction of a popular modern writer of science fiction and fantasy.

Contents: "Introduction"; "An Orson Scott Card Chronology"; "A. Books"; "B. Short Fiction"; "C. Poetry"; "D. Plays"; "E. Video and Audio Tapes"; "F. Science-Fiction Criticism, Theoretical Essays, and Reviews"; "G. Non-SF Articles, Relating to Computers and Computing, Mormonism, Writing as a Profession, etc."; "H. Editorial Credits"; "I. Honors and Awards"; "J. Secondary Sources"; "K. Unpublished Manuscripts"; "L. Miscellanea"; "Quoth the Critics"; Afterword: "Fantasy and the Believing Reader," by Card; appendix: "Contents of the Orson Scott Card Archives at the Harold B. Lee Library, Brigham Young University," compiled by Willard R. Card; "Index."

Collings arranges Card's works chronologically by publication date, separated into appropriate subject chapters. A typical book entry includes item number, title (boldfaced), byline (if different from normal usage), place of publication, publisher, year of publication, pagination, format (e.g., "cloth"), type of publication (e.g., "anthology"), and full bibliographical data on all known reprint editions, translations, republications, and anthologizations. The books are fully annotated, with complete contents listings for collections and anthologies, plot summaries for novels, and a list of chapter heads for nonfiction; also included is a list of "Secondary Sources and Reviews," arranged in alphabetical order by main entry (critic, if known, or by title or publication), with complete bibliographical data. Entries from other sections are selectively annotated as needed.

A typical short fiction entry includes item number, title (boldfaced quotes), magazine or anthology title (in italics), volume number, date of publication, and pagination (for magazine entries); or, for stories published in anthologies, editor, place of publication, publisher, format (paper or cloth), and pagination (for anthologies), with similar data for all subsequent reprints. Similar material is provided in the other sections. The brief introduction by Collings provides a general biographical to the author's life and career; Card's afterword, "Fantasy and the Believing Reader," an extensive critical essay on fantastic literature, is here published for the first time in book form. The chronology provides a year-by-year account of the author's professional and personal life in block paragraph format. "Secondary Sources" includes all known secondary works. The "Miscellanea" section includes information on pen names, book dedications, memberships, Library of Congress cataloging data, career highlights, and other data. "Quoth the Critics" includes selected excerpts of reviews and other comments by leading critics on the author's works, chronologically by title. Items in each section are numbered consecutively from the number one, prefixed by the letter of the alphabet associated with that chapter. The index correlates titles and item numbers only.

In the appendix, Card's father has provided a complete inventory of the twenty-one boxes of manuscripts, letters, and other Cardiana housed in the Brigham Young University Library; most of these materials (nineteen boxes) are available for examination by serious researchers, making this guide an important starting point for all future scholarship on this important writer. Coverage is complete through 1991. Complete and well-organized, *The Work of Orson Scott Card* provides an excellently rendered glimpse into the life and fiction of an author who is rapidly assuming a major role in the science-fiction world.

A. Bertram Chandler

313. Benson, Gordon, Jr. **Arthur Bertram Chandler, Master Navigator of Space: A Working Bibliography.** 2nd ed. Albuquerque, N.M., Galactic Central, 1989. [ii], v, 43 p. (Galactic Central Bibliographies for the Avid Reader, Vol. 3). ISBN 0-912613-07-6 (pbk.).

Benson's checklist of this popular Australian SF author's works is arranged by broad subject category, then alphabetically by title. Contents: Author's full name, date and place of birth and date of death, his pseudonyms, and his awards (listed in chronological order by date of award, giving year, award name, and title honored); "A. The Stories"; "B. Phantom Stories"; "C. The Books"; "D. Series and Related Stories" (arranged in proper reading order); "E. Book Reviews" (of Chandler's books, listed in alphabetical order by book title, then by magazine title, giving book title [boldfaced caps], magazine title [all caps], month and year of publication, reviewer); "F. Articles"; "G. Articles and Miscellaneous about A. B. Chandler"; "H. Chronological Listing of Stories and Books (First Appearances)"; "Reference Sources" (i.e., works Benson has consulted, divided into three parts: primary, secondary, tertiary). In each section materials are arranged in alphabetical order by title, each item being numbered consecutively from the number one in each section. For shorter works, Benson gives item number, title, category ("ss"=short story, "nt"=novelette, etc.), magazine or book in which the item appeared, month and year of publication (for magazines in the form "1-47" for January 1947), or year of publication (for books), and a list of subsequent reprints (for which title, publisher, year, and editor's last name are given), but no paginations. For book-length works, Benson provides item number, title (bold caps), publisher, stock number, month and year of publication (if known in the form "10-59" for October 1959), pagination, price, cover artist, and similar data for all known reprint editions. The book lacks an index. Benson's book is shot from clear word-processed copy and stapled through the spine. This volume has not yet been revised into the new series format.

Chandler died in 1984, making this volume essentially complete except for future reprintings of existing material. Benson reports that a definitive bibliography by Keith Curtis of Sydney, Australia, is currently in preparation; until that work appears, this book will provide a good starting place for scholars interested in researching Chandler's many space operas.

John Christopher

314. Stephensen-Payne, Phil. **Christopher Samuel Youd, Master of All Genres: A Working Bibliography.** 2nd ed. Leeds, West Yorkshire, England & Albuquerque, N.M., Galactic Central, 1990. 9, 33 p. (Galactic Central Bibliographies for the Avid Reader, Vol. 25). (pbk.).

This new checklist on Sam Youd, a British SF and children's book writer who writes as John Christopher, is organized by subject category, then alphabetically by title. Contents: Author's name, date and place of birth, pseudonyms, and awards (listed chronologically, a typical entry giving year of award, award name, and title of work being honored); "A. Stories"; "B. Fiction Books"; "C. Series"; "D. Poems and Songs (All as by C. S. Youd)"; "E. Poem and Song Collections"—none (empty section); "F. Articles"; "G. Miscellaneous (as by

C. S. Youd Unless Otherwise Indicated)" (includes letters, interviews, etc.); "H. Non-Fiction Books"—none; "I. Books Edited by C. S. Youd"—none; "J. Media Presentations"; "K. Articles on C. S. Youd"; "L. Reviews" (of the author's works, listed alphabetically by title of his books, then by magazine title, giving item number, book title [all caps], magazine title, month and year of publication, reviewer's name); "M. Books about C. S. Youd"; "N. 'Phantom' Titles"; "O. Related Items by Other Authors"—none; "P. Textual Variations"; "Q. Chronological Index" (arranged by year, books and other works being interfiled).

In each section Youd's works are arranged in alphabetical order by title, items being numbered consecutively from the number one in each section, prefixed by the identifying letter for that section. A typical book entry includes item number, title (all caps), pseudonym (where appropriate), contents for collections keyed to item number, and publication data (publisher, stock number [and occasionally, Library of Congress or British Library Catalog Card Number], month and year of publication [if known, in the form "7-56" for July 1956], pagination, price, cover artist), and similar data on known reprint editions. Each shorter work entry includes item number, title, category (e.g., "NT"=novelette), magazine or book in which the item appeared, month and year of publication (for magazines, in the form "12-54" for December 1954); or year of publication (for books), plus a list of subsequent reprints (for which title, editor, publisher, and year are given), but no paginations. There is no index. The book is shot from very clear word-processed copy and stapled through the spine.

An index and magazine paginations would be worthy additions to a future edition, but given the fact that each section is arranged alphabetically, these are relatively minor quibbles. As the only current guide to this enigmatic author's work, Stephensen-Payne's bibliography is a basic resource for both student and scholar.

Arthur C. Clarke

315. Samuelson, David N. **Arthur C. Clarke: A Primary and Secondary Bibliography**. Boston, G. K. Hall, 1984. xv, 256 p. index. (Masters of Science Fiction and Fantasy). LC 84-10762. ISBN 0-8161-8111-X.

Samuelson, author of *Visions of Tomorrow* and other works, here provides a complete and well-organized bibliography of this classic British SF writer. Contents: "Preface" (discussing the book's arrangement); "Introduction" (a very brief biographical guide to the author); "Part A: Fiction"; "Part B: Miscellaneous Media"; "Part C: Nonfiction"; "Part D: Biography, Bibliography, Criticism" (on Clarke); "Part E: Book Reviews" (of Clarke's books). Four appendices list "Manuscripts in Collections"; "Resources—People, Institutions, Publications"; "Honors and Awards"; "Radio and Television Broadcasts." Three indexes at the end of the book cover "Works by Arthur C. Clarke," "Works About Arthur C. Clarke," "Register of Names."

Each section except E is arranged chronologically from the earliest published material to the latest and numbered consecutively by section and item (e.g., A1, A2, etc., for Clarke's fiction). Books and shorter works are interfiled by year; reprints of books and stories are grouped as subsidiary entries under their first edition or appearance, chronologically by year of reprint; reprint editions of short stories include editor of anthology, title, place of publication, publisher, year, format (e.g., "paper"), but no paginations. Each book entry gives item number, title (underlined), place of publication, publisher, format ("paper"), but no paginations. Each shorter work entry provides item number, title (in quotes), magazine, volume number, issue number, date, pagination; or, for those published originally in books: book title, book editor, place of publication, publisher, format, and specific pagination. Story collections include complete contents listings, plus the years in which the original stories were published and references to the item numbers of the stories included. Some entries, particularly in Sections B-C, include bibliographical or descriptive notes but no other annotations; however, all of the entries in Part D are extensively annotated.

"Part B: Miscellaneous Media" includes a few audio tapes and recordings plus some video tapes; for each of these, Samuelson lists item number, title, city of publication, publisher or production company, stock number, and description of item (e.g., "32-minute audio cassette"). "Part C: Nonfiction" includes all the author's nonfiction publications (some 700 items) arranged chronologically, undated items being grouped at the very end. Parts D and E include secondary sources: D covers all known articles and books about Clarke, arranged chronologically, with author, title, bibliographical data, and summaries; most "Who's Who" publications are omitted after the author's first appearance in them. Part E indexes known book reviews of Clarke's books listed alphabetically by title and then chronologically under each work, providing magazine title (keyed to a letter code referenced to the abbreviations list at the front of this section), volume number and pagination, year and month of publication, and reviewer's name (when known). The indexes correlate titles, names, and item numbers only. Coverage is complete through 1980. The book is reproduced from typed copy and bound to academic library standards.

Samuelson's book is believed to have been the last of the fourteen volumes published in this series, and while it lacks the critical apparatus of, say, Pringle on Ballard (see #275) and is now a decade out-of-date, it remains a thoroughly good piece of work, an essential starting point for all future scholarship. Very little is missed here, with over 1,000 items in the primary bibliography alone. This is a worthy swan song of a notable set of bibliographies; and kudos are due both to Samuelson and to series editor Lloyd Currey.

Hal Clement

316. Benson, Gordon, Jr. **Hal Clement, Scientist with a Mission: A Working Bibliography**. Albuquerque, N.M., Galactic Central, 1989. [ii], v, 20 p. (Galactic Central Bibliographies for the Avid Reader, Vol. 4). ISBN 0-912613-08-4 (pbk.).

Benson's checklist of this American "hard" science fiction writer's works is arranged by general subject category, then alphabetically by title. Contents: Author's full name, date and place of birth, and his awards and honors arranged chronologically by date, giving year of award, award name, and title being honored; "A. The Stories"; "B. The Science Fiction Books"; "C. Non-Fiction Books and Edited Anthologies"; "D. Articles and Miscellaneous"; "E. Biography, Criticism, and Survey"; "F. Book Reviews" (listed alphabetically by title of the work being reviewed, then by review, giving book title [bold caps], magazine title, month and year of publication, reviewer). In each part Clement's works are arranged in alphabetical order by title, items being numbered consecutively from the number one in each section. A typical shorter work entry includes item number, title, category ("ss"=short story, "nt"=novelette, etc.), magazine or book in which the item appeared, month and year of publication (for magazines in the form "9-68" for September 1968) or year of publication (for books), plus a list of subsequent reprints (for which title, publisher, year, and editor's last name are given), but no paginations. Book-length works cite item number, title (bold caps), publisher, stock number, month and year of publication (if known, in the form "6-87" for June 1987), pagination, price, cover artist, and similar material on all known reprint editions. There is no index. The book is shot from very clear word-processed copy and stapled through the side. This volume has not been reworked into the new series format.

Clement (in real life science teacher Harry Stubbs) has never been a prolific writer, but his works have long been championed as exemplars of the "hard science fiction" school. This very comprehensive checklist should stay reasonably current for quite some time. The addition of an index and magazine paginations should be considered for future editions.

317. Drumm, Chris. **A Hal Clement Checklist**. Polk City, Ia., Chris Drumm Books, 1983. 8 p. ISBN 0-936055-00-6 (pbk.).

This small-sized (4.25" x 7") checklist of Clement's works is arranged in one straight chronological sequence. Entries are grouped by year and under each year by month; materials are numbered in order from the number one (through fifty-three). Books are underlined, short stories surrounded by quotation marks. A typical short fiction entry includes item number, title, magazine, category code (e.g., "s"=short story), and month of publication (or book title, if an anthology, plus editor's name, publisher, and year of publication). Subsequent reprintings are grouped under the original edition with similar data provided. No paginations are included. A typical book entry includes item number, title, category code ("n"=novel), publisher, stock number, month of publication (if known), pagination, price, and format (e.g., "pb"=paperback). See references and contents listings are keyed to item number. There are no paginations, secondary materials, or index. Data are complete through 1980; a one-leaf addendum is also available. The book is shot from typed copy and stapled through the spine; the text runs too close to the right-hand margin to allow rebinding by libraries. Prefer Benson's more current and complete bibliography, which also includes secondary sources (see #316).

Michael R. Collings

318. Reuben, Willard. **The Work of Michael R. Collings: An Annotated Bibliography & Guide**. San Bernardino, Calif., The Borgo Press, 1992. [160] p. index. (Bibliographies of Modern Authors, No. 22). ISBN 0-8095-0501-0; ISBN 0-8095-1501-6 (pbk.).

Michael R. Collings is a rising critic, poet, and bibliographer of fantastic literature, being known especially for his critiques on Stephen King. This new guide to his work includes the following chapters: "Introduction"; "A Michael R. Collings Chronology"; "A. Books"; "B. Short Nonfiction"; "C. Reviews"; "D. Poetry"; "E. Fiction"; "F. Screenplays"; "G. Professional Papers"; "H. Public Readings"; "I. Honors and Awards"; "J. Editorial Credits"; "K. Secondary Sources"; "L. Unpublished Manuscripts"; "M. Miscellanea"; "Quoth the Critics"; "Afterword" (by Collings); and an "Index."

In each section, works are listed chronologically by publication date from the earliest to the latest and are numbered consecutively from the number one, prefixed by the letter code associated with that chapter. A typical book entry includes entry number, title (boldfaced), place of publication, publisher, month and year of publication, pagination, format (paper or cloth), and category (e.g., "poetry collection"), with similar data for all known reprints, descriptive annotation, table of contents, and a list of secondary sources and reviews. The shorter works sections typically list item number, title (in boldfaced quotes), magazine or book title (in italics), volume number, dates, and paginations (for magazine listings), or book title, editor, series name, place of publication, publisher, month and year of publication, and pagination (for short pieces included in original anthologies or collections). Similar data are included for all known reprints. The chronology is a year-by-year listing of events and publications important to Collings's life and career. The introduction provides a basic overview of the author's life, while the afterword gives Collings's own response to the compilation of this bibliography. The index correlates titles and item numbers only. The book is shot from attractive and sophisticated word-processed copy and bound to library standards.

In just twenty years of work as academic and critic, Collings has penned nearly a thousand items, many of them relating to fantastic literature and all of them carefully recorded in this meticulously wrought bibliography. Complete and comprehensive, *The Work of Michael R. Collings* should be found on the shelves of every major research collection.

Glen Cook

319. Schlobin, Roger C., and Glen Cook. **A Glen Cook Bibliography**. [S.l., s.n.], 1983. [4] p. (pbk.).

This brief checklist by a well-known critic and bibliographer covers Cook's works through 1983, broken into discrete subject sections: "Novels," "Series Novels," "Short Fiction," "Nonfiction," "Secondary Studies & Interviews," and "Addenda." Each section is listed in chronological order or in series order for those novels and short stories which are parts of series (the majority of his works). A typical book entry provides title (in italics), city of publication, publisher, year of publication, but no paginations. A typical short story listing includes title, magazine, date of publication, pagination. A few reprints are noted, several in foreign languages. Scanty and outdated.

Jack Dann

320. Elliot, Jeffrey M. **The Work of Jack Dann: An Annotated Bibliography & Guide**. San Bernardino, Calif., The Borgo Press, 1990. 128 p. index. (Bibliographies of Modern Authors, No. 16). LC 88-34679. ISBN 0-8095-0506-1; ISBN 0-8095-1506-7 (pbk.).

Elliot's comprehensive guide to the works of this rising SF writer, editor, and critic includes "Introduction"; "A Jack Dann Chronology"; "A. Books"; "B. Short Fiction"; "C. Poetry"; "D. Nonfiction"; "E. Editorial Credits"; "F. About the Author"; "H. Public Appearances"; "G. Honors and Awards"; "I. Miscellanea"; "Quoth the Critics"; "Index."

In each section, the author's works are arranged chronologically and numbered consecutively from one, chapter by chapter (e.g., C1, C2, C3, etc.). A typical book entry includes item number, title (in boldface), byline, place of publication, publisher, month and year of publication, pagination, format (e.g., "cloth"), type of publication (e.g., "anthology), and similar data on reprint editions, translations, republications, etc. The books are fully annotated, with complete contents listings and/or plot summaries and other pertinent data and include a list of "Secondary Sources and Reviews" filed alphabetically by main entry after the annotation; entries from other sections are selectively annotated as needed. A typical short fiction entry includes item number, title (in boldface quotes), magazine or anthology title, volume number, month and year of publication, and pagination, or, for stories published in anthologies, title, editor, place of publication, publisher, year of publication, format (e.g., "paper"), pagination; similar data are included on all known reprints, including foreign editions. Elliot's interesting "Introduction" provides basic background material on Dann's life and works. The chronology provides a year-by-year account of the author's professional and personal life, in block paragraph format. "About the Author" includes all known secondary works arranged chronologically. The "Miscellanea" section includes information on pen names, book dedications, memberships, Library of Congress cataloging data, career highlights, and similar data. "Quoth the Critics" includes selected excerpts of reviews and other comments by leading critics on the author's work. The index lists titles and item numbers only.

Dann has been a Nebula Award finalist eleven times without having won the award; his work is held in great esteem by his fellow writers. Much of the material in this book derives from his own records; coverage is complete through the summer of 1989. Complete and well-organized, this guide will be an essential beginning point for all future researchers into the author's work.

L. Sprague de Camp

321. Laughlin, Charlotte, and Daniel J. H. Levack, with annotations by Loay H. Hall. **De Camp: An L. Sprague de Camp Bibliography**. San Francisco & Columbia, Penn., Underwood/Miller, 1983. 328 p. index. ISBN 0-934438-71-4; ISBN 0-934438-70-6 (pbk.).

A comprehensive, illustrated bibliography of L. Sprague de Camp's writings through mid-1982, Laughlin and Levack's work includes "Introduction," "Annotator's Introduction," and the bibliography proper "The Works of L. Sprague de Camp." The major part of the book is broken into appropriate chapters: "Books," "Edited Books," "Non-Book Appearances," "Translations," "Miscellaneous." Completing the guide are a series of indexes: "Fiction," "Verse," "Book Reviews," "Radio Scripts," "Other Non-Fiction"; a chronological list of "Pseudonym Appearances," "Connected Works—Continuing Characters—Series, Genres, Collaborations"; "Magazine Checklist"; "A Catherine Crook de Camp Checklist"; an alphabetical general index; "Acknowledgments."

Works are listed alphabetically by title and numbered consecutively from the number one in each section, with over 800 items included. A typical book entry includes item number, title (bold caps), series (when appropriate) or category (e.g., "Non-Fiction"), contents (if a collection) or one-paragraph annotation (if a novel) in boldface, publisher, stock number (for paperback editions), place of publication (with original price for paperback versions), year of publication, cover artist (for cloth editions), edition points, paginations. Reprints are listed in chronological order by publication date; many foreign editions are included, but few of the reprint editions list paginations. An asterisk after a specific edition indicates it has been viewed by the compilers.

A typical shorter work entry includes item number, title (in bold quotes), estimated wordage, type or other notes (e.g., "verse"), annotation (in bold type), magazine or book title, date, volume number, issue number, and occasionally the starting page number (only of the story). All subsequent reprint editions (including some foreign-language materials with foreign-language titles) are listed with similar data. Anthology appearances include title, editor, publisher, place of publication, price, year of publication, but no paginations. The indices by type include titles only, greatly reducing their effectiveness: one must refer to the bibliography proper or to the alphabetical index to locate specific items. The latter is itself organized quirkily, giving titles and abbreviated references to each chapter only (e.g., "B"=Books, "NBA"=Non-Book Appearances, etc.). Although the various sections of the bibliography are alphabetically arranged, there are no running heads to key the user into each chapter without having to page through the book. One wonders why the compilers bothered to number each item when those numbers were not used as quick reference points for the indices.

The book is beautifully typeset and designed and is illustrated throughout with reproductions of book and magazine covers featuring de Camp material. The addition of a mini-bibliography covering the writings of de Camp's wife (an increasingly frequent collaborator in the author's later years) is a nice touch. However, while one can applaud the enormous labor that went into this volume, and the immense amount of material thus made available to the scholar, one must also lament the missed opportunities that would have made this one of the finest bibliographies in the field. The lack of adequate indexing, the absence of complete paginations in the shorter works section, the utter absence of secondary materials, inevitably mean that somewhere, somehow, someone must do this work over again. And that's a real shame.

Samuel R. Delany

322. Peplow, Michael W., and Robert S. Bravard. **Samuel R. Delany: A Primary and Secondary Bibliography, 1962-1979.** Boston, G. K. Hall, 1980. xiv, 178 p. index. (Masters of Science Fiction and Fantasy). LC 80-20108. ISBN 0-8161-8054-7.

Delany, the first Black writer to attain "major-author" status in the field, has attracted a great deal of critical attention in the last decade; a detailed guide to his fiction was long overdue. Contents: "Preface" (discussing the book's arrangement); "Magazine and Journal Abbreviations," "Introduction" (a sixty-one-page biographical and critical guide to the author's life and work); "Part A: Fiction"; "Part B: Miscellaneous Media"; "Part C: Nonfiction"; "Part D: Critical Studies." Three appendices list "Part E. Juvenilia"; "Part F. Unpublished Speeches and Nonfiction"; "Part G. Collections of Delanyana." Two indexes cover "Works by Delany" and "Works about Delany."

Each section is arranged chronologically, from the earliest published material to the latest, and numbered consecutively by section from one (e.g., C1, C2, etc., for nonfiction). Books and shorter works are interfiled by year; reprints of books and stories are grouped as subsidiary entries under their first edition or appearance, chronologically by year of reprint (some foreign editions are listed, but none of the translated foreign-language titles); reprint editions of short stories include editor of anthology, title, place of publication, publisher, year, format (e.g., "paper"), but no paginations. Each book entry gives item number, title (underlined), place of publication, publisher, format ("paper"), but no pagination. Each shorter work entry gives item number, title (in quotations), magazine, volume number, date, pagination, or, for those published originally in books, book title, book editor, place of publication, publisher, format, pagination. Story collections include complete contents listings, plus the years in which the original stories were published. Some entries, particularly in Sections B-C, include bibliographical or descriptive notes but no other annotations; all of the entries in Part D are extensively annotated.

"Part B: Miscellaneous Media" includes screenplays, teleplays, interviews, recordings, poetry, and other material which does not specifically fit the other three categories; for Delany, there are only a handful of comic book adaptations and amateur films. "Part C: Nonfiction" includes all the author's nonfiction publications arranged chronologically. Part D includes known secondary sources, including some book reviews arranged chronologically, with author, title, bibliographical data, and extensive annotations; most "Who's Who" publications are omitted, but the authors still include some 274 items, making this a major resource. Parts E-G only cover twenty-eight items but do include mentions of two Delany manuscript collections of great potential value to researchers. The indexes reference titles, names, and item numbers only. The introduction by Peplow and Bravard provides extensive and little-known background material on the author's youth in New York City and is valuable in its own right. Coverage of Delany's books is complete through 1979. The volume is reproduced from typed copy and bound to library standards.

This thoroughly professional effort is now ten years outdated, lacking all of Delany's numerous and significant publications from the 1980s (particularly the Nevèrÿon Cycle), and should be revised into a second edition. In the interim, this is a sound piece of work in its own right, one of interest both to SF scholars and those researching modern Afro-American literature. Stephens's checklist (see #323) can serve as a supplement.

323. Stephens, Christopher P. **A Checklist of Samuel R. Delany**. Hastings-on-Hudson, N.Y., Ultramarine Publishing Co., 1991. 18 p. index. ISBN 0-89366-184-8 (pbk.).

The major Black writer in the SF field, Delany has written noteworthy criticism on fantastic literature in addition to his acclaimed novels and short stories. This new checklist is arranged chronologically by publication date and divided into two sections: "Part One: Books Written by Samuel R. Delany"; "Part Two: Books Edited by Samuel R. Delany." Materials in each section are numbered from the number one (A1-A31 and AA1-AA5). A typical entry provides year (as a floating head), item number, title (underlined), pseudonym, publisher, stock or ISBN number, pagination, format (e.g., "cloth with dust wrapper"), cover illustrator, price, and similar data for all known reprints (which are numbered, for example, A10a, A10b, A10c, etc., in descending order by publication date). The chapbook is shot from legible typed copy and bound with staples in stiff paper covers. The index correlates titles with years of publication only. Stephens's chapbook in no way supplants Peplow and Bravard's more extensive work (see #322), which, although now outdated, includes extensive secondary source listings, among others; however, until a newer version of that work is available, this brief guide will have to suffice.

August Derleth

324. Derleth, August. **August Derleth: Thirty Years of Writing, 1926-1956.** Sauk City, Wisc., Arkham House, 1956. 24 p. (pbk.). **100 Books by August Derleth**. [2nd ed.]. Sauk City, Wisc., Arkham House, 1962. 121 p. LC 63-4567 (pbk.).

These two versions of a developing personal bibliography were issued by Derleth through Arkham House, the publishing company he founded in 1939 to disseminate the writings of H. P. Lovecraft. Contents (*100 Books*): "Foreword," by Donald Wandrei; "Biographical" (background); "Bibliographical" (a list of magazines in which Derleth's work has appeared); "A Checklist of Published Books"; "Awaiting Publication"; "Work in Progress"; "Summary" (lists of Derleth's books by series and/or subject); "Recordings" (including contents, price, and bibliographical data); "Compilations" (single-author collections edited or introduced by Derleth, with no details other than titles and dates); "Anthologies/Textbooks" (in which Derleth stories have appeared with some bibliographical details but no paginations); "Publications" (issued by Arkham House—a skeletal listing); "Films" (adaptations of Derleth stories for motion pictures and television, with no production details); "Lectures" (topics only; no actual list of appearances); "Appraisals" (short critical excerpts on Derleth books); "From the Reviews" (more of the same); "Self-Appraisal" (Derleth's own list of his best books).

The bulk of this bibliography (sixty-one pages) is a chronological checklist of Derleth's books, numbered in order from one (strangely, original paperback editions are listed but not numbered). A typical entry includes item number, title (all caps), byline, publisher, place of publication, year of publication, contents (for collections and anthologies), cover artist, format (e.g., "paperbound"), pagination, and price; similar data are provided for all known English-language reprint editions. The remaining sections are much less bibliographically detailed, providing bare-bones listings of peripheral items. The book lacks a title index, making access relatively difficult for the uninitiated. Derleth died in 1971 having produced a number of works not included herein; however, in the absence of any definitive bibliography, *100 Books by August Derleth* must still be regarded as an essential starting point for all future scholarship. Compare with Wilson's guide (see #325).

325. Wilson, Alison M. **August Derleth: A Bibliography.** Metuchen, N.J. & London, The Scarecrow Press, 1983. xxvi, 229 p. index. (The Scarecrow Author Bibliographies, No. 59). LC 82-24020. ISBN 0-8108-1606-7.

Derleth, a well-known American writer, editor, and publisher, founded Arkham House in 1939 to disseminate the works of H. P. Lovecraft and others and died in 1971. Contents: "Preface"; "Introduction" (on Derleth's life and career); "Chronology" (two pages, year by year, in block paragraph format); "I. The Fantasy World: Mystery, Science Fiction, and Horror." "A. Short Stories"; "B. Anthologies of Derleth's Own Work"; "C. Posthumous Collaborations with H. P. Lovecraft"; "D. Collaborations with Mark Schorer"; "E. Collaborations: Books"; "F. The Pontine Canon"; "G. Judge Peck"; "H. Miscellaneous Mysteries"; "I. Books Edited by Derleth"; "J. Derleth Introductions." "II. Sac Prairie and the Real World." "A. Sac Prairie Saga: Short Stories"; "B. Collections"; "C. Novels"; "D. Miscellaneous Prose"; "E. Steve-Sim Juvenile Mysteries"; "F. Wisconsin Saga"; "G. Other Juvenile Literature"; "H. Poetry"; "I. Nonfiction: Books"; "J. Nonfiction: Articles, Reviews, Introductions"; "K. Representative Published Letters." "Index."

In each section Derleth's works are listed alphabetically by title; entries are in the book is numbered in consecutive order (1-736). A typical shorter work entry includes item number, title (in quotes), one- to two-sentence annotation, magazine, volume and issue number, date, pagination, pseudonym (where appropriate), plus a list of reprints in chronological order by date of publication. Reprints in anthologies include title (underlined), editor, place of publication, publisher, year of publication, pagination of story; reprints in collections of Derleth's own works include title (in caps), pagination. A typical book entry gives item number, title (underlined), place of publication, publisher, year of publication, contents (if a collection or anthology) or three- to four-sentence annotation (if a novel), brief list of reviews (two or three maximum), list of reprint editions (with similar data), but no paginations. Omitted are Derleth's poems (an estimated 1,000 items), most book reviews written by Derleth (estimated in the hundreds), plays (none of which were ever published), and all secondary sources save for a handful of book reviews. The index references titles and item numbers only. The book is shot from legible typed copy.

The lack of book paginations and secondary resources hamper what could have become a standard guide to the author's work. The annotations are valuable in their own right, but the book is so broken into subject-oriented sections that it is very difficult for the scholar to get an overview of Derleth's writings. The alphabetical arrangement in such circumstances can become almost irritating: one can get a chronological list of the Solar Pons stories or Judge Peck novels (surely a desirable datum!), for example, only by laboriously comparing several different sections and rearranging the data oneself. This is hardly the definitive work it should have been and can only be considered a beginning point for the study of this prolific author's life and career. Prefer Derleth's own guide to his work (see #324) for materials published prior to 1962.

Philip K. Dick

326. Levack, Daniel J. H., with annotations by Steven Owen Godersky. **PKD: A Philip K. Dick Bibliography.** Columbia, Penn., San Francisco, Underwood/ Miller, 1981. 158 p. **PKD: A Philip K. Dick Bibliography.** Rev. ed. Westport, Conn., Meckler Corp., 1988.

156 p. (Meckler's Bibliographies on Science Fiction, Fantasy, and Horror, No. 1). LC 88-15597. ISBN 0-88736-096-3.

Levack, who also compiled similarly formatted bibliographies on de Camp, Vance, and Zelazny for Underwood/Miller, as well as a more recent book on Herbert (see #321, #434, #455, and #347), prepared this book just prior to the author's sudden death (the book covers through mid-1981; Dick died in February of 1982). Contents: "Introduction," "Annotator's Note," "Books," "Stories," "Unpublished Manuscripts," "Other Media," "Pseudonyms," "Collaborations," "Connected Stories and Continuing Characters," "Non-Fiction Index," "Verse Index," "Chronological Order of Publication of Philip K. Dick's Work," "Magazine Checklist," "Works About Philip K. Dick," "Afterword" by Philip K. Dick, "Acknowledgements."

Works are listed alphabetically by title and numbered consecutively from one, section by section, with over 200 items included. A typical book entry includes item number, title (bold caps), series note (when appropriate) or category (e.g., "Non-Fiction"), contents (if a collection) or one-paragraph annotation (if a novel) in boldface, publisher, stock number (for paperback editions), place of publication (inconsistently; the price, in parentheses, is included for paperback versions), year of publication, edition points, but no paginations. Reprints are listed in chronological order by publication date; many foreign editions are included. An asterisk after a specific edition indicates it has been viewed by Levack. A typical shorter work entry includes item number, title (in bold quotes), estimated wordage, type or other notes (e.g., "verse"), one- to two-sentence annotation (in bold type), magazine or book title, date, volume number, issue number, but no paginations. All subsequent reprint editions (including some foreign-language materials with foreign-language titles) are listed with similar data. Anthology appearances include title, editor, publisher, stock number, price, year of publication, format (e.g., "paper"), but no paginations. The magazine checklist is an alphabetic listing of those publications in which Dick stories appeared, keyed to issue date and to item number in the short fiction section. There is also a master chronological checklist of Dick's work, year by year, with all publications interfiled, but no index.

The book is beautifully typeset and designed, bound to library standards, and illustrated throughout with reproductions of book and magazine covers featuring Dick's fiction. The brief (two-page) secondary bibliography only lists seventeen items and is lamentably incomplete and out-of-date. *Caveat emptor!*: the Meckler edition contains only very minor revisions at the end of the book and does not update the basic bibliography beyond 1981, specifically failing to include the many posthumous Dick novels published during the 1980s; it is in no sense the revised edition it claims to be. The lack of an index, the total absence of paginations, and the miserly list of secondary materials inevitably make this work much less than it should have been. Prefer Stephensen-Payne's more current and detailed checklist (see #328).

327. Stephens, Christopher P. **A Checklist of Philip K. Dick**. Hastings-on-Hudson, N.Y., Ultramarine Publishing Co., 1990. 46 p. index. ISBN 0-89366-174-0 (pbk.).

Stephens's brief bibliography of this late American writer's fiction is broken into two parts: "Books by Philip K. Dick" and "Stories by Philip K. Dick." Materials are arranged in chronological order by publication date in each section and are numbered, respectively, from 1-55 and 1-130. A typical book entry provides year (as a floating head), item number, title (underlined), pseudonym, publisher, stock or ISBN number, pagination, format (e.g., "cloth with dust wrapper"), cover illustrator, price, and similar data for all known reprints (which are numbered, for example, A30a, A30b, A30c, etc., in descending order by publication date). Short fiction entries include title (in quotes), magazine title (underlined), month and year of publication, pagination (provided on a very haphazard basis), and a list of all known reprints, with brief bibliographical data (but no paginations). The book is shot from legible typed copy and bound with staples in stiff paper covers. The index correlates titles with years of publication only. With the exception of a few story paginations for original magazine publications, there is nothing here that can't be found in Stephensen-Payne and Benson's more extensive (and equally current) guide (see #328).

328. Stephensen-Payne, Phil, and Gordon Benson, Jr. **Philip Kindred Dick, Metaphysical Conjurer: A Working Bibliography.** 3rd rev. ed. Leeds, West Yorkshire, England & Albuquerque, N.M., Galactic Central Publications, 1990. 9, 102 p. (Galactic Central Bibliographies for the Avid Reader, Vol. 18). ISBN 0-912613-09-2 (pbk.).

In an irony that the author would surely have appreciated, Philip K. Dick attained his greatest commercial success by dying in 1982, at which point all of the unpublished book manuscripts he had been unable to sell in the preceding decades suddenly became valuable commodities.

This comprehensive checklist of Dicks writings is arranged by category, then alphabetically by title. Contents: Author's full name, date and place of birth and date of death, his awards and honors; "A. Stories"; "B. Fiction Books"; "C. Series"; "D. Poems"; "E. Poem & Song Collections" ("none known"); "F. Articles"; "G. Miscellaneous"; "H. Non-Fiction Books"; "I. Edited Books" ("none known"); "J. Media Presentations"; "K. Articles on Philip K. Dick"; "L. Reviews" [of Dick's books]; "M. Books About Philip K. Dick"; "N. Phantom and Forthcoming Titles"; "O. Related Works by Other Authors"; "P. Textual Variations"; "Q. Chronological Listing of Fiction." Materials are arranged in alphabetical order by title, section by section, and are numbered consecutively from the number one, preceded by the letter code for that part (e.g., B1, B2, B3, etc.).

For shorter works, the authors provide item number, title, category ("ss"=short story, "nt"=novelette, etc.), magazine or book in which the item appeared, month and year of publication (for magazines in the form "1-59" for January 1959) or year of publication (for books), plus similar data for all known reprints (for which title, publisher, year, and editor's last name are given), but no paginations. For book-length works, the authors list item number, title, contents listing of collections (keyed to item number), publication data (publisher, stock number, month and year of publication [if known, in the form "10-59" for October 1959], pagination, price), and cover artist, plus similar data for all known reprint editions. There is no general index. Secondary monographs are listed in alphabetical order by main entry (usually critic's name), with similar data. Two hundred eighty-nine short nonfiction pieces are included, an impressive and very current list. Data are complete through the end of 1989. The checklist is shot from very legible word-processed copy and bound through the spine with staples.

Although Levack's book (see #326) is somewhat more complete and more explicit for the period covered (and certainly more physically attractive), Stephensen-Payne and Benson's guide includes Dick's important posthumous novels (most of them published in the 1980s) and far more secondary sources than Levack. Future editions would benefit from an overall index and the addition of magazine paginations. Serious researchers should have access to both books; SF fans and most libraries will find Stephensen-Payne/Benson's bibliography quite adequate.

Gordon R. Dickson

329. Benson, Gordon, Jr., and Phil Stephensen-Payne. **Gordon Rupert Dickson, First Dorsai: A Working Bibliography.** 4th rev. ed. Albuquerque, N.M., & Leeds, West Yorkshire, England, Galactic Central Publications, 1990. 9, 62 p. (Galactic Central Bibliographies for the Avid Reader, Vol. 2). ISBN 0-912613-10-6 (pbk.).

American SF writer Dickson is best known for his Dorsai Series. This checklist of his works is arranged by category, then alphabetically by title. Contents: Author's full name, date and place of birth, and his awards and honors; "A. Stories"; "B. Fiction Books"; "C. Series"; "D. Poems, Songs & Plays"; "E. Poem & Song Collections" ("none known"); "F. Articles"; "G. Miscellaneous"; "H. Non-Fiction Books" ("none known"); "I. Books Edited by Gordon R. Dickson"; "J. Media Presentations"; "K. Articles on Gordon R. Dickson"; "L. Reviews" [of Dickson's books]; "M. Books About Gordon R. Dickson"; "N. Phantom & Forthcoming Titles"; "O. Related Items by Other Authors"; "P. Textual Variations" ("no details known"); "Q. Chronological Index."

In each part the material is arranged in alphabetical order by title, items being numbered consecutively from the number one in each section. For shorter works, the authors provide item number, title, category ("ss"=short story, "nt"=novelette, etc.), magazine or book in which the item appeared, month and year of publication (for magazines in the form "9-60" for September 1960) or year of publication (for books), a list of subsequent reprints (for which title, publisher, year, and editor's last name are given), but no paginations. For book-length works, the authors give item number, title, publication data (publisher, stock number, month and year of publication [if known, in the form "10-59" for October 1959], pagination, price), cover artist, plus similar data for known reprints. There is no overall index. The book is shot from readable word-processed copy and stapled through the spine in paper covers. Materials are included through the end of 1989.

Although this basic checklist is not as detailed as Thompson's guide (see #330), it covers an additional decade of material, both primary and secondary, and serves quite well as a supplement. An index and magazine paginations should be added to future editions. Researchers and academic libraries should acquire both works.

330. Thompson, Raymond H. **Gordon R. Dickson: A Primary and Secondary Bibliography**. Boston, G. K. Hall, 1983. xix, 108 p. index. (Masters of Science Fiction and Fantasy). LC 82-12126. ISBN 0-8161-8363-5.

Canadian-born writer Dickson moved to the United States as a child; this bibliography was compiled by a well-known Canadian academic critic. Contents: "Preface" (discussing the book's arrangement); "Introduction" (a brief guide to the author and his work); "Abbreviations List"; "Part A: Fiction"; "Part B: Miscellaneous Media"; "Part C: Nonfiction"; "Part D: Critical Studies." Five appendices list "A. An Overview of MSS 39, The Gordon R. Dickson Papers, Manuscript Division, University of Minnesota Libraries"; "B. Chronological Checklist of Novels, Collections, and Anthologies by Dickson"; "C. Series by Dickson"; "D. Translations of Dickson's Works"; "E. Reviews Excluded." Two indexes complete the book, correlating Dickson's works and secondary sources with item numbers.

Each section is arranged chronologically, from the earliest published material to the latest, and numbered consecutively from one, section by section (e.g., A1, A2, for fiction). Books and shorter works are interfiled by year; reprints of books and stories are grouped as subsidiary entries under their first edition or appearance, chronologically by year of reprint; reprint editions of short stories include editor of anthology, title, place of publication, publisher, year, format (e.g., "paper"), but no paginations. A typical book entry provides item number, title (underlined), place of publication, publisher, format ("paper"), contents (for collections and anthologies), but no pagination. Each shorter work entry gives item number, title (in quotations), magazine, volume number, date, pagination, or, for those published originally in books, book title, book editor, place of publication, publisher, format, pagination. Story collections include complete contents listings, plus the years in which the original stories were published. Some entries, particularly in Sections B-C, include bibliographical or descriptive notes, but no other annotations; all of the entries in Part D are extensively annotated.

"Part B: Miscellaneous Media" include screenplays, teleplays, interviews, recordings, poetry, and other material which does not specifically fit the other three categories. "Part C: Nonfiction" includes all the author's nonfiction publications, arranged chronologically. Part D includes all known articles, reviews, and books about Dickson, arranged chronologically, with author, title, bibliographical data (in the same form as the other sections), and one- to five-sentence annotations; most "Who's Who" publications are omitted. Appendix D, "Translations," is arranged by language, and then in item number order as correlated with Section A (the original item number appears in brackets at the end of the entry). The indexes include titles, names, and item numbers only. Coverage is complete through the first part of 1981. The book is reproduced from typed copy and bound in sturdy library cloth.

Thompson's volume is soundly organized and constructed, the author demonstrating a clear familiarity with (and sympathy for) Dickson's work. Although now out-of-date, this will be an essential starting point for all future research on this popular writer. A new edition would be warranted, although Benson and Stephensen-Payne's checklist (see #329) provides very adequate coverage of the intervening decade.

Thomas M. Disch

331. Drumm, Chris. **A Tom Disch Checklist: Notes Toward a Bibliography**. Polk City, Ia., Chris Drumm Books, 1983. [22] p. index. ISBN 0-936055-02-2 (pbk.).

Disch, an American science fiction writer, has received great critical acclaim from academic circles. Drumm's 4.25" x 7" checklist of the author's works is arranged in one straight chronological sequence. Entries are grouped by year, and under each year by month; each item is numbered in order from 1 to 194. Books are underlined, short stories appear in quotation marks. A typical short fiction entry includes item number, title, magazine, category code (e.g., "s"=short story), date of completion by the writer, month of publication (or book title, if an anthology, plus editor, publisher, and year of publication). Subsequent reprintings are grouped under the original edition, with similar data provided. No paginations are provided. A typical book entry includes item number, title, category code ("n"=novel), publisher, stock number, month of publication (if known), pagination, price, format (e.g., "pb"=paperback), contents of collections. See references, index, and contents listings are keyed to item number. No secondary materials are included. Data are complete through 1982; a one-leaf addendum sheet is also available. The book is shot from typed copy; the text runs too close to the right-hand margin to allow rebinding by libraries. Although Drumm's coverage is comparable to Nee's (see #332), the latter bibliography does list some secondary sources. However, Stephens's more current guide is preferable to either (see #333).

332. Nee, Dave. **Thomas M. Disch: A Preliminary Bibliography**. Berkeley, Calif., The Other Change of Hobbit, 1982. ii, 30 p. (pbk.).

Nee, owner of a well-known science fiction shop, assembled this short checklist of Disch's work, arranged by category and then alphabetically by title. Sections include "Prefatory Note"; "B. Books"; "C. Anthologies Edited"; "F. Fiction"; "N. Non-Fiction, Reviews, Criticism" (i.e., secondary sources); "P. Poetry." Materials are numbered consecutively in each section from the number one. The "Books" section includes item number, title, publisher, ISBN or stock number, exact month of publication (when known). The short fiction section lists item number, story title, magazine, date plus all known reprints with title of the reprint anthology and year and month of publication. The "Non-Fiction, Reviews, Criticism" section includes articles, biographies, and reviews on Bishop and his works, and interviews with the author, but does not mention the book(s) being reviewed. The book is reproduced from rather faint 8.5" x 11" computer printout, using hanging indents to set off specific entries. This volume includes considerably less data than the second book in this series on Michael Bishop (see #279), overlapping to a great extent with Drumm's work (see #331); however, the addition of secondary sources makes this slightly the more valuable guide of the two. Stephens's checklist (see #333), although it lacks secondary works, is far more current.

333. Stephens, Christopher P. **A Checklist of Thomas M. Disch**. Hastings-on-Hudson, N.Y., Ultramarine Publishing Co., 1989. 22 p. index. ISBN 0-89366-183-X (pbk.).

This new checklist is arranged chronologically by publication date, in two sections covering books written by Disch and volumes edited by him, numbered separately from A1-A41 and from AA1-AA5. A typical entry provides year (as a floating head), item number, title (underlined), pseudonym, publisher, stock or ISBN number, pagination, format (e.g., "cloth with dust wrapper"), cover illustrator, price, and similar data for all known reprints (which are numbered, for example, A12a, A12b, A12c, etc., in descending order by publication date). The chapbook is shot from legible typed copy and bound with staples in stiff paper covers. The index correlates titles with years of publication only. Disch deserves better bibliographical treatment than any of these three checklists provide; however, the currency of Stephens's guide makes it slightly preferable to Drumm (see #331) or Nee (see #332).

Jeffrey M. Elliot

334. Clarke, Boden. **The Work of Jeffrey M. Elliot: An Annotated Bibliography & Guide**. San Bernardino, Calif., The Borgo Press, 1984. 50 p. index. (Bibliographies of Modern Authors, No. 2). LC 84-21745. ISBN 0-89370-381-8; ISBN 0-89370-481-4 (pbk.).

Although not himself a science-fiction writer, Elliot, a well-known political scientist, has been extensively involved with the genre as an SF interviewer, critic, anthologist, and bibliographer. Contents: "Introduction" (by Clarke); "Section A: Books"; "Section B: Articles"; "Section C: Book Reviews"; "Section D: Letters to the Editor"; "Section E: Speeches and Papers"; "Section F: Television Productions and Appearances"; "Section G: Radio Appearances"; "Section H: Other Media"; "Section J: Honors and Awards"; "Section K: About the Author"; "Section L: Unpublished Works"; "Quoth the Critics"; "Index."

In each section, the author's works are arranged chronologically and numbered consecutively chapter by chapter. A typical book entry includes item number, title (underlined), place of publication, publisher, year of publication, pagination, format (e.g., "paper"), and type of publication (e.g., "children's story), with similar data on all reprint editions, translations, republications, etc. Book entries are fully annotated with complete contents listings and plot summaries; entries from other sections are selectively annotated as needed. A typical shorter work entry includes item number, title (in quotes), magazine title (underlined), volume or issue number, date, pagination. A brief introduction provides background material on the author's life and works. "About the Author" includes all known secondary works. "Quoth the Critics" includes selected excerpts of reviews and other comments by leading critics on the author's work. The index lists titles and item numbers only.

Although listed as the second volume in the set, Clarke's was the first actually published in the Bibliographies of Modern Authors series and was used as the pattern volume for the first half-dozen books (the style was extensively reworked in 1986 and 1988). The format used in this bibliography was somewhat cramped, employing a small typeface (word-processed copy) with minimal spacing between lines. Thus, a great deal of information is crammed into these fifty pages. Data on this author are provided through the fall of 1984; a completely revised and expanded second edition is reportedly underway. This extremely thorough and comprehensive bibliography was based in large part on Elliot's own records and files.

Harlan Ellison

335. Swigart, Leslie Kay. **Harlan Ellison: A Bibliographical Checklist.** Dallas, Tex., Williams Pub. Co., 1973. vi, 117 p. index. LC 74-159836 (pbk.). **Harlan Ellison: A Bibliographical Checklist.** 2nd ed. in *Fantasy Research & Bibliography* no. 1-2 (December 1980-February 1981/March 1981-May 1981): 24-94. (pbk.).

Ellison, a popular fantasy and screen writer, was well treated in this early bibliography by librarian Swigart. Contents: "Preface"; "Harlan Ellison" (biographical background); "In Re Ellison," by Isaac Asimov; "Harlan Ellison," by Ben Bova; "A Fagin Walks Among Us," by Edward Bryant; "Partners in Wonder," by Joanna Russ; "Harlan Ellison: An Appreciation," by Robert Silverberg; "Harlan Ellison: An Appreciation," by James Sutherland; "Section A: Books"; "B. Scripts"; "C. Fiction"; "D. Articles and Essays"; "E. Introductions and Afterwords"; "F. Reviews"; "G. Published Letters"; "H. Interviews with Harlan Ellison"; "I. Fanzines" edited by Harlan Ellison; "J. Titles Announced But Not Yet Published"; Afterword: "Thoughts on Turning Eighteen," by Ellison; "Index."

The introductory pieces provide insights into Ellison's character and life. The bibliography proper is arranged in chronological order, section by section, materials being numbered from one in each part. A typical book entry includes item number, title (in caps), category (e.g., "anthology"), plus complete bibliographical data for each edition and printing, in chronological order by release date. Each edition listing includes title, subtitle, byline (as shown in the book), illustrators, city of publication, publisher, year of publication, collation, size in centimeters, series title, price, other notes, and contents listings (for the first printing only unless contents have changed). Short fiction and nonfiction are listed by year, then alphabetically under each year by title; each short fiction entry includes item number, byline, title, magazine (underlined), volume and issue number, date of publication, pagination. Reprints in this and the nonfiction section are shown as new entries whenever they appear and are numbered accordingly without see references (but can be accessed through the master index). Some foreign-language titles are included. Section B lists scripts in order by air date, with item number, byline, title, TV series title, and first known air date. The index correlates all data in the bibliography, including titles, names, and non-Ellisonian publications by entry number.

Swigart's 8.5" x 11" volume is attractively illustrated with dozens of author photos and reproductions of book and magazine covers. The book is shot from typed copy with limp paper covers that cannot withstand heavy use. The constant repetition of short story titles in Section C is unfortunate, making it difficult for the casual user to trace reprints of the same story or even to determine how many stories Ellison has actually penned. Still, Swigart's guide is a remarkable bibliographical achievement for its time period, one which provides a sound base for the greatly revised, much expanded third edition currently in progress.

Philip José Farmer

336. Knapp, Lawrence J. **The First Editions of Philip Jose Farmer**. Menlo Park, Calif., David G. Turner, Bookman, 1976. ii, 8 p. (Science Fiction Bibliographies, 2). (pbk.).

This very brief checklist focuses on Farmer's first edition books and uncollected short stories, with a few secondary sources and a series index. The books are listed chronologically by year of publication and numbered from one; a typical entry includes item number, title (in underlined caps), publisher, place of publication, year of publication, stock number, format (e.g., "wraps"). Collections include complete contents listings; there are other occasional bibliographical notes but no paginations. The uncollected stories are listed alphabetically by title, with magazine and date of publication but no paginations. The brief list of secondary sources is arranged in alphabetical order by critic. Now completely superseded by Stephensen-Payne/Benson's guide (see #337).

337. Stephensen-Payne, Phil, & Gordon Benson, Jr. **Philip José Farmer, Good-Natured Ground Breaker: A Working Bibliography.** 2nd rev. ed. Leeds, West Yorkshire, England & Albuquerque, N.M., Galactic Central Publications, 1990. 9, 63 p. (Galactic Central Bibliographies for the Avid Reader, Vol. 23). ISBN 0-912613-11-4 (pbk.).

Farmer is the highly regarded American author of the Riverworld stories. Stephensen-Payne and Benson's guide to his work is arranged by category, then alphabetically by title. Contents: Author's full name, pseudonyms, date and place of birth, and his awards and honors; "A. Stories"; "B. Fiction Books"; "C. Series"; "D. Poems & Songs"; "E. Poem & Song Collections" ("none known"); "F. Articles"; "G. Miscellaneous"; "H. Non-Fiction Books"; "I. Books Edited by Philip José Farmer"; "J. Media Presentations"; "K. Articles on Philip José Farmer"; "L. Reviews" [of Farmer's books, alphabetical by book title]; "M. Books About Philip José Farmer"; "N. Phantom & Forthcoming Titles"; "O. Related Items by Other Authors"; "P. Textual Variations"; "Q. Chronological Index."

Materials are arranged alphabetically by title and are numbered consecutively from the number one in each section. For shorter works, Benson gives item number, title, category ("ss"=short story, "nt"=novelette, etc.), magazine or book in which the item appeared, month and year of publication (for magazines in the form "12-54" for December 1954) or year of publication (for books), a list of subsequent reprints (for which title, publisher, year, and editor's last name are given), but no paginations. For book-length works, Benson provides item number, title, publication data (publisher, stock number, month and year of publication [if known, in the form "10-59" for October 1959], pagination, price), cover artist, and similar information on all known reprints. There is no general index. The book is shot from very legible word-processed copy and stapled into paper covers. Data are complete through mid-1990.

These checklists have developed considerably with each new edition, both in terms of content and style; the second edition is three times the size of the first (1987), and includes over seventy secondary sources, plus more than a hundred book reviews in addition to a very comprehensive primary bibliography. An index and magazine paginations would be attractive additions to future editions. Any scholar researching Farmer's work would be well advised to consult this checklist first.

John Russell Fearn

338. Harbottle, Philip. **John Russell Fearn: An Evaluation.** Wabash, Ind., Coulson Publications, 1963. 10 p. (pbk.). **John Russell Fearn: The Ultimate Analysis.** [2nd ed.]. Wallsend, Northumberland, England: Philip Harbottle, 1965. 94 p. (pbk.). **The Multi-Man: A Biographic and Bibliographic Study of John Russell Fearn (1908-60).** [3rd ed.]. Wallsend, Northumberland, The Author, 1968. iv, 69 p. LC 68-135425 (pbk.).

Harbottle, Fearn's literary executor, has compiled three different versions of an illustrated biography, analysis, and bibliography of this prolific British pulp writer, each expanding upon the previous edition. Contents (*The Multi-Man*): "The Ultimate Analysis" (a thirty-four-page biographical and critical background on the author); "Part One: Science Fiction and Fantasy"; "Part Two: Detective and Mystery"; "Part Three: Westerns"; "Part Four: Romances"; "Part Five: Film Magazines." In each section and subdivision, materials are arranged by pseudonym and then in alphabetical order by title. The major section, Part One, is subdivided into "Non-Fiction," "SF Fanzine Articles," "Fanzine Fiction," "Magazine Stories," "Miscellaneous and Associated Magazine Items," "Unconfirmed Pseudonyms," and "Science Fiction Novels." A typical short fiction entry includes title, category code (e.g., "s"=short story), magazine title, date of publication, illustrator, one-sentence annotation, but no paginations.

A typical book entry includes title, publisher, pagination, price, format ("pb"=paperback), reprint editions (including some foreign, with foreign-language titles and similar bibliographical details), plus a one- to five-sentence annotation. There is no index, making location of any specific title difficult for the casual user; the many textual subdivisions also tend to overwhelm the data, making an overall evaluation of Fearn's enormous output inordinately difficult. Harbottle has included a number of generally well-reproduced black-and-white illustrations taken from the covers of Fearn's paperbacks and from the drawings accompanying his pulp stories. As the only guide to Fearn's work currently available, this is a valuable introduction to a little-known period of British publishing; however, a completely revised and updated edition with better internal organization and index plus individual story paginations would certainly be justified.

Raymond Z. Gallun

339. Elliot, Jeffrey M. **The Work of Raymond Z. Gallun: An Annotated Bibliography & Guide.** San Bernardino, Calif., The Borgo Press, 1992. [140] p. index. (Bibliographies of Modern Authors, No. 24). ISBN 0-8095-0503-7; ISBN 0-8095-1503-2 (pbk.).

Elliot, who edited Gallun's recent autobiography *Starclimber*, here has assembled what will become the definitive guide to this American pulp writer's many works. Contents: Introduction: "Riding the Star Wings," by Elliot; "A Raymond Z. Gallun Chronology"; "A. Novels"; "B. Short Fiction"; "C. Short Nonfiction"; "D. Unpublished Works"; "E. Editorial Credits"; "F. Philosophical Statement," by Gallun; "G. Honors and Awards"; "H. Secondary Sources"; "I. Miscellanea"; "Quoth the Critics"; Afterword: "Journey's Retrospect," by Gallun; "Around the Curve: An Interview with Raymond Z. Gallun," conducted by Elliot;

"The Restless Tide" (a story), by Gallun; "Title Index"; "About Jeffrey M. Elliot"; and selected photographs from Gallun's life.

In each section, materials are arranged in chronological order by publication date and numbered anew from the number one. A typical book entry includes item number, title (boldfaced), place of publication, publisher, month and year of publication, pagination, format (paper or cloth), type (e.g., novel), and similar data on all known reprint editions in all languages, plot summary, and all known secondary sources and reviews. A typical shorter work entry provides item number, title (in quotes), magazine title (italics), volume number, month and year of publication, pagination, plot summary, and similar data on all known reprints, foreign and domestic. The chronology provides a very detailed guide to the author's personal and creative life. "Quoth the Critics" includes excerpts from selected critical reaction. The index correlates titles and item numbers only. The book is nicely printed and bound to library standards.

The supplemental materials which have been added to the recent volumes in this continuing bibliographical series provide glimpses into the author's creative life unlike anything else currently available. Gallun's own autobiographical essay, his statement of philosophy, the lengthy and very revealing interview, the inclusion of a Gallun story which has not been reprinted in forty years, the photographs from his early life, all combine with the very complete bibliographical data to summarize in a very succinct way one man's sixty-year career as a writer. Gallun is not well-known outside the SF field, and there may be those who question the need for this volume. That misses the point. There are a great many writers and other artists who have had lengthy and very worthy careers in their respective fields but who have failed for one reason or another to grab the public's interest. This kind of literary guide, when properly accomplished, freezes into a specific time and place an overview of a life spent immersed in creativity. Dr. Elliot has once again with this book accomplished that task very well indeed.

James Gunn

340. Drumm, Chris. **A James Gunn Checklist**. Polk City, Ia., Chris Drumm Books, 1984. [24] p. index. LC 84-212825. ISBN 0-936055-13-8 (pbk.).

Gunn, a respected American English professor, critic, and science fiction writer, is the featured target of this brief 4.25" x 7" checklist. The author's works are arranged in one straight chronological sequence. Entries are grouped by year and under each year by month; each item is numbered in order from 1 to 142. Books are underlined, short stories listed in quotation marks. A typical short fiction entry includes item number, title, category code (e.g., "s"=short story), magazine, month of publication—or book title, if the first appearance is in an anthology, plus editor, publisher, and year of publication. Subsequent reprintings are grouped under the original edition, with similar data provided. No paginations are included. A typical book entry includes item number, title, category code (e.g., "c"=collection), publisher, stock number, month of publication (if known), pagination, price, format (e.g., "pb"=paperback), contents of collections. See references, index, and contents listings are keyed to item number. A few secondary materials are mentioned in passing in their appropriate years but are not easily retrievable. Data are complete through mid-1984. The book is shot from typed copy; the text runs too close to the right-hand margin to allow rebinding by libraries. A four-page critical essay, "Of Dreams and of Nightmares," by Stephen H. Goldman, provides a basic introduction to the author and his work. A good starting point for future scholarship on this writer, but a new edition of this outdated pamphlet would now be warranted.

H. Rider Haggard

341. Scott, J. E. **A Bibliography of the Works of Sir Henry Rider Haggard, 1856-1925.** Takeley, England, Elkin Matthews, 1947. 258 p. index. LC a48-430. Limited to 500 copies.

This thorough and very carefully rendered bibliography is organized into nine chapters: "Preface"; "A Note Concerning the Late Mr. Allan Quatermain" (a detailed examination of the chronology of the Quatermain tales); "I. First Editions"; "II. Articles in Newspapers, Periodicals, Etc."; "III. Letters to *The Times*"; "IV. Letters to Newspapers, Periodicals, Etc."; "V. Reports of Haggard's Speeches"; "VI. Reviews by H. Rider Haggard"; "VII. Dramatisations of Haggard's Novels"; "VIII. Parodies, Etc., of Haggard's Books"; "IX. Interviews, Biographical Sketches, Critical Articles, Etc."; plus an index.

The section on Haggard's books accounts for 132 pages (and eighty-five first editions), more than half the bibliography, and is arranged chronologically by publication date. A typical entry includes item number, title (boldfaced caps), year of publication, and exact transcription of title page copy, collation, description of binding cloth and style, publication date, number of copies published, contents (where appropriate), details on previous serialization (where appropriate), background information, and notes. Second editions and first American editions are described immediately following the first British versions, as separate entries, being numbered (in the case of *Mr. Meeson's Will*, for example) 9A and 9B. Materials are numbered consecutively throughout the book from 1-732. No attempt has been made to cover the myriad reprints of Haggard's popular novels.

The remaining sections are also recorded chronologically by date of publication or filming. A typical shorter work entry provides year of publication, item number, date of publication title (small caps), magazine title (italics), and occasional descriptive notes but no paginations. The chapter on dramatizations is broken into two sections covering play adaptations of Haggard's work (including date of first production, theatre name, principal stars, author, etc.), and motion picture versions (giving production company, director, writer, date of first showing, and the names of actors and other principals). The section on parodies is notably incomplete, lacking all of the American parody novels which appeared in the late 1880s. The valuable final chapter, on secondary sources, includes references to and descriptions of many materials which would be nearly impossible to locate today. The index correlates titles (including periodicals) and entry numbers. A few facsimiles of Haggard manuscript pages are included. The book is beautifully typeset and bound to library standards.

One very obvious omission from this otherwise excellent bibliography is a section covering Haggard's ten or twenty short stories. Some information on the previous publication of these works is buried at the end of the several collections issued in book form (*Smith and the Pharoahs*, for example), and the individual story titles do appear in the index; nonetheless, one can gain no unified overview of these materials without a great deal of flipping back and forth between different monograph entries. Compare with Whatmore's more recent guide (see #342).

342. Whatmore, D. E. **H. Rider Haggard: A Bibliography.** London, Mansell Publishing Ltd., 1987. xix, 187 p. index. ISBN 0-7201-1806-9. Also: Westport, Conn., Meckler Publishing Corp., 1987. xix, 187 p. index. LC 86-33272. ISBN 0-88736-102-1.

Whatmore generally follows Scott's format (see #341), with further divisions and amalgamations. Contents: "Preface"; "Introduction"; "Guide to the Bibliography"; "Sources and Acknowledgements"; Bibliography: "1. Principal Works [i.e., books]: Fiction"; "2. Principal Works"; "3. Pamphlets and Reports"; "4. The African Review"; "5. Miscellaneous

Writings"; "6. Letters to Newspapers and Periodicals"; "7. Selected Reports of Haggard's Speeches"; "8. Films, Plays and Radio Broadcasts Based on Haggard's Work"; "9. Books and Articles About Haggard and His Works"; "10. Parodies and Lampoons"; "11. Theses" [about Haggard's works]; Appendixes: "1. Some Popular Editions of Note"; "2. Haggard Manuscripts in the Norfolk Record Office"; "Subject Index"; "Index to Newspapers and Periodicals."

Materials in each section are listed in chronological order by publication date and numbered anew from one, chapter by chapter. A typical monograph entry provides item number, title, year of publisher, publisher, identification features (binding, spine, front cover, end papers, preliminaries, text, supplements, illustrations, errors), technical data (format, edges, collation), number of copies in first edition (with exact date of publication), earlier publication in magazine form, other editions of note (chiefly the first American edition, early large paper editions, and other contemporaneous variants of significance; no later editions are noted, and relatively few bibliographical details are provided), "Notes," "Some Haggard Notes" (comments by Haggard himself). The two book sections account for 93 pages out of 187.

A typical short work entry includes year of publication, item number, month (and day, where appropriate) of publication, title (in quotes), magazine title (italics), pagination (where known). The first appendix lists fourteen series (British and American) which included significant numbers of Haggard titles, including the early unauthorized U.S. dime novel versions, with dates of publication and series number (where appropriate), but no other bibliographical data. The second appendix is a very useful guide to the major collection of surviving Haggard manuscripts in the Norfolk Record Office; included are the originals of some of his best-known novels. The "Subject Index" correlates titles, authors, and some subjects to item numbers; the "Index to Newspapers and Periodicals" is organized by country (the United Kingdom is listed first, then all others alphabetically by country name), then alphabetically by magazine title, with a list of entry numbers following each title. The book is very clearly typeset and bound to library standards. Data are complete through part of 1986.

Both Whatmore's bibliography and Scott's (see #341) lack any specific section covering Haggard's short fiction. Scott provides more details on first American editions, while Whatmore includes somewhat more explicit data on first British editions. Whatmore also lists far more secondary sources (359 items, plus seven unpublished academic theses, versus ninety-one records for Scott), but not all of the entries from Scott are repeated in Whatmore. Whatmore is also more complete in his coverage of the Haggard parodies and far more complete in his listings of dramatizations, movie versions of Haggard's works, and other media adaptations; but he misses the 1978 American republication (in two omnibuses) of six Haggard parodies by Arno Press and the reprint of eight Haggard titles between 1973-80 in the Newcastle Forgotten Fantasy Library (and a half dozen others by Arno Press), among others. Libraries will probably find Whatmore adequate for most purposes, but scholars seriously interested in researching Haggard's fiction will require both volumes and then some.

Edmond Hamilton

Benson, Gordon, Jr. **Leigh Douglass Brackett and Edmond Hamilton: A Working Bibliography**. *See the entry for Leigh Brackett* (see #288).

Harry Harrison

343. Benson, Gordon, Jr., and Phil Stephensen-Payne. **Harry Maxwell Harrison, Stainless Steel Talent: A Working Bibliography.** 4th rev. ed. Albuquerque, N.M., Galactic Central Publications, 1989. 9, 71 p. (Galactic Central Bibliographies for the Avid Reader, Vol. 9). ISBN 0-912613-12-2 (pbk.).

Harry Harrison, author of the Stainless Steel Rat stories and the Eden series, is an American SF writer turned Irish emigré. Contents: Author's full name, date and place of birth, and pseudonyms; "A. Stories"; "B. Fiction Books"; "C. Series"; "D. Poems & Songs"; "E. Poem & Song Collections" ("none known"); "F. Articles"; "G. Miscellaneous"; "H. Non-Fiction Books"; "I. Edited Books"; "J. Media Presentations"; "K. Articles on Harry Harrison"; "L. Reviews" [of Harrison's books]; "M. Books About Harry Harrison"; "N. Phantom Titles and References"; "O. Related Works by Other Authors" ("none known"); "P. Textual Variations" ("no details known"); "Q. Chronological Index."

In each section materials are arranged alphabetically by title and numbered consecutively from the number one. A typical shorter work entry gives item number, title, category ("ss"=short story, "nt"=novelette, etc.), magazine or book in which the item appeared, month and year of publication (for magazines in the form "4-64" for April 1964) or year of publication (for books), plus similar data for all known reprints (for which title, publisher, year, and editor's last name are given), but no paginations. Book entries provide item number, title (all caps), contents (where applicable, listing the item numbers of the stories as recorded in Section A), publication data (publisher, stock number, month and year of publication [if known, in the form "10-59" for October 1959], pagination, price, and cover artist), plus similar information on all known reprints. There is no general index. The book is shot from very legible word-processed copy and stapled into paper covers. Data are complete through mid-1989.

Although Benson and Stephensen-Payne's work is not as comprehensive or revelatory as the massive Tomlinson volume (see #345), it remains a sound piece of bibliography and will provide most students with a firm beginning point for their research.

344. Biamonti, Francesco. **Harry Harrison: Bibliographia (1951-1965).** Trieste, Italy, Printed by Editoriale Libraria, 1965. [11] p. (pbk.).

Biamonti's brief guide to Harrison's work uses the same format developed by Margaret Aldiss for her bibliographical chapbooks, *Item Forty-Three* and *Item Eighty-Three* (see #265). Forty-six items are listed (and numbered) in alphabetical order by title. A typical entry includes item number, title (in bold caps), estimated wordage, pen name (where appropriate), [for short fiction:] magazine title, date of publication, [for novels:] publisher, date of publication, plus all known reprints (including some foreign-language editions, with translated titles), and occasional one- to two-sentence annotations by Harrison himself in italics at the end of the entry. Beautifully typeset but now outdated and subsumed by both Benson (see #343) and Tomlinson (see #345).

345. Tomlinson, Paul. **The Work of Harry Harrison: An Annotated Bibliography & Guide.** San Bernardino, Calif., The Borgo Press, 1992. [224] p. index. (Bibliographies of Modern Authors, No. 20). ISBN 0-8095-0515-0; ISBN 0-8095-1515-6 (pbk.).

Harry Harrison attained great popularity in the 1980s with his Eden stories of an alternate world in which dinosaurs developed an intelligent species that dominated the Earth. Contents: "Introduction," by Tomlinson; "A Harry Harrison Chronology"; "A. Books"; "B. Short Fiction"; "C. Short Nonfiction"; "D. Reviews"; "E. Editorial Posts"; "F. Fanzines";

"G. Media Adaptations"; "H. Unproduced Scripts"; "I. Secondary Sources"; "J. Miscellanea"; "Quoth the Critics"; Afterword: "Just a Few Words...," by Harrison; "Acknowledgments"; "Notes on Sources"; "Index."

In each chapter materials are listed chronologically by publication date and are numbered anew from the number one, prefixed by the letter code identifying that section (e.g., B1, B2, B3, etc.) for the author's short fiction. A typical book entry provides item number, title (bold italics), place of publication, publisher, month and year of publication, pagination, format (paper or cloth), type (novel), plus similar data for all known reprints, including foreign-language editions, a detailed plot synopsis or contents listing (for collections and anthologies), and a list of secondary sources and reviews specific to that work. A typical shorter work entry includes item number, title (in quotes), pseudonym (where appropriate), magazine title (italics), volume number, month and year of publication, pagination, and complete bibliographical data for all known reprints, foreign and domestic, including republication in Harrison's own collections. Stories appearing first in anthologies include item number, story title, book title (in italics), editor's name, place of publication, publisher, year of publication, format (e.g., paper), and specific pagination.

Tomlinson's introduction includes a number of autobiographical quotations from Harrison, and the detailed Chronology records major events in Harrison's life in block paragraph format, year by year. Harrison's afterword comments specifically on the meaning of this bibliography to the author, and reminisces about his career as a writer. The "Quoth the Critics" chapter reproduces critical commentary about specific works by Harrison, in chronological order by publication date. The detailed index coordinates titles and item numbers only. The book is shot from clear well designed word-processed copy and bound to library standards.

British librarian Tomlinson has done the scholarly world a service by compiling this very detailed and thoroughly professional guide to a writer whose work has been consistently overlooked by the critics. All major research libraries in Britain and America should obtain a copy.

Robert A. Heinlein

346. Owings, Mark. **Robert A. Heinlein: A Bibliography**. Baltimore, Croatan House, 1973. xii, 23 p. ISBN 0-88358-000-4 (pbk.).

Astonishingly, this is the only bibliographical monograph published to date on a man considered by many *the* major science fiction writer of the twentieth century. A seven-page critical introduction by Fred Lerner frames Heinlein's life and work. The bibliography proper is organized in one alphabetical sequence by title with books being underlined. Each title is flush to the left-hand margin, the remainder of the entry being indented three spaces to set it off. There are no line breaks between entries (but several lines are skipped between letters of the alphabet). A typical short fiction entry includes title, magazine title, month and year of publication (in the form 5/48 for May 1948), and known reprint editions (with book title, editor, publisher, place of publication, stock number [for paperbacks], year of publication, format [e.g., "wpps"=paperback], total pagination of the book, price, but no specific paginations for the story). A typical book entry includes title, publisher, place of publication, year of publication, pagination, price, with similar data for known reprint editions. Many foreign-language editions are shown with translators and foreign-language title equivalents (such data are very difficult to locate). The book is shot from sometimes faint typed copy. Data are included through part of 1973. Even with Heinlein's recent death, the book is wholly out-of-date, and the scholarly world now awaits a comprehensive, definitive bibliography on the works of this classic SF writer.

Frank Herbert

347. Levack, Daniel J. H., with annotations by Mark Willard. **Dune Master: A Frank Herbert Bibliography**. Westport, Conn., Meckler Corp., 1988. xx, 176 p. (Meckler's Bibliographies on Science Fiction, Fantasy, and Horror, No. 2). LC 87-25034. ISBN 0-88736-099-8.

Levack has authored four other similarly formatted bibliographies on de Camp, Dick, Vance, and Zelazny (see #321, #326, #434, #455); this new work has many of the same faults as its brethren. Contents: "Introduction," "Annotator's Introduction"; "Books"; Edited Books"; "Non-Book Appearances" (i.e., short fiction and nonfiction); "Manuscript Collection"; "Series and Connected Stories"; "Pseudonyms"; "Chronological Order of Publication of Frank Herbert's Work"; "Fiction Checklist"; "Non-Fiction Checklist"; "Verse Checklist"; "Other Media Checklist"; "Magazine Checklist"; "Works About Frank Herbert"; "Appendix: Illustrations of Covers."

Works are listed in the major sections alphabetically by title and numbered consecutively from the number one, section by section, with over 160 items included. A typical book entry includes item number, title (bold caps), series note (when appropriate) or category (e.g., "Non-Fiction"), contents (if a collection) or one- to three-page annotation (if a novel) in boldface, publisher, stock number (for paperback editions), place of publication (inconsistently), price (in parentheses), year of publication, edition points, but no paginations. Reprints are listed in chronological order by publication date; many foreign editions are included with foreign-language titles. An asterisk after a specific edition indicates it has been viewed by Levack.

A typical shorter work entry gives item number, title (in bold quotes), category (e.g., "non-fiction"), one- to fifteen-paragraph annotation (in bold type), magazine or book title, date, issue number (inconsistently), but no paginations. All subsequent reprint editions (including some foreign-language materials with foreign-language titles) are listed with similar data. Anthology appearances include title, editor, publisher, stock number, price, year of publication, format (e.g., "paper"), but no paginations. This section also includes some media publications (sound recordings, for example). The magazine checklist is an alphabetical listing of those publications in which Herbert stories appeared, keyed to issue date and to item number in the "Non-Book Appearances" section.

Levack also includes a master chronological checklist of Herbert's work, year by year, with all publications interfiled (but their titles here are keyed to none of the item numbers in the main bibliography). A "Fiction Checklist" (and non-fiction and verse lists) provide quick, alphabetical sequences for each category, but again fail to refer the reader to specific item numbers in the main bibliography. There is no index as such. The book includes twenty pages of b&w book and magazine cover reproductions (four to a page), an attractive feature. The brief (two-page) secondary bibliography includes just eleven items, five monographs and six articles, and is lamentably incomplete. Coverage extends through early 1987, and with Herbert's recent death, should remain reasonably current for some time.

The absence of an index, of all paginations, of most secondary sources, is inexcusable in a production of this magnitude from a major publisher. Thus, while Levack contains a great deal of useful information, it can serve as no more than a starting point for the serious researcher and is in no way "definitive." Compare with Stephensen-Payne's more current checklist (see #348).

348. Stephensen-Payne, Phil. **Frank Herbert, a Voice from the Desert: A Working Bibliography.** Leeds, West Yorkshire, England & Albuquerque, N.M., Galactic Central, 1990. 9, 48 p. (Galactic Central Bibliographies for the Avid Reader, Vol. 36). (pbk.).

The late Frank Herbert is best known for his six novels revolving around the planet Dune. Contents: Author's full name and dates of birth and death; dates and names of awards received; "A. Stories"; "B. Fiction Books"; "C. Series"; "D. Poems, Songs & Plays"; "E. Poem, Song & Play Volumes" ("none known"); "F. Articles"; "G. Miscellaneous"; "H. Non-Fiction Books"; "I. Books Edited by Frank Herbert"; "J. Media Presentations"; "K. Articles on Frank Herbert"; "L. Reviews" (of Herbert's books listed alphabetically by book title, then alphabetically by magazine title); "M. Books About Frank Herbert"; "N. Phantom & Forthcoming Titles"; "O. Related Items by Other Authors"; "P. Textual Variations"; "Q. Chronological Index."

Materials are listed in each section alphabetically by title, and are numbered anew from one, prefixed by the identifying letter for that chapter (e.g., P1, P2, P3, etc.). A typical book entry provides item number, title (all caps), contents (where appropriate, by item number), publisher, format (e.g, "pb"=paperback), stock number, month and year of publication (in the form "12-70" for December 1970), pagination, price, cover artist, a list of subsequent printings from the same publisher (with similar data), and all other known reprints from other publishers, listed chronologically by initial publication date. No foreign language editions are included.

A typical shorter work entry gives item number, title, type (e.g., "N-3"=a serialized novel in three parts), magazine title, month and year of publication (in the form "7-55" for July 1955), and brief bibliographical data on all known reprints. Reprints in anthologies include book title (all caps), editor's last name, publisher, and year of publication. Ninety-seven secondary sources are listed, plus over a hundred book reviews. Coverage is complete through mid-1990. The checklist has no overall index, but the alphabetization of individual sections makes materials relatively easy to find. The book is shot from dark, clear word-processed copy and stapled into paper covers.

Levack's guide (see #347) includes some foreign-language editions of Herbert's books, provides minimal annotations, and reproduces numerous illustrations of paperback and magazine covers of interest to the Herbert collector, making it more attractive physically, but in virtually every other respect is deficient to Stephensen-Payne's more concise checklist. Scholars interested in intensively researching the author's life and works should have access to both bibliographies; all others, including libraries, will find Stephensen-Payne more than adequate.

William Hope Hodgson

349. Bell, Joseph. **William Hope Hodgson, Night Pirate; Volume One: An Annotated Bibliography of Published Works, 1902-1987.** Toronto, Canada, Soft Books, 1988 (?). viii, 41 p. (pbk.).

Bell has also compiled bibliographies with similar formats on Clive Barker and H. P. Lovecraft (see #276, #368, and #369). This new work covers the publications of a classic British horror writer killed in World War I. The main section, on the author's books, is arranged in chronological order by publication date and includes title (large bold type), publisher, place of publication, pagination, price, binding, date of publication, information on edition priority states, contents (for collections), other notes, and similar data on all known reprintings and subsequent editions. A second section covers periodical and anthology appearance(s) of Hodgson's stories and essays, in alphabetical order by title. A typical shorter work entry includes title (bold caps), category (e.g., "nf"=non fantasy), magazine title, month and year of publication, but no paginations, and a list of all known reprint editions, including in Hodgson's own books. Anthology appearances include book title, editor, publisher, place of publication, format (e.g., "paper cover" for paperback), year of publication, but no paginations. As usual with Bell's bibliographies, there is no overall title index.

This volume is intended primarily as a collectors' guide, not a literary bibliography, and contains no information on the content of the books or stories and very little on Hodgson himself. Nicely designed and typeset and stapled into 8.5" x 11" paper covers. Note: the remaining five volumes in this series include a biography of Hodgson, three collections of stories by Hodgson, and a concluding book (not yet published) containing addenda to the first two volumes, plus a bibliography covering Hodgson's works in translation.

Robert E. Howard

350. Lord, Glenn. **The Last Celt: A Bio-Bibliography of Robert Ervin Howard**. West Kingston, R.I., Donald M. Grant, Publisher, 1976. 416 p. index. LC 77-351659. Also: New York, A Berkley Windhover Book, Berkley Books, 1976. 415 p. index. LC 77-154974. ISBN 0-425-03630-8 (pbk.).

This 7" x 10" volume was published for the fan and collectors' market to commemorate the life and works of a well-known American pulp fantasy writer who took his own life in 1936 at the age of thirty. Contents: "Introduction," by E. Hoffmann Price; "Foreword" (by Lord), "I. Autobiography" (various pieces by Howard); "II. Biography" (essays on Howard's life and career by different hands); "III. Bibliography" (p. 103-352); "IV. Miscellanea" (reproductions of several Howard manuscripts and magazine covers featuring Howard stories, and photographs of the author and his family). The bibliography proper includes "Introduction"; "Books"; "Fiction"; "Verse," (with "Title Index," "First Line Index," and "Headings"); "Articles"; "Letters"; "Index by Periodicals"; "Translations: Books, Fiction, Verse, Headings, Articles, Letters"; Unpublished Fiction"; "Unpublished Verse" (with "Title Index" and "Headings"); "Unpublished Articles"; "Series Index"; "Lost Manuscripts"; "Unborn Books"; "Comics"; "Television Adaptations"; "The Junto"; "About the Author: Books, Amateur Publications, Robert E. Howard Press Association, Articles, Conan Pastiches."

Monographs are listed in chronological order by publication data. A typical book entry includes title (caps), contents (for collections), publisher, place of publication, year of publication, pagination, price, in-print status, binding details, cover artist (if known), other bibliographical notes. Howard's short fiction is organized by pseudonym, then alphabetically by story title. Each entry provides title, magazine title, month and year of publication, and all known reprints but no paginations. Reprints in anthologies include book title, editor, publisher, place of publication, year of publication. Verse and nonfiction are arranged similarly to short fiction, by pseudonym and title; a separate index correlates the first lines of Howard's poems with their titles. Howard's letters are arranged in alphabetical order by recipient. The index by periodicals provides magazine title, then titles of Howard stories which appeared in each, by date. Translations of books are organized chronologically by date of publication; translations of stories, however, are arranged by country, pseudonym and English-language title, with publication data and foreign-language titles. The secondary bibliography covers a paltry three books and two additional pages of articles (nineteen items) arranged by critic, including Howard's original newspaper obituaries and some rather obscure fan articles.

The Last Celt is beautifully printed and designed, typical of Grant's fine press editions, but the absence of an index is a major flaw in a volume with so much text and so many internal subdivisions. Finding a specific title can require much paging through many non-relevant sections. One also laments the lack of page number data for anything except book publications. A revised, expanded edition is overdue.

351. McHaney, Dennis, and Glenn Lord. **The Fiction of Robert E. Howard: A Pocket Checklist**. [S.l.], D. McHaney & T. Foster, 1975. [22] p. (pbk.).

Just what it says, this small (4.25" x 5.5") checklist of Howard's short stories is alphabetically arranged by title, listing the first appearances of each in published form either by magazine title, with month and year of publication, or by book title (in caps) and year. There is also a separate two-and-one-half-page list of Howard's "Unpublished Fiction" and eight pages of very amateurish drawings of Howard heroes. The booklet is shot from typed copy. Clearly something to carry with you wherever you go.

352. Weinberg, Robert. **The Robert E. Howard Fantasy Biblio**. Newark, N.J., Mike Deckinger and Robert Weinberg, 1969. 7 p. (pbk.).
[not seen].

Dean Ing

353. Burgess, Scott Alan. **The Work of Dean Ing: An Annotated Bibliography & Guide**. San Bernardino, Calif., The Borgo Press, 1990. 82 p. index. (Bibliographies of Modern Authors, No. 11). LC 87-827. ISBN 0-89370-395-8; ISBN 0-89370-495-4 (pbk.).

Dean Ing is best known for his tales of a post-nuclear holocaust America and for his bestselling near-future techno-thrillers. Contents: Introduction: "Talking with Dean Ing" (an original interview conducted by Burgess); "A Dean Ing Chronology"; "A. Books"; "B. Short Fiction"; "C. Nonfiction"; "D. Unpublished Works"; "E. Editorial Credits"; "F. Radio and Television Appearances"; "G. Honors and Awards"; "H. About the Author"; "I. Miscellanea"; "Quoth the Critics"; Afterword: "Excuse the Shouting...," by Ing (comments on his philosophy of writing and living); "Index"; "About Scott Alan Burgess."

In each section, Ing's works are arranged chronologically and numbered consecutively from the number one, chapter by chapter, prefixed by the appropriate letter code (e.g., C1, C2, C3, etc.). A typical book entry includes item number, title (in boldface), place of publication, publisher, year of publication, pagination, format (e.g., "cloth"), and type of publication (e.g., "novel"); full bibliographical data are also included for all known reprint editions, translations, republications, etc. The books are annotated with complete contents listings and/or plot summaries and other pertinent data; entries from other sections are selectively annotated as needed.

A typical shorter work entry includes item number, title (in bold quotes), magazine, volume number, month and year of publication, pagination, and complete bibliographical data for all known reprints, including foreign publications. The nonfiction chapter lists over a hundred of Ing's little-known writings for survivalist publications. The chronology provides a year-by-year account of the author's professional and personal life in block paragraph format. "About the Author" lists all known secondary works chronologically by publication date. "Miscellanea" includes information on pen names, book dedications, memberships, Library of Congress cataloging data, career highlights, and other data. "Quoth the Critics" includes selected excerpts of reviews and other comments by leading critics on the author's work. The index correlates titles and item numbers only. The book is nicely typeset and the cloth version bound to library standards.

Much of the material in this volume was compiled directly from Ing's own files and personal library of his works. Coverage is complete through late 1990. Although Ing is not well-known outside the SF field, his reputation is growing rapidly; Burgess's guide will provide the scholar with everything he or she needs to know about this rising Oregon author. For larger library collections.

Carl Jacobi

354. Smith, R. Dixon. **Lost in the Rentharpian Hills: Spanning the Decades with Carl Jacobi.** Bowling Green, Ohio, Bowling Green State University Popular Press, 1985. 146 p. index. LC 84-72634. ISBN 0-87972-287-8; ISBN 0-87972-288-6 (pbk.).

Both a biography and bibliography of this American pulp writer's life and works, Smith's guide includes the following sections: "Acknowledgments"; "Foreword," by Robert Bloch; "Foreword," by Joseph Payne Brennan; "Lost in the Rentharpian Hills" (biography); "Notes"; "Appendix I, Carl Jacobi: A Bibliography" (p. 75-119); "Appendix II, Selected Letters to Carl Jacobi"; "Index."

The forty-five-page bibliography is organized into several sections: "I. High School and College Publications" (further divided into two parts, "A. Central High School" and "B. University of Minnesota"); "II. Magazine Publications" (the bulk of the entries); "III. Fan Magazine Publications": "A. Fiction," "B. Non-Fiction"; "IV. Book Publications": "A. [stories in] "Anthologies," "B. Collections" [of fiction by Jacobi himself], "C. Non-Fiction" [books by Jacobi]; "V. Selected Foreign Publications": "A. Magazines," "B. Anthologies," "C. Collections"; "VI. Miscellaneous Publications": "A. Interviews," "B. Autobiographical Sketches," "C. Letters to Editors," "D. Humorous Sketches," "Anecdotes," and "Poems," "E. Book Reviews," "F. Articles Written as a Reporter on the *Minneapolis Star*," "G. Other Writings"; "VII. Unpublished Works."

In each section, materials are arranged chronologically by publication date. A typical book entry includes author (even when it's Jacobi himself!), title (italics), place of publication, publisher, year of publication, pagination, price, cover illustrator, and a list of the stories included in that volume by Jacobi, with title of the magazine where the piece originally appeared and year and month of original publication. A typical short fiction entry provides title (in quotes), magazine title (in italics), volume and issue number, month and year of publication, pagination, category (e.g., "Borneo adventure"), wordage, submission and title change history, amount Jacobi was paid for sale. The book is nicely typeset and designed, featuring some reproductions of magazine covers and interior illustrations and bound to library standards. The items are indexed within the body of Jacobi's own index entry, then alphabetically by title, keyed to page numbers within all parts of the book (not just the bibliography).

One major problem with the bibliography is the absence of any coordinated list of reprints for a particular story or collection. This is less burdensome in the book section, where the overall number of monograph titles and reissues by Jacobi are small enough that the eye can encompass virtually the entire list at a glance; but Jacobi was also responsible for the publication of many dozens of pulp stories, and tracking these items is difficult without constant references back and forth to the index. Scholars will welcome the publication of this volume but will lament the unnecessarily cumbersome structure of the bibliography section.

K. W. Jeter

355. Joyce, Tom, and Christopher P. Stephens. **A Checklist of K. W. Jeter**. Hastings-on-Hudson, N.Y., 1991. 13 p. index. ISBN 0-89366-200-3 (pbk.).

This brief guide to American SF writer Jeter's works is arranged in two sections: "Books" and "Short Stories." In both parts materials are arranged in chronological order by publication date, and numbered anew from the number one (books from A1-A14, short fiction from B1-B5). A typical book entry includes year (as a floating head), item number, title (underlined), publisher, stock or ISBN number, pagination, format (e.g., "paper over boards"), cover illustrator, price, and similar data for all known reprints (which are numbered, for example, A9a, A9b, A9c, etc., in descending order by publication date). A typical short fiction entry gives year (header), item number, title (in quotes), magazine title (underlined) and month and year of publication, or book title (if an anthology; underlined), editor's name, publisher, year of publication, but no paginations. The booklet is shot from legible typed copy and bound with staples in stiff paper covers. The index correlates titles with years of publication only. Joyce and Stephens have provided an inexpensive introduction to Jeter's work, one which will be primarily of use to fans and collectors.

Stephen King

356. Collings, Michael R. **The Annotated Guide to Stephen King: A Primary and Secondary Bibliography of the Works of America's Premier Horror Writer**. Mercer Island, Wash., Starmont House, 1986. vi, 176 p. (Starmont Reference Guide, No. 8). LC 86-1854. ISBN 0-930261-81-X; ISBN 0-930261-80-1 (pbk.).

Collings, author of a half dozen critical monographs on America's premier writer of horror fiction, here has produced the first comprehensive bibliography of King's work. Contents: "Foreword" (by Collings); "List of Abbreviations"; "Part One: Primary Bibliography: A. Book-Length Fiction"; "B. Collections of King's Fiction"; "C. Short Fiction and Poetry"; "D. Non-Fiction, Criticism, and Reviews"; "E. The Audio-Visual King." "Part Two: Secondary Bibliography": "F. Bibliographical Studies"; "G. Book-Length Critical Studies and Newsletters"; "H. Selected Critical Articles, Reviews, and Interviews"; "List of Works Cited."

Entries are numbered anew from one in each chapter (e.g., A1, A2, A3, for the first three book titles). The primary bibliography lists King's works in alphabetical order by title, section by section. A typical book entry includes item number, title (underlined boldface), place of publication, publisher, format (e.g., paperback), brief data on reprint editions and translations, plot summary, list of book reviews (by magazine title, with date and page number). No paginations are supplied for monographs. The collections also include contents listings in addition to analytical annotations. A typical shorter work entry includes item number, title (in bold quotes), magazine (underlined), date, pagination, and an abbreviated title of King collection in which the piece is included (where appropriate), with year of publication of the collection and the exact pagination of the story or article in the first edition of the collection; one-paragraph annotations are also included for all short fiction and essays. Section E includes item number, title, production company, date, whether the film is available on tape (and in what format), number of minutes, film rating (G, R, etc.), critical evaluation, list of principals (producer, director, etc.), and cast. Also included are computer games, audio tapes, calendars, with brief summaries of each.

The secondary bibliography is arranged by author or main entry, section by section, with approximately 600 secondary sources listed. A typical entry includes item number, author, title, publication, date, pagination, critical evaluation.

Collings's coverage is thorough, and his knowledge of King's work is unsurpassed; the list of secondary sources is particularly valuable for researchers. However, the book is crowded and somewhat cramped, particularly in Sections C, D, and H, where the items are jammed together with no spaces between the entries. Also, the constant use of abbreviations is both irritating and unnecessary. The lack of a comprehensive title index is very noticeable, and one also misses having paginations for King's monographs. Still, Collings's work, outdated as it is, remains a good beginning guide to a modern literary phenomenon, which should be owned by all academic (and all large public) libraries. See also the second (much revised) version (see #357).

357. Collings, Michael R. **The Work of Stephen King: An Annotated Bibliography & Guide.** San Bernardino, Calif., The Borgo Press, 1992. [400] p. index. (Bibliographies of Modern Authors, No. 25). ISBN 0-8095-0520-7; ISBN 0-8095-1521-2 (pbk.).

In little more than a decade and a half Stephen King has become one of the world's bestselling authors, and certainly the best-known horror writer since H. P. Lovecraft. Contents: Introduction: "Not So Much to Tell, as to Let the Story Flow Through," by Collings; "A Stephen King Chronology"; "A. Books"; "B. Short Fiction"; "C. Nonfiction"; "D. Poetry"; "E. Screenplays" [by King]: "EA. Produced Screenplays," "EB. Unproduced Screenplays"; "F. Public and Screen Appearances": "FA. Public Appearances and Speeches," "FB. Screen Appearances"; "G. Visual Adaptations": "GA. Feature-Length Films," "GB. Teleplays and Television Adaptations," "GC. Musical Adaptations," "GD. Stage Adaptations," "GE. Videocassettes"; "H. Audiocassettes"; "I. Secondary Sources: Books and Book-Length Studies"; "J. Secondary Sources: Newsletters"; "K. Secondary Sources: Bibliographic Studies"; "L. Secondary Sources: Profiles and Bio-Bibliographical Sketches"; "M. Secondary Sources: Interviews": "MA. Print Interviews," "MB. Non-Print Interviews"; "N. Secondary Sources: Scholarly, Critical, and Interpretive Articles"; "O. Secondary Sources: Popular Magazines and Journals, News Magazines"; "P. Secondary Sources: Media, Specialty, and Fan Magazines"; "Q. Secondary Sources: *Castle Rock: The Stephen King Newsletter*"; "R. Secondary Sources: Newspaper Articles"; "S. Secondary Sources: Professional and Trade Journals"; "T. Secondary Sources: Selected Reviews"; "U. The Stephen King Archives"; "V. Unpublished Works": "VA. Novels," "VB. Short Fiction"; "W. Parodies, Pastiches, Cartoons, Etc.": "WA. Cartoons About Stephen King," "WB. Contents and Puzzles," "WC. Parodies and Satires," "WD. Pastiches," "WE. Stories and Poems About King," "WF. Conferences," "WG. Miscellaneous Secondary Items"; "X. Honors and Awards"; "Y. Miscellanea"; "Quoth the Critics"; "Index."

In each section and subsection materials are arranged chronologically by publication date and numbered anew from the number one, with the appropriate letter prefix (e.g., MB1, MB2, MB3, etc.). A typical book entry includes item number, title (bold italics), place of publication, publisher, year of publication, pagination, format (e.g., cloth), and type (e.g., collection), plus similar data on all known reprints, foreign and domestic, a plot synopsis and/or list of contents, references to motion picture or other versions of the work, and a comprehensive list of reviews and/or articles about that specific title arranged in alphabetical order by main entry (critic, if known, or title or magazine, in that order, if no byline has been credited). A typical shorter work entry gives item number, title (boldfaced, in quotes), magazine title, volume number, month and year of publication, and pagination, or, if the publication has first appeared in an anthology or collection: book title (in italics), editor or author, place of publication, publisher, month and year of publication, format, and specific pagination. Similar data are provided for all known reprints. The media sections give title (bold italics), production company, producer, director, screenwriter, running time, rating (e.g., "R"), cast, and a comprehensive list of reviews. The index correlates all data with item numbers. The book is beautifully typeset and is bound to library standards.

Collings has assembled an incredibly large number of citations, carefully arranged and logically organized. For example, some 1,521 secondary sources are noted, plus another thousand reviews of King's novels and film adaptations of his work, all made easily accessible through the index. It is difficult to imagine how any serious researcher of Stephen King's fiction could bypass this extremely comprehensive guide. Recommended for all university and large public library collections.

Dean R. Koontz

358. Stephens, Christopher P. **A Checklist of Dean R. Koontz**. Hastings-on-Hudson, N.Y., Ultramarine Publishing Co., 1987. 14 p. index. ISBN 0-89366-133-3 (pbk.). **A Checklist of Dean R. Koontz**. [3rd ed.]. Hastings-on-Hudson, N.Y., Ultramarine Publishing Co., 1990. 19 p. index. ISBN 0-89366-133-3 (pbk.).

Koontz has achieved wide popularity in recent years with his horror and suspense novels, although his beginnings as a writer were deeply rooted in the science-fiction field. Stephens's checklist (both editions) is organized in chronological order by publication date, books being numbered from A1-A61. A typical entry provides year (as a floating head), item number, title (underlined), pseudonym, publisher, stock or ISBN number, pagination, format (e.g., "cloth with dust wrapper"), cover illustrator, price, and similar data for all known reprints (which are numbered, for example, A40a, A40b, A40c, etc., in descending order by publication date). The chapbook is shot from legible typed copy and bound with staples in stiff paper covers. The index correlates titles with years of publication only. Koontz deserves fuller treatment than this brief guide provides, but until a complete bibliography is available, Stephens's checklist will suffice for most fans.

C. M. Kornbluth

359. Stephensen-Payne, Phil, and Gordon Benson, Jr. **Cyril M. Kornbluth, the Cynical Scrutineer: A Working Bibliography.** 2nd rev. ed. Leeds, West Yorkshire, England & Albuquerque, N.M., Galactic Central Publications, 1990. 9, 39 p. (Galactic Central Bibliographies for the Avid Reader, Vol. 29). ISBN 1-871133-03-3 (pbk.).

Kornbluth, who died tragically young in 1958, left over a hundred vivid stories and novels, and an abiding literary legacy. Stephensen-Payne and Benson arrange this new bibliography by subject category, then alphabetically by title. Contents: Author's full name, date and place of birth and date of death, awards, and pseudonyms; "A. Stories"; "B. Fiction Books"; "C. Series"; "D. Poems"; "E. Poetry Collections" ("none known"); "F. Articles"; "G. Miscellaneous"; "H. Non-Fiction Books" ("none known"); "I. Edited Books" ("none known"); "J. Media Presentations"; "K. Articles on C. M. Kornbluth"; "L. Reviews"; "M. Books About C. M. Kornbluth" ("none known"); "N. Phantom Titles"; "O. Related Books by Other Authors"; "P. Textual Variations"; "Q. Chronological Index." In each part the material is arranged in alphabetical order by title, the author's works being numbered anew from the number one in each.

For shorter works, the authors give item number, title, category ("ss"=short story, "nt"=novelette, etc.), pseudonym (where appropriate), magazine or book in which the item appeared, month and year of publication (for magazines in the form "7-50" for July 1950) or year of publication (for books), a list of subsequent reprints (for which title, publisher, year, and editor's last name are given), but no paginations. For book-length works, they provide item number, title (in caps), pseudonym, contents for collections, keyed to item number, and publication data (publisher, LC card number, month and year of publication [if known, in the form "10-59" for October 1959], pagination, price, stock number, with dates of reissues by the same publisher), plus cover artist and similar data for all known reprints. The list of secondary sources includes thirty-four items and more than a hundred book reviews. There is no general index. The book is shot from very clear word-processed copy and bound with staples in paper covers. Data are complete through 1989.

The addition of an index and magazine paginations to future editions would be useful. As the only current guide to this neglected writer's fiction, Stephensen-Payne and Benson's bibliography will be an essential starting point for all future scholarly investigations of Kornbluth.

Katherine Kurtz

360. Clarke, Boden. **The Work of Katherine Kurtz: An Annotated Bibliography & Guide.** San Bernardino, Calif., The Borgo Press, 1992. [100] p. index. (Bibliographies of Modern Authors, No. 7). LC 85-31401. ISBN 0-89370-386-9; ISBN 0-89370-486-5 (pbk.).

Kurtz is a popular American writer of historical fantasy novels, now living in Ireland. Contents: "Introduction"; "A Katherine Kurtz Chronology"; "A. Books"; "B. Short Fiction"; "C. Short Nonfiction"; "D. Songs"; "E. Editorial Credits"; "F. Scripts"; "G. Cassette Tapes"; "H. Unpublished Works"; "I. Honors and Awards"; "J. Secondary Sources"; "K. Miscellanea"; "Quoth the Critics"; Afterword: "Speaking of Katherine Kurtz," by Jeffrey M. Elliot and Robert Reginald; "Index."

In each section, the author's works are arranged chronologically and numbered consecutively chapter by chapter. A typical book entry includes item number, title (in boldface), place of publication, publisher, year of publication, pagination, format (e.g., "paper"), type of publication (e.g., "novel"), with full bibliographical data for all reprint editions, translations, republications, etc. The books are fully annotated, with complete contents listings or plot summaries and other pertinent data; entries from other sections are selectively annotated as needed. A typical short work entry includes item number, title (bold quotes), magazine title, volume or issue number, date, pagination, with bibliographical data on all known reprints. The introduction provides background material on the author's life and works. The chronology provides a year-by-year account of the author's professional and personal life in block paragraph format. "About the Author" includes all known secondary works. The "Miscellanea" section includes information on book dedications, memberships, Library of Congress cataloging data, career highlights, and other data. "Quoth the Critics" includes selected excerpts of reviews and other comments by leading critics on the author's work. The afterword consists of a lengthy written interview with Kurtz conducted originally by Dr. Elliot, updated and expanded by Reginald. The index correlates titles and item numbers only. The book is nicely designed and typeset and bound to library standards. Coverage is complete through 1991.

Kurtz has a large and loyal following for whom this volume will provide the first organized guide to her life and work. Much of the material is derived from Kurtz's own files and personal library, supplemented by follow-up questions and later correspondence. Clearly presented, well designed, and comprehensive.

Henry Kuttner

361. Anderson, Karen. **Henry Kuttner: A Memorial Symposium**. Berkeley, Calif., Sevagram Enterprises, 1958. 34 p. (pbk.).

Kuttner died in 1958 in his forties after a twenty-year career during which he produced hundreds of short stories and several dozen novels. Immediately after his death, a number of his California friends put together a memorial volume, which includes a number of reminiscences by his colleagues, a Kuttner story, and a brief bibliography of his SF works compiled by the well-known Australian bibliographer Donald H. Tuck. Although Tuck covers Kuttner's periodical and monographic fictions in the science-fiction field, none of his mystery novels or stories are mentioned, or his work in other genres, and the guide shows signs of hasty composition. Prefer Utter and Benson's more current bibliography (see #387).

Utter, Virgil, and Gordon Benson, Jr. **Catherine Lucille Moore and Henry Kuttner: A Working Bibliography**. *See the entry for C. L. Moore* (see #387).

R. A. Lafferty

362. Drumm, Chris. **An R. A. Lafferty Checklist: A Bibliographical Chronology with Notes and Index**. Polk City, Ia., Chris Drumm Books, 1983 (1984). [31] p. index. ISBN 0-936055-04-9 (pbk.).

Lafferty, an eccentric, iconoclastic engineer-turned-science fiction writer, is the focus of this brief 4.25" x 7" checklist. The author's works are arranged in one straight chronological sequence. Entries are grouped by year and under each year by month; items are numbered in sequence from 1 to 192. Books are underlined, short stories listed in quotation marks. A typical short fiction entry includes item number, title, category code (e.g., "s"=short story), magazine, month of publication, paginations, and estimated wordage—or book title if the first appearance is in an anthology, plus editor, publisher, year of publication, paginations, and estimated wordage. Subsequent reprintings are grouped under the original edition, with similar data provided. A typical book entry includes item number, title, category code (e.g., "c"=collection), publisher, stock number, month of publication (if known), pagination, price, format (e.g., "pb"=paperback), contents of collections. See references, title index, and contents listings are keyed to item number. A few secondary materials are mentioned in passing in their appropriate years but are not easily retrievable. Data are complete through early 1984. The book is shot from typed copy; the text runs too close to the right-hand margin to allow rebinding by libraries. A long one-paragraph autobiographical essay by Lafferty on page (3) provides a brief introduction to the author and his work. Drumm has published many of Lafferty's collections and novels since this bibliography first appeared; a second, more elaborate edition would clearly be justified.

Keith Laumer

363. Stephensen-Payne, Phil, and Gordon Benson Jr. **Keith Laumer, Ambassador to Space: A Working Bibliography**. 2nd rev. ed. Leeds, West Yorkshire, England and Albuquerque, N.M., Galactic Central Publications, 1990. 9, 41 p. (Galactic Central Bibliographies for the Avid Reader, Vol. 30). (pbk.).

Ex-diplomat Laumer is best known for his tales of Retief, ambassador to the stars and rogue extraordinaire. This new checklist arranges the data by subject, then alphabetically by title. Contents: Personal data on the author; "A. Stories"; "B. Fiction Books"; "C. Series";

"D. Poems & Songs" ("none known"); "E. Poem & Song Collections" ("none known"); "F. Articles"; "G. Miscellaneous" (introductions and interviews); "H. Non-Fiction Books"; "I. Edited Books"; "J. Media Presentations"; "K. Articles on Keith Laumer"; "L. Reviews" [of Laumer's books]; "M. Books About Keith Laumer" ("none known"); "N. Phantom and Forthcoming Titles"; "O. Related Books by Other Authors"; "P. Textual Variations" ("no details known"); "Q. Chronological Index."

A typical book entry provides item number, title (all caps), contents (where appropriate, keyed to item number), publisher, format (e.g., "hb"=hardback), stock number, month and year of publication ("8-76"=August 1976), pagination, price, cover artist, plus similar data for all known reprints and reissues. A typical shorter work entry gives item number, title, type (e.g., "ss"=short story), magazine title and month and year of publication, or, for anthology appearances, book title (all caps), editor's last name, publisher, and year of publication, but no paginations; similar data are provided for all known reprints. Materials are numbered anew from the number one in each section, prefixed by the letter associated with that chapter (e.g., A44, A45, A46, etc.). The eighteen secondary sources are listed alphabetically by critics' name, reviews alphabetically by Laumer book title, then by magazine title. There is no overall index. The book is shot from very clear word-processed copy and bound through the side with staples.

Laumer has received little attention from the critics, even within the SF genre, despite his prolific output; this bibliography represents the first attempt to synthesize his literary career. SF scholars and major academic libraries should both include copies in their collections.

Ursula K. Le Guin

364. Cogell, Elizabeth Cummins. **Ursula K. Le Guin: A Primary and Secondary Bibliography**. Boston, G. K. Hall & Co., 1983. xl, 244 p. index. (Masters of Science Fiction and Fantasy). LC 82-12071. ISBN 0-8161-8155-1.

Le Guin is generally regarded as one of the most literate SF writers of the last two decades and has thus generated a flood of critical articles and commentaries. Cogell's well-constructed bibliography contains "Preface" (discussing the book's arrangement); "Introduction" (an excellent twenty-eight-page guide to the author's life and work); "Part A: Fiction"; "Part B: Miscellaneous Media": "Section One: Works by Le Guin," "Section Two: Adaptations of and Creative Responses to Le Guin's Work"; "Part C: Nonfiction"; "Part D: Critical and Bio-Bibliographical Studies"; "Indexes: I. Writings by Le Guin"; "II. Writings About Le Guin."

Each section is arranged chronologically, from the earliest published material to the latest, and numbered consecutively from one, section by section (e.g., C1, C2, C3 for nonfiction). Books and shorter works are interfiled by year; reprints of books and stories are grouped as subsidiary entries under their first edition or appearance, chronologically by year of reprint; reprint editions of short stories include editor of anthology, title, place of publication, publisher, year, format (e.g., "paper"), but no paginations. Each book entry gives item number, title (underlined), place of publication, publisher, format ("paper"), contents (for collections and anthologies, with years of original publication), but no paginations. Each shorter work entry gives item number, title (in quotations), magazine, volume number, date, pagination, or, for those published originally in books, book title, book editor, place of publication, publisher, format, and pagination. Some entries, particularly in Sections B-C, include bibliographical or descriptive notes but no other annotations; all of the entries in Part D are extensively annotated.

"Part B: Miscellaneous Media" includes screenplays, teleplays, interviews, recordings, poetry, and other material which do not specifically fit the other three categories; for Le Guin, most of the 147 entries are poems or collections of verse. "Part C: Nonfiction" includes all the author's nonfiction publications, arranged chronologically. "Part D" includes all known articles, reviews, and books about Le Guin, arranged chronologically, with author, title, bibliographical data (in the same form as the other sections, except that paginations are provided for books), and one- to five-paragraph annotations; most "Who's Who" publications are omitted. There are 761 secondary items noted, making this a substantial and extraordinarily valuable resource for the scholar. The indexes include titles, names, and item numbers only. Coverage is complete through the first part of 1981. The book is reproduced from typed copy.

Cogell clearly is familiar with and sympathetic to Le Guin's work; thus, although her guide is now a decade out-of-date, this bibliography must still be regarded as the essential starting point for all scholarly examinations of the author's fiction. A new edition is badly needed.

Fritz Leiber

365. Benson, Gordon, Jr., and Phil Stephensen-Payne. **Fritz Leiber, Sardonic Swordsman: A Working Bibliography.** 2nd rev. ed. Albuquerque, N.M., and Leeds, West Yorkshire, England, Galactic Central Publications, 1990. 9, 90 p. (Galactic Central Bibliographies for the Avid Reader, Vol. 22). ISBN 0-912613-23-8 (pbk.).

Fritz Leiber, a science fiction and fantasy author of the classic period, is second only to Harlan Ellison as a winner of Hugo and Nebula Awards. This guide to Leiber's work is arranged by subject category, then alphabetically by title. Contents: Author's full name, date and place of birth, pseudonyms, and awards and honors; "A. Stories"; "B. Fiction Books"; "C. Series"; "D. Poems, Songs & Plays"; "E. Poem, Song & Play Volumes"; "F. Articles"; "G. Miscellaneous"; "H. Non-Fiction Books"; "I. Books Edited by Fritz Leiber"; "J. Media Presentations"; "K. Articles on Fritz Leiber"; "L. Reviews" [of Leiber's books]; "M. Books About Fritz Leiber"; "N. Phantom & Forthcoming Titles"; "O. Related Items by Other Authors" ("none known"); "P. Textual Variations"; "Q. Chronological Index."

Materials are numbered consecutively from the number one in each section. For shorter works, the authors give item number, title, category ("ss"=short story, "nt"=novelette, etc.), magazine or book in which the item appeared, month and year of publication (for magazines in the form "6-57" for June 1957) or year of publication (for books), plus a list of all known reprints (for which title, publisher, year, and editor's last name are given), but no paginations. Monographic entries provide item number, title (in caps), contents (for collections and anthologies, keyed to item number), publication data (publisher, stock number, month and year of publication [if known, in the form "10-56" for October 1956], pagination, price, with dates of reissues by the same publisher), cover artist, plus similar data for all known reprint editions. Seventy-five secondary sources are listed and well over a hundred book reviews. There is no general index. The book is shot from clearly legible word-processed copy and bound with staples in paper covers. Data are complete through mid-1990.

The second edition of this bibliography represents a substantial improvement over the first, both quantitatively (increasing the page count from 35 to 90 pages) and qualitatively (adding substantial numbers of secondary sources and other works and improving physical appearance and organization). The addition of an index and magazine paginations in future editions would be helpful. Compared to Morgan's guide (see #366), *Fritz Leiber, Sardonic*

Swordsman includes considerably more information arranged in a superior format and is a decade more current, making it clearly the better of the two.

366. Morgan, Chris. **Fritz Leiber: A Bibliography, 1934-1979.** Birmingham, Morgenstern, England, 1979. 36 p. index. (pbk.).

Morgan, a British fan with several other pamphlet-length bibliographies to his credit, here provides a brief chronological checklist of this well-known American fantasist and essayist. Contents: "Brief Biography," by David Langford; "Notes"; "Books"; "Bibliography" (i.e., sources consulted); "Special Magazine Issues"; "Awards"; "Articles"; "Key to Photographs"; "Stories"; two pages of jacket photographs; "Media"; "Index." Each section is arranged by date of publication. Books are numbered in order from 1 to 37; a typical book entry includes item number; title (underlined caps); subject and type (e.g., "horror novel); contents (for collections); previous serialization of novels (if applicable); and a list of all known English-language editions in order of publication. Bibliographical entries are lettered in chronological order from "a" and include country, format (e.g., "hardcover"), publisher, month and year of publication, stock number, price, cover artist, other notes. No foreign-language versions or paginations are shown.

Materials in other sections are unnumbered and are listed year-by-year, the year being centered at the head of each sub-section, and then by month of publication. A typical shorter work entry includes title (in quotes); alternate titles (where applicable); magazine title (italics) and month of publication; or book title (for stories appearing originally in anthologies), and editor. Subsequent appearances of each piece in English, including stories or essays reprinted in Leiber's own books, are listed chronologically thereafter. No paginations—and no bibliographical data for anthologies—are provided. The index is oddly arranged, referencing titles and item numbers for books, but titles and years and months of publication for all other materials; essays are distinguished from short stories by having "ART" appended to each title. Materials are included through August 1979. The book is shot from fairly legible typed copy. Although Morgan's guide includes illustrations not found in Benson/Stephensen-Payne's bibliography (see #365), the latter contains far more data in a much more usable format and should be preferred by researchers and libraries.

Murray Leinster

367. Owings, Mark. **Murray Leinster (Will F. Jenkins): A Bibliography.** Washington, D.C., Washington Science Fiction Association, 1970. [9] p. (pbk.).

Owings was a well-known bibliographer of science fiction during the early 1970s, producing several significant checklists with similar formats (see #270, #346, #373, #409, #415). This booklet, the first of the series, is organized into one alphabetical sequence by title, with books being underlined. Each title is flush to the left-hand margin, the remainder of the entry being indented to set it off. There are no line breaks between entries, but several lines are skipped between letters of the alphabet. A typical short fiction entry includes title, magazine title, month and year of publication (in the form "6/58" for June 1958), and known reprint editions (with book title, editor, publisher, place of publication, stock number [for paperbacks], year of publication, format [e.g., "wpps"=paperback], total pagination of book, price, but no pagination). A typical book entry includes title, publisher, place of publication, year of publication, pagination, price, with similar data for known reprint editions. Some foreign-language editions are shown with translators and foreign-language title equivalents (such data are very difficult to locate elsewhere). The book is shot from sometimes faint typed copy which is now yellowing with age. Data are included through 1969, the year Leinster's last book was published. Despite its poor production values, this brief bibliography remains essentially a complete record of the SF output of this very prolific pulp writer. Leinster now deserves a fuller treatment, of both his life and his works.

H. P. Lovecraft

368. Bell, Joseph. **Howard Phillips Lovecraft: A Chronology** (title varies slightly from section to section). Toronto, Soft Books, 1984-87. 8 v. index. (Les Bibliotheques, Parts 1-8). (pbk.).

Bell has prepared an interesting chronological checklist, year by year (and in the earlier sections, month by month), of the publications of Howard Phillips Lovecraft, America's premier horror writer of the first half of the twentieth century. Publications are arranged year by year, then alphabetically under each year by title. Bell mentions *all* Lovecraft publications in his schematic, including reprints, reissues, and republications of stories and books previously issued elsewhere; thus, many of the popular collections (e.g., *At the Mountains of Madness and Other Novels*) or the frequently anthologized shorter works are repeated again and again, some of them dozens of times. Short stories (in lower case boldface), include numbers after the title indicating how many times this particular tale has been reprinted to the date of that particular entry. A typical shorter work entry includes title, printing number, title of book or magazine (in italics), and (for anthologies) editor, publisher, place of publication, pagination of book (but not of story within that book), reissue data.

Book entries include title (all caps), item number (correlated with Bell's checklist of Lovecraft's books, listed below), publisher, place of publication, pagination. An entry in all caps with boldface type indicates this is the first separate publication of this item. Part Six is an index to the preceding five sections; a title index to Parts Seven and Eight appears at the end of the latter volume, correlating title, part number of the chronology in which it appears, page number, and type (e.g., "essay"). Since many of the individual pieces of this long-running chronological bibliography are now out-of-print, a reprint in one volume with the indexes merged into one alphabetical sequence, would prove of great value to the collecting community.

369. Bell, Joseph. **Howard Philips Lovecraft: The Books (4), 1915-1986**. 2nd ed. Toronto, Soft Books, 1987. v, 63 p. index. (pbk.).

This latest edition of a collectors' guide to Lovecraft's monographs arranges (and numbers) his monographs in chronological order by year of publication, then alphabetically by title. A typical entry includes item number, title (large boldface letters), publisher, place of publication, pagination, binding style, price, year of first printing, other bibliographical notes, complete contents listing. Similar details are provided about subsequent printings with enough detail to identify edition states. Two separate indexes are provided, of book titles and individual story titles, keyed to both item number and page number. The book is attractively printed in 8.5" x 11" format. Bell's guide is designed primarily for collectors, providing enough edition points so that the experienced bookman can find his or her way through the labyrinthine maze of Lovecraftiana. Libraries should prefer Joshi's more substantial literary bibliography (see #370).

370. Joshi, S. T. **H. P. Lovecraft and Lovecraft Criticism: An Annotated Bibliography.** Kent, Ohio, Kent State University Press, 1981. xxxiv, 473 p. index. (The Serif Series: Bibliographies and Checklists, No. 38). LC 80-84662. ISBN 0-87338-248-X. Joshi, S. T., and L. D. Blackmore. **H. P. Lovecraft and Lovecraft Criticism: An Annotated Bibliography Supplement, 1980-1984.** West Warwick, R.I., Necronomicon Press, 1985. iv, 72 p. (pbk.).

Joshi's excellent bibliography covers the work of a particularly difficult writer, one who published his stories in a wide variety of amateur and semi-professional outlets. Contents: "Introduction"; "Explanatory Notes"; "Abbreviations"; "I. Works by Lovecraft in English": "A. Books by Lovecraft"; "B. Contributions to Periodicals": "i. Fiction," "ii. Nonfiction," "iii. Poetry," "iv. Revisions and Collaborations," "v. Letters"; "C. Material Included in Books by Others"; "D. Works Edited by Lovecraft": "i. Books," "ii. Periodicals"; "E. Apocrypha and Other Miscellany": "i. Apocrypha," "ii. Lost Works," "iii. Works Destroyed," "iv. Items Included Within Published Works by Lovecraft," "v. Award-Winning Stories by Lovecraft," "vi. Miscellany"; "II. Works by Lovecraft in Translation": "A. Books by Lovecraft"; "B. Contributions to Periodicals": "i. Fiction," "ii. Nonfiction," "iii. Poetry," "iv. Revisions and Collaboration," "v. Letters"; "C. Material Included in Books by Others"; "III. Works about Lovecraft": "A. News Items and Encyclopedias"; "B. Bibliographies and Glossaries"; "C. Books and Pamphlets About Lovecraft"; "D. Criticism in Books or Periodicals"; "E. Academic Theses and Unpublished Papers": "i. Academic Theses," "ii. Unpublished Papers"; "F. Book Reviews": "i. Books in English," "ii. Books in Languages Other than English"; "G. Special Periodicals and Unclassifable Data": "i. Periodicals Devoted Exclusively or Largely to Lovecraft," "ii. Single Issues of Periodicals Devoted to Lovecraft," "iii. Amateur Press Associations," "iv. Unclassifiable Data"; "Supplement"; "IV. Indexes": "A. Works by Lovecraft"; "B. Works by Others"; "C. Names"; "D. Periodicals"; "E. Foreign Languages."

Monographs are listed in chronological order by date of publication, shorter works alphabetically by title. Entries are numbered consecutively from one in each section. A typical book entry includes item number, title (in italics), year of publication, title page (occasionally cover page) copy, collation, binding, size (in centimeters), edition notes and points. Similar data are provided on all subsequent printings and editions, in chronological order by date of publication. A typical shorter work entry includes title (in quotes), magazine title (italics), volume and issue number, month and year of publication, pagination, and occasional notes. "Material Included in Books by Others" is arranged in alphabetical order by main entry (usually editor), with item number, editor, book title (italics), place of publication, publisher, month and year of issue, total pagination of book, title of Lovecraft work included, pagination of Lovecraft work, and similar data on subsequent reprintings (including any changes in paginations of the Lovecraft item).

Translations are arranged chronologically for books and in alphabetical order by the original English-language title for shorter works; bibliographical data are arranged similarly to preceding sections except that the shorter works chapters also include the title of the work in the foreign language and the translator (when known). Secondary sources are arranged by critic, except for book reviews, which are listed by book reviewed, then by critic. Complete bibliographical data are provided for all. Joshi lists roughly 1,000 items in this section, making his book an immensely valuable resource for the student of Lovecraft's work (Joshi even includes reviews of the critical monographs!). The indexes are keyed to item number. Coverage is complete through 1979 (extended to 1984 with the supplement). The book is beautifully typeset and designed. The *Supplement* is arranged in exactly the same format as the original except that it lacks an overall index and is shot from legible typed copy, being bound with staples into stiff paper covers.

H. P. Lovecraft and Lovecraft Criticism is one of the finest single-author bibliographies ever produced in fantastic literature, on a par with Ashley's guide to

Blackwood's works (see #280): comprehensive, knowledgeable, logically arranged, and beautifully executed. Everything that a researcher would ever want to know about Lovecraft's publications is here, carefully indexed and easily accessible to even the most obtuse user. Kudos to Joshi and his publisher for a first-class effort. Every university library should own a copy.

371. Joshi, S. T. **An Index to the Selected Letters of H. P. Lovecraft.** West Warwick, R.I., Necronomicon Press, 1980. 77 p. (pbk.).

Joshi's book indexes the five volumes of Lovecraft's *Selected Letters* (which were published by Arkham House between 1965 and 1976) in one straight alphabetical sequence by author, title, and subject. Items are correlated to the volume and page number of the respective book (e.g., "III.73"=Volume III, page 73). Five appendices provide "I. A Brief Chronology of the Life of H. P. Lovecraft (1914-1937)"; "II. List of Lovecraft's Correspondents" (alphabetically by surname, keyed to letter number); "III. Index to Illustrations and Photographs" (alphabetically by artist's name, keyed to volume and page number); "IV. Prose and Poetry Excerpts in the *Selected Letters*" (alphabetically by writer's name, keyed to volume and page number); "V. Errata in the *Selected Letters*" (by volume, page, and line number, listing the original error and the corrected text). The book is shot from legible typed copy and bound with staples in stiff paper covers. Lovecraft was a prolific (even obsessive) letter writer, covering a broad array of subjects that are now made accessible for the first time. Researchers seriously interested in examining Lovecraft's writings will find this index a literary gold mine.

372. Laney, Francis T., and William H. Evans. **Howard Phillips Lovecraft (1890-1937): A Tentative Bibliography.** Los Angeles, An "Acolyte" Publication, FAPA, 1943. 12 p. (pbk.). Brennan, Joseph Payne. **A Select Bibliography of H. P. Lovecraft.** New Haven, Conn., [Joseph Payne Brennan], 1952. 8 p. LC 52-24147. (pbk.). Brennan, Joseph Payne. **H. P. Lovecraft: A Bibliography.** [rev. ed.]. Washington, D.C., Biblio Press, 1952. 13 p. LC 52-32856 (pbk.). Wetzel, George T., ed. **Howard Phillips Lovecraft—Memoirs, Critiques, & Bibliographies.** North Tonawanda, N.Y., SSR Publications, 1955. 88 p. LC 55-9424 (pbk.). Chalker, Jack L., *et al.* **The New H. P. Lovecraft Bibliography.** Baltimore, Md., An Anthem Press Chapbook, 1962. 40 p. (pbk.). Owings, Mark, with Jack L. Chalker. **The Revised H. P. Lovecraft Bibliography.** Baltimore, Md., Mirage Press, 1973. viii, 43 p. LC 72-85408. ISBN 0-88358-010-1 (pbk.).

Each of these bibliographies was more or less pyramided upon its predecessor, with internal printed acknowledgments (page vi in Owings), and so they have been treated as one work here despite some differences in content and format (it should be noted in particular that Wetzel includes, in addition to separate bibliographies by Wetzel and Robert E. Briney, six essays on Lovecraft's life and work). Contents (of Owings's guide): "Using This Bibliography"; "Preface"; "Essays"; "Verse"; "Fiction"; "Fiction Collaborations"; "Collections"; "Foreign-Language Collections"; "Revisions"; "Mythos Stories"; "Comic Book Adaptations"; "Material on Lovecraft." Each section through the "Fiction" section is arranged in alphabetical order by title. A typical entry provides title (small caps), magazine title (italics), month and year of publication, and details of all known reprints, including in Lovecraft's collections, anthologies, and foreign-language materials, but no paginations. Reprints in anthologies include title (boldface), editor, publisher, place of publication, stock number (for paperbacks), format (e.g., "wpps"=paperback), total pagination of the book, price, but no specific paginations of the Lovecraft story. Reprints in foreign-language collections and anthologies include the foreign-language title of the book but not of the individual stories.

Collaborations and revisions are listed by collaborator name, then alphabetically by title with similar bibliographical data. Collections are arranged in alphabetical order by book title with title (small caps), publisher, place of publication, year of publication, exact pagination, price, reissues, contents. The foreign-language section includes book-length collections translated into other languages, arranged by language, then by title, with similar bibliographical data, *including* lists of the stories with their translated titles (because these are not given under the individual story listings, above, matching them with their correct English-language versions may not be easy in some instances). Cthulhu Mythos stories are also arranged by author. Comic book adaptations are arranged by comic book title. The secondary bibliography is very scanty, including only six items.

Owings's bibliography is attractively and professionally printed in 8.5" x 11" format; however, the format seems excessively jumbled, with no line breaks between entries, making the data crowd together on the pages; the absence of an index does not help matters. All of these booklets have now been completely superseded by Joshi's definitive bibliography (see #370).

373. Owings, Mark, and Irving Binkin. **A Catalog of Lovecraftiana: The Grill/Binkin Collection**. Baltimore, Mirage Press, 1975. 71 p. LC 73-93645. ISBN 0-88358-122-1; ISBN 0-88358-020-9 (pbk.).

This published catalog of the Lovecraft collection of Philip Jack Grill (1903-1970) serves as a kind of substitute bibliography of Lovecraft books, manuscripts, and other materials. Contents: "Professional Periodicals"; "Amateur Press Works"; "Books by Lovecraft"; "Anthologies"; "Novels"; and "Author Collections with HPL Material"; "Books About Lovecraft"; "Letters"; "Photographs"; and "Miscellaneous"; "Recent Additions" (subdivided into the same sections as above). Materials are numbered consecutively from 1 to 668. The first two sections, comprising the majority of the text, are arranged by magazine title, then chronologically by date, providing item number, magazine title, date, volume and issue number, title of Lovecraft story (in quotes), a list of the other authors featured in the same issue, cover artist, condition of item. The books section is arranged in alphabetical order by book title and includes publisher, place of publication, year of publication, format (e.g., "wpps"=paperback), pagination, condition of item. The letters are arranged by sender (to Grill) in the first section or by recipient (from HPL) in the second; each of these entries includes date, subject matter, and other notes. The book features twenty-four pages of photographic plates inserted in the middle of the volume, reproducing items from the collection (keyed to item number), including rare photos of Lovecraft himself. The absence of an index makes anything more than idle browsing impossible. An intriguing guide to much peripheral Lovecraftiana, but basically of interest only to collectors.

Brian Lumley

374. Blackmore, Leigh. **Brian Lumley: A New Bibliography**. Penrith, N.S.W., Australia, Dark Press Publication, 1984. 53 p. ISBN 0-9590367-0-9 (pbk.). Also: San Bernardino, Calif., The Borgo Press, 1987. 53 p. LC 87-33842. ISBN 0-89370-541-1.

This illustrated checklist covers the works of a popular British horror writer. Contents: "Explanatory Notes"; "Acknowledgments"; "I. Works by Lumley in English": "A. Books"; "B. Contributions to Periodicals": "i. Fiction," "ii. Nonfiction," "iii. Poetry," "iv. Letters"; "II. Works by Lumley in Translation": "A. Books"; "B. Contributions to

Periodicals": "i. Fiction," "ii. Nonfiction"; "C. Material Included in Books by Others"; "A Portfolio of Early Fanzine Artwork by Lumley"; "III. Works about Lumley": "A. Reference Works"; "B. Bibliographies"; "C. Criticism in Books or Periodicals"; "D. Book Reviews": "i. Books in English," "ii. Books in Languages Other than English"; "E. Special Periodicals and Unclassifiable Data": "i. Single Issues of Periodicals Devoted to Lumley"; "Unclassifiable Data"; "Brian Lumley: A Chronology of His Fiction and Poetry"; "IV. Indexes": "A. Works by Lumley"; "B. Names"; "C. Periodicals."

Blackmore's format is very similar to that of Joshi's bibliography on Lovecraft (see #370—Blackmore co-authored the *Supplement* to that work). Materials are numbered anew from one in each section. Books are listed in chronological order by publication date. A typical book entry includes item number, title (in italics), year of publication, exact title page transcription, collation, exact publication date, contents (where appropriate), with paginations of each section, binding, size (in centimeters), cover artist, price, ISBN or stock number, plus other bibliographical or literary notes. Translated books are similarly listed in a separate section of their own.

Shorter works are filed alphabetically by title in each section, with item number, title (in quotes), magazine title (italics), volume and issue number, date, pagination, other notes. Reprints in anthologies include item number, main entry of anthology (usually editor), book title (in italics), place of publication, publisher, year of publication, total pagination of book, title of Lumley story included, pagination of Lumley story in the book. Book reviews are arranged by work covered, then alphabetically by critic; full bibliographical data are provided. The list of secondary sources is probably complete, although only nine items are included. Chronological lists of the fiction and poetry show Lumley's development as a writer. The indexes are keyed to item number. The book is shot from legible typed copy and is illustrated throughout with reproductions of covers and a few of Lumley's own illustrations. Coverage is completed through part of 1984. One of the better author checklists we have seen: thorough, logically arranged, well-indexed, and very easy to use.

Arthur Machen

375. Danielson, Henry. **Arthur Machen: A Bibliography.** London, Henry Danielson, 1923. x, 59 p. LC 23-10829.

This interesting bibliography features an introduction by Henry Savage, "Arthur Machen: An Appreciation," and extensive commentaries by Machen himself. The bibliography proper lists Machen's books in chronological order by publication date. A typical entry provides book title (all caps) and year of publication (as part of the header), an exact transcription of the title page of the first edition, edition points, a detailed description of the binding and paper, contents listing (where appropriate), plus Machen's remarks on the volume. The latter range in size from one brief paragraph to seven pages and provide much insight into each book's literary origins—and to Arthur Machen himself. Coverage is complete through 1922. The book is nicely designed and typeset but lacks an index or table of contents. The bibliographical data have largely been duplicated in Goldstone and Sweetser's much more complete and current guide (see #376), but researchers will still find this book of interest for the author's sidepieces.

376. Goldstone, Adrian, and Wesley Sweetser. **A Bibliography of Arthur Machen**. Austin, Tex., University of Texas, 1965. 180 p. LC 65-63475.

Adapted from Sweetser's Ph.D. disssertation, this bibliography of the highly touted British horror and fantasy writer's works includes "Introduction"; "Explanations &

Acknowledgments"; "Books and Pamphlets"; "Translations"; "Contributions"; "Periodicals"; "Criticism and Commentary" (i.e., secondary sources, divided into "Books & Pamphlets," and "Periodicals"); and "Index."

Most sections are arranged chronologically by publication date. A typical book entry includes item number, title (all caps), year of publication, transcription of the title page copy, an exact collation of the text, description of the binding and end papers, publication date, price, and similar data on all known reprint editions. A typical shorter work entry in the "Contributions" section, which includes materials by Machen published in books by other authors, provides item number, book title (italics), bibliographical description, specific pagination of the Machen contribution, and a description of what it contains, with similar data for all known reprints. The "Periodicals" chapter is organized alphabetically by magazine title, then chronologically by publication date. A typical entry includes magazine title (small caps, as a running head for the section), Machen contribution (in italics), volume number, publication date, with specific pagination of the Machen item. Fiction and nonfiction materials are interfiled without any indication of subject matter, making it difficult for the user who is not already familiar with the author's work to identify his short stories (for example). Materials are numbered in the first three sections consecutively from 1 to 131; items listed in the fourth chapter are unnumbered (for no apparent reason).

The chapter on secondary sources ("Criticism and Commentary") includes "Books & Pamphlets," arranged in alphabetical order by name and giving author or editor, title (italics), place of publication, publisher, year of publication, and an exact citation to and brief description of the reference to Machen or his work; and "Periodicals," arranged alphabetically by periodical title, then chronologically by publication date, providing magazine title (small caps), title of article (in italics), author's name, volume number, publication date, and specific pagination. The index coordinates the titles of Machen's works with page numbers; the secondary source section is not indexed, nor are the names of anthologies or their editors included. The book is nicely typeset and bound to library standards.

Goldstone and Sweetser have produced a sound if somewhat quirky guide to an equally odd writer. Their coverage of Machen's writings seems thorough, and the section on secondary materials is remarkably complete, including books which have even a passing reference to the author or his work. However, the organization of periodical contributions, both primary and secondary, is less than ideal and will cause the casual user immediate problems. Specifically, the arrangement of articles about Machen by periodical title and date of publication, rather than by critic's name, without any additional indexing, makes this section almost unusable. A new edition correcting these flaws and updating the basic data base would certainly be warranted.

George R. R. Martin

377. Stephensen-Payne, Phil. **George R. R. Martin, the Ace from New Jersey: A Working Bibliography**. 2nd rev. ed. West Yorkshire, Leeds, England & Albuquerque, N.M., Galactic Central Publications, 1989. 9, 23 p. (Galactic Central Bibliographies for the Avid Reader, Vol. 27). ISBN 0-871133-01-7 (pbk.).

George Martin is a well-regarded American SF writer, author of *Nightflyers* and other works. This new bibliography is organized by subject category, then alphabetically by title. Contents: Author's name, date and place of birth, and awards; "A. Stories"; "B. Fiction Books"; "C. Series" ("none known"); "D. Poems & Songs" ("none known"); "E. Poem & Song Collections" ("none known"); "F. Articles"; "G. Miscellaneous"; "H. Non-Fiction

Books" ("none known"); "I. Books Edited by George R. R. Martin"; "J. Media Presentations"; "K. Articles on George R. R. Martin"; "L. Reviews of Books by George R. R. Martin"; "M. Books About George R. R. Martin" ("none known"); "N. Phantom and Forthcoming Titles"; "O. Related Books by Other Authors" ("none known"); "P. Textual Varitiations" ("no details known"); "Q. Chronological Index."

In each section materials are numbered anew from the number one. A typical shorter work entry includes item number, title, category ("ss"=short story, "nt"=novelette, etc.), magazine or book in which the item appeared, month and year of publication (for magazines in the form "11-77" for November 1977) or year of publication (for books), a list of subsequent reprints (for which title, publisher, year, and editor's last name are given), but no paginations. A typical book entry includes item number, title (in caps), pseudonym, contents for collections keyed to item number, and publication data (publisher, stock number, month and year of publication [if known, in the form "10-59" for October 1959], pagination, price, with dates of reissues by the same publisher), plus cover artist and similar data for all known reprint editions. The list of secondary sources includes just ten items but is probably complete; there are roughly a hundred book reviews noted. The book lacks an overall index. The bibliography is shot from very clear word-processed copy and bound with staples into paper covers. Data are complete through the end of 1989.

One would hope for the addition of an index and magazine paginations to future editions. As the only current guide to this rising author's work, Stephensen-Payne's bibliography is a logical starting point for future scholarship on this writer.

Richard Matheson

378. Rathbun, Mark, and Graeme Flanagan. **Richard Matheson: He Is Legend: An Illustrated Bio-Bibliography.** Chico, Calif., Mark Rathbun, 1984. 55 p. (pbk.).

This brief illustrated checklist focuses on a popular American SF, fantasy, and television writer. Contents: "The Curious Child: A Preface" (by Rathbun); "Bon Homme Richard," by Robert Bloch; "Writing the Nightmare" (Rathbun); "SF Unlimited" (by Matheson); "Comment," by Jack Finney; "Blood Son: Comments," by Richard Christian Matheson (the author's son, also a writer); Bibliography; "Comment," by William F. Nolan; "Filmography"; "Richard Matheson: The Early Years," by William Campbell Gault; "One for the Books: The Genesis of 'Duel'," by Jerry Sohl.

The bibliography proper includes "Novels," "Short Story Collections," "Short Stories," "Television Scripts" (published), "Interviews," "Foreign Translations," "Miscel-lanea," "Adaptations." Material in each of these sections is arranged alphabetically by title. A typical book entry includes title (bold caps), publisher, stock number (for paperbacks), place of publication, year of publication, pagination, and price, with similar data for all subsequent reprints (listed in chronological order under the main entry). A typical short work entry includes title (bold caps), magazine title, month and year of publication, but no paginations, plus known reprint editions. Reprints in anthologies include title (boldface), editor, and year of publication, but no other bibliographical data.

The "Filmography" includes "Films," "Television," "Other Television Work," "Unproduced Motion Picture and Television Scripts." In the first two sections, Matheson's screen- and teleplays are arranged in chronological order by date of production date, with the following data: title (bold caps), production company, year of production, script credits, one-sentence annotation, major stars, director's name; TV programs add the name of the series and season number. The book is attractively illustrated with photos of the author, of his book and magazine covers, and with stills from selected Matheson movies. While this checklist provides a beginning point for future scholarship, the absence of both an index and any secondary sources (outside of nine interviews) is unfortunate. Matheson deserves a more extended treatment of his many works.

Julian May

379. Dikty, Thaddeus, and R. Reginald. **The Work of Julian May: An Annotated Bibliography & Guide**. San Bernardino, Calif., The Borgo Press, 1985. 66 p. index. (Bibliographies of Modern Authors, No. 3). LC 84-21705. ISBN 0-89370-382-6; ISBN 0-89370-482-2 (pbk.).

May, an extraordinarily prolific children's book writer and SF novelist with nearly 300 book credits in her forty-year career, is here profiled by her husband and agent, the well-known editor, T. E. Dikty. Contents: "Introduction" (by Dikty); "A. Books"; "B. Articles"; "C. Short Fiction"; "D. Study Prints"; "E. Lesson Plans"; "F. Kits"; "G. Audio Cassettes"; "H. Audio Recordings"; "I. Music"; "J. Maps"; "K. Media Productions"; "L. About the Author"; "M. Unpublished Works"; "N. Miscellanea"; "Title Index."

In each section, the author's works are arranged chronologically and numbered anew from one, chapter by chapter. A typical book entry includes item number, title (underlined), byline, place of publication, publisher, year of publication, pagination, format (paper or cloth), type of publication (novel, nonfiction, etc.), with full bibliographical data on reprint editions, translations, republications, etc. The books are annotated with brief plot summaries and other pertinent data; entries from other sections are selectively annotated as needed. A typical shorter work entry includes item number, title (in quotes), magazine title, volume number, date, pagination. Similar data are included for all reprint editions; a typical anthology listing includes place of publication, publisher, year of publication, format ("cloth"), and pagination. Dikty's introduction provides a nostalgic look back at May's life. "About the Author" includes all known secondary works. The "Miscellanea" section includes information on pen names, memberships, Library of Congress cataloging data, career highlights, and other data. The index lists titles and item numbers only.

The format for this book, one of the first issued in the series, was somewhat cramped: the lack of line breaks between entries jumbles the data together despite hanging indents. The book is shot from eight- or nine-point size word-processed copy and is sometimes hard to read. Coverage is complete through the end of 1984. A much expanded and revised second edition is reportedly in progress.

Bruce McAllister

380. Bourquin, David Ray. **The Work of Bruce McAllister: An Annotated Bibliography & Guide**. San Bernardino, Calif., The Borgo Press, 1985. 30 p. index. (Bibliographies of Modern Authors, No. 10). LC 85-22400. ISBN 0-89370-389-3; ISBN 0-89370-489-X (pbk.). **The Work of Bruce McAllister: An Annotated Bibliography & Guide.** [Rev. ed.]. San Bernardino, Calif., The Borgo Press, 1986. 32 p. All other data the same as above.

McAllister, a well-known SF writer, poet, and American academic, sold his first story at the age of seventeen. This new bibliography is the first detailed guide to his work. Contents (both versions): "Introduction" (by Bourquin); "A. Books"; "B. Short Fiction"; "C. Nonfiction"; "D. Poetry"; "E. Graphic/Experimental Work"; "F. Papers"; "G. Editorial Posts"; "H. Media Appearances"; "I. Awards and Prizes"; "J. About the Author"; "Critical Comments"; "Title Index."

In each section, the author's works are arranged chronologically and numbered consecutively from the number one, chapter by chapter, prefixed by the appropriate letter code (e.g., B1, B2, B3, etc.). A typical book entry includes item number, title (in italics), place of publication, publisher, year of publication, pagination, format (e.g., "paper"), type of publication (e.g., "anthology"), with full bibliographical data on reprint editions, translations, republications, etc. The books are fully annotated with complete contents listings or plot summaries and other pertinent data; entries from other sections are selectively annotated as needed. A typical short fiction or verse entry includes item number, title (in quotes), magazine title, volume number, date, pagination. Similar data are included for all reprint editions; a typical anthology listing includes place of publication, publisher, year of publication, format ("cloth"), and pagination. Bourquin's introduction provides an informal look at the author's background. "Media Appearances" includes interviews on television and radio, participation in conferences, and speeches. "About the Author" includes all known secondary works. "Critical Comments" includes selected excerpts of reviews and other comments by leading critics on the author's work. The index correlates titles and item numbers only.

Academic librarian Bourquin worked extensively with McAllister in the preparation of this guide. The original edition, shot from word-processed copy, was complete through mid-1985; the revised version was completely reworked and reset into a new, more legible (and readable) format and style and extended the data base by eight months. The result is well-organized, legible, easy-to-read, and comprehensive. A second edition is reportedly underway.

Anne McCaffrey

Arbur, Rosemarie. **Leigh Brackett, Marion Zimmer Bradley, Anne McCaffrey: A Primary and Secondary Bibliography.** *See the entry for Leigh Brackett (# 288).*

381. Stephensen-Payne, Phil, and Gordon Benson, Jr. **Anne McCaffrey, Dragonlady and More: A Working Bibliography.** 3rd rev. ed. Leeds, West Yorkshire, England, & Albuquerque, N.M., Galactic Central Publications, 1989. 9, 30 p. (Galactic Central Bibliographies for the Avid Reader, Vol. 13). (pbk.).

McCaffrey, author of the Dragonriders of Pern series, is a popular American fantasy writer who has resettled in Ireland. Benson's guide to her work is arranged by subject category, then alphabetically by title. Contents: Author's full name, date and place of birth, and awards; "A. Stories"; "B. Fiction Books"; "C. Series"; "D. Poems & Songs" ("none known"); "E. Poetry & Song Collections"; "F. Articles"; "G. Miscellaneous"; "H. Non-Fiction Books" ("none known"); "I. Books Edited by Anne McCaffrey"; "J. Media Presentations"; "K. Articles on Anne McCaffrey"; "L. Reviews" [of McCaffrey's books]; "M. Books About Anne McCaffrey"; "N. Phantom and Forthcoming Titles"; "O. Related Books by Other Authors"; "P. Textual Variations" ("no details known"); "Q. Chronological Index."

In each section materials are arranged alphabetically by title, the author's works being numbered consecutively from one and prefixed with the letter code appropriate to that part (e.g., B1, B2, B3, etc.). A typical shorter work entry provides item number, title, category ("ss"=short story, "nt"=novelette, etc.), magazine or book in which the item appeared, month and year of publication (for magazines in the form "12-73" for December 1973) or year of publication (for books), plus a list of subsequent reprints (for which title, publisher, year, and editor's last name are given), but no paginations. Monograph entries include item number, title (in caps), contents (for collections), publication data (publisher, stock number, month and year of publication [if known, in the form "10-59" for October 1959], pagination, price, with dates of reissues by the same publisher), cover artist, and similar data for all known reprints. There is no overall index. The authors list thirty-two secondary sources (including three monographs) and another hundred book reviews arranged alphabetically by title of the book being reviewed, then alphabetically by magazine title. The book is shot from legible word-processed copy and bound with staples into paper covers. Data are complete through early 1989.

Arbur's guide (see #288) gives short fiction paginations (first appearances only) but lacks book paginations. Both her guide and Stephensen-Payne contain roughly the same number of secondary sources (Arbur shows 165 items, most of them book reviews). Arbur's data base continues through 1980; Stephensen-Payne and Benson's work adds almost a decade of additional entries. Completists and scholars will need both works; libraries will find *Anne McCaffrey, Dragonlady and More* current, complete, and more than adequate for their needs.

J. T. McIntosh

382. Covell, Ian. **J. T. McIntosh: Memoir & Bibliography**. Polk City, Ia., Chris Drumm Books, 1987. 32 p. (plus one-page insert). index. ISBN 0-936055-28-6 (pbk.); ISBN 0-936055-29-4 (signed ed.). Also: San Bernardino, Calif., The Borgo Press, 1989. 32 p. index. ISBN 0-8095-4305-2.

Covell's book is organized differently from Drumm's usual format for this series. McIntosh, a well-known British SF writer, provides a fourteen-page memoir-*cum*-interview, giving much insight into his life and work, and detailing why he stopped writing in 1979. The bibliography proper includes "Abbreviations List"; "Pseudonyms Used"; "List A. Science Fiction"; "B. Contemporary Fiction"; "C. Non-Fiction"; plus a "Chronological List of Published Works," in turn broken into "Stories" and "Novels." Lists A-C are arranged in alphabetical order, interfiling book-length and shorter works. A typical book entry includes title (underlined caps), publisher, nationality, stock number (for paperbacks), year of publication (abbreviated to last two digits—e.g., "54"=1954), and similar data for all known reprints. A typical short fiction entry includes title, abbreviated magazine title, month and year of publication (in form "1.61" for January 1961). No paginations are included and no index; the book is reproduced from typed copy. The memoir is fascinating, but the bibliography section needs paginations and organizations. A one-page corrigenda sheet is included in most copies.

A. Merritt

383. Wentz, W. Jas. **A. Merritt: A Bibliography of Fantastic Writings**. Roseville, Calif., George A. Bibby, 1965. 33 p. (pbk.).
[not seen]

Michael Moorcock

384. Bilyeu, Richard. **The Tanelorn Archives: A Primary and Secondary Bibliography of the Works of Michael Moorcock, 1949-1979**. Altona, Manitoba, Canada, Pandora's Books, 1981. 108 p. ISBN 0-919695-04-3; ISBN 0-919695-05-1 (pbk.).

Bilyeu's illustrated checklist of this popular British fantasy author's publications contains: "Introduction"; "Books"; "Stories"; "Non-Fiction"; "Reviews"; "Editorials"; "Self-Published"; "Letters"; "Blurbs for Others' Books"; "Comic Books and Strips"; "Music";

"Films"; "Manuscripts"; "Influenced Fiction"; "Influenced Non-Fiction"; "Posters, Portfolios, Art Books"; "War Games"; "Appendix 1—Avon and DAW"; "Appendix 2—Notes." Most sections are arranged in alphabetical order by title. A typical book entry includes title (in capital letters), series, publisher, stock number (for paperbacks), place of publication, year of publication, and similar data for all known reprintings. Shorter work entries give title, magazine title, volume and/or issue number, month and year of publication, or (for anthology listings) book title (caps), editor, publisher, year of publication, occasional notes. No paginations are included for either type of fiction. A valuable, detailed inventory of the Moorcock manuscripts at the Texas A&M University is also provided. There is a three-page (incomplete) list of secondary sources, including book reviews. The book is shot from legible typed copy and is illustrated throughout with reproductions of magazine and book covers and one photo of Moorcock.

Bilyeu's book is the most complete and best realized of the three Moorcock bibliographies published to date but it still is far from definitive, lacking both an index as well as many bibliographical details. Moorcock deserves a complete, well-organized guide to his many works.

385. Callow, A. J. **The Chronicles of Moorcock.** Worcester, England, A. J. Callow, 1978. 43 p. (pbk.).

This amateurish hodgepodge is so badly organized that, short as it is, it must still be read completely through to locate a specific item. Lacking both a contents page or index, the guide arranges its data by series and then in chronological *series* (not publication) order; non-series books are grouped after the series listings, in chronological order by publication date. No bibliographical details are provided other than publisher, year of publication, and format (e.g., "paperback"). All of the books have one- to two-sentence annotations or contents listings (for collections). The rest of the book is a similar mass of miscellaneous, often uncorrelated data, jumbled onto pages with no sense of why anything is where it is. The booklet is photocopied from barely discernible typed copy. Abominable drivel. Prefer Bilyeu's bibliography (see #384).

386. Harper, Andrew, and George McAulay. **Michael Moorcock: A Bibliography.** Baltimore, T-K Graphics, 1976. 3-29 p. (pbk.).

Harper and McAulay's booklet is little better than Callow's. Covering only Moorcock's books, it provides not one iota more of additional bibliographical data than its competitors. Materials are arranged in chronological order by publication date. A typical entry includes title (bold caps), one-line annotation or contents listing, publisher, date of publication and format (e.g., "paperback"), and similar information on reprints. A few foreign editions are mentioned with their translated titles. Books by Moorcock published under pseudonyms are omitted, although the authors seem to indicate their awareness of these items (so why are they omitted?). A brief checklist of Moorcock's series concludes the book. There is no index, of course. About all one can say of this wholly amateurish effort is that at least the typeset copy is legible. Prefer Bilyeu (see #384).

C. L. Moore

387. Utter, Virgil S., and Gordon Benson, Jr. **Catherine Lucille Moore & Henry Kuttner, A Marriage of Souls and Talent: A Working Bibliography.** 3rd rev. ed. Albuquerque, N.M. and Leeds, West Yorkshire, England, Galactic Central Publications, 1989. v, 92 p. (Galactic Central Bibliographies for the Avid Reader, Vol. 21). ISBN 0-912613-04-1 (pbk.).

Like Brackett and Hamilton, Catherine Moore and Henry Kuttner were two science-fiction writers (both now deceased) who married after each had established a reputation separately; unlike the Hamiltons, however, the Kuttners almost immediately began to collaborate literarily on a scale never before seen in the genre, to the point where virtually all their work after 1940 cannot be separated. This new bibliography is broken into two sections (Moore and Kuttner), then arranged by subject category and alphabetically by title. Contents (Moore): "Pseudonyms and Awards"; "A. The Stories" (alone); "B. The Series"; "C. The Books" (predominantly her work alone); "D. Biographical Material"; "E. Criticism and Commentary and Survey"; "F. Interviews"; "G. Television Credits"; "H. A Miscellany"; "I. Book Reviews" [on Moore's work]; "J. Chronological Listing of Stories and Books" (First Appearance).

Contents (Kuttner): Author's full name, date and place of birth and date of death, pseudonyms; "A. The Stories" (alone and in collaboration); "B. Stories of Uncertain Parentage"; "C. Further Speculations" (the James Hall mystery stories); "D. Some Unused Story Titles"; "E. The Story Behind the Story Department in *Thrilling Wonder Stories*"; "F. The Series" (alone and in collaboration); "G. The Poems"; "H. The Books" (alone and in collaboration); "I. Books: Non-English Editions"; "J. Book Reviews" [on Kuttner's books]; "K. Fanzine Articles and Miscellany"; "L. Partial List of Additional Letters"; "M. Biography, Commentary and Criticism"; "N. Obituaries"; "O. A Miscellany"; "P. Chronological Listing of Stories and Books (First Appearance)"; Appendix 1: "Kuttner: Fading Masks," by Utter; "Reference Sources."

In each section the material is arranged in alphabetical order by title, the author's works being numbered anew from one (unlike the other books in the Galactic Central series, however, the numbers are not prefixed by letter codes). A typical shorter work entry provides item number, title, category ("ss"=short story, "nt"=novelette, etc.), magazine title, month and year of publication (in the form "1-39" for January 1939), but no paginations, with similar data for all known reprints. For book-length works, Utter and Benson give item number, title (in caps), publication data (publisher, stock number, month and year of publication [if known, in the form "10-59" for October 1959], pagination, price, with dates of reissues by the same publisher), cover artist. There is no overall index, but some secondary sources and obituaries are provided for both writers, plus a few foreign-language editions, virtually unique for this series. Data are complete through mid-1989. The book is shot from very clear word-processed copy and bound with staples through the spine into paper covers.

Utter's afterword provides much information on Kuttner's many pseudonymous works, including a review of various speculations on other names he may or may not have used in the SF and mystery genres. An index is badly needed in future editions; the split of data between two authors makes the location of specific items unnecessarily difficult despite the alphabetical arrangement of each section. In general, however, Utter and Benson's volume is authoritative, thorough, and probably as complete as humanly possible given the morass of works generated by these authors, singly and jointly, from the 1930s to 1958. No serious researcher of Kuttner and Moore's fiction should be without this volume.

Kenneth Morris

Zahorski, Kenneth J., and Robert H. Boyer. **Lloyd Alexander, Evangeline Walton Ensley, Kenneth Morris: A Primary and Secondary Bibliography.** *See the entry for Lloyd Alexander (#268).*

Talbot Mundy

388. Day, Bradford M. **Talbot Mundy Biblio: Materials Toward a Bibliography of the Works of Talbot Mundy**. New York, Science-Fiction & Fantasy Publications, 1955. 28 p. (pbk.).

Day's brief checklist of this classic fantasy adventure writer's fiction follows the format used in his other author bibliographies. The book section is arranged alphabetically by title, a typical entry including title (caps), publisher, place of publication, year of publication, pagination, brief cover copy quote, mention of magazine serialization, with magazine name and dates, plus binding color style. The short fiction section is arranged in chronological order by date of publication and lists title (caps), magazine title, year of publication, month of publication, list of reprints in Mundy's books. There are also three series listings. The book is mimeographed from typed copy. The basic bibliography was slightly updated in Day's later bibliography, *Bibliography of Adventure* (see #202).

389. Grant, Donald M., ed. **Talbot Mundy: Messenger of Destiny**. West Kingston, R.I., Donald M. Grant, 1983. 253 p. LC 83-243379. ISBN 0-937986-46-1.

This nicely illustrated bio-bibliography focuses on adventure and fantasy writer Talbot Mundy (1879-1940), whose real-life identity of William Lancaster Gribbon was only recently discovered by Peter Berresford Ellis (a major contributor to this volume). Contents: "Introduction," by Grant; "Autobiography," by Mundy; "Willie—Rogue and Rebel," by Ellis; "Talbot Mundy," by Dawn Mundy Provost (Mundy's widow); "Ghosts Walk...," by Darrel Crombie; "Talbot Mundy in *Adventure*" [the first of the bibliographic chapters]; "The Glory of Tros," by Fritz Leiber; "Books"; "Magazine Appearances"; "*The Jerusalem News*"; "*The Theosophical Path*"; "*The New York Times*."

The bibliography occupies exactly half of the volume, the section on Mundy's contributions to *Adventure* magazine itself running fifty pages. This chapter is organized chronologically by publication date, a typical subsection including year (as a running head), a list of the Mundy stories, novels, and essays published during that year, in descending order by issue date (but no paginations), plus extensive commentary. The book section is arranged alphabetically by title, a typical entry providing book title (bold caps), place of publication, publisher, year of publication, pagination, format (e.g., "paperback"), plus similar data on all known reprint editions, original title (if any), and notes of previous magazine publication and title(s). The "Magazine Appearances" chapter includes fiction and nonfiction interfiled into one A-Z arrangement. A typical entry gives title (bold caps), pseudonym (if any), magazine title (in italics; appearances in *Adventure* are also included), month and year of publication, and mentions of subsequent book reprintings; no paginations are included. The short end chapters mention Mundy's contributions to three unusual periodicals. As usual with Grant publications, the book is copiously illustrated with clear black-and-white reproductions of book and magazine covers. The absence of an index is unfortunate.

Grant's bio-bibliography is more current than Day's checklist (see #388), although the latter does include more detailed information on binding states and other points of potential interest to collectors. Scholars and libraries will probably be satisfied with Grant; completists will want access to both volumes.

Robert Nathan

390.   Laurence, Dan H. **Robert Nathan: A Bibliography**. New Haven, Conn., Yale University Library, 1960. xi, 97 p. index. LC 61-2221.

Nathan is best known for *Portrait of Jennie* and other works of haunting fantasy; this is the first bibliography of his works. Contents: "Introduction"; "A. Books and Pamphlets"; "B. Contributions to Books"; "C. Periodical Publications"; "D. Works in Translation"; "E. Musical Contributions"; "Acknowledgment"; "Index of First Lines of Poetry"; "General Index."

In each section materials are listed chronologically by publication date and numbered anew from one, prefixed by the letter associated with that chapter (e.g., C1, C2, C3, etc.). A typical book entry provides item number, title (all caps), year of publication, an exact transcription of the title page copy, collation, size, price, description of binding, cover artist, number of copies published, exact publication date, similar data on the first British edition of each volume, plus a sketchy list of further reprints (giving place, publisher, and year of publication only), and notes, including complete contents listings of collections. Section B lists Nathan's contributions to books in chronological order by date, arranged similarly to the first chapter but excluding collation and binding data and including specific pagination and identification of the Nathan piece(s).

Chapter C, giving Nathan's contributions to periodicals (poetry, stories, and plays), is also organized chronologically by publication date. A typical entry records item number (from C1-C207), title (prose contributions in all caps), magazine title (italics), volume number, month and year of publication, and specific pagination, with occasional bibliographical notes, including mentions of further reprintings in other sources. The fourth section, "Works in Translation," is arranged alphabetically by language of translation, then separated into category (books, anthologies, periodicals) and listed chronologically by publication date, with bibliographical data and English-language titles. No paginations are given for monographs. The final chapter, "Musical Contributions," is broken into three subsections: "Translations of Lyrics from the German or the Italian" (with musical settings by Richard Hageman); "Musical Settings of Lyrics by Robert Nathan"; and "Miscellaneous" (notes for the jacket liner of Beethoven's *Sixth Symphony*). Each of the twenty-two items in this section gives item number, title, original title (where applicable) or first lines, the names of other artists associated with the project, place of publication, publisher, year of publication, and price. Both indexes correlate the data with item numbers only. The book is professionally typeset and bound to library standards.

Laurance's guide is complete, well organized, and attractively presented. Nathan continued to write for another fifteen years after this volume was published (his last book was published in 1975), dying in 1985. A final bibliographical accounting of his many publications would certainly be appropriate.

Larry Niven

391.   Drumm, Chris. **A Larry Niven Checklist**. Polk City, Ia., Chris Drumm Books, 1983. [24] p. index. ISBN 0-936055-07-3 (pbk.). Guptill, Paul, and Chris Drumm. **The Many Worlds of Larry Niven**. [2nd ed.]. Polk City, Ia., Chris Drumm Books, 1989. ii, 63 p. index. ISBN 0-936055-44-8 (pbk.).

Niven is a well-known American "hard SF" author of the Ringworld series. In both editions of this 4.25" x 7" volume, the author's works are arranged in one straight chronological sequence. Entries are grouped by year and under each year by month; items are numbered in order from 1 to 198 (in the second edition). Books and short stories are both listed in boldface, without distinction. A typical short fiction entry includes item number, title, category code (e.g., "ss"=short story), magazine, month and year of publication, and paginations—or book title if the first appearance is in an anthology, plus year and month of publication, paginations, and price. Subsequent reprintings are grouped under the original edition, with similar data provided.

A typical book entry includes item number, title, series key, category code (e.g., "coll"=collection), format (e.g., "pb"=paperback), publisher, nationality (e.g., American), month and year of publication, price, contents of collections. See references, title index, series index, and contents listings are keyed to item number. Foreign-language editions are arranged in order by the item numbers assigned to the English-language original versions; a typical entry provides English title, category code, language of translation, foreign-language title, format, year, publisher, cover artist. The awards section is similarly arranged in item number order. Secondary materials (twenty-four items) are arranged in chronological order by publication, as are the sixteen interviews. Data are complete through 1988. The book is produced from very clear word-processed copy, with good margins, and is generally a great improvement over the somewhat primitive first edition (and the other books in this series). However, the lack of a clear differentiation between novels and stories (until one examines the bibliographical data), and the lack of specific data for book publications, limit the effectiveness of what could have been a first-class effort. Future editions should offset short story titles with quotation marks and provide exact paginations for monographs.

William F. Nolan

392. Clarke, Boden, and James Hopkins. **The Work of William F. Nolan: An Annotated Bibliography & Guide**. San Bernardino, Calif., The Borgo Press, 1988. 224 p. index. (Bibliographies of Modern Authors, No. 14). LC 87-6334. ISBN 0-89370-393-1; ISBN 0-89370-493-8 (pbk.).

This comprehensive guide to the 1,200+ works of the prolific SF, mystery, and horror novelist, short story writer, bibliographer, and critic, who is best known for his Logan Trilogy, includes Introduction: "The Multi-Media Man," by Dr. Jeffrey M. Elliot; "William F. Nolan: A Chronology"; "A. Books"; "B. Short Fiction"; "C. Verse"; "D. Personality Profiles"; "E. Reviews"; "F. Other Nonfiction"; "G. Screenplays"; "H. Teleplays"; "I. Film and Television Outlines"; "J. Radio"; "K. Stage"; "L. Comics"; "M. Letters"; "N. Juvenilia"; "O. Interviews"; "P. Speeches and Public Appearances"; "Q. Television and Radio Appearances"; "R. Other Media"; "S. Artwork"; "T. Editorial Posts"; "U. Honors and Awards"; "V. About the Author"; "W. Unpublished Works"; "X. Miscellanea"; "Quoth the Critics"; "Index."

In each section, the author's works are arranged chronologically and numbered consecutively from one, chapter by chapter, prefixed by the appropriate letter code (e.g., P1, P2, P3, etc.). A typical book entry includes item number, title (italics), place of publication, publisher, month and year of publication, pagination, format (e.g., "cloth"), type of publication (e.g., "novel"), with complete data on reprint editions, translations, republications, etc., in all languages. The books are fully annotated, with contents listings, plot summaries, and other pertinent data; entries from other sections are selectively annotated as needed. A typical shorter work entry includes item number, title (in quotes), magazine title, volume number, pagination, plus detailed information on all known reprints in all languages; entries for stories reprinted in anthologies include book title, editor, place of publication, publisher, year of publication, format (cloth or paper), and specific pagination. Elliot's entertaining introduction tells us something about Nolan the man as well as Nolan the writer. The chronology provides an extensive year-by-year account of the author's professional and personal life. "About the Author" includes all known secondary works, in chronological order by publication date. The "Miscellanea" section records information on pen names, book dedications, memberships, Library of Congress cataloging data, career highlights, and other data. "Quoth the Critics" includes selected excerpts of reviews and other comments by the leading critics. The index correlates titles and item numbers only. The book includes eight pages of black-and-white plates reproducing Nolan book covers.

This volume represented a major style change for the Bibliographies of Modern Authors series and with two later upgrades (the boldfacing of all title entries, and the additional of book review sources for individual monographs) has been used as the paradigm for all later volumes in the series. The amount of material included in this volume is enormous, much of it deriving directly from the author's personal library and files. Complete data on Nolan's works are provided through the summer of 1988. This exceptionally comprehensive and well-designed bibliography should be a part of all major research collections.

Andre Norton

393. Schlobin, Roger C. **Andre Norton: A Primary and Secondary Bibliography**. Boston, G. K. Hall & Co., 1980. xxxii, 68 p. index. (Masters of Science Fiction and Fantasy). LC 79-18477. ISBN 0-8161-8044-X.

Schlobin's contribution to this series covers the work of a librarian-turned-science fiction writer who attained great popularity in the 1960s and '70s. Contents: "Preface"; "Introduction"; "Part A: Fiction"; "Part B: Miscellaneous Media"; "Part C: Nonfiction"; "Part D: Criticism, Biography, and Selected Reviews"; "Appendix I: Genres"; "Appendix II: Series, Sequels, and Related Works"; "Primary Index"; "Secondary Index."

Schlobin's twenty-page introduction provides a very sound critical and biographical introduction to Norton's work. The bibliography is arranged chronologically, section by section, from the earliest published material to the latest, and numbered consecutively (e.g., A01, A02, for fiction). Books and shorter works are interfiled. No reprint editions or paginations are listed for monographs. Reprints of stories are listed under the main entry, chronologically by year of reprint with the editor of the anthology, title, place of publication, publisher, year, format (e.g., "paper"), but no paginations. Each book entry gives title, place of publication, and publisher. Entries of shorter works published originally in magazines provide title (in quotations), magazine, volume number, date, pagination; those published originally in books give title (in quotations), editor, book title, place of publication, publisher, format, but no paginations. Story collections include complete contents listings, plus the years in which the original stories were published. Some items include bibliographical notes but no other annotations.

Part B includes screenplays, teleplays, interviews, recordings, poetry, and other material which does not specifically fit the other three categories. Part C includes all nonfiction works by the author with occasional annotations. Part D lists fifty-seven secondary works, including published book reviews, fan commentaries, critiques, and bibliographies, with author, title, bibliographical data, and extensive subject annotations. Appendix I categorizes Norton's works by genre, listing title and item number; Appendix II lists series and other works in sequence. The main index cites title and item number only, the second index (to critical studies) author, title, and item number. Unlike most other volumes in the series (which are shot from typed copy), this guide is nicely typeset and bound to library standards.

Schlobin's was one of the first volumes published in this fourteen-volume series, and unfortunately, it shows signs of not having all the format bugs quite worked out. The lack of reprint editions and the absence of book paginations are particularly noticeable for an author who owes much of her popularity to widely circulated paperback editions; thus, even though Norton has published well over a hundred books, the fiction section comprises just under twelve pages of text. Coverage is complete through 1979, making the book considerably out-of-date for this still-active writer; an updated edition with some design changes would definitely be warranted.

394. Turner, David G. **The First Editions of Andre Norton**. Menlo Park, Calif., David G. Turner, Bookman, 1974. 12 p. (Science Fiction Bibliographies, 1). (pbk.).

This very brief checklist to a popular SF writer's work includes "Books," "Magazine Fiction," "Anthologies," "Articles," and "Series Listings." Items are numbered anew from one in each part. In each section materials are arranged in chronological order by year of publication and under each year in alphabetical order by title. A typical book entry includes item number, title (caps), publisher, place of publication, year of publication (in parentheses), pagination, brief categorization ("adventure novel"). Per the title, first editions only are listed. The last three chapters are very short, since Norton has done most of her work in book-length formats. A typical shorter work listing includes item number, title (caps), pseudonym, magazine, volume and issue number, month and year of publication, but no paginations. The series listings are arranged by series title and proper series order. There is no index or list of secondary sources. Now partially superseded by Schlobin's bibliography (see #393), which should be generally preferred—the latter does *not*, however, include the book paginations recorded in Turner's guide.

Chad Oliver

395. Hall, Hal W. **Chad Oliver: A Preliminary Bibliography**. Bryan, Tex., Dellwood Press, 1985. vi, 86 p. (pbk.).

This preliminary version of *The Work of Chad Oliver* (see #396) includes "Introduction," "Books," "Short Stories," "Letters," "Secondary Material," "News Releases," "Book Reviews," "Interview," "Second Thoughts." Each section is arranged in alphabetical order by title. A typical book entry includes title (boldface), place of publication, publisher, year of publication, pagination, format (e.g., "pb"=paperback), Library of Congress Catalog Card Number, cover artist, stock number (for paperback editions), price, contents (for collections), some bibliographical notes, and similar information on all known reprints, including foreign-language editions. A typical shorter work entry includes title (in quotes), magazine, volume and issue number, pagination, month and year of publication, and all known reprints. Reprints in anthologies include editor, book title, place of publication, publisher, year of publication, pagination. Oliver's numerous fan letters to professional SF magazines are arranged by magazine title, then chronologically by date, with full bibliographical data. Secondary sources are listed alphabetically by critic, with title of article or review, plus bibliographical data in the same formats as above. The text is shot from word-processed copy. There is no index. *Chad Oliver* was produced in a 100-copy edition to commemorate the author's appearance as a guest of honor at a local science-fiction convention. Prefer the newer reorganized version (see #396).

396. Hall, Hal W. **The Work of Chad Oliver: An Annotated Bibliography & Guide**. San Bernardino, Calif., The Borgo Press, 1989. 88 p. index. (Bibliographies of Modern Authors, No. 12). LC 86-2288. ISBN 0-89370-391-5; ISBN 0-89370-491-1 (pbk.).

Hall, a well-known librarian and bibliographer, here contributes a comprehensive guide to the works of American SF and Western writer and anthropologist, Dr. Chad Oliver. Contents: Introduction: "The Voice Out of the Whirlwind," by Howard Waldrop; "A Chad Oliver Chronology"; "A. Books"; "B. Short Fiction"; "C. Nonfiction"; "D. Letters"; "E. Other Media"; "F. Unpublished Works"; "G. About the Author"; "H. Honors and Awards"; "I. Miscellanea"; "An Interview with Chad Oliver," conducted by Hall and Richard D. Boldt; Afterword: "Second Thoughts," by Oliver; "Index."

In each section, the author's works are arranged chronologically by publication date and numbered anew from one, chapter by chapter, with the appropriate letter prefix (e.g., H1, H2, H3, etc.). A typical book entry includes item number, title (boldfaced), place of publication, publisher, year of publication, pagination, format (e.g., "paper"), cover artist, stock number and price (for paperbacks), category (e.g., "science fiction novel"), and full bibliographical data for all known reprint editions, translations, and republications. Monographs are fully annotated, with complete contents listings, plot summaries, and other pertinent data; entries from other sections are selectively annotated as needed. A typical shorter work entry includes item number, title (bold quotes), magazine title (in italics), volume number, month and year of publication, pagination, plus complete data on all subsequent reprints. Reprints in anthologies include title, editor, place of publication, publisher, year of publication, format (e.g., "cloth"), and specific pagination.

Waldrop's introduction provides a very personal look at Oliver and his life. The chronology gives a year-by-year account of the author's professional and personal life in block paragraph format. "About the Author" includes all known secondary works; a second subdivision of this section lists University of Texas, Austin news releases relating to Oliver's professional career as an anthropology professor. The "Miscellanea" section includes information on Oliver's fanzine, education, professional career, and Library of Congress cataloging data. The lengthy interview with and afterword by Dr. Oliver provide much insight into his character and thoughts. The index correlates titles and item numbers only.

Hall worked closely with the author over a period of years (see his previous bibliography on Oliver [#395]), using Oliver's files and personal library to gather much of the data. Coverage is complete through mid-1989. This comprehensive, well-organized, and attractive professional effort by an experienced bibliographer is a particularly fine example of a literary guide.

Edgar Pangborn

397. Benson, Gordon, Jr. **Edgar Pangborn: A Bibliography**. Albuquerque, N.M., Galactic Central Publications, 1985. i, 4 p. (Galactic Central Bibliographies for the Avid Reader, Vol. 5). ISBN 0-912613-14-9 (pbk.).

The late Edgar Pangborn wrote a number of poignant science-fiction novels and stories set in a post-holocaust America. This guide to his work is arranged by subject category, then alphabetically by title. Contents: Author's full name, date and place of birth and date of death, and pseudonym; "A. The Stories"; "B. The Books." In each part the material is arranged in alphabetical order by title, the author's works being numbered anew from one in each section. For shorter works, Benson gives item number, title, category ("ss"=short story, "nt"=novelette, etc.), magazine or book in which the item appeared, month and year of publication (for magazines in the form "6-51" for June 1951) or year of publication for books, plus a list of subsequent reprints (for which title, editor's last name, publisher, and year are given), but no paginations. For book-length works, Benson provides item number, title (in caps), pseudonym, contents (for collections, by item number), publication data (publisher, Library of Congress Catalog Card Number [inconsistently], stock number, month and year of publication [if known, in the form "10-59" for October 1959], pagination, price, with dates of reissues by the same publisher), cover artist. There are no indexes or list of secondary sources.

The book is shot from typed copy, and some of the text runs into the right margin, making potential rebinding of these volumes impossible for libraries. Data are complete through March 1985. The absence of an index in this short bibliography is not noticeable, but the addition of magazine paginations and secondary sources in a future edition would be helpful. Note: this guide has not yet been reworked into the new series format.

H. Beam Piper

398. Benson, Gordon, Jr. **Henry Beam Piper**. Albuquerque, N.M., Galactic Central Publications, 1985. 5 p. (Galactic Central Bibliographies for the Avid Reader, Vol. 6). ISBN 0-912613-15-7 (pbk.).

H. Beam Piper, an avid gun collector, mystery novelist, and SF writer, eventually took his own life in 1964; ironically, his career rebounded in the 1980s with the republication of all his early work and the appearance of at least one previously unpublished novel. Benson's checklist is arranged by subject category, then alphabetically by title. Contents: Author's full name, dates of birth and death; "A. The Stories"; "B. The Books"; "C. Fuzzy Books by Others"; "D. Lord Kalvan Books by Others"; "E. Space Viking Books by Others"; "F. Selected Articles About H. Beam Piper." In each part the material is arranged in alphabetical order by title, the author's works being numbered consecutively from one in each section. For shorter works, Benson gives item number, title, series code (e.g., "*"=Paratime Series), category ("ss"=short story, "nt"=novelette, etc.), magazine or book in which the item appeared, month and year of publication (for magazines, in the form "6-57" for June 1957), or year of publication (for books), plus a list of subsequent reprints (for which title, publisher, year, and editor's last name are given), but no paginations.

For book-length works, Benson provides item number, title (in caps), publication data (publisher, Library of Congress Card Number [inconsistently], stock number, month and year of publication [if known, in the form "10-59" for October 1959], pagination, price, with dates of reissues by the same publisher), cover artist. The list of pastiches is useful for this long-deceased author, but the secondary source listings are minimal, including only three items. There is no index. As with the other early books in this series, the book is shot from typed copy, and some of the text runs into the right margin, making potential rebinding of these volumes difficult at best. Data are complete through early 1985. This volume has yet to be reworked into the new series format, which should provide additional lists of secondary sources and reprints.

Frederik Pohl

399. Stephensen-Payne, Phil, and Gordon Benson Jr. **Frederik Pohl, Merchant of Excellence: A Working Bibliography.** Leeds, West Yorkshire, England & Albuquerque, N.M., Galactic Central, 1989. 9, 109 p. (Galactic Central Bibliographies for the Avid Reader, Vol. 34). (pbk.).

Frederik Pohl has had a long and distinguished career as an SF editor, award-winning writer, and critic. This new guide includes full name, date and place of birth, list of awards won (with dates and book or story titles), and pseudonyms; "A. Stories"; "B. Fiction Books"; "C. Series"; "D. Poems"; "E. Poem & Song Collections" (""none known"); "F. Articles"; "G. Miscellaneous" (including letters, interviews, afterwords, etc.); "H. Non-Fiction Books"; "I. Books Edited by Frederik Pohl"; "J. Media Presentations"; "K. Articles on Frederik Pohl"; "L. Reviews" [of Pohl's books]; "M. Books About Frederik Pohl"; "N. Phantom & Forthcoming Titles"; "O. Related Books by Other Authors" ("none known"); "P. Textual Variations" ("no details known"); "Q. Chronological Index."

In each section materials are arranged alphabetically by title and numbered anew from the number one, chapter by chapter. A typical shorter work entry gives item number, title, type ("NT"=novelette), magazine title, month and year of publication (in the form "11-41" for November 1941), pen name (where appropriate), and a list of all reprints, including the author's own collections. Reprints in anthologies provide book title (all caps), editor's last name, publisher, and year of publication. No paginations are given for any short fiction entries. A typical book entry records item number, title (all caps), collaborator's name and/or pen name (where appropriate), contents (where appropriate, correlated to item numbers), publisher, format (e.g., "hb"=hardback), stock number, month and year of publication (in the form "5-57" for May 1957), pagination, price, cover artist, and similar data for all known reprints. Sixty-six secondary sources are listed, and hundreds of book reviews, arranged alphabetically by title of the work being reviewed, then alphabetically by magazine title. There is no overall index. The book is shot from very clear word-processed copy and bound with staples into paper covers.

Although Stephensen-Payne and Benson's bibliography is extremely thorough and very professionally organized, the rigidity of the format forces the authors generally to gloss over Pohl's extensive career as a science-fiction magazine editor, summarizing dates and titles in entry #G17. This should be expanded in any second edition. Nonetheless, this bibliography will be an essential starting point for for all future scholarship on this important author.

Tim Powers

400. Stephens, Christopher P., and Tom Joyce. **A Checklist of Tim Powers**. Hastings-on-Hudson, N.Y., Ultramarine Publishing Co., 1991. 15 p. index. ISBN 0-89366-198-8 (pbk.).

Powers is a rising SF and fantasy writer, author of *The Drawing of the Dark*. This new checklist is organized into two sections ("Books" and "Short Stories"), then chronologically by publication date, with the books being numbered from A1-A11, and the stories from B1-3. A typical book entry provides year (as a floating head), item number, title (underlined), pseudonym, publisher, stock or ISBN number, pagination, format (e.g., "cloth with dust wrapper"), cover illustrator, price, and similar data for all known reprints (which are numbered, for example, A10a, A10b, A10c, etc., in descending order by publication date). A typical short fiction entry gives year (floating head), item number, story title (in quotes), magazine title (underlined), month and year of publication, but no paginations. The chapbook is shot from legible typed copy and bound with staples in stiff paper covers. The index correlates titles with years of publication only, not item numbers. This is a good introductory checklist of Powers's works, one which will chiefly be of interest to fans and collectors.

Robert Reginald

401. Burgess, Michael, and Jeffrey M. Elliot. **The Work of R. Reginald: An Annotated Bibliography & Guide**. San Bernardino, Calif., The Borgo Press, 1985. 48 p. index. (Bibliographies of Modern Authors, No. 5). LC 84-21672. ISBN 0-89370-384-2; ISBN 0-89370-484-9 (pbk.). Burgess, Michael. **The Work of Robert Reginald: An Annotated Bibliography & Guide**. 2nd ed., rev. and expanded. San Bernardino, Calif., The Borgo Press, 1992. 176 p. index. (Bibliographies of Modern Authors, No. 5). LC 87-6306. ISBN 0-8095-0505-3; ISBN 0-8095-1505-9 (pbk.).

This comprehensive guide to the works of a prolific SF publisher, bibliographer, editor, and critic includes (first edition): "I Fear the Greeks...: An Introduction," by Dr. Jeffrey M. Elliot; "A. Books"; "B. Articles and Reviews"; "C. Periodicals, Serials, and Publishing Companies"; "D. Juvenilia"; "E. Radio and Television Appearances"; "F. About the Author"; "G. Honors and Awards"; "H. Unpublished Works"; "J. Miscellanea"; "Index." Contents (second edition): "A Robert Reginald Chronology"; "Introduction," by William F. Nolan; Foreword: "It Was Twenty Years Ago Today...," by Dr. Fran J. Polek; "Preface," by Jack Dann; "A. Books"; "B. Articles and Reviews"; "C. Editorial Credits"; "D. Juvenilia"; "E. Documents"; "F. Catalogs"; "G. Public Appearances"; "H. Secondary Sources"; "I. Honors and Awards"; "J. Unpublished Works"; "K. Miscellanea"; "Quoth the Critics"; "Afterthoughts," by Reginald; "Afterword," by Jack Dann; "Index."

In each section, the author's works are arranged chronologically and numbered consecutively from one, chapter by chapter. A typical book entry includes (second edition) item number, title (in bold type), byline, place of publication, publisher, month and year of publication, pagination, format (e.g., "cloth"), type of publication (e.g, "anthology"), and full bibliographical data on reprint editions and translations. The books are fully annotated with complete contents listings or plot summaries and other pertinent data; entries from other sections are selectively annotated as needed. A typical shorter work entry includes (second edition) item number, title (bold quotes), magazine title (italics), volume number, month and year of publication, pagination. The introductions and afterwords provide background material (from different points of view) on Reginald's life and works. The chronology gives a year-by-year account of the author's professional and personal life, in block paragraph format. There are fifty-five secondary works listed, plus about a hundred and fifty individual book reviews listed after the monographs in Chapter A. The "Miscellanea" section includes information on pen names, book dedications, memberships, Library of Congress cataloging data, career highlights, and similar data. "Quoth the Critics" includes selected excerpts of reviews and other comments by leading critics on the author's works, arranged in chronological order by book title. Coverage is complete through 1991. The index references titles and item numbers only.

Reginald has been responsible as writer, editor, or publisher, for publication of approximately 1,750 volumes; this bibliography provides a timely look at this rising author's career. Well-organized, clear, and comprehensive, this guide should be included in all major research collections. A much-expanded second edition appeared early in 1992.

Mack Reynolds

402. Drumm, Chris, and George Flynn. **A Mack Reynolds Checklist: Notes Toward a Bibliography.** Polk City, Ia., Chris Drumm Books, 1983. 24 p. index. ISBN 0-936055-01-4 (pbk.).

Reynolds was a socialist SF writer who died in 1983 just before this checklist was released. This brief 4.25" x 7" checklist arranges his works in one straight chronological sequence. Entries are grouped by year, and under each year by month; items are numbered in order from 1 to 242. Books are underlined, short stories listed in quotation marks. A typical short fiction entry includes item number, title, category code (e.g., "s"=short story), series note, magazine title, month of publication—or book title, if the first appearance is in an anthology, plus editor, publisher, and year of publication. There are no paginations for short stories. Subsequent reprintings are listed chronologically under the original edition, with similar data provided. A typical book entry includes item number, title (underlined), category code (e.g., "c"=collection), place of publication, publisher, stock number (for paperbacks), month of publication (if known), pagination, price, format (e.g., "pb"=paperback), and contents of collections. See references, title index, and contents listings are keyed to item number. A few secondary materials are mentioned in passing in their appropriate years but are not easily retrievable. Data are complete through mid-1983; a one-sheet corrigenda page is also included in some copies. The volume is shot from typed copy; the text runs too close to the margins to allow rebinding by libraries. This booklet will provide a basic starting point for future research on the author, but a new, more elaborate edition would certainly be justified. Although Reynolds died the same year this checklist was published, he left over a dozen unpublished books, many of which were reworked or revised by other writers for subsequent publication.

Kim Stanley Robinson

403. Joyce, Tom, and Christopher P. Stephens, **A Checklist of Kim Stanley Robinson**. Hastings-on-Hudson, N.Y., Ultramarine Publishing Co., 1991. 28 p. index. ISBN 0-89366-204-6 (pbk.).

Robinson achieved immediate fame and popularity with the publication of his first novel, *The Wild Shore*, in 1984; this is the first bibliography of his work. Joyce and Stephens's checklist is arranged chronologically by publication date in two sections covering the author's books and short stories. A typical monograph entry provides year (as a floating head), item number, title (underlined), pseudonym, publisher, stock or ISBN number, pagination, format (e.g., "cloth with dust wrapper"), cover illustrator, price, and similar data for all known reprints (which are numbered, for example, A1a, A1b, A1c, etc., in descending order by publication date). A typical short fiction entry gives year (floating head), item number, title (in quotes), magazine title (underlined) and month and year of publication, or book title (for original anthology appearances; underlined), editor's name, publisher, and year of publication. No paginations are listed for short stories. Items are numbered consecutively from A1-A14 in the book section and from B1-B34 in the short fiction chapter. Robinson also has provided an illuminating eight-page autobiographical introduction. The book is shot from legible typed copy and bound with staples in stiff paper covers. The index correlates titles with years of publication only. This is a good beginning checklist of this popular writer's works, one which is intended primarily for the fan and collectors market.

Ross Rocklynne

404. Menville, Douglas. **The Work of Ross Rocklynne: An Annotated Bibliography & Guide**. San Bernardino, Calif., The Borgo Press, 1989. 70 p. index. (Bibliographies of Modern Authors, No. 17). LC 88-34360. ISBN 0-8095-0511-8; ISBN 0-8095-1511-3 (pbk.).

Rocklynne, an American SF writer of the pulp era, died in 1988; this is the first extended work ever published on his life and works. Contents: Introduction: "A Man for All Magazines," by Arthur Jean Cox; "A Ross Rocklynne Chronology"; "A. Books"; "B. Short Fiction"; "C. Nonfiction"; "D. Fanzine Contributions"; "E. Radio"; "F. Juvenilia"; "G. About the Author"; "H. Unpublished Works"; "I. Miscellanea"; "Quoth the Critics"; "Index."

The author's works are arranged chronologically by publication date in each section and numbered anew from one, chapter by chapter; the numbers are prefixed by the appropriate chapter letter (e.g., B1, B2, B3, etc.). A typical book entry includes item number, title (bold type), place of publication, publisher, month and year of publication, pagination, format (e.g., "paper"), type of publication (e.g., "novel"), and full bibliographical data on reprint editions, including foreign. The books are fully annotated, with complete contents listings and plot summaries; entries from other sections are selectively annotated as needed. Rocklynne worked primarily in the short fiction market; a typical story entry includes item number, title (bold quotes), magazine title (italics), volume number, month and year of publication, pagination, with complete bibliographical details on all known reprints (including those in Rocklynne's own books).

Reprints in anthologies include book title (italics), editor, place of publication, publisher, year of publication, format (e.g., "paper"), pagination. Cox's introduction provides a sympathetic discussion of Rocklynne's life and works. The chronology provides a year-by-year account of his professional and personal life. "About the Author" includes all known secondary works. The "Miscellanea" section includes information on pen names, book dedications, memberships, Library of Congress cataloging data, career highlights, and other data. "Quoth the Critics" includes selected excerpts of reviews and other comments by leading critics on the author's work. The "Index" lists titles and item numbers only.

Menville, a well-known film critic and editor, has produced a complete and sympathetic guide to the author's work, much of it deriving from Rocklynne's own files, gathered just before his untimely death. Complete data on this author's works are provided through mid-1989. The result is a thoroughly professional and attractive literary bibliography, one which is likely to remain current for years to come.

Sax Rohmer

405. Day, Bradford M. **Sax Rohmer: A Bibliography**. Denver, N.Y., Science-Fiction & Fantasy Publications, 1963. 34 p. LC 63-4431 (pbk.).

This checklist of the classic British horror writer's work is presented in the same format as Day's previous bibliographies on Burroughs and Mundy (see #303 and #388). The book section is arranged alphabetically by title, a typical entry including title (caps), publisher, place of publication, year of publication, pagination, mention of other editions (publisher and year only), brief cover copy quote, notes on previous magazine serialization (in parentheses), with magazine name and dates, plus binding color style. The short fiction section is arranged in chronological order by date of publication, and lists title (all caps), magazine title, year of publication, month of publication, a list of reprints in Mundy's books, but no paginations. There is a brief biography and checklist of film adaptations, but no index. The book is mimeographed from typed copy and has begun to yellow. The basic bibliography was slightly updated in Day's later book, *Bibliography of Adventure* (see #202). In the absence of a comprehensive bibliography of Rohmer's work—long overdue—Day's work is the only guide currently available to the scholar or researcher.

Eric Frank Russell

406. Stephensen-Payne, Phil. **Eric Frank Russell, Our Sentinel in Space: A Working Bibliography**. 2nd rev. ed. Leeds, West Yorkshire, England & Albuquerque, N.M., Galactic Central Publications, 1988. 9, 35 p. (Galactic Central Bibliographies for the Avid Reader, Vol. 24). ISBN 1-871133-06-8 (pbk.).

The late Eric Frank Russell was a "hard" British science fiction writer who died in 1978. Stephensen-Payne's guide to his work is arranged by subject category, then alphabetically by title. Contents: Author's full name, date and place of birth and date of death, pseudonyms, and awards; "A. Stories"; "B. Fiction Books"; "C. Series"; "D. Poems"; "E. Poem Collections" ("none known"); "F. Articles"; "G. Miscellaneous"; "H. Non-Fiction Books"; "I. Books Edited by Eric Frank Russell" ("none known"); "J. Media Presentations"; "K. Articles on Eric Frank Russell"; "L. Reviews" [of Russell's books]; "M. Books About Eric Frank Russell"; "N. Phantom Titles"; "O. Related Books by Other Authors" ("none known"); "P. Textual Variations"; "Q. Chronological Checklist." In each part the material is arranged in alphabetical order by title, the author's works being numbered anew from one in each section.

For shorter works, Stephensen-Payne gives item number, title, category ("ss"=short story, "nt"=novelette, etc.), magazine or book in which the item appeared, month and year of publication (for magazines, in the form "5-55" for May 1955) or year of publication for books, plus a list of subsequent reprints (for which title, editor's last name, publisher, and year are given), but no paginations. A typical monograph entry includes item number, title (in caps), publication data (publisher, Library of Congress Catalog Card Number [inconsistently], stock number, month and year of publication [if known, in the form "10-59" for October 1959], pagination, price, with dates of reissues by the same publisher), cover artist. There are no indexes. Thirty-three secondary sources are listed and about eighty book reviews (arranged by title of the volume being reviewed, then alphabetically by magazine title). Data are complete through the end of 1988. The book is shot from very clear word-processed copy and bound with staples into paper covers.

This bibliography should remain relatively current for some time to come; with the absence of any new material from Russell, the only future additions will be reprints of previously published works. Scholars will find this guide a necessary beginning point for any future research on Russell's fiction.

Fred Saberhagen

407. Stephensen-Payne, Phil. **Fred Saberhagen, Berserker Man: A Working Bibliography**. Leeds, West Yorkshire, England & Albuquerque, N.M., Galactic Central Publications, 1991. 9, 28 p. (Galactic Central Bibliographies for the Avid Reader, Vol. 37). (pbk.).

Saberhagen, best known for his Berserker series and his modern adaptation of the Dracula mythos, is the target of this new addition to the Galactic Central Series. Contents: "A. Stories"; "B. Fiction Books"; "C. Series"; "D. Poems & Songs"; "E. Poem & Song Collections" ("none known")"; "F. Articles"; "G. Miscellaneous"; "H. Non-Fiction Books" ("none known"); "I. Books Edited by Fred Saberhagen"; "J. Media Presentations"; "K. Articles on Fred Saberhagen"; "L. Reviews" [of Saberhagen's books]; "M. Books About Fred Saberhagen" ("none known"); "N. Phantom & Forthcoming Titles"; "O. Related Items by Other Authors"; "P. Textual Variations"; "Q. Chronological Index."

Materials are arranged in each section alphabetically by title. A typical shorter work entry provides item number, title, type ("ss"=short story), magazine title and month and year of publication, or (for an original anthology appearance) book title (all caps), editor's surname, publisher, and year of publication, but no paginations. Similar data are provided for all known reprints. A typical monograph entry gives item number, title (all caps), contents (correlated by item number), publisher, format (e.g., "pb"=paperback), stock number, month and year of publication (in the form "10-81" for October 1981), pagination, price, and cover artist, with similar data on all known reprints. Items are numbered from the number one in each section, prefixed by the letter code assigned to that chapter (for example, B1, B2, B3, etc., for the Books section). Seventeen secondary sources are listed and about a hundred book reviews. The book is shot from legible word-processed copy and bound with staples through the spine into paper covers. There is no index.

This is a good introductory guide to Saberhagen's writings. Future editions should add short fiction paginations and a comprehensive index.

Pamela Sargent

408. Elliot, Jeffrey M. **The Work of Pamela Sargent: An Annotated Bibliography & Guide**. San Bernardino, Calif., The Borgo Press, 1990. 80 p. index. (Bibliographies of Modern Authors, No. 13). LC 88-34361. ISBN 0-89370-394-X; ISBN 0-89370-494-6 (pbk.).

Sargent is a rising star in the SF field, with many award-winning credits as novelist, short-story writer, children's writer, and editor. Contents: Introduction: "Let the Rest Take Care of Itself" (by Elliot); "A Pamela Sargent Chronology"; "A. Books"; "B. Short Fiction"; "C. Nonfiction"; "D. Unpublished Works"; "E. Editorial Credits"; "F. Other Media"; "G. Juvenilia"; "H. Public Appearances"; "I. Honors and Awards"; "J. About the Author"; "K. Miscellanea"; "Quoth the Critics"; Afterword: "Though the Looking Glass," by Sargent; "Index."

In each section, the author's works are arranged chronologically and numbered consecutively from one, chapter by chapter, prefixed by the appropriate letter code. A typical monograph entry includes item number, title (boldface), place of publication, publisher, month and year of publication, pagination, format (e.g., "cloth"), cover artist, series designation, type of publication (e.g., "novel"), and full bibliographical data on all known reprint editions and translations. The books are annotated with complete contents listings or plot summaries, and other pertinent data; entries from other sections are selectively annotated as needed. A typical shorter work entry gives item number, title (bold quotes), magazine (italics), volume number, month and year of publication, pagination, and similar data on all known reprints. Reprints in anthologies include title (italics), editor, place of publication, publisher, year of publication, format (e.g., "cloth"), pagination. Elliot's introduction provides a personal look at the author's life. The chronology provides a year-by-year account of the author's professional and personal life, in block paragraph format. "About the Author" includes all known secondary works. The "Miscellanea" section includes information on pen names, book dedications, memberships, Library of Congress cataloging data, career highlights, and other data. "Quoth the Critics" includes selected excerpts of reviews and other comments by leading critics on the author's work. Sargent's short original afterword tells why and how she became a writer and how her nearsightedness led her into the world of literature. The index correlates titles and item numbers only. Coverage is complete through 1989.

Sargent is closely associated with two other upstate New York writers, George Zebrowski and Jack Dann, on whom Elliot also prepared bibliographies (see #320 and #454).

This comprehensive guide, much of it based on material provided by the author, provides a good base for future scholarship on this rising star, and should be acquired by all libraries interested in modern American women writers.

James H. Schmitz

409. Owings, Mark. **James H. Schmitz: A Bibliography**. Baltimore, Croatan House, 1973. [33] p. (Croatan House Bibliographies). ISBN 0-88358-902-8 (pbk.).

Owings's brief checklist of the late American science fiction writer's works includes a nineteen-page critical introduction, "The Natural Heroine of James H. Schmitz," by novelist Janet Kagan. The bibliography proper, which consists of just six pages of copy, is arranged by title in one alphabetical sequence, book titles being underlined. A typical short fiction work entry gives title, abbreviated magazine title (an abbreviations list appears on page [3]), month and year of publication (in the form 7/49 for July 1949), but no paginations, plus known reprint editions. Reprints in anthologies include book title (underlined), editor, publisher, place of publication, year of publication, total book pagination, price, but no individual story paginations.

A typical book entry includes title (underlined), publisher, place of publication, year of publication, pagination, price, and similar data on all known reprint editions. A complete contents listing is provided for collections. The book is shot from very legible typed copy. Two appendices provide an alphabetical list of the author's books and a chronological checklist of all his publications by year and month. Schmitz published relatively little between 1973-81 (the year of his death), so this concise guide to his work still remains fairly current. A larger, more elaborate bibliographical synthesis of Schmitz's work would now be warranted.

Bob Shaw

410. Stephensen-Payne, Phil, Chris Nelson, and Gordon Benson, Jr. **Bob Shaw, Artist at Ground Zero**. 4th rev. ed. Leeds, West Yorkshire, England & Albuquerque, N.M., Galactic Central Publications, 1989. 9, 32 p. (Galactic Central Bibliographies for the Avid Reader, Vol. 14). ISBN 0-912613-17-3 (pbk.).

Bob Shaw, a native of Northern Ireland, is known for his "hard SF" stories and novels. This new checklist, earlier versions of which were authored by just Nelson and Benson, arranges by subject category, then alphabetically by title. Contents: Author's full name, date and place of birth, and awards; "A. Stories"; "B. Fiction Books"; "C. Series"; "D. Poems & Songs" ("none known"); "E. Poem & Song Collections" ("none known"); "F. Articles"; "G. Miscellaneous"; "H. Non-Fiction Books"; "I. Edited Books" ("none known"); "J. Media Presentations" ("none known"); "K. Articles on Bob Shaw"; "L. Reviews" [of Shaw's books]; "M. Books About Bob Shaw"; "N. Phantom Titles"; "O. Related Books by Other Authors" ("none known"); "P. Textual Variations" ("none known"); "Q. Chronological Index."

Each section arranges the material alphabetically by title, the author's works being numbered anew from one in each section and prefixed by the appropriate letter code. For shorter works, the authors give item number, title, category ("ss"=short story, "nt"=novelette, etc.), magazine or book in which the item appeared, month and year of publication (for magazines in the form "4-82" for April 1982) or year of publication (for books), plus a list of subsequent reprints (for which title, editor's last name, publisher, and year are given), but no paginations. A typical book entry provides item number, title (in caps), publication data (publisher, stock number, month and year of publication [if known, in the form "10-59" for October 1959], pagination, price, with dates of reissues by the same publisher), cover artist. There is no general index. Seventeen secondary sources are listed and about a hundred book reviews. Coverage is complete through late 1989. The book is shot from very dark and clear word-processed copy and bound with staples in paper covers.

The inclusion of an index and short fiction paginations would be desirable additions to future editions of this useful bibliography. Even with its limitations, this guide provides a wealth of hard-to-locate data organized into an easily accessible format. Research libraries should acquire a copy.

Lucius Shepard

411. Joyce, Tom, and Christopher P. Stephens. **A Checklist of Lucius Shepard**. Hastings-on-Hudson, N.Y., Ultramarine Publishing Co., 1991. 18 p. index. ISBN 0-89366-203-8 (pbk.).

Shepard began publishing poetry in the 1960s but first achieved popularity in the SF field with *Green Eyes*, a novel published in 1984. Joyce and Stephens's checklist arranges the data into two sections covering his books and short stories, then chronologically by publication date. Items are numbered consecutively, books from A1-A9, short fiction from B1-B41. A typical book entry provides year (as a floating head), item number, title (underlined), publisher, stock or ISBN number, pagination, format (e.g., "cloth with dust wrapper"), cover illustrator, price, and similar data for all known reprints (which are numbered, for example, A8a, A8b, A8c, etc., in descending order by publication date). Shorter work entries include item number, title (in quotes), magazine title (underlined) and month and year of publication, or (for original anthology appearances) book title (underlined), editor's name, publisher, and year of publication, with similar data for all known reprints. There are no paginations for the short stories. The booklet is shot from legible typed copy and bound with staples in stiff paper covers. The index correlates titles with years of publication only. Shepard's fiction and verse has found a solid following who will appreciate this carefully compiled checklist.

M. P. Shiel

412. Morse, A. Reynolds. **The Works of M. P. Shiel: A Study in Bibliography**. Los Angeles, Fantasy Publishing Co. Inc., 1948. xvii, 170 p. index. LC 49-1086. Originally published in cloth, but some unbound sheets were later issued in paper covers. **The Works of M. P. Shiel Updated: A Study in Bibliography, Including "About Myself," by M. P. Shiel, 1865-1947 (New Revised Version), with a New Appendix on Louis Tracy (1863-1928).** 2nd and updated ed. Dayton, Ohio, Reynolds Morse Foundation in Association with JDS Books, 1980. 858 p. in 2 v. index. (The Works of M. P. Shiel, Vols. 2-3). LC 79-88144. ISBN 0-934236-01-1.

Morse's comprehensive guide to this somewhat obscure British fantasy writer was obviously a labor of love. Shiel worked mainly in book-length form, and the basic bibliography of monographs is arranged in chronological order by publication date. Each entry includes title (caps), lengthy annotation (from one-to-two pages covering both the plot or contents of the book and other items of interest), bibliographical data for each known edition of the work, including publisher, place of publication, month and year of publication, exact title page transcription, collation, physical size, binding (all known variations, with edition states and priorities). Similar data are provided about Shiel's short stories, articles, translations, and poems, without annotations, as they have appeared in magazines, newspapers, and known book reprints (with paginations). Morse also includes a list of the books in Shiel's personal library, a guide to the known manuscripts, proofs, and typescripts, and a complete bibliographical guide to the eight mystery novels of "Gordon Holmes," a house pseudonym which included several Shiel collaborations. The autobiographical "About Myself" and several similar pieces provide much background information on the author's life. Morse's secondary list is exhaustive, including many sources that are difficult to locate, with complete bibliographical data and brief annotations summarizing the Shiel material. A title index (correlated to page number) completes a very well organized and presented bibliography.

The second edition subsumes, expands upon, and corrects the earlier work, but is otherwise arranged very similarly. Contents: "1. A Checklist of the Various Editions of the Novels and Short Stories of M. P. Shiel"; "2. The Collations": "a) "Notes on Collations," "b) 1895-1901," "c) 1901-1914," "d) 1923-1937," "3. The Short Stories of M. P. Shiel"; "4. Miscellaneous Works by M. P. Shiel": a) and b) in Books, Anthologies, etc., c) in Periodicals and Newspapers, "d) M. P. Shiel and Arthur Machen"; "5. Known Manuscripts, Corrected Texts, Proofs, Typescripts, Published and Unpublished, of M. P. Shiel"; 6. Bibliography": "M. P. Shiel [i.e., Secondary Sources] a) in Books, b) in Periodicals, etc. (arranged chronologically); 7. a) "About Myself," by M. P. Shiel, "b) Biographical Notes," "c) The Personal Library of M. P. Shiel," "d) An Epilogue: The Address of Edward Shanks at the Funeral of Matthew Phipps Shield," "e) Bohemia in London," "f) Introduction to the Original Edition of 1948"; "8. The Shielography Update" (an essay on the years 1948-1979); "9. The Conquest of M. P. Shiel's Redonda"; "10. New Appendix on Louis Tracy (Including the Novels of "Gordon Holmes" and the Lamb-Morse Bibliography on the Works of Tracy)"; "11. Acknowledgments"; "12. Index."

Both books are nicely typeset and illustrated, and the second edition is bound to library standards. Clearly, no scholar could even begin to think of researching Shiel without consulting Morse's extraordinarily complete guide.

Robert Silverberg

413. Clareson, Thomas D. **Robert Silverberg: A Primary and Secondary Bibliography**. Boston, G. K. Hall & Co., 1983. xxx, 321 p. index. (Masters of Science Fiction and Fantasy). LC 83-154. ISBN 0-8161-8118-7.

Robert Silverberg is one of the most prolific writers of modern fantastic literature, having authored (as writer or editor) over a hundred SF books and over a hundred additional monographs in other categories, some under pseudonyms, plus several hundred short stories. Clareson is an acknowledged expert on Silverberg's work, having previously published a critique of his work. Contents: "Preface"; "Acknowledgments"; "Introduction"; "Comprehensive Short-Title List of Silverberg's Books"; "A. Science Fiction and Fantasy"; "B. Miscellaneous Fiction"; "C. Edited Anthologies"; "D. Nonfiction"; "E. Silverberg on Science Fiction"; "F. Other Media"; "G. Reviews and Critical Studies of Silverberg's Works"; "Appendix 1: Silverberg's Articles in the *Bulletin of the Science Fiction Writers of America*"; "Appendix 2: Silverberg's Pseudonymous Works Listed by Pen Name"; "Appendix 3: Awards and Nominations"; "Indexes: The Works of Robert Silverberg"; "Reviews and Critical Studies."

Clareson's brief introduction provides a cursory critical and biographical introduction to Silverberg's work. The bibliography is arranged chronologically from the earliest published material to the latest and numbered consecutively (e.g., A1, A2, A3, for his science fiction). Books and shorter works are interfiled. Each book entry gives title, place of publication, publisher, and contents (for collections), with years of publication of the individual stories and their entry numbers. Reprints of monographs are arranged in chronological order by year of publication under the primary entry and include place of publication, publisher, year of publication, and an indication of whether the book was issued in paperback format. Shorter works published originally in magazines provide title (in quotes), magazine, volume number, month of publication (in parentheses), and pagination; those published originally in books give title (in quotes), editor, book title, place of publication, publisher, format (e.g., "paper"), and paginations. Reprints of stories are listed under the main entry, chronologically by year of reprint, with the editor of the anthology, title, place of publication, publisher, year, format (e.g., "paper"), but no paginations. Story collections include complete contents listings, plus the years in which the original stories were published. Some entries include bibliographical notes, but no other annotations.

In Part B Clareson summarizes Silverberg's many soft-porn titles, reportedly numbering in the hundreds, providing a skeletal listing without complete bibliographical details; also mentioned in this chapter are ten titles Silverberg wrote in other genres, arranged in the same format as Part A. Part C lists sixty-seven anthologies edited by Silverberg in chronological order by date, with title, place of publication, publisher, and date, but no contents listings. Part D includes ninety-one nonfiction pieces by Silverberg, most of them juvenile or young adult books on science, biography, and history. Part E lists all of Silverberg's nonfiction essays on fantastic literature, plus his fanzines contributions, with lengthy annotations. Part F, "Other Media," includes four records and filmstrips. The secondary bibliography is extensive, covering almost 800 items, including published book reviews, fan commentaries, critiques, biographies, and bibliographies, with author, title, bibliographical data, and subject annotations, many of them lengthy and analytical. Appendix 1 lists Silverberg's essays in the *SFWA Bulletin*; Appendix 2 provides a checklist of his pseudonymous work, alphabetically by pen name and then by title, with references to the main-entry item numbers of each; Appendix 3 is a useful list of the author's awards and award nominations in chronological order by year. The main index cites title and item number only, the second index (to critical studies) author and title (separately), plus item number. The book is shot from generally clear typed copy and bound to library standards.

The lack of book paginations in this volume is very noticeable, as is the absence of anthology contents; Silverberg was one of the leading editors of original and reprint anthologies in the field for the ten-year period from 1970-1980, and inclusion of such data (with appropriate indexes) would have provided scholars with a much better sense of his contributions to this area. Coverage is complete through 1981. An extended and updated edition with additional material on the earlier works would definitely be warranted.

Clifford D. Simak

414. Becker, Muriel R. **Clifford D. Simak: A Primary and Secondary Bibliography**. Boston, G. K. Hall & Co., 1980. xliii, 149 p. index. (Masters of Science Fiction and Fantasy). LC 79-18124. ISBN 0-8161-8063-6.

The late Clifford Simak was a well-regarded writer of pastoral science fiction stories that combined his love of nature and the Wisconsin countryside with a sense of wry nostalgia. Becker's bibliography provides a good basic introduction to this American author's works. Contents: "Preface"; "Acknowledgments"; "Introduction"; "Clifford D. Simak Interviewed"; "Documents Consulted"; "Brief Chronology"; "Awards and Honors"; "Part A: Science Fiction"; "Part B: Miscellaneous: Westerns, Air War Stories, and Media";

"Part C: Nonfiction"; "Part D: Critical and Bio-Bibliographical Studies"; "Appendix A: Periodical Reviews Excluded"; "Appendix B: Overview of MSS44, the Clifford D. Simak Papers"; "Appendix C: Title Changes"; "Appendix D: Anthologies in Which Simak's Stories Appear"; "Appendix E: Works in U.S. Science Fiction Book Club Editions"; "Index I: The Writings of Clifford D. Simak—Parts A, B., C"; "Index II: About Clifford D. Simak—Part D."

The introduction provides a broad critical and biographical introduction to Simak's work. The bibliography is arranged chronologically, from the earliest published material to the latest, and numbered consecutively (e.g., D1, D2, D3, etc.). Books and shorter works are interfiled. Each book entry gives title, place of publication, publisher, but no paginations. Reprints of books are listed chronologically under the main entry, with place of publication, publisher, year of publication, and format (e.g., "paper"). Story collections include complete contents listings, plus the years in which the original stories were published. Shorter works published originally in magazines give title (in quotations), magazine, volume and issue number, month of publication (in parentheses), and pagination; those published originally in books give title (in quotations), editor, book title, place of publication, publisher, format, and pagination. Reprints of stories are listed under the main entry, chronologically by year of reprint, with the editor of the anthology, title, place of publication, publisher, year, format (e.g., "paper"), and paginations. Some entries include bibliographical notes, but no other annotations.

Part B includes fiction in other genres, most of it published during the pulp era, and a few interviews and speeches. Part C lists all nonfiction works by the author, including fanzine contributions, with occasional annotations. Part D lists roughly 200 secondary works, including published book reviews, fan commentaries, critiques, and bibliographies, with author, title, bibliographical data, and extensive subject annotations. Appendix A indexes otherwise unrecorded reviews of individual Simak works alphabetically by book title, then chronologically by review, with abbreviated magazine title, volume, pagination, date of publication, and reviewer; Appendix B is a detailed itemization of the seventeen boxes of the Clifford D. Simak papers at the University of Minnesota Libraries; Appendix C correlates title changes in Simak's fiction; Appendix D indexes the anthologies in which Simak's stories have appeared, alphabetically by editor and book title, with the item number (but not the title) of the Simak story—the lack of story titles makes this section difficult to use; Appendix E is a chronological checklist of Simak's books selected by the American version of the Science Fiction Book Club. The main index cites title and item number only, the second index (to critical studies) author, title, and item number. Unlike most books in this series, Becker's volume is attractively typeset and bound to library standards.

Data are complete through 1978; however, Simak's recent death means this book will remain relatively current indefinitely, lacking only the author's last few books and a handful of short stories, plus subsequent reprintings. The absence of monograph paginations, a standard feature of this series, is unfortunate, but could easily be restored in a revised and updated "definitive" edition. Until then, this guide must remain the essential starting point for all future scholarship on Simak's writings.

415. Owings, Mark. **Clifford D. Simak**. Baltimore, Alice & Jay Haldeman, 1971. [11] p. (The Electric Bibliograph, Part 1). (pbk.).

This brief 8.5" x 11" checklist of Simak's science fiction stories, novels, and collections is arranged in the standard Owings format, alphabetically by title in one master sequence. A typical short fiction entry includes title, abbreviated magazine title, month and year of publication (in the form "3/51" for March 1951), and bibliographical data on all known reprints in other collections and anthologies, with title, editor, publisher, place of publication, year of publication, total pagination of book (but not of the individual story), price, format (e.g., "wpps"=paperback). A typical book entry includes title (in italics), original magazine serialization information (where appropriate), publisher, place of publication, year of publication, pagination, price, and similar data on all known reprint editions, including some foreign-language versions (with foreign-language titles and translators). A brief afterword mentions one story collaboration and three nonfiction books written or edited by Simak. The booklet was reproduced on sometimes faint mimeographed sheets which are now yellowing. Although largely superseded by Becker's more current and complete work (see #414), Owings's bibliography does provide paginations and prices for the early books and can be used as a supplement to the former. This was the first volume of a series that sputtered along for a few volumes before dying.

John Sladek

416. Drumm, Chris. **A John Sladek Checklist: Pre-Publication Version.** Polk City, Ia., Chris Drumm Books, 1984. [26] p. index. (pbk.).

Sladek's experimental and sometimes controversial SF is aptly chronicled in this new 4.25" x 7" checklist. The author's works are arranged in one chronological sequence. Entries are grouped by year and under each year by month; items are numbered in order from 1 to 114. Books are listed in bold italics, short stories in quotation marks. A typical short fiction entry includes item number, title, category code (e.g., "s"=short story), series note, magazine title (in italics), month of publication—or book title (in italics) if the first appearance is in an anthology, plus editor, publisher, and year of publication. There are no paginations listed for short stories. Subsequent reprintings are listed chronologically under the original edition, with similar data provided. A typical book entry includes item number, title (bold italics), type (e.g., "story collection"), place of publication, publisher, stock or ISBN number, pagination, price, format (e.g., "pb"=paperback), contents of collections. Similar data are provided on all reprint editions, including a few foreign monographs, with foreign-language titles and translators. Contents listings of collections include original year of publication with each story title. The index correlates titles and years of publication only. A few secondary materials are mentioned in passing in their appropriate years but are not easily retrievable. Data are complete through part of 1984. The book is shot from very legible word-processed copy; margins are much wider than in earlier books from this publisher. A revised and expanded edition of this well-organized checklist would definitely be justified (but has not yet been issued, despite the title).

Clark Ashton Smith

417. Bell, Joseph, and Roy A. Squires. **The Books of Clark Ashton Smith.** Toronto, Soft Books, 1987. 28 p. index. ("Old Masters" Series, Number Two). (pbk.).

Bell's bibliographies of Lovecraft and other weird fiction writers are essentially collectors' guides to the authors' books. Contents: "Index of Book Titles" (with title, publisher, year of publication, and page number of entry); "Information Is Given as Follows" (Bell's description of the basic entry format); "The Books of Clark Ashton Smith"; "Alphabetical Index of Fiction" (an index to the short stories, correlated to Smith collections in which they are included and year of book publication); and "A Chronological Listing of Book Titles" (essentially the first section rearranged by year). The bibliography proper is arranged chronologically by year of publication. A typical entry includes, for all known editions title (bold underlined caps), publisher, place of publication, pagination, number of copies printed, cover artist, printer's name, binding and paper states (arranged in priority order), original price, month of publication, and contents (for collections). For a writer like Smith who has had many of his works issued in small press chapbook editions, this kind of guide is useful to establish first-edition points, but as a bibliography it can only be considered a brief supplement to Sidney-Fryer's much more complete work (see #419).

418. Cockcroft, T. G. L. **The Tales of Clark Ashton Smith: A Bibliography**. Lower Hutt, N.Z., Thomas G. L. Cockcroft, 1951. vi p. (pbk.). **The Tales of Clark Ashton Smith: A Bibliography**. Rev. ed. Lower Hutt, N.Z., Thomas G. L. Cockcroft, 1959. vii p. (pbk.).

This brief checklist of Smith's works was professionally printed and produced by an early bibliographer of the field and is typical of the best of fan scholarship. Contents: "Collections"; "In Preparation"; "Anthology Representations"; "Stories; "Addenda" (1959; pages [vi-vii]). Smith's story collections are listed chronologically by year of publication; a typical entry includes title (italics), publisher, place of publication, year of publication, pagination, format (e.g., "wraps"), with physical dimensions measured in inches. "Anthology Representations" is also arranged chronologically, and includes book title (italics), editor, publisher, place of publication, year of publication, and the title of the Smith story included (in italics). The story section is arranged alphabetically by story title, a typical entry giving title (italics), magazine of publication, the Smith collection in which the story is included (keyed to three-letter codes; e.g., "TDS"=*The Double Shadow*), and month and year of publication. The addendum includes materials published through the 1950s and additional stories not previously mentioned. Now wholly superseded by Sidney-Fryer (see #419).

419. Sidney-Fryer, Donald. **Emperor of Dreams: A Clark Ashton Smith Bibliography**. West Kingston, R.I., Donald M. Grant, 1978. 303 p. LC 79-103877.

Sidney-Fryer's immense bibliography includes practically anything any scholar might want to know about this well-regarded American poet and fantasy writer, but its size, complexity, and lack of an index make it unnecessarily difficult to use. Contents: "Introduction"; "Acknowledgements"; "Principal Facts of Biography"; "Collections"; "Clark Ashton Smith—In Memory of a Great Friendship," by Eric Barker; "Poems"; "Poems in French"; "Poems in Spanish"; "Translations of Poems: From the French, From the Spanish"; "Prose Translations of Verse"; "Contents of Poetry Collections"; "Uncollected Poems"; "Appearances of Poems in Anthologies," etc.; "Poems in Prose"; "Collections of Poems in Prose"; "Tales"; "Addendum"; "Contents of Prose Collections"; "Uncollected Tales"; "Appearances of Tales in Anthologies"; "Epigrams and Pensées"; "Miscellaneous Prose"; "Juvenilia"; "Periodicals"; "Published Letters"; "*The Auburn Journal* and *Weird Tales*"; "About Clark Ashton Smith"; "Library Holdings of Smith Mss."; "Pseudonyms"; "Five Approaches to the Achievements of Clark Ashton Smith—Cosmic Master Artist," by Marvin R. Hiemstra; "Index to First Lines of Poems"; "The Sorcerer Departs," by Clark Ashton Smith. Also included are fourteen tribute or biographical letters from well-known writers and/or friends of Smith and eight pages of photographs.

Shorter works are arranged alphabetically by title, chapter by chapter; monographs are organized in chronological order by date of publication. A typical shorter work entry includes title (bold caps), date of composition, magazine title, month and year of publication, plus a list of books in which the story or poem has been collected or anthologized (giving book title [all caps] and year only). No paginations are included for magazine publication of shorter works. A typical book entry includes title (bold caps), publisher, place of publication, year, pagination, cover artist, price, format (e.g., "paperbacked"), number of copies printed, and an exact collation of the contents. Reprints are interfiled by publication year; see references refer the reader back to the original edition but not forward *from* the original. Some foreign-language materials are included. The list of secondary sources is excellent as far as it goes; materials are arranged chronologically by year of publication. The volume is beautifully designed and printed, as is customary with Don Grant's books, and bound to library standards.

However, although Sidney-Fryer clearly knows his material well and includes an enormous amount of carefully gathered data, the absence of an index is fatal to what could have been *the* standard book on Smith. The complicated format makes immediate access to any particular title almost impossible without extensive reading of the text. A reorganized and updated version would clearly be desirable.

Cordwainer Smith

420. Bennett, Mike. **A Cordwainer Smith Checklist**. Polk City, Ia., Chris Drumm Books, 1991. [28] p. index. (Drumm Booklet #37). ISBN 0-936055-49-9 (pbk.).

Under his real name, Paul M. A. Linebarger, Smith was a well-known intelligence officer and political scientist; his science-fiction works have long been praised for their insights into war, politics, and sociology. This new checklist organizes the author's works into two sections covering his SF output as Cordwainer Smith and his real-life career as political scientist and novelist as Linebarger, "Felix C. Forrest," and "Carmichael Smith."

In each section materials are arranged chronologically by publication date. A typical monograph entry includes item number, title (in quotes, underlined), type (e.g., "n"=novel), contents (referring to other item numbers), publisher, stock number, month and year of publication, pagination, price, and similar data for all known reprints. A typical shorter work entry gives item number, title (in quotes), magazine title (underlined), month and year of publication, specific pagination, and similar data for all known reprints, including the author's own collections. Reprints in anthologies note anthology title (underlined), editor's name, publisher, year of publication, and specific pagination. Books and stories are interfiled in their respective sections; materials in the first section are numbered from 1 to 43, and in the section half from 1 to 24. There are separate indexes for each section, correlating titles and item numbers. The booklet is shot from legible typed copy and bound with staples into limp paper covers. A one-page addenda runs on the last page of text.

This guide will provide a good starting point for all future scholarship on this intriguing writer. Future editions should attempt to include secondary sources and should combine the indexes into one straightforward list.

Margaret St. Clair

421. Benson, Gordon, Jr. **Margaret St. Clair**. Albuquerque, N.M., Galactic Central Publications, 1986. 10 p. (Galactic Central Bibliographies for the Avid Reader, Vol. 15). ISBN 0-912613-16-5 (pbk.).

Margaret St. Clair wrote numerous science fiction stories and novels during the 1940s-'60s. Benson's checklist arranges her work by subject category, then alphabetically by title. Contents: Author's full name, date and place of birth, and pseudonyms; "A. The Stories"; "B. The Books"; "C. The 'Oona & Jik' Series." In each part the material is arranged in alphabetical order by title, the author's works being numbered anew from one in each section. A typical short fiction includes item number, title, category ("ss"=short story, "nt"=novelette, etc.), magazine or book in which the item appeared, month and year of publication (for magazines in the form "1-60" for January 1960), or year of publication (for books), plus a list of subsequent reprints (for which title, editor's last name, publisher, and year are given), but no paginations. A typical book entry provides item number, title (in caps), publication data (publisher, stock number, month and year of publication [if known, in the form "10-59" for October 1959], pagination, price, with dates of reissues by the same publisher), cover artist. Collections include contents lists referenced to the item numbers in the first section. There are no indexes or secondary sources. Coverage is complete through early 1986.

The early books in this series were shot from typed copy, with some of the text running into the right margin, making potential rebinding of these volumes impossible for libraries. The inclusion of an index, secondary sources, and short fiction paginations would be desirable additions to future editions. Note: this volume has not yet been reorganized into the new series format.

Olaf Stapledon

422. Satty, Harvey J., and Curtis C. Smith. **Olaf Stapledon: A Bibliography**. Westport, Conn., London, Greenwood Press, 1984. xxxviii, 167 p. index. (Bibliographies and Indexes in World Literature, No. 2). LC 84-6549. ISBN 0-313-24099-X.

This very well-organized and comprehensive bibliography of the English SF writer and philosopher's work is a major contribution to the scholarship of the genre. Contents: "Preface"; "Acknowledgments"; "Abbreviations"; "Location Symbols"; "Introduction"; "The Peak and the Town," by Olaf Stapledon; "A. Books and Pamphlets"; "AA. Omnibus Collections and Complete Novel Reprints"; "B. Contributions to Books and Pamphlets"; "BB. Reprinted Contributions to Books"; "C. Contributions to Periodicals and Newspapers"; "CC. Reprinted Contributions to Periodicals"; "D. Contributions to Periodicals, Newspapers, and Pamphlets in Collaboration with Others"; "E. Manuscripts of Published Writings in Public Archives"; "EE. Manuscripts of Unpublished Writings in Public Archives"; "F. Translations"; "G. Bibliographies"; "Selected Secondary Bibliography"; "Addenda"; "Index."

Each section is arranged chronologically by date of publication, Stapledon's works being numbered consecutively from one in each chapter (e.g., A1, A2, A3, etc., for books). A typical book entry includes item number, title (all caps), exact transcriptions of title page, copyright page, and cover or jacket copy, collation, contents collation, typography, paper and binding details, month of publication, price, number of copies printed, exact physical proportions of the book and jacket in millimeters, plus a list of libraries known to have copies (vastly incomplete) as taken from the *National Union Catalog*, and other notes. Similar data are provided for all known issues and binding states. A typical shorter work contribution to periodicals includes title (in quotes), magazine title (italics), volume and issue number, year and month of publication, pagination, plus some subject annotations. Contributions to books include data similar to the books section. Reprints appear in separate sections, with see references back to the original listings. The guide to Stapledon's manuscripts will prove most useful to scholars, and the list of secondary sources, although noted as selective, seems very complete. All internal references and the index correlate the data with item number only. The book is shot from very clear word-processed copy and bound to library standards. Data are complete through early 1984.

Satty and Smith have provided an immeasurable resource here, one that will benefit students of Stapledon's work for generations to come. The data are well presented, easily accessible, and very complete. Kudos to both authors for this excellent bibliographic guide.

Bram Stoker

423. Dalby, Richard. **Bram Stoker: A Bibliography of First Editions**. London, Dracula Press, 1983. [xii], 81 p. index. LC 84-242632. ISBN 0-7212-0643-4 (pbk.).

Dalby's brief but valuable guide to this English horror writer's work contains "Quest for Stoker" (Dalby's informative introduction); [The Books]; "Articles, Short Stories, and Serials"; "Biographies of Bram Stoker"; "Index." Each section is arranged chronologically by date of publication. A typical book entry includes item number (consecutively from the beginning of this section), title (all caps), place of publication, publisher, year of publication, collation, binding details, and notes, including price, month of publication, and contents (for collections) or brief description (for novels). Similar data are provided for notable reprint editions. Many reproductions of the original title pages of the books are also included, together with several drawings of Stoker from contemporary sources. Brief checklists are also included of Stoker's magazine publications (fiction and nonfiction in one chronological list) and of major biographies and miscellanea relating to Stoker and his best-known creation, Count Dracula. The index correlates titles and page numbers. Dalby's bibliography will provide a very good beginning point for students of this popular author's works; a revised edition should add a more comprehensive list of secondary sources and pastiches.

Theodore Sturgeon

424. Diskin, Lahna F. **Theodore Sturgeon: A Primary and Secondary Bibliography**. Boston, G. K. Hall, 1980. xxvii, 105 p. index. (Masters of Science Fiction and Fantasy). LC 79-18120. ISBN 0-8161-8046-6.

This early volume in the Masters series by the author of a critical monograph on Sturgeon covers the works of the late American SF and fantasy writer. Contents: "Preface"; "Primary and Secondary Source Documents"; "Abbreviations"; "Theodore Sturgeon: Toward a Chronology"; "Introduction"; "Part A: Science Fiction"; "Part B: Miscellaneous Media"; "Part C: Nonfiction"; "Part D: Critical Studies"; and six separate indexes.

Diskin's introduction provides a brief critical introduction to Sturgeon's work. The bibliography is arranged chronologically, from the earliest published material to the latest, and numbered consecutively (e.g., A1, A2, A3, etc., for fictional works). Books and shorter works are interfiled. Each book entry gives title, place of publication, publisher, but no paginations. Reprints of books are listed chronologically under the main entry, with place of publication, publisher, year of publication, and format (e.g., "paper"). Story collections include complete contents listings, plus the years in which the first stories were published. Shorter works published originally in magazines give title (in quotations), magazine code (full title is given in the abbreviations list at the front of the book; some codes are not obvious), month of publication (in parentheses), and pagination; those published originally in books give title (in quotations), editor, book title, place of publication, publisher, format, and pagination. Reprints of stories are listed under the main entry, chronologically by year of reprint, with the editor of the anthology, title, place of publication, publisher, year, format (e.g., "paper"), and paginations. Some entries include bibliographical notes but no other annotations.

Part B includes radio, television, and stage plays and some comic book adaptations and audio recordings. Section C lists all nonfiction works by the author, with occasional annotations. Part D lists 116 secondary works, including published book reviews, critiques, and bibliographies, with author, title, bibliographical data, and extensive subject annotations. The six indexes correlate the data by item number only; they include a general index to

Sturgeon's works, separate indexes for each of the four sections, and a rearrangement of the book reviews covered in Section D by the title of the Sturgeon book being reviewed. Unlike most later books in this series, this volume is attractively typeset and is bound to library standards.

Data are complete through 1978; since Sturgeon had largely stopped writing fiction by 1975 and has now died, Diskin's book remains relatively current, lacking only a handful of the author's last essays, reprints, and additional critical works. A definitive revision and updating would certainly be justified, but until then, this bibliography will provide students and scholars with plenty of access points to Sturgeon's writings.

425. Stephensen-Payne, Phil, and Gordon Benson, Jr. **Theodore Sturgeon, Sculptor of Love and Hate: A Working Bibliography.** Leeds, West Yorkshire, England & Albuquerque, N.M., Galactic Central Publications, 1989. 9, 75 p. (Galactic Central Bibliographies for the Avid Reader, Vol. 32). (pbk.).

Stephensen-Payne and Benson's bibliography covers works by and about American SF writer Sturgeon. Contents: Author's full name, dates of birth and death, awards, and pseudonyms; "A. Stories"; "B. Fiction Books"; "C. Series"; "D. Poems and Songs"; "E. Poem and Song Collections" ("none known"); "F. Articles"; "G. Miscellaneous" (including reviews, editorships, forewords, interviews, introductions, etc.); "H. Non-Fiction Books" ("none known"); "I. Books Edited by Theodore Sturgeon" ("none known"); "J. Media Presentations"; "K. Articles on Theodore Sturgeon"; "L. Reviews [of Sturgeon's books]"; "M. Books About Theodore Sturgeon"; "N. Phantom Titles and Editions"; "O. Related Items by Other Authors" ("none known"); "Textual Variations" ("no details known"); "Chronological Index."

Materials in each section are arranged alphabetically by title and numbered anew from one, prefixed by the appropriate letter code for that chapter. A typical book entry gives item number, title (all caps), contents (keyed to item number), publisher, format (e.g., "pb"=paperback), stock number, month and year of publication (in the form "12-66" for December 1966), pagination, price, cover artist, and similar data for all known reprints. A typical shorter work entry includes item number, title, type (e.g., "NA"=novella), magazine title, month and year of publication (in the form "1-58" for January 1958), pseudonym (where applicable), and similar data for all known reprints, including the author's own books. Stories appearing in anthologies give book title (all caps), editor's surname, publisher, and year of publication. No paginations are listed for short fictions. Ninety-seven secondary sources are listed and about a hundred book reviews, arranged alphabetically by title of the book being reviewed, then alphabetically by magazine title. The book is shot from very clear word-processed copy and bound with staples into paper covers. Data are complete through the end of 1988.

In comparing this bibliography with Diskin's (see #424), Stephensen-Payne and Benson's volume is a decade more current and includes book paginations which Diskin's work lacks (but lacks the story paginations which Diskin's work includes) and lists more secondary works. Researchers and libraries will want access to both volumes; fans will find Stephensen-Payne and Benson's guide more than adequate.

Thomas Burnett Swann

426. Collins, Robert A. **Thomas Burnett Swann: A Brief Critical Biography and Annotated Bibliography.** Boca Raton, Fla., Thomas Burnett Swann Fund, College of Humanities, Florida Atlantic University, 1979. [ii], 29 p. (pbk.).

American academic and novelist Thomas Burnett Swann died at the age of forty-seven in 1976; this booklet was intended as a memorial to the man and his work. Collins's eighteen-page introduction provides an excellent biographical and critical background on Swann the writer and teacher. The bibliography proper (Collins acknowledges Roehm's conributions; see #427) is arranged in one chronological sequence, year by year, and then by month. A typical book entry includes title (in italics), category (e.g., "novel," in parentheses), place of publication, publisher, pagination, contents (for collections), one paragraph of plot summary (averaging four sentences), and a list of reviews (with reviewer, magazine title, issue number, date, pagination). A typical shorter work entry provides title (in quotes), category (e.g., "novelette," in parentheses), magazine title (italics), volume and issue number, month and year of publication, pagination, and plot summary (two or three sentences). Some translations are also included, with foreign-language titles and translators, in addition to other data. A chronological table of Swann's fictional worlds is provided by Bob Roehm. The absence of an index in this brief bibliography is unnoticeable. The book is beautifully typeset and produced and serves generally as an excellent introductory guide to Swann's writings.

427. Roehm, Bob. **A Thomas Burnett Swann Bibliography.** Rev. ed. Clarksville, Ind., Bob Roehm, 1978 (originally 1976). [4] p., plus one-page supplement. (pbk.).

This brief checklist of the late American fantasy writer's works is arranged by category ("Short Fiction," "Novels & Collections," "Poetry," "Non-Fiction," "Anthology Appearances," "and "Foreign Publications"), then chronologically by publication date. Shorter work entries include title (in quotes), magazine title (underlined), and month and year of publication (British magazines include issue numbers). Book entries include title (underlined), references to magazine serializations and original titles (if any), contents, publisher, year of publication, cover artist. No paginations are included. An unnumbered one-page insert supplements the original, with data complete through the end of 1977. The booklet is shot from clear typed copy. Now subsumed into Collins's bibliography (see #426).

William Tenn

428. Benson, Gordon, Jr. **William Tenn (Philip Klass).** Albuquerque, N.M., Galactic Central Publications, 1987. 7 p. (Galactic Central Bibliographies for the Avid Reader, Vol. 7). (pbk.).

This brief checklist of the American author's SF work is arranged by subject category, then alphabetically by title. Contents: Author's full name, date and place of birth, and pseudonyms; "A. The Stories"; "B. The Books"; "C. Books Edited" (two entries). The material is arranged in alphabetical order by title, category by category, the author's works being numbered anew from one in each section. A typical short fiction entry includes item number, title, category ("ss"=short story, "nt"= novelette, etc.), magazine or book in which the item appeared, month and year of publication (for magazines in the form "7-51" for July 1951) or year of publication (for books), plus a list of subsequent reprints (for which title, editor's last name, publisher, and year are given), but no paginations. A typical book entry provides item number, title (in caps), publication data (publisher, stock number, month and year of publication [if known, in the form "10-59" for October 1959], pagination, price, with dates of reissues by the same publisher), plus cover artist. Collections include lists of the stories collected, referenced to the item numbers in the first section. There are no indexes or secondary sources. Coverage is complete through 1987.

As with the other early volumes in this series, the book is shot from typed copy, and some of the text runs into the right margin, making potential rebinding by libraries very difficult. Since Tenn is now inactive as a fiction writer, Benson's bibliography is probably complete except for future reprintings of his stories and books. This guide has not yet been reworked into the new series format for the Galactic Central bibliographies.

James Tiptree, Jr.

429. Stephensen-Payne, Phil, and Gordon Benson, Jr. **James Tiptree, Jr., A Lady of Letters: A Working Bibliography**. Leeds, West Yorkshire, England & Albuquerque, N.M., Galactic Central, 1989. 9, 26 p. (Galactic Central Bibliographies for the Avid Reader, Vol. 31). (pbk.).

Tiptree, the professional name of the late Alice Sheldon, was one of the best regarded SF writers during her relatively brief career. This new guide to her work includes full name and dates of birth and death, awards, and pen names; "A. Stories"; "B. Fiction Books"; "C. Series" ("none known"); "D. Poems & Songs" ("none known"); "E. Poem & Song Collections" ("none known"); "F. Articles"; "G. Miscellaneous"; "H. Non-Fiction Books" ("none known"); "I. Edited Books" ("none known"); "J. Media Presentations"; "K. Articles on James Tiptree, Jr."; "L. Reviews" [of Tiptree's books]; "M. Books About James Tiptree, Jr."; "N. Phantom Titles"; "O. Related Books by Other Authors" ("none known"); "P. Textual Variations" ("no details known"); "Q. Chronological Index."

In each section, materials are arranged alphabetically by title and numbered from one, chapter by chapter, with the appropriate letter prefix. A typical story entry includes item number, title, type (e.g., "NT"=novelette), magazine title and month and year of publication (in the form "12-85" for December 1985), or (for stories appearing in anthologies) book title (all caps), editor's last name, publisher, and year of publication, plus similar data for all known reprints. No paginations are listed for shorter works. A typical monograph entry records item number, title (all caps), contents (where applicable, with materials listed by item number), publisher, format ("hb"=hardback), stock number, month and year of publication (in the form "4-86" for April 1986), pagination, price, and cover artist, plus similar information for all known reprint editions. Thirty-four secondary sources are noted and about thirty reviews of Tiptree's works. The book is shot from word-processed copy and bound with staples through the spine into paper covers. Data are included through 1988.

Tiptree died in 1987, so this guide will likely remain current for quite some time. Future editions should add short fiction paginations and a comprehensive index.

J. R. R. Tolkien

430. Johnson, Judith A. **J. R. R. Tolkien: Six Decades of Criticism**. Westport, Conn. & London, Greenwood Press, 1986. viii, 266 p. index. (Bibliographies and Indexes in World Literature, No. 6). LC 85-27248. ISBN 0-313-25005-7.

This annotated checklist of Tolkien's work and Tolkien criticism is a good example of valuable research buried beneath a terrible format. Contents: "Preface"; "Introduction"; "Chapter I: The First Three Decades, 1922-1953"; "II: The Fourth Decade, 1954-1963"; "III. The Fifth Decade, 1964-1973"; "IV. The Sixth Decade, 1974-1984"; "V. The Future"; "Appendix: Tolkien-Related Organizations, Societies, and Publications"; "Index of Critics"; "Index of Tolkien's Works and Critical Response to Them." Each of the four main chapters is further subdivided into two sections: "A. Works by Tolkien"; "B. Critical Response" (by far the larger portion of the book). Works by Tolkien are arranged in each chapter alphabetically by title.

A typical book entry includes item number, title (underlined), place of publication, publisher, year of publication. Shorter works (interfiled with books) record item number, title (in quotes), magazine (underlined), volume and issue number, month and year of publication, pagination; shorter works published in books include item number, title (quotes), book title (underlined), editor, place of publication, publisher, year of publication, pagination. The 1,649 secondary works are listed chronologically, year by year, then alphabetically by main entry (usually critic), and provide similar information. Tolkien's works are numbered consecutively from A1; secondary sources consecutively from B1. The indexes correlate critics and item numbers; and Tolkien's works, critics, and item numbers (the latter index provides a very useful guide to what the critics have said about specific Tolkien novels or stories). The book is shot from typed copy and bound to library standards.

Astonishingly, however, there is no general index to secondary source titles, making it extraordinarily difficult to locate a specific work if the critic in question has been at all prolific; for example, under Richard West, author of the book listed below (see #431), one finds some fifteen items, none distinguishable from each other without separate examination. Even worse is the division of data into annual components, a particularly bad choice for the arrangement of secondary sources. Instead of having one (or even four) places to search for materials about Tolkien, we are left with dozens of mini-bibliographies crammed into one book. Thus, despite Johnson's plethora of material, her book is virtually impossible to access without hours to dig out the data. An English Department chairperson should know better. Compare with West's guide (see #431).

431. West, Richard C. **Tolkien Criticism: An Annotated Checklist**. Kent, Ohio, Kent State University Press, 1970. xv, 73 p. index. (The Serif Series: Bibliographies and Checklists, No. 11). LC 71-626235. ISBN 0-87338-052-5. **Tolkien Criticism: An Annotated Checklist**. Rev. ed. Kent, Ohio, Kent State University Press, 1981. xiv, 177 p. index. (The Serif Series: Bibliographies and Checklists, No. 39). LC 81-8135. ISBN 0-87338-256-0.

West's checklist of publications by and about this popular British fantasy writer and academic includes (revised edition) "Introduction"; "List of Abbreviations"; "I. Tolkien's Writings, Arranged Chronologically"; "II. Critical Works on Tolkien"; "III. Book Reviews: A. Reviews of Tolkien's Writings"; "B. Reviews of Critical Works on Tolkien"; "IV. Indexes: A. Tolkien's Writings, Arranged by Title"; "B. Anthologies, Books, Monographs on Tolkien, Arranged by Author"; "C. Critical Works on Tolkien, Arranged by Title"; "D. Doctoral Dissertations and Master's Theses"; "E. Tolkien-Related Groups and Publications." Materials in Part I are arranged in chronological order by year of publication; those in Part II are arranged in alphabetical order by name of critic; "Book Reviews" in Part III is arranged in alphabetical order by title of the book being reviewed, then alphabetically by critic (with see references to the more complete entries in section II). Items in each section are consecutively numbered anew from one (e.g., II-1, II-2, II-3, etc., for Part II); the indexes coordinate titles and item numbers only.

Section I covers all of Tolkien's known writings, fiction and nonfiction, monographs and short pieces, through 1980. A typical book entry includes item number, title (in italics), place of publication, publisher, year of publication, but no paginations, and a short annotation. A typical shorter work entry provides item number, title (in quotes), magazine (italics), volume and issue number, month and year of publication, pagination, and a short annotation; shorter works appearing in books include item number, title (in quotes), book title (italics), editor, place of publication, publisher, year of publication, pagination, short annotation. Similar data are included for the 755 secondary sources, except that the annotations tend to be longer and more analytical. The book is nicely designed and typeset and bound to library standards.

Compared to Johnson's guide (see #430), the latter includes more entries but fewer annotations and is more current; however, Johnson's peculiar format makes finding material in her book considerably more difficult than in West. Thus, neither book now has a decided advantage over the other, but any new edition of West would probably be preferable. It is astonishing to note, however, that two such major Tolkien bibliographies by self-acknowledged experts cannot supply even basic bibliographical details such as the paginations for Tolkien's famous *Lord of the Rings* Trilogy or a complete listing of all English-language printings (though West does mention several paperback editions), not to mention foreign-language materials. *O bibliographia, O mores!*

Wilson Tucker

432. Benson, Gordon, Jr. **Arthur Wilson "Bob" Tucker**. Albuquerque, N.M., Galactic Central Publications, 1985. 5 p. (Galactic Central Bibliographies for the Avid Reader, Vol. 8). ISBN 0-912613-19-X (pbk.).

Wilson Tucker wrote a number of interesting SF and mystery stories and novels during a thirty-five-year period beginning in the 1940s. This new checklist of his work is arranged by subject category, then alphabetically by title. Contents: Author's full name, date and place of birth, pseudonyms, and list of awards; "A. The Stories"; "B. The SF Books"; "C. Mystery Books"; "D. Miscellaneous." In each section materials are arranged alphabetically by title, the author's works being numbered anew from one in each part. A typical short fiction entry includes item number, title, category ("ss"=short story, "nt"=novelette, etc.), magazine or book in which the item appeared, month and year of publication (for magazines in the form "10-59" for October 1959) or year of publication (for books), plus a list of subsequent reprints (for which title, editor's last name, publisher, and year are given), but no paginations. A typical book entry provides item number, title (in caps), publication data (publisher, LC card number, stock number, month and year of publication [if known, in the form "10-59" for October 1959], pagination, price, with dates of reissues by the same publisher), cover artist. There are no indexes; Section D includes just a handful of secondary sources, all of them minor. None of Tucker's many fan publications (most under the name "Bob Tucker") are listed. Coverage is complete through April 1985.

The early books in this series were shot from typed copy, with some text running into the right margin, making potential rebinding difficult at best. Future editions should include an index, story paginations, contents for Tucker's several story collections, more secondary sources, and as many of his fan articles and edited fanzines as can be located. This guide has not yet been reformatted into the revised series style.

433. Stephens, Christopher P. **A Checklist of Wilson Tucker**. Hastings-on-Hudson, N.Y., Ultramarine Publishing Co., 1991. 13 p. index. ISBN 0-89366-211-9 (pbk.).

Tucker is best known for his time-travel novels. Stephens's checklist records Tucker's monographs in chronological order by publication date, books being numbered consecutively from one. A typical entry provides year (as a floating head), item number, title (underlined), pseudonym, publisher, stock or ISBN number, pagination, format (e.g., "cloth with dust wrapper"), cover illustrator, price, and similar data for all known reprints (which are numbered, for example, A2a, A2b, A2c, etc., in descending order by publication date). The chapbook is shot from legible typed copy and bound with staples in stiff paper covers. The index correlates titles with years of publication only. Stephens's brief guide is more current than Benson's (see #432) but provides very little additional data; Benson's revision, when published, will undoubtedly be preferred by researchers and librarians.

Jack Vance

434. Levack, Daniel J. H., and Tim Underwood. **Fantasms: A Bibliography of the Literature of Jack Vance**. San Francisco and Columbia, Penn., Underwood/Miller, 1978. 91 p. cloth and pbk. Cockrum, Kurt, Daniel J. H. Levack, and Tim Underwood. **Fantasms II: A Bibliography of the Literature of Jack Vance**. [Rev. ed.]. Riverside, Calif., Kurt Cockrum, 1979. vi, 99 p. (paper printout).

Levack has produced a series of similary formatted bibliographies on de Camp, Dick, Herbert, and Zelazny (see #321, #326, #347, #455). All are attractive books, but all also lack paginations, indexes, and secondary sources. Contents: "Introduction"; "Books"; "Notes on Books"; "Stories"; "Series and Connected Stories"; "Pseudonyms"; "Chronological Order of Publications of Vance's Work"; "Television Appearances"; "Acknowledgments."

Materials are listed alphabetically by title and numbered consecutively from one in each section, with some 150 total items included. A typical book entry includes item number, title (bold caps), series (when appropriate) or category (e.g., "Mystery"), manuscript title (if different), byline (if under some other name than Jack Vance), contents (if a collection), publisher, stock number (for paperback editions), place of publication (not included for paperbacks), year of publication, format (e.g., "paper"). Reprints are listed in chronological order by publication date; some foreign editions are included, with foreign-language titles, but no translators. A typical shorter work entry includes item number, title (in quotes), estimated wordage, series note, magazine or book title, month and year of publication; stories in anthologies include title, editor, publisher, place of publication, year of publication, but no paginations. All subsequent reprint editions (including Vance's own collection) are listed in chronological order beneath the first printing of each story, with similar data. The series index and chronological checklist of Vance's writings are both useful guides to the writer's work. Materials are included through early 1978.

The book is beautifully typeset and designed and is illustrated throughout with reproductions of book and magazine covers featuring Vance's novels and stories. Unfortunately, despite its attractive appearance, this volume lacks such basic features as an index, story and book paginations, and secondary sources, making it much less the standard source it should have become. Prefer Stephensen-Payne and Benson's bibliography (see #435).

435. Stephensen-Payne, Phil, and Gordon Benson, Jr. **Jack Vance, a Fantasmic Imagination: A Working Bibliography**. 2nd rev. ed. Leeds, West Yorkshire, England & Albuquerque, N.M., Galactic Central Publications, 1990. 9, 61 p. (Galactic Central Bibliographies for the Avid Reader, Vol. 28). ISBN 1-871133-02-5 (pbk.).

Vance is a well-regarded American SF and mystery writer whose exotic characters and worlds have long been regarded with affection by aficionados. Stephensen-Payne and Benson's volume contains author's full name, date and place of birth, awards won, and pseudonyms; "A. Stories"; "B. Fiction Books"; "C. Series"; "D. Poems & Songs"; "E. Poem & Song Collections" ("none known"); "F." Articles"; "G. Miscellaneous"; "H. Non-Fiction Books" ("none known"); "I. Books Edited by Jack Vance" ("none known"); "J. Media Presentations"; "K. Articles on Jack Vance"; "L. Reviews" [of Vance's works]; "M. Books

About Jack Vance"; "N. Phantom and Forthcoming Titles"; "O. Textual Variations" ("no details known"); "P. Related Items by Other Authors"; "Q. Chronological Index."

In each part the author's works are arranged alphabetically by title and numbered anew from one, with the appropriate letter prefix. A typical short fiction entry includes item number, title, category ("ss"=short story, "nt"=novelette, etc.), magazine or book in which the item appeared, month and year of publication (for magazines in the form "12-50" for December 1950) or year of publication (for books), plus a list of subsequent reprints (for which title, editor's last name, publisher, and year are given), but no paginations. A typical book entry provides item number, title (all caps), publication data (publisher, stock number, month and year of publication [if known, in the form "10-59" for October 1959], pagination, price, with dates of reissues by the same publisher), cover artist, and similar data for all known reprint editions. Collections include lists of the stories referenced to the item numbers in the first section. The secondary sources chapter records eighty-two fan and professional books and articles and roughly 250 book reviews. Coverage is complete through early 1990. The text is shot from very legible word-processed copy and bound with staples into paper covers.

Levack *et al.*'s guide (see #434) is more attractively designed, with numerous cover reproductions, and it also includes some data (chiefly foreign-language reprints and estimated word counts) not found in the later work. In every other respect, however, *Jack Vance, a Fantasmic Imagination* is more current, complete, and bibliographically sound and should be preferred by both librarians and researchers alike.

Jules Verne

436. Gallagher, Edward J., Judith A. Mistichelli, and John A. Van Eerde. **Jules Verne: A Primary and Secondary Bibliography**. Boston, G. K. Hall, 1980. xxi, 387 p. index. (Masters of Science Fiction and Fantasy). LC 80-20206. ISBN 0-8161-8106-3.

Verne has always been a particularly difficult writer to track, because so many of his works were either reworked, cut, divided, or retitled for their English-language editions, the same novel going through many differing reincarnations from various American and British publishers. This carefully researched bibliography of both the author's French and English editions is the first real guide to his work ever published in English, and as such, it will be heartily welcomed both by scholars and students of this seminal French SF writer.

Contents: "Preface"; "Introduction"; "Abbreviations"; "Part A: Fiction"; "Part B: Miscellaneous Media"; "Part C: Nonfiction"; "Part D: Critical Studies in English"; "Part E: Critical Studies in French"; "Index to Verne's Work"; "Index to Critical Studies." The introduction provides a brief biographical and critical evaluation of Verne. The bibliography proper is arranged chronologically, from the earliest published material to the latest, items being numbered consecutively in each section from one (e.g., A1, A2, A3, etc., for Verne's fiction). Books and shorter works are interfiled; reprint editions of books are listed under the first edition in chronological order by publication date; both French- and English-language printings are included, with appropriate titles, but many paperback editions are omitted. A typical monograph entry gives item number, title (underlined), place of publication, publisher, but no paginations.

Shorter works published originally in magazines include item number, title (in quotes), magazine (underlined), volume number, date, but no paginations. Reprints of stories are listed under the main entry, chronologically by year of reprint, with the editor of the anthology, title, place of publication, publisher, year, format (e.g., "paper"), but no paginations. Story collections include complete contents listings plus the item numbers of the original stories (if published previously).

Part B includes mostly plays and songs (twenty-one items). Part C includes all known nonfiction works by the author, with occasional annotations (thirty-two items). Parts D and E, covering secondary works, make up the greater part of the book, providing an immense resource for the scholar, listing some 450 sources in English and almost 900 in French, including complete bibliographical data and extensive subject annotations. The indexes reference titles, authors (of critical works), and item numbers only, ensuring quick access to the material. Coverage is complete through 1979. The book is shot from legible typed copy and bound to library standards.

This is perhaps the most bibliographically significant book in the entire fourteen-volume Masters series, a long-overdue guide to Verne's many works: well-conceived and -executed, generally a first-rate piece of work. One laments, however, the lack of paginations for books, particularly when they are so hard to find for many of Verne's novels, both originals and translations. A future edition should restore these missing data. Other than this minor *caveat*, *Jules Verne* is nearly flawless and should be on the shelves of every academic library in the country. Highly recommended.

437. Margot, Jean-Michel. **Bibliographie Documentaire sur Jules Verne: Catalogue par Mots-Clés et par Auteurs**. Paris, Société Jules Verne, 1978. 142 p. (pbk.). Also: Ostermundigen, Chez l'Auteur [i.e., published by the author], 1978. 4, 35, 21, 109, 8, 64 p. LC 79-365008 (pbk.).

This peculiarly arranged bibliography to secondary sources on or about French author Jules Verne quickly stumbles headlong over its own data. Contents: "Introduction"; "Nombre de Documents Publiés par Année"; "Catalogue par Mot-Clés"; "Catalogue par Auteurs"; "Catalogue par Cote"; "Oeuvres de Jules Verne"; "Thesaurus."

The first section, "Nombre de Documents," records 1,300 items in a statistical table, year by year, with a series of asterisks representing each item. The "Catalogue par Mot-Clés" indexes the documents section alphabetically by key word (e.g., "albatros"), correlating them with item numbers, and, at the end of this chapter, by year and item number. The "Catalogue par Auteurs" rearranges the data alphabetically by author surname and item number. The "Catalogue par Cote" records items in chronological order by publication name, numbering the materials consecutively from the number one. A typical entry includes item number, author's name (inverted), title, magazine title, month and year of publication, pagination, volume number, type (e.g., "article"), key words, and a series of two-letter codes referring to the specific Verne works mentioned in the book or essay. Monographic entries give item number, author (name inverted), title, place of publication, publisher, year of publication, pagination, type, key words, and letter codes. One thousand three hundred items are recorded in this largest (109-page) chapter of the volume.

The section "Oeuvres de Jules Verne" correlates the two-letter codes referencing the master's own publications, with title and type (e.g., "roman"). The "Thesaurus" correlates key words with other related, broader, or narrower terms, with other see references. Data are complete through 1978. The book is shot from primitive computer-generated copy, photoreduced from the original; parts of the documents section are often difficult to read or discern. This, combined with the overwrought design of the volume, should send the reader forthwith to the better-organized and much more reader-friendly bibliography by Gallagher *et al.* (see #436).

438. Myers, Edward, and Judith Myers. **A Bibliography of the First Printings of the Writings of Jules Verne in the English Language, Together with Information on Numerous Reprints, and a Key to Title Interpretation**. New Hartford, Conn., Country Lane Books, 1989. 68, [5] p., [6] p. of plates, plus [5]-page addendum. (pbk.).

This new guide to Verne's English-language editions is organized alphabetically by title (using the earliest known English-language title as a key). A typical entry gives item number, title (all caps, underlined), place of publication, publisher, year of publication, pagination, description of binding and dust jacket, series name and number (where appropriate), and other notes providing information necessary for discovering specific printings. Similar data are provided for all other early significant printings in the U.S. and U.K. The main entries of Verne's monographs are numbered consecutively from 1 to 60; subsidiary editions are unnumbered. A final entry records the "Collected Works of Jules Verne" (five different sets). End matter includes a brief bibliography of "Works about Jules Verne," and an "Index of Titles," correlated with item and page numbers. Five pages of addenda sheets are inserted loosely into the rear of the book. The plates and frontispiece display thirty-nine book covers in clear black-and-white reproductions, plus several illustrated title pages of early Verne editions. The bibliography itself is shot from sometimes faint typed copy and rather poorly bound in paper covers (sheets were coming loose from the binding on the specimen examined). Myers's guide will be useful primarily to collectors and book dealers; scholars and libraries should prefer Gallagher's more complete literary bibliography (see #436).

Karl Edward Wagner

439. Marek, Joe. **"Death Angel: A Bibliography of Karl Edward Wagner,"** in *One More Barbarian* 2 (Sept. 1979): 1-32.

This checklist of the American fantasy writer's work appeared as an entire single issue of a fan magazine. Contents: "Foreword"; "Books"; "Fiction"; "Poetry"; "Non-Fiction"; "Series Index"; "Index to Periodicals"; "About the Author"; "One Letter" (from Wagner); "Afterword." Wagner's books are listed chronologically by year of publication. A typical entry includes title (all caps), publisher, place of publication, month and year of publication, pagination, price, format (e.g., "paperbound"), stock number and/or ISBN, printing size, cover artist; similar data are provided on all known reprint editions, including some foreign, with foreign-language titles and translators. The rest of the primary bibliography is arranged section by section in alphabetical order by title. A typical shorter work entry includes title, magazine title (italics), volume and issue number, month and year of publication, but no paginations; shorter works appearing in books include title, book title (italicized), publisher, editor, year of publication, but no paginations. All known reprint editions (including some foreign) are listed in chronological order under the original publication data. Secondary sources in the "About the Author" section are arranged by main entry (usually critic) and include mostly book reviews and fan commentary, with similar bibliographical data. The two indexes (to series and works appearing in periodicals, by periodical name) are useful but do not substitute for a full title index. There are a dozen reproductions of Wagner covers and other fan illustrations, but the 8.5" x 11" booklet is so badly mimeographed that many of the covers are faint (as is part of the text). A one-sheet insertion page includes material through early 1980. An updated, more professionally produced version of this bibliography would definitely be warranted.

Evangeline Walton

Zahorski, Kenneth J., and Robert H. Boyer. **Lloyd Alexander, Evangeline Walton Ensley, Kenneth Morris: A Primary and Secondary Bibliography**. *See the entry for Lloyd Alexander (see #268).*

Ian Watson

440. Mackey, Douglas A. **The Work of Ian Watson: An Annotated Bibliography & Guide**. San Bernardino, Calif., The Borgo Press, 1989. 148 p. index. (Bibliographies of Modern Authors, No. 18). LC 88-36646. ISBN 0-8095-0512-6; ISBN 0-8095-1512-1 (pbk.).

British writer Watson has produced a number of interesting philosophical SF novels over the past two decades; this is the first published bibliography on his work. Contents: Introduction: "Elementary Watson" (by Mackey); "An Ian Watson Chronology"; "A. Books"; "B. Short Fiction"; "C. Nonfiction"; "D. Letters"; "E. Poetry"; "F. Campaign Literature"; "G. Other Media"; "H. Unpublished Manuscripts"; "I. Awards"; "J. Editorial Posts"; "K. Public Appearances"; "L. Interviews"; "M. About the Author"; "N. Miscellanea"; "Quoth the Critics"; Afterword: "Dancing on a Tightrope," by Watson; "Index."

In each section, the author's works are arranged chronologically and numbered consecutively from one, chapter by chapter, with the appropriate letter prefix. A typical monographic entry includes item number, title (boldface), place of publication, publisher, month and year of publication, pagination, format (e.g., "paper"), type of publication (e.g., "collection"), and full bibliographical data on all known reprint editions and translations, including foreign, with foreign-language titles and translators. The books are fully annotated, with complete contents listings and/or plot summaries and other pertinent data; entries from other sections are selectively annotated as needed. Each book entry also includes all known secondary sources and reviews, arranged in alphabetical order by critic, with complete bibliographical data.

A typical shorter work entry includes item number, title (bold quotes), magazine title (in italics), volume number, month and year of publication, pagination, and similar data on all known reprints. Reprints in anthologies include title (italics), editor, place of publication, publisher, year of publication, format (e.g., "cloth"), pagination. Mackey's short introduction provides an excellent critical introduction to the author's work, one that is certain to be cited by all future critics. The chronology provides a year-by-year account of the author's professional and personal life, in block paragraph format. "About the Author" includes all known secondary works except individual reviews of specific titles, which are listed in Section A under those works. The "Miscellanea" section lists "Books Dedicated to Ian Watson," with complete bibliographical data and verbatim transcriptions of the dedications; "Library Holdings of Ian Watson's Papers"; "Memberships"; and Library of Congress cataloging data. "Quoth the Critics" includes selected excerpts of reviews and other comments by leading critics on the author's work. Watson's concluding essay, original to this book, provides a fascinating autobiographical glimpse into the author's life and politics (Watson has been a Labour Party candidate for local council offices). The index correlates titles and item numbers only. Coverage is complete through mid-1989. The book is nicely typeset and bound to library standards.

This is an excellently conceived and compiled bibliography by a well-known critic who clearly sympathizes with his subject. The format is spacious and easy to access, the data complete and well organized. With publication of this volume, the Bibliographies of Modern Authors series is beginning to develop into the most consistently *realized* and complete set of bibliographical tools currently available on individual science fiction and fantasy authors.

Manly Wade Wellman

441. Benson, Gordon, Jr. **Manly Wade Wellman, the Gentleman from Chapel Hill: A Memorial Working Bibliography.** Albuquerque, N.M., Galactic Central Publications, 1986. 18 p. (Galactic Central Bibliographies for the Avid Reader, Vol. 17). (pbk.).

Manly Wade Wellman (1903-1986), brother of well-known historical novelist Paul I. Wellman, was a science-fiction and fantasy writer who began writing during the pulp era. This new checklist arranges his writings by subject category, then alphabetically by title. Contents: Author's full name, date and place of birth and death, pseudonyms, awards won, abbreviations used; "A. The Shorter Works"; "B. The Stories of Mrs. Manly Wade Wellman" (as Frances Garfield); "C. The Books of Fantasy and Science Fiction"; "D. The Mysteries"; "E. Juvenile Books"; "F. Non-Fiction and Miscellaneous" (adult); "G. Addenda" (there is also a section called "Further Addenda" on page 18). In each part the material is arranged by title, the author's works being numbered anew from one in each section. A typical short fiction entry includes item number, title, category ("ss"=short story, "nt"=novelette, etc.), magazine or book in which the item appeared, month and year of publication (for magazines in the form "12-40" for December 1940) or year of publication (for books), plus a list of subsequent reprints (for which title, editor's last name, publisher, and year are given), but no paginations. A typical book entry provides item number, title (in caps), series info, publication data (publisher, stock number, month and year of publication [if known, in the form "10-59" for October 1959], pagination, price, with dates of reissues by the same publisher), cover artist, and similar data on all known reprint editions. There are no indexes and only a minimal list of secondary sources (four items) in the "Miscellanea" section. Coverage is complete through 1986.

The book is shot from typed copy, and the text runs too close to the right-hand margin to allow potential rebinding of these volumes by libraries. Even with these defects, Benson's checklist remains the only detailed bibliographical guide to the author's work, an essential starting point for all future research on his fiction. A revised edition should include an index, contents listings for collections, magazine paginations, and a considerably expanded list of secondary materials. Note: this volume has not yet been revised into the new series format.

H. G. Wells

442. H. G. Wells Society. **H. G. Wells: A Comprehensive Bibliography.** Edgware, England, The H. G. Wells Society, 1966. viii, 61 p. LC 67-87305 (pbk.). **H. G. Wells: A Comprehensive Bibliography.** 2nd ed. London, H. G. Wells Society, 1968. vi, 69 p. LC 68-114049 (pbk.). **H. G. Wells: A Comprehensive Bibliography.** 3rd ed. London, H. G. Wells Society, 1972. vi, 74 p. LC 73-156022. ISBN 0-902291-65-3 (pbk.). **H. G. Wells: A Comprehensive Bibliography.** 4th ed. London, H. G. Wells Society, 1986. 58 p. ISBN 0-903592-08-8 (pbk.). The foreword to the fourth edition mentions that "this edition has been prepared by Patrick Parrinder, A. H. Watkins, and J. R. Hammond."

This brief but very handy guide to Wells's works is organized by broad subject chapters. In the fourth edition the first section, devoted to the author's monographs, is arranged chronologically by publication date. A typical book entry includes item number, year of publication (as a centered head), title (italicized), notes on illustrations, introductory material, etc., pagination, publisher, place of publication, binding height in centimeters, and a one-paragraph descriptive annotation, with notes referencing other significant tie-in editions. First editions only are described, and only partial contents are given for story collections. Section II covers posthumous works, also organized chronologically by publication date, and similar data. Part III lists Wells's short stories in the same order in which they appear in *The Complete Short Stories of H. G. Wells* (1927). A typical shorter work entry provides item number, title (in italics), magazine title (in single quotes), and month and year of original publication, but no paginations and no list of subsequent reprintings. Nineteen additional stories from the posthumous collection, *The Man with a Nose and Other Uncollected Stories of H. G. Wells*, are listed at the end of this section.

Part IV records the materials published in The Atlantic Edition of the Works of H. G. Wells (1924) in volume-number order. Section V, "Miscellaneous Writings of H. G. Wells" (mostly essays), is presented in chronological order by publication date, with similar data to Part III and no paginations; the second half of this section records prefaces by H. G. Wells in the works of other writers chronologically by date, giving item number, year of publication, author (in inverted order, surname in all caps), title, place of publication, publisher, but no paginations. Section VI covers biographies of Wells in book form, arranged alphabetically by main entry (usually author), with item number, author, title (in italics), publisher, and year of publication, but no paginations. Chapter VII lists "Bibliographies and Dictionaries," organized similarly to the previous section. Part VIII records "Other Writings on H. G. Wells" (critical monographs, but no articles), arranged similarly to the previous section but adding (for no apparent reason) pagination and volume size (measured in centimeters)—if these were regarded by the authors as worth noting for *some* secondary sources, why were they not included for all? The final chapter gives "Films, Radio, and Stage Productions During Wells's Lifetime," arranged chronologically by production date and listing item number, year of production, title (in italics), production company, producer's name, director's name, and principal actors; a brief note comments generally on film productions since 1946 but does not provide credits (another anomaly). A brief subsection mentions radio adaptations through 1946.

Materials are numbered consecutively throughout the book from 1 to 472. The index correlates titles and authors with item numbers but uses such small type (about a six-point level) that it is virtually unusable by anyone over the age of forty. The volume is professionally typeset and bound in paper covers. This bibliography will provide a useful introductory guide to Wells's works; although it does record three posthumous collections not mentioned in Hammond's more complete work (see #443), plus early media adaptations, the latter will still be preferred by most libraries and scholars.

443. Hammond, J. R. **Herbert George Wells: An Annotated Bibliography of His Works.** New York & London, Garland Publishing, 1977. xvi, 257 p. index. (Garland Reference Library of the Humanities, Vol. 84). LC 76-52667. ISBN 0-8240-9889-7.

John Hammond founded the H. G. Wells Society in 1960 and co-authored the checklist mentioned above (see #442). This comprehensive bibliography includes "Preface"; "Part One, Fiction": "A. Novels," "B. Romances," "C. Short Stories," "D. Essays"; "Part Two, Non-Fiction": "E. Books," "F. Pamphlets"; "Part Three, Collected Editions": "G. The Atlantic Edition," "H. Other Editions"; Part Four: "I. Posthumously Published Works"; Part Five: "J. Letters"; Part Six: "K. Books by Other Writers Containing Prefaces by Wells"; Part Seven: "L. Books by Other Writers Containing Contributions by Wells"; Part Eight: "M. Illustrations"; Appendices: "I. The Works of H. G. Wells, Chronologically Arranged"; "II.

Note on Unreprinted Writings"; "III. Critical, Biographical, and Bibliographical Studies"; "IV. Principal Collections of H. G. Wells Material"; "V. The H. G. Wells Society"; "Index."

In each section materials are arranged chronologically by publication date and numbered anew from one, the numbers being prefixed by the appropriate letter code associated with that chapter. A typical book entry includes item number, title, and year of publication as centered headings; exact title-page transcription; printing description, physical height of the volume (in centimeters), pagination, and detailed itemization of the contents; detailed description of the binding; mention of previous appearances and significant bibliographical variants in later publications; and other notes as needed. Unusually, the "Short Stories" section is organized around Wells's book collections, each entry providing complete contents listings in addition to the bibliographical data recorded in earlier chapters; but only item #C8, *The Short Stories of H. G. Wells* (1927), which collects together most of his short fiction into one volume, provides details of previous publications of these works, giving magazine title and month and year of publication for each but no specific paginations and certainly no coordinated list of the collections or anthologies into which each of these pieces has been gathered. Thirteen additional uncollected tales are mentioned at the end of C8, with previous publication data. This seems a very odd arrangement indeed.

The chapters recording Wells's contributions to other books provide item number and year of publication (centered heads), book title, author, publisher, place of publication, category (e.g., "introduction"), and specific pagination of the Wells's piece. The final chapter lists Wells's drawings as they appear in his books, showing specific page numbers on which they are reproduced. The end matter includes a chronology of Wells's works (but only the books), with years of publication and item numbers. There are also sections on the unreprinted writings of Wells, a list of "Critical, Biographical, and Bibliographical Studies" (monographs only, also arranged by publication date, a particularly bad format choice for this kind of material), and a very useful guide to the "Principal Collections of H. G. Wells Material" in library archives around the world. A description of the aims of the H. G. Wells Society founded by Hammond represents the last section of the text. The index correlates titles with item numbers. No attempt has been made to record Wells's dozens (or hundreds) of unreprinted journalistic essays or to give a comprehensive listing of the hundreds (or thousands) of short critical pieces which have been penned about this influential author and his work. The text is shot from sometimes faint typed copy and bound to library standards.

There is no doubt that Hammond knows his material, and also no doubt that his volume represents the best Wells bibliography currently available. However, the book's format is unnecessarily cumbersome, coming between the text and the user and making any overall assessment of Wells's development as a writer extraordinarily difficult. Also, Garland's decision to produce a major bibliography on a major author without typesetting the text must certainly be questioned by any scholar and librarian: some of the material is very dense and difficult to distinguish. A revised and expanded second edition is now needed.

444. Watkins, A. H., ed. **Catalogue of the H. G. Wells Collection in the Bromley Public Libraries**. Bromley, England, London Borough of Bromley Public Libraries, 1974. xi, 196 p., [4] p. of plates. LC 75-316320. ISBN 0-901002-02-X.

Wells was born at Bromley in 1866, so it is not surprising that the public library there began collecting Wellsiana beginning in 1952, using a large 1958 purchase as the core of its collection. Materials in this catalog are ordered into broad subject categories: "Introduction"; "Acknowledgements"; "I. The Works of H. G. Wells": "(a) Collected Works," "(b) Individual Books and Articles," "(c) Books Containing Writings by Wells," "(d) Introductions and Prefaces by Wells"; "II. Bibliographies, Catalogues, Dictionaries";

"III. Biography": "(a) H. G. Wells and Family," "(b) Obituaries, Tributes, The Will," "(c) 13 Hanover Terrace," "(d) Wells As a Character in Fiction," "(e) People Who Knew Wells"; "IV. Books and Articles Relating to Wells, Other Than Biography"; "V. Review": "(a) Of Books by Wells," "(b) Of Books About Wells"; "VI. Periodicals"; "VII. Letters": "(a) Wells's Letters," "(b) Letters Written by Mrs. Wells on Behalf of Her Husband," "(c) Letters by Other Hands," "(d) Correspondence with Dr. Henry Hick and Family," "(e) Fabian Society, Correspondence and Papers"; "VIII. Pictorial Material": "(a) Portraits and Photographs of Wells," "(b) Cartoons," "(c) Picshuas," "(d) Places," "(e) H. G. Wells Centenary, 21 September 1966"; "IX. Miscellany"; "Index of Wells's Writings"; "General Index."

Materials in most sections are listed in alphabetical order by title. A typical monograph entry provides item number (boldfaced), title, place of publication, publisher, year of publication, pagination, height of book (in centimeters), and notes of interest. A typical shorter work entry (in the "Periodicals" chapter) gives item number (boldfaced), magazine title, volume and/or issue number, month and year of publication, pagination, and notes. Secondary sources are arranged alphabetically by main entry (usually author's surname); a typical entry records item number, author (inverted, surname in all caps), title, and bibliographical data (for books: place of publication, publisher, year of publication, pagination, and notes; for articles: magazine title [in italics], month and year of publication, specific pagination, and notes). Two indexes, to Wells's own works and to all other references, are keyed to item numbers. The materials in the book are numbered consecutively throughout the bibliography from 1 to 1,290. The catalog is professionally typeset and bound to library standards.

This guide will be most useful to those scholars of Wells's life and work who are interested in travelling to Bromley. However, there is also much of interest here for other researchers, since the catalog records many peripheral items not mentioned in Hammond's more complete bibliography (see #443). Recommended for major research collections.

445. Wells, Geoffrey H. **The Works of H. G. Wells, 1887-1925: A Bibliography, Dictionary, and Subject-Index.** London, George Routledge & Sons, 1926. xxv, 274 p. index. LC 26-14925. Also: New York, Burt Franklin, 1970. xxv, 274 p. index. LC 77-20335.

Geoffrey Wells, who apparently is not related to H. G. or his paramour, Rebecca West, also used the name Geoffrey West in later life. Contents: "Introduction"; "Addenda"; "Part One: Books and Pamphlets"; "Part Two: Books and Pamphlets Containing Miscellaneous Publications"; "Part Three: Books by Other Writers with Prefaces"; "Appendix i: Chronological List of Unreprinted Writings"; "ii. Letters to the Press"; "iii. Translation into Foreign Languages"; "iv. Parodies by Various Writers"; "v. Critical Studies of H. G. Wells"; "A Dictionary of the Works of H. G. Wells"; "A Subject-Index to the Works of H. G. Wells."

In each section materials are listed chronologically by publication date. A typical monograph entry provides item number, title (all caps italics), and year of publication as centered headings; exact title page transcription; an exact description of the interior of the book, including pagination, number of advertisements, etc.; a careful description of the binding, including mention of variations in later issues; and other bibliographical notes (usually one long paragraph), giving details of previous publication, contents (for collections), and a plot description. Materials are numbered consecutively from 1 to 89, the last item being "The Atlantic Edition of the Works of H. G. Wells." Part II gives books including Wellsiana, a typical entry providing year of publication (centered head), title, author or editor, publisher, place of publication, year of publication, specific pagination of the Wells's piece, and a brief descriptive note. Part III is similarly arranged and presented.

The first appendix provides a chronological list of the author's unreprinted essays and stories, with no bibliographical data beyond year of publication (as a centered heading). Appendix ii includes a selection of Wells's letters to newspapers and magazines, giving title (actually subject theme, in italics), magazine title, and month and year of publication, but no paginations. Appendices iii-iv are both slight and sketchy. The last appendix is subdivided into three parts: "(a) Books"; "(b) Essays in Books"; "(c) Essays in Periodicals." Each section is arranged chronologically by publication date. A typical book entry gives title (italics), author, publisher, place of publication, year of publication, and series name (where appropriate). Section (b) lists book title (italics), author or editor, publisher, place of publication, year of publication, essay title (in italics), and specific pagination of the piece. Section (c) gives essay title (italicized), author, magazine title, and month and year of publication, but no paginations.

The dictionary section actually comprises the bulk of the book (163 pages). It provides an A-Z record of the author's works, fictional and nonfictional, plus mentions of all the major and significant minor characters. A typical character entry gives name (small caps), occupation, physical description, the work in which he or she appears, and a description of his or her fate. The remaining entries (about half) concern Wells's essays, stories, novels, pamphlets, etc., typically giving item number, title (small caps), a reference (where appropriate) to the item number in the bibliography section where the item occurs or bibliographical data (usually for short pieces, providing magazine title and month and year of publication, but no paginations), and detailed description or plot summary. Only those entries describing Wells's individual works are numbered (from 1 to 753). The subject index correlates names, titles, and subjects with the item numbers in the dictionary chapter (not those from the bibliography section). The book is beautifully typeset and designed and bound to library standards.

Although much of these data are subsumed into Hammond's more current and comprehensive bibliography (see #443), the serious researcher will also want access to this earlier guide, which provides much first-hand background information on Wells's books (obviously derived from the author himself), plus detailed descriptions of so many of the minor works in the dictionary section—much of the latter data cannot be located in any other single source. Hammond's volume (see #443) should be acquired by all four-year academic and all large public libraries; research collections should have all four works herein described (see #442-#444). Also compare the dictionary chapter with Ash's and Connes's dictionaries of Wells's characters (see #491 and #492).

James White

446. Benson, Gordon, Jr. **James White, Doctor to Aliens: A Working Bibliography.** Albuquerque, N.M., Galactic Central Publications, 1986. 9 p. (Galactic Central Bibliographies for the Avid Reader, Vol. 12). ISBN 0-912613-21-1 (pbk.).

James White, a native of Northern Ireland, has penned a number of science fiction tales of future medics and doctors interfacing with alien patients. This new checklist is arranged by subject category, then alphabetically by title. Contents: Author's full name and date and place of birth; "A. The Stories"; "B. The Books"; "C. The Series"; "D. Articles, Non-Fiction, Misc." (by and about White). In each part materials are arranged by title, White's works being numbered anew from one. A typical short fiction entry includes item number, title, category ("ss"=short story, "nt"=novelette, etc.), magazine or book in which the item appeared, month and year of publication (for magazines in the form "11-55" for November 1955) or year of publication (for books), plus a list of subsequent reprints (for which title, editor's last name, publisher, and year are given), but no paginations. A typical book entry provides item number, title (in underlined caps), publication data (publisher, stock number, month and year of publication [if known, in the form "10-59" for October 1959], pagination, price, with dates of reissues by the same publisher), cover artist, and similar data for known reprints. Collections include lists of the stories referenced to the item numbers in the first section. There are no indexes and only a handful of secondary sources (included in Section D). Coverage is complete through early 1986.

The book is shot from typed copy, and some of the text runs into the right margins, making rebinding of these volumes very difficult. White is not well known outside the SF field, but scholars mining the back veins of fantastic literature will welcome this brief checklist and hope for a future expansion that will include more secondary sources, paginations, and better production values. Note: this volume has not yet been reworked into the new series format.

Charles Williams

447. Glenn, Lois. **Charles W. S. Williams: A Checklist.** Kent, Ohio, Kent State University Press, 1975. viii, 128 p. index. (The Serif Series: Bibliographies and Checklists, No. 33). LC 75-17277. ISBN 0-87338-179-3.

Charles Williams (1886-1945) was a friend and colleague of both J. R. R. Tolkien and C. S. Lewis and a well-known British fantasy writer in his own right. This new bibliography includes "Introduction"; "I. Williams's Works": "A. Books" (divided into "Poetry," "Novels," "Plays," "Criticism," "Theology," "Biographies"); "B. Poems and Stories"; "C. Articles and Letters"; "D. Reviews"; "E. Edited Works"; "II. Works About Williams": "A. Books"; "B. Articles, Chapters, and Dissertations"; "C. Reviews" (subdivided into Williams's individual books, which are arranged in chronological order by publication date); "D. Dissertations"; "III. Indexes": "A. Index of Names"; "B. Index of Titles of Williams's Works"; "C. Index of Titles of Works About Williams."

The arrangement in Section I is chronological by date of each of Williams's works, but Section II, secondary sources, is arranged alphabetically by main entry (usually critic's name); in both sections, materials are further divided into many different subdivisions, as indicated by the chapter titles, and are numbered anew from one in each *sub*-section. A typical book entry includes item number, title (in italics), place of publication, publisher, year of publication, and pagination, with similar data on all known reprint editions, plus a short (one- to two-sentence) annotation.

A typical shorter work entry includes item number, title (in quotes), magazine title (italics), volume number, month and year of publication, pagination; or, for works appearing originally in anthologies, book title (italics), editor, place of publication, publisher, year of publication, pagination within the book, and brief one-sentence (or several-word) annotation. Similar data are included for all known reprints. Secondary works are similarly recorded, with one- to two-sentence annotations. Section II, Chapter D, on dissertations, essentially excerpts those entries from their original appearances in II-B. The three indexes are keyed to item numbers (in the form "I-A-iv-6" or "II-B-178," for example). The book is nicely designed and typeset and bound to library standards.

The author appears familiar with her material, and the data appear complete. However, one must question the wisdom of breaking a relatively small book into so many subdivisions. For example, separating Williams's books into six sections in just eleven pages of text, each chronologically arranged, makes overall comprehension of his monographic work extraordinarily difficult to any but the most intensive user. However, in partial compensation, the material *is* easily accessed through the indexes, and Glenn's volume will provide a sound beginning point for both the scholar and student. It should also be on the shelves of every research library.

Jack Williamson

448. Benson, Gordon, Jr. **Jack (John Stewart) Williamson, Child and Father of Wonder**. Albuquerque, N.M., Galactic Central Publications, 1985. 14 p. (Galactic Central Bibliographies for the Avid Reader, Vol. 10). ISBN 0-912613-22-X (pbk.).

Dr. Jack Williamson, who began writing SF in the 1920s, later became one of the first academics to teach classes in fantastic literature at the university level. Benson's checklist supplements Myers (see #449), arranging the author's work by subject category, then alphabetically by title. Contents: Author's full name, date and place of birth, pseudonyms, and awards; "A. The Stories"; "B. The Books"; "C. Books: Non-Fiction"; "D. Articles, Editorials, Introductions, etc."; "E. Miscellaneous." In each part the material is arranged by title, the author's works being numbered anew from one. A typical shorter work entry includes item number, title, category ("ss"=short story, "nt"=novelette, etc.), magazine or book in which the item appeared, month and year of publication (for magazines in the form "2-39" for February 1939) or year of publication (for books), plus a list of subsequent reprints (for which title, editor's last name, publisher, and year are given), but no paginations. A typical book entry provides item number, title (in underlined caps), publication data (publisher, stock number, LC card number, month and year of publication [if known, in the form "10-59" for October 1959], pagination, price, with dates of reissues by the same publisher), cover artist. There are no indexes; a half dozen secondary sources are included in Section E. Coverage is complete through early 1985.

The volume is shot from typed copy, with some of the text running occasionally into the right margin, and is stapled through the spine into paper covers. Benson's guide is more current than Myers's (see #449) and includes the book paginations the latter omits but omits the magazine paginations Myers includes, making both essential to the student of Williamson's work.

449. Myers, Robert E. **Jack Williamson: A Primary and Secondary Bibliography**. Boston, G. K. Hall & Co., 1980. xiii, 93 p. index. (Masters of Science Fiction and Fantasy). LC 79-18471. ISBN 0-8161-8158-6.

Myers here covers the work of a respected American science fiction writer of the pulp era who later earned his Ph.D. in English Literature with a dissertation on the works of H. G. Wells. Contents: "Preface"; "Introduction"; "Part A: Fiction"; "Part B: Miscellaneous Media"; "Part C: Nonfiction"; "Part D: Criticism and Reviews"; "Part E: A Selection of Non-English Editions and Publications of Williamson's Works"; "Appendix: A Selected List of Additional Reviews and Criticism"; "Index I: Subject-Author Index, Listing Titles in Parts A, B, C and English Titles in Part E"; "Index II: Listing of Criticism-Reviews in Part D."

The introduction provides a very brief biographical and critical introduction to Williamson's work. The bibliography proper is arranged chronologically, from the earliest published material to the latest, and numbered consecutively (e.g., A1, A2, A3, etc., for Williamson's fiction). Books and shorter works are interfiled; reprint editions are listed under the first edition in chronological order. Each book entry gives item number, title (in italics), place of publication, publisher, but no paginations. Shorter works published originally in magazines list item number, title (in quotations), magazine, volume number, date, and paginations; those published originally in books give title (in quotes), book title (italics), editor, place of publication, publisher, format, but no paginations. Story collections include complete contents listings, plus the years in which the original stories were published.

Part B includes a handful of teleplay adaptations and audio tapes. Part C includes all nonfiction works by the author, with occasional annotations. Part D lists all known secondary works (ninety-nine items), including some published book reviews, profiles, critiques, and bibliographies, with author, title, bibliographical data, and extensive subject annotations. Part E includes known foreign editions of Williamson's works (particularly books), listed alphabetically by English-language title, then in chronological order by date of publication of the foreign edition, with all known bibliographical data, including foreign-language titles and translators. The main index cites title or subject and item number only, the second index (to critical studies) author, title, and item number. The book is nicely type-set and bound to library standards.

Myers's data are complete only through 1978 (with one entry from 1979), making the book somewhat out-of-date for a writer who remains moderately active, and his guide lacks the book paginations which Benson's more current bibliography (see #448) supplies. A revised and expanded edition with the missing bibliographical information would be more than justified. Libraries and researchers will require both volumes for their collections.

Colin Wilson

450. Stanley, Colin. **The Work of Colin Wilson: An Annotated Bibliography & Guide**. San Bernardino, Calif., The Borgo Press, 1989. 312 p. index. (Bibliographies of Modern Authors, No. 1). LC 84-11181. ISBN 0-89370-817-8; ISBN 0-89370-917-4 (pbk.).

This massive, extremely comprehensive guide to the works of the well-known British novelist and philosopher is the flagship volume of the Bibliographies of Modern Authors series, delayed in publication until 1989. Contents: "Acknowledgments and Note"; Introduction: "The Quest for Colin Wilson" (by Stanley); "A Colin Wilson Chronology"; "A. Books"; "B. Short Fiction"; "C. Nonfiction"; "D. Introductions and Afterwords"; "E. Book Reviews"; "F. Other Media"; "G. Editorial Credits"; "H. About the Author: Monographs"; "I. About the Author: Critiques, Profiles, Interviews"; "J. About the Author: Short Bio-Bibliographies"; "K. About the Author: Other Materials"; "L. Miscellanea"; "Quoth the Critics"; Afterword: "Inside Outside: Reflections on Being Bibliographed," by Colin Wilson; "Title Index to Colin Wilson's Works"; "Subject Index with Author/Title Index."

In each section, the author's works are arranged chronologically and numbered consecutively, chapter by chapter, with the appropriate letter prefix. A typical book entry includes item number, title (boldface), place of publication, publisher, year of publication, pagination, format (e.g., "paper"=paperback), type of publication (e.g., "novel"), and similar data on reprint editions, translations, republications, anthologizations, etc., which are listed chronologically under the main entry. The books are fully annotated, with completely analyzed and very detailed contents and subject listings and/or plot summaries, lists of book reviews and other secondary sources (in alphabetical order by critic), and other pertinent data (for example, verbatim transcriptions of the dedications at the front of each Wilson title); entries from other sections are selectively annotated as needed.

A typical shorter work entry includes item number, title (in boldfaced quotes), magazine title (italics), volume or issue number, month and year of publication, and paginations; shorter works appearing originally in books include item number, title (boldface quotes), book title (italics), editor, place of publication, publisher, format (e.g., "cloth"), and paginations. Similar data are provided on all known reprints, including foreign editions, with foreign-language titles and translators. Stanley's introduction provides an excellent introductory guide to the author's life and works. The chronology gives a year-by-year account of the author's professional and personal life, in block paragraph format. "About the Author" includes all known secondary works, which are so numerous in this volume that they have been further subdivided into four chapters by type; reviews of individual Wilson books are included, however, under their respective entries in Section A.

The "Miscellanea" section includes information on library holdings of Wilson manuscripts, spurious titles, screenplays adapted from Wilson novels, books dedicated to Wilson (with verbatim transcriptions of the dedications and full bibliographical data), Wilson's plays and unpublished works, and Library of Congress cataloging data. "Quoth the Critics" includes selected excerpts of reviews and other comments by leading critics on the author's work, arranged chronologically by Wilson book title. The very comprehensive indexes correlate Wilson's titles with their item numbers and (in the second index) all other references to authors, titles, and subjects, again by item number. Wilson's original twenty-page afterword sums up the philosophical basis for his entire career.

This is a major literary reference work. Particularly important are Stanley's extensive annotations and descriptive contents listings, which not only delineate Wilson's development as a writer and philosopher but also provide much background information for future researchers through numerous quotations from specific Wilson titles, as well as contemporary critical reactions *to them*. Much of the material derives directly from Wilson's own files and personal library of his works, with coverage complete through the end of 1988. It is difficult to see how any serious student of Colin Wilson could possibly ignore this absolutely superb condensation of his life and career. Recommended for all major academic collections.

Richard Wilson

451. Drumm, Chris. **A Richard Wilson Checklist**. Polk City, Ia., Chris Drumm Books, 1986. 13, 20 p. Index. Bound upside down with *Adventures in the Space Trade: A Memoir*, by Richard Wilson. LC 90-108879. ISBN 0-936055-24-3 (pbk.); ISBN 0-936055-25-1 (ltd. ed.).

The late Richard Wilson, who died just before this 4.25" x 7" booklet was published, was a well-regarded American SF writer and academic. Drumm's checklist arranges the author's works in one straight chronological sequence. Entries are grouped by year and under each year by month; items are numbered consecutively in order from 1 to 100. Books are underlined, short stories listed in quotation marks. A typical shorter work entry includes item number, title, category code (e.g., "s"=short story), magazine (underlined), month of publication, but no paginations; or book title, if the first appearance is in an anthology, plus editor, publisher, and year of publication. Subsequent reprintings are grouped chronologically under the original edition, with similar data provided.

A typical book entry includes item number, title (all caps), category code (e.g., "c"=collection), publisher, stock number, month of publication (if known), pagination, price, format (e.g., "pb"=paperback), contents of collections. See references, title index, and contents listings are keyed to item number. A few secondary materials are mentioned in passing in their appropriate years but are not easily retrievable. Data are complete through 1986. The book is shot from typed copy; the text runs too close to the right-hand margin easily to allow rebinding by libraries. The original autobiographical memoir by Wilson provides a poignant (he died shortly after it was written) look back at the author's life and career. An expanded edition with further primary and secondary resources would certainly be justified.

Gene Wolfe

452. Stephens, Christopher P. **A Checklist of Gene Wolfe.** Hastings-on-Hudson, N.Y., Ultramarine Publishing Co., 1990. 37 p. index. ISBN 0-89366-181-3 (pbk.).

Wolfe is best known for his tetralogy, *The Book of the New Sun*. This new checklist to his works is organized into two sections, "Books" and "Stories," then chronologically by publication date. Books are numbered consecutively from A1 to A29, short stories from B1 to B125. A typical monograph entry provides year (as a floating head), item number, title (underlined), pseudonym, publisher, stock or ISBN number, pagination, format (e.g., "cloth with dust wrapper"), cover illustrator, price, and similar data for all known reprints (which are numbered, for example, A12a, A12b, A12c, etc., in descending order by publication date). A typical short fiction entry gives item number, title (in quotes), pagination, magazine title, month and year of publication, volume and issue number; or, for materials appearing in anthologies: book title (underlined), editor's name, publisher, and year of publication, but no paginations. Similar data are provided for all known reprints. The book is shot from legible typed copy and bound with staples in stiff paper covers. The two indexes (to books and stories) correlate titles with years of publication only; these would be more useful if amalgamated into one alphabet list and correlated with specific item numbers. Wolfe is well-regarded in academic circles; research libraries should consider purchasing this introductory checklist to his works.

John Wyndham

453. Stephensen-Payne, Phil. **John Wyndham, Creator of the Cosy Catastrophe: A Working Bibliography.** 2nd rev. ed. Leeds, West Yorkshire, England & Albuquerque, N.M., Galactic Central Publications, 1989. 9, 39 p. (Galactic Central Bibliographies for the Avid Reader, Vol. 16). (pbk.). The first edition appeared under the title *John Wyndham Parkes Lucas Beynon Harris: A Bibliography.*

The late John Wyndham, the pseudonym of John Beynon Harris (1903-1969), was the premier British exponent of the near-future disaster novel. Contents: Author's full name, date and place of birth and death, and pseudonyms; "A. Stories"; "B. Fiction Books"; "C. Series"; "D. Poems and Songs" ("none known"); "E. Poem and Song Collections" ("none known"); "F. Articles"; "G. Miscellaneous"; "H. Non-Fiction Books" ("none known"); "I. Books Edited by John Beynon Harris" ("none known"); "J. Media Presentations"; "K. Articles on John Beynon Harris"; "L. Reviews" [of Wyndham's books]; "M. Books About John Beynon Harris"; "N. Phantom Titles and Editions"; "O. Related Books by Other Authors"; "P. Texual Variations"; "Q. Chronological Index."

In each part the material is arranged by title, the author's works being numbered anew from one in each section. A typical shorter work entry includes item number, title, category ("ss"=short story, "nt"=novelette, etc.), magazine or book in which the item appeared, month and year of publication (for magazines in the form "4-32" for April 1932) or year of publication (for books), plus a list of subsequent reprints (for which title, editor's last name, publisher, and year are given), but no paginations. A typical book entry provides item number, title (in underlined caps), publication data (publisher, stock number, month and year of publication [if known, in the form "10-59" for October 1959], pagination, price, with dates of reissues by the same publisher), cover artist, and similar data for all known reprint editions. Collections include complete contents listings, referenced by item number to the stories in Section A. There is no general index. Forty-one secondary sources are listed (included two unpublished theses in Section M and roughly seventy book reviews arranged by Wyndham book title, then alphabetically by magazine title. Coverage is complete through mid-1989. The book is shot from very clear word-processed copy and bound with staples into paper covers.

This volume is one of the better Galactic Central bibliographies, one which will become *the* essential reference tool for any student of Wyndham's writings. For larger research collections.

George Zebrowski

454. Elliot, Jeffrey M., and R. Reginald. **The Work of George Zebrowski: An Annotated Bibliography & Guide**. San Bernardino, Calif., The Borgo Press, 1986. 54 p. index. (Bibliographies of Modern Authors, No. 4). LC 84-24239. ISBN 0-89370-383-4; ISBN 0-89370-483-0 (pbk.). **The Work of George Zebrowski: An Annotated Bibliography & Guide**. 2nd ed., rev. and expanded. San Bernardino, Calif., The Borgo Press, 1990. 118 p. index. (Bibliographies of Modern Authors, No. 4). LC 89-7093. ISBN 0-8095-0514-2; ISBN 0-8095-1514-8 (pbk.).

Zebrowski is the acclaimed writer of *Macrolife,* in addition to being a highly regarded SF editor. Contents (first edition): "Introduction" (by Elliot); "A. Books"; "B. Short Fiction"; "C. Translations"; "D. Articles and Reviews"; "E. Journals and Publishing Series"; "F. Juvenilia"; "G. About the Author"; "H. Honors and Awards"; "I. Public Appearances"; "J. Unpublished Works"; "K. Miscellanea"; "Quoth the Critics"; "Title Index." Contents (second edition): Introduction: "Between Sensitivity and Concern," by Elliot; "A George Zebrowski Chronology"; "A. Books"; "B. Short Fiction"; "C. Nonfiction"; "D. Translations"; "E. Juvenilia"; "F. Editorial Credits"; "G. Unpublished Works"; "H. Other Media"; "I. Honors and Awards"; "J. Public Appearances"; "K. About the Author"; "L. Miscellanea"; "Quoth the Critics"; Afterword: "6,250 Bits of Immortality," by Zebrowski; "Index"; "About the Authors."

In each section, the author's works are arranged chronologically and numbered consecutively, chapter by chapter, with the appropriate letter prefix. A typical entry includes (second edition) item number, title (bold type), place of publication, publisher, month and year of publication, pagination, format (e.g., "cloth"), type of publication (e.g., "anthology"), similar bibliographical details on known reprint editions, including foreign versions, with foreign-language titles and translators, and a list of secondary sources and reviews, arranged alphabetically by main entry (usually critic). The books are fully annotated, with complete contents listings and/or plot summaries and other pertinent data; entries from other sections are selectively annotated as needed. A typical shorter work entry includes item number, title (bold quotes), magazine title (italics), volume number, month and year of publication, and paginations; a shorter work appearing in an anthology lists item number, title (bold quotes), book title (italics), editor, place of publication, publisher, and paginations, with similar data on all known reprintings.

Elliot's introduction provides an interesting and entertaining introduction to the author's life and works. The chronology provides a year-by-year account of the author's professional and personal life, in block paragraph format. "About the Author" includes all known secondary works, arranged chronologically by publication date, with full bibliographical data. The "Miscellanea" section includes information on pen names, book dedications, memberships, Library of Congress cataloging data, career highlights, and other data. "Quoth the Critics" includes selected excerpts of reviews and other comments by leading critics on the author's work, arranged in chronological order by book title. Zebrowski's original afterword comments perceptively on the function of bibliography and the state of the author at mid-life. The index correlates titles and item numbers only. Coverage is complete through mid-1989.

This is the first volume in the Bibliographies of Modern Authors series to reach a second edition; the revised version includes considerable changes in the format (better organization and more spaciousness), plus expanded annotations, book reviews, and many other new data, with other major and minor tinkerings to the format. The size of the revision is more than double that of the original. An excellent introductory guide to the work of a rising SF star.

Roger Zelazny

455. Levack, Daniel J. H., with annotations by Darrell Schweitzer. **Amber Dreams: A Roger Zelazny Bibliography**. San Francisco, Calif. & Columbia, Penn., Underwood/Miller, 1983. 151 p. ISBN 0-934438-40-4; ISBN 0-934438-39-0 (pbk.). Also: Westport, Conn., Meckler Publishing, 1986. 151 p. ISBN 0-88736-098-X.

Levack, who compiled similarly formatted bibliographies on de Camp, Dick, Herbert, and Vance (see #321, #326, #347, #434), has produced another attractive but bibliographically insipid volume. Contents: "Introduction"; "Books"; "Edited Books"; "Stories"; "Magazine Checklist"; "Works About Roger Zelazny"; "Miscellaneous"; "Connected Stories and Continuing Characters"; "Pseudonyms"; "Collaborations"; "Verse Index"; "Non-Fiction Index"; "Chronological Order of Publication of Roger Zelazny's Work"; "Acknowledgments."

Works are listed alphabetically by title and numbered consecutively from one, section by section, with 251 items included. A typical book entry includes item number, title (bold caps), series note (when appropriate), previous magazine serialization data (title, magazine title, parts, dates of publication), awards won, award nominations, contents (if a collection) or one-paragraph annotation (if a novel), both in boldface type, publisher, stock number (for paperback editions), place of publication (inconsistently for paperbacks), price (in parentheses), year of publication, edition points, but no paginations. Reprints are listed in chronological order by publication date; many foreign editions are included, with foreign-language titles. An asterisk after a specific edition indicates it has been viewed by Levack.

A typical shorter work entry includes item number, title (in bold quotes), estimated wordage, type or other notes (e.g., "verse"), one- to two-sentence annotation (in bold type), magazine or book title, date, volume number, issue number, but no paginations. All subsequent reprint editions (including some foreign-language materials, with foreign-language titles) are listed with similar data. Anthology appearances include title, editor, publisher, stock number, price, year of publication, format (e.g., "paper"), but no paginations. The magazine checklist records those publications in which Zelazny stories have appeared, alphabetically by title, keyed to issue date and to item number in the short fiction section. There is also a master chronological checklist of Zelazny's work, year by year, with all publications interfiled, and a brief list of twenty-five secondary sources in alphabetical order by title. There is no overall title index.

As usual with this series, the book is beautifully typeset and designed and is illustrated throughout with reproductions of book and magazine covers featuring Zelazny's fiction. The cloth edition is bound to library standards but is otherwise a facsimile reprint, with no additional data. Levack's guide includes three more years of data than Sanders's bibliography (see #456) plus illustrations and edition points, but lacks an overall index (which Sanders includes) and story or book paginations. (Stephens [see #458] includes these data, but does not list shorter works.) Levack's bibliography records only twenty-five secondary sources, as compared with over 300 in Sanders, and none in Stephens. For the serious scholar and the academic librarian, all three titles will be necessary complements, but Sanders is far the superior bibliographically.

456. Sanders, Joseph L. **Roger Zelazny: A Primary and Secondary Bibliography.** Boston, G. K. Hall, 1980. xxx, 154 p. index. (Masters of Science Fiction and Fantasy). LC 80-20253. ISBN 0-8161-8081-4.

Zelazny is the well-known American author of the Amber Series and other major SF and fantasy novels and stories. Contents: "Preface"; "Introduction"; "Acknowledgments"; "A: Fiction"; "B: Poetry"; "C: Nonfiction"; D: "Critical Studies"; "Appendixes: A. Nominations, Awards, and Honors"; "B. Foreign Language Editions"; "C. Manuscripts and Papers"; "Index to Primary Works"; "Index to Secondary Sources."

Sanders's introduction provides a brief biography to and broad critical evaluation of Zelazny's life and work. The bibliography itself is arranged chronologically, from the earliest published material to the latest, and numbered consecutively (e.g., A1, A2, A3, etc., for Zelazny's fiction). Books and shorter works are interfiled; reprint editions of books are listed under the first edition, in chronological order. A typical book entry gives item number, title (underlined), place of publication, publisher, but no paginations. Shorter works published originally in magazines list item number, title (in quotations), magazine, volume number, date, paginations; those published originally in books give item number, title (in quotations), book title (underlined), book editor, place of publication, publisher, format (e.g., "paper"), and paginations. Reprints of stories are listed under the main entry, chronologically by year of reprint, with the editor of the anthology, title, place of publication, publisher, year, format (e.g., "paper"), but no pagination. Story collections include complete contents listings, plus the years in which the original stories were published. A few entries include bibliographical notes, but no other annotations.

Part B includes Zelazny's many published poems. Part C includes all nonfiction works by the author, with occasional annotations. Part D lists some 300 secondary works, including published book reviews, fan commentaries, critiques, and bibliographies, with author, title, bibliographical data, and extensive subject annotations. The appendices list Zelazny's awards (chronologically); selected foreign editions (by language, then chronologically, with foreign-language title, English-language title, place of publication, publisher, year of publication, and format); and a complete description of the Roger Zelazny manuscripts and papers held by two library collections, a potentially major resource for future scholarship. The primary index cites title and item number only, the secondary index (to critical studies) author, title, and item number. Coverage is complete through 1979. The book is shot from sometimes faint typed copy and bound to library standards.

This is an excellent bibliographical guide to Zelazny's works, but given the fact that the author has remained very active, it has aged more rapidly than most volumes in this series and badly needs an expanded and updated edition. Nonetheless, it remains the best available introduction to the writer's many works, superior in every respect to two more recent bibliographies of Zelazny's writings (see #455 and #457). Stephens's checklist (see #457) can be used as a supplement.

457. Stephens, Christopher P. **A Checklist of Roger Zelazny**. Hastings-on-Hudson, N.Y., Ultramarine Publishing Co., 1990. 20 p. index. ISBN 0-89366-166-X (pbk.).

Stephens's checklist (both editions) is organized into two sections covering books written by Zelazny and anthologies edited by him, then chronologically by publication date. Materials are numbered consecutively from A1-A47 (first section), and B1 (the single entry in part two). A typical entry provides year (as a floating head), item number, title (underlined), pseudonym, publisher, stock or ISBN number, pagination, format (e.g., "cloth with dust wrapper"), cover illustrator, price, and similar data for all known reprints (which are numbered, for example, A46a, A46b, A46c, etc., in descending order by publication date). The chapbook is shot from legible typed copy and bound with staples in stiff paper covers. The index correlates titles with years of publication only. Although Stephens's guide is a decade more current than Sanders's (see #456) and includes monograph paginations the latter omits, it will be useful primarily as a supplement to Sanders's more scholarly work and as a brief checklist of Zelazny's very collectible books for fans and collectors.

ARTIST BIBLIOGRAPHIES

SCOPE NOTE: This chapter includes guides to art work produced by individual artists (in alphabetical order by name of the artist) and general works indexing SF art by many artists. Biographies of some of these artists can be found in general encyclopedias (see the first section of this book) or in Weinberg's *A Biographical Dictionary of Science Fiction and Fantasy Artists* (see #48).

GENERAL WORKS

458. Page, Bill. **Index to SF Cover Art.** Bryan, Tex., Dellwood Press, 1979-80. 3 v. index. (pbk.).

Page attempts to index artwork used on the covers of science-fiction and fantasy paperbacks; a fourth volume indexing the dustjacket art on hardcover books and Science Fiction Book Club editions was also announced but has not been seen. The arrangement is similar in each volume: works are indexed alphabetically by artist surname, then alphabetically by surname of the author of the work on which the art has appeared. A typical entry includes artist name (inverted, surname first), item number (materials are numbered consecutively from one in the first volume through 1,502 in the third volume), author's name (inverted, surname first), book title (underlined), publisher, stock number, month and year of publication. Most of the books covered were published in the 1960s and '70s; however, each volume includes a random selection of paperbacks from this time period, with no obvious criterion for selection; major artists such as Jack Gaughan appear in all three volumes. The books are shot from occasionally faint typed copy but are generally readable, line breaks and hanging indents serving to set the entries off from each other quite clearly and legibly.

Page's idea is sound, but the absence of an overall artist index, or of author and title indexes for the works mentioned, limits the usefulness of what could have been a major resource guide for future study. A comprehensive reference guide to SF paperback art is badly needed.

BIBLIOGRAPHIES OF INDIVIDUAL ARTISTS

Vaughn Bodé

459. Beahm, George W., and Vaughn Bodé. **Vaughn Bodé Index.** Newport News, Va., Distributed by C. W. Brooks, Jr., 1976. 64 p. LC 76-371310 (pbk.).

This bibliography of Bodé's works was already underway before his tragic death in 1975 and was converted into a tribute to his life and art. Contents: "Dedication"; "Genesis of an Index," by Beahm; "Chronology of Important Events"; "Bodé Consciousness," by Bodé; "Daydream" (a cartoon by Bodé); "Bodé's Cartoon Concert" (unsigned critique); "Bodé's Milestone Cartoons" (reproductions of artwork); "Vaughn Bodé Index"; "Two Portraits" (photographs of the artist).

The bibliography proper is organized into eleven sections: "I. Books"; "II. Periodicals"; "III. Newspapers"; "IV. Convention Material"; "V. Comic Books"; "VI. Bodé Oriented Projects"; "VII. Posters"; "VIII. Stationary"; "IX. Flyers"; "X. Miscellaneous Publications"; "XI. Bodé's Cartoon Concert." The material is arranged roughly chronologically, but each of the major sections (particularly I-II) is so broken up into subdivisions that discovering any real order to this mass of data can only be serendipitous. Complete bibliographical details are provided, including paginations, and many of the entries include illuminating comments by Bodé himself. The book is attractively typeset and designed, featuring numerous reproductions of Bodé drawings and photos of the artist and his family. However, the absence of an index plus the difficult structure of the book make access to the material virtually impossible without reading entire sections. A better-organized version would definitely be desirable.

Hannes Bok

460. Brooks, C. W., Jr. **Interim Hannes Bok Illustration Index.** Newport News, Va., Purple Mouth Press, 1967. [16 leaves]. (pbk.). Brooks, Ned [i.e., C. W., Jr.], and Don Martin. **Hannes Bok Illustration Index.** Newport News, Va., National Fantasy Fan Federation, 1970. 22 p. (pbk.). Brooks, C. W., Jr. **The Revised Hannes Bok Checklist.** Baltimore, T-K Graphics, 1974. [45] p. (with one-page addendum). (pbk.).

American writer and artist Hannes Bok (1904-1964) is justly regarded as one of the finest SF illustrators of the 1940s and '50s. These are three successive versions of the same index to his published artwork (no attempt has been made to record unpublished drawings or paintings). Contents: "I. Magazines"; "II. Books"; "III. Artfolios"; "IV. Fanzines"; "V. Miscellaneous Items"; "VI. Collaborations with Dolgov"; "VII. Non-SF Sources"; "Addendum." Materials are arranged alphabetically by publication title, chapter by chapter, then chronologically by date.

In Section I, Bok's work for the professional SF magazines is organized by magazine title, then chronologically by issue number. A typical entry includes magazine title (all caps), month and year of publication, paginations of Bok drawings or paintings (with the story title and author for the illustrated work). The books section lists monographs illustrated by Bok in alphabetical order by title, giving title (underlined), author, publisher, place of publication, year of publication, and the page numbers on which the Bok illustrations appear. Other chapters are similarly organized. Some of the entries include explanatory annotations by Brooks. An index would have been useful, but its absence is not fatal to this strongly organized artist's guide. A definitive version covering all known Bok artwork, as well as his published fiction, is long overdue and badly needed.

Virgil Finlay

461. Bell, Ian. **Virgil Finlay Indexed: The Eighth Book of Virgil Finlay.** Chalgrove, Oxfordshire, England, Bell, 1986. 40 p. (pbk.).
　　　[Not seen.]

Tim Kirk

462. Beahm, George, and Tim Kirk. **Kirk's Works.** Newport News, Va., Heresy Press, 1980. 121 p. LC 81-116969. ISBN 0-9603276-2-2; ISBN 0-9603276-1-4 (pbk.).

This lavishly illustrated guide to this American artist's work was published in an oversized 9" x 12" format. Contents: "Introduction"; "Foreword," by William Rotsler; "Tim Kirk: An Appreciation," by George Barr; "Tim Kirk: Wizard of Whimsey," by Mike Glicksohn; "The Making of Monsters," by Kirk (autobiographical); "A Conversation with Tim Kirk," conducted by George Beahm; "Kirk's Works: An Annotated Index": "Index of Books"; "Professional Periodicals"; "Fanzines"; "Semi-Professional Periodicals";

"Convention Material"; "Apa Material"; "Portfolios"; "Calendars"; "Greeting Cards"; "Flyers"; "Games"; "Miscellaneous Items."

Most sections are organized alphabetically by title of the work illustrated, although a few (the books chapter, for example) vary from this slightly, dumping miscellaneous titles or publishers at the beginning of the chapter without apparent reason. Complete bibliographical data are provided, including specific page numbers on which Kirk artwork appears. The book is beautifully typeset and designed and is filled with dozens of black-and-white illustrations of Kirk paintings and drawings, plus photos of the artist himself. The introductory materials, particularly the Kirk interview, provide much background material on the artist and his life. An overall title index would have been very helpful in locating specific works. Unlike the other artists covered in this section (all of whom died before their indexes were published), Tim Kirk remains quite active as an artist, and so this guide to his work is now very much out-of-date; an updated version should be contemplated.

CHARACTER DICTIONARIES

SCOPE NOTE: This section includes general dictionaries or directories of one or more authors' works, the primary focus being on the author's created world and/or characters, arranged alphabetically by name or place. Books whose primary intent is to provide a guide to the created place names in the author's fictional world are included in the "Atlases and Gazetteers" section.

GENERAL WORKS

463. Hamilton, Frank, and Link Hullar. **Amazing Pulp Heroes**. Brooklyn, N.Y., Gryphon Publications, 1988. 59 p. ISBN 0-936071-09-5 (pbk.).

This poorly organized, written, and presented publication features biographies of created fictional heroes and villains from the pulp magazine era. Descriptions range in size from one short paragraph to several pages and typically include background, attributes, lists of companions (and the villains who regularly oppose him), and brief mentions of the magazine(s) which featured his adventures (but with no bibliographical details). There is no discernible arrangement in the book, entries appearing haphazardly; without an index, access is difficult. Hamilton's full-page drawings of each hero accompany the text by Hullar. The idea behind this booklet is laudable, but Rovin has done it better (see #466).

464. Pringle, David. **Imaginary People: A Who's Who of Modern Fictional Characters**. London & Glasgow, Grafton Books, 1987. x, 515 p. ISBN 0-246-12968-9. Also: New York, World Almanac, 1988. x, 518 p. LC 88-60375. ISBN 0-88687-364-9. Also: London, Paladin, Grafton Books, 1989. x, 518 p. ISBN 0-586-08744-3 (pbk.).

Pringle, former editor of the British publication *Foundation* and current editor of the magazines *Interzone* and *Million*, has assembled an annotated alphabetical directory of 1,300 well-known literary, motion picture, television, and comic-book heroes and other characters dating from the dawn of the modern novel, in the early 1700s through the 1980s.

A typical entry includes name (boldface all caps), and a description which ranges from one sentence to four pages in length, focusing on the character's life, attributes, career, and real name, with details of the publication(s) and/or films and television productions featuring the character, their authors, and the years of publication or release. Internal cross-references in the entries (names mentioned in all caps) lead the reader to other names of interest. Many of the fictional personages derive from genre literature and perhaps one-fourth relate directly or indirectly to fantastic fiction, making this book a valuable guide to major characters in the field, including such worthies as The Prisoner, Mad Max, Dracula, Han Solo, Titus Groan, Lemuel Gulliver, Jules de Grandin, James Bond, Bomba, Sumuru, "Carrie" White, The Wolf Man, Zorro, Indiana Jones, Fafhrd and the Gray Mouser, and many others. The volume is attractively illustrated throughout with movie and TV stills and black-and-white reproductions of book and magazine covers and previously published drawings. A six-page bibliography of works consulted completes the book. There is a slight British bias, as might be expected, but Pringle's coverage seems complete, objective, and highly literate and includes many American heroes little known in Britain.

465. Rovin, Jeff. **The Encyclopedia of Monsters**. New York, Oxford, Facts on File, 1989. ix, 390 p. index. LC 89-30417. ISBN 0-8160-1824-3; ISBN 0-8160-2303-4 (pbk.).

Rovin's guide to the monsters of film, comic books, and literature shares the faults and high points of its two predecessors (see #466 and #467). The basic arrangement is alphabetical by creature name (some of the appellations are well-known or self-evident, but others have been created by Rovin himself). A typical entry includes name (bold caps), medium (e.g., "C"=comic books), first appearance, species, gender, size, features and powers, biography, and comment. An Appendix covers "Monstrous Lands," listed in alphabetical order by country or regional name, with appearance, location, history, and flora and fauna. The book is illustrated throughout with black-and-white movie stills and reproductions of comic book and magazine covers. The index includes references to every name and title, with boldface references to main entry essays. As usual in this series, Rovin draws heavily from motion pictures and comics while including relatively few entries from science fiction or fantasy literature. This particular volume restricts its coverage to mutated humans, beasts, and other critters with horrible aspects; villains as such are covered in the companion volume (see #467). Thorough but lightweight.

466. Rovin, Jeff. **The Encyclopedia of Superheroes.** New York & Oxford, Facts on File Publications, 1985. xi, 443 p., 32 p. of plates. index. LC 85-10329. ISBN 0-8160-1168-0.

This alphabetical guide to superheroes, their careers and attributes, focuses primarily on comic book characters with superhuman powers. Contents: "Introduction"; "Entries A-Z"; Appendices: "A. Superhero Teams"; "B. Obscure or Borderline Golden Age Comic Book Superheroes," "C. Foreign Superheroes"; "D. Minor Superheroes"; "E. Superheroes Featured in "Dial 'H' for Hero""; "Late Arrivals" (i.e., addenda); "Index."

A typical entry includes superhero name (all caps), medium in which the hero has appeared (e.g., "C"=comics), alter ego (the real-life identity of the hero), first appearance, occupation, costume, tools and weapons, biography, quote ("profound or characteristic declarations from the lips of the superhero"), comment (additional miscellaneous information). Although some characters from the pulp magazines of the 1920s and '30s are included, plus other fictional and motion picture superheroes, the vast majority of the more than 1,000 entries derive ultimately from comic-book sources. The appendices include heroes who don't quite fit the parameters in the main section: superhero teams, foreign heroes, and borderline cases; although all of these characters can be found through the index, it might have been wiser to interfile them with their other crime-fighting brothers and sisters rather than separate them into seventy extra pages with five separate alphabetical sequences. The index correlates all names and publishers with page numbers. The book is beautifully typeset and designed and includes black-and-white cover reproductions and movie stills throughout, as well as thirty-two four-color plates illustrating classic comic book and pulp magazine covers.

Rovin clearly knows his subject well: his book is complete and detailed, with all the information an aficionado might want to know. There is, however, an occasional problem with locating particular individuals, since Rovin regards appelations (Captain, Doc, Mr., etc.) as part of each hero's name and files them accordingly; with no see references and no reverse entries in the index, one can easily get lost. See also the companion *Encyclopedia of Super Villains* (#467).

467. Rovin, Jeff. **The Encyclopedia of Super Villains.** New York & Oxford, Facts on File Publications, 1987. ix, 416 p. 32 p. of plates. index. LC 87-8831. ISBN 0-8160-1356-X; ISBN 0-8160-1899-5 (pbk.).

Rovin's companion volume to *The Encyclopedia of Superheroes* (see #466) is organized much the same way, alphabetically by name of super-character. Contents:

"Introduction"; "Entries A-Z"; Appendix: "Super Villain Teams"; "Index." A typical entry includes name (all caps), source (e.g., "TV"=television), real name, first appearance, costume, weapons, chief henchman, biography, quote, comment. As with the book on heroes, the majority of entries derive from comic-book sources, but the percentage in this volume is much less than in the earlier work. The volume is nicely designed and typeset and includes numerous black-and-white cover illustrations and movie stills and thirty-two pages of color plates, mostly reproducing comic book and pulp covers. The index references individuals and publishers to title pages.

Super Villains appears less focused than Rovin's earlier work, perhaps because it covers a wider range of sources; for example, Rovin includes Freddy Krueger from *The Nightmare on Elm Street* movie series but not Jason from the *Friday the 13th* series—why? Similarly, the book lists "The Wolf" from "Little Red Riding Hood," and The Wolf Man from the serial *The Lightning Warrior* but not the Wolf Man of motion picture fame. Various vampire villains are included, but not all. The problem of locating specific individuals is also more pronounced in this new volume: Freddy appears in the alphabetical sequence under his *first name* and is indexed under both first and last name, making it possible to find him either way; but Superman's perennial foe, Lex Luthor (similarly alphabetized by first name), is *not*. Captain Nemo appears in the "C" section, and is so indexed, but "Nemo" is not. Dr. Gregory Gruesome is listed in the "D" part of the alphabet, for "Doctor," but is not indexed under either of his names. The absence of cross references either in the text or in the index makes searching these villains unnecessarily difficult, unless one checks entries several different ways, and is an inexcusable lapse in a book published by a major publisher with major production values. Pretty as this volume is, it is less than it could be.

DICTIONARIES ON INDIVIDUAL AUTHORS

Lloyd Alexander

468. Tunnell, Michael O. **The Prydain Companion: A Reference Guide to Lloyd Alexander's Prydain Chronicles**. New York, Westport, Conn., & London, Greenwood Press, 1989. xvii, 257 p. LC 88-7705. ISBN 0-313-26585-2.

Alexander's Prydain Chronicles, a five-novel fantasy series written for the young adult market, received much acclaim when it was published in the 1960s. Contents: "Foreword," by Alexander; "Lloyd Alexander: A Biographical Sketch"; "How to Use the Companion"; "The Prydain Companion"; "Appendix: Category of Entry Headings"; [Bibliographical] "References."

The companion proper is an A-Z guide to the people, places, and things in Alexander's created universe, which is loosely adapted from the Welsh epic *The Mabinogion*. Major entries are preceded by double asterisks (**); single asterisks are used throughout the text to refer the reader to other names or terms which have separate entries (there are also numerous see references scattered throughout the text). Entries range in size from one sentence to fifteen pages (for the chief character of the saga, Taran Wanderer) and tend to be descriptive, utilizing excerpts from the stories themselves to illustrate plot developments and physical descriptions of characters or places. References are keyed to an abbreviations list on page xvi, citing the five main books of the Prydain Chronicles, three peripheral books, and two other sources: Charlotte Guest's translation of the *Mabinogion* and Robert Graves's classic guide to mythology, *The White Goddess*; the citations use a one- to three-letter code plus page number (e.g., "HK 162+"=*The High King*, page 162 and following). There are some additional references which cite authors and works listed in the three-page bibliography by surname, year of publication, and pagination (e.g., "Jacobs, 1978:281-282," referencing pages 282-82 of James S. Jacobs's "Lloyd Alexander: A Critical Biography," an unpublished 1978 doctoral dissertation). Also included are numerous quotations from Alexander himself, taken from letters, published interviews or essays, and from personal communications with the author; these add a great deal of insight into the author's work and into the origins of Prydain and its characters. Many entries also feature a pronunciation guide to help those readers unfamiliar with Alexander's orthography.

The final section, "Categories of Entry Headings," is a very useful subject guide to the entries by general topic: for example, "common folk," "characters," "potters," "female characters," "realms," etc. The book is beautifully typeset and arranged, illustrated with very clear black-and-white reproductions of the covers of the eight Prydain books and a Prydain map, and is bound to library standards. Tunnell's work is authoritative, well written, well referenced, and very well organized. All collections with an interest in modern children's and/or recent fantasy literature should own a copy, as should all research collections. A current bibliography of Alexander's work is also badly needed.

Piers Anthony

469. Anthony, Piers, and Jody Lynn Nye. **Piers Anthony's Visual Guide to Xanth**. New York, Avon Books, 1989. 236 p. LC 89-91277. ISBN 0-380-75749-4 (pbk.).

This beautifully designed and copiously illustrated potpourri includes descriptive chapters on various aspects of Anthony's created world, together with numerous alphabetical lists of characters, places, things, flora, and fauna relating to Xanth. Contents: "Introduction to Xanth: Great Events in the History of Xanth"; "Xanth, The Demon X(A/N)th and the Balance of Existence"; "People of Xanth: Magic and Customs of the People of Xanth, Magicians and Kings, Harpies and Goblins, Demons, Centaurs, Other Races of Equine Descent, Fairies, Imps, Elves, and Gnomes, Ogres, Voles, Zombies, Nymphs and Fauns, Other Human and Humanlike Folk, Other Individuals"; "Places in Xanth: North of the Gap, North Village, The Gap, South of the Gap, Good Magician Humfrey's Castle, Castle Roogna, Centaur Isle, The Gourd"; "Hazards of Xanth"; "The Bestiary of Xanth"; "The Best Things in Xanth Are Free: Flowers, Plants, Trees; Magical Things of Xanth"; "Calendar of Xanth"; "Afterword"; "Appendix: Crewel Lye, Chapter I."

The maps and illustrations by Todd Cameron Hamilton and James Clouse are both appropriate and illuminating. The short alphabetical listings of characters, etc., following many of the sub-sections include the term (in boldface or italics) with a one-sentence to three-paragraph description. The book's main fault is its relative inaccessibility: an index would have made it useful both as a browser's guide to the author's work and as a reference source for future literary scholarship. Similarly, a brief bibliography of the Xanth books, with a listing of their various editions, would have added another dimension to the volume. When such items are so relatively easy to compile, their absence from a book of this type is inexcusable. The result is a superficially attractive guide that's as lightweight as the fiction it covers. The book is nicely typeset and perfect bound in paper covers.

Note: *The Xanth Encyclopedia*, mentioned internally as one of Nye's other book credits, is *not* a reference volume but one of a series of fictional interactive game pastiches of the Xanth universe created with Anthony's approval.

Arthurian Romances

470. Lerond, Dennis. **An Arthurian Concordance**. [Baltimore, T-K Graphics], 1974. [51] p. (pbk.).

This alphabetical guide to Arthurian characters, places, implements, and events provides a good general introduction to this legendary character and his associated mythological world. A typical entry includes name (all caps) and brief description (in italics, ranging in size from several words to five sentences). No sources are cited (Malory's *Le Morte d'Arthur*, for example), making it difficult to identify the level of Lerond's research. The book is shot from legible typed copy and bound with staples through the spine into stiff paper covers.

Marion Zimmer Bradley

471. Breen, Walter. **The Darkover Concordance: A Reader's Guide**. Berkeley, Calif., Pennyfarthing Press, 1979. ix, 163 p. LC 79-84472. ISBN 0-930800-10-9; ISBN 0-930800-07-9 (pbk.).

Bradley's former husband here contributes, with the cooperation of the author and the "Friends of Darkover," a fan group, an excellent alphabetical guide to the Darkover universe. Contents: "Foreword," by Bradley; "To the Reader," by Breen; "Chronological Sequence of the Darkover Novels"; "Guide to Pronunciation of Darkover Words"; "Concordance" [141 pages]; Appendices: "The Ballad of Hastur and Cassilda"; "The Ballad Commonly Called 'The Outlaw'"; "The Oath of the Comhi-Letzii"; "Darkovan Proverbs and Proverbial Expressions"; "Some Notes on the New Hebrides Communal Songs"; "The Darkover Novels: Publishing Histories and Story Summaries"; "Darkovan Genealogies."

A typical entry includes character name (boldfaced; italics signify words of Darkover origin, while those in all caps are characters who actually appear in the story in question); a description ranging in length from a few words to a double-columned page; citation (boldfaced, in the form "**WW 97**" for page 97 of *The World Wreckers*). There are excellently rendered line drawings by Melisa Michaels scattered throughout the text. The book is exceptionally detailed, referencing even typographical errors and misspellings of names in the original texts and noting various inconsistencies in the saga; and the appendices provide very useful supplemental materials, including a complete bibliography of the Darkover books, with all known English-language and foreign-language reprint editions and complete bibliographical data. A new edition including the Darkover novels of the last decade would certainly be justified; even without the recent books in the series, Breen's volume will be an essential starting point for any student of this well-known author's work.

Edgar Rice Burroughs

472. Harwood, John, and Allan Howard. **Tarzan Encyclopedia**, in *Burroughs Bulletin* no. 45/46 (January/February, 1975): [1-41]. (pbk.).

This alphabetical guide to the persons, places, and things of the Tarzan mythos was issued as a special double issue of this well-known Burroughs fanzine, with both the magazine and book title appearing on the front cover. A typical entry includes term (all caps), brief description (one to ten sentences, but occasionally extending to several paragraphs for major entries), and book reference (in the form "(LION)" for *Tarzan and the Lion Man*). Included in the main alphabetical sequence are the Tarzan books, under the second element of the title (for example, *Tarzan at the Earth's Core* is referenced as EARTH'S CORE, TARZAN AT THE).

A typical book entry includes title (all caps), brief bibliographical data (first magazine serialization, with magazine title and date, and first book publication, with publisher and year), and extensive plot summary (ranging in size from one to two full columns of text). An interesting and very useful feature of this guide is a series of brief dictionaries of the main languages used in the Tarzan saga, gathered together under the generic term "LANGUAGE," and subarranged by language and then alphabetically by word, each with its English-language equivalent. The volume is shot from legible typed copy arranged in double 8.5" x 11" columns and stapled through the spine. Entries in both Harwood and Howard's dictionary and McWhorter's (see #474) contain about the same level of description; however, the former's inclusion of mini-dictionaries, as well as extensive separate plot summaries of the Tarzan books, and a guide to the Clayton (i.e., Tarzan's) family, makes the *Encyclopedia* valuable in its own right. A more elaborate and updated version, with better production values, should be contemplated; the original is virtually impossible to locate.

473. Kudlay, Robert R., and Joan Leiby. **Burroughs' Science Fiction, with an Analytical Subject and Name Index**. Geneseo, N.Y., School of Library and Information Science, State University College of Arts and Science, 1973. 236 p. index. (Geneseo Studies in Library and Information Science, No. 5). LC 74-172705 (pbk.).

This curious set of indexes was evidently produced as a library science school project. Contents: "Preface"; "Introduction" (by Kudlay); "Introduction to the Indexes"; "I. Pellucidar"; "Symmes' Hole"; "Synopsis of the Pellucidarian Saga"; "Animal Kingdom of Pellucidar"; "Tribes of Pellucidar"; "People of Pellucidar"; "A Note on Aging and Ages"; "Burroughs' Social Thought"; "How to Use the Index"; "Index to Pellucidar"; "II. Other Science-Fiction Romance": "Synopsis"; "Indexes: Caspak, Cave Girl, Lost Continent, Moon, Poloda"; "III. Bibliographies"; "Burroughs in the Literature"; "Bibliography"; "Symmes' Bibliography"; "IV. Illustrations."

The section on Pellucidar, the underworld kingdom created by Burroughs in a seven-book series, comprises about half the text (110 pages). This chapter is broken into various sub-sections, each dealing with a specific theme (e.g., "Tribes of Pellucidar"), under which terms or names are listed in alphabetical order, in chart format, with related terms such as "Description" and "Ruler(s)" (in the tribes section), or individual "Names," "Title(s)," "Native Land," and "Relatives" (in the people section), sorted into their respective columns. Each world (Pellucidar, Caspak, etc.) is then indexed separately at the end of its respective section or chapter to an abbreviation representing book title and page and/or chapter number of the Burroughs's work from which it derives (e.g., "P(15)"=*Pellucidar*, page 15). There are several amateurishly drawn maps and illustrations, and a much outdated bibliography of secondary sources on Burroughs. The book is shot from typed copy, printed on now-yellowing paper, and poorly bound in paper covers.

A one-alphabet dictionary format would have been much more useful here, together with a single index, but the volume still provides some hard-to-find data for the diehard Burroughs fan. Prefer McWhorter's guide (#474).

474. McWhorter, George T. **Burroughs Dictionary: An Alphabetical List of Proper Names, Words, Phrases, and Concepts Contained in the Published Works of Edgar Rice Burroughs**. Lanham, Md. & New York, University Press of America, 1987. xiii, 446 p. LC 87-14266. ISBN 0-8191-6512-3.

This long overdue guide to a master fantasy writer's many works organizes into one alphabetical sequence every place, person, and term appearing in Burroughs's seventy-seven published works, omitting only those general geographical locations (such as "Africa") for which no explanation is necessary.

A typical entry includes name (boldface), description, and citation (keyed to a one- to three-letter code, in the form [TC] for *Tarzan and the Castaways*). The descriptions often include brief illuminating quotations from Burroughs's original text. The citations lack page or chapter numbers; short stories included in larger collections are separately cited. In addition to the alphabetical directory which comprises the vast majority of the work, there is an introductory section of explanatory notes and a two-page Edgar Rice Burroughs chronology at the end. The author also cites many other reference works throughout the text, both as explanation to terms and personages no longer part of the current American consciousness and to demonstrate Burroughs's antecedents. Roughly 6,500 entries are included, a number far exceeding the combined total of all other available sources. The book is shot from very legible word-processed copy and bound to library standards, the only one of the four Burroughs dictionaries suitable for library use.

Although McWorter's descriptions are not as detailed as some of those appearing in Roy's more limited work on the eleven Martian books (see #475), or in Harwood and Howard's comprehensive guide to the Tarzan series (see #472), the *Dictionary* includes so many more works—and so many more entries—that it will become *the* essential starting point (with Heins's standard bibliography [see #305]) for all future scholarship on Burroughs's fiction.

475. Roy, John Flint. **A Guide to Barsoom: Eleven Sections of References in One Volume, Dealing with the Martian Stories Written by Edgar Rice Burroughs.** New York, A Del Rey Book, Ballantine Books, 1976. [viii], 200 p. LC 76-11849. ISBN 0-345-28595-6 (pbk.).

Roy, a long-time Burroughs fan, compiled this mass-market guide to the Martian tales as a tribute to the author and his work. Contents: "Introduction"; "I. A Brief History of Pre-Carter Barsoom"; "II. A Geography of Barsoom, Including a Gazetteer-Index and Hemispheric and Polar Maps of Its Surface"; "III. A Biography of Barsoom, Including a Dictionary of People, Past and Present, Whose Names Appear in the Barsoomian Sagas"; "IV. The Flora and Fauna of Barsoom, Including a Dictionary of Barsoomian Plants and Animals"; "V. Measurements on Barsoom—Linear, Time, Monetary—and a List of Barsoomian Numbers"; "VI. The Language, Religions, and Customs of Barsoom"; "VII. A General Barsoomian Glossary: Terms, Titles, Organizations, Games, Weapons, Buildings, Streets, Etc."; "VIII. Quotations, Proverbs, and Expletives—From the Rich Heritage of Barsoom and the Pen of John Carter"; "IX. Barsoomian Science and Invention"; "X. Through Space to Barsoom?"; "XI. Edgar Rice Burroughs: A Brief Biographical Sketch"; "Acknowledgments and Sources"; "From the Author."

Each chapter includes three to five pages of narrative background materials on the topic in question, followed by alphabetically arranged guides at the end of most chapters providing details about specific places, characters, things, concepts, and flora and fauna of Burroughs's imagined Mars. A typical entry includes name (boldface), citation (with two- to three-letter keys to the eleven book titles, plus chapter number, in the form "*PM*/18,19" for *A Princess of Mars*, Chapters 18-19), and an annotation ranging in size from a few words to several pages. For individuals, Roy generally gives their complete history and background as described in the books, including parentage, associates, family members, noble titles, and an exact account of what they accomplished during the saga. It is obvious that Roy has contributed some of the "history" to this volume, particularly in the narrative sections; this is perhaps inevitable given the inconsistencies of the original books. The descriptions are generally better wrought and more fully fleshed than those in McWhorter's dictionary (see #474). However, the lack of an overall index, and the split nature of Roy's guides (four separate alphabetical lists as opposed to one A-Z sequence in McWhorter's volume), makes the latter much more accessible. *A Guide to Barsoom* is nicely illustrated throughout with line drawings by Neal MacDonald.

Alan Dean Foster

476. Teague, Robert (text), and Michael Goodwin (illustrator). **A Guide to the Commonwealth: The Official Guide to Alan Dean Foster's Humanx Commonwealth Universe**. Roy, Utah, Galagraphics, 1985. 70 p. (pbk.).

This interesting and well-illustrated reference book focuses on the fictional future created by American SF writer Foster over the past two decades in a series of a dozen novels and several short stories. Following an introduction by Foster and forewords by Teague and Goodwin, the first section, "Galographics," provides a guide to place names in the "known universe," with separate alphabetical listings of worlds in the AAnn Empire, The Blight, and the Humanx Commonwealth (including physical descriptions, brief histories, and lists of races, etc.). This section also includes maps of the three empires, and of the universe as known and explored by mankind. Part Two, "Natural History," gives two alphabetical lists of flora and fauna in the known universe, with the worlds on which they occur, and chief attributes.

Section Three, "Intelligence," lists alien races (alphabetically), extinct races, a rendition of the Thranx alphabet, diagrams (drawings) of aliens, and the Commonwealth T-Standard Calendar. Part Four, "Technology," includes drawings and lists of the spacecraft and weaponry employed by the intelligent races known to man. A final section, "General," provides "Commonwealth Chronology"; "Classification of Planets"; "Measurement Standards"; "Chemicals, Drugs, Medicines, and Poisons"; and "Mineralogy." The book is attractively designed and typeset in 8.5" x 11" format and bound with staples into paper covers. Although an index would have been desirable, plus a brief bibliography of Foster's works (the authors only include a bare list of books consulted, without further data), Teague and Goodwin's excellent guide provides virtually everything that the fan and scholar would want to know about Foster's fictional world.

Robert A. Heinlein

477. Downing, Nancy Bailey. **A Robert A. Heinlein Cyclopedia: A Guide to the Persons, Places, and Things in the Fiction of America's Most Popular Science Fiction Author**. San Bernardino, Calif., The Borgo Press, 1992. [500] p. index. (Borgo Literary Guides, No. 5). LC 87-714. ISBN 0-89370-814-3; ISBN 0-89730-914-X (pbk.).

This massive guide to the late SF writer's work provides an enormous amount of information in an attractive, well-organized format. All of Heinlein's fictions, novels as well as short stories, are covered in one alphabetical sequence encompassing the characters, place names, and concepts mentioned in the writer's work.

A typical entry includes name (boldface), description, and citation (in the form "FRI, 6," for the paperback edition of *Friday*). The body of the entry includes both background material on the character and an account of what happens to each individual in the stories in which he or she appeared; the use of hanging indents and copious see references makes this section both readable and easy to use. In addition to the main section, Downing also provides an abbreviations list; an alphabetical guide to each story or novel covered, with detailed plot summaries; and (at the end of the book) a primary bibliography. There are numerous see and see also references scattered throughout the text, from alternate forms of a name to the main entry, and to other names or places of interest. The book is nicely typeset and bound to library standards.

Heinlein's death in 1988 marked the end of the career of the best-known SF author of his time; although several unexpurgated versions of previously issued novels have been published in the intervening years (particularly *Stranger in a Strange Land*), no more original stories have appeared. Thus, this *Cyclopedia* is very likely complete as it stands, and its thousands of entries will become the standard guide to this writer's many fictional creations.

Frank Herbert

478. McNelly, Willis E., ed. **The Dune Encyclopedia**. New York, G. P. Putnam's Sons, 1984. ix, 526 p. LC 84-4824. ISBN 0-399-12950-2. Also: New York, Berkley Books, 1984. ix, 526 p. ISBN 0-425-06813-7 (pbk.). Also: London, Corgi Books, 1984. ix, 526 p. ISBN 0-552-99131-7 (pbk.).

McNelly's book differs from the other guides included in this section in two respects: it includes contributions from forty-three fans and scholars, arranged in an alphabetical, encyclopedic format; and much of the material is invented, though based upon the future world created by Frank Herbert in his six Dune sagas. Thus, not all the characters or places mentioned by Herbert in the Dune books may be listed; and those which do have entries feature a combination of "factual" (i.e., based upon Herbert's story lines) and supplemental material created by the contributors. Thus, the list of "Emperors of the Known Universe" contributed by Robert Reginald, although it incorporates the few emperors actually mentioned by Herbert, and was used by McNelly to coordinate the "history" of the Dune mythos in this *Encyclopedia*, is largely invented out of whole cloth and relatively useless to the student of Herbert. Even the bibliographical citations at the end of each article, and the bibliography proper at the end of the book, both feature nonexistent titles and authors, as well as legitimate cross references to other articles of interest. The result, while amusing, is more an exercise in literary pastiche than a real guide to the author's work.

Robert E. Howard

479. Weinberg, Robert. **The Annotated Guide to Robert E. Howard's Sword & Sorcery**. West Linn, Ore., Starmont House, 1976. vii, 152 p. LC 76-16708. ISBN 0-916732-20-7; ISBN 0-916732-00-2 (pbk.). The cloth edition was not produced until 1980. Also: San Bernardino, Calif., The Borgo Press, 1980. vii, 152 p. LC 80-19169. ISBN 0-89370-029-0.

Although the reference value of this guide is minimal, it is mentioned here because it complements *A Gazeteer of the Hyborian World of Conan*, by Lee N. Falconer (i.e., Julian May; see #13). Contents: "Introduction"; "Solomon Kane"; "King Kull"; "Bran Mak Morn and the Picts"; "James Allison"; "Turlogh Dubh"; "Non-Series Stories"; "Conan"; "The Chronological Conan"; "The Conan Saga" (as written by Robert E. Howard).

Each chapter covers a specific Howard fantasy hero. Several pages of narrative text at the beginning of each section give background information on the character, a physical description of his attributes, a brief account of his life as described in Howard's stories, a chronological listing of those fictions, and other material of interest. The remainder of each chapter lists the stories chronologically by publication date, or occasionally in reading order, a typical entry providing title (all caps), magazine title (in italics) and month and year of publication, or book title (in all caps), publisher, and year of publication, for those stories which appeared first in anthologies or collections; a list of the principal characters featured in that tale; several paragraphs of plot summary; and a one-to-three-paragraph commentary. The book is nicely typeset and the cloth edition bound to library standards.

The absence of an index makes access to the material in this volume unnecessarily difficult, requiring the reader to peruse whole sections to find specific character references. Although May's book (see #13) does include an excellent A-Z guide to the geographical names and principal tribes and states of Hyboria (the Conan fictional universe), but not to the rest of Howard's creations, the world is still waiting for a concise one-volume alphabetical guide to the proper names in Howard's entire canon.

C. S. Lewis

480. Ford, Paul F. **Companion to Narnia**. New York, Harper & Row, 1980. xxxii, 313 p. LC 80-7734. ISBN 0-06-250340-5 (pbk.). **Companion to Narnia**. 2nd ed. San Francisco, Harper & Row, 1983. xxxix, 448 p. LC 82-21172. ISBN 0-06-250341-3 (pbk.). **Companion to Narnia**. 3rd ed. New York, Collier Books, Macmillan Publishing Co., 1986. xli, 450 p. LC 86-5352. ISBN 0-02-084940-0 (pbk.).

Ford has continued to expand this very detailed guide to Lewis's fantasy septology through three separate editions. Contents (third edition): "List of Illustrations and Maps"; "Foreword," by Madeleine L'Engle; "Preface to the Third Edition"; "Acknowledgements"; "Introduction"; "Using the Companion"; "The Companion from A to Z";" Appendix One: Chronology of the Composition and Publication of *The Chronicles*"; "Appendix Two: List of Comparative Ages"; "Appendix Three: A Comparison of Narnian and Earth Time"; "About the Author."

The main section of the book (450 pages) is an A-Z rendering of the people, places, and things in Lewis's fictional creation. Entries range in size from one sentence to thirty pages (for Aslan, the Lion King of Narnia), and typically include term (all caps, boldfaced), single-sentence description (e.g., "one of the Seven Noble Lords"), physical attributes, a detailed accounting of the events which have affected the person or place, a list of references (keyed to the abbreviations recorded on pages xl-xli, in the form "PC 16, *15*" for *Prince Caspian*, page 16 of the Collier mass-market edition, and page 15 of the trade paperback edition), and footnotes. There are numerous see references scattered throughout the text; see also references to other terms of interest for which entries exist are noted by an asterisk following the term. The book is very nicely typeset, illustrated with maps of Narnia and black-and-white reproductions of full-page drawings from Lewis's original volumes, and perfect bound.

Ford knows his material, and his work is far more complete and detailed than Sammons's guide (see #482). However, the absence of running heads sometimes results in unnecessary difficulty in finding one's way through the alphabet; for example, the intrusion of thirty pages of unlabelled text into the "A" section for the entry on Aslan makes searching entries in this area extraordinarily difficult. Also, the latter entry includes twelve pages of very intrusive footnotes in small type; if this material was worth including, it should have been integrated into the text, or, at the very least, gathered together at the end of the volume into a footnotes section. Fortunately, most sections of the book do not suffer unduly from these design problems, and the *Companion* can be recommended to all research libraries and to any scholar studying Lewis's fiction.

481. Sammons, Martha C. **A Guide Through C. S. Lewis' Space Trilogy**. Westchester, Ill., Cornerstone Books, 1980. 189 p. LC 80-68329. ISBN 0-89107-185-7 (pbk.).

Sammons, author of a companion volume to Narnia (see #482), covers Lewis's Perelandra Trilogy in both narrative and dictionary formats. Contents: "Introduction"; "Chapter 1: Maker of Myths: C. S. Lewis and Science Fiction"; "Chapter 2: The Myth of Deep Heaven"; "Chapter 3: Medieval Perspectives and the Trilogy"; "Chapter 4: Mythology, Arthurian Legend, and the Trilogy"; "Chapter 5: Myth Became Fact: Science and Spirit in the Trilogy"; "Chapter 6: Man and His World in the Trilogy"; "Chapter 7: Maleldil and His Reign: Biblical Background and Themes"; "Appendix: A Summary of the Trilogy"; "The Languages in the Trilogy"; "A Dictionary of Deep Heaven"; "Notes."

The narrative sections (140 pages) cover major topics, themes, and characters in their respective chapters, in one or two pages of descriptive and evaluative text. The chapter on languages (four pages) gives brief summaries of Malacandrian, Hrossan, Pfifiltriggian, and Surnibur, with short lists of words and their English-language equivalents. The "Dictionary of Deep Heaven" (thirty-seven pages) is an A-Z listing of the people, places, and things in the Perelandra mythos. A typical entry provides term (boldfaced), citation ("OSP"=*Out of the Silent Planet*, "P"=*Perelan-dra*, "THS"=*That Hideous Strength*), and a brief (one sentence to one paragraph) description of the person or item, plus its significance to the stories, with internal see also references to other terms of interest (indicated with an asterisk before the term). Roughly 300 items are listed. The book is professionally typeset and designed but not made to withstand library use.

Sammons has provided enough material here to guide any beginning student into the world of Lewis's fictional universe, but her work is no substitute for the kind of full-length alphabetical guide Ford has produced on The Narnia Chronicles (see #480). Future editions should include a general index, without which access to anything but the dictionary itself is unnecessarily difficult.

482. Sammons, Martha C. **A Guide Through Narnia**. Wheaton, Ill., Harold Shaw Publishers, 1979. 164 p. LC 78-26476. ISBN 0-87788-325-4 (pbk.). Also: London: Hodder & Stoughton, 1979. 164 p.

Sammons's guide, like her companion volume on the Perelandran tales (see #481) consists of broad narrative chapters plus a character and place dictionary at the end of the volume. Contents: "Introduction"; "Chapter 1: The Creator of the Narnia Chronicles"; "Chapter 2: The Creation of the Narnia Tales"; "Chapter 3: The Chronicles of Narnia"; "Chapter 4: The Country of Narnia"; "Chapter 5: The Creator of Narnia—Aslan"; "Chapter 6: Characters of Narnia"; "Chapter 7: Creations of Evil"; "Chapter 8: Christian Concepts in the Narnia Tales—A Summary"; "Index of Names and Places"; "A Note on Names and Creatures"; "Notes."

The narrative chapters are further subdivided into one- to three-page sections covering specific characters, places, and concepts, in no apparent order. Without an index, these mini-essays, while interesting in themselves, remain basically inaccessible to the average reader. The "Index of Names and Places" is a twenty-six-page A-Z guide to the major persons and sites in the Narnia Saga. A typical entry gives term (bold all caps), citation (in the form "HHB" for *The Horse and His Boy*), and a brief one-paragraph description. The "Note on Names and Creatures" describes the different kinds of men and creatures found in Narnia and the given names with which C. S. Lewis honored them. The book is nicely designed and typeset, but the paperback binding will not withstand library usage.

Sammons appears to know her material well, but her brief introductory guide to the Narnia series is clearly outshown by Ford's much more comprehensive and copiously referenced dictionary (see #480).

H. P. Lovecraft

483. Weinberg, Robert E. **A Reader's Guide to the Cthulhu Mythos**. Hillside, N.J., Robert Weinberg, 1969. [Pagination unknown]. (pbk.). Weinberg, R[obert] E., and E. P. Berglund. **Reader's Guide to the Cthulhu Mythos**. 2nd rev. ed. Albuquerque, N.M., The Silver Scarab Press, 1973. 88 p. index. (pbk.).

American writer Howard Phillips Lovecraft (1890-1937) based many of his horror tales around a common background which he invited many of his young correspondents to share. This shared milieu gradually became known as the "Cthulhu Mythos" after the name of one of the Elder Gods featured as a background "character" in the stories. This brief checklist of Cthulhu Mythos stories includes (second edition): a two-page "Introduction" by the authors, a "Chronological Listing by Publication Dates"; "Alphabetical Listing by Title"; "Alphabetical Listing by Author"; "Series Listing"; "Alphabetical Listing by Author of Non-Fiction"; "Alphabetical Listing by Author of Parodies"; "Alphabetical Listing by Author of Poetry" [including many by Lovecraft himself]; "Alphabetical Listing by Title of Books, Pamphlets, Brochures, etc."; "Non-English Publications"; "Errata"; and "Addenda."

The chronological checklist includes an abbreviations guide at the beginning of the listing, then arranges the data by publication date. A typical entry gives year of publication, month of publication, title, author, and an abbreviation signifying the magazine name or book publisher. Items considered an integral part of the Cthulhu Mythos are so indicated with an asterisk following the entry (this is true throughout the book). The title listing correlates titles and authors only. The author index lists author's name, title, magazine title (in italics), month and year of publication, or (for monograph appearances) book title (all caps), publisher, and year of publication (in the form "45" for 1945), plus similar data for all known reprints. No paginations for books or periodical listings are given anywhere in the volume.

The alphabetical listings give book title (all caps), author or editor, publisher, year of publication, and complete contents for anthologies and single-author collections (many of the entries), each separate edition of the book being listed completely separately. The foreign-language section is arranged alphabetically by translated title, giving title (all caps), author or editor, translator, publisher, place of publication, year of publication, and complete contents for anthologies and collections, with original, English-language titles in parentheses. The book is attractively designed, but the binding tends to disintegrate with usage.

Although now two decades out-of-date, Weinberg and Berglund's book remains the only guide to the horrors spawned by Lovecraft's pen and those of his imitators. A new edition without so many subdivisions would definitely be warranted.

Julian May

484. May, Julian. **A Pliocene Companion, Being a Reader's Guide to The Many-Colored Land, The Golden Torc, The Nonborn King, The Adversary**. Boston, Houghton Mifflin Co., 1984. xiii, 219 p. LC 84-9124. ISBN 0-395-36516-3. Also: New York, A Del Rey Book, Ballantine Books, 1985. xiii, 219 p. ISBN 0-345-32290-8 (pbk.). Also: London,

Collins, 1985. xiii, 219 p. ISBN 0-00-222970-6. Also: London & Sydney, Pan Books, 1985. xiii, 220 p. ISBN 0-330-28986-1 (pbk.).

Although the vast majority of character dictionaries are compiled by fans of a writer's work, May comes well qualified to produce this dictionary of her own created world of Pliocene Exile, having previously authored (under the pen name Lee N. Falconer) a similar book on Robert E. Howard (see #13). The main section of the book (118 pages) is an alphabetical guide to the persons, places, and implements of the quatrology, a typical entry including name (boldfaced), pronunciation guide, description (ranging in size from a few words to an entire page), and see references (all caps).

This is followed by "A Chronology of the Saga"; "The Remillard Family Tree" (a genealogical chart); "The Ocala Rebels and Their Offspring" (table); "Author's Three Original Maps of Pliocene Europe"; "Two Maps of Ocala Island and Vicinity"; "The Good Ship Killikki" (description and diagram); "The Double Ourobouros" (description and drawing); "Music in My Head—Science Fiction As Opera" (an article by May on the musical background of the Saga); "Certain Poems Quoted in the Saga"; "The Pliocene Wildcat Lives!" (on cats); "Three Interviews with Julian May"; "A Selective Bibliography" [of materials used by May to research the saga]. There are also several photographs of May near the end of the book. The book is well designed and typeset and bound to library standards.

A Pliocene Companion provides an excellent introduction to May's popular fictional creation. Indeed, this attractive and comprehensive guide is a paradigm of what a character dictionary should be and is recommended as a model to prospective compilers of such volumes.

Anne McCaffrey

485. Nye, Jody Lynn, with Anne McCaffrey. **The Dragonlover's Guide to Pern**. New York, A Del Rey Book, Ballantine Books, 1989. xi, 178 p. LC 89-6715. ISBN 0-345-35424-9.

This beautifully designed volume was intended for fans of McCaffrey's popular Pern Cycle. Contents: "Introduction"; "I. Overview"; "II. Fit for Human Habitation"; "III. The Red Star"; "IV. From Dragonets to Dragons"; "V. Weyrlings"; "VI. Training and Fighting Dragons," by Todd Johnson; "VII. Threadfall Charts"; "VIII. Fort, the First Hold"; "IX. Benden, the Second Weyr"; "X. Holds, Crafthalls, and Weyrs"; "XI. Pronunciation Guide to Names on Pern"; "Sources" (i.e., bibliography).

Each narrative chapter is organized around a specific topic, then broken into subdivisions covering specific subjects. For example, Chapter IX, on "Benden Weyr," includes sections on "The Queen's Weyr," "The Support Structure of the Weyr," "Duties," "Benden Hold," "Benden Wine," plus scattered interpolated sections giving recipes, oaths, and other material. Other chapters are similarly broken into component pieces. Some of the material is taken directly from McCaffrey's fiction, but Nye has also clearly added text of her own, with or without the author's connivance. The distinction between the two is deliberately blurred, so that one is never sure whether or not the customs or places described are actually derived from the tales themselves. The pronunciation guide, while useful, does not cover every character from the Pern books. The absence of an index makes the material virtually inaccessible without extensive reading. The book is nicely typeset and is bound to library standards.

A complete A-Z guide to the persons, places, and things in McCaffrey's fictional universe has yet to be produced. Compare with Fonstad's *Atlas of Pern* (see #15), which shares some of the same problems.

John Myers Myers

486. Lerner, Fred, ed. **A *Silverlock* Companion: The Life and Works of John Myers Myers.** Center Harbor, N.H., Niekas Publications, 1988. 52 p. ISBN 0-910619-02-6 (pbk.). Also: San Bernardino, Calif., The Borgo Press, 1989. 52 p. LC 89-861. ISBN 0-8095-6850-0.

Myers wrote many works of Western Americana but is best known in fantastic literature for his rousing fantasy adventure *Silverlock*. Contents: "Preface"; "John Myers Myers: A Brief Biography," by James M. Crane; "John Myers Myers: A Tribute," by Lerner; "Recollections," by Edmund R. Meskys; "*Silverlock* and *The Moon's Fire-Eating Daughter*: An Appreciation," by Charlotte Moslander; "A Reader's Guide to the Commonwealth: A Glossary of Literary, Mythological, and Geographical Allusions in *Silverlock*," by Lerner and Anne J. Braude; "The *Silverlock* Library," by Lerner; "The Western Writings," by James M. Crane; "The Inside Scoop on John Myers Myers," by Myers; "A Bibliography," by Crane; "The Makers' Muse," by Myers.

The reader's guide, which occupies twenty-eight pages of text, is an A-Z listing of the people, places, and things which fill the allusion-strewn pages of *Silverlock*. A typical entry gives term (boldfaced all caps), page number (referenced to the 1949 E. P. Dutton cloth edition of the book), identification of the reference (with one paragraph of description), its role in the narrative, and (in parentheses) the author, title (both in English and in the original language, if the work was first published overseas), nationality and genre, and original date of publication.

Crane's "Bibliography" is broken into "Part I: The Books"; "Part II: Essays and Articles"; "Part III: The Poems"; "Part IV: Unpublished Writings." In each section materials are arranged chronologically by publication date, each printing of a title being listed separately. A typical book entry provides year of publication (boldfaced), book title (boldfaced), place of publication, publisher, year of publication, pagination, first edition points, height of the book in centimeters, and a list of all printings, with months and years noted, and other notes. Crane includes translations into other languages when known. The shorter works sections give year of publication (boldfaced), title (boldfaced, in quotes), magazine title (in italics), month and year of publication, specific pagination, and bibliographical notes. The list of unpublished writings gives date and manuscript page count. The guide is very attractively typeset and designed, filled with illustrations, and bound with staples into paper covers; the Borgo edition is bound to library standards.

Myers died shortly after this book was produced, and it is unlikely much will be added to his bibliography in the future. Students of this important regional writer will use this guide as an essential starting point for their research.

Mervyn Peake

487. Metzger, Arthur. **A Guide to the Gormenghast Trilogy.** [Baltimore, T-K Graphics], 1976. 35 p. (pbk.).

This brief guide to Peake's best-known fictional creation includes a poignant introduction by Michael Moorcock adapted from his 1969 obituary of Peake in *New Worlds*. The dictionary section is arranged alphabetically by main entry (persons, places, or things), a typical entry including name (bold caps), citation (to book and chapter number), and description. Entries range in size from one sentence to several pages (for Titus Groan, the key figure in the Trilogy). Many items feature illustrative quotations from Peake's original text, as, for example, the entry for Mr. Gumshaw: "His polished pate reflects a brace of candles." Nicely typeset, this very readable but exceedingly brief guide deserves wider circulation than it originally received.

Cordwainer Smith

488.   Lewis, Anthony R. **Concordance to Cordwainer Smith**. Boston, New England Science Fiction Association, 1984. [iv], 90 p. LC 84-236060. ISBN 0-915368-24-2 (pbk.).

Intended as a preliminary version of a larger dictionary index to Smith's work (which has never appeared), the *Concordance* provides a guide to the people, places, and things of the author's fictional future history but excludes his early mainstream and spy novels, *Ria*, *Carola*, and *Atomsk*. Following a brief preface and a key to the works cited, Lewis arranges the material in alphabetical order by name; a typical entry includes term, line break, description, title code (in the form "UP" for *The Underpeople*), double line break. The entries tend to be short (a few words to two brief paragraphs) and straightforward; however, Lewis does include references to known or extrapolated sources for Smith's often punning or deliberately derivative names (e.g., "Englok, Lord. Built the Brown and Yellow Corridor as a thoughtproof shelter during the ancient wars. [DL] eng + loch (German) = narrow gate, opening. 'Enter by the Narrow Gate'—Gospels.").

Interfiled with the descriptive entries are the titles of Smith's books and stories; a typical book entry includes title (underlined), contents (if a collection), publisher, place of publication, pagination, year of publication, cover artist, and price (if a paperback). A typical short story entry includes title (all title entries are followed by the word "story"), category, magazine title, month and year of publication, and brief description (i.e., time, setting, broad story line). There are numerous see references from similar names or terms to other entries scattered throughout the text. The book is shot from very legible double-columned word-processed copy and is bound with staples into paper covers.

Lewis's book is a good beginning guide to this well-known author's stories; however, the descriptions are sometimes so terse as to be incomprehensible to someone unfamiliar with Cordwainer Smith's work. A more elaborate version, perhaps including the missing books, with the bibliographical data separated into their own section, would certainly be appropriate.

J. R. R. Tolkien

489.   Foster, Robert. **A Guide to Middle-Earth**. Baltimore, Mirage Press, 1971. xiii, 283, [8] p. LC 72-94777. Cloth and pbk. Also: New York, Ballantine Books, 1974. 283 p. (pbk.). **The Complete Guide to Middle-Earth, from the Hobbit to the Silmarillion**. Rev. and enlarged ed. New York, A Del Rey Book, Ballantine Books, 1978. xvi, 575 p. LC 77-26825. ISBN 0-345-27320-9; ISBN 0-345-30974-X (trade pbk.); ISBN 0-345-27975-1 (mass market pbk.). Also: London, George Allen & Unwin, 1978. xii, 441 p. ISBN 0-04-803002-3; ISBN 0-04-803001-5 (pbk.).

Foster's comprehensive guide to Tolkien's works was expanded in 1978 to encompass the then-recent publication of *The Silmarillion*. Contents: "Introduction"; "Sources and Abbreviations"; "Complete Guide"; "Appendix A: A Chronology of the First Age"; "Appendix B: Genealogical Tables"; "Appendix C: Conversion of Page References to Houghton Mifflin Editions."

The main section (555 pages in the revised edition) is an A-Z guide to the persons, places, and things in Tolkien's Lord of the Rings Trilogy, *The Hobbit*, and *The Silmarillion*. A typical entry gives term (bold all caps); language abbreviation (e.g., "S"=Sinhardin) and

English-language meaning of the word, where appropriate; brief description; significance; and citation (e.g., "I 206"=*The Fellowship of the Ring*, revised Ballantine edition, p. 206). The descriptions range in size from one sentence to several pages, averaging one paragraph. Roughly 2,500 terms are covered. There are numerous see and see also references scattered throughout the text. The book is shot from nicely designed typeset copy, and the cloth versions are bound to library standards.

Although both Foster and Tyler (see #490) cover essentially the same territory at comparable lengths, Foster's copious use of citations makes his work more useful for scholars and researchers and is generally to be preferred. Curiously, neither of these works has been updated to include the eight Tolkien collections of previously unpublished Tolkien material released during the 1980s.

490. Tyler, J. E. A. **The Tolkien Companion**. London, Macmillan, 1976. 531 p. ISBN 0-333-19633-3. Also: New York, St. Martin's Press, 1976. 10, 531 p. LC 76-5203 (pbk.). Also: New York, Avon, 1977. 10, 530 p. ISBN 0-380-00901-3 (pbk.). Also: New York, Bell Publishing Co., 1979. 10, 530 p. ISBN 0-517-27914-2. **The New Tolkien Companion**. [2nd ed.]. New York, St. Martin's Press, 1979. xiii, 649 p. LC 79-22773. ISBN 0-312-57066-X. Also: London, Macmillan, 1979. xiii, 649 p. ISBN 0-333-27532-2. Also: London & Sydney, Pan Books, 1979. xiii, 651 p. LC 79-32311. ISBN 0-330-25801-X (pbk.). Also: New York, Avon, 1980. xiii, 649 p. LC 79-89235. ISBN 0-380-46904-9 (pbk.).

As with Foster's guide (see #489), Tyler updated his work when Tolkien's last major work, *The Silmarillion*, was published in 1978 but has not revised it since, despite the publication of a half dozen additional posthumous collections. Contents: "Acknowledgements"; "Preface"; "Compiler's Note"; "The Companion."

Materials are arranged alphabetically by term. A typical entry includes term (boldfaced), dates (if the term describes an individual whose dates of reign or of birth and death are known), description, and significance. Items range in length from a few words to four pages, averaging one paragraph; about 2,500 terms are covered. A few citations appear in the notes sections following the last term for each letter of the alphabet, but verification of sources is much more difficult in this work than in Foster's very carefully compiled guide. The book is nicely typeset, and the cloth editions are bound to library standards.

Both Foster's *Complete Guide* (see #489) and this volume contain specific entries which cover their topics in greater depth than in the competing volume, and both have about the same number of entries and describe the same Tolkien works. Completists or intensive researchers will undoubtedly want access to each of the two books, but libraries can be satisfied with Foster's work (see #489), which cites all references and is the more scholarly of the two.

H. G. Wells

491. Ash, Brian. **Who's Who in H. G. Wells**. London, Elm Tree Books, Hamish Hamilton, 1979. xvii, 299 p. LC 79-311512. ISBN 0-241-89597-9.

Ash's work is an A-Z guide to the significant peoples and characters in Wells's fiction. A typical entry includes term (all caps), description, significance, a record of the events affecting the person or place, and a citation (giving the title of the Wells story or novel and original year of publication, but no paginations). Most entries run one-to-two middle-sized paragraphs. Ash also includes two appendices: the "Bibliography of Novels" records Wells's book-length fictions (including *The Time Machine*, which is sometimes listed among his shorter works) in chronological order by publication date, giving year of publication, title (in italics), publisher, place of publication, author's dedication, and the name of the chief character covered in the dictionary part of the book. The "Bibliography of Short Stories," Appendix Two, lists the author's short stories in the same order in which they appear in *The Complete Short Stories of H. G. Wells* (1927), a typical entry providing title (in quotes), magazine title in which the story first was published (in italics), month and year of original publication, and the name of the principal character who is covered in the first section of Ash's book. A "Select Bibliography of Studies of Wells's Life and Fiction" completes the volume. The book is nicely typeset and bound to library standards.

Curiously and unfortunately, Ash's book has never found an American publisher, which makes the location of copies difficult for the average researcher. Ash's dictionary includes a wider range of characters than Wells's (see #445) and provides more detailed descriptions than Connes's (see #492). All three works include some entries not found in the others, and Ash covers a number of the relatively minor fictions published in the last two decades of H. G. Wells's life. Serious researchers of Wells's characters and characterizations will require all three works; most libraries will find Ash's volume sufficient as a character dictionary, although academic collections should also retain Geoffrey Wells's guide for its bibliographical data (see #445).

492. Connes, G. A. **A Dictionary of the Characters and Scenes in the Novels, Romances, and Short Stories of H. G. Wells.** Dijon, France, M. Darantiere, 1926. 489 p. LC 27-21949. Also: New York, Haskell House Publishers, 1971. 489 p. LC 73-174698. ISBN 0-8383-1353-1.

Georges Connes covers fictions published by H. G. Wells through 1924. The first section of his book annotates the author's novels and stories in chronological order by publication date. A typical short story entry provides title (small caps), abbreviation code, magazine title (in italics), month and year of publication (but no paginations), and a one-paragraph annotation. A typical book entry gives abbreviation code, item number, title (all caps), publisher, place of publication, month and year of publication, book dedication, and a plot summary that averages one page in length. The annotations are descriptive rather than evaluative.

The main text of the volume consists of an A-Z dictionary of the people and things mentioned in Wells's stories and novels through the mid-1920s. A typical entry includes term (in italics), citation (in the form "WW" for *The War of the Worlds*), and a one-sentence to one-paragraph descriptive annotation. Connes is compulsively complete: there are six short separate entries, for example, for "Agent," who, for example, "Procured Trafford and Marjorie their house" in Marriage. The majority of entries run no more than ten-to-twenty words. Thus, while Connes's dictionary covers more "persons" (including many individuals who consist only of labels like "agent") than Ash's guide (see #491), Ash describes characters from an additional two decades of Wells's works and provides more detailed annotations for the persons he does cover. Serious students of Wells's fiction will want both works for comparison; most libraries can "make do" with Ash's dictionary (#491).

Roger Zelazny

493. Zelazny, Roger, and Neil Randall. **Roger Zelazny's Visual Guide to Castle Amber**. New York, Avon Books, 1988. 218 p. LC 88-18860. ISBN 0-380-75566-1 (pbk.).

Randall adapted this guide from Zelazny's nine Amber novels and from four days of intensive interviews with the author. The first hundred pages provide detailed descriptions of the fictional Castle Amber itself, its environs, rooms, apartments, library, etc., including floor plans. Pages 119-169 cover The Greater Trumps (i.e., the chief characters of the Amber saga), with brief biographies of each of the Princes of Amber, plus their portraits on facing pages. The rest of the book provides chapters on such topics as "The Pattern of Amber," "The Arts," "Religion and Mythology," "Flora and Fauna," etc. The appendix is a genealogical chart of the liaisons and descendants of Oberon, first King of Amber. The book is beautifully typeset and designed and is illustrated throughout with black-and-white drawings by Todd Cameron Hamilton and maps by James Clouse. There is no index. Designed for fans of the Amber series, this lightweight volume has minimal reference value.

FILM AND TELEVISION CATALOGS

SCOPE NOTE: This chapter includes general film and TV catalogs and guides, as well as handbooks on individual programs or motion pictures, alphabetically by film or series title. Additional information on some SF pictures and television programs can be found in the encyclopedias covered in the first chapter of this book.

GENERAL WORKS

494. Anderson, Craig W. **Science Fiction Films of the Seventies**. Jefferson, N.C. & London, McFarland & Co., 1985. ix, 261 p., [32] p. of plates. index. LC 83-42898. ISBN 0-89950-086-2 (pbk.).

Anderson provides a chronological look at the good, the bad, and the ugly of SF films released during a seminal decade for motion pictures. Materials are arranged in chapters corresponding to the ten years 1970-79 and organized by release date. A typical entry provides film name (boldfaced head), production company, running time, color process, other technical information (for example, whether the film used 70mm cameras and Dolby sound), month and year of release; "Synopsis"; "Commentary"; and "Cast and Credits." The "Synopsis" summarizes the major plot elements in about a page of text. Anderson's perceptive "Commentary" adds another two-to-four pages of evaluation. The "Cast and Credits" section includes lists of all major characters and technical crew.

Two questions must be asked of this kind of book: 1) does it indeed cover all the noteworthy films of the decade? 2) are the author's comments fair and balanced? The answers to both of these queries are positive. Anderson tries to walk a middle line between the pretentious and folksy, keeping a colloquial style suited for the average reader while providing serious comments on why these films worked or did not work. Most importantly, he tries very conscientiously to sprinkle comments of other reviewers (taken from periodical articles and film books) throughout his own material, showing different sides of each question, and, with controversial movies such as *Zardoz*, displaying a variety of opinions at opposite ends of the critical spectrum. The reader is thus able to gain a perspective beyond the author's own very clearly stated position. It should also be noted that Anderson's commentaries average 1,500 words each, generally running much longer (and providing more details) than those in competing works.

Unlike many film books, this guide has a very thorough index to every name and film mentioned in the volume, keyed to page number. The book is nicely typeset; unfortunately, the publisher chose not to issue it in cloth form. The forty-three black-and-white illustrations, although relatively common, are very clearly reproduced on good quality stock. On the whole, this is an excellent introductory guide to this key decade in the genre's film development. For many of these pictures, Anderson's comments are the longest and most thorough evaluations available in book form.

495. Benson, Michael. **Vintage Science Fiction Films, 1896-1949**. Jefferson, N.C. & London, McFarland & Co., 1985. ix, 219 p. index. LC 83-42889. ISBN 0-89950-085-4.

This new guide from the McFarland stable covers in narrative style the development of the fantastic film through its early decades. Contents: "Acknowledgements"; "Silents"; "Sound"; "Serials"; "Filmography"; "Bibliography"; "Index."

"Science fiction" is here interpreted in the broadest possible terms, including such monster films as *Mighty Joe Young* and *King Kong*, the horror flick *The Hands of Orlac*, and other borderline pictures. Coverage is more or less chronological by release date, a typical entry providing title (in italics), production year, a detailed plot summary, and analysis. The longest entry runs three pages (about 1,500 words) and tends to be descriptive, although some attempt at evaluation is included, particularly for the better films.

A separate filmography occupies fifty-two pages of text, arranged alphabetically by film title. A typical entry includes title (boldfaced italics), production year, color or black and white, running time, production company, principal staff (director, producer, screenwriter, cinematographer, special effects technicians, art director, editor, make-up artist, and composer), and actors with their assigned roles. A three-page bibliography of other film books, organized alphabetically by author, gives author, title (in italics), place of publication, publisher, year of publication, pagination, notation of index, and one- to two-sentence annotation; the listing lacks some of the titles covered below and must be considered incomplete. The very detailed index correlates all references in the volume to page numbers. The book is nicely typeset, illustrated throughout with black-and-white stills, and bound to library standards.

In reality, there were not very many good SF films made during this period, unless one stretches the definition, as Benson (and many other historians) have been forced to do. One can count on the fingers of one hand the serious, significant attempts to depict a future civilization in motion pictures made prior to 1950. Benson does about as good a job as any of his fellow critics given the limitations of the genre, covering roughly the same number of films as *Things to Come* (see #508) at greater length, although with fewer and less significant stills. Recommended for research collections.

496. Frank, Alan. **The Horror Film Handbook.** Totowa, N.J., Barnes & Noble Books, 1982. 194 p. index. LC 81-22882. ISBN 0-389-20260-6. Also: London, B. T. Batsford, 1982. 194 p. index. ISBN 0-7134-2724-8.

Frank's catalog is divided into three main sections: "Films," "People," and "Themes." The major part of the book (138 pages) is an A-Z description of all the major (and many minor) horror films from the age of the silents through 1980. A typical entry records title (boldfaced caps), country and year of production, production company, principal credits (producer, director, screenwriter, etc.), cast, a one-paragraph plot synopsis, and from one-to-five brief quotations from other critical sources. Roughly 350 films are covered. The second section is an alphabetical biographical directory of the major actors and film makers, giving name (boldfaced), occupation (e.g., "make-up artist"), date and place of birth, highpoints of the individual's career, and a genre filmography (listing film title and production date only). The final chapter lists basic themes of the horror film (e.g., "Baron Frankenstein"), with a one-paragraph history of the development of that theme and a detailed chronological filmography which gives film title, alternate titles, chief star, nationality of film, and year of production. There is a separate checklist of alternate titles and a personal name index keyed to page number. The book is well designed and typeset, illustrated with 232 postage stamp-sized stills, and bound to library standards.

This is a handy one-volume guide to this ever-popular genre, although Hardy (see #499), Stanley (see #511), and Willis (see #514) all cover many more films, sometimes in greater depth. Libraries can pass.

497. Frank, Alan. **The Science Fiction and Fantasy Film Handbook**. Totowa, N.J., Barnes & Noble Books, 1982. 187 p. index. LC 82-8802. ISBN 0-389-20319-X. Also: London, B. T. Batsford, 1982. 187 p. index. ISBN 0-7134-2726-4.

Like his companion volume on horror films (see #496), Frank's guide is divided into three sections covering "Films," "People," and "Themes." In the "Films" chapter materials are listed alphabetically by title, a typical entry providing title (boldfaced caps), nationality (an abbreviation), release year, production company, producer, director, screenwriter(s), and other major production credits, cast (actors and the characters they play), a one-paragraph plot summary, and a synthesis of critical reactions from other previously published sources. Roughly 400 films are covered, including some foreign-language flicks. The longer entries, dealing with several of the major SF motion pictures from the late 1970s, run two pages. The twenty-five-page section on "People" is an A-Z guide to the major stars, directors, writers, and other principals who have made significant contributions to SF cinematography. A typical entry gives name (boldfaced caps), place and date of birth, one-paragraph bio- graphical summary, and principal SF film credits, listed chronologically by title. The final section groups the films by major theme (e.g., "Apocalypse and After," "Time Travel," etc.), then chronologically by year of release. Seven unnumbered pages at the end of the book provide a list of alternative movie titles and an index to persons mentioned in the book, arranged by profession (e.g., "Producers," "Art Directors,": etc.), then alphabetically by surname. The book is nicely designed and illustrated throughout with small-sized stills and bound to library standards.

The liberal inclusion of critical quotes gives the reader an immediate choice of sometimes diverse opinions on every film, but the small number of motion pictures covered severely limits this book's usefulness. Also, the quirky arrangement of the index impedes access for the average user. Prefer Hardy's much more comprehensive work (see #500) as a reference guide and Stanley's book (see #511) as a filmgoer's guide.

498. Gerani, Gary, with Paul H. Schulman. **Fantastic Television**. New York, Harmony Books, 1977. 192 p. index. LC 76-56821. ISBN 0-517-52646-8; ISBN 0-517-52645-X (pbk.).

Amidst a cornucopia of guides to fantastic films of all kinds, this is the only catalog of fantastic television programs, long out-of-print and out-of-date, but still a worthy acquisition for any library. The main section is arranged by series name, in chronological order by initial production date from "The Adventures of Superman" (1953-57) through "Space: 1999" (1975-77). A typical entry gives a two- to eight-page history of the series; a summary of continuing credits (seasons produced, total number of episodes, production company, network on which it was aired, usual running time, medium (color or black and white), regular cast, and continuing production credits); and an index of episodes, listed season by season, chronologically by production date, giving episode title (bold caps), writer, director, guest cast, and a one- to two-sentence plot summary.

The second section of the volume (thirty-seven pages) includes chapters on "American Telefantasy," an A-Z guide to minor programs with fantastic content, listing series title (bold caps), seasons, network name, continuing cast, brief series premise and history; "British Telefantasy," organized similarly to the preceding chapter, but covering series which were produced in the U.K.; "Kid Stuff," listing children's live and animated series, with the same data as before; and "Made-for-TV Movies," an alphabetical checklist of all known fantastic films produced for television through 1977. The index coordinates titles and personal names with page numbers. The book is attractively designed, copiously illustrated with many rare stills, and the cloth edition is bound to library standards.

Gerani and Schulman cover thirteen series in depth and many others peripherally. Any future book of this type should include original air dates for the series episodes and should expand the original base to cover other shows of importance. However, the thirteen programs summarized here are all important to the development of the genre, and the plot details provided by the authors on individual episodes are virtually impossible to locate in any other source (Lentz's checklist of credits [see #503] does list air dates for all episodes, and the names of the actors and actresses who starred in them, but no specifics about content). An updated guide is badly needed; until one arrives, libraries should retain copies of this book. Compare with Javna's fan-oriented catalog (see #501).

499. Hardy, Phil, ed., Tom Milne and Paul Willemen, writers. **Horror**. London, Aurum, 1986. 408 p. Index. (The Aurum Film Encyclopedia, Volume 3). As: **The Encyclopedia of Horror Movies.** New York, Harper & Row, 1987. 408 p. index. LC 86-45718. ISBN 0-06-055050-3; ISBN 0-06-096146-5 (pbk.). Also: London, Octopus Books, 1986. 408 p. index. LC 88-161097. ISBN 0-7064-2771-8.

This chronological guide to major and minor horror films released between 1896 and 1985 is organized by year of release date, then alphabetically by title. A typical entry gives title (boldfaced), English-language title (for foreign films, also boldfaced), production company, nationality, color or black and white, running time, a one- to two-paragraph annotation, and major production and casting credits ("d"=director, "p"=producer, "s"=screenwriter, "c"=cinematographer, "lp"=leading players). The annotations are descriptive rather than evaluative, although the final sentence usually provides a summation of a sort (e.g., "sluggishly directed and very wordy"). The appendices include "All-Time Horror Rental Champs" (now out-of-date), "Critics' Top Tens" (nine writers list their favorite films and provide a paragraph of general critical commentary), "Horror Oscars," and "Select Bibliography" (one page). The index coordinates titles and page numbers. The book is illustrated throughout with small but clearly reproduced black-and-white stills and is attractively typeset and designed; the cloth version is bound to library standards.

Hardy, Milne, and Willemen have produced one of the most comprehensive guides to the horror film yet published, detailing some 1,300 motion pictures dating from the very beginnings of the film era. In particular, the authors' coverage of foreign-language titles is unsurpassed in any other source and provides sufficient justification in itself for all research libraries to include this volume in their collections. Compare with John Stanley's guide (see #511).

500. Hardy, Phil, ed. **Science Fiction**. London, Aurum Press, 1984, 400 p. index. LC 85-145954. (The Aurum Film Encyclopedia, Volume 2). ISBN 0-906053-82-X (pbk.). Also: New York, William Morrow, 1984. 400 p. index. LC 84-60579. ISBN 0-688-00842-9. As: **The Encyclopedia of Science Fiction Movies.** Minneapolis, Minn., Woodbury Press, 1986. 408 p. index. ISBN 0-8300-0436-X. Also: London, Octopus Books, 1986. 408 p. index. ISBN 0-7064-2557-X.

This companion volume to Hardy's *Horror* (see #499) is similarly arranged and organized. Films are listed chronologically by year of release, then alphabetically by title. A typical entry provides movie title (boldfaced), production company, film stock (e.g., "b/w"=black and white), running time, one- to three-paragraph annotation, and major production and casting credits (using the same abbreviations as in the volume on horror films [see #499]). The annotations average 150-200 words in length and are both descriptive and evaluative, with a one- to two-sentence critical summation. Coverage is complete through 1983. Appendices include "1. All-Time Science Fiction Rental Champs" [now woefully out-of-date]; "2. Most Successful Science Fiction Films: Inflation Adjusted" [also out-of-date]; "3. Critics' Top Ten" [top ten lists from eleven SF critics, with a paragraph each of discussion]; "4. Science Fiction Oscars"; "5. The Trieste Festival of Science Fiction Films"; "6. Select Bibliography." The title index is keyed to production year only, not page numbers, and is reproduced in rather difficult-to-read, six-point type. The volume is illustrated throughout with hundreds of small-sized black-and-white stills (averaging three inches square), with one insert of sixteen full-sized pages of color illustrations between pages 200-201. *Science Fiction* is nicely designed and printed and the cloth edition is bound to library standards.

Hardy's coverage of foreign films is excellent, providing plot details on many hard-to-locate SF motion pictures from Europe and Asia. Roughly 1,200 movies are delineated in this volume, less than in Stanley's guide (see #511) or in Willis's three-volume set (see #514), but more than in the average pictorial history. A good acquisition for those medium-sized public libraries or smaller academic collections which can afford just one volume on the subject.

501. Javna, John. **The Best of Science Fiction TV: The Critics' Choice from Captain Video to Star Trek, from The Jetsons to Robotech.** New York, Harmony Books, 1987. 144 p. LC 87-21120. ISBN 0-517-56650-8 (pbk.).

Javna's book is fun to read but has very little reference value. The first section of the volume lists the top fifteen SF television series of all time, as voted upon by a group of over a hundred critics, science-fiction writers, fans, and other experts. "Science fiction" is here defined very loosely, with anthology programs such as "Night Gallery" (which usually featured horror and fantasy stories) being included. A typical four-page entry provides title, history and development of the series, flashback (well-known quotes taken from various episodes), "Vital Stats" (background setting, brief biographies of the continuing characters, and other basic data), and "Critics' Comments," original mini-critiques by the voting experts on why the series worked or failed. The section part of the book covers "The Worst Ten" SF programs of all time. Additional chapters cover: "The Classics," "Cult Favorites" (subdivided into: "It Came from Japan," "British Science Fiction," "Super-Marionation," "Anthologies," "Cartoons" [in two sections: "The Best and The Worst", and "Golden Age Science Fiction TV"]. A final chapter on sources lists: "Recommended Reading," "Photos & Collectibles," and "Fan Clubs." The book is nicely illustrated and designed, but the paperbound version will disintegrate rapidly on library shelves.

Javna's guide covers many more series in far less depth, while *Fantastic Television* (see #498) provides far more detailed technical information and episode guides. The absence of an index in Javna's book is unfortunate, although the very detailed table of contents on pages 4-5 does provide some access. Completists will want both books; libraries can be satisfied with the older (albeit out-of-date) work by Gerani and Schulman.

502. Lee, Walt, and Bill Warren. **Reference Guide to Fantastic Films: Science Fiction, Fantasy, & Horror.** Los Angeles, Chelsea-Lee Books, 1972-74. xli, xviii, xxii, 559, 80, 38, 14 p. in 3 v. LC 72-88775. ISBN 0-913974-04-8 (set); ISBN 0-913974-01-3 (v.1); ISBN 0-913974-02-1 (v.2); ISBN 0-913974-03-X (v.3) (pbk.).

This immense compilation is divided into three sections in each volume: the reference guide proper, "Problems" (printed on blue sheets), and "Exclusions" (printed on yellow sheets), plus front and end matter. Materials are arranged alphabetically by title, the first book covering the letters A-F, the second G-O, and the third P-Z. A typical entry includes title (underlined), original title (if first released in a foreign country), year of release, production company, color or black and white, running time, production credits (director, producer, screenwriter, art director, cinematographer, editor, score), cast (but not the roles each played), subject categorization (e.g., "SF"=science fiction—"white man's brain transplanted into black man's body"), and references to reviews in the film and SF media, and to critical coverage in books (e.g., "MPW 12:150"=*Motion Picture World*, Vol. 12, p. 150), plus see references to sequels or other related pictures.

The second (blue-colored) section in each book lists "problems," including motion pictures which may or may not have fantastic content or which may not exist. The third (yellow-colored) part of each volume lists titles which have been listed in other sources as fantastic or whose titles make them sound fantastic, but which have been verified as having no fantasy content. The introductory sections of each volume provide detailed instructions on how to use the book, with duplicate abbreviations' lists. Volume Three contains an original afterword by Forrest J Ackerman at the end of the work, plus a detailed bibliography of sources consulted. There are numerous see also references from one title to another scattered throughout the text, and each book includes a number of clearly reproduced black-and-white stills.

The books are shot from typed copy which is generally legible but has been reduced to such an extent (to about a six-point level, in four columns per page) that it is difficult for the older user to read. The paper binding will not withstand heavy use. This is one of the most detailed A-Z guides to fantastic films yet published, covering in excess of 2,000 titles. Hardy's two catalogs (see #499 and #500) are more current, better produced physically, and include plot details not listed in Lee and Warren's work, but lack the latter's subject categories, review sources (very valuable for further study), or lists of peripheral and unverified titles. Libraries and serious researchers into the SF film should own both sets; libraries are advised to rebind the *Reference Guide* immediately into cloth before its heavy weight damages it beyond repair.

503. Lentz, Harris M., III. **Science Fiction, Horror, & Fantasy Film and Television Credits: Over 10,000 Actors, Actresses, Directors, Producers, Screenwriters, Cinematographers, Art Directors, and Make-Up, Special Effects, Costume, and Other People; Plus Full Cross-References from All Films and TV Shows.** Jefferson, N.C., McFarland & Co., 1983. xx, 1,374 p. in 2 v. index. LC 82-23956. ISBN 0-89950-071-4 (set); ISBN 0-89950-069-2 (v.1); ISBN 0-89950-070-6 (v.2). **Science Fiction, Horror, & Fantasy Film and Television Credits Supplement 1987.** Jefferson, N.C., McFarland & Co., 1989. xii, 924 p. index. LC 88-42646. ISBN 0-89950-364-0.

This detailed guide is very simply arranged. Volume 1 is broken into two sections, providing alphabetical listings of "Actors and Actresses," and of "Directors, Producers, Screenwriters, Cinematographers, Special Effects Technicians, Make-Up Artists, Art Directors, and Others." A typical actor entry includes name (all caps), years of birth and death (if known), film credits, and television credits. Only roles in SF, fantasy, or horror movies or TV shows are included, giving (for films) title (in quotes), year of production (which may also be coupled with the initials "TVM" for a "made for TV movie," or with an abbreviation indicating nationality for overseas flicks), and name of character portrayed; and/or (for television roles) series name (underlined), episode name (in quotes), air date, and character name. Credits are listed in both sections in descending order by release date.

Volume 2 is also divided into two parts, a "Film Index" and a "Television [program] Index." The first section is arranged alphabetically by movie title, typically including title (all caps), year of production, nationality (if other than American), alternate title(s), director's name (but no other production credits), and a list of all major and most minor acting credits, plus the name of the character being portrayed by each. The TV section is organized alphabetically by series name, then chronologically by episode air date, providing series title (all caps), production years, continuing series regulars and the characters portrayed by each (with seasons, if they did not serve the entire span); plus a record of each episode, listed chronologically and giving teleplay title (in quotes), first air date, and the actors and actresses (other than series regulars) who appeared in that episode, with the characters played by each. The supplement is similarly arranged.

The book is shot from very clear typed copy and bound to library standards. There are several minor problems with this set: 1) the layout of the "Television Index" in Volume 2 often results in multi-seasonal series being listed in long columns of unbroken text that tend to blend together for the average user—the absence of boldfaced heads, the use of line breaks only between series entries, and the lack of contrast among the typed text poorly serves this section; 2) the "Film Index" fails to include any production credits other than directors, although the other principals are indexed in the latter half of Volume 1. Although these data are available elsewhere (see particularly Lee's [#502], Hardy's [#499 and #500] and Willis's [#514] catalogs), their absence here forces the user to seek other sources for very basic information. It perhaps would have been wiser to cross reference the data in both directions. Still, these are relatively minor quibbles, for the main indexes in Volume 1, by actor and by production personnel, are generally not available in any other source and provide the user with quick and invaluable access to this material. These volumes should be owned by all major research libraries and all large public library systems.

504. Lucas, Tim. **Your Movie Guide to Horror Video Tapes and Discs**. New York, Signet Books, New American Library, 1985. 128 p. ISBN 0-451-13929-1 (pbk.).

One of six such guides prepared by Lucas for *Video Times Magazine*, this book is arranged alphabetically by film title. A typical entry gives title (bold caps), release year (boldfaced), C[olor] or B[lack and]/W[hite], director, stars, running time (boldfaced), motion picture industry rating (PG, R, etc.), format availability (Beta, VHS, etc.), price, vendor, Lucas's quality rating (one to four asterisks, four being best), and a one-paragraph plot summary. The annotations are descriptive rather than evaluative, although a tag line at the end of each entry makes some effort at summation. There are scattered see references throughout the text to alternative titles. The book is typeset with ragged-right paragraphs and illustrated throughout with postage stamp-sized stills that reproduce very murkily on the poor-quality paper. A brief list of video vendors and their addresses complete the text. All of these data are, of course, laughably out-of-date, and this guide is now only marginally useful.

505. Lucas, Tim. **Your Movie Guide to Science Fiction/Fantasy Video Tapes and Discs**. New York, Signet Books, New American Library, 1985. 128 p. ISBN 0-451-13930-5 (pbk.).

Lucas prepared six of these slight video guides, two of them on fantastic films and the others on other genres. Data are arranged alphabetically by film title. A typical entry gives title (bold caps), release year (boldfaced), C[olor] or B[lack and]/W[hite], director, stars, running time (boldfaced), motion picture industry rating (PG, R, etc.), format availability (Beta, VHS, etc.), price, vendor, Lucas's quality rating (one to four asterisks, four being best), and a one-paragraph plot summary. The annotations are descriptive rather than evaluative, although a tag line at the end of each entry makes some effort at summation. There are scattered see references throughout the text to alternative titles. The book is typeset with ragged-right paragraphs and illustrated throughout with postage stamp-sized stills that reproduce very murkily on the poor-quality paper. A brief list of video vendors and their addresses completes the text. Although the video data are now long out-of-date, Lucas's guide remains marginally useful for the individual descriptions he provides of SF television episodes (particularly for the series *Star Trek* and *The Prisoner*) marketed as separate cassettes.

506. McCarty, John. **Video Screams 1983: The Official Source Book to Horror, Science Fiction, Fantasy, and Related Films on Videocassette and Disc.** Albany, N.Y., FantaCo Enterprises, 1983. xxxix, 253 p. ISBN 0-938782-02-9 (pbk.).

This basic guide to horror and SF flicks available on videocassette and videodisc arranges its data in alphabetical order by film title. A typical entry gives motion picture title (boldfaced), rating (one to four screaming head logos, four being best), production year, color or b&w, running time, director, major casting credits, one-paragraph plot summary (ten to one hundred words), and a list of video vendors and availability codes (e.g., "VC"=videocassette). The appendices include "1. Additional Titles"; "2. Video Sources" (addresses and phone numbers of the vendors); "3. Directors and Their Films" (arranged alphabetically by director's name). The book is illustrated throughout with poorly reproduced black-and-white stills, and cheaply printed on yellowing paper. Now severely outdated and not much good for anything else.

507. Menville, Douglas, and R. Reginald, with Mary A. Burgess. **Futurevisions: The New Golden Age of the Science Fiction Film.** North Hollywood, Calif., A Greenbriar Book, Newcastle Publishing Co.; San Bernardino, Calif., The Borgo Press, 1985. 192 p. index. LC 85-20098. ISBN 0-89370-681-7; ISBN 0-87877-081-X (pbk.).

This sequel to *Things to Come* (see #508) is organized very similarly. Contents: "Introduction," by William F. Nolan; "Foreword," by Reginald; "Chapter 1: "Futures Past" (1897-1976—a summary of *Things to Come*); "Chapter 2: Starships and Superheroes" (1977-1979); "Chapter 3: Telepaths and Time Travelers" (1980-1981); "Chapter 4: Horrors and Holocausts" (1982-1983); "Chapter 5: Dreams and Dimensions" (1984-1985); "Selected Bibliography"; "Title Index."

In each section films are listed chronologically by release date. A typical entry gives title (boldfaced italics), production year, director, production, production company, and principal actors, embedded within the narrative text. The entries are both descriptive and evaluative, ranging in size from 150-1,500 words (averaging 250) and focusing around each motion picture's integrity to its story and fictive world. The index coordinates titles and page numbers only, principal entries being indicated with boldfaced numbers. The 8.5" x 11" book is beautifully illustrated with black-and-white stills which are clearly reproduced in sizes sufficiently large that the connoisseur can distinguish even the smallest details; the cloth edition is bound to library standards.

This is not a major book, but it does provide a good introductory guide to the genre during a period of time when some of the best-known flicks in SF film history were released on an unsuspecting public.

508. Menville, Douglas, and R. Reginald. **Things to Come: An Illustrated History of the Science Fiction Film.** New York, Times Books, 1977. [xii], 212 p. index. LC 77-79033. ISBN 0-8129-0710-8; ISBN 0-8129-6287-7 (pbk.).

This basic film guide includes "Introduction," by Ray Bradbury; "Foreword"; "1. Moon Voyages and Metal Maidens" (1895-1929); "2. Serials and Scientists" (1930-1949); "3. Monsters and Menaces" (1950-1959); "4. Monoliths and Monkeys" (1960-1969); "5. Wars and Wizards" (1970-1977); "Selected Bibliography"; "Index of Titles."

In each section materials are arranged chronologically by release date. A typical entry includes title (boldfaced), production company, release year, and principal actors, embedded in a continuous narrative style. The annotations are both descriptive and evaluative, ranging in size from 50-1,500 words, averaging 150, with entries in the earlier sections being shorter than those in the latter three chapters (the modern period). The 8.5" x 11" book is beautifully illustrated with many rare black-and-white stills, including many running half a page or more in size, with every detail obvious to the devotee. The index coordinates page numbers and titles, principal entries being indicated with italicized numbers. The cloth edition is bound to library standards.

Public libraries will find this volume a good introduction to the history and chronology of SF film making. Note also the sequel, *Futurevisions* (see #507), which continues the narrative through 1985.

509. Parish, James Robert, and Michael R. Pitts. **The Great Science Fiction Pictures**. Metuchen, N.J., Scarecrow Press, 1977. viii, 382 p. LC 77-5426. ISBN 0-8108-1029-8. **The Great Science Fiction Pictures II**. Metuchen, N.J. & London, Scarecrow Press, 1990. x, 489 p. LC 89-24058. ISBN 0-8108-2247-4.

Both of these volumes are similarly organized. The unnumbered Volume 1 includes "Authors' Note and Acknowledgments"; "The Great Science Fiction Pictures"; "Science Fiction Shows on Radio and Television," by Vincent Terrace; "A Select Bibliography of Science Fiction Bibliographies, Indexes and Checklists," by Stephen Calvert; "About the Authors and Staff." Volume 2 contents: "Acknowledgments"; "Introduction"; "Great Science Fiction Pictures II"; "Science Fiction on Radio and TV"; "About the Authors."

In each volume, the main section is arranged alphabetically by film title. A typical entry provides title (all caps), production company, year of release, running time, all major (and many minor) production credits, all major (and many minor) casting credits, with the names of characters each actor portrays, a one-to-two-paragraph plot summary (running 100 to 250 words), and one-to-two paragraphs of analysis and critique, including excerpts from previously published reviews of the film. The critical bibliography at the end of Volume 1 is now wholly outdated and utterly useless. The brief checklists of fantastic radio and TV series at the rear of both volumes (in alphabetical order by series title) provide a skeletal and incomplete guide that lists title (all caps), network, first and last air dates, and series cast regulars (but without the names of the characters they portray); prefer Gerani (see #498) and Javna (see #501) for information on SF television series. The first volume is shot from clear typed copy; the second volume is nicely typeset, and both are bound to library standards. Both books are illustrated throughout with clearly reproduced but rather small film stills.

Roughly 350 films are covered in Volume 1, and 450 in Volume 2. Although the second work generally focuses on motion pictures produced from 1977-86, approximately one-fourth of the entries consist of older flicks not covered in the first guide, spanning the entire history of fantastic films; and since the second book fails to include a list of the titles covered in Volume 1, one must constantly flip back and forth between the two to determine if a particular work has been analyzed by the authors. This is just bad design, and the problem will only get worse when the projected third volume is published. As far as content is concerned, Parish and Pitts make an effort in their guides to provide analyses as well as descriptions, sprinkling their own opinions with numerous quotations from other critics, some excerpted from published reviews, some from other film histories and catalogs. The result provides the reader with a good mixture of favorable and unfavorable views from a wide variety of sources. This set should be acquired by most academic and all large public libraries. The projected third volume should include a master checklist of films covered, referencing the appropriate volume number.

510. Pickard, Roy. **Science Fiction in the Movies: An A-Z**. London, Frederick Muller, 1978. 139 p., [16] p. of plates. index. ISBN 0-584-10442-1.

This curious little volume covers actors, directors, characters, terms, and films in one alphabetical sequence. A typical film entry gives title (boldfaced), year of production (italics), one-paragraph plot summary, production company, major credits, nationality, and running time. A typical personal entry provides name (boldfaced), years of birth and death (where available, when appropriate), nationality, occupation, and a one-paragraph summary of his or her career in SF films. Other entries include places ("Sorgo, a space-age Gomorrah..."), things ("The Space Gun, a vertical gun of vast dimensions..."), and a hodgepodge of other irrelevancies. Sixteen pages of plates grouped between pages 68-69 clearly reproduce rather common black-and-white movie stills. There is also a brief bibliography of eight items and a three-page index listing names and film titles with page numbers. Obviously issued to capitalize on the *Star Wars* phenomenon, this wholly forgettable guide has absolutely nothing unique to offer either the researcher, fan, or librarian.

511. Stanley, John. **The Creature Features Movie Guide; or, An A to Z Encyclopedia to the Cinema of the Fantastic; or, Is There a Mad Doctor in the House?** Pacifica, Calif., Creatures at Large, 1981. 208 p. LC 81-67664. ISBN 0-940064-00-6 (pbk.). **The Creature Features Movie Guide; or, An A to Z Encyclopedia to the Cinema of the Fantastic; or, Is There a Mad Doctor in the House?** [2nd] rev. ed. New York, Warner Books, 1984. xv, 304 p. LC 83-23574. ISBN 0-446-38006-7 (pbk.); ISBN 0-446-38008-3 (pbk.; Canada). **Revenge of the Creature Features Movie Guide; or, An A to Z Encyclopedia to the Cinema of the Fantastic; or, Is There a Mad Doctor in the House?** 3rd rev. ed. Pacifica, Calif., Creatures at Large Press, 1988. xxiv, 420 p. LC 87-91426. ISBN 0-940064-05-7; ISBN 0-940064-04-9 (pbk.).

This continuing reference guide had expanded to almost 4,000 mini-reviews of fantastic films by the third edition (1988), making it the largest single-volume catalog of science-fiction, fantasy, and horror films yet published. Materials are arranged alphabetically by film title. A typical entry includes title (boldfaced caps), year of release (parentheses), and a one-paragraph annotation. Made-for-TV flicks are included with the rest and so indicated in the body of the text. The descriptions include both plot summaries and evaluations, plus mention of the leading players; the director is usually listed at the end of the entry, and occasionally the screenwriter. Following the entry (in the third edition only) is a code ("VC") indicating whether the film is available on videocassette. All three editions are illustrated with different black-and-white stills, well reproduced (if small in size) from the original motion pictures. The books are nicely typeset and designed, and the cloth version of the third edition is bound to library standards.

Stanley's guides are intended to provide quick reference sources for the TV and VCR viewer and SF film fan and in no way supplant the more detailed volumes covered herein, particularly Hardy's two books (see #499 and #500), or Willis's catalog (see #514). The author obviously intends to keep his work current and to continue expanding and developing earlier entries (for example, the entry for *The Bamboo Saucer*, a very forgetable 1967 flick, has been wholly recast in the third edition, expanding its size to three times the original version and providing many more details). A useful addition to a potential fourth edition would be a rating system (one to four stars) similar to that employed by Leonard Maltin in his comprehensive TV movie guide. Meanwhile, Stanley's handy book should be purchased by all large public library systems.

512. Strickland, A. W., and Forrest J Ackerman. **A Reference Guide to American Science Fiction Films, Volume 1**. Bloomington, Ind., T.I.S. Publications Division, 1981. xvii, 397 p. index. LC 81-158697. ISBN 0-89917-268-7.

Projected as a four-volume set (of which only one was ever published), *A Reference Guide to American Science Fiction Films* organizes its data chronologically by publication date, year by year, then alphabetically by title within each year. Contents: "Foreword"; "Preface"; "List of Illustrations"; "Explanation Key and Abbreviations"; "Acknowledgements"; "Films: 1897-1909"; "1910-1919"; "1920-1929"; "Filmography"; "Summary Classification of Films"; "Summary Releasing Companies"; "References"; "Bibliography"; "Index."

A typical entry provides title (bold caps, centered), release date, production company, description (e.g., "silent" or "sound"), number of feet of film, classification (e.g., "SF"=science fiction), references (keyed to a list of numbered secondary sources on pages 385-87, and giving item number, volume number, and page number), production credits, casting credits, and an annotation ranging in size from fifty words (for some early silent shorts) to over 2,000 words for several of the major pictures of the 1920s. The descriptions include detailed plots summaries, historical notes, evaluations, and extensive excerpts from contemporaneous critical reviews (with exact citations of sources). The entries are illustrated with very rare full-page stills carefully reproduced in black and white; very few of these are available in any other source.

Each chapter includes at the end of that decade's films a classification list, arranging films by subject and production year, and an index to production companies and the SF films they released, year by year. End matter includes a detailed filmography arranged in chronological order, giving film titles and production years, an overall classification of SF movies from 1897-1929 (arranged similarly to the chapter classifications), an overall index to production companies and their films (arranged as above), a list of references and the reference numbers assigned to each by the authors, a detailed bibliography of periodical sources, and a title index coordinating films with page numbers for their entries.

The amount of data on early SF motion pictures is unsurpassed in any other source. The combination of Ackerman's knowledge of the origins of the fantastic film and his immense collection of early film memorabilia and stills, and the academic documentation brought to the project by Dr. Albert Strickland, make this *the* standard resource volume on SF pictures of the silent era. All research libraries should own copies of this outstanding guide.

513. Warren, Bill; research associate, Bill Thomas. **Keep Watching the Skies! American Science Fiction Movies of the Fifties**. Jefferson, N.C. & London, McFarland & Co., 1982-86. xvi, 467, xx, 839 p. in 2 v. index. LC 81-19324. ISBN 0-89950-191-5 (set); ISBN 0-89950-032-3 (v.1); ISBN 0-89950-170-2 (v.2).

Warren attempts to annotate every science-fiction film released in America between 1950 and 1962 inclusive, Volume 1 covering 1950-57, and Volume 2 the years 1958-62. Contents (v.1): "Acknowledgments"; "The Chapter Illustrations"; "1950"; "1951"; "1952"; "1953"; "1954"; "1955"; "1956"; "1957"; "Appendix I: Cast and Credits"; "Appendix II: Films in Order of Release"; "Appendix III: Announced (But Not Produced) Films"; "Appendix IV: SF Serials of the 1950s"; "Index." Contents (v.2): "Acknowledgments"; "The Illustrations"; "A Note on Quotations in the Text"; "Preface"; "1958"; "1959"; "1960";

"1961"; "1962"; "Addenda" (to Volume 1); "Selected Bibliography" (for Volumes I and II); "Appendix I: Credits and Cast"; "Appendix II: Films in Order of Release"; "Appendix III: Announced (But Not Produced) Titles"; "Index; A Final Word."

The motion pictures are organized in chronological order by release date, year by year, then alphabetically by title. Main entries include no credits, which are grouped together in an alphabetically arranged appendix at the end of each book. A typical credits entry gives title (boldfaced), production credits, casting credits (characters' names in italics), production company, color or black and white, running time, alternate titles, and other details of interest. The annotations in the main section of each volume are quite lengthy, running from 400-6,000 words (averaging 1,500), and are simultaneously descriptive, analytic, and historical, providing extensive information on how the film was made, how well it was received (both contemporaneously and by present-day critics, with selected quotations), and Warren's own reactions to it.

The books are illustrated throughout with clearly reproduced full and half-page black-and-white stills from the pictures. At the end of each volume, in addition to the extensive lists of credits, are appendices providing chronological checklists of the exact release dates of each motion picture (so far as they are known), and lists of movie projects which were announced but never completed. Serials are not covered in these guides, but a brief checklist of serial productions appears at the end of Volume 1. Both books contain comprehensive indexes correlating all personal names and film titles with page numbers, photo pages being indicated with boldfaced type. The set is nicely typeset and bound to library standards.

These are immense productions, filled with data and background details that are just not available in any other single source. Warren's mini-essays represent in most cases the lengthiest critical analyses generally available on each of these motion pictures. This set should be purchased by every research library worthy of the name and by any film critic seriously interested in the development of the SF film.

514. Willis, Donald C. **Horror and Science Fiction Films: A Checklist**. Metuchen, N.J., Scarecrow Press, 1972. xi, 612 p. LC 72-3682. ISBN 0-8108-0508-1. **Horror and Science Fiction Films II**. Metuchen, N.J. & London, Scarecrow Press, 1982. xiv, 474 p. LC 81-23295. ISBN 0-8108-1517-6. **Horror and Science Fiction Films III**. Metuchen, N.J. & London, Scarecrow Press, 1984. xiii, 335 p. LC 84-13885. ISBN 0-8108-1723-3.

Willis's guides cumulatively provide the most comprehensive reference work yet published on the fantastic film, although they suffer somewhat from being broken into three separate alphabetical sequences. Contents (v.1): "Introductory Notes and Acknowledgments"; "Explanatory Notes"; 'Abbreviations"; "Horror and Science-Fiction Films: A Checklist"; "Titles Announced for Release in 1971-1972"; "Shorts (1930-1971), and Animated and Puppet Films"; "Out List" (i.e., borderline or misleading titles, those with only slight SF elements, or items which cannot be verified); "References." Contents (v.2): "Introduction"; "Explanatory Notes"; "Abbreviations"; "Horror and Science Fiction Films II: Main List"; "Peripheral and Problem Films"; "Principal References"; "Addenda." Contents (v.3): "Introduction"; "Explanatory Notes"; "Abbreviations"; "Horror and Science Fiction Films III: 1982-1983: Main List"; "Peripheral and Problem Films"; "Alternate Titles" (Volumes I & II); "Principal References"; "Addenda."

The bulk of each book consists of one alphabetical list of film titles. A typical entry provides title (all caps), production company, year of release, color or black and white, running time, alternate title(s), director, screenwriter, and other production credits, references to the publication (listed in the bibliography at the end of the volume) from which verification was cited, casting credits, and annotation. The annotations in Volume I are either nonexistent (for many early silent shorts) or very brief (for later films), usually consisting of no more than one or two sentences (e.g., "Men on Mars and the moon in the year 2021"). Volume II expands the annotations into a full paragraph, although comments on lesser films remain brief. In Volume III Willis has increased his annotations up to several pages of text for better films, the average being two paragraphs, although some entries remain very short. End matter for each book includes unverified titles (listed alphabetically by title, with the source of reference indicated), bibliography, and (for II and III) brief addenda sections. The books are shot from sometimes faint typed copy and bound to library standards; the volumes are not illustrated.

Willis includes an enormous amount of data in these books, covering 4,400 titles in Volume I, 2,350 in II, and 760 in III, for a total of roughly 7,500 foreign and domestic motion pictures with some fantastic content. Many of the films are peripheral by anyone's standards, and few are important to the development of the field; yet it is still necessary that they be recorded. The major problem with these volumes, other than the fact that an important library publishing company has once again issued a set of major reference sources "on the cheap" without bothering to have them professionally typeset, lies in their organization. The user must run through five alphabetical sequences (the three main sections, plus two addenda; titles from the first addenda have not been incorporated into the text of Volume III) to locate a potential title. This is because the second and third volumes include, in addition to many new titles, numerous "fill-ins" missing from the original guide. Without a coordinating index, there is no easy way for the reader to determine where a title may be found—or indeed *if* it will be located in any of the three books. Perhaps this problem is insurmountable given the nature of this type of guide, but it should be addressed in any potential fourth volume. In the meantime, these books will provide the scholar with an immense amount of research material and should be included in every large academic collection.

515. Willis, Donald C., ed. *Variety*'s **Complete Science Fiction Reviews**. New York & London, Garland Publishing Co., 1985. xiv, 479 p. index. LC 85-25257. ISBN 0-8240-6263-9; ISBN 0-8240-8712-7 (pbk.).

Willis has compiled contemporaneous reviews of fantastic films reproduced facsimile from the weekly movie industry journal *Variety*. The first essay, from the November 23, 1907, issue of the magazine, discusses *Liquid Electricity*, and the last, dated December 26, 1984, evaluates the Mexican film *Historias Violentas*. Approximately 1,200 motion pictures are covered, in essays ranging in size from 100 to 1,000 words, averaging 300. The annotations are both descriptive and evaluative and include casting and production credits, running time, MPAA rating, and other particulars of interest. For those who have not previously seen *Variety*, the emphasis here is on the marketability of the films being reviewed and not necessarily on their art or literacy, although such factors are often mentioned in passing.

The essays are shot facsimile from the original publications and pasted onto a three-column format, with some type (particularly from the early years) being very small (around a six-point level) and/or faint and difficult to read. A dozen full-page illustrations are sprinkled throughout the text; the cloth edition is bound to library standards. The index coordinates film titles and page numbers only. The reviews tend toward the dyspeptic, but this is a refreshing change from the often adulatory critiques featured in many film guides. All research libraries should acquire copies, whether or not they own a complete run of *Variety*.

516. Wingrove, David, ed. **The Science Fiction Film Source Book**. Harlow, Longman, 1985. vi, 312 p. LC 86-215261. ISBN 0-582-89239-2; ISBN 0-582-89310-0 (pbk.).

Wingrove, the author of an earlier volume on SF authors and their works, *The Science Fiction Source Book* (see #82), here provides a similarly designed rating guide to SF films. Materials are arranged alphabetically by film title. A typical entry includes title (boldfaced), production year, description, ratings, director, writer, major cast credits, and an abbreviation indicating which of the entries were contributed by the editor's panel of five judges (a majority of entries were penned by Wingrove himself). The annotations are both descriptive and evaluative, typically running 150 words and including a one-sentence critical summation; selected entries on major films range up to 500 words in length.

A unique feature of this guide is a series of four ratings for each motion picture, evaluating Plot (P), Technical Merit (T), Enjoyment (E), and Artistic Merit (A), using a five-star system, five being best. Roughly 1,350 films are covered, from earliest times through 1984. There are a few postage stamp-sized black-and-white stills scattered throughout the text. Other matter includes a "Foreword" by Brian W. Aldiss; a one-page "Chronology of Important Films" (through 1984); "The SF Serials, 1913-1956"; "Creators of SF on Screen" (brief biographies and filmographies of the major directors, actors, and others, arranged in alphabetical order by name); "The Literary Sources: Books into Film" (a very useful guide, arranged alphabetically by surname, to the authors and their stories or novels which have been adapted into SF films); "Special Effects in Science Fiction Cinema" (a ten-page essay by well-known critic John Brosnan); "All-Time Rental Figures for SF Films" (now outdated); and "Select Bibliography." There is no index. The book is attractively designed and typeset and the cloth edition is bound to library standards.

Unfortunately, Wingrove's guide never achieved U.S. publication, making it one of the least known works covered in this section. It deserved better. The judgments here are sound and balanced, and the ratings fairly apportioned; the section delineating SF "Books into Film" provides a unique perspective unavailable in any other source. A new edition would definitely be warranted.

517. Wright, Gene. **The Science Fiction Image: The Illustrated Encyclopedia of Science Fiction in Film, Television, Radio, and the Theater**. New York, Facts on File Publications, 1983. 336 p., [16] p. of plates. LC 82-2348. ISBN 0-87196-527-5. As: **Who's Who & What's What in Science Fiction Film, Television, Radio, & Theater**. New York, Bonanza Books, 1985. ix, 336 p. LC 85-14680. ISBN 0-517-48886-8. Includes a new introduction, "The S.F. Success," by Isaac Asimov, but is otherwise identical.

Like Pickard's guide (see #510), Wright's encyclopedia tries to be all things to all people and suffers from similar problems. *The Science Fiction Image* mixes entries on SF films, television programs, radio series, writers, directors, actors, and other terms in one alphabetical sequence. A typical film entry gives title (boldfaced caps), type (e.g., "TV film"), release year, nationality, running time, color or black and white, annotation, production credits, and casting credits. A typical personal entry provides name (boldfaced caps), years of birth and death (if known), a description of his or her career, and a brief filmography (listing motion pictures [in italics] and release years). The annotations range in size from 50 to 1,000 words (averaging 200) and are both descriptive and evaluative. See also references are noted by highlighting text within an entry in boldfaced type; Wright also includes some see references from alternate titles to main entries. The book is illustrated throughout with 200 clearly reproduced black-and-white stills, plus sixteen pages of color stills, and is bound to library standards.

There are several problems with this book. The volume shows signs of having been thrown together with great haste. For example, an entry header is missing on page 111, the entries on pages 237-38 are way out of alphabetical sequence, the *Millennium Falcon* entry is misspelled, at least one photo on the color plates is completely miscredited, etc. There is simply no excuse for these kinds of lapses appearing in a reference work from a major publisher. One must also question the selection criteria employed by Wright. On what basis were some films or filmmakers covered—and not others? The selection seems haphazard at best: *Star Trek* (both television series and motion pictures) is covered in great detail, with separate entries on Mr. Spock (under "M"), Ensign Pavel Chekhov (under "E" in the alphabet, with no see references), Leonard Nimoy, the Klingons, the Romulas, the *Enterprise*, Gene Roddenberry, Transporter Room, Tricorder, Phaser, etc., but *not* on William Shatner, Capt. James T. Kirk, Leonard McCoy (or DeForest Kelley), or any of the other characters or principals. Why? One can get a better idea of the problem by noting that the halfway point in the text (pages 168-69) features entries covering the early "G" part of the alphabet, when we would expect it to find terms from the "Ls" or "Ms." In fact, the last one hundred pages of text, less than a third of the entire book, feature entries from Ma-Z, more than half of the alphabet. One has the clear impression that the author was forced at the last minute to cull a significant amount of wordage from this section to make the book fit into a preconceived size.

The result is a hodgepodge, occasionally entertaining or enlightening (Wright's comments are usually sound), but more often than not simply frustrating to the potential user. If extensively reworked and expanded, this volume has the potential to become a true SF film encyclopedia but cannot be recommended in its present form.

SPECIFIC MOVIES, TV PROGRAMS, OR SUBJECTS

Battlestar Galactica

518. Kraus, Bruce. **Encyclopedia Galactica: From the Fleet Library Aboard the *Battlestar Galactica*.** New York, Windmill Books and E.P. Dutton, 1979. [57] p. LC 79-4649. ISBN 0-525-61039-1.

This illustrated A-Z guide to the persons, places, and things in the "Battlestar Galactica" universe was designed for the adolescent market. Entries cover the principal characters (Adama, Starbuck, Imperious Leader, etc.), worlds visited by the *Galactica* (Kobol, Borallus), and other terms (Viper, Warrior, etc.). A final page provides "A Chronology of Major Events in Human [i.e., Twelve Colonies] History." The book is nicely illustrated throughout with color stills from the television series and bound to library standards. Some of the entries include fictional elaborations which may or may not be based on the series "Bible" or on events which were mentioned during the course of the program's short run. For "Galactica" fans only.

Dark Shadows

519. Gross, Edward, and James Van Hise. ***Dark Shadows* Tribute.** Las Vegas, Nev., Pioneer Books, 1990. 144 p. ISBN 1-55698-234-8 (pbk.).

"Dark Shadows" was a popular gothic soap opera from 1966-71, which also spun off two separately produced motion pictures and a reworked nighttime television series during the 1990/91 season. Contents: "Introduction"; "Origins: Dan Curtis, Art Wallace, Robert Costello"; "What It Is..."; "Jonathan Frid"; "The Reluctant Vampire"; "Barnabas Collins";

"Collinwood Memories: Louis Edmonds, Grayson Hall, Jerry Lacy, Alexandra Moltke"; "Star Panel: John Sedwick, Ron Sprout"; "Appendix: The Episodes"; "A Gallery of *Dark Shadows.*" The narrative sections have little reference value, but the episode guide, occupying pages 68-131, provides one-paragraph plot summaries of the 600 episodes beginning with the introduction of Barnabas Collins (Jonathan Frid) as a continuing vampire character (the sequence actually begins with the 210th program of the series, the previous segments having occupied themselves with more-or-less standard gothic fare). The book is illustrated throughout with black-and-white full- and partial-page illustrations of the characters and sets. Gross and Van Hise's plot descriptions are a little fuller than Scott's (see #520), but their book provides summaries for less than half of the episodes actually televised. Prefer Scott's more comprehensive guide.

520. Scott, Kathryn Leigh. **The *Dark Shadows* Companion: 25th Anniversary Collection.** Los Angeles & London, Pomegranate Press, 1990. 208 p. LC 90-62402. ISBN 0-938817-26-4; ISBN 0-938817-25-6 (pbk.).

Scott was one of the principal actresses on the "Dark Shadows" television series from 1966-71 and previously published *My Scrapbook Memories of Dark Shadows.* Contents: "Acknowledgements"; "Dedication"; "Introduction," by Scott; "Foreword," by Jonathan Frid; "Out of Angélique's Shadow," by Lara Parker; "*Dark Shadows* and Me," by Matthew Hall; "A Word from Me," by Sam Hall; "The *Dark Shadows* History," by Melody Clark, Kathleen Resch, and Marcy Robin: "Picture Gallery," "The Journey Continues," "The Cousin from England," "When Every Day Was Opening Night," "That Year of Insanity," "A Werewolf with a PhD," "Rain, Snow, and a Drafty Old House," "The Last Days at Collinwood"; "Episode Guide," by Jim Pierson; "Update: Where Are They Now?"; "Collectibles"; "In Memoriam."

The narrative sections are both interesting and informative and copiously illustrated with full-page black-and-white and color stills and personal photographs of the series and the stars. The very detailed episode guide provides one-sentence plot summaries of each of the 1,225 programs; the plot developments are so complicated and convoluted, involving travels back and forth in time and into parallel dimensions, that the reader is advised to use the guide in conjuction with the detailed history of the series by Clark, Resch, and Robin, who show exactly how each plot segment segued into the next. The update section gives brief biographies of each of the principals involved in the series (including actors, directors, writers, and others), listing other credits and the names of the character(s) each of the cast portrayed (again, because of the complex array of plot lines, most of the actors played more than one character in the Collins family). The "Collectibles" chapter lists the thirty-two "Dark Shadows" novelizations, plus other monographs, recordings, videos, periodicals, merchandise, and the addresses of two fan clubs. The book is beautifully designed, printed on high-quality glossy paper, and the cloth edition is bound to library standards.

This is a superior tribute to a TV program that remains popular in syndication. Future editions should include original air dates in the episode directory and an overall index to the book.

Doctor Who

521. Haining, Peter. ***Doctor Who*: The Time-Travelers' Guide.** London, W. H. Allen, 1989. 272 p. ISBN 0-86379-188-3 (pbk.).

Haining's guide is one of several publications he has produced on this long-running British SF series. Contents: "Introduction"; "1. The Science that Inspired *Doctor Who*"; "2.

Back in the Mists of Time Travel"; "3. Time and the Lords of Gallifrey"; "4. Regeneration—The Mystery of Ages"; "5. A Who's Who of Enemies"; "6. A Tourist's Guide to Alien Worlds"; "7. Space Craft Checklist"; "8. Time Travel Update."

The main sections of reference value are Chapters 5-8. "A Who's Who of Enemies" is further subdivided into three sections: "I. Villainous Humanoids"; "II. Dangerous Robots"; "III. Evil Monsters." In each section villains are arranged alphabetically by name or type. A typical entry gives name (bold caps), episode(s) in which it appeared, telewriter, year of production, actor(s), and a one-paragraph description. Chapter 6 is an A-Z listing of the worlds and places visited by Doctor Who in his travels through time and space. A typical entry provides place name (bold caps), location, and the role it played in the saga. The guide to spacecraft (Chapter 7) is arranged chronologically by appearance date, giving type of craft (bold caps), first sighting date, and the part each played in the plot. The final chapter includes a detailed programme log from 1983-86 by Jeremy Bentham, with over a thousand words of plot summary for each.

The book is beautifully illustrated with full- and partial-page black-and-white and color stills and photographs. All fans of "Doctor Who" will want a copy of this guide; libraries will probably prefer Haining's 25th anniversay tribute (see #522), which includes a complete episode log from 1963-87.

522. Haining, Peter. *Doctor Who*: **25 Glorious Years: XXV**. London, Virgin, 1988. 224 p., [12] p. of plates. ISBN 0-86369-324-5 (pbk.).

"Doctor Who" is the longest-running science-fiction television series in history, the first episodes having been shown in 1963. Well-known horror anthologist and critic Peter Haining has here produced a marvelously detailed tribute to the program and its stars. Contents: "The Legend Begins"; "Introduction"; "The Great Whovian Mystery"; "The Silver Decade"; "Inside the World of *Doctor Who*"; "The Seven Faces of *Doctor Who*"; "Who Are These Doctors!"; "The Doctor We Presume?"; "Stories of Intergalactic Guest Stars"; "*Doctor Who* and the Merchandisers"; "The Doctor in the Comics"; "The Lost Stories of *Doctor Who*"; "Time Travels: The Seven Doctors' 150 Adventures in 25 Years."

The narrative sections which comprise the bulk of the book delineate the history of the program, the careers of the seven fictional Doctor Whos and the lives of the seven actors who have played him, and other material of interest. "The Doctor We Presume?" records in chronological order the characters (and actresses) who have portrayed the Doctor's female companions, giving details of their fictional and factual lives. The "Time Travels" section provides a chronological checklist of the 150 "Doctor Who" mini-series, giving producer, episode number, title, telewriter, director, guest stars, and original air dates, season by season. The metamorphosis of each Doctor Who into his regenerated new body (i.e., portrayal by a new actor) is also noted, in large bold letters. The book is beautifully illustrated with reproductions of black-and-white and color stills from the original series and is nicely typeset and designed.

"Doctor Who" has seen a resurgence of critical interest in recent years; this carefully compiled tribute will provide a useful starting point for all future scholarship.

Dracula Films

523. Glut, Donald F. **The Dracula Book.** Metuchen, N.J., Scarecrow Press, 1975. xx, 388 p. index. LC 75-4917. ISBN 0-8108-0804-8.

Although Glut also covers Dracula books, comic books, and other media, the primary emphasis here is on film adaptations. Contents: "Acknowledgments"; "Preface";

introductions by Christopher Lee and William Marshall; "1. Vlad Dracula, the Impaler"; "2. The Vampire Image"; "3. The Ancestors of Dracula"; "4. Bram Stoker's Classic"; "5. Dracula Dramatized"; "6. Dracula on the Silent Screen"; "7. Dracula Haunts Universal"; "8. The Hammer Horrors of Dracula"; "9. Dracula Flies Again"; "10. Stay Tuned for Dracula"; "11. Other Dracula Books"; "12. Dracula Meets the Comics"; "13. Dracula Eternal"; "Afterword" ; " Index."

The narrative chapters having reference value include 5-12, which delineate in chronological order stage adaptations, motion pictures, television and radio appearances, novels and short stories featuring Dracula and other Dracula-like vampires (but also those books having the word "Dracula" in the title, even when no vampire is actually present), comic book adaptataions, and other media. Some foreign-language books and films are covered (with the original titles followed by their English-language translations). The annotations range in size from 50-500 words, averaging 250, and tend to be descriptive, with some evaluation at the end of each summary. Motion picture production and casting credits (generally the producer, director, screenwriter, and major stars) are buried in the narrative text, each film's title being highlighted in all-capital letters (book titles are underlined). Materials are covered through 1974. The comprehensive index correlates all names and titles with page numbers. The book is shot from legible typed copy, illustrated throughout with clearly reproduced black-and-white stills and cover illustrations, and bound to library standards.

Glut clearly knows his material, and his judgments seem sound. Any scholar doing research on the vampire myth in film and literature will want a copy of this book. A new edition with better production values (and possibly reorganized along the lines of Glut's *Frankenstein Catalog* [see #524]) would definitely be warranted.

Frankenstein Films

524. Glut, Donald F. **The Frankenstein Catalog: Being a Comprehensive Listing of Novels, Translations, Adaptations, Stories, Critical Works, Popular Articles, Series, Fumetti, Verse, Stage Plays, Films, Cartoons, Puppetry, Radio & Television Programs, Comics, Satire & Humor, Spoken & Musical Recordings, Tapes, and Sheet Music Featuring Frankenstein's Monster and/or Descended from Mary Shelley's Novel.** Jefferson, N.C. & London, McFarland & Co., 1984. xiii, 525 p. index. LC 81-6026. ISBN 0-89950-029-3.

In this companion volume to *The Dracula Book* (see #523), Glut again covers all media in his exploration of the Frankenstein theme, although the dramatic presentations occupy half the book. Contents: "Acknowledgments"; "Preface"; "Chapter One: Mary Shelley's *Frankenstein*"; "Chapter Two: The Frankenstein Chronicles"; "Chapter Three: Frankenstein on Stage"; "Chapter Four: Frankenstein on Film"; "Chapter Five: Frankenstein on Radio and Television"; "Chapter Six: Frankenstein in the Comics"; "Chapter Seven: Frankenstein Recordings, Music, and Lyrics"; "Name Index"; "Title Index."

Most publications sections are arranged alphabetically by main entry; most film sections are arranged chronologically by publication date. Chapters are subdivided into as many as nine sections, covering such topics as "Frankenstein Fiction"; "Film Series"; "Writings About *Frankenstein*" [the novel]; "Television Movies"; Newspaper Strips"; etc. Both primary and secondary sources are included; particularly in Chapters One and Two, there are extensive lists of articles and books about Mary Shelley's work and on the Frankenstein theme in general. Foreign-language materials are interfiled with the rest, with an English-language translation in brackets. A typical film entry gives item number, title (italicized), production company, year of release, running time, color or black and white, alternate (or English-language) title, production and casting credits, and one-paragraph plot summary, with occasional additional notes and/or see references to other items of interest.

A typical book entry provides item number, author, title (italicized), place of publication, publisher, pagination, similar data for all known reprint or variant editions, and a one-paragraph plot summary. A typical short prose work entry gives item number, author, title (in quotes), magazine title (italicized), month and year of publication, and pagination. Materials are numbered consecutively throughout the book from 1-2,666. The book is nicely typeset and designed, illustrated throughout with clearly reproduced black-and-white stills and cover shots, and bound to library standards. The indexes correlate names and titles to specific item numbers.

It is difficult to imagine how any researcher even remotely interested in the Frankenstein theme in literature or film could bypass this work. Every datum that might possibly be desired is present, well-organized, and easily accessible through the indexes. Kudos to Glut on a job well done. All four-year college libraries and all research institutions should own a copy.

The Outer Limits

525. Schow, David J., and Jeffrey Frentzen. *The Outer Limits*: **The Official Companion**. New York, Ace Science Fiction Books, 1986. 406 p. index. LC 87-400050. ISBN 0-441-37081-0 (pbk.).

"The Outer Limits" was one of the most imaginative of the SF anthology series to run on television during the 1960s, exceeded, perhaps, only by individual episodes of "The Twilight Zone." Contents: "Introduction"; "Part One: The Awe and Mystery of the Universe"; "Part Two: We Are Controlling Transmission"; "Part Three: Fear of the Unknown"; "Part Four: The Devil's Puppeteer"; "Part Five: Man's Endless Thirst for Knowledge"; "Part Six: Beyond the Outer Limits"; "Appendixes"; "Index."

The annotations for each of the episodes are interspersed throughout the narrative part of the text, arranged in chronological order by production (not broadcast) date. A typical entry includes episode title (bold caps), broadcast date, writer, director, assistant director, director of photography, cast (characters and players), voiceover introduction from that episode, one- to two-paragraph plot summary, and several pages of background material, including excerpts from selected dialogue, interviews with the principals, and other material of interest. The appendices include: "The Canons of *Please Stand By*" (the original title for the series), "*The Outer Limits* That Never Were: Unfilmed Episodes," "Production & Broadcast Schedules" (showing exact dates of filming for each episode, and air dates), "End Credits" (a list of the executive staff at Daystar Productions, producers of the series). The detailed index correlates all names and titles with page numbers. The book is illustrated throughout with sometimes fuzzy stills from the programs, printed on poor-quality paper that is already beginning to yellow, and rather cheaply bound.

Which is unfortunate, because this guide deserves permanent preservation as a homage to a program that stretched the limits of both the imagination and of special-effects technology. Everything the fan or scholar would want to know about the program is here, easily accessed through the index. Any library collection with an interest in the history of television should acquire this book, and immediately have it rebound in cloth and deacidified.

Prehistorical Creatures in Films

526. Kinnard, Roy. **Beasts and Behemoths: Prehistoric Creatures in the Movies.** Metuchen, N.J. & London, Scarecrow Press, 1988. xi, 179 p. index. LC 87-23424. ISBN 0-8108-2062-5.

Kinnard annotates thirty-seven motion pictures featuring primitive beasties, from the early silents to *Baby* (1985). Materials are arranged in chronological order by publication date. A typical entry provides item number, title (all caps), production company, release year, principal production credits, cast, and critique. The annotations range in size from 200-4,000 words (the longest entry covers *King Kong*), averaging 400, and are both descriptive, historical, and evaluative, including much background information on the making of each film. The book is nicely illustrated with little-seen stills from the motion pictures and shot from word-processed copy. The appendices add "Feature Film Checklist," listing all known prehistoric creature pictures in chronological order by release date, with asterisks following those titles which are *not* annotated in this guide; and a "Japanese Feature Film Checklist," including the Godzilla series and related titles. Two indexes, to names and titles, coordinate these data with page numbers; underlined page numbers indicate illustrations.

Kinnard certainly knows his material, but his guide can only be a rather peripheral acquisition for most personal and institutional collections. For larger research libraries only.

The Prisoner

527. White, Matthew, and Jaffer Ali. **The Official *Prisoner* Companion.** New York, Warner Books, 1988. ix, 244 p. LC 88-5606. ISBN 0-446-38744-4 (pbk.); ISBN 0-446-38745-2 (pbk.; Canada). Also: London, Sidgwick & Jackson, 1988. ix, 244 p. ISBN 0-283-99598-X (pbk.).

When "The Prisoner" first aired on television in 1968, it created a great deal of puzzlement among viewers, and little else, but later developed a cult following. Many critics now regard it as the finest TV series ever broadcast. Contents: "Acknowledgments"; "Introduction"; "Chapter One: *Prisoner* Episode Guide"; "Chapter Two: Notes, Anecdotes, and Nonsense"; "Chapter Three: The Great Debates"; "Chapter Four: What Does It All Mean?"; "Chapter Five: Talking with McGoohan"; "Patrick McGoohan Films"; "Appendix A: Sources of Information"; "Appendix B: The Shooting Scripts."

The first half of the book consists of a detailed guide to the individual programs in the official order established by the production company. A typical entry provides title (boldfaced caps), writer, script editor, producer, director, executive director, cast (players and characters), crew, synopsis, and observations. The synopsis usually runs 800-1,000 words, the observations 500-600. Other material of reference value includes the Patrick McGoohan filmography, listing his motion picture roles in chronological order by date, and giving title (boldfaced), nationality, release year, and one-paragraph synopsis. The "Sources of Information" section lists fan clubs and addresses, books about "The Prisoner" series, conventions, videotapes, and sources of memorabilia. There are some very valuable excerpts from the program's shooting scripts, highlighting key moments from the series. The book is nicely illustrated throughout with black-and-white stills and nicely typeset; the binding will not withstand library use.

Both the scholar and fan will welcome this very complete handbook on a TV series that seems likely to endure the test of time. Recommended for all collections with an interest in the history of television.

Star Trek

528. Asherman, Allan. **The *Star Trek* Compendium**. New York, A Wallaby Book, Simon & Schuster, 1981. 187 p. LC 81-140016. ISBN 0-671-79145-1 (pbk.). **The *Star Trek* Compendium**. [Rev. ed.]. London, A Star Book, W. H. Allen & Co., 1983. 194 p. ISBN 0-352-31355-2 (pbk.). **The *Star Trek* Compendium**. [Rev. ed.]. New York, Pocket Books, 1986. 184 p. index. LC 87-400763. ISBN 0-671-62726-0 (pbk.). **The *Star Trek* Compendium**. [Rev. ed.]. New York, Pocket Books, 1989. 182 p. index. LC 89-199904. ISBN 0-671-68440-X (pbk.).

Each of these books has been updated from the previous version, usually by adding coverage of an additional *Star Trek* movie (the 1989 edition covers through *Star Trek V, The Final Frontier*) but are otherwise similarly organized. Contents (1989 edition): "Introduction"; "The Beginnings"; "The Episodes"; "The Long Road Back"; "Indices."

The first chapter discusses the origins of the series, including credits and plot summaries for the two different pilots, "The Cage" and "The Menagerie." More than half of the volume is concerned with "The Episodes," arranged chronologically by production date (not air date). A typical entry provides episode title (bold caps), episode number, writer(s), director, characters, a one- to two-paragraph plot summary, and roughly 500-600 words of commentary giving background information on how technical problems were solved, sidelights on guest stars and the principal actors, changes made in the story line from the original script, etc. The episodes are organized into three chapters corresponding to the three seasons the television series was in production; Asherman provides a general introduction at the beginning of each chapter. "The Long Road Back" includes coverage of the animated episodes of "Star Trek," the five *Star Trek* movies, and the abortive television series, "Star Trek II," but nothing on "Star Trek—The Next Generation." There are two indexes, to the series episodes (giving production number and original air date in addition to title), and to characters, correlated with episode number and actor's name; there is no separate index to the actors' real names. The book is nicely typeset and illustrated throughout with black-and-white stills from the television programs and motion pictures.

Asherman's continuing work is the most current guide to the *Star Trek* universe, and is generally recommended over all other competing volumes listed below, although Jones and Trimble's *Concordance* (see #529) does provide more detailed coverage of the original series.

529. Jones, Dorothy; edited by Bjo Trimble. **Star Trek Concordance of People, Places, & Things**. Berkeley, Calif., Mathom House Publications, 1969. 84 p. (pbk.). Trimble, Bjo, and Dorothy Jones. **The Third Season Supplement to the *Star Trek* Concordance**. Los Angeles, Calif., Mathom House Publications, 1973. [70] p. (pbk.). Trimble, Bjo; based on a concept by Dorothy Jones Heydt. **The *Star Trek* Concordance**. [Rev. ed.]. New York, Ballantine Books, 1976. 256 p. index. LC 76-9778. ISBN 0-345-25137-7 (pbk.).

The first version of this guide to the *Star Trek* universe, together with its *Supplement*, were both produced in rather amateurish fashion, offset from typed copy and bound through the spine with metal clasps. The much more professional revised version is broken into two major sections.

The first half of the book discusses the individual episodes from both the original and animated series in chronological order by air date. A typical entry provides title (bold caps), writer(s), stardate, air date, plot summary (400-600 words), characters and players, and "Lexicon" references. The second half of the work, the "Lexicon," provides an A-Z guide to the people, places, and things mentioned in the television series. The entries range in size from one sentence to 650 words and reference the specific episode in which the item appears (in the form TSP for "This Side of Paradise"), keyed to "An Index of Episode Abbreviations" on page 256. The latter is not quite as useful as it might be, referencing page numbers only and not listing the actual episode titles. Trimble has also provided a "Star Trek" time line (listing each episode in chronological order by "stardate"), and an index to episode titles on pages 14-15. A portfolio of amateurish "Fan Art" fills pages 17-31; other black-and-white line drawings are sprinkled throughout the text.

Trimble and Jones's guide is the most detailed concordance yet published on the original television series, but it does not, of course, cover the *Star Trek* motion pictures or "Star Trek—The Next Generation." Asherman's *Compendium* (see #528) is more current.

530. Peel, John; edited by Hal Schuster. **The *Trek* Encyclopedia**. Las Vegas, Nev., Pioneer Books, 1988. 365 p. ISBN 1-55698-205-4 (pbk.).

Peel has written dozens of nonfiction works on SF television programs and motion pictures. This new guide is broken into four sections: "The Characters," "The People" (i.e., actors), "The Planets," and "Appendix: Ships & Devices."

The first chapter is an A-Z listing of the characters, peoples, and things filling the *Star Trek* universe. A typical character entry provides name, actor's name, title of episode(s) in which the character appeared (in chronological order), and description, ranging in size from one sentence to several paragraphs. The other entries feature creatures or national groups; the entry for the "Klingons," for example, lists each of the Klingon characters featured in the series, episode by episode, with the actors who portrayed them, see references to specific character names covered elsewhere in the *Encyclopedia*, plus a two-page narrative description of the Klingon Empire, Klingon attributes, and interactions with Federation personnel.

The second section indexes actors and actresses, directors, and writers featured in the "Star Trek" television series and the first four *Star Trek* motion pictures, alphabetically by surname, a typical entry providing person's name, episode title(s), role, and biography, including a brief filmography of each. The third chapter is an alphabetical guide to the planets mentioned (or visited) in the *Star Trek* saga, a typical entry giving planet name (bold caps), story title, and one-to-two-paragraph description. The appendix provides a narrative description of *The Enterprise* itself, and a separate section detailing (in no particular order) some of the devices used in the series. The book is rather poorly designed and printed (on cheap paper which will oxidize within a few years), and the entry heads are sometimes difficult to read. Prefer Jonas Trimble (see #529) and Asherman (see #528).

531. Turnbull, Gerry, ed. **A *Star Trek* Catalog**. New York, Grosset & Dunlap Publishers, 1979. 160 p. LC 77-71296. ISBN 0-448-14053-5 (pbk.).

This catalog tried to provide the *Star Trek* fan with a basic guide to the series and its spin-offs. Contents: "Introduction"; "An Interview with Gene Roddenberry"; "The Cons"; "The Clubs and Organizations"; "The Crew"; "The Episodes"; "The Animated *Star Trek*"; "The Marketspace"; "The Bookcase"; "The Future Voyages."

The "Clubs and Organizations" chapter lists fan groups alphabetically by state, then by city of location, giving group name, address, meeting schedule, and other data. The "Crew" section provides biographies of the principal continuing actors of *Star Trek*, with brief filmographies. The "Episodes" and animated chapters give a chronological checklist (by air date) of the programs from the main and animated series, a typical entry providing title (boldfaced), episode number, telewriter, one-paragraph plot summary, and air date. The "Marketspace" section is an A-Z rendering of the business firms selling *Star Trek* memorabilia. The "Bookcase" provides an annotated guide to the *Star Trek* books published through 1977. The book is illustrated thoughout with stills and photos; there is no index.

All of this is, of course, wholly outdated and now only of peripheral interest to the diehard fan. Prefer Gibson-Downs and Gentry's more current and complete catalog (see #538), and Van Hise's *Fan's Handbook* (see #532).

532. Van Hise, James. **The *Trek* Fan's Handbook**. Las Vegas, Nev., Pioneer Books, 1990. 109 p. ISBN 1-55698-271-2 (pbk.).

One of a series of rather trashy guides to films and television mass produced by this Las Vegas firm, the *Handbook* contains "Introduction"; "Brief History of *Star Trek* Fandom"; "The *Star Trek* Welcommittee"; "Guide to *Star Trek* Fan Clubs"; "Books About *Star Trek*"; "*Star Trek* Fan Fiction"; "Guide to *Star Trek* Fan Publications"; "*Star Trek* Conventions"; "A Guide to *Star Trek* Merchandise"; "*Star Trek* on Home Video."

The most useful sections of this guide include Chapter Three, which provides a comprehensive list of fan clubs, arranged alphabetically by state and city; Chapter Four (by Wendy Rathbone), an alphabetical index of nonfiction works about *Star Trek* and its characters, including fanzine and magazine publications in addition to monographs, with partial bibliographical data; Chapter Six, the bibliography of *Star Trek* fan fiction, in alphabetical order by title, including both fanzines and self-published novels, with names and addresses of authors and/or proprietors; and Chapter Eight, "A Guide to *Star Trek* Merchandise," which lists such materials in alphabetical order by type (e.g., "Audio Cassette," "Belt Buckle," etc.), but provides no vendor names. The book is printed on better-quality paper than is usual from this publisher.

Trekkers will welcome this guide, but most libraries and researchers can safely pass.

Star Wars

533. Velasco, Raymond L. **A Guide to the *Star Wars* Universe**. New York, A Del Rey Book, Ballantine Books, 1984. xlvii, 215 p. index. LC 84-90943. ISBN 0-345-31920-6 (pbk.).

The major part of this book is an A-Z guide to the people, places, and things in the *Star Wars* universe. A typical character entry provides name (listed under given name, not surname), brief description, a more detailed account of his or her life and career as derived from the canon, and a set of letter codes referencing original sources (e.g., "SW"=*Star Wars*). Other entries focus on places, creatures, devices, weapons, etc. The front matter includes indexes to "Alien Creatures and Species," "Characters and Character Names," "Devices and Things," "Droid Names and Types of Droids/Automata," "Historical Events," "Slang/Colloquialisms," "Social Customs and Institutions," "Technical Concepts and Other Abstractions," "Vehicles/Vessels," "Weaponry," and "Worlds and Places," all of them used as entries in the main dictionary. A list of abbreviation codes on pages lxv-lxvii references twenty-seven published *Star Wars* books and associated items (including map and art portfolios).

Velasco's definitions are based upon these printed sources and not directly on the three motion pictures themselves; there are a number of discrepancies between the movies and their novelized adaptations, and some of the other printed spin-off items include fictional elaborations not mentioned elsewhere. The book is nicely typeset, illustrated with postage stamp-sized black-and-white drawings, and printed on poor-quality paper. For fans only.

The Twilight Zone

534. Prouty, Howard H. **TZX: The *Twilight Zone* Index.** North Hollywood, Calif., [Howard H. Prouty], 1985. 40 p. index. (pbk.).

Designed as a supplemental index to Zicree's work (see #535), this guide is broken into four sections: "Directors," "Writers/Authors," "Selected Performers," and "Episode Titles." In each part materials are arranged alphabetically by person or title. A typical Directors entry gives director (all caps), episode title, network, original air date, and format (e.g., "FB/30"=film, black and white, thirty-minute running time). A typical entry from the writers' section includes name (all caps), episode, network, original air date, credit (e.g., "ot"=original teleplay), story source (where applicable; "ps"=published story), and format (e.g., "TB/30"=videotape, black and white, thirty-minute running time). A typical performers' entry gives name (all caps), episode title, network, original air date. The guide to episode titles provides title, network, original air date, format, and the page number in Zicree's book (see #535) which annotates that episode (however, episode titles *are* indexed in the latter volume). The booklet is shot from clearly reproduced typed copy and bound with staples into paper covers.

Students of this ever-popular television series will want copies of this index; all others may safely pass.

535. Zicree, Marc Scott. **The *Twilight Zone* Companion.** Toronto & New York, Bantam Books, 1982. 447 p. index. LC 82-90326. ISBN 0-553-01416-1 (pbk.). **The *Twilight Zone* Companion.** 2nd ed. New York & Toronto, Bantam Books, 1989. 466 p. index. LC 89-6754. ISBN 0-553-34744-6 (pbk.).

Zicree's book pays homage to this long-running and critically acclaimed television series in a marvelously well-wrought guide to the programs and to the writers and other principals who contributed to its success. Individual episodes are arranged in chronological order by production date. A typical entry gives title (bold caps), air date, writer, producer, director, director of photography, music, cast (characters and actors), a transcription of Serling's introduction (in italics), one-paragraph plot summary, Serling's coda, and background details on the development of the story, on the characters, etc., including occasional excerpts from the script. Interspersed throughout the text are separate sections on the major writers, actors, directors, and other principals involved in "The Twilight Zone," usually associated with their first appearance on the program and including snippets of interviews, either with the individuals themselves or with those who knew them, and much other associational information of importance. The book is very well designed and typeset and illustrated with rare black-and-white stills from the television program. Unfortunately, the quality of paper used by Bantam means that the text will yellow and oxidize within five years. The index correlates all names and titles with page numbers.

This is one of the best TV series guides yet published: Zicree is knowledgeable, informative, never intrusive. Fans and scholars alike will welcome this volume; research libraries should immediately rebind and deacidify their copies.

CALENDARS AND CHRONOLOGIES

SCOPE NOTE: This section includes chronologies of fantastic literature arranged by year and month in descending order, and historical calendars in book form arranged by month and day and year.

536. Post, Joyce. **Let's Drink to That, Being a Compendium of Events, Real & Imaginary, of Interest to the Reader of Science, Fiction, & Science Fiction.** Philadelphia, The Terminus, Owlswick, & Ft. Mudge Electrick Street Railway Gazette, 1970. 58 p. (pbk.).

Post, wife of map compiler J. B. Post, has here assembled a literary calendar of science fiction and related topics. The basic arrangement is by month, then by date. Under each day events which occurred on that date in history are listed in descending order by year, from the earliest to the latest. January 1st, for example, includes entries for 1879, 1889, 1921, 1923, 1928, and 1948, noting the births of E. M. Forster and Seabury Quinn, the release of the serial version of *Around the World in 18 Days*, the opening of the first air-conditioned office building, and the formation of The Spectator Club. Entries average from one-to-two lines each, and there are two to fifteen entries per date. Post mentions the dates of birth and death of all major SF authors and editors, scientific advances of all kinds, space exploration, the production or release of major fantastic films, etc. The booklet is shot from legible typed copy, illustrated throughout by Roy Krenkel, and bound with staples into paper covers.

Post's calendar can be most entertaining but is now two decades out-of-date. An updated version with better production values would be highly desirable.

QUOTATIONS DICTIONARIES

SCOPE NOTE: This section includes reference books which feature quotations from works of fantastic literature.

537. Gaiman, Neil, and Kim Newman. **Ghastly Beyond Belief**. London, Arrow Books, 1985. 343 p. ISBN 0-09-936830-7 (pbk.).

Gaiman and Newman have compiled a collection of unintentionally humorous SF quotations taken from mostly bad science-fiction and fantasy novels and films, and including enough passages from even the top-name writers to make one wonder how the field has ever survived to this day. Contents: "Foreword and Acknowledgements"; "Introduction," by Harry Harrison; "Part One—The Books": "Attention Please"; "Characters, Human and Otherwise"; "Language!"; "Preoccupations"; "Special Effects"; "Writers and Rules"; "Part Two—The Movies": "For Starters"; "Expectations"; "The Nasties"; "SF Styles"; "The Cast"; "Science"; "Funny Bits"; "Countdown"; "Just Testing."

Each of these chapters is further subdivided into specific subjects ("Love and Marriage," for example), with quotations randomly listed thereunder. A typical entry includes quotation, book author (all caps) and title (italics), or film title (italics) and year of release. The quotations range in size from one line to several paragraphs and have been chosen for their out-of-context amusement value, with appropriate remarks by the editors (in boldfaced type preceding the quote). The book is nicely typeset and the text most amusing. However, the absence of an index makes the volume almost completely unusable as a reference work.

COLLECTORS' AND PRICE GUIDES

SCOPE NOTE: Included in this section are price and collectors' guides to science-fiction and fantasy books, films, and memorabilia. Catalogs of one author's works are included in the Author Bibliographies chapter. Also covered herein are lists of SF bookstores and dealers.

538. Gibson-Downs, Sally, and Christine Gentry. **Encyclopedia of Trekkie Memorabilia: Identification and Value Guide**. Florence, Ala., Books Americana, 1988. iii, 269 p., [8] p. of plates. LC 88-208326. ISBN 0-89689-066-X (pbk.).

This very detailed guide to *Star Trek* collectibles is arranged in alphabetical order by subject category, then alphabetically by title or description. Categories include: "Artwork and Cels," "Blueprints," "Clothing and Accessories," "Film and Photography," "Games," "Hobby Kits," 'Housewares," "ID's," "Printed Wallhangings," "Jewelry," "Literature," "Music," "Posters and Posterbooks," "Props," "School and Office Supplies," "Scripts," "Toys," "Trading Cards," "Promoting *Star Trek*" (in two sections, covering special promotions, contents, display/exhibits, offers and specials, premiums, publicity releases, souvenirs; and conventions and live performances), and "Bibliography." Introductory chapters cover "What's It All About," "Your *Star Trek* Collection," and "Storing Your Collection."

A typical entry gives item or title (boldfaced), publisher or production company, description, original issue price (in dollars), current price range (in dollars). The volume includes numerous black-and-white illustrations of the products and books described, and eight pages of color reproductions. Serious Trekkers will welcome this guide, although the price listings are already out-of-date; libraries will probably find the book too limited in scope to add to their collections; researchers may find the "Literature" chapter of interest, since it provides, in essence, a complete bibliography of all *Star Trek* fiction and nonfiction published through 1987. Compare with Cornwell and Kott's price list (see #540).

539. Halpern, Frank M. **International Classified Directory of Dealers in Science Fiction and Fantasy Books and Related Materials**. Haddonfield, N.J., Haddonfield House, 1975. x, 90 p. index. LC 74-22449. ISBN 0-88366-003-2.

The main section of this directory is arranged alphabetically by dealer name. A typical entry gives business name, proprietor (if different), address, phone number, hours, specializations. Two indexes reference the dealers' names by subject and geographically, by country or state and city. There are also brief lists of dealers who accept want lists, dealer appraisers, and search services. The book is shot from very clear typed copy and bound to library standards. Lamentably, this guide is so far out-of-date as to be completely useless; a continuously updated version is badly needed.

540. **The Official Price Guide to *Star Trek* and *Star Wars* Collectibles**. 2nd ed. Orlando, Fla., House of Collectibles, 1984. 236 p. LC 82-84639. ISBN 0-87637-437-2 (pbk.). **The Official Price Guide to *Star Trek* and *Star Wars* Collectibles**. 3rd ed. Orlando, Fla., House of Collectibles, 1985. 257 p. LC 82-84639. ISBN 0-87637-494-1 (pbk.). Cornwell, Sue, and Mike Kott. **The Official Price Guide to *Star Trek* and *Star Wars* Collectibles**. 1st ed. New York, House of Collectibles, Ballantine Books, 1986. 377 p. Cornwell, Sue, and Mike Kott. **The Official Price Guide to *Star Trek* and *Star Wars* Collectibles**. 2nd ed. New York,

House of Collectibles, Ballantine Books, 1987. 415 p. Cornwell, Sue, and Mike Kott. **The Official Price Guide to *Star Trek* and *Star Wars* Collectibles.** 3rd ed. New York, House of Collectibles, Ballantine Books, 1991. 277 p. LC 84-644977 (pbk.). ISSN 0748-1128.

The early versions of this price guide were unattributed, although Cornwell and Kott are acknowledged in the 1985 edition as having been contributors. Ballantine Books purchased and reworked the House of Collectibles list in 1986, established Cornwell and Kott as editors of this series, and called the heavily reworked volume a "1st edition."

Contents (1987 edition): "Market Review"; "*Star Trek*: From the Beginning"; "The *Star Trek* Movies"; "The Creation of *Star Wars*"; "*Revenge (Return) of the Jedi*"; "Building a Collection"; "Condition and Care"; "Conventions"; "Dealer Directory"; "Publications"; "About the Prices in This Book"; "How to Use This Book"; *Star Trek*: "Action Figures," "Artwork," "Blueprints," "Books," "Bumper Stickers," "Buttons," 'Calendars," "Cels and Storyboards," "Ceramics," "Certificates and Diplomas," "Clothing and Accessories," Comic Books," "Convention Program Books," "Costumes and Uniforms," "Decals and Stickers," "Fan Clubs," "Fanzines," "Games and Accessories," "Greeting Cards," "Household Wares," "Jewelry," "Magazines," 'Medallions," "Model Kits," "Patches," Postcards," "Poster Books," "Posters," "Promotional Items," "Puzzles," "Scripts," School and Office Supplies," "Sheet Music," "Stills, Slides and Photographs," "Toys, Trading Cards," and "Video Cassettes." *Star Wars*: "Action Figures and Accessories," "Artwork," "Badges," "Buttons and Bumper Stickers," "Blueprints," "Books," "Cards," "Clothing and Accessories," "Collector Plates," "Comic Books," "Cosmetics," Costumes," "Fan Clubs," "Fanzines," "Figurines," "Films and Video Cassettes," "Games," "Greeting Cards," "Household Wares," "Jewelry," "Magazines," "Models," "Party Goods," "Patches," "Posters," "Promotional Items" (Studio), "Puzzles" (Jigsaw), "Records and Tapes," "Scripts," "Sheet Music," Stationery and School Supplies," "Toys," "Toys" (Action-Figure Related), and "Video Games."

In each section materials are listed alphabetically by description or title. A typical entry gives item (boldfaced), description, and price range. The book is illustrated with a small number of black-and-white reproductions of the items described and printed on poor-quality paper. Gibson-Downs and Gentry's guide (see #538), is generally much more helpful for *Star Trek* items; for example, both catalogs list Blish's early fictionalizations of *Star Trek* episodes (*Star Trek 1-Star Trek 12*), but the *Encyclopedia* gives contents listings, pagination, and a complete rundown of changes in ISBN numbers and original prices, changes in cover art, etc. However, Cornwell and Kott's guide will be helpful to *Star Wars* collectors, and no doubt collectors will want to compare prices anyway. Libraries can safely pass.

541. Resnick, Michael D. **Official Guide to the Fantastics.** Florence, Ala., House of Collectibles, 1976. 212 p. (pbk.). **Official Guide to Comic Books and Big Little Books.** [2nd ed.]. Florence, Ala., House of collectibles, 1977. ii, 264 p. **Official Price Guide to Comic and Science Fiction Books.** [3rd ed.]. Orlando, Fla., House of Collectibles, 1979. 422 p. (pbk.). Hugdeons, Thomas E., III. **The Official 1981 Price Guide to Comic and Science Fiction Books.** [4th ed.]. Orlando, Fla., House of Collectibles, 1981. 437 p. (pbk.). Hudgeons, Thomas E., III, and William Roger. **The Official 1982 Price Guide to Comic and Science Fiction Books.** [5th ed.]. Orlando, Fla., House of Collectibles, 1982. 501 p. (pbk.). **The Official Price Guide to Science Fiction and Fantasy Collectibles.** [6th ed.] Orlando Fla., House of Collectibles, 1983. 526 p. Hudgeons, Thomas E., III. **The Official Price Guide to Science Fiction and Fantasy Collectibles.** [7th ed.]. Orlando, Fla., House of Collectibles, 1985. 537 p. (pbk.). Thompson, Don, and Maggie Thompson. **The Official Price Guide to Science Fiction and Fantasy Collectibles.** 3rd ed. [*sic*]. New York, House of Collectibles, Ballantine Books, 1989. viii, 482 p., [8] p. of plates. index. LC 84-647218. ISBN 0-87637-754-1 (pbk.). ISSN 8755-2787.

This guide has gone through a variety of styles and formats in its history but was reworked extensively when Ballantine Books bought out House of Collectibles in the late 1980s; Ballantine has chosen to call the first version of its revised publication the "Third Edition." Contents (1989 edition): "Acknowledgments"; "Introduction"; "Getting to Know Science Fiction and Fantasy"; "Collecting Science Fiction and Fantasy"; "Evaluating Science-Fiction and Fantasy Collectibles"; "History of the Field"; "The Market"; "Science-Fiction and Fantasy Names"; "American Fiction Magazines"; "British Fiction Magazines"; "Science Fiction and Fantasy in Comic Books"; "Science-Fiction and Fantasy Drama"; "Filksongs and Other Recordings"; "Collecting the Best"; "You Can't Have It All"; "Science-Fiction and Fantasy Glossary"; "Non-Fiction/Reference Material"; "Afterword"; "Index."

The main section of the book, "Names," is an A-Z bibliography of major science fiction authors. A typical entry gives author's name (bold caps), real name (if a pseudonym, in parentheses), years of birth and death (when known), brief one-paragraph biography, a list of the awards the author has received (with years and titles of the fiction being honored), and a checklist of the writer's major book publications, in ascending, chronological order by publication date, giving year of publication, and title (in italics, plus any alternate titles in parentheses), and some prices (but many items are unpriced). No bibliographical data are recorded, making identification of first editions virtually impossible.

The two chapters on magazines are each arranged in alphabetical order by magazine title, a typical entry providing title (bold caps), alternate titles, years of publication, brief history (one to two paragraphs), and a checklist of issues and prices, year by year and month by month. The drama chapter includes brief sections on "Doctor Who," "Star Trek," *Star Wars*, "The Man from U.N.C.L.E.," and other programs and motion pictures, but again provides little in the way of identification beyond title. The book is illustrated with a handful of black-and-white reproductions of some of the items described, plus eight pages of seemingly randomly chosen color plates and is printed on poor-quality paper.

It is difficult to see how the neofan or beginning collector could ever make sense of this catalog, which provides no edition points, very little in the way of descriptions, and a paucity of pricing data in the book section. In fact, this is one collectible that need not be collected by anyone (including the earlier editions, which are even worse).

542. Rovin, Jeff. **The Science Fiction Collector's Catalog**. San Diego, A.S. Barnes & Co., 1982. 181 p., [8] p. of plates. LC 81-3593. ISBN 0-498-02562-4 (pbk.). Also: London, The Tantivy Press, 1982. 181 p., [8] p. of plates. (pbk.).

Rovin's collector's guide includes "Foreword," by Adam West; "Preface"; "1. Where to Collect"; "2. Pulp Magazines"; "3. Big Little Books"; "4. Comic Books"; "5. Comic Strips"; "6. Books"; "7. Motion Pictures"; "8. Film Stills and Posters"; "9. Movie Props"; "10. Record Albums"; "11. Science Fiction Magazines"; "12. Picture Cards"; "13. Edgar Rice Burroughs"; "14. *Star Trek*"; "15. Toys"; "16. "SF Wargames"; "Bibliography."

Each chapter provides a very basic introduction to its subject, with a list of major dealers, and mentions of a handful of major collectibles, with tentative prices (now a decade out-of-date). The chapter on books, for example, gives two pages of introductory material, lists twenty-seven major authors and roughly a hundred hardcover titles, gives years of publication and suggested prices, but no other bibliographical data; a separate subsection lists roughly a hundred paperbacks grouped by price category and then alphabetically by title (the previous section was arranged by author). None of the other sections are any better organized. The book is illustrated throughout with well-reproduced black-and-white covers and stills, plus eight pages of color illustrations, and attractively typeset.

This outdated guide provided little of value even in 1982.

FAN GUIDES

SCOPE NOTE: Among the items featured in this chapter are fan guides, convention guides, and other reference books relating to fandom, except directories, which are included in the Directories section of this book.

543. Speer, Jack Bristol. **Fancyclopedia**. Los Angeles, Los Angeles Science Fiction Society, 1944. 97 p. (pbk.). Eney, Dick, ed., based on the work of Jack Speer. **Fancyclopedia II**. Alexandria, Va., Operation Crifanac, 1959. 186 p. (pbk.).

These rare guides were mimeographed from typed copy and bound into paper covers. Both books are arranged alphabetically by term. A typical entry includes term (all caps) and description (running one sentence to one page). Items include fan groups, faanish names, club name abbreviations, and much else that defies description (e.g., "Kehli. Lee Hoffman's horse, which sparked her first retirement from fandom"; "KTP. Kaj tiel plu; Esperanto and so forth, equivalent to Latin etc. and Deutsch usw"). None of this is particularly important, of course, but libraries with collections of fantastic literature will want to have these volumes for their historical value as SF memorabilia. Some of the original pages are faint and yellowed, as might be expected, and both books were produced in runs of less than 500 copies; existing copies are fragile and now very hard to find.

544. Strauss, Erwin S. **The Complete Guide to Science Fiction Conventions**. Port Townsend, Wash., Loompanics Unlimited, 1983. 56 p. (pbk.).

Erwin "Filthy Pierre" Strauss, compiler of MIT's *Index to the S-F Magazines, 1951-1965* (see #138), here provides a brief guide to attendance at and production of SF conventions (cons). Contents: "What Goes on at a Science Fiction Convention, Anyway?"; "Filthy Pierre Steps Out to a Con"; "A Bestiary of Conventions"; "Here's What Goes On at an SF Con"; "So You Want to Run a Con"; "Access" [i.e., bibliography and directory]. Most of the sections provide very general but sound advice on various aspects of con functions, fan language, and what the neofan might expect to see at his or her first con. The "Access" chapter, now outdated, includes addresses of basic publications and convention registration services or groups (the Star Trek Welcommittee, for example). The book is nicely typeset but not designed for library usage. The narrative parts of this guide remain valid; the reference section badly needs updating. Libraries can pass.

545. Tucker, Bob. **Neo-Fan's Guide to Science Fiction Fandom**. Hartford City, Ind., Robert & Juanita Coulson, 1966. 16 p. (pbk.).

[Not seen.]

CORE PERIODICALS

SCOPE NOTE: Relatively few SF periodicals, fanzines, or newsletters have had any consistent reference value. Those listed herein are grouped into appropriate categories:

546. Newsletters and Newspapers.

The principal newszines of the SF field have included *Fantasy Times/SF Times* (1941-69), *Luna Monthly* (1969-77), *Locus* (1968-DATE), and *Science Fiction Chronicle* (1979-DATE). Each of these publications has featured contemporaneous news items, obituaries of authors and other figures important to the field, film columns, convention reports, and much other material of interest. *Locus* also includes (since the early 1980s) a monthly register of the books published in the field, arranged alphabetically by author with complete bibliographical data, and (in more recent years) a similar listing of SF monographs published in Great Britain. Some of this information has been cumulated since 1984 into the annual volumes of *Science Fiction, Fantasy, & Horror* (see #24).

547. Review Magazines.

Those professionally produced nonfiction magazines having significant numbers of reviews of science-fiction and fantasy works include *Delap's F & SF Review** (1975-77), *Fantasy Newsletter/Fantasy Review** (1978-87), *Luna Monthly* (1969-77), *Locus* (1968-DATE), *Science Fiction & Fantasy Book Review** (1979-80, 1982-83), *Science Fiction Chronicle* (1979-DATE), *SF Booklog** (1975-77), *SFRA Newsletter* (1971-DATE).

Those titles with asterisks were primarily review journals (all now defunct). The *SFRA Newsletter* has become primarily a review publication within the last five years. *Locus* and *Science Fiction Chronicle* run approximately twenty-five reviews of new books per issue, although their primary focus remains the reporting of news events. All of these reviews are indexed in Hal W. Hall's *Science Fiction Book Review Index* (see #92).

548. Scholarly Magazines.

Scholarly journals devoted specifically to science fiction and fantasy include *Extrapolation* (1959-DATE), *Foundation* (1972-DATE), *Journal of the International Association for the Fantastic in the Arts* (1985?-DATE), *Science-Fiction Studies* (1973-DATE).

Very few articles with reference value have been published in these journals. *Extrapolation* did run in its first issue a bibliography of early American science fiction by Founding Editor Thomas D. Clareson, an article which later became the basis of his book, *Science Fiction in America* (see #199). In addition, Tymn's annual guide to nonfiction works about SF, *The Year's Scholarship in Science Fiction and Fantasy* (see #105) was first published each year in *Extrapolation*, and later in *Journal of the International Association for the Fantastic in the Arts*. Since none of the annuals after 1982 have yet been issued in book form, researchers and librarians should have access to the magazine issues containing the supplements.

549. Other Publications of Interest.

Science-Fiction Collector (1976-81) occupies a unique position among semi-professional fanzines, being filled with a cornucopia of bibliographies, checklists, and bibliographical articles on a wide variety of subjects. Often published on poor-quality paper, the issues include single-author bibliographies, subject bibliographies, publisher checklists, and much else of interest to the SF collector and bibliographer. One hundred fifty three-volume sets were bound into cloth in 1980 and 1981 by Editor-Publisher Grant Thiessen; however, the issues in Volume One badly need deacidification (later issues were published on better stock).

One issue of *Fantasy Research & Bibliography* (dated December, 1980-February, 1981/March, 1981-May, 1981) was produced by Editor-Publisher Leslie Kay Swigart in 1981, including two articles: "Starguide," by Larry Roeder, an attempt at defining the genre through very detailed subject headings; and Swigart's Second Edition of *Harlan Ellison: A Bibliographical Checklist*, covered elsewhere in this volume (see #335). Lamentably, the journal ceased after its maiden outing.

PROFESSIONAL ORGANIZATIONS

550. Professional Writers' Groups.

Two organizations for writers serve the field of fantastic literature: Horror Writers of America (HWA) and Science Fiction and Fantasy Writers of America, Inc. (SFWA). Both are open to active membership only by professionals working in their respective genres, although both do provide separate rates for institutional and affiliate memberships. Each organization publishes a variety of public and private newletters, journals, and directories (the latter are covered elsewhere in this book; see #29 and #32). Neither specifically sponsors publications outside of these directories which contain anything of reference value.

551. Scholarly Groups.

Two groups service scholars in the science-fiction and fantasy fields: International Association for the Fantastic in the Arts (IAFA; founded by Dr. Marshall B. Tymn) and The Science Fiction Research Association (SFRA; founded by Dr. Thomas D. Clareson). Both produce a journal, a newsletter, and a directory (the latter are covered in #30-#31). As mentioned in #548, several of these publications have produced articles or features having reference value, but the bulk of these organizations' efforts have been directed toward the publication or dissemination of criticism, not bibliographies or indexes. Both groups also sponsor a series of annual awards honoring scholarship in the field; a handful of the honorees have been bibliographers (for example, SFRA's Pilgrim Award for 1991 was presented to Pierre Versins).

CORE COLLECTIONS

SCOPE NOTE: Excluded from these lists are books limited to very specific topics (for example, single-author bibliographies, guides to particular television series, etc.), since selection of these materials will depend much more heavily on individual collection orientation. Very large research libraries may wish to gather as many of these materials as possible, particularly those produced to higher bibliographical standards and/or by major reference publishing houses. This section is divided into three levels covering academic libraries, public libraries, and individual research collections; entries are keyed to item number and title.

ACADEMIC LIBRARIES

Research University Collections

4. *The New Encyclopedia of Science Fiction.*
7. *The Encyclopedia of Science Fiction/The Science Fiction Encyclopedia.*
9. *The Penguin Encyclopedia of Horror and the Supernatural.*
10. *The Encyclopedia of Science Fiction and Fantasy Through 1968.*
11. *Encyclopédie de l'Utopie, des Voyages Extraordinaires, et de la Science Fiction.*
12. *Critical Terms for Science Fiction and Fantasy.*
18. *The Dictionary of Imaginary Places.*
19. *An Atlas of Fantasy.*
21. *A Guide to Science Fiction & Fantasy in the Library of Congress Classification Scheme.*
24. *Science Fiction, Fantasy, & Horror.*
25. *Science Fiction & Fantasy Book Review Annual.*
30. *International Association for the Fantastic in the Arts Membership Directory.*
31. *Science Fiction Research Association Annual Directory.*
33. *Illustrated Book of Science Fiction Lists.*
34. *The Complete Book of Science Fiction and Fantasy Lists/The SF Book of Lists.*
38. *Science Fiction and Fantasy Awards.*
39. *The Pendex.*
40. *Science Fiction and Fantasy Pseudonyms.*
41. *Who's Hugh?*
42. *Who's Who in Science Fiction.*
43. *Who's Who in Horror and Fantasy Fiction.*
44. *Twentieth-Century American Science-Fiction Writers.*
45. *Contemporary Science Fiction, Fantasy, and Horror Poetry.*
46. *Stella Nova/Contemporary Science Fiction Authors, First Edition.*
47. *Twentieth-Century Science-Fiction Writers.*
48. *A Biographical Dictionary of Science Fiction and Fantasy Artists.*
49. *More Than 100: Women Science Fiction Writers.*
51. *Anatomy of Wonder.*

52. *Fantasy Literature.*

53. *Horror Literature.*

54. *The Guide to Supernatural Fiction.*

55. *Science Fiction, the Early Years.*

56. *Science Fiction Writers.*

57. *Supernatural Fiction Writers, Fantasy and Horror.*

58. *Benchmarks.*

59. *Fantasy: The 100 Best Books.*

61. *Reader's Guide to Twentieth-Century Science Fiction.*

63. *Horror: 100 Best Books.*

65. *Women of the Future.*

67. *Fantasy for Children/Fantasy Literature for Children and Young Adults.*

68. *Survey of Modern Fantasy Literature.*

69. *Survey of Modern Science Fiction Literature.*

71. *A Reference Guide to Modern Fantasy for Children.*

72. *Modern Fantasy: The Hundred Best Novels.*

73. *Science Fiction: The 100 Best Novels.*

74. *The Ultimate Guide to Science Fiction.*

75. *A Reader's Guide to Fantasy.*

76. *A Reader's Guide to Science Fiction.*

77. *Fantasy Literature: A Core Collection and Reference Guide.*

78. *Horror Literature: A Core Collection and Reference Guide.*

79. *The Science Fiction Reference Book.*

80. *The Hills of Faraway.*

81. *Images in a Crystal Ball.*

82. *The Science Fiction Source Book.*

83. *Shadowings.*

84. *Horror.*

86. *SF Bibliographies.*

87. *Science Fiction Criticism.*

89. *The Gothic's Gothic.*

90. *Gothic Fiction.*

91. *A Guide to the Gothic.*

92. *Science Fiction Book Review Index.*

93. *Science Fiction and Fantasy Reference Index/Science Fiction and Fantasy Research Index.*

94. *Science Fiction, Fantasy, and Horror Reference.*

95. *Science Fiction Master Index of Names.*

98. *The Eighteenth-Century Gothic Novel.*

100. *The English Gothic.*

103. *A Research Guide to Science Fiction Studies.*

104. *Survey of Science Fiction Literature: Bibliographical Supplement.*

105. *The Year's Scholarship in Science Fiction, Fantasy, and Horror.*

106. *Science/Fiction Collections.*

109. *Dictionary Catalog of the J. Lloyd Eaton Collection of Science Fiction and Fantasy Literature.*
111. *Science Fiction, Fantasy, and Weird Fiction Magazines.*
112. *Index to the Science Fiction Magazines.*
115. *Index to the Weird Fiction Magazines.*
116. *A Checklist of Science-Fiction Anthologies.*
117. *Index to Science Fiction Anthologies and Collections.*
121. *Index to the Science-Fiction Magazines, 1926-1950.*
125. *The Science Fiction Magazines.*
128. *The Index of Science Fiction Magazines, 1951-1965.*
129. *Index to the Science Fiction Magazines (and Original Anthologies).*
130. *Monthly Terrors.*
133. *The Pulp Magazine Index.*
134. *Science Fiction and Fantasy Magazines, 1923-1980.*
136. *Science Fiction Story Index.*
138. *The MIT Science Fiction Society's Index to the S-F Magazines, 1951-1965.*
140. *Index to Stories in Thematic Anthologies of Science Fiction.*
177. *Paralittératures.*
178. *The Checklist of Fantastic Literature.*
179. *The Supplemental Checklist of Fantastic Literature.*
181. *A Spectrum of Fantasy.*
182. *Science Fiction and Fantasy Literature.*
184. *The Science Fiction and Heroic Fantasy Author Index.*
186. *CDN SF & F.*
196. *Russian Science Fiction.*
199. *Science Fiction in America, 1870s-1930s.*
200. *American Fantasy and Science Fiction.*
202. *Bibliography of Adventure.*
208. *The Literature of Fantasy.*
210. *Science Fiction and Fantasy Authors.*
212. *The Tale of the Future.*
213. *Voices Prophesying War, 1763-1984.*
214. *Future War Novels.*
215. *The First Gothics.*
216. *Gothic Novels of the Twentieth Century.*
217. *A Gothic Bibliography.*
218. *The Gothic Novel, 1790-1830.*
219. *The Imaginary Voyage in Prose Fiction.*
220. *Nuclear Holocausts.*
221. *The Checklist of Fantastic Literature in Paperbound Books.*
223. *Who Goes There.*
225. *Science Fiction and Fantasy Series and Sequels.*
226. *Uranian Worlds.*
227. *Voyages in Space.*
231. *Utopian Literature.*

232. *British and American Utopian Literature.*

233. *The Vampire in Literature.*

234. *The Transylvanian Library.*

235. *Vampires Unearthed.*

236. *Urania's Daughters.*

237. *Index to the Science-Fantasy Publishers.*

260. *Bibliographies of Modern Authors.*

263. *Masters of Science Fiction and Fantasy.*

464. *Imaginary People.*

494. *Science Fiction Films of the Seventies.*

495. *Vintage Science Fiction Films, 1896-1949.*

496. *The Horror Film Handbook.*

497. *The Science Fiction and Fantasy Film Handbook.*

498. *Fantastic Television.*

499. *Horror/The Encyclopedia of Horror Movies.*

500. *Science Fiction/The Encyclopedia of Science Fiction Movies.*

502. *Reference Guide to Fantastic Films.*

503. *Science Fiction, Horror, & Fantasy Film and Television Credits.*

507. *Futurevisions.*

508. *Things to Come.*

509. *The Great Science Fiction Pictures.*

511. *The Creature Features Movie Guide/Revenge of the Creature Features Movie Guide.*

512. *A Reference Guide to American Science Fiction Films.*

513. *Keep Watching the Skies!*

514. *Horror and Science Fiction Films.*

515. Variety's *Complete Science Fiction Reviews.*

517. *The Science Fiction Image.*

State University Collections

4. *The New Encyclopedia of Science Fiction.*

7. *The Encyclopedia of Science Fiction/The Science Fiction Encyclopedia.*

9. *The Penguin Encyclopedia of Horror and the Supernatural.*

10. *The Encyclopedia of Science Fiction and Fantasy Through 1968.*

12. *Critical Terms for Science Fiction and Fantasy.*

18. *The Dictionary of Imaginary Places.*

19. *An Atlas of Fantasy.*

21. *A Guide to Science Fiction & Fantasy in the Library of Congress Classification Scheme.*

24. *Science Fiction, Fantasy, & Horror.*

25. *Science Fiction & Fantasy Book Review Annual.*

33. *Illustrated Book of Science Fiction Lists.*

38. *Science Fiction and Fantasy Awards.*

41. *Who's Hugh?*

43. *Who's Who in Horror and Fantasy Fiction.*

44. *Twentieth-Century American Science-Fiction Writers.*
45. *Contemporary Science Fiction, Fantasy, and Horror Poetry.*
47. *Twentieth-Century Science-Fiction Writers.*
48. *A Biographical Dictionary of Science Fiction and Fantasy Artists.*
51. *Anatomy of Wonder.*
52. *Fantasy Literature.*
53. *Horror Literature.*
54. *The Guide to Supernatural Fiction.*
55. *Science Fiction, the Early Years.*
56. *Science Fiction Writers.*
57. *Supernatural Fiction Writers, Fantasy and Horror.*
59. *Fantasy: The 100 Best Books.*
61. *Reader's Guide to Twentieth-Century Science Fiction.*
63. *Horror: 100 Best Books.*
65. *Women of the Future.*
67. *Fantasy for Children/Fantasy Literature for Children and Young Adults.*
68. *Survey of Modern Fantasy Literature.*
69. *Survey of Modern Science Fiction Literature.*
72. *Modern Fantasy: The Hundred Best Novels.*
73. *Science Fiction: The 100 Best Novels.*
74. *The Ultimate Guide to Science Fiction.*
79. *The Science Fiction Reference Book.*
84. *Horror.*
87. *Science Fiction Criticism.*
89. *The Gothic's Gothic.*
90. *Gothic Fiction.*
92. *Science Fiction Book Review Index.*
93. *Science Fiction and Fantasy Reference Index/Science Fiction and Fantasy Research Index.*
95. *Science Fiction Master Index of Names.*
100. *The English Gothic.*
103. *A Research Guide to Science Fiction Studies.*
104. *Survey of Science Fiction Literature: Bibliographical Supplement.*
105. *The Year's Scholarship in Science Fiction, Fantasy, and Horror.*
111. *Science Fiction, Fantasy, and Weird Fiction Magazines.*
112. *Index to the Science Fiction Magazines.*
117. *Index to Science Fiction Anthologies and Collections.*
121. *Index to the Science-Fiction Magazines, 1926-1950.*
125. *The Science Fiction Magazines.*
128. *The Index of Science Fiction Magazines, 1951-1965.*
129. *Index to the Science Fiction Magazines (and Original Anthologies).*
130. *Monthly Terrors.*
133. *The Pulp Magazine Index.*
140. *Index to Stories in Thematic Anthologies of Science Fiction.*
178. *The Checklist of Fantastic Literature.*

182. *Science Fiction and Fantasy Literature.*
184. *The Science Fiction and Heroic Fantasy Author Index.*
199. *Science Fiction in America, 1870s-1930s.*
208. *The Literature of Fantasy.*
210. *Science Fiction and Fantasy Authors.*
212. *The Tale of the Future.*
213. *Voices Prophesying War, 1763-1984.*
214. *Future War Novels.*
215. *The First Gothics.*
216. *Gothic Novels of the Twentieth Century.*
217. *A Gothic Bibliography.*
219. *The Imaginary Voyage in Prose Fiction.*
220. *Nuclear Holocausts.*
225. *Science Fiction and Fantasy Series and Sequels.*
226. *Uranian Worlds.*
227. *Voyages in Space.*
231. *Utopian Literature.*
232. *British and American Utopian Literature.*
233. *The Vampire in Literature.*
234. *The Transylvanian Library.*
236. *Urania's Daughters.*
260. *Bibliographies of Modern Authors.*
263. *Masters of Science Fiction and Fantasy.*
464. *Imaginary People.*
494. *Science Fiction Films of the Seventies.*
495. *Vintage Science Fiction Films, 1896-1949.*
498. *Fantastic Television.*
499. *Horror/The Encyclopedia of Horror Movies.*
500. *Science Fiction/The Encyclopedia of Science Fiction Movies.*
502. *Reference Guide to Fantastic Films.*
503. *Science Fiction, Horror, & Fantasy Film and Television Credits.*
507. *Futurevisions.*
508. *Things to Come.*
509. *The Great Science Fiction Pictures.*
511. *The Creature Features Movie Guide/Revenge of the Creature Features Movie Guide.*
512. *A Reference Guide to American Science Fiction Films.*
513. *Keep Watching the Skies!*
514. *Horror and Science Fiction Films.*
515. Variety's *Complete Science Fiction Reviews.*

Small Private and Community College Collections

7. *The Encyclopedia of Science Fiction/The Science Fiction Encyclopedia.*
9. *The Penguin Encyclopedia of Horror and the Supernatural.*

499. *Horror/The Encyclopedia of Horror Movies.*
500. *Science Fiction/The Encyclopedia of Science Fiction Movies.*
503. *Science Fiction, Horror, & Fantasy Film and Television Credits.*
511. *The Creature Features Movie Guide/Revenge of the Creature Features Movie Guide.*
514. *Horror and Science Fiction Films.*

PUBLIC LIBRARIES

Large City Systems

1. *The Visual Encyclopedia of Science Fiction.*
2. *The Encyclopedia of Horror.*
4. *The New Encyclopedia of Science Fiction.*
5. *Encyclopedia of Science Fiction.*
7. *The Encyclopedia of Science Fiction/The Science Fiction Encyclopedia.*
9. *The Penguin Encyclopedia of Horror and the Supernatural.*
10. *The Encyclopedia of Science Fiction and Fantasy Through 1968.*
12. *Critical Terms for Science Fiction and Fantasy.*
18. *The Dictionary of Imaginary Places.*
19. *An Atlas of Fantasy.*
24. *Science Fiction, Fantasy, & Horror.*
25. *Science Fiction & Fantasy Book Review Annual.*
28. *Fandom Directory.*
33. *Illustrated Book of Science Fiction Lists.*
34. *The Complete Book of Science Fiction and Fantasy Lists/The SF Book of Lists.*
38. *Science Fiction and Fantasy Awards.*
39. *The Pendex.*
40. *Science Fiction and Fantasy Pseudonyms.*
41. *Who's Hugh?*
42. *Who's Who in Science Fiction.*
43. *Who's Who in Horror and Fantasy Fiction.*
44. *Twentieth-Century American Science-Fiction Writers.*
45. *Contemporary Science Fiction, Fantasy, and Horror Poetry.*
46. *Stella Nova/Contemporary Science Fiction Authors, First Edition.*
47. *Twentieth-Century Science-Fiction Writers.*
48. *A Biographical Dictionary of Science Fiction and Fantasy Artists.*
49. *More Than 100: Women Science Fiction Writers.*
51. *Anatomy of Wonder.*
52. *Fantasy Literature.*
53. *Horror Literature.*
54. *The Guide to Supernatural Fiction.*
55. *Science Fiction, the Early Years.*

56. *Science Fiction Writers.*
57. *Supernatural Fiction Writers, Fantasy and Horror.*
58. *Benchmarks.*
59. *Fantasy: The 100 Best Books.*
61. *Reader's Guide to Twentieth-Century Science Fiction.*
63. *Horror: 100 Best Books.*
64. *Supernatural Fiction for Teens.*
65. *Women of the Future.*
67. *Fantasy for Children/Fantasy Literature for Children and Young Adults.*
68. *Survey of Modern Fantasy Literature.*
69. *Survey of Modern Science Fiction Literature.*
71. *A Reference Guide to Modern Fantasy for Children.*
72. *Modern Fantasy: The Hundred Best Novels.*
73. *Science Fiction: The 100 Best Novels.*
74. *The Ultimate Guide to Science Fiction.*
75. *A Reader's Guide to Fantasy.*
76. *A Reader's Guide to Science Fiction.*
77. *Fantasy Literature: A Core Collection and Reference Guide.*
78. *Horror Literature: A Core Collection and Reference Guide.*
79. *The Science Fiction Reference Book.*
80. *The Hills of Faraway.*
81. *Images in a Crystal Ball.*
82. *The Science Fiction Source Book.*
83. *Shadowings.*
84. *Horror.*
87. *Science Fiction Criticism.*
89. *The Gothic's Gothic.*
90. *Gothic Fiction.*
91. *A Guide to the Gothic.*
92. *Science Fiction Book Review Index.*
93. *Science Fiction and Fantasy Reference Index/Science Fiction and Fantasy Research Index.*
94. *Science Fiction, Fantasy, and Horror Reference.*
95. *Science Fiction Master Index of Names.*
98. *The Eighteenth-Century Gothic Novel.*
100. *The English Gothic.*
103. *A Research Guide to Science Fiction Studies.*
104. *Survey of Science Fiction Literature: Bibliographical Supplement.*
105. *The Year's Scholarship in Science Fiction, Fantasy, and Horror.*
106. *Science/Fiction Collections.*
111. *Science Fiction, Fantasy, and Weird Fiction Magazines.*
112. *Index to the Science Fiction Magazines.*
115. *Index to the Weird Fiction Magazines.*
116. *A Checklist of Science-Fiction Anthologies.*
117. *Index to Science Fiction Anthologies and Collections.*

121. *Index to the Science-Fiction Magazines, 1926-1950.*

125. *The Science Fiction Magazines.*

128. *The Index of Science Fiction Magazines, 1951-1965.*

129. *Index to the Science Fiction Magazines (and Original Anthologies).*

130. *Monthly Terrors.*

133. *The Pulp Magazine Index.*

134. *Science Fiction and Fantasy Magazines, 1923-1980.*

136. *Science Fiction Story Index.*

138. *The MIT Science Fiction Society's Index to the S-F Magazines, 1951-1965.*

140. *Index to Stories in Thematic Anthologies of Science Fiction.*

177. *Paralittératures.*

178. *The Checklist of Fantastic Literature.*

179. *The Supplemental Checklist of Fantastic Literature.*

181. *A Spectrum of Fantasy.*

182. *Science Fiction and Fantasy Literature.*

184. *The Science Fiction and Heroic Fantasy Author Index.*

186. *CDN SF & F.*

196. *Russian Science Fiction.*

199. *Science Fiction in America, 1870s-1930s.*

200. *American Fantasy and Science Fiction.*

202. *Bibliography of Adventure.*

208. *The Literature of Fantasy.*

210. *Science Fiction and Fantasy Authors.*

212. *The Tale of the Future.*

213. *Voices Prophesying War, 1763-1984.*

214. *Future War Novels.*

215. *The First Gothics.*

216. *Gothic Novels of the Twentieth Century.*

217. *A Gothic Bibliography.*

218. *The Gothic Novel, 1790-1830.*

219. *The Imaginary Voyage in Prose Fiction.*

220. *Nuclear Holocausts.*

221. *The Checklist of Fantastic Literature in Paperbound Books.*

223. *Who Goes There.*

225. *Science Fiction and Fantasy Series and Sequels.*

226. *Uranian Worlds.*

227. *Voyages in Space.*

231. *Utopian Literature.*

232. *British and American Utopian Literature.*

233. *The Vampire in Literature.*

234. *The Transylvanian Library.*

235. *Vampires Unearthed.*

236. *Urania's Daughters.*

237. *Index to the Science-Fantasy Publishers.*

260. *Bibliographies of Modern Authors.*

263. *Masters of Science Fiction and Fantasy.*
464. *Imaginary People.*
494. *Science Fiction Films of the Seventies.*
495. *Vintage Science Fiction Films, 1896-1949.*
496. *The Horror Film Handbook.*
497. *The Science Fiction and Fantasy Film Handbook.*
498. *Fantastic Television.*
499. *Horror/The Encyclopedia of Horror Movies.*
500. *Science Fiction/The Encyclopedia of Science Fiction Movies.*
502. *Reference Guide to Fantastic Films.*
503. *Science Fiction, Horror, & Fantasy Film and Television Credits.*
507. *Futurevisions.*
508. *Things to Come.*
509. *The Great Science Fiction Pictures.*
511. *The Creature Features Movie Guide/Revenge of the Creature Features Movie Guide.*
512. *A Reference Guide to American Science Fiction Films.*
513. *Keep Watching the Skies!*
514. *Horror and Science Fiction Films.*
515. Variety's *Complete Science Fiction Reviews.*
517. *The Science Fiction Image.*

Medium County and City Libraries

7. *The Encyclopedia of Science Fiction/The Science Fiction Encyclopedia.*
9. *The Penguin Encyclopedia of Horror and the Supernatural.*
18. *The Dictionary of Imaginary Places.*
19. *An Atlas of Fantasy.*
28. *Fandom Directory.*
33. *Illustrated Book of Science Fiction Lists.*
38. *Science Fiction and Fantasy Awards.*
41. *Who's Hugh?*
43. *Who's Who in Horror and Fantasy Fiction.*
47. *Twentieth-Century Science-Fiction Writers.*
51. *Anatomy of Wonder.*
52. *Fantasy Literature.*
53. *Horror Literature.*
56. *Science Fiction Writers.*
57. *Supernatural Fiction Writers, Fantasy and Horror.*
63. *Horror: 100 Best Books.*
64. *Supernatural Fiction for Teens.*
65. *Women of the Future.*
67. *Fantasy for Children/Fantasy Literature for Children and Young Adults.*
72. *Modern Fantasy: The Hundred Best Novels.*
73. *Science Fiction: The 100 Best Novels.*

74. *The Ultimate Guide to Science Fiction.*
75. *A Reader's Guide to Fantasy.*
76. *A Reader's Guide to Science Fiction.*
87. *Science Fiction Criticism.*
90. *Gothic Fiction.*
92. *Science Fiction Book Review Index.*
93. *Science Fiction and Fantasy Reference Index/Science Fiction and Fantasy Research Index.*
103. *A Research Guide to Science Fiction Studies.*
105. *The Year's Scholarship in Science Fiction, Fantasy, and Horror.*
117. *Index to Science Fiction Anthologies and Collections.*
121. *Index to the Science-Fiction Magazines, 1926-1950.*
125. *The Science Fiction Magazines.*
128. *The Index of Science Fiction Magazines, 1951-1965.*
182. *Science Fiction and Fantasy Literature.*
208. *The Literature of Fantasy.*
210. *Science Fiction and Fantasy Authors.*
214. *Future War Novels.*
216. *Gothic Novels of the Twentieth Century.*
217. *A Gothic Bibliography.*
219. *The Imaginary Voyage in Prose Fiction.*
220. *Nuclear Holocausts.*
225. *Science Fiction and Fantasy Series and Sequels.*
226. *Uranian Worlds.*
232. *British and American Utopian Literature.*
234. *The Transylvanian Library.*
464. *Imaginary People.*
498. *Fantastic Television.*
499. *Horror/The Encyclopedia of Horror Movies.*
500. *Science Fiction/The Encyclopedia of Science Fiction Movies.*
503. *Science Fiction, Horror, & Fantasy Film and Television Credits.*
507. *Futurevisions.*
508. *Things to Come.*
509. *The Great Science Fiction Pictures.*
511. *The Creature Features Movie Guide/Revenge of the Creature Features Movie Guide.*
514. *Horror and Science Fiction Films.*

Small Public and County Libraries

7. *The Encyclopedia of Science Fiction/The Science Fiction Encyclopedia.*
9. *The Penguin Encyclopedia of Horror and the Supernatural.*
18. *The Dictionary of Imaginary Places.*
19. *An Atlas of Fantasy.*
33. *Illustrated Book of Science Fiction Lists.*

43. *Who's Who in Horror and Fantasy Fiction.*
47. *Twentieth-Century Science-Fiction Writers.*
51. *Anatomy of Wonder.*
52. *Fantasy Literature.*
53. *Horror Literature.*
63. *Horror: 100 Best Books.*
67. *Fantasy for Children/Fantasy Literature for Children and Young Adults.*
72. *Modern Fantasy: The Hundred Best Novels.*
73. *Science Fiction: The 100 Best Novels.*
74. *The Ultimate Guide to Science Fiction.*
103. *A Research Guide to Science Fiction Studies.*
117. *Index to Science Fiction Anthologies and Collections.*
182. *Science Fiction and Fantasy Literature.*
210. *Science Fiction and Fantasy Authors.*
464. *Imaginary People.*
498. *Fantastic Television.*
499. *Horror/The Encyclopedia of Horror Movies.*
500. *Science Fiction/The Encyclopedia of Science Fiction Movies.*
511. *The Creature Features Movie Guide/Revenge of the Creature Features Movie Guide.*

PERSONAL RESEARCH LIBRARIES

7. *The Encyclopedia of Science Fiction/The Science Fiction Encyclopedia.*
9. *The Penguin Encyclopedia of Horror and the Supernatural.*
10. *The Encyclopedia of Science Fiction and Fantasy Through 1968.*
18. *The Dictionary of Imaginary Places.*
24. *Science Fiction, Fantasy, & Horror.*
30. *International Association for the Fantastic in the Arts Membership Directory.*
31. *Science Fiction Research Association Annual Directory.*
33. *Illustrated Book of Science Fiction Lists.*
38. *Science Fiction and Fantasy Awards.*
41. *Who's Hugh?*
43. *Who's Who in Horror and Fantasy Fiction.*
45. *Contemporary Science Fiction, Fantasy, and Horror Poetry.*
47. *Twentieth-Century Science-Fiction Writers.*
48. *A Biographical Dictionary of Science Fiction and Fantasy Artists.*
51. *Anatomy of Wonder.*
52. *Fantasy Literature.*
53. *Horror Literature.*
54. *The Guide to Supernatural Fiction.*
55. *Science Fiction, the Early Years.*
59. *Fantasy: The 100 Best Books.*

63. *Horror: 100 Best Books.*

65. *Women of the Future.*

71. *A Reference Guide to Modern Fantasy for Children.*

72. *Modern Fantasy: The Hundred Best Novels.*

73. *Science Fiction: The 100 Best Novels.*

74. *The Ultimate Guide to Science Fiction.*

75. *A Reader's Guide to Fantasy.*

76. *A Reader's Guide to Science Fiction.*

87. *Science Fiction Criticism.*

90. *Gothic Fiction.*

92. *Science Fiction Book Review Index.*

93. *Science Fiction and Fantasy Reference Index/Science Fiction and Fantasy Research Index.*

95. *Science Fiction Master Index of Names.*

105. *The Year's Scholarship in Science Fiction, Fantasy, and Horror.*

111. *Science Fiction, Fantasy, and Weird Fiction Magazines.*

117. *Index to Science Fiction Anthologies and Collections.*

121. *Index to the Science-Fiction Magazines, 1926-1950.*

125. *The Science Fiction Magazines.*

128. *The Index of Science Fiction Magazines, 1951-1965.*

129. *Index to the Science Fiction Magazines (and Original Anthologies).*

130. *Monthly Terrors.*

133. *The Pulp Magazine Index.*

178. *The Checklist of Fantastic Literature.*

182. *Science Fiction and Fantasy Literature.*

199. *Science Fiction in America, 1870s-1930s.*

208. *The Literature of Fantasy.*

210. *Science Fiction and Fantasy Authors.*

212. *The Tale of the Future.*

213. *Voices Prophesying War, 1763-1984.*

214. *Future War Novels.*

216. *Gothic Novels of the Twentieth Century.*

217. *A Gothic Bibliography.*

219. *The Imaginary Voyage in Prose Fiction.*

225. *Science Fiction and Fantasy Series and Sequels.*

226. *Uranian Worlds.*

232. *British and American Utopian Literature.*

233. *The Vampire in Literature.*

234. *The Transylvanian Library.*

236. *Urania's Daughters.*

237. *Index to the Science-Fantasy Publishers.*

260. *Bibliographies of Modern Authors.*

263. *Masters of Science Fiction and Fantasy.*

464. *Imaginary People.*

495. *Vintage Science Fiction Films, 1896-1949.*

498. *Fantastic Television.*
499. *Horror/The Encyclopedia of Horror Movies.*
500. *Science Fiction/The Encyclopedia of Science Fiction Movies.*
502. *Reference Guide to Fantastic Films.*
503. *Science Fiction, Horror, & Fantasy Film and Television Credits.*
509. *The Great Science Fiction Pictures.*
511. *The Creature Features Movie Guide/Revenge of the Creature Features Movie Guide.*
514. *Horror and Science Fiction Films.*

AUTHOR INDEX

References are to item numbers.

TITLE INDEX

References are to item numbers.

SUBJECT INDEX

References are to item numbers.